THE

WORKS

OF

JOHN WHITGIFT, D.D.,

ARCHBISHOP OF CANTERBURY.

THE

WORKS

OF

JOHN WHITGIFT, D.D.,

MASTER OF TRINITY COLLEGE, DEAN OF LINCOLN, &c.
AFTERWARDS SUCCESSIVELY
BISHOP OF WORCESTER AND ARCHBISHOP OF CANTERBURY.

THE FIRST PORTION,

CONTAINING

THE DEFENCE OF THE ANSWER TO THE ADMONITION,
AGAINST THE REPLY OF THOMAS CARTWRIGHT:

TRACTATES I—VI.

EDITED FOR

The Parker Society,

BY THE

REV. JOHN AYRE, M.A.

OF GONVILLE AND CAIUS COLLEGE, CAMBRIDGE, MINISTER OF ST JOHN'S
CHAPEL, HAMPSTEAD.

WIPF & STOCK · Eugene, Oregon

Wipf and Stock Publishers
199 W 8th Ave, Suite 3
Eugene, OR 97401

The Works of John Whitgift
The First Portion, Containing the Defense of the Answer to the Admonition,
Against the Reply of Thomas Cartwright: Tractates I - VI.
By Whitgift, John
ISBN 13: 978-1-60608-430-4
Publication date 6/5/2009
Previously published by Cambridge University Press, 1851

CONTENTS.

	PAGE
ADVERTISEMENT	vii
Preface to the Godly Reader	3
Cartwright's Epistle to the Church of England	13
Answer to the Epistle to the Church	14
Cartwright's Address, The Author to the Reader	45
Whitgift's Reply	46
Epistle to the Church of England	49
Cartwright's Answer to the Whole Epistle to the Church	52
Whitgift's Reply	53
A brief Examination of the Reasons used in the book called an Admonition to the Parliament	58
To the Christian Reader	75
An Exhortation to such as be in Authority	76
Cartwright's Answer to the Exhortation	77
Certain Notes and Properties of Anabaptists, collected out of Zuinglius and others	125
The Preface of the Admonition	140
Answer to the Preface	141
Cartwright's Reply unto the Answer of the Preface	144
Tract. I. Whether Christ forbiddeth Rule and Superiority unto the Ministers	148
— II. Of the Authority of the Church in things indifferent	175
— III. Of the Election of Ministers	296
— IV. Of Ministers having no pastoral charge; of Ceremonies used in ordaining Ministers; of Apostles, Evangelists, and Prophets	469
— V. Of the Residence of the Pastor	506
— VI. Of Ministers that cannot preach; and of giving Licences to preach	538

ADVERTISEMENT.

THE present Volume contains a portion of archbishop Whitgift's Defence of the Answer to the Admonition. Of this there appear to have been at least two editions bearing the date of 1574. The text of one of these, designated Def. B., has been adopted, and that of another frequently consulted. The two editions, bearing date 1572 and 1573, of Whitgift's Answer to the Admonition have been collated; as also the first and second editions of Cartwright's Reply. These are distinguished respectively as (when the readings vary) Answ. 1 and 2; and as Repl. 1 and 2. A copy of the Admonition has, moreover, been collated; and its various readings marked Adm. It is in the University Library, Cambridge: it is not, however, the first edition; but another, probably the first, is in the Bodleian library at Oxford, and has been referred to.

There have been added in the notes some extracts from Cartwright's Second Reply, which was a Rejoinder to the Defence. That Second Reply is a bulky quarto: it was therefore impossible to introduce any large portion of it; but the editor has thought it desirable to give the reader some notion of the mode in which Cartwright retorts upon his antagonist. Where practicable, his own words are quoted; elsewhere it has been attempted to give briefly the scope of his argument. The editor has endeavoured to discharge this part of his task with as much impartiality as possible.

The writings of archbishop Whitgift will, it is expected, occupy two more volumes. The last will be accompanied by an index and a biographical account of the author.

J. A.

April, 1852.

ADDENDA ET CORRIGENDA.

P. 64, note 1. A MS. copy of the conference alluded to is in the possession of Sir Thomas Phillips; who has obligingly granted a transcript to the Parker Society. Ridley there says: "For how is it possible to receive the holy communion but thou must either sit, stand, kneel, or lay? Thou must either take it at one time or another, fasting or after meat, clothed or naked, in this place or in another. Without the sum of these circumstances it is impossible to do that that the Lord biddeth thee. But none of all these circumstances are commanded in scripture."

pp. 181, 2, note 6, last line, *for* cap. 2, *read* cap. 1.

p. 253, note 4, last line, *for* p. 8, *read* fol. 8.

THE DEFENCE

OF THE

ANSWER TO THE ADMONITION,

AGAINST THE

REPLY OF T. C.

1. Cor. 8. 2.
If any man thinke that he knoweth any thing, he knoweth nothing yet as he ought to knowe.

¶ THE DEFENSE
of the Aunswere to
the Admonition, against the Replie of *T. C.*

BY IOHN VVHITGIFT
Doctor of Diuinitie.

In the beginning are added these .4. Tables[1].
1 Of dangerous doctrines in the Replie.
2 Of Falsifications and Untruthes.
3 Of matters handled at large.
4 A table generall.

If any man be contentious, we haue no such custome, neyther the Churches of God. 1. Cor. 11. 16.

* Printed at London by Henry Binneman, for Humfrey Toye. *Anno.* 1574[2].

Gal. 5. 26.
Let vs not be desirous of vaineglorie, prouoking one another, enuying one another.

[1 Of these four tables, three will be printed in the concluding volume: the fourth will be replaced by a new index.]

[2 There were two impressions, bearing the same date; they differ very slightly. One has a table of errata; most of them being corrected in the other, which was probably the later of the two. This, of which the text has been generally followed, the editor has designated as "Def. b."; while the former, "Def. a.", has been also consulted, and its readings (due notice being always given) occasionally adopted.]

TO THE GODLY READER[3].

It were but a needless labour to make any particular recital of those points of doctrine which this church of England at this day doth hold and maintain; for they be at large set out in sundry English books, and especially in the Apology of the Church of England, and the Defence of the same; summarily also collected together in the book of Articles agreed upon in the Convocation at London, Anno 1562, &c. This I dare boldly affirm, that all points of religion necessary to salvation, and touching either the mystery of our redemption in Christ, or the right use of the sacraments and true manner of worshipping God, are as purely and perfectly taught, and by public authority established, in this church of England at this day, as ever they were in any church sithence the apostles' time, or now be in any reformed church in the world: the which to be true, those that be learned (even among the mislikers of this present state) can not nor will not deny.

Likewise, that all heresies, all corrupt doctrines, all superstitious and papistical opinions, have been and be by the prince and the realm banished, by the learned bishops and preachers in word and in writing confuted, who is so blinded with malice that he cannot see, or so froward and wilful that he will not confess?

[[3] To Whitgift's "Defense" Cartwright rejoined, in a work entitled "The second replie of Thomas Cartwright: agaynst Maister Doctor Whitgiftes second answer, touching the Churche Discipline. Imprinted M.D.LXXV." It was followed by "The rest of the second replie of Thomas Cartvurihgt: against Master Doctor Vuhitgifts second ansvuer, touching the Church discipline. Imprinted M.D. LXXVII." In this "Second Replie" Cartwright thus notices Whitgift's preface:

"The answer, unto the doctor's preface: entitled 'To the godly reader,'

"To all here in controversy, considering they are barely said without proof; if they be affirmations, one yea, if they be denials, one nay, shall be enough; seeing they are all handled at large in this book. Except that of ceremonies used in popery, whereof how untruly he speaketh, when he saith that the rejecting of them standeth upon this, 'that we may not use in any wise, or in any consideration retained in the church anything that hath been abused under the pope'; both hath manifestly in my former book, and further shall (God willing) in the later part of my reply appear."]

or the things themselves, because they be abused by some men.

But to let this pass, and come to the purpose: this Reply of T. C. (which is of some counted so notable a piece of work) consisteth of two false principles and rotten pillars; whereof the one is, that we must of necessity have the same kind of government that was in the apostles' time, and is expressed in the scriptures, and no other; the other is, that we may not in any wise, or in any consideration, retain in the church anything that hath been abused under the pope: if these two posts be weak, yea rotten (as I have proved them to be in this my Defence), then must the building of necessity fall. Touching the first, it is to be understanded that there is a double government of the church, the one spiritual, the other external. Christ only, and none other, by the operation of his Spirit and direction of his word, spiritually governeth his church, and reigning in the consciences of the faithful guideth their minds in all matters of devotion, faith, and holiness; and this is the spiritual kingdom of Christ, so much spoken of in the scriptures, and specially in the prophets: of this kind of government I mean not. The external government hath both a substance and a matter about which it is occupied, and also a form to attain the same, consisting in certain offices and functions, and in the names and titles of them. The substance and matter of government must indeed be taken out of the word of God, and consisteth in these points, that the word be truly taught, the sacraments rightly administered, virtue furthered, vice repressed, and the church kept in quietness and order. The offices in the church, whereby this government is wrought, be not namely and particularly expressed in the scriptures, but in some points left to the discretion and liberty of the church, to be disposed according to the state of times, places, and persons, as I have further declared in my Answer, and Defence following. Of the second principle I have also spoken at large there; so that I shall not need to trouble the reader any further in these matters.

The proofs that T. C. useth in this his Reply are grounded only upon untrue allegations and interpretations of the scriptures, vain and childish reasons, falsifying the authorities of doctors and other writers, untruly ascribing that unto them which they wrote not; as shall be evidently declared in this Defence, by the grace of God: and surely I have not read many books wherein so many gross untruths are to be found, or wherein there is so many manifest arguments uttered, to prove the ignorance of the author, and lack of reading ancient and learned writers.

Touching his manner of writing I shall not need to say much; for any man of judgment that readeth his book may easily perceive, with what haughtiness of mind, what contempt and disdain of others, in what slanderous and opprobrious manner it is written. How oft doth he repeat "M. Doctor," in contempt either of the degree or of the person! 370 times is the least. What other speeches of disdain and reproach doth he utter! But I do nothing at all marvel at it; for I consider it hath been the usual practice of sectaries and disquieters of the church. It is true, that St Augustine saith, *Lib.* I. *contra Donatist. cap.* xi. *Nulli...schismata facerent, si fraterno odio non excæcarentur*[1]: "None would make schisms, if they were not blinded with hatred of their brethren." And again: *Annon est in schismate odium fraternum? quis hoc dixerit, cum et origo et pertinacia schismatis nulla sit alia, nisi odium fraternum*[2]? "Is there not hatred of brethren in schisms? Who would say so? seeing that the beginning and continuance of schisms proceedeth from no other cause, than from hatred of our brethren." I must therefore say with M. Zuinglius: *Scio quibus conviciis et quantis furoribus illorum hic me exponam*[3]: "I know to what reproaches and to how great rages of theirs I make myself subject." And I will conclude with him: *Quamvis miris conviciis nos perstringere, et novis quotidie clamoribus mordere non desinant, &c.*[4]: "Although they marvellously slander us, and daily with new clamours revile and backbite us, yet will I never leave off the defence of the truth before their contumacy be made known to all men." Whoso peruseth

Aug. Lib. I. contra Donatist.

Lib. de Baptismo.

Eodem.

[1 August. Op. Par. 1679—1700. De Bapt. contr. Donat. Lib. I. cap. xi. 16. Tom. IX. col. 88.]

[2 Id. ibid.; where *nisi odium fratris.*]

[3 Huld. Zvingl. Op. Tigur. 1581. De Bapt. Lib. Tract. II. Pars II. fol. 83.]

[4 Quamvis denique miris &c. quotidie calumniis mordere ... non desinant, nunquam tamen veritatis patrocinium deserturus sum,...donec illorum contumacia omnibus innotescat.—Ibid. fol. 82. 2.]

such learned authors as had great experience of the like kind of men, he shall find that their especial grace, both in speaking and writing, hath been in bitter invectives against other, whom they have envied and hated for some special causes. M. Zuinglius, in an epistle that he writeth before his book *de Baptismo*, speaking of the anabaptists, saith thus: *Hypocritica illorum humilitas illis satis nota et perspecta est, qui cum his aliquando sermones contulerunt; quam scilicet sit illorum oratio omni felle amarulentior*[1]: "Their hypocritical humility is very well known to those which have had conference with them, how that their talk is more bitter than gall." And in his book *de Baptismo*, he earnestly protesteth that he never found anything in them, *quam saturninam quandam et melancholicam ingeniorum contumaciam, &c.*[2]; and in his book against Baltasar he saith that, "by dispraising and reviling others, they seek to win credit unto themselves[3]." How this quality agreeth with some of our men, and especially with the author of this Reply, I am content that other men judge. If I myself have in writing, and in this Defence, spoken something more sharply, it must be imputed to mine infirmity; and yet am I thereunto greatly provoked: but herein, as in many other matters, I submit myself to the judgment of those that have authority to judge, and of those that be learned; for I am content still to make this the foot of my song: *Errare possum, hæreticus esse nolo*[4].

To those that be in authority I only speak as M. Zuinglius did to the magistrates in his time upon the like occasion:

In Ecclesiast. *Quod si hoc cuivis hominum impune facere licebit, ut quæ privato suæ rationis consilio adinvenit in vulgus spargat, inconsulta, imo resistente etiam universa totius ecclesiæ auctoritate, brevi plus errorum, quam fidelium et Christianorum in ecclesia erit cernere*[5]: "If it be lawful for every

---

[1 Id. Epist. præf. de Bapt. Libr. ibid. fol. 57. 2.]

[2 ...testor, me in omnibus istis rebaptismi auctoribus nihil unquam aliud, quam &c., contumaciam, vel insatiabilem honoris et gloriæ cupiditatem deprehendisse.—Id. de Bapt. Lib. Tract. II. fol. 83.]

[3 ...convitiis et calumniis tuis plusquam mordacibus favorem aliquem conciliare voluisti.—Epist. præf. ad Libell. Baltaz. Huebm. Respons. ibid. fol. 99. 2.]

[4 This sentence is ascribed to Augustine; but it does not appear literally in his works. See Works of Bishop Jewel, Park. Soc. Edit. Vol. III. p. 210, note 6.]

[5 Epist. præfat. de Bapt. Libr. ubi supr. fol. 57.]

man to publish abroad among the people those things which he hath devised of his own head, before he hath consulted with the church, nay, against the authority of the whole church, in short time we shall see more errors in the church than there be faithful men and Christians." And again: *Si* Lib. de Baptis. *enim hoc permittamus ut capitosus quisque et male feriatus homo, mox ut novum aliquid et insolens animo suo concepit, &c.*[6]*:* "If we suffer every heady and brainless fellow, so soon as he hath conceived any new thing in his mind, to publish it abroad, gather disciples, and make a new sect, in short time we shall have so many sects and factions, that Christ, which scarce with great pain and labour is brought to unity in every church, should be divided again into many parts." Wherefore, as you have singularly, and with great wisdom and labour, already restored the true religion of Christ, and banished all superstition and erroneous doctrine; "so likewise (as the same Zuinglius saith) in those perilous times, In his epistle before his book de Baptismo. wherein Satan seeketh so busily to entrap us (so that, with new contentions about external things, he goeth about to trouble those whom the sword of persecution either moved not, or terrified not), look well about you, note the crafts and subtilties of them, take heed of the pestilent winds of divers doctrine, let none trouble the gospel amongst you, or set you at strife and variance[7]." And remember that, "as the stream that cometh down from the high mountains, being caused by much rain and snow, taking every thing that it meeteth with before it, the further it goeth the greater strength and the more abundance of water it gathereth, and first removeth out of their places small stones, after with greater violence casteth down strong bridges, yea, huge and mighty rocks, and increaseth to that strength that nothing, be it of never so great force, can resist or withstand it, and in

[6 Si enim &c. concepit, illud in publicum spargens discipulos colligat, et sectam instituat novam, brevi tot sectas et factiones videre licebit, ut Christus, qui vix multo negotio et summis laboribus ad unitatem redactus est, in singulis ecclesiis in partes quam plurimas denuo scindatur.—Id. de Bapt. Lib. Tract. I. fol. 72. 2.]

[7 ...hisce periculosis temporibus, quibus tantis studiis curisque nobis insidias struit Satan, ut novis contentionibus de rebus externis concitatis eos turbare conetur, quos gladius persecutionis vel non movet, vel nondum territat, diligenter rebus vestris prospicite, notate dolos et imposturas omnium, cavete ventos variæ doctrinæ nocentissimos, ne quis evangelium vobis interturbet, vel discordes reddat.—Id. Epist. præf. de Bapt. Libr. fol. 58. 2.]

the end leaveth nothing else behind it, *quam inutilem luctum, querelas inanes, et miseram vastatorum agrorum et segetum formam*[1], but unprofitable mourning, vain complaints, and a miserable form of the spoiled fields ;" even so *contentionum pestis* [*et impia hæresis, eodem modo progrediens*], *non quicquam aliud quam turpem et calamitosam rerum faciem in florentissimo ante ecclesiæ agro post se relinquit*[2], "the plague of contention, and wicked heresy, proceeding in like manner, leaveth nothing after it but a miserable and pitiful face and shew of things in that place, which was before the flourishing field of the church." Consider what the wise man saith, Proverbs xvii. "The beginning of strife is as one that openeth the waters." It had been well if the beginning had been withstanded; but, seeing that was neglected, and rather by some furthered than stopped, yet now it is time to make up the breach. This is sufficient to you, whose wisdom and carefulness is well known to all those that be not with sinister affection blinded.

Those that be in the ecclesiastical state, and desirous to keep the peace of the church, I have only to admonish, that they be not discouraged from doing their duties, because of the slanderous reports and unchristian taunts and contumelies that our unquiet brethren lade them with; knowing that it hath been the usual practice of all sectaries, and especially of anabaptists, who count them all as wicked and ungodly, as worldings and men-pleasers, as idle and slothful, that conspire not with them in their confused platform. I may use the same exhortation to you, that M. Zuinglius used in the like time: *Nec quicquam vos moveant atroces illæ calumniæ, &c.*[3]:

Zuinglius in Ecclesiast.

[1 Ut enim torrens inundans obvia quæque rapiens quo longius progreditur, eo majores vires et undas colligit; et primo quidem minores calculos loco movens, mox frequenti impetu majores quoque lapides, imo immanes petras abripit, et effractis omnium aggerum claustris tanto fragore fertur, ut nihil tam solidum sit et constans, quod non hujus impetu fractum succumbat; nec quicquam post sese quam &c., formam relinquit.—Id. de Bapt. Lib. Tract. i. fol. 59.]

[2 Id. ibid.; where *post sese relinquat.*]

[3 Nec quicquam vos moveant atroces illæ calumniæ, quibus vos et catabaptistæ et reliqui seditionum studiosi homines deprimunt, eo quod Christi potius quam illorum partes sectemini. Licet enim vos impios et infideles nominent, interim tamen, quis vobis sit animus et quæ in Deum unum fiducia, ignorare non potestis. Quoties ergo aliquem e vobis firma fide uni Deo innitentem infidelitatis et impietatis insimulant, toties argumentum de sese produnt, quo spiritum horum ex patre mendaciorum esse videre liceat.—Id. Ecclesiast. Pars II. fol. 56.]

"Let not those bitter reproaches and cavilling speeches, wherewith the anabaptists and others studious of contention and discord oppress you, move you anything at all, because you rather follow Christ than them; for, although they call you wicked and infidels, yet yourselves best know what your confidence in God is, and what is your meaning and purpose: so that, so often as they accuse you of impiety or of infidelity, so oft do they minister manifest proofs unto you, that their spirit proceedeth from the father of lies." And marvel not at those bitter contentions: you know it to be true, that the same Zuinglius also saith: *Nec enim aliud est communis illius hostis nostri ingenium, &c.*[4]: "This is the subtilty of our common enemy, this is his manner, hereunto doth he bend himself wholly, and sleepeth not; that, as soon as the Lord hath revealed the light of his word, he also by and by soweth darnel: this do almost all the epistles of St Paul teach us, wherein it is manifestly declared that there hath been always some men, *pietatis simulatores potius quam cultores*, rather feigners of holiness than embracers of it, who, for certain external and unprofitable things, doubt not to lay (as it were) grievous stumbling-blocks to the doctrine of the gospel." Only let us be diligent in our vocation, earnest against all kind of enemies, fervent in prayers for the preservation of the queen's majesty, and for the peace of the church, with the good success of the gospel, and vigilant that errors be not published without controlment; and God will, ere it be long (if our sins deserve not the contrary), give peace to this church, as he hath done to other disturbed in like manner.

To conclude, I do charge all men before God and his angels, as they will answer at the day of judgment, that under the pretence of zeal they seek not the spoil of the church; under the colour of perfection they work not confusion; under the cloak of simplicity they cover not pride, ambition, vain-glory, arrogancy; under the outward shew of

[[4] Nec &c., ingenium, hic mos, huic denique rei unice intentus nunquam dormit: sed ut primum verbi sui lumen revelarit Dominus, ipse quoque zizania sua illico aspergit. Argumento nobis sunt hac in re omnes fere divi Pauli epistolæ, in quibus clarissime demonstratur, semper fuisse homines aliquot, pietatis &c. cultores, qui propter externa quædam et inutilia evangelicæ doctrinæ graves remoras objicere non dubitarunt.—Id. Epist. præf. de Bapt. Libr. ibid. fol. 56. 2.]

godliness they nourish not contempt of magistrates, popularity, anabaptistry, and sundry other pernicious and pestilent errors. The Lord make us thankful for his infinite mercies and singular goodness bestowed upon us, in thus long continuing his gospel, preserving our most gracious and loving queen, and overthrowing all the conspiracies and devices that the devil hath hitherto invented to molest this state and church.

¶ *To the Church of England,
and all those that love the truth in it,
T. C. wisheth mercy and peace, from God our
Father, and from our Lord Jesus Christ*[1].

As our men do more willingly go to warfare, and fight with greater courage, against strangers than against their countrymen; so it is with

[1 The following is the title to Cartwright's Reply:
A
REPLYE TO AN
anſvvere made of M.
Doctor VVhitgifte.
AGAYNSTE THE ADMONITION
to the Parliament.
By T. C.
ISAY. 62. ver. 1.
For Syons sake / I will not holde my tonge / and for Jerusa‑
lems sake / I will not rest / vntill the righteousnes
thereof / breake forthe as the lighte / and the
saluation thereof / be as a
burning lampe.
ver. 6. & 7.
Ye that are the Lordes remembrancers / kepe not
silence / and giue hym no rest / vntill he
repayre / and set by Jerusalem
the praise of the worlde.

There is no date to this book; but it was probably printed in 1573. A second impression afterwards came out with the same title-page, there being only a few slight variations of spelling, and with this advertisement:
"The Printer to the Reader.

"Some perhaps will marvel at the new impression of this book, and so much the more will they wonder because they shall see that with great confidence and boldness (notwithstanding our most gracious prince's late-published proclamation, procured rather by the bishops than willingly sought for by her majesty, whose mildness is such that she were easier led to yield to the proclamation of the Highest than drawn to proclaim anything against him, were it not for the subtile persuasions and wicked dealings of this horned generation, as by their false doctrine and cruel practices is to be seen) and by the special motion of God's Spirit and his protection it hath been both attempted and ended. But cease to muse, good christian reader, whosoever thou art; and learn to know that no laws, were they never so hard and severe, can put out the force of God's Spirit in his children, nor any cruelty, though it stretched itself so far as to shedding of blood (from which kind of dealing the bishops are not clear (as the prisons in London,

me in this spiritual warfare. For I would have wished that this controversy had been with the papists, or with other (*if any can be*) *more pestilent and professed enemies of the church; for that should have been less grief to write, and more convenient to persuade that which I desire. For, as the very name of an enemy doth kindle the desire of fighting, and stirreth up the care of preparing the furniture for the war; so I cannot tell how it cometh to pass, that the name of a brother slaketh that courage, and abateth that carefulness, which should be bestowed in defence of the truth. But, seeing the truth ought not to be forsaken for any man's cause, I enforced myself, considering that, if the Lord might lay to*[1] *my charge, that I was not, for certain considerations, so ready as I ought to have been to publish the truth, he might more justly condemn me, if, being impugned and slandered by others, I should not, according to that measure which he hath dealt unto me, and for my small ability, defend it, and deliver it from the evil report that some endeavour to bring upon it.*

An Answer to the Epistle dedicated by T. C. to the Church of England, &c.[2]

It doth not appear by the style and manner of writing used in this your book, that there remaineth any portion of such natural affection or brotherly love in you, as you would bear the world in hand and seem to have by these your words. For, if you should have written against the veriest papist in the world, the vilest person, the ignorantest dolt, you could not have used a more spiteful and malicious, more slanderous and reproachful, more contemptuous and disdainful kind of writing, than you use throughout your whole book: and truly, if you had not these two letters T. C. for your name, yet could I have easily conjectured by the haughtiness of the style, and contemptuous speeches, who had been the author of the book; so well am I acquainted with your

the Gatehouse at Westminster, &c., can witness) the Lord forgive them and us our sins), can discharge the saints and servants of the Lord from going forward in that which is good. For the profit therefore of the godly and their instruction have we hazarded ourselves, and as it were cast ourselves into such dangers and troubles as shall be laid upon us if we come into the hands of the persecuting bishops. From the which pray the Lord, if it be his will, to deliver us; if not, yet that it would please him to give us both patience to bear whatsoever he shall give them power and liberty to lay upon us, and constancy also to continue in his truth and the profession thereof unto our lives' end. Farewell in the Lord, and praise God for this work. J. S."

[1 Lay it to, T. C.'s Repl. 1 & 2.]

[2 In the second Reply Cartwright observes: "For the four first sections, being either false accusations, bare repetitions of my words, or proofs of things which I have set down and confess, I will not answer."—Sec. Repl. p. 1.]

modesty, and such experience have I of your mildness. But it is well; for now such as before have thought that you had been *sine felle,* "without gall," and that butter would not melt in your mouth, may perceive that all is not untrue that hath been reported of you. But what would they farther think, if they should compare (you being that T. C. that I take you to be) your oath which you once took when you were admitted fellow into T. C. (*Item me huic collegio fidelem et benevolum futurum; ei et omnibus sociis ac discipulis, atque etiam magistro ejusdem, non solum dum in eo vixero, sed etiam postea, pro virili, cum opus sit, benevolentiam et opem præstiturum, &c.*[3]) with this your good-will uttered throughout your whole book? Verily you might have answered as well as you have done, and had better regard both to your oath and to your brethren. But to let that pass, I doubt whether you mean good faith or no, when you would make us believe that you take us for brethren; for surely that doth not appear either by the first or second Admonition, or by this your book, if a man consider the fierceness and fiery heat, almost in every line of them, uttered against us. In the second Admonition, fol. 35, speaking of the bishops which be now, and their confederates (as you call them), these words in most spiteful manner be uttered: "And take them for better who shall, they are no other[4] but a remnant of antichrist's brood, and God amend and[5] forgive them, for else they did battle to Christ and his church, and it must bid defiance[6] to them, till they yield. And I protest before the eternal God I take them so, and thereafter will use[7] myself in my vocation, and many more too no doubt, which be careful of God his glory, and the church's liberty, will use themselves against them, as the professed enemies of the church of Christ, if they proceed in this course, and thus persecute as they do." And therefore these be but words of dalliance, when you say that you "cannot tell how it cometh to pass, that the name of a brother slaketh that courage and abateth that carefulness, which should be bestowed in the defence of the truth." Indeed it ought to have abated your outrageous and disdainful speeches, if old rancour, and desire of revenge-

The oath which the fellows of Trinity College in Cambridge do take at their admission.

2. Admo. fo. 35.

[3 Liber Statut. Coll. Trin. cap. xii. *De Sociorum electione.*]
[4 None other, Sec. Adm.]   [5 Amend them and, Sec. Adm.]
[6 Bid the defiance, Sec. Adm.]   [7 Will I use, Sec. Adm.]

ment, had not gotten in you the upper hand. For whether you deal with me like a brother, or like an utter enemy, let the indifferent reader judge.

What truth you have on your side, and how it is oppugned and slandered by such as you mean, shall (I trust) appear, when your Reply is diligently compared with my Answer. If you had meant the truth in good earnest, you would have dealt more plainly in replying than you have done: you would have set down my book, as I have done the Admonition, that the reader might have compared both together, and not have mangled it, depraved it, falsified it, and untruly collected of it, as you have done, and almost nothing else, as (God willing) shall appear. God grant that it be not laid to your charge, that you have hindered truth, slandered it, and given the common adversaries occasion to speak evil of it!

T. C.

And, as unto other parts of the gospel, so soon as the Lord openeth a door for them to enter in, there is for the most part great resistance; so in this part, concerning the government and discipline of the church, which is the order which God hath left, as well to make the doctrine most effectual, and to give as it were a sharper edge unto the preaching of the word, as also to be a wall to keep it, and make it continue amongst[1] us, I see there be sundry lets, which do, as it were with weapons, stand up to stop the passage, and to hinder that it should not be settled amongst us.

John Whitgift.

It is true that there is great resistance so soon as the Lord openeth any door to his gospel, and that by sundry means and divers kinds of men, as the stories of the church from time to time declare, and daily experience teacheth: it is also true that many, under this pretence of right government and restoring of discipline, have and do disturb the churches wherein the gospel is sincerely preached, and the sacraments rightly ministered; for further proof whereof, and avoiding of tediousness, I refer you to Master Bullinger, *Lib.* VI. *cap.* 10, *adversus Anabaptist.*[2]; to Master Calvin *adversus Anabaptist.*[3]; to Master Gualter in his epistle de-

[1 Among: T. C.'s Repl. 2.]

[2 H. Bullinger. adv. Anabapt. Libri VI. Tigur. 1560. Lib. VI. cap. x. foll. 233, &c.]

[3 Calvin. Op. Amst. 1667–71. Inst. adv. Anabapt. Tom. VIII. pp. 355, &c. See particularly pp. 360, 3, &c.]

dicatory before his commentary upon the first to the Corinthes[4]. Therefore this pretence of restoring the right government of the church, with so great disquietness of the same, is but a cover to hide the further purposes of Satan, the enemy of the peace and quietness of the church.

The pretence of restoring the right government, but a cloak for farther mischief.

T. C.

With the which albeit I wrestle hand to hand in this book, yet, forasmuch as we have all drunk so deep of the cup of untruth, that we do not only stumble at blocks, which other men lay in our way, but oftentimes we gather lets unto ourselves in framing a prejudice against the truth; I thought good to note shortly what those stumbling-blocks are, and, although I cannot remove them, yet to give warning of them, and to lend my hand to the weaker and simpler sort to help to overstride them.

Jo. Whitgift.

What these stumbling-blocks are, and how you will help the weaker and simpler sort to overstride them, we shall see in the discourse that followeth.

The Epistle of T. C. Sect. 2.

The offences which are taken herein be either in respect of the cause, or in respect of those which seek to defend and promote the cause. The cause is charged first with newness and strangeness, then as author of confusion and of disorder, and last of all as enemy to princes, magistrates, and commonwealths. For the first, besides that it is no sufficient challenge to say it is new and strange, there is no cause why it should be counted new, which is confessed of those which mislike it to have been for the most part used in the apostles' times; nor why it should be esteemed strange, which is used now far and near, of this and that side the sea, and of no strangers, but of those which are of the household of faith. And it shall more largely appear in this book, that this is no innovation, but a renovation, and the doctrine not new, but renewed, no stranger, but born in Sion, whereunto it (being before unjustly banished) ought now of right to be restored.

Jo. Whitgift.

Surely the offences are taken both in respect of the persons and of the cause: neither is, either the persons, or the cause, charged with anything by me, but I am ready either to prove it or to retract it. The antiquity of it and the strangeness we must refer to be judged of the reader when we have both written what we can. In the mean time I suppose that your devices, with the circumstances, will

[4 R. Gualther. In Prior. ad Corinth. Epist. Hom. Tigur. 1578. Præf. foll. a 3, &c.]

appear not only not to be ancient, but very strange and lately devised: although in such matters antiquity is not sufficient to prove a thing convenient, except it agree with the circumstances of time, place, and persons; much less necessary, unless it be in matters pertaining to salvation, as shall hereafter, God willing, more largely be declared; where also it will appear, that many of your assertions tend not to renovation, but innovation, and that they were never either born in Sion, or meet for Sion.

The Epistle of T. C. Sect. 3.

And of confusion and disorder it is yet more untruly accused. For justice may be as well accused for doing wrong, as this doctrine for bringing in disorder, whose whole work is to provide that nothing be done out of place, out of time, or otherwise than the condition of every man's calling will bear; which putteth the people in subjection under their governors, the governors in degree and order one under another, as the elder underneath the pastor, and the deacon underneath the elder; which teacheth that a particular church shall give place unto a provincial synod, where many churches are, and the provincial to a national, and likewise that unto the general, if any be, and all unto Christ and his word. When, on the contrary part, those which stand against this doctrine are thereby compelled to bring into the church great confusion and marvellous disorder, whilst the pastor's office is confounded with the deacon's; whilst women do minister the sacraments, which is lawful only for men; whilst private men do that which belongeth unto public persons; whilst public actions are done in private places; whilst the church is shuffled with the commonwealth; whilst civil matters are handled by ecclesiastical persons, and ecclesiastical by those which be civil; and, to be short, whilst no officer of the church keepeth his standing, and one member doth take upon it the office of another: which things as they hazard the army, and destroy the body, so they do presently hinder, and will shortly (if remedy be not provided) utterly overthrow the church. And therefore, unless good order be in that which was brought into the church by popery, and confusion in that which was left unto the church by the apostles; and that it be order, that public actions should be done in private places by private persons, and by women that is appointed to be done by men, and confusion when the contrary is observed; and, finally, unless order have another definition or nature than hitherto hath been read or heard of, there is no cause why this doctrine, which containeth the discipline and government of the church, should be thus shamefully slandered with confusion and disorder.

Jo. Whitgift.

Whereunto their opinions tend.

It will fall out, I think, that your opinions now in question tend in deed to confusion, respect neither time, place, nor persons, confound degrees, bring such in contempt as be in authority, make the ignorant subject lofty and arrogant, take from princes their due authority in ecclesiastical matters; when as present experience and the peace and quietness of this church since the beginning of the queen's majesty's reign (until you and your company began to broach these your fantasies) declareth that the doctrine maintained by those whom you count as your adversaries is most agreeable to order, preserveth peace, keepeth every man in his degree and calling. And truly, if the government of the church, now allowed by public authority, be compared with your new devised policy, the difference of them both will easily appear. For, I pray you, tell me how many of you which have been permitted as preachers in several places have consented in one kind of government, nay, which of you have not troubled, not only the town where you have remained, but the whole country round about also? so that, undoubtedly, though you be not anabaptists (as I hope you be not), yet doth this property of theirs most aptly agree unto you, that wheresoever you come you make contention and kindle the fire of discord: take it as you list, experience doth teach it to be so.

The admonitors agree not in their government.

Whether we confound the pastor's office with the deacon's or no, otherwise than it hath been in the apostles' time and primitive church; whether private men, women, civil, or ecclesiastical persons, do more than they ought to do or no; to be short, whether order, according to the true nature and definition thereof, be observed or no, I shall have better occasion hereafter to discuss. Now my meaning is to answer words with words, although in no such deriding and opprobrious manner.

The Epistle of T. C. Sect. 4.

For the third point, which is, that it is an enemy to magistrates and the commonwealth; if it be enough to accuse without proof, say[1]*, and shew no reason, innocency itself shall not be guiltless. This doctrine was in times past, even by their confession which write against it, a friend unto princes and magistrates, when princes and magistrates were enemies unto it; and can it now be an enemy unto princes and magistrates which are friends unto it? It helped and upholded the commonwealths which were governed by tyrants; and can it hinder those which are governed by godly*

[1 Proof to say, Repl. 1 & 2.]

princes? And in what is it an enemy to princes and magistrates? Note the variance, set down the enemity. If the question be, whether princes and magistrates be necessary in the church, it holdeth that the use of them is more than of the sun, without the which the world cannot stand. If it be of their honour, it holdeth that, with humble submission of mind, the outward also of the body, yea, the body itself and all that it hath, if need so require, are to be yielded for the defence of the prince, and for that service, for the which the prince will use them unto, for the glory of God, and maintenance of the commonwealth.

Jo. Whitgift.

These be but glorious words, the truth whereof shall appear when we come to the more particular declaration of the several points; and, if we accuse without proof, say and shew no reason, take your remedy against us as slanderers, and bring us to our trial[1]. Indeed, the doctrine of the gospel, which is the doctrine of salvation, hath been, is, and will be, a friend to princes and magistrates, yea, though they persecute the same; but you have not yet proved your doctrine now in question to be that doctrine of the gospel and of salvation. These words might well have been spoken of the gospel against Mahometism, Judaism, papism; but you do injury to that doctrine of life, when you confound with the same your erroneous contentions about ceremonies and the kind of government, which all being external things, I think not many will make them to be *de necessitate salutis*, "of necessity unto salvation." You have here said nothing of your doctrine but that which the Arians, the Pelagians, the papists, the Turks, yea, almost the anabaptists, will say of theirs: for many, even of the anabaptists, confess that magistrates be necessary, but yet not to be lawful for Christians to be magistrates; and, for proof thereof, they use divers of the self-same places that the Admonition hath alleged, and you allowed, against superiority in the clergy. And (except I be deceived) you come very near to them, for you will have the ecclesiastical and civil government so distinct, that they can by no means concur in one and the self-same persons; whereby

[1 Cartwright accuses Whitgift here of "falling to railing," and goes on: "For himself cannot deny but the government by elders, the choice of the ministers by the church, the most of those things which he especially supposeth to have war with the civil magistrate, and are in controversy between us, were in the times of the apostles, when they, being trodden under feet of the civil magistrate did never lift up their heel against his power."—Sec. Repl. p. 1.]

you take from the civil magistrate authority in ecclesiastical matters, and by that means spoil him of the one half of his jurisdiction. But of this matter more at large hereafter, as occasion shall be ministered by you. In the mean time, I admonish the reader to believe your words no farther than he shall see just proof of them.

T. C.

If it be asked of the obedience due unto the prince and unto the magistrate, it answereth that all obedience in the Lord is to be rendered; and, if it come to pass that any other be asked, it so refuseth that it disobeyeth not, in preferring obedience to the great God before that which is to be given to mortal man. It so resisteth, that it submitteth the body and goods of those that profess it, to abide that which God will have them suffer in that case.

Jo. Whitgift.

All this is truly spoken of the doctrine of the gospel, but not of the doctrine in controversy amongst us: and verily this is not plain dealing[2] to make the reader believe that we do withstand the doctrine of the gospel, when we only resist your contentions about external matters, whereby the doctrine of the gospel is hindered, and the church of Christ disturbed.

T. C.

And, if it be shewed that this is necessary for the church, it cannot be but profitable for the commonwealth: nay, the profit of it may easily appear, for that by the censures and discipline of the church, as they are in this book described, men are kept back from committing of great disorders, of stealing, adultery, murder, &c.; whilst the smaller[3] faults of lying, and uncomely jesting, of hard and choleric speeches, which the magistrate doth not commonly punish, be corrected.

Jo. Whitgift.

If it be necessary for the present state of the church, it is also profitable for the present state of the commonwealth; for I perceive no such distinction of the commonwealth and the church that they should be counted, as it were, two several bodies, governed with divers laws and divers magis-

---

[2 "He needed not to have charged us with want of plain dealing, seeing we offer to shew the discipline to be a part of the gospel."—Sec. Repl. p. 1.]

[3 Smallest, Repl. 2.]

What ecclesiastical functions the civil magistrate may not take upon him.

trates, except the church be linked with an heathenish and idolatrous commonwealth. The civil magistrate may not take upon him such ecclesiastical functions as are only proper to the minister of the church, as preaching of the word, administering of the sacraments, excommunicating, and such like; but that he hath no authority in the church to make and execute laws for the church, and in things pertaining to the church, as discipline, ceremonies, &c. (so that he do nothing against the word of God), though the papists affirm it never so stoutly, yet is the contrary most true, and sufficiently proved by men of notable learning, as Master Jewel, bishop of Salisbury, Master Horne[1], bishop of Winchester, Master Nowel[2], dean of Paul's, in their books written against papists holding your assertion; to whose painful and learned writings I refer the reader, for the avoiding of too much prolixity.

I do not well understand what is meant by these words, "Nay, the profit of it may easily appear, for that by the censures and discipline of the church, as they are in this book described, men are kept back from committing of greater disorders, of stealing, adultery, murder, &c.; whilst the smaller faults, of lying, and uncomely jesting, of hard and choleric speeches, which the magistrate doth not commonly punish, be corrected." Do you not think the punishment for stealing and murder to be sharp enough? or do you think that the fear of the discipline of the church will more terrify men from these vices than the fear of death? or do you doubt whether the civil magistrate hath authority to appoint any other punishment for these, and such like crimes, than is prescribed in the judicial law of Moses? (for this is now called in controversy, and beginneth to be table-talk;) or are you persuaded that the civil magistrate either may not, or will not, correct "lying, uncomely jesting, hard and choleric speeches?" or that, if these were punished by the discipline of the church, men would rather be terrified from the greater crimes than they will be if they be punished with civil correction? Truly I think that the civil magistrate hath sufficient authority to provide remedies for all such mischiefs,

[1 Bishop Horne wrote "An Answeare made by Rob. Bishoppe of Wynchester to a Booke, &c, by M. Iohn Fekenham, Lond. 1566."]

[2 Nowel was engaged in controversy with Dorman: a list of his writings may be seen in Churton's Life of Nowel, Sect. vi.]

without altering the state, either of the church, or of the commonwealth. But let the indifferent reader judge whether you go about to wring the sword out of the magistrate's hand or no, or, at the least, so to order the matter, that it be never drawn out to punish vice, but with the consent, and at the appointment of you and your seigniory[1].

T. C.

And, undoubtedly, seeing that the church and commonwealth do embrace and kiss one another, and seeing they be like unto Hippocrates' twins, which were sick together and well together, laughed together and weeped together, and always like affected; it cannot be but that the breaches of the commonwealth have proceeded from the hurts of the church, and the wants of the one from the lacks of the other: neither is it to be hoped for that the commonwealth shall flourish, until the church be reformed.

Jo. Whitgift.

All this I grant (and God be thanked therefore): if we shall measure the state of the church with the flourishing estate and wise government of the commonwealth, we shall have no great cause to complain, but to burst out into most hearty thanks unto God for the same, and most humbly desire the continuance thereof.

I do not say that the church is without fault, for then should I affirm an impossibility; but I think the faults that are, rather to be in the persons than in the laws, rather in the governors than in the kind of government: neither would I have men (either puritans, Donatists, or anabaptists) to dream of such a church, as Plato did of a commonwealth, Aristotle of felicity, and the Stoics of their just man; much less to make contention in the church, or divide themselves from the same if all things go not according to their fantasy; for then shall they never be quiet with any church, no, not long with that church which they themselves do presently best like of. Surely, if this rule be certain, that "the common- *The rule of T. C.* wealth shall not flourish, until the church be reformed," then *returned against* this may be a good token unto us that this church of En- *himself.*

[¹ Cartwright in reply coarsely accuses Whitgift of misrepresenting him, declares that he meant that ecclesiastical censures being joined with civil punishments "have more force to resist sin than the civil punishments only," and denies that he wrings "the sword by these words out of the magistrate's hand."—Sec. Repl. pp. 2, 3.]

gland is reformed, because the commonwealth doth flourish[1]. Neither do I speak this to flatter the magistrates, and to sew cushions under their elbows (as it pleaseth some to report), but I speak it before God, I speak it as I think; and the rather I utter it, to deliver both the state of the church, and also of the commonwealth of England, from the unthankful, unnatural, and slanderous tongues of such as seek to deface and deprave them both.

I will not defend the vice, the negligence, the security of any man; I shall be as bold and as ready to tell even the best thereof in time and place (as occasion is ministered, and my duty shall require), as any of those shall be which would seem to be farthest from all kind of flattery.

T. C.

And it is also certain, that as the church shall every day more and more decay, until it be made even with the ground, unless the walls be builded, and the ruins repaired; so the weight of it (if it fall) will either quite pull down the commonwealth, or leave it such as none which fear God will take any pleasure in it. For, seeing Salomon saith that Prov. viii. 15.[2] *"by wisdom (which is the word of God) kings do govern, and princes do bear rule;" it cannot be but, as that wisdom is either contemned, or[3] neglected, or otherwise abridged of her free and full course, so princes and magistrates, and consequently their commonwealths, either go to wrack, or decay, or, at the least, want so much of the[4] flourishing estate, as there wanteth of that word of God which he hath appointed to be their stay. And, howsoever (before the coming of our Saviour Christ) amongst the Athenians, Lacedæmonians, and Romans, and since his coming in divers places where this wisdom hath not been heard of, there may seem to have been some shews of either flourishing or tolerable commonwealths, yet neither have those endured, but, according to the prophecy of* Dan. ii. 34.[2] *Daniel, have been broken all to pieces; so that there is not so much of them left as a sherd to fetch fire in: neither yet can those kingdoms which have the knowledge of the gospel revealed unto them look for that long-suffering and patience of God towards them, wherewith those[5] ignorant kingdoms have been borne with. For, as the benefit is greater towards these than towards the other, so is the judgment swifter against them than against the other, if that grace which was not offered unto them, being offered unto these, be refused and made light of. And in these especially is, and shall be, fulfilled that which the prophet Esay*

[1 Cartwright insinuates in his Reply, that there were "divers cracks in the commonwealth."—Sec. Repl. p. 4.]
[2 These references are inserted from Repl. 2.]
[3 *Or* is not in Repl. 2.]
[4 Their, Repl. 1 & 2.]   [5 These, Repl. 1 & 2.]

Isai. lx. 12. saith, that it shall be in the later days, that "every nation and kingdom which shall not serve the church shall be destroyed:" as, of the other side, the full and whole placing of our Saviour Christ in his throne is the perpetual stay and stayed perpetuity of all princes in their seats.

Jo. Whitgift.

All this is true; for, if any nation shall refuse the word of God offered unto it, or not suffer Christ wholly to be placed in his throne, no doubt God will pour upon that nation his plagues, as he hath done upon all other that have run into the same contempt[6]. But would you make your reader believe that, because this church of England doth not admit your kind of government, therefore the walls of it be broken, the word of God contemned, and Christ not suffered wholly to be placed in his throne? We admit the gospel wholly; and in government the magistrates take upon them no office only proper to Christ, neither yet any authority which is not by the word of God limited unto them. These words might aptly have been spoken, if you had written against the state of the church in France, or any such like kingdom as refuseth the gospel offered unto it, and most cruelly persecuteth the true professors of the same. I do not excuse such in the church of England as contemn the word of God, neither do I justify the whole church for not receiving the gospel offered, by bringing forth the fruits thereof as it ought to do. But I exhort every man, from the highest to the lowest, even in the bowels of Jesus Christ, to have a better regard thereunto, lest it be said unto us, as it is said unto the church of Ephesus, *Apoc.* ii. *Sed habeo adversum te,* Rev. ii. *quod caritatem tuam pristinam, &c.:* "I have something against thee, because thou hast forsaken thy former love, &c.;" and to the Hebrews, vi.: "For the earth, which drinketh in Heb. vi. rain that cometh oft upon it, and bringeth forth herbs meet for them by whom it is dressed, receiveth blessing of God. But that which beareth thorns and briers is reproved, and is near unto cursing, whose end is to be burned." For surely even these contentions, stirred up in the church where the gospel is truly preached, are arguments that we be void

[6 Cartwright rejoins that the discipline is "a part of the gospel," and therefore the refusal of it "must needs arm the Lord against the refusers."—Sec. Repl. p. 4.]

of love and peace, the chief and principal tokens and fruits of the gospel.

T. C.

And therefore, if this book shall come into the hands of any that have access unto her majesty, the head of this commonwealth, and[1] unto her most honourable council, the shoulders thereof, my humble suit and hearty request in the presence of God is that, according as their callings will suffer them, they will put them in remembrance of these things, which otherwise they know better than I; and that they would set before them the example of Moses, who was not contented to have brought the Deut. iii. 25.[2]

T. C. maketh greater account of the government than of the gospel itself; for he likeneth the state of this church to the wandering in the wilderness.[3]

people out of Egypt, but would very fain also have conducted them into the land of Canaan, that is, would gladly have been the instrument of the full and whole deliverance of the people; and, seeing that the Lord doth offer them[4] this honour, which he denied unto his servant Moses, that they would not make themselves guilty of so great unthankfulness, as will follow of the forsaking of so incomparable a benefit; that her majesty especially, and her most honourable council, would set before them the example of David, who although he made a great reformation of those things which were defaced by Saul, yet he 2 Sam. vii. 2.[2] *was not content that the ark of the Lord should dwell under* Psal. cxxxii.[2] *a tabernacle, and therefore desired marvellously that he might build the temple unto the Lord. And, seeing that the Lord hath granted unto[5] them (which he denied unto his servant), that they would not be narrow and strait in themselves, seeing the Lord openeth the treasures of his goodness so largely unto them; that they would set before them the zeal of Zerubbabel, who, although he had (after the return out* Ezra iii. 3, *of captivity) abolished idolatry, laid the foundations of the* 10.[2] *temple, and set up an altar unto God, whereupon the morning and evening sacrifice was daily made; yet, being admonished by the prophet Agge, that God would not be pleased, unless the temple also* Hag. i. 14.[2] *were fully builded, did (all fear of the nations round about and other business[6] laid aside) cause it forthwith, and with all possible speed, to be made an end of. Finally, that it would please them to consider the examples of Josias, Ezechias, and Jehoshaphat, who are there-* 2 Kings xxii. xxiii.[2] *fore, to their everlasting commendation, praised of the Holy* 2 Kings *Ghost, for that they made whole and thorough reformations;* xviii.[2] 2 Chron. *whereas the honour of other some (albeit they were otherwise* xvii.[2]

That is, they suffered manifest idolatry; wherewith you can by no means charge this church of England; and therefore your application is unfit.

good) is stained, and carrieth the mark of their imperfection by this and like exception, that, although they did such good things and such, yet they left also such and such undone.

[1 Or, Repl. 1, 2, & Def. A.]
[2 These references are inserted from Repl. 2.]
[3 Cartwright calls this "a manifest untruth, for I speak of the discipline as of a part of the gospel, and therefore neither under nor above the gospel, but the gospel."—Sec. Repl. p. 5.]
[4 Offer unto them, Repl. 1 & 2.]
[5 Granted that unto, Repl. 1 & 2.]   [6 Businesses, Repl. 1 & 2.]

Jo. Whitgift.

And why is not her majesty the head of this church also, as well as of this commonwealth[7]? For I must give thee to understand, good reader, that T. C. maketh the church and the commonwealth two such distinct and several bodies, as must of necessity have distinct and several magistrates and governors, and that the civil magistrate hath not to meddle in ecclesiastical matters, except his aid be required by the pastor and seigniory, or such like cases: wherein he flatly joineth with the papists, who say that the civil magistrate hath only *potestatem facti*, and not *juris*, that is, authority to execute such things as they decree, but not authority to make any laws in ecclesiastical matters. And, lest you should think that I feign this, consider the whole scope of his book, and particularly his words before-mentioned in this leaf, where as he accuseth the government of this church, now in practice, of confusion, because "civil matters are handled by ecclesiastical persons, and ecclesiastical matters by those which be civil[8];" also that which he speaketh of this matter, foll. 144 and 154, and especially that which the second Admonition hath, foll. 8, 9, 57, 60. I know not how he could have made a greater difference betwixt the church and the commonwealth, in those places where the princes be enemies unto the church. Indeed true it is, that in the apostles' time princes did not meddle in causes ecclesiastical, except it were by persecuting, &c. For they were then infidels, not Christians, persecutors, not professors; and therefore, if all ought of necessity to be reduced to the form of government used in the apostles' time, christian princes must be delivered from that care, and be content to forego that portion of their authority. But hereof more in the due place: this I only here note, that you may the better consider the same in the perusing of his book.

The rest of that which is contained in this part may have some use, if it be rightly applied; for godly princes have to follow such godly examples, and to be diligent in reforming such things as are to be reformed, either in substance, circumstances, or persons.

[7 Here Cartwright declares that Whitgift "hath broken his bridle again," and denies that there is any "head of the church but only Christ."—Sec. Repl. pp. 4, 5.]   [8 See before, page 18.]

T. C.

Which I do not speak, as though we had not already, by her majesty especially, and afterward by their honours' hands, received a singular benefit; but that we, having the whole, might have our hearts and mouths filled with the praise of God, and continue the possession of that which we have, which otherwise, for our unthankful refusal, shall be taken away. Wherein, as we have especial regard that the name of God should be magnified, not by us alone, but by our posterity unto[1] the world's end; so it is[2] not the smallest part of our care, that her majesty and your honours, to whom we are so deeply bound, and of whom we have received so singular benefits of peace and preaching of the gospel, might with your successions continue and flourish amongst us for ever. But the desire of reformation, and fear of God's heavy wrath to come upon us, hath carried me further herein than I purposed. I will therefore make an end of these points, considering that the untruth of these accusations, of newness and strangeness, of disorder and confusion, of being enemy to princes and commonwealths, shall better appear in the discourse of this book.

Jo. Whitgift.

These be smooth words to win credit by; but they agree not with the rest of your book; wherefore I doubt not but that they will be considered of accordingly. I would to God that you did indeed acknowledge that "singular benefit" that you have received "by her majesty and their honours:" then truly would you have shewed yourself more thankful than you have done, neither would you have maintained libels which seek utterly to deface all that is done, as will manifestly hereafter by further examination appear. Whatsoever accusations have been made of your doctrine, if they be not justified, then let the authors of them suffer the shame. Surely you have as slenderly answered these accusations hitherto, as may be.

The Epistle of T. C. Sect. 5, 6, 7.

Amongst the offences taken by occasion of those which prefer the[3] doctrine, this is the chiefest, that, comparison being made betwixt[4] those excellent men, both in virtue and learning, which suffered for the testimony of the truth, and between us of the one side, also between the archbishops, bishops, deans, and archdeacons, which now are, and us on the other side, it seemeth unto many that it is not like to be good which was not found out by those excellent personages, and which, being now propounded by men of no great

[1 To, Repl. 1 & 2.]   [2 Is it, Repl. 1 & 2.]
[3 This, Repl. 1 & 2.]   [4 Between, Repl. 1 & 2.]

shew, is either misliked, or, at the least, by no open approbation allowed, of those which carry greater countenances, and be in greater dignities.

Unto the first, although answer is made more at large in this book, yet I will add thus much, that as, for my part, I confess myself to be a great deal inferior unto the least of them; so the omitting of these necessary things ought to be no more prejudice against them, or against those that prefer them, than the omitting of the celebration of the feast of tabernacles so many hundred years, by so many good high priests, in the reigns of so many good kings, was prejudicial unto the ministers which caused it to be celebrated when the people returned out of their captivity; for it appeareth Chap. viii. *in the book of Nehemias, that the feast of tabernacles, which* 17, 18.[5] *was commanded of the Lord to be celebrated every year, was not celebrated[6] from the days of Josua, the son of Nun, until the return of the people from their captivity. And yet were there in this space divers both judges and kings, both priests and prophets, singularly zealous and learned.* This is a manifest untruth, as shall appear.

If therefore the omitting of so necessary a thing so many hundred years, by such godly, zealous, learned persons, could not bring any prescription against the truth; the lack of this necessary discipline by the space of thirty years, through the oversight of a few (if they be compared with that multitude), ought not to be alleged to keep it out of the church.

Jo. Whitgift.

Surely the inequality of the persons, and great difference betwixt them, both in godliness, zeal, learning, experience, and age (though it seem a small matter to some), yet it ought to be well considered; for it is well known that the first sort of men here mentioned did excel in all those forenamed qualities, and have continued in the same even to the death[7]; and the latter sort, many of them singular in learning, zeal, wisdom, and experience, having also knowledge of other churches reformed more than you (howsoever it pleaseth you and some of your companions undutifully to contemn them): wherefore, as I said, this comparison is something, and not so lightly to be esteemed, as you would make the reader

[[5] The verses are inserted from Repl. 2.]

[[6] Here Repl. 2 adds, *in such sort as it was commanded in the law.*]

[[7] Cartwright rejoins, that "it ought not seem strange unto us if those famous martyrs were ignorant of some principal point commanded by the word of God." He urges that Justin and Cyprian were martyrs and yet maintained erroneous doctrines, and asserts the same of some of those who had lately suffered: "I have not the book by me, but I well remember there mentioned of a notable man, and of the later martyrs, which affirmeth a very gross descent of our Saviour Christ into hell; which is an error in one of the articles of our faith. Another granting such a purgatory after this life as the papists do imagine, and others also divers failing in substantial points of doctrine."—Sec. Repl. pp. 6, 7.]

believe. For my part I think the worse of you, because you think so well of yourselves, that you dare be so bold, as not only to compare yourselves with them, but to prefer yourselves before them. As for this humility, and abasing yourself in saying, that you confess yourself "to be a great deal inferior to the least of them," he that will take pains but to peruse your book, shall easily understand that you think nothing less. For truly your style is so big and lofty, and your taunts such towards them and others, that a man would think you not only to have cast off all modesty, but utterly to have forgotten all good manners, civility, and duty. But it is rhetoric common to you with other of your companions, as appeareth in divers places of the first Admonition, and in the second throughout the whole; which I would wish the reader to consider, that he may thereby partly know and discern your spirit.

But say you, "the omitting of these necessary things ought to be no more prejudice against them," &c. Surely, if you can prove that they have omitted any thing expressly against the commandment of God, then is it true that you say; but, if you cannot do so, then do you unjustly charge these learned and godly martyrs. But what if you have *The feast of tabernacles was not so long omitted.* abused the place in the 8 chapter of Nehemias? What if you understand it not truly? What if there can be no such thing gathered of it, as you would make the reader believe? Shall I triumph over you, and say, that either "you have not read it," or "you do not understand it," or that "you wittingly and willingly abuse it," or "that you received it in some notes from others," as it pleaseth you to deal with me, when no such occasion is offered unto you? I will not so requite you; but this only I say, that you have not set down the true sense of that place: for the meaning is not, "that the *The true interpretation of the place alleged out of the viii. of Nehemias.* feast of tabernacles was not celebrated from the time of Josua the son of Nun, until that day, which was almost a thousand years," but that it was not celebrated in that manner, that is, with such solemnity, so great rejoicing and gladness; as the very words themselves declare, both in the Hebrew text and in the best translations. And so doth Pellican *Pell. in Neh. viii.* expound that place, who saith that these words, "'since the time of Josua the son of Nun, &c.' be spoken in the respect of the greatness of the joy which then happened to the people¹." Lyra also expoundeth the same place much after the same sort, and presupposeth nothing less, than that the feasts were omitted all this time; for he affirmeth that they were "much more solemnly, and with greater cost, celebrated in the times of David and Salomon:" therefore, saith he, "the comparison is *secundum quid, et proportionaliter* (for I use his words), because, in all this time sithence Josua it is not read that the people were so generally gathered together in Hierusalem, as we read in the beginning of this chapter, that they were at this time²:" and again he saith, that "it was more for the people, newly returned from captivity, to celebrate such a feast with that solemnity, than it was to mighty kings and people, being in prosperity and settled in a kingdom, to celebrate the same day with much more cost and solemnity³." I might allege other expositors to the same effect; neither have I read any that doth expound that place otherwise⁴. _{Lyra in Neh. viii.}

The like kind of speech we have, 2 Reg. xxiii., where it is said, that "there was no passover holden like that (which Josias held) from the days of the judges that judged Israel, nor in all the days of the kings of Israel, and the kings of Juda:" which is only spoken in respect of the multitude and zeal of the people, with the great preparation; and not because the passover was not all this time celebrated. The like is also used, 2 Chron. xxx. ver. 26. Even so it is in this place; for there is no doubt but that the feast of taber- _{2 Kings xxiii.} _{2 Chron. xxx. 26.}

[¹ ...ut a tempore Josue per excessum dicatur amplius gaudium populo non contigisse. Sic enim loquitur scriptura, ut solent homines communiter loqui... Id enim significatur in fine versus, Et fuit lætitia magna valde.—Comment. Biblior. Op. C. Pellican. Tigur. 1536—46. Neh. cap. viii. Tom. II. fol. 270. 2.]

[² Non est intelligendum quod ista solennitas fuerit simpliciter major quam aliqua quæ fuerit intermedio tempore prædicto; quia temporibus quibus floruit regnum, scilicet tempore David et Salamonis, fuerunt pluries facta tabernaculorum festa solennior aquam istud: sed ista comparatio accipitur secundum quid: et proportionabiliter: quia tempore intermedio prædicto non legitur populus sic fuisse generaliter congregatus in Hierusalem quasi vir unus: ut dicitur in principio hujus capituli.—Bibl. cum Gloss. Ord. et Expos. N. de Lyra. Basil. 1502. Neh. cap. viii. Pars III. fol. 263.]

[³ ...majus fuit illis qui de captivitate redierant facere tale festum quam regibus potentibus et populo existenti in statu potentissimo facere festa multo majora simpliciter.—Id. ibid.]

[⁴ Cartwright replies that the keeping of the feast of tabernacles "with boughs" had been in times past omitted, and that there was "a general ignorance of the manner of solemnizing" it, " even in Ezra the high priest."—Sec. Repl. pp. 8, 9.]

nacles was celebrated both in David and Salomon's time; and it is manifest that it was celebrated not long before this time; as it is in plain words expressed, 1 Esdras cap. iii. ver. 4. Wherefore I might make much ado at this oversight of yours, or rather wilful depraving of the scriptures, if I were delighted with that kind of confuting. But, though my learning be small, and that I am "ignorant both of logic and philosophy, and have read so little in divinity," and you so mighty a man in the scriptures, and so profound in all kind of knowledge, as you persuade yourself to be; yet you must be content here to be admonished of me, that you have abused this place, and that it serveth not for your turn, to prove those godly men, which suffered martyrdom in queen Mary's time, to have permitted anything in this church of England (after it was reformed) expressly contrary to the commandment and word of God, as you untruly report "so many good high priests in the reigns of so many good kings, so many hundred years to have omitted the feasts of tabernacles, expressly by God commanded:" although I do not deny but such men also may sometimes be overseen in some points; but neither can you prove that they were deceived in any substantial point of doctrine, neither yet, if they were, is this place aptly or truly alleged.

Ezra iii. 4.

The Epistle of T. C. Sect. 8.

The dignity also and high estate of those which are not so earnest in this cause cannot hinder it, if we consider the wisdom of God almost from time to time to consist and to shew itself most in setting forth his truth by the simpler and weaker sort, by contemptible and weak instruments, by things of no value, to the end that, when all men see [1] *the baseness and rudeness of the instrument, they might the more wonder at the wisdom and power of the Artificer, which with so weak and foolish instruments bringeth to pass so wise and mighty things. And, if men will with such an eye of flesh look upon matters, they shall condemn that excellent reformation made under the godly king Josias*[2], *which the Holy Ghost doth so highly commend; in which it is witnessed that the Levites, which were a degree under the priests, were more forward and more zealous than the priests themselves; yea, wherein it is witnessed that the people were yet more earnest and more willing than either the Levites or the priests, which thing, if ever, is verified in our time.*

1 Cor. i. 27, 28.[1]

2 Chron. xxix. 34.[1]
2 Chron. xxx. 15.[1]

Josias is here alleged for Ezekias. This place is not rightly interpreted.

[¹ The verses are inserted from Repl. 2.]
[² Reformation under the godly king Ezechias, Repl. 2.]

For, when I consider the zeal for religion which sheweth itself in many, A manifest flattery, and *as well of the nobility and gentry of this realm, as of the people, their care* the scripture abused to *to continue it and advance it, their voluntary charges to maintain it, their* colour it. *liberality towards them which bend themselves that way; as I do thereby conceive some hope of the favourable countenance and continuance of God's goodness towards us, so I cannot be but ashamed of mine own slackness, and afraid of the displeasure of the Lord, for that those, whose proper work this is especially, and which should bear the standard and carry the torch unto the rest, are so cold and so careless in these matters of the Lord.*

JO. WHITGIFT.

I know none among us, which in the respect of his dignity and high estate seeketh or desireth to be preferred or believed before you, but in the respect of the cause, which is the peace of the church, suppression of schisms, and the truth itself. No man denieth but God of his wisdom, in the God useth not the beginning of the church of Christ, poured out his gifts more simple only, or always, to plenteously upon the simpler, contemptible, and weaker sort, set forth his truth. and that he choosed for his apostles fishermen, toll-gatherers, and ignorant persons, lest that should be ascribed to the wit, eloquence, and learning of man, which cometh only of the goodness, might, and power of God; as the apostle plainly declareth, 1 Cor. i. and ii. But will you therefore conclude that truth, zeal, and godliness, remaineth either only or especially in the simple, rude, and ignorant sort? and make this your conclusion, The learned, the honourable, men of great countenance or knowledge, be of this or that opinion; *ergo*, it is not true? Or, The simple, rude, and ignorant people are thus and thus persuaded; *ergo*, they must be followed; or to the like effect? Verily, this were to reason as the Franciscan friars do to excuse their ignorance: *Apostoli nesciebant literas; ergo, Franciscanis non est opus literis;* and like some other fantastical persons also, which think that no learned, rich, or honourable man shall be saved, but only beggars, and such as be ignorant, as M. Gualter testifieth Gualt. in 1 Cor. i. in his commentaries upon 1 Cor. i.[3] Hom. 7.

You know (as I suppose) that this place of the 1 Cor. i., quoted in your margent, doth not gather any such conclusion,

[[3] Nimis ergo odiose hoc loco fanatici quidam abutuntur, qui omnes damnationi obnoxios esse judicant, qui vel non stupidi prorsus, aut errones atque mendici fuerint.—R. Gualther. In Prior. ad Corinth. Epist. Hom. Tigur. 1578. cap. i. Hom. vii. fol. 16. 2.]

that therefore the doctrine is not true, because princes, nobles, wise and learned men, &c. do allow of it; or therefore it is true, because it pleaseth the simple, rude, and ignorant people. For Nicodemus, Joseph, Lazarus Betha., Sergius Paulus, Dionysius Areopagita, Crispus, Gaius, Erastus, with divers others, were politic, wise, wealthy, learned, and honourable men; and the prophet Esay saith that "kings and queens shall be the nursing fathers and mothers," the defenders and maintainers of the church. And Bullinger in his commentaries upon this place doth thus expound it: "He speaketh of the first calling especially, wherein fishermen and idiots[1] were especially called to the preaching of the gospel. For no man can deny but that, after the gospel was confirmed in the world, the best-learned embraced the truth. For first shepherds declared that Christ was born: then the *magi*, that is, the wise men of the east, came to salute him with gifts[2]." Wherefore, I pray you, let not the wealth, calling, or dignity, which you think we have, prejudice our cause. The simple and plain meaning of the place is, that God in his electing to eternal life hath neither respect to nobility, learning, riches, or any such thing[3].

I might here again trip you for alleging Josias instead of Ezechias, and say that you had not read the scriptures, or that you used other men's notes, and so dally with you as you use to do with others; but I will leave such kind of gibes to brabbling sophisters in the schools, and think that it was some light oversight, which in such a case may sometimes happen to him that is most circumspect.

Your collection upon that place, 2 Chron. xxix. and xxx., I cannot as yet allow, until I be better instructed therein: for, whereas you say that it is there witnessed "that the Levites, which were a degree under the priests, were more forward and more zealous than the priests themselves, and

[1 Idiots: ἰδιῶται—private, obscure men.]

[2 Loquitur autem de prima vocatione potissimum, qua piscatores et idiotæ ad evangelii prædicationem vocati sunt. Nemo enim negare potest confirmato jam in orbe evangelio doctissimos quosque accidisse veritati ecclesiasticæ. Primum quidem pastores Christum nunciant esse natum: deinde vero salutatum muneribus accedunt magi sive orientis sophi.—H. Bullinger. In Omn. Apostol. Epist. Comm. Tigur. 1558. In 1 ad Cor. cap. i. p. 131.]

[3 Cartwright denies that "the true and simple meaning of St James in this place is, that God in his eternal election hath no regard to riches or poverty."—Sec. Repl. p. 11.]

the people more earnest and more willing than either the Levites or the priests;" I see not how you can gather any such thing out of either of these two chapters: for, if there be any sentence to gather it of in the 29. chapter, it is the 34. verse; which, although in some translation it seem to insinuate some such thing, yet, if credit may be given to those that be notable learned men, and very well seen in the Hebrew tongue, the meaning of that place is nothing less. Pellican translateth the words thus: *Levitæ quippe faciliori ritu sanctificantur quam sacerdotes:* "For the Levites were sooner or easier sanctified than the priests;" which he expoundeth more plainly in his commentaries, saying: *Intelligitur sacerdotum numerum imminutum fuisse, &c.*[4]: "It is to be understood that the number of the priests was diminished, which should have sufficed for to prepare the sacrifices, and therefore they desired the help of the Levites, that all things might be done more diligently: there was also another cause of the Levites' help; for the sanctifying of the temple and the preparation of the sacrifice was so suddenly commanded, that many of the priests had not time to sanctify themselves according to the law, which required a certain space for the same; and the Levites might be sanctified with less ado, and in shorter time." And surely even the very circumstances of the place doth prove this to be the true understanding of it; for these be the words that immediately go before: "But the priests were too few, and were not able to flay all the burnt-offerings; therefore their brethren the Levites did help them until they had ended the work, and until other priests were sanctified."

Pell. in 2 Chion. xxxix.

2 Chron. xxix. 34.

Your second assertion, that is, "that the people were yet more earnest and more willing than either the Levites or the priests," I think is grounded upon the 15. verse of the 30. chapter, which is this: "Afterward they slew the passover the fourteen day of the second month; and the priests and

2 Chron. xxx. 15.

[4 Intelligitur sacerdotum numerum imminutum fuisse, qui pro parandis sacrificiis non suffecerint, ideoque Levitarum operas postulasse, quo omnia perficerentur diligentius. Alia quoque adjicitur ratio Levitici subsidii, quia negotium totum sacrificandi et templum reconciliandi subito imperatum fuerat et tentatum, ita ut sacerdotum multi non se legitime purificare potuerint, quod ea lapsu temporis fieret secundum legem. Levitæ autem minori opera levius et citius mundabantur, et suis functionibus parabantur.—Comment. Biblior. Op. C. Pellican. Tigur. 1536—46. 2. Paral. cap. xxix.T om. II. fol. 249.]

Levites were ashamed, and sanctified themselves, and brought the burnt-offerings into the house of the Lord." Truly I see not how you can collect any such thing out of these words[1]: I know that some do gather such a note of that place, but I do not understand the reason of it. Howsoever it be, and howsoever you abuse the scriptures to justify yourselves, I doubt not but that a great number of those whom you contemn and seek to deface do presently, and will to their lives' end, shew that zeal of religion, that diligence in their calling, that uprightness in conversation which becometh them, and which they are well assured pleaseth God: neither do I in so saying condemn the godly zeal of any; but I admonish all to take heed of a preposterous and affectionated zeal, such as is spoken of in the 30. page of the second edition of my Answer to the Admonition[2].

The Epistle of T. C. Sect. 9.

And I humbly crave, and most earnestly desire, of those which bear the chief titles in the ecclesiastical functions, that, as we do in part correct our negligence by the example of the forwardness and readiness of the people, so they would suffer themselves to be put in remembrance of their duties by us which are underneath them, and that they would not neglect this golden gift of God's grace, in admonishing them, because the Lord doth offer it in a treene[3] *or earthen vessel; but that they would first consider that, as Naaman, the Syrian prince, received great commodity by fol-* 2 Kings v. 4, *lowing the advice of his maid, and, after, of his man; and* 14.[4] *Abigail, being a wise woman, singular profit by obeying the* 1 Sam. xxv. 18.[4] *counsel of her servant; so they may receive oftentimes profitable advertisement by those which are in lower places than they themselves be. Then let them think that, as Naaman was never the less noble for obeying the voice of his servants, nor Abigail never the less wise, because she listened unto the words of her man, so it cannot diminish their true honour, nor impair the credit of their godly and uncounterfeit wisdom, if they give ear unto that which is spoken by their inferiors.*

Jo. Whitgift.

This humility appeareth to be counterfeit by the opprobrious speeches and great contempt that you shew towards them in the rest of this book.

What diligence you are provoked unto by the forward-

[[1] Cartwright in his Second Reply strongly insists upon his interpretation of the passages referred to.]
[[2] See below, page 138.]   [[3] Treene: wooden.]
[[4] These references are inserted from Repl. 2.]

ness and readiness of the people, I know not; but every man may see you are ready to shake off your calling upon every light occasion. Neither will you preach in those places where the gospel hath not been so well planted; but there only you loiter where there is less need, and where you easily may make stirs and move contention, as experience sufficiently teacheth.

I know none, no, not of the best, that refuseth to hear either you or any other modestly admonishing; neither have you any cause hereof to complain: but your stomachs are such, and your arrogancy so great, that you passingly abuse yourselves toward those whom indeed you ought to reverence and with all duty obey.

I marvel that you will confess yourself to be underneath them, seeing you so cry out against superiority in the clergy, and claim such interest in equality: but I may not stand in answering words.

The Epistle of T. C. Sect. 10.

And, last of all, that as, if they had not listened unto those simple persons, the one had perished in his leprosy, the other had been slain, with her family ;(*) even so, if they shall, for any worldly respect of honour, riches, or fear of being accounted either unadvised in taking this course, or light or inconstant in forsaking it, stop their ears against this loving admonition of the Lord, they provoke his anger, not against their health, or against their life, but against their own souls, by exercising of unlawful authority, and by taking unto them partly such things as belong by no means unto the church, and partly which are common unto them with the whole church, or else with other the ministers and governors of the same; whereof I beseech them humbly to take the better heed, for that the judgment of the Lord will be upon a great part of them by so much the heavier, by how much they have not only believed the gospel, but also have received this grace of God, that they should suffer for it. So that, if they will neither take example of divers their superiors, the nobles of this realm, nor be admonished by us of the lower sort (wherein we hope better of them), yet they would remember their former times, and correct themselves by themselves; and, seeing they have been content, for the gospel's sake, to quit the necessary things of this life, they would not think much, for the discipline, which is no small part of the gospel (having both things necessary and commodious), to part from that, which is not only in them superfluous, and hath nothing but a vain ostentation (which will vanish as the shadow), but also is hurtful unto them, and pernicious unto the church; which thing I do more largely and plainly lay forth in this book.

* This is glorious talk, builded upon a false ground.

Jo. Whitgift.

Surely if they do for any such respects refuse any admonition given unto them, for the avoiding of such things as be unlawful, and as they unjustly retain, then, no doubt, they are worthy of great reprehension: but, if your Admonition be not loving, but spiteful, not brotherly, but unchristian, nay, no admonition indeed, but a very scolding and uncharitable railing; if the things you would have them forsake be both lawful and convenient for them to use, and, contrariwise, the things that you move them unto tend to confusion and overthrow of the gospel and of the state (as they do); then truly have they to consider of such disturbers of the peace of the church, and, according to their office and duty, provide a convenient remedy for them; knowing that it is the extreme refuge of Satan, when by other means he cannot, then to seek the overthrow of the gospel through contention about external things.

The Epistle of T. C. Sect. 11.

Another exception against the favourers of this cause is taken, for that they propound it out of time, which is that the Jews said, that the time was not yet come to build the Lord's house; but it is known Hagg. i. 2, 3, *what the prophet answered. And, if no time were unseason-* 4.[1] *able in that kind of material building, wherein there be some times (as of summer) more opportune and fit than others; how can there be any untimely building in this spiritual house, where, as long as it is called to-day, men are commanded to further this work? And, as for those which say we come too late, and that this should have been done in the beginning, and cannot now be done without the overthrow of all for mending of a piece, they do little consider that St Paul compareth that which is good in the building unto gold, and silver, and precious stones, and that* 1 Cor. iii. 12, *which is evil laid upon the foundation, unto stubble, and hay,* 13.[1] *and wood. Likewise therefore as the stubble, and the hay, and the wood be easily by the fire consumed, without any loss unto the gold, or silver, or precious stones; so the corrupt things in this building may be easily taken away, without any hurt or hinderance unto that which is pure and sound. And, if they put such confidence in this similitude, as that they will thereby, without any testimony of the word of God, stay the further building, or correcting the faults of the house of the Lord, which by his manifest commandment ought to be done with all speed; then, besides that they be very uncunning builders, which cannot mend the faults without overthrow of all (especially when as the fault is not in the foundation), they must remember that, as the mean which is used to gather*

[[1] These references are inserted from Repl. 2.]

the children of God is called a building, so it is[2] *called a planting: and therefore, as dead twigs, riotous or*[3] *superfluous branches, or whatsoever hindereth the growth of the vine-tree, may be cut off without rooting up the vine, so the unprofitable things of the church may be taken away without any overthrow of those things which are well established. And,*
2 Cor. vi. 15.[1] *seeing that Christ and Belial cannot agree, it is strange that the pure doctrine of the one, and the corruptions of the other, should cleave so fast together, that pure doctrine cannot be, with her safety, severed from the corruptions, when as they are rather like unto*
Dan. ii. 42, *that part of Daniel's image, which was compounded of clay*
43.[1] *and iron, and therefore could not cleave or stick one with another.*

Jo. Whitgift.

They did not only propound it out of time (after the parliament was ended), but out of order also, that is, in the manner of a libel, with false allegations and applications of the scriptures, opprobrious speeches, and slanders; not to reform, but to deform the church, and to confound all. The rest in this part is *petitio principii*, "the petition of the principle;" for you take that as confessed and true which will not be granted unto you, as shall more at large hereafter appear.

The Epistle of T. C. Sect. 12.

It is further said, that the setters forward of this cause are contentious, and in moving questions give occasion to the papists of slandering the religion, and to the weak of offence. But, if it be found to be both true which is propounded, and a thing necessary about which we contend, then hath this accusation no ground to stand on. For peace is commended to us
Rom. xii. 18.[4] *with these conditions, if it be possible, if it lie in us. Now it is*
2 Cor. x. 8.[4] *not possible, it lieth not in us, to conceal the truth; we can do*
2Cor. xiii. 8.[4] *nothing against it, but for it. It is a profane saying of a profane man, that an unjust peace is better than a just war*[5]. *It is a divine saying of a heathen man,* ἀγαθὴ δ' ἔρις ἥδε βροτοῖσι[6]: "*It is good to contend for good things.*" *The papists have no matter of rejoicing, seeing they have greater and sharper controversies at home, and seeing this tendeth both to the further opening of their shame, and thrusting out of their remnants, which yet remain among us. The weak may not be offended, considering that even in the church of God and among those of the church there hath been as great varieties of judgments as these are.*

[[2] Is it, Repl. 1 & 2.]
[[3] And, Repl. 1 & 2.]
[[4] The verses are inserted from Repl. 2.]
[[5] Cicer. Epist. ad Famil. Lib. vi. Epist. vi.]
[[6] Hesiod. Op. et D. 24.]

For what weightier controversies can there be, than whether we shall rise again or no, whether circumcision were necessary to be observed of those which believed? And yet the first was amongst the church of the Corinths, the other was first in Hierusalem and Antioch, and after in the churches of Galatia, and yet they the churches, and that the true religion which was there professed.

_{These were offences, but woe to the authors.}

_{1 Cor. xv.1
Acts xv. 1, 2.
Gal. iii. 3.¹}

Jo. Whitgift.

It is very true and sufficiently proved in that Answer to the Admonition, that the authors thereof be contentious, and "give occasion to the papists of slandering the religion" professed, "and to the weak of offence." For whosoever troubleth the peace of the church, or divide themselves from the church for external things, they be contentious; but these men do so, therefore they be contentious. The major proposition is grounded upon the words of St Paul, 1 Corinth. 8, 9 and 10, but especially upon these words of the 11. chapter: "If any be contentious, we have no such custom, neither the churches of God²:" where as he purposely speaketh of such as be contentious for external matters; whereupon that is _{Bullinger.} grounded that Bullinger saith: "That those be contentious which trouble and divide the church for external things³;" and that also which Zuinglius, in his book *De Baptismo*, _{Zuinglius de Baptis.} speaking of contentious anabaptists, writeth: "They go about innovations of their own private authority in those churches where the gospel is truly taught, and that in external things⁴." And in his *Ecclesiastes* he calleth them _{Zuingl. in Ecclesiast.} "authors of contentions, and troublers of the church, which strive about external matters⁵." And surely this is an evi-

[¹ These references are inserted from Repl. 2.]

[² Cartwright inveighs for this against Whitgift: "it is not enough for you to corrupt the holy scripture sentence by sentence, but you must also overthrow at once the meaning of three whole chapters together."—Sec. Repl. p. 15.]

[³ H. Bullinger. adv. Anabapt. Libri vi. Tigur. 1560. See Lib. iii. cap. 1. fol. 78; where, as in other places, Bullinger exposes the groundlessness of the dissensions and separations caused by the anabaptists.]

[⁴ Hæc, hæc, inquam, diligentius expendite, quotquot hoc nostro seculo hujusmodi innovationes et motus in eas ecclesias inducitis, quæ Dei verbum attentis animis amplectuntur, audiunt, et pro gratia sibi divinitus concessa vitam omnem juxta hujus præscriptum emendant...Perpetuo autem de illis ecclesiis, in quibus evangelica veritas annunciatur, loquimur, et ad externa tantum quæ dicimus referri debent.—Huld. Zvingl. Op. Tigur. 1581. De Bapt. Lib. Tract. i. Pars II. fol. 72. 2.]

[⁵ Hi vero non nisi inter fideles propter externa quædam et inania turbas et rixas seminant...Certa ergo et infallibili ratiocinatione concludimus, eos non alios esse, quam seditiosos et rerum turbatores.—Id. Ecclesiast. ibid. fol. 54. 2.]

dent token that the accusation is true; because they and their companions (for the most part) make contention wheresoever they come, and especially in those places where the gospel hath with most diligence been taught, as experience sufficiently proveth. Furthermore, the time and manner of publishing their pamphlets argueth the same most evidently.

The truth and necessity of those things, for the which they contend, rest as yet in trial. Surely, if they be matters "necessary to salvation," then is there some just cause of breaking the peace of the church for them; but, if they be matters of no such weight, then can you not excuse either yourself or them.

Indeed the papists have no just matter of rejoicing, for they disagree both in more and also in far greater matters than these be, even in the chiefest points of their religion: but this is no sufficient excuse for us; we may not disagree in truth because they disagree in error. Neither ought the weak to be offended because such contentions have been usual in the church, as I have also shewed in mine Epistle dedicatory to the church of England[6]. But yet woe be unto those by whom such offences come!

T. C.

And it is to be remembered that these controversies, for the most part, are not between many. For sundry of those things which are comprehended in the Answer to the Admonition have (as I am persuaded) few favourers, of those especially which are of any staid or sounder judgment in the scriptures, and have seen or read of the government and order of other churches; so that in deed (the father of that Answer excepted) we have this controversy, oftentimes, rather with the papists, than with those that[7] *profess the gospel, as we do.*

Jo. Whitgift.

Certainly I do not willingly defend any thing against the word of God, or of mine own private persuasion, but I have either sufficient warrant of the word of God, or some godly-learned and zealous author's judgment for the same. If I have done otherwise, I trust I shall hear of it in this book: for I am fully persuaded that all men of "staid and sound judgment" join with me in these matters, and such especially as have had the best experience "of the order and government of other reformed churches;" for proof whereof I refer you to

[6 See below, page 50.] [7 Which, Repl. 1, 2, & Def. A.]

the wisest, godliest, and best-learned among the clergy in this land[1].

T. C.

And, whereas, last of all, it is said that this proceedeth of envy, of singularity, and of popularity, although these be no sufficient reasons against the truth of the cause, which is neither envious, singular, nor popular; and although they be such as might be severally by great likelihoods and probabilities refuted; yet, because the knowledge of these things pertaineth only to God, which is the searcher of the heart and reins, and for avoiding of too much tediousness, we will rest in his judgment, tarry *Acts i. 24.*[2] for the day wherein the secrets of hearts shall be made manifest. And yet all men do see how unjustly we be accused of singularity, which propound nothing that the scriptures do not teach, the writers both old and new for the most part affirm, the examples of the primitive churches, and of those which are at these days, confirm.

Notable untruths, as will fall out in trial.

Jo. Whitgift.

Whether it proceed of envy or no, let the manner both of their and your writings declare. Popularity you cannot avoid, seeing you seek so great an equality, commit so many things to the voices of the people, and in sundry places so greatly magnify and extol them; than the which three what can be more popular? It is singularity to divide yourself from that church which doth profess the word of God truly, and is not to be touched in any point of doctrine necessary to salvation. It is true that a godly-learned writer saith: "Charity knits together and reconcileth; singularity cutteth in pieces and divideth; it is the beginning and root of all heresy to hate and contemn the communion of the church." And a little after: "There be some contentious persons whom no church can please, always having something to blame in other, but nothing in themselves; which is a manifest sign of singularity [4]." But, because the minds and affections

Popularity.

Singularity and the properties thereof.

Musc. in xvi. Matt.[3]

[[1] Cartwright denies that Whitgift has "either scripture or godly-learned author" for his warrant. He afterwards says: "The estimation which you have of the learned may easily appear unto all men to be as they make for you or against you: so that when they make for you, they are as sharp of sight as eagles; afterward when they are against you, they see no more than jays."—Sec. Repl. pp. 17, 22.]

[[2] This reference is inserted from Repl. 2.]

[[3] This reference is not in Def. B.].

[[4] Caritas unit et conciliat: singularitas scindit ac dividit, mater non Christianorum, sed hæreticorum...Principium et radix omnis hæresis est odisse et contemnere communionem ecclesiæ. Reperias hodie...quibus nulla placet ecclesia, semper habentes quod causentur in reliquis, in se ipsis nihil. Apertissimum

of men are certainly known only to God, the determinate judgment hereof I also refer unto him.

As for this bold assertion, that you "propound nothing that the scriptures do not teach, &c.," how true it is, must hereafter by examination appear.

The Epistle of T. C. Sect. 13.

All these accusations as well against the cause, as the favourers thereof, albeit they be many and diverse; yet are they no other than which have[5] been long sithence in the prophets', apostles', and our Saviour Christ's, and now of late in our times, objected against the truth and the professors thereof. And therefore, as the sun of the truth then appeared, and brake through all those clouds which rose against it to stop the light of it; so no doubt this cause, being of the same nature, will have the same effect. And, as all those slanders could not bring the truth in disgrace with those that loved it; so the children of the truth, through these untrue reports, will neither leave the love of this cause, which they have already conceived, nor yet cease to inquire diligently, and to judge indifferently, of those surmises which are put up against it.

Jo. Whitgift.

These be but words of course, which men of any sect (though not truly) will apply unto themselves, if they be otherwise dealt with than they can well bear. The truth certainly cannot be kept under by any means; and yet sometime error overshadoweth the truth, even as the clouds do the sun. My hope also is that men will not be carried away with slanderous reports (for, if they should, then must you needs prevail), but with sound reasons, and the truth of the cause.

The Epistle of T. C. Sect. 14.

Moreover, seeing that we have once overcome all these lets, and climbed over them, when they were cast in our way to hinder us from coming from the gross darkness of popery unto the glorious light of the gospel; there is no cause why now they should stay our course to further perfection, considering that neither the stile is higher now than it was before (being the very self-same objections), and in all this time we ought so to have grown in the knowledge of the truth that, instead of being then able to leap over a hedge, we should now have our feet so prepared by the gospel, that they should be as the feet of a hind, able to surmount even a wall, if need were.

signum est, quod singularitatis, et non caritatis studio teneantur.—Wolf. Muscul. in Evang. Matt. Comm. Basil. 1611. cap. xvi. Tom. II. p. 385.]

[5 Hath. Def. B.]

Jo. Whitgift.

There is but one truth, and that is certain: when we have obtained it, we must therein remain constant without altering: whosoever shall overleap or overrun this "wall" must of necessity procure unto himself great danger, and therefore, according to the old proverb, "Look before thou leap."

We must grow in faith and knowledge, and always be growing and going forward; but it doth not therefore follow that we must daily invent new opinions, or broach new doctrines, and alter in judgment: we must grow in strength of faith, we must increase in practice and love of virtue, we must study to increase our knowledge, that we may be the more confirmed in the truth that we have learned out of the word of God. This is an evil collection: we must grow in the knowledge of the truth; therefore must always be altering and changing our religion.

The Epistle of T. C. Sect. ult.

The sum of all is, that the cause may be looked upon with a single eye, without all mist of partiality; may be heard with an indifferent ear, without the wax of prejudice; the arguments of both sides may be weighed, not with the changeable weights of custom, of time, of men, which notwithstanding (popish excepted) shall be shewed to be more for the cause than against it, but with the just balances of the incorruptible and unchangeable word of God. And I humbly beseech the Lord to increase in us the Spirit of knowledge and judgment, that we may discern things which differ one from another, and that we may be sincere and without offence until the day of Christ.

Jo. Whitgift.

This do I in like manner desire with all my heart, and to the latter end of it I say, Amen. The midst if you prove not, then shall you be blamed for making such a brag.

T. C.

THE AUTHOR TO THE READER.

I am humbly to crave at thy hand, gentle reader, that thou wouldest vouchsafe diligently and carefully to compare Master Doctor's Answer, and my Reply; both that thou mayest the better understand the truth of the cause, and that the untempered speeches of him (especially that whippeth other so sharply for them) which I have in a manner altogether passed by, and his loose conclusions, which I have (to avoid tediousness) not so fully pursued, may the better appear; which thing as I crave to be done through the whole book, so chiefly I desire it may be done in the beginning, where the reader shall not be able so well to understand what is said of me, unless he have M. D. book before him. The cause of which diversity rose of that, that I first purposed to set down his Answer before my Reply, as he did the Admonition before his Answer: but afterward, considering that (his book being already in the hands of men) it would be double charges to buy it again; and especially weighing with myself that, through the slowness of the print for want of help, the Reply by that means should come forth later than was convenient (for, although he might commodiously bring in the Admonition, being short, yet the same could not be done in his book, swelling in that sort which it doth); I say, these things considered, I changed my mind, and have therefore set down the causes which moved me so to do, because I know that those, if any be, which have determined to continue their fore-judged opinions against the cause, whatsoever be alleged, will hereupon take occasion to surmise that I have left out his Answer, to the end that it might the less appear wherein I have passed over any weight of his reasons; whereas, had it not been for these causes, which I have before alleged, my earnest desire was to have set his Answer before my Reply; whereof I call the Lord to witness, whom I know to be a sharp judge against those which shall abuse his holy name to any untruth[1].

He desireth that which (as much as he hath in him) he hath sought to hinder.

Vain and unsufficient excuses why he hath not set down the Answer to the Admonition.

[[1] In the first edition of Cartwright's Reply, there is here added the following advertisement:

"The Printer to the Reader:

"It is to be lamented that the noble science of printing, given of the Lord for the maintenance of the truth, should be readier to wait upon the defence of corruptions than upon the sincerity of the truth; whilst those which are cunning in it, and are enriched by it, (I know not upon what sinister respect) refuse to bestow their knowledge and employ their wealth wherewith God hath blessed them this ways. Whereupon it falleth out, gentle reader, that I neither having wealth to furnish the print with sufficient variety of letters have been compelled (as a poor man doth one instrument to divers purposes) so to use one letter for three or four tongues; and, being for want of long training up in this mystery not so skilful to spy a fault so soon as it is made, have left out, or ever I was aware, divers quotations in the margent, displaced other some, and committed some other faults in the text. Whereof also the cause hath been not only that I was sometimes for want of help driven both to work at the press, to set and to correct, but also that I

Jo. Whitgift.

You have well provided for the comparing of Master Doctor's Answer with your Reply; and, howsoever you protest that your earnest desire was to set it down before your Reply, yet the sequel will declare the contrary; for it shall evidently appear that therefore you have omitted it, because you are loth they should be compared together, lest your frivolous replies, your childish collections, your wilful depraving, your fraudulent dismembering of my book, should manifestly appear. Full well knew you that your fautors (in whose hands especially your books are kept) would not take pains to compare them both together, except they had been joined together, that they might have done it with one labour. And surely herein you have dealt very unhonestly with me, done me great injury, and not performed that towards me that you before required of me in one of your pamphlets, and do now again require of me in the end of this book. But wise and indifferent men will soon espy the causes, if it will please them to peruse this book with some diligence.

My "untempered speeches," if they be compared with your flouts, and disdainful phrases, or with either of the Admonitions, will seem, I am sure, very modest. And no doubt you would have set down some examples of some of them, if they had been such as you would make the reader believe. But in your book he may see the humbleness of your spirit, and judge whether that one quality be found in you or no, which Zuinglius in his book called *Elenchus contra Anabapt.* and in his books *De Baptismo*, and *Ecclesiast.*, and Bullinger, in his book *Adversus Anabapt.* do say, is common to the anabaptists, that is, "to revile the ministers of the word, and much more bitterly to inveigh against them (if they withstand their

The true causes why T. C. set not down the Answer.

Zuinglius.
Bullinger.

wanted the commodity that other printers commonly have of being near either unto the author, or to some that is made privy unto his book. Which may the better appear, for that, after the author came unto me, which was when the half of the book was printed, the faults neither are so many nor so great as before. In consideration whereof I will humbly desire thee, gentle reader, the rather to bear with me, considering that that which I do in this art I do not in respect of any gain, but only for the desire I have to advance the glory of God, and considering also that I have procured the grosser faults, and those wherein there is any danger of misleading the reader to be amended with the pen." There then follows a list of fifteen faults, " besides those which are amended with the pen."]

errors) than against the papists [1]." Truly, if you should have written against the doggedest papist, or the pestilentest heretic that ever was, you could not have invented how in more spiteful manner to deface him; but how truly, it resteth in the trial.

Touching "loose conclusions," it is unlike that you have omitted any, seeing that you have feigned those to be which are not: wherein your false dealing plainly appeareth, and shall be made manifest. Your excuses for omitting my book in your Reply be mere excuses; for why should you run in suspicion of corrupt dealing for saving 12d. in another man's purse? As for the volume of your book, it would not have been much bigger, if you had spared your superfluous digressions, cut off your vain words, and kept in your scornful and opprobrious speeches. What I think of your protestation, I have told you before.

[[1] Eos enim qui hodie ab evangelio stant longe acerbius proscindunt, quam qui a pontifice.—Huld. Zvingl. Op. Tigur. 1581. Epist. ad Lect. præf. Elench. contr. Catabapt. Pars II. fol. 6. 2. Conf. De Bapt. Lib. Tract. III. fol. 94; Ecclesiast. foll. 48, 9, 56; et H. Bullinger. adv. Anabapt. Libri VI. Tigur. 1560. Lib. I. cap. viii. fol. 18.]

¶ An answere to a

certen Libel intituled,

An admonition to the Parliament,

By Iohn VVhitgifte,
D. of Diuinitie.

I. COR. 8. 2.
If any man thinke that he knoweth any thing,
he knoweth nothing yet as he
ought to knowe.

I. COR. 11. 16.
If any man be contentious, we haue no
suche custome, neyther the
Churches of God.

GALA. 5. 26.
Let vs not be desirous of vayne glorie, prouoking one another, enuying
one another.

¶ Imprinted at London,
By Henrie Bynneman,
for Humfrey Toy.
Anno .1572.

[This is the title-page of the first edition of Whitgift's Answer: that of the second edition resembles it with the addition of "Newly augmented by the Authoure, as by conference shall appeare." It is dated 1573.]

To his loving Nurse, the Christian Church of
England, Jo. Whitgift, a member and minister of
the same, wisheth peace in Christ, and continuance of his glorious gospel, even
to the world's end.

THERE be divers things, and especially five, that, when I first took this labour in hand, had almost utterly dissuaded me from the same:

First, because I do with all my heart hate contention and strife, and especially in matters of religion, among such as profess the self-same gospel.

Secondly, for that I feared greatly lest some slander might redound to the gospel by this open contention, seeing that "God is not the author of contention or confusion, but of peace." [1 Cor. xiv.]

Thirdly, I doubted whether this kind of dealing by writing might minister matter to the common adversaries of the gospel to rejoice and glory, and to flatter themselves the more in their damnable errors.

Fourthly, I greatly suspected the slanderous reports of the backbiter, and of the unlearned tongue; the one, because he loveth to speak evil, and hear evil, of all those that be not in all points inclinable to his fancy, whereof I have great experience, being myself most unjustly slandered by that viperous kind of men; the other, because they be not able to judge of controversies according to learning and knowledge, and therefore are ruled by affection, and carried headlong with blind zeal into divers sinister judgments and erroneous opinions.

Lastly, because I know sundry (in all respects) worthy men, much more able to deal in such matters than I am.

But, when I considered my duty towards God, to his church, and to our most gracious lady and sovereign, Elizabeth her majesty (by whose ministry God hath given his gospel free passage unto us), the first stop and hindrance was answered. For I thought that that duty ought not to be omitted for any such cause, seeing God and not man shall be my judge; and also, that not he which defendeth the truth and confuteth errors, but he that impugneth the truth and spreadeth sects, is the author of contention.

Likewise, when I remembered that it was no new thing to have contentions, sects, and schisms in the church of Christ (especially when it enjoyeth external peace), and that we had manifest examples thereof from time to time (first in Peter and Paul *ad Gal.* ii., Paul and Barnabas, *Acto.* xv., then in the church of the Corinthians, 1 Cor. i. and iii.; afterwards betwixt the oriental church and occidental church, touching Easter and such like matters; betwixt the bishops of Africa and the bishops of Italy, for rebaptizing of heretics; and sundry times, yea, usually in the external peace of the church, as may be more at large seen in Eusebius, Lib. iv. Eccl. Hist. cap. vi, and Lib. v. cap. xxiv. xxv. xxvi, and Lib. viii. &c.[1]; likewise in Ruffinus, Lib. i. cap. i.[2]; in Sozom., Lib. vi. cap. iv.[3]; in Basilius Magnus, Ep. lxi. *Ad fratres et episcopos in occidente*, and Ep. lxix.[4]; and in sundry other ancient and learned histories and writers); for the second point I was satisfied; for I thought that that could be no slander to this church, which by the malice of Satan hath been practised in all churches even since the ascension of Christ.

Thirdly, when I perceived that these men against whom I now write did agree with the adversaries in defacing the state of religion, the order of common-prayers, the ministry, the sacraments, the kind of government, &c. used and allowed in this realm of England, and that in as opprobrious and spiteful manner as the adversaries do; likewise that they seek to overthrow the

[[1] Euseb. in Hist. Eccles. Script. Amst. 1695-1700. Lib. iv. cap. vii.; Lib. v. capp. xxiv., &c.; Lib. viii. capp. i., &c. pp. 96, &c., 155, &c., 238, &c.]

[[2] Hyst. Eccles. Par. Lib. x. capp. i. ii. fol. 105.]

[[3] Soz. in Hist. Eccles. Script. Lib. vi. cap. iv. pp. 520, &c.]

[[4] Basil. Op. Par. 1721-30. Ad Episc. Occid. Epist. xc.; ad Ital. et Gall. Epist. xcii. Tom. III. pp. 181, &c.]

self-same pillars of this church with the adversaries (although not by the self-same means); I thought that the confutation and overthrow of the one should be the confutation and overthrow of the other, and therefore the adversaries to have small cause indeed of rejoicing.

Against backbiters, slanderers, and unlearned tongues, I shall, by God's grace, arm myself with patience; for their talk is no sufficient cause for a man to abstain from doing his duty.

To conclude, I (although the unworthiest and unmeetest of a great number) was bold to take upon me this enterprise, partly to shew that the book called the Admonition is not such but that it may easily be answered, and especially to satisfy mine own conscience; for I considered that, if no man had taken upon him the envy of the common sort, in withstanding the enterprises and proceedings of the anabaptists, when they began in Germany, anabaptism had overrun those churches, and utterly destroyed them.

These were the reasons that satisfied the former objections, and especially moved me to take upon me this labour, wherewith if I can also satisfy others, I have my desire; if not, yet have I done my duty, and satisfied mine own conscience. And, forasmuch as the matter toucheth the state of the whole church of England, I thought it most meet to dedicate this my book rather unto the same generally, than to any one particular member thereof; protesting that, if I have affirmed anything therein, that by learning and good reasons may be proved erroneous, I will reform the same; for I wholly submit it to the rule of God's word, and the judgment of those that be learned, discreet, and wise. The Lord bless thee, O dear spouse of Christ, with the continuance of his gospel, of the queen's majesty, and of godly peace and quietness. Amen.

An Answer to the whole Epistle to the church.

T. C.

What causes either pulled you forward, or thrust you backward, to write, or not to write, and how, in this dispute with yourself, in the end you were resolved to write in this sort, I leave it unto the judgment of the Lord, who only knoweth the secrets of the heart, and will in his good time unseal them. But, if there be any place of conjecture, the hatred of contention, which you set down as the first and principal cause that beat you back from writing, might well have been put as the last and least, or rather none at all. For, if peace had been so precious unto you (as you pretend), you would not have brought so many hard words, bitter reproaches, enemy-like speeches (as it were sticks and coals), to double and treble the heat of contention. If the sharpness of the Admonition misliked you, and you think that they[1] outreached in some vehemency of words; how could you more effectually have confuted that, than to have in a quiet and mild spirit set them in the way, which (in your opinion) had left it? Now in words condemning it, and approving it in your deeds, I will not say that you do not so much mislike this sharpness as you are sorry that you are prevented, and are not the first in it: but this I may well say unto you, which he said: Quid verba audiam, cum facta videam? "What should I hear words, when I see the deeds?" In the fourth reason whereby you were discouraged to write, if, by "backbiters," and "unlearned tongues," "viperous kind of men," "not able to judge of controversies," "carried away with affections and blind zeal into divers sinister judgments and erroneous opinions," you mean all those that think not as you do in these matters; I answer for myself, and for as many as I know of them, that they are they which first desire (so it be truly) to hear and speak all good of you. But if that be not, through your perseverance in the maintenance of the corruptions of this church (which you should help to purge), then the same are they that desire that both the evil which you have done, and that which you have yet in your heart to do, may be known, to the less discredit of the truth and sincerity which you with such might and main do strive against.

A charitable figure.

A manifest perverting of the words and meaning of the Epistle.

Touching our "unlearned tongues," we had rather a great deal they were unlearned than they should be as theirs which have taught their tongues to speak falsely. And how unlearned soever you would make the world believe that we and our tongues be, I hope (through the goodness of God) they shall be learned enough to defend the

Jer. ix. 5.

[¹ Think they, Repl. 1 and 2.]

Isai. liii. 8. truth against all the learning that you shall be able to assault it with. If those be the generation of Christ which you call viperous kind of men, know you that you have not opened your mouth against earth, but you have set it against heaven; and, for all indifferent judgment, it will easily perceive that you are as far from the spirit of John Baptist as you are near to his manner of speech which you use: *Matt. iii. 7.* whether it be " affection" or " blind zeal" that we follow and are driven by, it will then appear, when the reasons of both sides, being laid out, shall be weighed indifferently. Whereas you say that your duty towards God, and the queen her majesty, moved you to take this labour in hand, it will fall out, upon the discourse, that, as you have not served the Lord God in this enterprise and work of yours, so have you done nothing less than any godly duty which you owe unto her majesty; so that the best that can be thought of you herein is that, where in an evil matter you could yield no duty, yet now you have done that which you thought a duty: which judgment we will so long keep of you, until you shall, by oppugning of a known truth, declare the contrary; which we hope will not be. What truth it is, that we impugn, and you defend, let it in the name of God appear by our several proofs and answers of both sides. And, as for the slanderous surmises, whereby in your third and last consideration, you set the papists of the one side of us, and the anabaptists of the other, and us in the midst, reaching out our hands (as it were) to them both; first, it ought not to be strange unto us, miserable sinners, seeing that the Lord himself, without all sin, was placed in the midst of two grievous malefactors, as though he had been worse than they both. Then, for answer of these[2] slanderous speeches, I will refer the reader to those places where these general charges are given out in more particular manner.

Slanderous and cursed speakers be not the generation of Christ.

Jo. Whitgift.

It is well that you are content to rest in his judgment until the time come; for so indeed ought we to do, as the apostle admonisheth, 1 Cor. iv., *Nolite ante tempus quicquam judicare:* "Judge not before the time, until the Lord come, &c."

1 Cor. iv.

Your conjecture is a mere conjecture indeed; for undoubtedly these so many "hard words" of mine, "bitter reproaches," &c., would not have been kept so secret of you, if you could have had them forthcoming. But be it so, as you will needs have it; yet have I not in like bitterness of speech spoken against them, as Zuinglius, Bucer, Calvin, Bullinger, Gualter, &c., have done against the like troublers of the church; who had notwithstanding all these pretences and cloaks to shadow their contentions with, which either you, or the authors of the Admonition, do allege; for they

[² Those, Repl. 2.]

pretend the glory of God, the purity of religion, the safety of the church, as Master Bucer witnesseth in his Comment. upon the Ephesians, cap. iv.; Master Calvin, in his book *Adversus Anabapt.*; Gastius in his book *De exordio et erroribus Catabaptist.*; Zuinglius in his book called *Ecclesi.*; and Bullinger in his book *Adversus Anabaptist.*; as I have, by setting down their very words more at large, declared in the second edition of my Answer to the Admonition[1]. But grant that, for the love of peace, and hatred of contention, and earnest zeal that I bear to this church of Christ in England, and dutiful affection to my sovereign, I have sometimes passed the bounds of modesty (wherein I will neither accuse nor excuse myself); yet are my speeches in bitterness far inferior to those opprobries, slanders, and disdainful words uttered either in the first or second Admonition, or in your Reply. And where have you learned to espy a mote in another man's eye, and not to see the beam that is in your own? or what point of rhetoric do you call it, to charge me in the beginning of your book with that that you yourself most outrageously fall into sundry times, almost in every leaf? or how unwise are you to give unto me that counsel which you yourself in no respect observe! But of both our modesties, and manners of writing, we must be content that other men judge which shall read our books; and therefore it is but in vain either for you to accuse, or me to excuse. God grant us both the spirit of modesty and humility.

In my fourth reason, by "backbiters," I mean all such as are ready to hear evil, and speak evil of all men that be not of their judgment, and such as cease not continually to deprave those especially that be of any countenance and calling; the which vice doth abundantly reign (I will not say in all, but) in a great sort of your sect, and those learned also. I could name some which go from place to place for that purpose especially, although under other pretences: and in this quality they agree with the anabaptists; as may appear more plainly in the notes of the anabaptists' qualities, contained in the second edition of mine Answer to the Admonition, to the which, for brevity's sake, I refer you[1].

By "unlearned tongues" I mean such of the common people as you have deluded, who indeed are carried away by

[1 See below, pages 125, &c.; especially, 129, 33, 8.]

a blind and preposterous zeal, and therefore the rather to be excused. I know there be some (both of the learned and unlearned sort) among you, that have milder spirits than the rest: such I do not blame in this point; I would other would follow their modesty.

As for the "good" that you and other would so gladly "speak" of me, it evil appeareth in this book, where you do but devise how possibly you may deface me: indeed both you, and some others (if you considered your duties towards me, and my dealings towards you, whilst you kept yourselves within your bonds), have small occasion to whisper of me in corners as you do, or otherwise to deal so unchristianly with me. The evil that you know by me, utter it and spare not: I desire no silence; so that it be done where I may come to the answering of it. And surely he that shall read this your book cannot but conceive that, if you knew any evil thing by me, it would not be concealed. But to all reproaches I will answer, as they come in order, and proclaim defiance against you, for anything that you can justly charge me with.

I intend not to maintain any "corruptions of this church:" I will seek for the redress thereof as earnestly as you shall, and more orderly, and therefore I trust more effectually. But I neither can, nor may suffer that, which is lawfully and by due order established, unlawfully and out of order by you to be defaced. This your pretence of cleansing the church from corruptions is but the accustomed excuse of the Novatians, Donatists, and anabaptists, as you know well enough; and therefore, before you condemn me to be a defender of the corruptions of this church, you must first prove them to be corruptions; and, when you have so done, you must also declare them to be such corruptions, as deserve this stir and hurly-burly for them: for there were great corruptions in the church of the Corinthes; and yet the apostle greatly misliked such as stirred up contentions for the same: so hath there been always imperfections in the church, especially in external things; and yet such as therefore did break the peace of it were always counted as contentious, and condemned as schismatics. Look the writers before of me mentioned, in their books against the anabaptists.

As I said before, so I say again, let the evil which I have done, and that which you say I have yet in my heart to do (wherein you take upon you the office of God), be proclaimed at the standard in Cheap[1], or elsewhere, so it be done publicly that I may answer it, and not in corners as it hath been; and, if I fail in my purgation, let me sustain the pain due for the same. I ask no favour, I fear no accuser, I refuse no indifferent judge. And, if you have any thing to say against me, do it orderly, do it lawfully, not in corners, not in libels. This I speak not to justify myself before God (for in that respect I know more imperfections in myself than I do in any other, because I know myself better than I know any man else), but before man, in doing my duty, in observing laws, in walking in my vocation, &c.

I do not accuse you all for lack of learning; neither can you, or any man else, gather any such thing of my words: God grant you may use your learning to better purpose than to the disturbing of the church, and stirring up of contentions, where the gospel is truly preached. This is but a slender collection to say that therefore I accuse you all of unlearnedness, because I say that I greatly suspected "the slanderous reports of backbiters," and "of the unlearned tongue." Surely there be both learned and unlearned tongues among you too much given to backbiting and slandering, as it is well known; and yet I accuse not all. Let them which find this imperfection in themselves, in the name of God, amend it; for it is a foul fault.

Matt. v.

In that they, like "vipers," with slanderous reports sting men privily, they be not the generation of Christ, but of Christ's adversary, howsoever otherwise they seem to be godly and zealous: for Christ doth will them "to love their enemies, to pray for them that curse them, &c.;" so far would he have them from backbiting and slandering of their brethren, and of such as profess the name of Christ with them. He that speaketh against slanderous tongues doth not open his mouth "against heaven," but against that vice which is earthly, yea, hellish: neither must you think that your church is so pure, but that it hath in it a number such as well deserve this reprehension. And therefore these great speeches of yours might well have been forborne: your learning and reasons, which you so oft boast of, must be left to the judgment of others.

[1 Cheapside.]

What "duty" I have performed "towards God and her majesty," lieth not in your power to judge. I am fully persuaded that I have done that which my duty towards them both requireth of me, and urgeth me unto in this behalf; and I doubt not but that therein I have done good service to them both. Your judgment of me I do not greatly regard, so long as you are affected as you are. I will die rather than impugn a known truth; neither will I cease from defending of that which I am fully persuaded to be a truth.

In my third and last consideration, all is true that I said; neither can you deny it. Most true it is that, in defacing this present state of religion, that is, the order of common prayers, the ministry, the sacraments, the kind of government, you join with the papists, although you use in some points contrary reasons; and, in disquieting the church for external things, you join with the anabaptists: and in opprobrious speeches and taunts you are inferior to neither of them both. And yet I do not say that you be either papists or anabaptists. Prove that I herein speak untruly of you; and I will willingly make you amends.

A brief Examination of the reasons used in the book called an Admonition to the Parliament.

Jo. Whitgift.

First, in that book the scripture is most untolerably abused, and unlearnedly applied, quoted only in their margent to delude both such as for lack of learning cannot, and such as either for slothfulness or some prejudicate opinion will not, examine the same; as I have particularly declared in my answer following.

T. C.

An answer to that which is called, A brief examination of the reasons used in the Admonition to the Parliament.

<small>Vain shifts to colour the unapt allegations of scriptures by the Admonition.</small>
If the scriptures had been applied to the maintenance of the abomination of the mass, and some other of the grossest of antichristianity, you could have said no more, nor used vehementer speech than this, that they are "most untolerably abused, and unlearnedly applied." And then where is

<small>Charity doth not cover open and notorious faults.</small>
charity, which "covereth the multitude of faults," especially in brethren, when you do not only not cover them, but also take <small>Prov. x. 12.[1]</small> away their garments whereby they are covered? I will not deny but that there be some few places quoted, which might have been spared; but there are[2] a great number, which M. Doctor tosseth and throweth away so lightly, which he shall perceive to sit nearer him than he is, or at the least seemeth to be, aware of. And, to bring to pass that the quotations in the margent might appear to the reader more absurd, M. Doctor hath, besides

<small>There is no such advantage taken.</small>
the advantage which he taketh of the faults of the printer, used two unlawful practices especially: whereof the one is that, whereas the Admonition doth quote the scripture, not only to prove the matters which it handleth, but sometimes also to note the place from whence the phrase of speech is taken,

<small>Scriptures alleged for proof of the phrase.</small>
M. Doctor doth go about to make his reader believe that those places, which be alleged for proof of the phrase, are quoted for proof of the matter. The other practice is that, where the Admonition for the shortness which it promiseth, and was necessary in that case, could not apply the places, M. Doctor, presuming too much of the ignorance of his reader, thought he might make him believe that any thing else was meant by those places, than that which they meant indeed, and for which they were alleged. And,

[1 This reference is not in Def. B: the verse is supplied from Repl. 2.]
[2 Repl. 1. omits *are*.]

where you say the quotations are only " to delude such, &c.," I see you hold it no fault in yourself, which you condemn so precisely in others, that is, to judge before the time, to sit in the conscience, to affirm definitely of their thoughts, contrary to their own protestation. But, seeing you lift up our[3] *imperfections so high, and set them as it were upon a stage for all men to be looked of, to the discredit of the truth which we do maintain, you shall not think much if your poverty be pointed unto, in those things wherein you would carry so great countenance of store.*

Jo. Whitgift.

THE abusing of the scriptures, and the unjust applying of them, is to be maintained neither in papist nor other, and least of all in such as, seeming to give most authority unto them, do by that means give occasion to the adversary to contemn them. What just occasion might the papists have of triumphing, if they should understand that we as licentiously wring and wrest the scriptures to serve our turn, as they do to serve theirs! And truly as well may they apply the scriptures that they use in the defence of their transubstantiation, purgatory, merits, images, &c. as the authors of the Admonition can do to prove those things for the which they do oftentimes allege them. And therefore I think that my speech in that point against them cannot be too sharp.

Charity doth not so cover open and manifest sins, that it suffereth them to be unreprehended: but it remitteth private offences, it doth not publish secret sins at the first; neither doth it disclose all things that it knoweth to the defamation of a brother, when he may be otherwise reformed. But this fault of theirs in abusing the scriptures is public, printed in books, in every man's hand, used to discredit and deface this church of England, which no true member of the same ought to suffer. Wherefore in detecting this untrue dealing, I have not broken any rule of charity, but done my bounden duty.

If there be so many of their quotations "tossed and thrown away" by me, &c., I trust you will let me understand of them as occasion is offered; which surely you have done in very few places, and, in those wherein you have done it, you have done it very slenderly and loosely, as will appear. I take very little or no "advantage at all of the printer," but salve that as much as I can: and, whereas you say that "where the Admonition quoteth the scripture, not only to prove

[3 Your, Def. B.]

The abusing of scripture is to be maintained in none.

the matter, but to note the place from whence the phrase of speech is taken, &c.," that is a very feeble excuse, and far-fetched; for to what purpose should they so do? or why do you not by some examples declare unto us that they have so done? This is but a shift, and argueth that you are not purposed to acknowledge any fault, be it never so manifest: and therefore little hope there is of any amendment. And, whereas you also say that "the Admonition, for the shortness which it promiseth, &c.;" to that I answer as before, and I add that it was very uncircumspectly done of them, to quote places which could not be applied to that purpose for the which they were quoted. In such matters men ought to have such regard unto the time, that they abuse not the word of God. But I have (as you say) otherwise applied their quotations "than they meant indeed." I think you will let me hear of it, when you come to those places, and then shall I shape you an answer.

To what purpose should the margent of their book be pestered with such unapt quotations, but only to delude the reader, and to make him believe that all things there contained be grounded of the express word of God? Where things be open and manifest, there a man may judge, though he sit not in the conscience of him of whom he judgeth. As for protestations, they be now so usual and common in every matter, and the sequel so many times contrary to the same, that it is hard for a man to give credit at all times to all persons protesting: there is experience of it; and I could allege examples, if I were disposed.

Set out my "poverty" as much as you can, and spare it not; but take heed lest in so doing you shew yourself poor indeed, and that in those things especially wherein you seem most to complain of my poverty.

A brief Examination, &c.

Secondly, their proofs consist especially of these arguments. The first is *ab eo quod est secundum quid, ad id quod simpliciter est;* as, Such and such things were not in the apostles' time; *ergo*, they ought not to be now. Which kind of argument is very deceitful, and the mother and well-spring of many both old and new

Argu. a secundum quid ad simpliciter.

schisms; of old, as of them that called themselves *Apostolicos*, and of the Aërians[1]; of new, as of the anabaptists[2], who, considering neither the diversity of times concerning the external ecclesiastical policy, nor the true liberty of the christian religion in extern rites and ceremonies, in matters neither commanded nor forbidden in God's law, nor the authority of christian magistrates in the christian congregation concerning the same, have boldly enterprised to stir up many and heinous errors. For, if these reasons should take place, The apostles used it not; *ergo*, it is not lawful for us to use it: or this either, They did it; *ergo*, we must needs do it; then no Christians may have any place to abide in, they may have no christian princes, no ministration of sacraments in churches, and such like; for the apostles had no place to abide in, they had no christian princes to govern them, no churches to minister sacraments in, &c. Likewise we must have all things common: we must depart with all our possessions when we be converted to the gospel, baptize abroad in the fields, minister the communion in private houses only, be always under the cross and under tyrants, and such like: for the apostles had all things common, departed from their possessions, baptized abroad in fields, ministered the communion in private houses, were always under persecutors and tyrants, &c.

Acts ii. & iv.
Matt. xix.
Acts viii.
Acts ii. & xx.

Jo. WHITGIFT.

To this kind of argument and that which is here spoken, T. C. maketh no answer at all in this place: what he doth hereafter, we shall understand when we come to it.

A brief Examination, &c.

Another kind of argument is much like unto this, and is taken *ab auctoritate negative*, which in matters of salvation and damnation holdeth when we reason *ab auctoritate scripturæ*, "from the authority of the scripture," but not else: for this argument, It is not com-

Ab auctoritate negative.

[¹ See August. Op. Par. 1679-1700. Lib. de Hæres. xl. liii. Tom. VIII. cols. 11, 18.]
[² Of anabaptists, Answ.]

manded in the scripture to be done, nor there expressed; *ergo*, it ought not to be done, is so far out of the way and so erroneous, that it is not tolerable; for it taketh away the most part of all due circumstances, without the which, either after one manner or other, the very institutions of Christ cannot be observed. For how is it possible to receive the holy communion, but either sitting, standing, kneeling, walking, or lying; either at one time or other; in the morning or at night; before meat or after meat; clothed or naked; in this place or in that place, &c.? and yet none of these circumstances are in scripture commanded, or by necessary collection may thereof be gathered. The same is to be said of the observation of times, of common prayers, and other convenient and necessary orders in the church. If this argument were good, then all good laws and ordinances made for the advancing of true religion and establishing of good orders were to be abolished; which were the very root and well-spring of stubbornness, obstinacy, sedition, disobedience, and confusion.

T. C.

For the arguments themselves, they shall be seen what they be in their places; so shall also that be answered, which M. Doctor bringeth here for the confutation, being straightway after, and in sundry other places, repeated in this book. I will touch that which is not repeated, and that is,

A wrangling cavil.

that M. Doctor maketh it an indifferent thing for men and women to receive the supper of the Lord clothed or naked. This savoureth strongly of the sect of the Adamites[1].

Superfluous proofs.

St Paul, which commendeth the preservation of godliness and peace unto the civil magistrate, doth also commend unto him 1 *Tim.* ii. 2.[2]

Where found you these words?

the providing that honesty be kept; and M. Doctor maketh it an indifferent thing, to come either naked or clothed unto the Lord's table: verily there is

It is less honesty in charging M. Doctor falsely.

small honesty in this. And, if the heathen, which knew not God, did account it a filthy thing for a stage-player to come upon the stage without a slop, how much more filthy is it for a Christian to come naked unto the Lord's table! and the contrary thereof is necessarily collected of the scripture, notwithstanding that M. Doctor saith otherwise. They which have

A digression from the matter to the person.

heard M. Doctor read in the schools can tell that he, being there amongst learned men, never used to reduce the contrary arguments of the adversaries

[1 See August. Op. Par. 1679-1700. Lib. de Hæres. xxxi. Tom. VIII. col. 11. A similar sect existed in Bohemia in the fifteenth century.]

[2 This reference is inserted from Repl. 2.]

to the places of the fallations; and yet that was the fittest place for him to have shewed his knowledge in, because there they should have been best understood: now that he professeth himself to be a doctor of the people, which because they have not learned these things cannot understand them, he dasheth out his logic. What may be probably gathered hereof, I leave to every man's consideration: this is certain, that circumstances of place and persons, which he so often urgeth, are not well observed of him, when logic speaketh in the church, and is mute in the schools; when things are handled more learnedly amongst the people, and more popularly amongst the learned. It is truly said, Κακόν ἐστι τὸ καλὸν ἥν τι μὴ καιροῦ τύχῃ· "A good thing is evil when it cometh out of season." But to observe what art here is shewed, I would gladly know what place of the falla- tions either an argument Ab auctoritate negative is, or of negatives by comparison. Aristotle, setting forth places whereunto all fallations may be called, maketh no mention of these; and, if these were fallations, and were such as he imagineth them, they should be referred unto the former place, Ab eo quod est secundum quid, ad id quod est simpliciter: for these reasons, The scripture hath it not; therefore it ought not to be; or, The minister was known by doctrine; therefore by doctrine only, and not by apparel—if, I say, they be fallations, they be referred unto that place; and whether they be or no, and also how corruptly, and otherwise than is meant, they be gathered, it shall afterward appear. In the mean season, in a small matter here is a great fault, not only to invent new places, but of one place to make three, and may as well make a thousand.

Where be they called fallations? you cannot deny them to be false arguments.

JO. WHITGIFT.

The arguments are left unanswered, because indeed they cannot be answered. Wherefore T. C. picketh other quarrels, and here beginneth his vein of gibing and jesting. Who would have made this ado about "clothed or naked," but such a one as is delighted in quarrelling? or who can gather that, by using this example, I would have men to receive the communion naked, or once surmise that I think it lawful for them so to do, and therefore to "savour strongly of the sect of the Adamites," but he that is disposed to piece out his Reply with such imagined toys? I pray you, where do I "make it an indifferent thing to come either clothed or naked unto the Lord's table?" Set down my words; but, if I say no such thing, if I have not so much as once named this word "indifferent" in that place, then surely have you dealt with me, not only not indifferently, but very dishonestly, in laying this thing to my charge. The example is apt, and proveth that thing manifestly that I allege it for; that is, that the most part of the due circumstances (without the which the very institutions of Christ in his sacraments cannot be observed) be not commanded particularly, nor expressed in the scriptures, but left to the church to determine. I do not say, that it is "an indifferent thing," I know it doth necessarily appertain to comeliness; but I deny it to be particularly expressed in the scriptures; and therefore I say that, although all things necessary to salvation be in the scriptures manifestly contained, yet all things necessary to order and comeliness are not there expressed, much less such things as according to time, place, and persons may be altered. If this doctrine be not true, why do you not overthrow the other examples also? why can you find no other faults in this argument? If this example so trouble you, I will tell you plainly from whom I had it, even from that famous martyr, and notable learned man, D. Ridley, sometime bishop of London, who used the same example to the same purpose in his conference by writing with M. Hooper exhibited up to the council in the time of king Edward the sixth, the true copy whereof I have[1]. Surely he was no "Adamite," but a man of singular judgment and learning.

Touching my reading in the schools (which you here opprobriously object unto me), though I know that the university had a far better opinion of me than I deserved, and that there were a great many which were in all respects better able to do that office than myself, yet I trust I did my duty and satisfied them. What logic I uttered in my lectures, and how I read, I refer to their judgments; who surely, if they suffered me so long to continue in that place, augmented the stipend for my sake[2], and were so desirous to have me still to remain in that function (reading so unlearnedly, as you would make the world believe I did), may be thought either to be without judgment themselves, or else to have been very careless for that exercise. Well, I will not speak that which I might justly speak by this provocation of yours; for I count this either[3] an heathenish or a childish kind of confuting, to fall from the matter to the depraving of the person. God grant that

[1 Cartwright, in his Second Reply, reiterates his charge that Whitgift made it indifferent (though not using the particular word) whether persons received the sacrament clothed or naked: he denies that Ridley ever used such an argument, but adds that, if he did, he is sure he would be "well content that as stubble it should pass through the fire."—Sec. Repl. pp. 24, 5.]

[2 Strype, Life of Whitgift. Book I. chap. ii.]   [3 Either this, Def. B.]

we both may so know our gifts and ourselves, that we may acknowledge them to be his, and employ them to the edifying of the church, not to the disgracing one of another. *Scientia* [1 Cor. viii. 1.] *inflat, &c.*

I did know that this my book should come into the hands both of the learned and unlearned; and therefore (as near as I could) I did frame myself to serve them both. And, because all, or the most part, of your proofs consist of these or the like kind of arguments, I thought it convenient to set down a note of them before my book, and that for the learned sake; whereof I do not repent me, neither do I think that it cometh out of place.

"But to observe what art is here shewed, you would gladly know (you say) what place of the fallations either an argument *ab auctoritate negative* is, or of negatives by comparison, &c." I marvel that you will so openly dally. I entitle this treatise, "A Brief Examination of the Reasons used in the Book, &c." And afterwards I call them arguments, I do not call them fallations (which notwithstanding I might have done in some respect); but, seeing you cavil about words, tell me where I call either an argument *ab auctoritate negative,* or of negatives by comparison, "fallations?" Do you not blush to trifle on this sort, and to seek occasion of cavilling in so small matters? I am sure that you are not so ignorant in logic, but that you know there be many false arguments, which be not amongst the fallations. What say you to an argument *a specie negative,* and such like? What say you to an argument *ex solis negativis,* or *ex solis particularibus?* or to that that otherwise doth offend in any mood or figure? or, to be short, to such as be in any place of logic negative or affirmative, when the nature of the place will not bear it? For you know that in some places only negative reasons hold, in some other places only affirmative.

Concerning an argument *ab auctoritate negative,* that it is no good argument all logicians confess; neither is he to be thought to have any skill in logic at all that will deny it. Only the authority of the scripture is to be excepted in matters pertaining to salvation or damnation, because therein it is perfect and absolute; as I have declared in my Answer to the Admonition. Arg. ab auctoritate negative.

Touching the argument "of negatives by comparison," Arg. of negatives by comparison.

which you think to be so strange, it is most usual in the scriptures, and most consonant to reason. When God said unto Samuel, 1 Sam. viii. "They have not refused thee, but me;" he meant not absolutely, that they had not rejected Samuel, but, by that one negative by comparison, he understandeth two affirmatives; that is, that they had rejected Samuel, and not him alone, but chiefly they had rejected God. But of this kind of argument, look the 2. book, and 12. chapter of worthy Cranmer, archbishop of Canterbury, which he writeth of the sacrament; where he, answering the objections of the papists out of Chrysostom, touching transubstantiation, handleth this argument at large, and setteth it out by many examples[1]: to the which place I refer the reader, and you too, that you may see your lack of discretion in finding fault where none is[2]. Those be but slender answers to these arguments: except you quit yourself better in the rest of your Reply, it had been much safer for your cause to have still kept silence.

Jo. Whitgift.

A brief Examination, &c.

<small>Arg. a petitione principii.</small>

The third kind of argument is called *petitio principii*; which is, when a man frameth unto himself principles of his own device, grounded neither upon authority, neither yet upon substantial reason, and then upon the same will conclude his purpose, which is *vitiosissimum genus argumentandi*, "a very erroneous kind of reasoning;" as these men do in using these two false principles; the one, when they say that to be invented by an antichristian pope which was not so invented; the other, when they say that nothing may be used in the church of Christ which was invented by the pope, or used in the pope's church; which cannot be true, as in sundry places of the book I have declared. The self-same reasons moved the Aërians to forsake the order of the church, and to command their disciples to do the contrary of that that the church did[3]. We borrow good laws

[1 Cranmer's Works, Park. Soc. Edit. Vol. I. pp. 312, &c.]

[2 Cartwright accuses Whitgift of doing Cranmer "great injury to be compelled to communicate with this absurdity."—Sec. Repl. p. 26.]

[3 Epiph. Op. Par. 1622. Adv. Hær. Lib. III. Hær. lxxv. Tom. I. pp. 904, &c. See especially pages 907, 8.]

of the gentiles; and we use the churches, bells, pulpits, and many other things used of papists, &c.

The fourth kind of reason is of "negatives by comparison;" as this, Priests and ministers are to be known by their doctrine, not by their apparel; *ergo*, they ought not to have distinct apparel from other men. This argument followeth not: for negatives by comparison are not simply to be understanded, but by the way of comparison; and therefore of the former sentence thus we may conclude, that the apparel is not to be esteemed as a note of difference in comparison to learning and doctrine, and yet a note: as when Paul saith, that Christ sent him "not to baptize, but to preach the gospel," 1 Cor. i.; and God by his prophet, "I will have mercy, and not sacrifice," Osee vi. and Matt. ix. *[margin: Arg. a negativis per comparationem.]*

The fifth is: *Ab eo quod est non causam ut causam ponere:* "when that is taken for the cause of anything which is not the cause;" as when they condemn the Book of Common Prayer, and a prescript form of service, because (as they say) it maintaineth an unlearned, or (as they term it) a reading ministry: when as the book is not the cause of it, neither yet a prescript form of prayer, but either the parties themselves that be unlearned, or they that do admit them, or else both. This kind of argument is usual in the Admonition. *[margin: Arg. a non causa pro causa.]*

There be other unlearned[4] and unskilful reasons used in this book, which may easily be discerned, even of children; and therefore I here omit them.

Thus much I thought good generally to write, which being duly considered, the book itself needeth no other kind of confutation.

Jo. Whitgift.

To all this T. C. answereth nothing, but only to that of negatives by comparison, whereof I have spoken before.

T. C. Fol. 1, Sect. 1.

And, to the end the pith and weight of M. Doctor's arguments may be the better seen, I will likewise give the reader a say of them, noting the places of the fallations, whereunto they be referred. Which I do against my will, and compelled; for that M. Doctor, to discredit the truth, would

[4 Learned, Def. B.]

make his reader believe that those which think not as he doth in these matters are not only unlearned, but contemners of good[1] learning. Indeed there is no great learning in these small things, and they are of that sort, which although it be a great shame not to know, yet is it[2] no great commendation to have knowledge of them.

Jo. Whitgift.

It had been plain dealing to have set down M. Doctor's arguments in the same form that he hath written them; then might the reader better have judged of your collections: but you were too wise for that; for then should either your forgery have been manifest, or else your book should have been less by all this portion. I seek "to discredit" errors and contentious doctrine, and not the truth. Such learning there is even in those small things, that whoso is ignorant of them may easily be deceived, both in speaking, writing, and reasoning.

T. C. Fol. 1, Sect. 2.

In the 40.[3] page he reasoneth thus: "The ministers must learn; therefore they must learn catechisms:" which is a fallation of the consequent. For, although he that must learn a catechism must learn, yet it followeth not that whosoever must learn must by and by learn a catechism.

An untrue collection.

Jo. Whitgift.

My words in that place be these: "If they that find some want of learning in themselves, or that be crept into the ministry unlearned, either of their own accord or by commandment of their ordinary, read and learn godly and learned catechisms, they are to be commended, and so is he that provoketh them thereunto.

"That catechism which you in derision quote in the margent is a book fit for you to learn also; and I know no man so well learned but it may become him to read and learn that... necessary book. But some arrogant spirits there be that think themselves of all men best learned, and disdain to learn of any.

"That place of the fourth chapter of the first to Timothy doth not forbid a man to learn. He that is a good and modest preacher will not disdain as well to be taught as to teach."

[1 Of all good, Repl. 1 and 2.]   [2 It is, Repl. 1, 2, and Def. A.]
[3 The references here and in what follows are to the pages of the first edition of the Answer.]

Now how any man can gather of these words any such argument as T. C. frameth unto himself, let the reader judge. He might well have thus concluded: Ministers that find some want of learning in themselves, &c. ought to read and learn such books as may better instruct them; *ergo*, they may read and learn godly and learned catechisms. And again: M. Nowel his catechism is godly and learned; *ergo*, godly and learned men may read and learn it. Last of all: A godly and modest preacher will not disdain as well to be taught as to teach; *ergo*, he will be as well content to read other men's books, although they be catechisms, as he will be to have other men to read his. Now, I pray you, judge of the sequel of these reasons, and compare them with T. C. his wayward collection, and tell me truly whether he dealeth simply or no. It is true that, although a man must learn, it followeth not that he must of necessity learn a catechism; because there be other books besides catechisms to be learned, whereby a man may be instructed: but this is also true, that if a man must learn, he may learn catechisms. Surely T. C. is driven to a hard shift, when he is thus constrained to feign fallations where none are[4].

T. C. Page 1, Sect. 3.

In the 55. page he reasoneth that, forsomuch as the civil magistrate may appoint some kind of apparel, therefore he may appoint any, and so the popish apparel; which is ab eo quod est secundum quid ad id quod est simpliciter; *of which sort he hath divers others: as, women may baptize and preach, because such a one and such a one did; and, the ministers execute civil government, because Elias and Samuel did.*

Another forged argument of T. C. his own framing.

Jo. Whitgift.

The words in that page be these: "May not therefore christian magistrates in christian commonweals, for order and decency, appoint a several kind of apparel as well to ministers as to other states of men? Judges, serjeants, aldermen, and citizens, are known by their apparel; and why may not the ministers be so likewise? are they not under subjection? be they not subject to civil laws and ordinances? ought they not to obey their governors in all things not against

[4 Cartwright persists that if Whitgift has made any argument at all, it must be as he has gathered it—Sec. Repl. p. 27.]

the word of God?" If it had pleased T. C. to have set apart dallying, he might have seen, that from the last section of the 54. page unto the fourth section of the 56. page my drift is to prove that ministers may differ from other by their apparel, and that they may have a distinct kind of garments from laymen, and that the civil magistrate hath authority, for order and decency, to appoint a several kind of apparel to ministers. Now, if he would have gathered truly, he should have framed his argument thus: Christian magistrates have authority in christian commonweals, for order and decency, to appoint a several kind of apparel to ministers; *ergo*, ministers may differ and be known from other by their apparel. Whether that the civil magistrate may appoint them to wear such apparel as was used in the pope's time or no, that I handle at large, even from the 4. section of the 56. page to the portion of the Admonition in the 62. If T. C. had marked this mine order, he would not so confound himself and delude his reader by such untrue collections of my arguments.

Touching the other examples of baptizing by women, and civil offices in ecclesiastical persons, because he hath not quoted the page (which argueth he knoweth not where to find them, or that he is loth the reader by searching the places should perceive his corrupt dealing in the gathering), I will defer answering of them until I come where they, or any similitude of them, may be found. In the mean time with the first he chargeth me untruly, and the second I intend to justify.

T. C. Fol. 1, Sect. 4.

It is proved sufficiently in the treatise of archbishops.

In the 69. page he saith, "*Cyprian speaking of the office of an archbishop,*" *which is a manifest petition of the principle. For, it being that which should have been proved, M. Doctor taketh it for granted. And in divers places, speaking of the archbishop, he goeth about to deceive his reader with the fallation of the equivocation, or divers signification of the word*[1]. *For whatsoever he findeth said of archbishop and bishop in times past he bringeth to establish our archbishops and bishops, when notwithstanding those in times past were much different from ours, and are not of that kind, as shall appear afterward.*

[1 World, Def. B.]

Jo. Whitgift.

As though Cyprian may not speak "of the office of an archbishop," except he express his name; or as though the circumstance of the place may not declare that he speaketh of such an office. But how justly I am here charged with a manifest "petition of a principle," I shall have better occasion to declare, when I come to answer the manifest cavil which T. C. useth touching that place of Cyprian.

How also "in divers places, speaking of the archbishop, I go about to deceive my reader with the fallation of equivocation" (which is only said in this place without any manner of proof or any one example), shall likewise appear, when I come to answer the Reply touching that matter; where it will evidently fall out that T. C. is greatly deceived, in that he supposeth the archbishops and bishops in times past so much to differ from ours, especially if he mean the difference to be in authority and office.

T. C. Fol. 1, Sect. 5.

In the 239. page he reasoneth that, forsomuch as those which wear the apparel do edify; therefore they edify by reason of the apparel: which is to make that the cause which is not, but only cometh with the cause. Another untrue collection.

Jo. Whitgift.

You deal in this as you have done in the rest, that is, corruptly; for the second reason which I there use, to prove that the apparel doth edify, is this: "That such as have worn the[2] apparel, and do wear it, by the ministry of the word have greatly edified, and do daily." In the which argument I make not the apparel the efficient or substantial cause of edifying, but an accidental cause. For you know that it is an order and law in the church of England, that none should either administer the sacraments, or preach, except he receive the apparel appointed: forasmuch therefore as he that refuseth to wear the apparel, by order of this church, may not preach, and therefore cannot that way "edify;" and he that weareth that apparel may preach, and so "edify," therefore the apparel, *per accidens*, doth "edify;" even as the church, the pulpit, and such other things do, which

[2 This, Answ.]

"edify" not *per se*, "of themselves," but *per accidens*, "accidentally," as all other accidental ceremonies do.

T. C. Page 1, Sect. 6.

In the 240. *page he reasoneth thus, that the surplice, &c., be notes, and notes of good ministers; therefore they be good notes of ministers: which is a fallation of composition, when a man thinketh that whatsoever is said of a thing by itself may be said of it when it is joined with another.*

Jo. Whitgift.

The Admonition saith, that "cap, gown, tippet, &c. have the shew of evil, seeing the popish priesthood is evil[1]." To the which I answering say on this sort: "When they were a sign and token of the popish priesthood, then they were[2] evil, even as the thing was which they signified; but now they be signs and tokens of[3] the ministers of the word of God, which are good; and therefore also they be good." What can you say to this manner of speaking? is it not true to say that they were signs of evil, when the things that they signified were evil, and now they be signs of good, seeing the things they signify be good? and, as they were evil signs when they signified evil things, so they be now good signs because they signify good things. Do we not commonly call the signs and notes good or evil, even as the things signified be good or evil? None is so ignorant that knoweth not this; and therefore my reason is good, but your collection is like itself. I have used no other manner of reasoning or speaking in this place than M. Bucer doth in the same matter, fol. 59. and 60[4]. And therefore this is rather spoken against him than against me.

T. C. Page 1, Sect. 7.

In the 149. *page he reasoneth thus: Those which authorised the book of Common Prayer were studious of peace, and building the church; therefore those which find fault with it are pullers down of the church, and disturbers of the peace: which is a fallation of the accident, when a man thinketh that every thing which is verified of the subject may be likewise verified of that which is annexed unto it. The further confutation of the which[5] arguments I refer unto their places.*

[1 There is a slight variation here, and in the next page, from the words of the Admonition.]
[2 Were they, Answ.]   [3 The tokens and the signs of, Answ.]
[4 See below, Tract. VII. Chap. v. Div. 5.]   [5 Of which, Repl. 1 & 2.]

Jo. Whitgift.

The Admonition saith that those persons, "in which and by whom the book of Common Prayer was first authorised, were studious of peace, and of building up of Christ's church[6]." Whereupon I conclude that, if that be true, then the defacers of the[7] book "be disturbers of the peace." Which I gather of that that they themselves have granted, and as I am persuaded truly; neither do I understand how it can be made a fallation *ab accidente*. For I think that the meaning of the authors of the Admonition is, that these men shewed themselves "desirous of peace, and of building up the church," even in collecting and authorising that book (or else to what purpose should they make any mention of them?); which if it be true, as it is, then the argument must of necessity follow.

T. C. Page 1, Sect. 8.

There be divers other which he hath, which are so far from just conclusions, as they have not so much as any colour of likelihood of argument, which I cannot tell where to lodge unless I put them in the common inn, which is that which is called the "ignorance of the elench." As in the 68.[8] *page, when he concludeth thus, that Cyprian speaketh not of the bishop of Rome; ergo, he speaketh of an archbishop.* An untruth, for there is no such argument.

Jo. Whitgift.

I might here justly quarrel with you for leaping so disorderly, sometimes forward and sometimes backward, as from the 240. page to the 149., and from that to the 68., &c. But I let all such things pass, and come to the matter. In the 68. page as you quote it, but indeed the 69., after I have declared the true meaning of Cyprian, I add, that Cyprian there "speaketh not of the usurped authority of the bishop of Rome over all churches, but against the insolency of some which, despising their metropolitan or archbishop, did with their factiousness trouble the church." Which words I added, to declare how untruly the papists do abuse

[[6] Cartwright rejoins that Cranmer and Ridley were so studious of peace that they would have had the princess (afterwards queen) Mary in Edward VI.'s time indulged with the exercise of the mass; and that they allowed certain popish ceremonies in their book to draw the papists to the gospel; hence that "they were studious of peace and building of the church, but yet erred in the mean." —Sec. Repl. pp. 29, 30.]

[[7] That, Def. A.]   [[8] 69, Repl. 2.]

that place of Cyprian, to prove the pope's authority over all the churches, when he only speaketh of the authority of an archbishop or bishop in his own province or diocese[1]. True it is that Cyprian doth not speak of the authority of the bishop of Rome over all churches, but of the authority that Cornelius, then bishop of Rome, or Cyprian himself, had in his own province; neither will any deny this but papists. Now, to pervert this my plain meaning, and to father on me, whether I will or no, this argument, "he speaketh not of the bishop of Rome, and therefore of an archbishop," argueth a mind disposed to contend, and a stomach desirous rather to deface the person, than to give ear to the matter.

T. C. Page 1, Sect. 9.

Other untruths.

And in the 71. page: There must be superiors; ergo, one minister must be superior unto another. There must be degrees; therefore there must be one archbishop over a province.

Jo. Whitgift.

There are no such reasons; those that be in that place alleged are only out of Hierome and Chrysostom, and of greater force than will be truly answered.

T. C. Page 1, Sect. 10.

Another untruth.

And in the 73.: There was one over every congregation; therefore there was one over all the ministers in the province. These, and a number like unto these, M. Doctor hath scattered throughout his book, which, as Nero said of his master Seneca's works[2], cleave together like sand; and thus let it be seen whose arguments are most justly concluded, those of the Admonition or these of M. Doctor's.

Jo. Whitgift.

It is a shame to lie of the devil. Where find you in all that page any such argument, or similitude of it? But surely you have done me a great pleasure, who, searching my book so diligently for arguments to quit the Admonition, have not

[1 Cartwright sneers at Whitgift for saying that "Cyprian's place was abused by the papists," taunts him with using a "headless arrow," and says that the papists "have found you their champion to fight for them whilst they look on." —Sec. Repl. p. 30.]

[2 It is told of Caligula. See Sueton. Calig. 53.]

found one, but most vainly and untruly feigned those to be which be not. Truly, I do not think myself in every circumstance to be so circumspect, but that I may minister sometime matter to a quarreller; howbeit, as yet you have not found any thing for your purpose. And I shall most heartily desire the reader to judge of the rest of your doings even according to these beginnings.

TO THE CHRISTIAN READER[3].

I am not ignorant to what dangers (especially of uncharitable and slanderous tongues) I have made myself subject by taking upon me this work: notwithstanding, my reckoning is made, and I have armed myself against the worst, being taught so to do by the opprobrious speech of divers, who, as busy-bodies intermeddling in other men's matters more than it becometh them, do thereof judge most unchristianly, and report most untruly; believing as partial judges whatsoever is reported, howsoever falsely and unjustly. But, as I with all my heart for my part forgive them, and wish unto them more christian hearts, indifferent ears, and charitable mouths, so do I exhort thee, christian reader, to abstain from all such rancour, and other partial and sinister affections in reading of this my book; and think of me as of one that, to speak the truth, to testify his conscience, to maintain the peace and quietness of the church, to withstand erroneous opinions or contentious doctrine, will neither spare his labour nor his fame; and yet not so stiffly addicted to his own opinion, but that he can be contented to submit himself to better authority and reasons than he himself hath. And, I beseech thee, receive this admonition at my hand: Try before thou trust: believe not lightly every report: as thou hast two ears, so use them both: condemn no man before he be heard: abstain from speaking evil of any when he is not present to make thee answer (for that is a great injury): respect not the person, but the cause, and let not every pretensed zeal carry thee headlong thou knowest not whither; and suspend thy judgment of this book, until thou hast advisedly and indifferently read the same.

Necessary admonitions.

Respect of persons lay aside.

[3 This is inserted from the Answer: it is omitted in the Defence.]

An Exhortation to such as be in authority, and have the government of the Church committed unto them, whether they be Civil or Ecclesiastical Magistrates.

Jo. Whitgift.

Considering the strangeness of the time, the variety of men's minds, and the marvellous inclinations in the common sort of persons (especially where the gospel is most preached) to embrace new-invented doctrines and opinions, though they tend to the disturbing of the quiet state of the church, the discrediting and defacing of such as be in authority, and the maintaining of licentiousness and lewd liberty; I thought it good to set before your eyes the practices of the anabaptists, their conditions and qualities, the kind and manner of their beginnings and proceedings, before the broaching of their manifold and horrible heresies, to the intent that you, understanding the same, may the rather in time take heed to such as proceed in like manner, lest they, being suffered too long, burst out to work the same effect. I accuse none, only I suspect the authors of this Admonition, and their fautors: what cause I have so to do, I refer to yourselves to judge, after that I have set forth unto you the anabaptistical practices, even as I have learned in the writings of such famous and learned men, as had themselves experience of them, when they first began in Germany, and did both personally reason with them, and afterwards very learnedly write against them; neither will I in this point write one word, which I have not my[1] author to shew for.

[1 Mine, Answ.]

An Answer to the Exhortation to the Civil Magistrates.

T. C. Page 2, Sect. 1.

It is more than I thought could have happened unto you, once to admit into your mind this opinion of anabaptism of your brethren, which have always had it in as great detestation as yourself, preached against it as much as yourself, hated of the followers and favourers of it as much as yourself. And it is yet more strange, that you have not doubted to give out such slanderous reports of them, but dare to present such accu- Big words. *sations to the holy and sacred seat of justice, and thereby (so much as in you lieth) to corrupt it, and to call for the sword upon the innocent (which is given for their maintenance and safety), that, as it is a boldness untolerable, so could I hardly have thought that it could have fallen into any that had carried but the countenance and name of a professor of the gospel, much less of a doctor of divinity. Before you will join with us in this cause, you will place us, whether we will or no, in the camp of the anabaptists, to the end you might thereby both withdraw all from aiding us which are godly minded, as for that you, fearing (as it seemeth) the insufficiency of your pen, might have the sword to supply your want other ways. And, if we be found in their camp, or be such disturbers of the quiet estate of the church, defacers of such as be in authority, maintainers of licentiousness and lewd liberty, as you do seem to charge us with, we refuse not to go under those punishments that some of that wicked sect received, for just recompence of their demerits. You say you will not accuse any. I* A charitable judgment, and yet before he reproved the like. *know it is for want of no good-will that you do not accuse them, of whose condemnation and extreme punishment we might be sure, if your hand were as strong as your heart. But you "suspect the authors of the Admo-*

1 Cor. xiii. 5. *nition, and their fautors." Charity is not suspicious. Let us therefore see whether there be just matter to bear out and to uphold this suspicion. You will bear men in hand that, if we be not already full anabaptists, yet we are in the way thither: the footsteps whereby you trace us must be considered.*

Jo. Whitgift.

There is no cause why you should so marvel at the matter, all things well considered; neither do I think that the anabaptists do so greatly detest and hate them as you would make us believe. I do not accuse them of the doctrine of anabaptism (as you yourself in the end of this section do acknowledge), but I declare that I greatly suspect them, because they come so near unto the qualities and practices of the anabaptists, and use the same beginnings: whether this my suspicion be true or no, I refer it to the judgment of others. If the reports be slanderous, let them take their lawful remedy against me; but, if they be most manifest, then it is convenient that the magistrates have understanding thereof. Your great words do not answer the matter. I "fear" not "the insufficiency of my pen" (I thank God); neither is there any cause why I should; for the truth hath always a plentiful defence, whereas error and schism is compelled to use arrogant, opprobrious, and contemptuous speeches to maintain itself.

Of all other, T. C. hath least cause to complain of such extremity, or to speak in this manner. I have much more cause to accuse his undutiful and unthankful nature. If "charity be not suspicious," why do you then thus not suspect, but directly give sentence, that "it is not for want of good-will that I do not accuse them of anabaptism?" Is it not lawful for me to suspect, and is it lawful for you to condemn? You took upon you to reprove me before for judging, and can you fall so soon into it yourself? Indeed "charity is not suspicious" without just and lawful causes; but, whether the causes be just or no, let those judge to whom it doth especially appertain.

Jo. Whitgift.
The First Article, Page 2, Sect. 1.

Bull.adversus Anabap.fol.1.

First, "anabaptism tendeth to this end, that, in those places where the gospel hath been for a time preached, and where churches be reformed, the gospel may be hindered, the churches disquieted, the simple brought to doubt of the religion that hath been taught them, contentious and unquiet minds may have matter to work on, the preaching of the gospel become odious; finally, that magistrates, and such as be in authority, may be contemned and despised of their subjects and inferiors[1]."

[1 Anabaptismum e malo principio ortum huc tendere, ut illis in locis in quibus evangelium jam primum prædicari cœpit, vel ab aliquo jam tempore annuntiatur, ecclesias Christi turbet, simpliciores dubios et incertos faciat, contentiosos autem et inquietos animos adhuc inquietiores reddat, et ut prædicationem

T. C. Page 2, Sect. 2.

It is all true you here allege of the anabaptists: God be praised there is nothing of it true in us. If through these questions moved the church be disquieted, the disquietness riseth in that the truth and sincerity which is offered is not received. We seek it in no tumultuous manner, but by humble suit unto them to whom the redress of things pertain, and by teaching as our callings will suffer. If all those are to be counted in the way to anabaptism, which move controversies when the gospel is preached, Acts xi. 19 [2]. *then those that taught that the gentiles were to be preached unto, when as the most of the believing Jews (which likewise preached the gospel) thought otherwise, are to be counted in the way of* [3] *anabaptism; likewise, those that preached that circumcision was not necessary unto salvation, when as a great number of Christians at the first thought it necessary. Then Master Zuinglius and Œcolampadius smelt of anabaptism, which went about to overthrow divers things which Master Luther held. I could go further with this, but I content myself with these examples. If any be brought in doubt or hatred of the truth hereby, or any man take occasion to be contentious, it is not in the nature of the doctrine which is taught, but in the corruption of their minds; nor it is not offence given, but taken; nor this doctrine can be no more charged than* Matt. x. 34. Luke xii. 49. *the rest of the gospel, which is a sword that cutteth a city or kingdom in sunder, and setteth a fire where there was none, and putteth contention between the father and the son. But what is to give an incurable offence unto the simple, and matter to the enemy to rejoice in, to all good Christians of tears and weeping, if this be not, to make the world think that numbers of those which profess the gospel are infected with the poison of anabaptism, which cannot be touched with the smallest point of it? As for the magistrate, and authority, we acknowledge the lawfulness, necessity, and singular commodity of it, we commend it in our sermons to others, we pray for them, as for those of whose good or evil estate hangeth the flourishing or decay of the commonwealth and church both. We love them as our fathers and mothers, we fear them as our lords and masters, and we obey them in the Lord, and for the Lord. If there be any thing wherein we do not according to that which is commanded, it is because we cannot be persuaded in our consciences that we may so do (whereof we are ready to render a reason out* [4] *of the word of God); and, if that will not serve, forthwith to submit ourselves to that punishment that shall be awarded against us. And herein, we first call the Lord God to witness of our meaning, and then we refer ourselves to the consciences of all men in the sight of God.*

The case is nothing like.

A good saying if unfeigned.

evangelii omnibus suspectam, ingratam, et exosam faciat: præterea ut subditos cum suis dominis committat.—H. Bullinger. adv. Anabapt. Libri VI. Tigur. 1560. Lib. I. cap. i. fol. 1.]

[2 This reference is inserted from Repl. 2.]
[3 To, Repl. 1 and 2.]   [4 Def. B. omits *out*.]

Jo. Whitgift.

Nothing is here said of you in the defence of the authors of the Admonition, but the anabaptists will say the same in theirs. Let the like effects, proceeding from the like causes, and in like manner, judge the likelihood betwixt the anabaptists and them. One of the chief notes that are given of anabaptists by Zuinglius, in his book called *Ecclesiastes*, and in his other books where he speaketh of them, is, "that they sow discord and contention in those churches, where the gospel hath been truly preached, and that about external matters[1];" as it may more at large appear in the second edition of my Answer to the Admonition. And tell me, I pray you, what church hath any of them settled themselves in, but in such wherein the gospel hath been well planted before? or in what place have they for any time remained, where they[2] have not with contention and factions troubled, not that place only, but the whole country round about in like manner? Surely, if they preached doctrine necessary to salvation (that is the gospel), and in those places wherein the gospel is not received; then, if contentions should arise, the cause were not to be ascribed unto them, but unto their hearers only: but, seeing they cannot teach the gospel more sincerely than it is taught, and seeing the matters they contend for be not of such necessity, that the churches should for them be disquieted, seeing also that they seek reformation (as they call it) neither in due time, due place, nor before meet persons; and, finally, seeing contentions are raised by them in those places where the gospel is received, I see not how they can avoid the just accusation of contentious persons and disturbers of the peace of the church. For if you ask of the time; the Admonition was published after the parliament, to the which it was dedicated, was ended. If you speak of the place; it was not exhibited in parliament (as it ought to have been), but spread abroad in corners, and sent into the country. If you inquire of the persons; it came first to their hands who had least to do in reforming. Likewise your sermons of these matters: when preach you them? Surely even in this troublesome and tumultuous time, when there is especial occasion to move men to prayer, to

Zuinglius.

The admonitors justly accused of contention.

Their disorder in publishing the Admonition.

Their disorder in preaching.

[¹ See below, pages 125, &c.]   [² Thy, Def. B.]

unity, and to the embracing of the substance of religion, which by all means is sought to be overthrown. Where preach you them? Even where they do least good and most harm; in places where the gospel hath been already planted, yea, and oftentimes in secret conventicles and corners, which the truth never seeketh, but upon extreme necessity. And before whom preach you? Not before such as have authority to redress, but before the common people, who (although some of them be godly and sober) yet for the most part be greatly delighted with novelties, love such schoolmasters as teach liberty, and continually inveigh against superiors. All this being true, as you cannot deny it to be true, there is no cause why you should be offended with the setting down of the first article.

To preach the gospel is a thing necessary unto salvation; to preach that circumcision and such like ceremonies be not matters of salvation is a necessary doctrine, and of the substance of religion. Zuinglius and Œcolampadius, and other, differed from Luther in some matters of substance; and yet did they orderly and lawfully, with the consent of their magistrates, proceed in these matters: wherefore these examples help you nothing; for the matters you contend for be not of the same nature, neither do you proceed in like manner[3]. The same answer may be made to all other like examples that you can use in these matters. But, because I will not lean only to mine own judgment in this case, let it not grieve you if I set down M. Zuinglius' opinion touching the same, who in his book called *Ecclesiastes*, speaking against the anabaptists, saith on this sort: "If they were sent of God, and endued with the Spirit of God, they would have construed in the best part these external things which be not as yet rightly reformed, they would have become all things to all men, that they might have won all to Christ, &c.[4]" M. Calvin also in his book against the anabaptists saith, that "when, under the colour of a zeal of perfection, we can bear no imperfection, either in the body, or in the

_{Zuingl. in Eccles.}

_{Calvin adversus Anabap.}

[3 Cartwright rejoins that he is ready to prove that the matter which he and his party insist on is "also of the substance of religion," and asks what Zuinglius "should have done, if the magistrate would not have suffered him to answer."—Sec. Repl. p. 31.]

[4 H. Zvingl. Op. Tigur. 1581. Ecclesiast. Pars II. fol. 49. 2. See below, page 128, note 2.]

members of the church, it is the devil which puffeth us up with pride, and seduceth us with hypocrisy to make us forsake Christ's flock[1]."

T. C. useth the same defence for his contention, that the anabaptists do. Zuingl. in Eccles.

Whatsoever you allege for the salving of your contentious doctrine out of the x. of Matth. ver. 34, the same do the anabaptists use for their excuse also; as Zuinglius testifieth in his *Ecclesiastes:* his words be these: "Their doctrine bringeth forth nothing but contention and tumults; in the defence whereof they allege that Christ said, 'I came not to send peace, but the sword:' to whom we answer, that his

The sword which Christ sendeth is not between the faithful.

sword hath no place among the faithful; for it divideth the faithful from infidels; but they make contention and brawling among the faithful, and that for external things[2]." Hitherto Zuinglius; which is sufficient answer to you also using the same excuse, and moving contentions in like manner and matters. The same sense have the words of Christ, Luke xii. ver. 49[3]; for the gospel is a sword that divideth the faithful from infidels, but not the faithful among themselves[4]. It is the greatest " offence to the simple," and most worthy of christian " tears and weeping," that men should cloak and colour their arrogancy, contention, and errors, with a false pretence of godly zeal for the " purity of faith," the "sincerity of the gospel, and the reformation of the church," as Master Bucer in iv. *ad Ephes.* saith that some did even in his time[5].

Bucer in v. Eph.

What you think and teach of "the authority of the civil magistrate" will appear hereafter more plainly in some other parts of your book: your additions to your protestation of allowing magistrates, and of your obedience to them, may colour your abridging of their authority; for, if they command you any thing wherein you intend not to obey, you may say, they commanded not that "in the Lord," and that it is against your "conscience." These exceptions or excuses be very general, and may with you (who in all things pretend the word of God and "conscience") straiten the

[1 Calvin. Op. Amst. 1667—71. Instr. adv. Anabapt. Tom. VIII. p. 363. See below, page 138, note 2.]

[2 H. Zvingl. Op. Tigur. 1581. Ecclesiast. Pars II. fol. 54. See below, pages 128, 9, note 3.]   [3 94, Def. B.]

[4 Cartwright rejoins that it appears from John vi. that " the truth may sometimes divide the faithful amongst themselves."—Sec. Repl. pp. 31, 32.]

[5 M. Bucer. Prælect. in Epist. ad Ephes. Basil. 1562. cap. iv. p. 152. See below, page 138, note 4.]

authority of the magistrate to your own purpose. But hereof we shall something more plainly (although not fully) understand your opinion hereafter. The same protestation that you make it may appear that the anabaptists made also in the beginning; as Zuinglius declareth in his *Ecclesiastes*[6].

Jo. WHITGIFT.
The Second Article, Page 2, Sect. 2.

Secondly, "they bitterly inveighed against ministers and preachers of the gospel, saying that they were not ordinarily and lawfully called to the ministry, because they were called by the magistrate and not by the people; that they preached not the gospel truly; that they were scribes and Pharisees; that they had not those things which Paul required in a minister, 1 Tim. iii.; that they did not themselves those things which they taught unto other; that they had stipends and laboured not, and therefore were ministers of the belly; that they could not teach truly, because they had great livings, and lived wealthily and pleasantly; that they used not their authority in excommunication; that they attributed too much unto the magistrate[7]."

Bull. fol.1,11, 18, 87, 102, 244.

T. C. Page 3 and 4.

There was never heretic so abominable, but that he had some truth to cloak his falsehood: should his untruths and blasphemies drive us from the possession of that which he holdeth truly? No, not the devil himself, saying

[6 H. Zving. Op. Ecclesiast. Pars II. fol. 54. See below, pages 128, 9, note 3.]
[7 ... doctrina ipsius [Munceri] tota ardebat, et primum contra evangelii ministros...Thomas Muncerus...docebat...concionatores...neque a Deo missos esse, neque verum Dei verbum prædicare, sed esse scribas.—H. Bullinger. adv. Anabapt. Libri VI. Tigur. 1560. Lib. I. cap. i. fol. 1. 2. Quidam ipsorum in ministros ecclesiæ et magistratum invehebantur.—Id. ibid. cap. iv. fol. 11. Deinde aiunt...quod non legitime et ordinarie ad ministerium sint vocati. Quod non sint præditi his rebus quas Paulus 1 Tim. iii. in ministro requirit. Quod ea quæ alios docent, ipsi non faciant. Quod stipendia habeant, et non laborent, atque ideo ventris ministri sint.—Id. ibid. cap. viii. fol. 18. Conf. Lib. III. cap. iv. fol. 87. Libere enim dicunt, concionatores qui stipendium accipiant non esse veros Dei ministros, neque posse docere veritatem...qui otiose accipiant ingentia stipendia...et ex his divitiis splendide et luxuriose vivant.—Id. ibid. Lib. III. cap. ix. fol. 102. 2. Multa etiam ipsos [concionatores] magistratui tribuere, cujus tamen nullus inter Christianos usus sit....Concionatores nulla uti separatione, et peccatores non arcere a cœna Domini, neque ullam excommunicationem habere.—Id. ibid. Lib. I. cap. viii. foll. 18. 2, 19. Conf. Ejusd. Apolog. Anabapt. ibid. fol. 244.]

that God had given his angels charge over his, can thereby wring this sentence from us, why we should not both believe it, and speak it, being a necessary truth to believe and speak. You may as well say we are anabaptists, because we say, there is but one God, as they did, one Christ, as they did, &c. And here I will give the reader a taste of your logic, that you make so much of in your book. The anabaptists say that the churches should choose[2] their ministers, and not the magistrate; and you say so: therefore you are anabaptists, or in the way to anabaptism[3]. The anabaptists complained that the Christians used not their authority in excommunication; and so do you complain: therefore you are anabaptists, or in the way to them. I will not lay to your charge, that you have not learned Aristotle's Priorums, which saith it is ἀσύστατον, as often as the mean in any syllogism is consequent to both the extremes[4]. But have you not learned that which Seton, or any other halfpenny logic, telleth you, that you cannot conclude affirmatively in the second figure[5]? And of this sort are every one of your surmises contained in this treatise, which you entitle, "An Exhortation, &c." And, if I liked to make a long book of little matter (as you do), I would thus gather your arguments out of every branch which you ascribe as common unto us with the anabaptists, as you make ado upon every place which is quoted by the Admonition to the parliament. But answer, I pray you, in good faith: are you of that judgment, that the civil magistrate should ordain ministers? or that there should be no excommunication, as it was, and is used[6] in certain the Helvetian churches? If you be, your controversy is not so much with us as with the bishops, which both call ministers, and excommunicate. If you be not, why is that anabaptistical in us which is christian and catholic in you? and why do you go about to bring us in hatred for those things which you do no more allow, than those[7] whom you thus endeavour to discredit? We do not say that there is no lawful or no ordinary calling in England; for we do not deny but that he may be lawfully called, which is not ordinarily, as M. Luther, Melancthon, Zuinglius, Œcolampadius[8]. And there be places in England, where the ministers be[9] called by their parishes, in such sort as the examples of the scripture do shew to have been done, before the eldership and government of the church be established. I know not any that saith that the gospel is not truly preached in England, and by those also that are not of the same judgment that the Admonition to the parliament is of. But if it be said, that it is not generally of every

Psal. xci. 11.[1]
Matt. iv. 6.[1]

This is your own logic, and these be arguments of your own framing.

No: but that may be the true church of Christ wherein there is no excommunication; the contrary whereof the anabaptists affirm.

By what authority presume those parishes so to do? What scriptures, or where? will you not quote one?

[1 These references are inserted from Repl. 2.]
[2 Churches ought to choose, Repl. 2.]
[3 Anabaptistrie, Repl. 1.]   [4 Aristot. Analyt. Priora, I. c. 28.]
[5 Nulla est conclusio affirmativa in secunda figura.—Joh. Seton. Dialect. Lond. 1572. Lib. III. De Syllogism. Reg. 24. fol. Q. 2. John Seton was a fellow of St John's College, Cambridge. His Dialectica he dedicated to bishop Gardiner, chancellor of the university. It was frequently reprinted.]
[6 As in the primitive and is used, Repl. 1; which we know was in the primitive and is used, Repl. 2.]
[7 These, Repl. 1 and 2.]   [8 Œcolampadius, &c. Repl. 1 and 2.]
[9 Are, Repl. 1 and 2.]

one of them, and in all points, or not so often, or not there where their duty bindeth them and they are called unto, or not so sincerely or without mixture as it ought to be; then there is nothing said but that which, we fear, may be too easily proved. If it be said of some, that in certain there are found some of those things that were reprehended in the Pharisees, what is that to prove that they be anabaptists that speak of it[10]*? Yourself, in one place of your book, call the authors of the Admonition, and their favourers, Pharisees, who do all things to be seen of men, and therefore they sigh, and hold down their heads, &c. And this you speak against them that preach the gospel. Therefore by your reason you give sentence of anabaptism against yourself. You promised you would not write one word, whereof you had not your author for it. First, you have perverted the meaning of the anabaptists, in that wherein they accused the godly ministers, that they were not according to that which is written in the third of the 1. Epistle to Timothy, and all because you would multiply the number of your likelihoods. For they charged the ministers, by that place, of dissoluteness, and looseness of life, and corruption of manners; and we allege it to prove that they should be able to teach and instruct, against the dumb ministry that is abroad. But that which followeth uttereth not only great untruth and falsification of the author, but sheweth a mind desirous to slander, and sorry (as it seemeth) that those which you so grievously discredit are no liker the anabaptists than they be. I will set down the words, as they are written in the* 102. *leaf, that it may appear how faithfully you have dealt.* Libere enim dicunt concionatores qui stipendium accipiunt non esse veros Dei ministros, neque posse docere veritatem, sed esse ventris ministros, qui otiose accipiant ingentia stipendia ex illis rebus quae simulachris immolatae fuerunt, et ex divitiis splendide et luxuriose vivant; cum tamen Christus dixit, Gratis accepistis, gratis date; et prohibuit duas tunicas, peram, et pecuniam habere. Praeterea Paulum aiunt manibus suis laborasse, et mandasse reliquis ut idem faciant,...itaque concludunt... nulla debere stipendia habere sui officii, sed laborare et gratis ministrare, et quia hoc non faciunt, non posse ipsos veritatem docere.[11] : *" They say freely (speaking of the anabaptists) that the preachers which take stipends cannot be the true ministers of God, nor teach the truth, but are ministers of the belly, which, to live idly, take great stipends of those things which were offered to images, and do of their riches live gorgeously and riotously; when notwithstanding Christ said,* Ye have received freely, give freely; *and forbade them to have two coats, or a scrip, or money. Besides that, they say that Paul laboured with his own hands, and gave commandment to the rest of the ministers that they should do so; and therefore they conclude, that they should have no stipend for their office, but labour and minister for nought; and, because they do not so, they*

Marginal notes: This is untrue. If it be not so, what may be said of you? What other thing is affirmed in the second article?

[10] Speak it, Repl. 1 and 2.]
[11] H. Bullinger. adv. Anabapt. Libri vi. Tigur. 1560. Lib. iii. cap. ix. fol. 102. 2; where *stipendium accipiant, ex his divitiis, Christus dixerit, prohibuerit, reliquis ministris ut,* and *hoc non faciant.*]

cannot teach the truth." Now let all men judge whether it be one thing to say, that they ought not to have stipends that labour not, or to say, as the anabaptists said, that it was not lawful to have any stipend, or to say, they could not teach truly because they had great livings, or because they had any livings at all. Although I never read nor heard any of those that you mean say, that those which had great stipends and livings could not preach truly. It may be that divers have said, that it were meet the ministers should be content with competent stipends, and that the overplus of that might go to the supply of the wants of other ministers' livings, and to the maintenance of the poor, or of the university, and that that excess is the cause of divers disorders in those persons that have it; but that they could not preach truly (when they preached) which had great livings, I for my part never heard it. I think you would not be exempted from reprehension of that wherein you fault, and therefore I know not what you mean by these words, *"that they did not those things themselves which they taught others."* We profess no such perfection in our lives, but that we are oftentimes behind a great deal in doing of that which is taught to be our duties to do, and therefore think it necessary that we should be reprehended, and shewed our faults. Whereas you say that the anabaptists accused the ministers for giving too much to the magistrates, I have shewed what we give; and, if it be too little, shew us, and we will amend our fault. I assure you it grieveth me, and I am even in the beginning weary of turning up this dung, and refuting so vain and frivolous slanders, without all shew and face of truth, and therefore I will be brief in the rest.

<small>Note his modest and mannerly speeches.</small>

Jo. Whitgift.

I speak not here of the doctrine of the anabaptists, which is the certain note whereby they may be known; but of their other qualities and manner of talk and preaching. The words be M. Bullinger's, they be not mine. The arguments framed be yours, and neither his nor mine.

<small>They seek not the reformation, but the defamation of ministers.</small> Your disciples magnify you, because your usual talk, both public and private, is against the ministers of the church, against their calling, against their preaching, against their life, &c., which you do not to reform them (for you do it in their absence, and to the people), but to deface them, and to discredit them; not to promote the gospel (which they preach as diligently and sincerely as you do), but to bring them into hatred with the people, whereby you might the rather prevail in your enterprises; not to reform their manners (for they may compare with you in all kind of honesty and duty), but to express your malice and wrath; for that which Zuinglius in *Elench. contra Anabap.* speaketh

<small>Zuingl. in Elench. cont. Anabap.</small> of them (" It is melancholy and wrath, not true zeal of which

they glory[1]"), may be truly verified of you; and thereof let this your book be judge.

Now, if I say that in this point you agree with the anabaptists, I do not therefore straightway conclude that you are anabaptists; but this I conclude, that you are not for such invectives to be esteemed as more pure in deed than your brethren, nor they thorough such slanderous speeches of yours to be discredited; because herein you speak or practise nothing against the true ministers of the word of God, but that which the anabaptists have done in the self-same form and manner before you. And that these be qualities worthy to be observed in the anabaptists, and such as proceed in like manner, it may appear, not only by this observation of M. Bullinger, but of other learned and godly men also, that have written against them, and given notes of their qualities. Zuinglius, in his book before-named, saith, that "they speak evil both of the civil magistrate and of the ministers of the church, that, if at any time either of them, according to their office, reprove them, then they straightway say that therefore they be enemies unto them, because they tell them of their faults[2]." And in his *Ecclesiastes* he saith thus of them: "They so slander, revile, and backbite the ministers of the word, and of the church, that they ought to be suspected and hated of all godly men, even for their slanderous and cursed speaking. But their end and purpose is by this means to win credit unto themselves, and to discredit such as set themselves against them and detect their errors[3]." The like saying he hath in his book *De Baptismo*. To the same effect also speaketh Gastius of them in his book *De Exordio et Erroribus Catabap.*; where among other sentences he hath this: "Their talk uttereth nothing else but reprehension of the ministers of the word, and liberty in external things[4]." Now judge, I pray you, whether this hath been a quality worthy to be observed in the anabaptists, or no?

Ibidem. Why the anabaptists speak evil of magistrates and ministers.

Idem in Eccles.

Gastius.

[1 H. Zvingl. Op. Tigur. 1581. Elench. contr. Catabapt. Pars II. fol. 23. See below, page 126, note 2.]

[2 Id. ibid. fol. 8. See below, pages 125, 6, note 6.]

[3 Id. Epist. præf. Ecclesiast. fol. 40. 2. See below, page 126, note 5; also pages 129, 30.]

[4 J. Gast. De Anabapt. Exord. Error. &c. Basil. 1544. Lib. I. p. 143. See below, page 135, note 9.]

I do not speak against such as modestly, and according to the rule of the apostle, 1 Tim. v., do reprove any; but against those that have nothing else in their mouths but invectives against the ministers of the word, observing neither place, time, nor any other circumstances, whom I still say in this point to be fitly compared to the anabaptists.

Now whether it be my "logic" or yours that you give "a taste of" in this place, let the learned reader judge; to whom also I commit the trial of this spirit of yours, which bursteth out in such unseemly manner upon the consideration of your own devised arguments, to feed your contempt and disdain with. Indeed, if you make arguments where I make none, and if you frame them as it pleaseth you, no marvel it is, though you make a long book, and cause your reader to believe that my logic is as simple as you would have it. But deal with me uprightly and honestly, and then set down my unskilfulness, and spare not, as I trust you would do to the uttermost in every point, if you could, seeing that you do it where there is no occasion at all offered unto you by me, but imagined of yourself. Well, let these quarrels go, more meet to be among boys than among men. *Gratia Dei sum quod sum;* neither have I any thing but that which I have received of him from whom cometh all good things.

Both of the election of ministers, and of excommunication, what I think I will declare, God willing, in their proper places. The words here by me alleged (as I have said) are M. Bullinger's, and they be truly spoken, and to good purpose, as there it shall appear. In the meanwhile I refer you, for that of the magistrate in electing of ministers, to the 87. and 88. leaves of that his book, *Adversus Anabap.*, and for that of excommunication, to the 233. and 234. leaf of the same book[1].

First Admonition contrary to T. C. You deny that you say, "there is no lawful or no ordinary calling of ministers in England:" which is a strange hearing to me; for whereunto then tendeth all that which is written in your book touching the electing and calling of ministers? or that which is written in the first Admonition, folio 9, where they say in plain terms, that we have "neither a right minister of God, nor a right government of his

[¹ H. Bullinger. adv. Anabapt. Libri vi. Tigur. 1560. Lib. iii. cap. iv. foll. 87, 8; ibid. Lib. vi. cap. x. foll. 233, 4.]

church[2]?" and folio 34, 35, 36, &c., folio 157, where they say, that " this prescript form of service, used in this church of England, maintaineth an unlawful ministry;" or that which is so bitterly spoken against the book of ordering ministers and deacons, which they call the "pontifical?" But you say that "he may be lawfully called, which is not ordinarily." I would have you to speak plainly. Is our calling to the ministry here in England lawful, but not ordinary? If it be lawful, then is it not against the word of God, neither is there any law in the scriptures to the contrary, as you would make us to believe[3]. But truly I think that you were not here well advised; or else have you some subtle meaning; for you add immediately, that "there be places in England where the ministers are called by their parishes, &c." So that I suppose you mean that in some parishes of England there is a lawful calling of ministers: if it be so, then is it notwithstanding truly said, that you deny the manner of calling ministers in this church of England to be lawful; for that manner of calling is not to be ascribed to this church, which is used in some conventicles and secret congregations, but that which is allowed by public and common authority.

Your distinction of "lawful" and "ordinary" is not simply good; for, whatsoever is lawful in a church established, that is ordinary: I think that even very common reason doth teach this to be true. Wherefore certainly, if our ministry be lawful, it is ordinary[4]. If any parish in England do elect or call their ministers otherwise than the orders and laws of this church doth permit, I cannot see how that parish can excuse itself of schism, and I think verily that such parishes ought to be looked to in time.

Lawful is ordinary in a church established.

I do not well understand what you mean by these words, "in such sort as the examples of the scripture do shew to have been done, before the eldership and government of the

[2 See below, page 140. It may be observed that the quotations from the Admonition, here and below, page 93, are not quite literally accurate.]

[3 Cartwright censures Whitgift for not being able to see "how the ministry of England may be commonly and for the most part unlawful and not right, and yet some found which either may have their calling according to the word of God, diverse from that which is commonly used; or else (the lawful calling by the church ceasing) have it by an immediate calling from God."—Sec. Repl. p. 33.]

[4 Cartwright rejoins that "the distinction is good," and instances "it is not ordinary for a woman to bring forth three or four children at once and yet it is lawful."—Ibid. pp. 33, 4.]

church be established." What examples be these? You quote no places where to find them. Or when was the government of the church and eldership established? If you had more plainly expressed these two things, we might have the better understood your meaning[1]. But belike these parishes do not call their ministers in all points according to the rule that you would have prescribed; and therefore you make an "interim" of it, until your government be fully finished. This is your dealing to allow of all things done out of order; yea, though it be against your own order, so that it tend to the derogation of public and common order.

The admonitors deny the gospel to be truly preached in England.
Second Admonition, page 6.

Whether they say, that "the gospel is not truly preached in this church of England," or no, look in the whole discourse of their book; and in the second Admonition, page 6, where you may find these words: "I say that we are so scarce come to the outward face of a church rightly reformed, that, although some truth be taught by some preachers, yet no preacher may, without great danger of the laws, utter all truth comprised in the book of God; it is so circumscribed and wrapped within the compass of such statutes, such penalties, such injunctions, such advertisements, such articles, ... such sober caveats, and such manifold pamphlets, that in manner it doth but peep out from behind the screen." What say you to these words? how can you salve them?

Whether they generally call all the ministers of the gospel which be not on their sect Pharisees, or no, let the whole discourse of both the Admonitions judge, and that pamphlet intituled, "An Exhortation to the bishops to deal brotherly with their brethren[2]:" in my answer to which pamphlet I prove that this name Pharisee doth much more aptly agree unto the authors thereof, and such like, than to the bishops and other ministers, whom they so often call by that name, and so odiously compare them together in that pamphlet.

I must once tell you again, that I make no arguments here, I do but only compare their qualities and conditions: I have performed my promise; if I have not, shew me wherein. I pervert not the meaning of the anabaptists, but set down

[1 Cartwright replies, "I nothing doubt but a child of nine years old doth understand it: you cannot yet comprehend it."—Ibid. p. 36.]

[2 This pamphlet was replied to by Whitgift at the end of his Answer. For an account of it, see Strype, Life of Whitgift, Book I. chap. vii. It will be further noticed hereafter.]

the very words of M. Bullinger, word for word, without any addition, diminution, or alteration: it had been well if you had examined the places better.

Touching the falsification and untruth you charge me with, I think you be not in good earnest; it is but because you could no longer temper your heat: for you make many of these outcries; but I suppose you use them only as means to cast up your melancholy, which you call "zeal." Whatsoever I there speak of the anabaptists, I find it in the same form of words in those leaves of M. Bullinger's book, which I have quoted in the margent. Peruse with a little more diligence folio 18., where he hath these words: *Quod stipendia habeant, et non laborent, atque ideo ventris ministri sunt;* and the 102[3]: and, if you find not there, word for word, all this that I have here spoken touching the stipends and livings of ministers, and in the same form of words, then use your hot rhetoric; but I know they be there, and you reprove you cannot tell what. If this so greatly trouble you, I will tell you what Zuinglius also saith of this matter in his *Ecclesiastes*, where he, speaking of anabaptists, saith thus: "They teach that such cannot preach the gospel sincerely, which have benefices; but their hope is to have the true pastors expelled, that they may succeed in their places, and yet they publicly protest that they seek for no living[4]." Now whether you or your men agree with them in this point, or no, I neither deny nor affirm: if you be pricked, I cannot blame you though you kick. Neither do I say, that those ought to have stipends which labour not, I do but report Bullinger's words of the anabaptists: I would have no man exempted from due reprehension: I only report this, to shew the malicious spirits of the anabaptists against the ministers of the word, that it may be known of what society they may be suspected to be, whose talk is wholly bent against the ministers of the word of God.

That you give too little to magistrates, it shall be shewed in place.

Though you be weary, it is no marvel, for it grieveth

Bull. advers. Anab. fol. 18. Idem, fol. 102.

Zuingl. in Eccles.

[3 H. Bullinger. adv. Anabapt. Libri VI. Tigur. 1560. Lib. I. cap. viii. fol. 18. 2; where *sint;* Lib. III. cap. ix. fol. 102. 2.]

[4 H. Zvingl. Op. Tigur. 1581. Epist. præf. Ecclesiast. Pars II. fol. 41. See below, page 127, note 6.]

you to be touched so narrowly. And surely, if you use no cleanlier terms than you do in this place, or continue in pouring out your choler in such abundance, you will tire me also, or ever I make an end[1].

Whatsoever I have here spoken of the anabaptists is most true, and therefore no slander.

Jo. Whitgift.
The Third Article, Page 2, Sect. 3.

<small>Bull fol. 9, 18.</small>

Thirdly, "the whole reformation that was then in the church displeased them, as not spiritual enough and perfect. For the sacraments were not (as they said) sincerely ministered, things were not reduced to the apostolic church, excommunication not rightly used, no amendment of life appeared since the preaching of the gospel; therefore the church then reformed no more the[2] true church of Christ, than was the papistical church[3]."

T. C. Page 4, Sect. 1.

We praise God for this reformation, so far forth as it is agreeable unto the word of God: we are glad the word of God is preached, that the sacraments are ministered; that which is wanting we desire it may be added, that which is overmuch cut off; and we are not ashamed to profess that we desire it may be done according to the institution of the churches in the apostles' time: you yourself confess that excommunication is abused; that no amendment of life appeareth since the preaching of the gospel, it[4] is an old and general complaint of all godly ministers, in all churches, and in all times. Isay preached this in the church, and of the whole <small>Isai. v. 1.</small> *church, and, further, that they brought forth rotten fruit; David,* <small>&c.[5]</small>

[1 Cartwright says to this: "As for the cleanliness of my terms which I use, they are not so foul as the things whereunto they are applied," and refers to Mal. ii. 3, and Phil. iii. 8.—Sec. Repl. p. 38.]

[2 No more to be the, Answ. 2.]

[3 ...tota reformatio quæ tum instituebatur, illis displicebat, ut nimis angusta et exilis, non satis spiritualis, alta et perfecta.—H. Bullinger. adv. Anabapt. Libri vi. Tigur. 1560. Lib. i. cap. iv. foll. 9, 10. Ecclesias enim nostras non esse veras ecclesias Christi, non magis quam papistarum aut aliorum...prædicari quædam ex evangelio, neminem tamen emendari, ac omnem populum impœnitentem et peccatis ac sceleribus obnoxium esse....In ministerio...multa desiderari aiunt, cum in doctrina tum in administratione sacramentorum...Concionatores nulla uti separatione, et peccatores non arcere a cœna Domini, neque ullam excommunicationem habere.—Id. ibid. cap. viii. foll. 18, 9.]

[4 Repl. 2 omits *it*.]

[5 This reference is inserted from Repl. 1 and 2.]

Psal. xii. 1.[6] that "*the faithful people were diminished out of the land,*" *Psal. xiv.* 3.[6] *that there was "none that did good, no not one." And divers other of the prophets have made grievouser complaints, and great charges against the people of God, and yet were no anabaptists, nor in the way to anabaptism. If there be none that either have written or spoken, that the church of England "is no more the true church of Christ than the papistical church," then, besides that there is no truth in your tongue, there seemeth to be no shame in your forehead; if there be any, it standeth your good name in hand that you bring them out.*

Jo. Whitgift.

What is thought by some of you of the reformation of this church, let both the Admonitions and your book also bear witness. The second Admonition doth call it a "deformed reformation." I will say no more of that matter in this place; for our whole controversy is about it. You and yours seek to deface and abase this reformation as much as in you lieth; and surely you do but colourably seem in part to allow of it here. For your "so far forth" may include and exclude what pleaseth you: howbeit, I confess that it is no reformation, except it be agreeable to the word of God. The controversy is, what part of it is agreeable to the word of God, and what is not; also, what it is to be agreeable to the word of God. But of this more is to be spoken hereafter. *Second Admonition, fol. 37.*

It is true, that godly preachers have always complained of lack of amendment of life, where the gospel hath been preached. But the anabaptists use this as a reason to deface the church of Christ, and to condemn it; as it may appear in that place of M. Bullinger: even so likewise do the authors of the Admonition. *The difference betwixt the complaints of godly preachers and of anabaptists.*

Though they have not spoken so slanderously of this church of England in the very same words, yet have they done it by circumstance. For whereunto tend so many bitter words against the state of it in both the Admonitions, and in your book also? Both the Admonitions say, that "it is scarce come to the outward face of a church rightly reformed;" and the second Admonition addeth that "the truth in this church doth (in a manner) but peep out from behind the screen," fol. 6. And, fol. 38, it saith further, that there be "untolerable abuses in the communion book," and doth there deface it almost from the beginning even to the end. And, fol. 42, *Both the Admonitions speak slanderously of the church of England. Second Admonition, fol. 6. Fol. 38. Fol. 42.*

[[6] These references are inserted from Repl. 2.]

that "the sacraments are wickedly mangled and profaned;" fol. 43, that "the word of God is negligently, fantastically, profanely, and heathenishly preached, and the sacraments wickedly ministered." Every line of that book is almost nothing else but such untemperate speeches of the whole church of England, and everything therein used. I omit to recite the particular phrases of the first Admonition, and your modest speeches of this book; because I have already in my Answer laid out the one, and the other I intend not to omit, as occasion is offered. Now, therefore, I do boldly affirm that of the authors of the Admonition, which before I did but set down of the anabaptists, that they do with as spiteful words and bitter speeches condemn the church of England, as they do the papistical church; nay truly, I think they have nowhere so outrageously spoken against that church, as they have done against this; more outrageously I am sure they can speak against nothing.

Jo. Whitgift.
The Fourth Article, Page 3, Sect. 1.

Bull. fol. 9, 18, 77.

Fourthly, "they had their private and secret conventicles, and did divide and separate themselves from the church, neither would they communicate with such as were not of their sect either in prayers, sacraments, or hearing the word[1]."

T. C. Page 5, Sect. 1.

If some of those which favour this cause have been overcarried in part to do things which might have been more conveniently ordered, it is against reason that you should therefore charge those which favour this cause which[2] you oppugn. You would think you had wrong, if, because some of those that favour that which you favour in this matter be either free-will men, or hold consubstantiation in the sacrament, you should be chal-

It standeth your good name in hand to bring them out.

[1 Hi omnes simul conspirabant, ac multa clandestina colloquia habebant.— H. Bullinger. adv. Anabapt. Libri vi. Tigur. 1560. Lib. i. cap. iv. fol. 9, 2. ...docent...non debere ullam communionem habere cum evangelicis et christianis nostris ecclesiis, aut cum aliis quibusvis.—Id. ibid. cap. viii. fol. 18. ...omnia sua dicta, consilia et facta, huc dirigunt...quo [homines] coetus ecclesiasticos non amplius adeant, sacras conciones non audiant a suis pastoribus, neque in illis coetibus preces suas Deo per Christum offerant et eum adorent, ac sacramenta in suis ecclesiis et a suis pastoribus non percipiant.—Id. ibid. Lib. iii. cap. i. fol. 77.]

[2 That, Repl. 1 and 2.]

lenged as free-will men, or maintainers of consubstantiation. If those meetings which they had were permitted unto them by them that have authority, I see nothing why they may not seek to serve God in purity and less mixture of hurtful ceremonies. If they were not permitted, yet your name of " conventicles," which agreed to the anabaptists, is too light and contemptuous to set forth those assemblies, wherein I think you will not deny but that the word of God and his sacraments were ministered; and take you heed that these so reproachful speeches, which you throw out against men, reach not unto God. A softer word would have better becomed you. Schismatical meetings are aptly called conventicles.

JO. WHITGIFT.

I declare what the anabaptists did, and I use M. Bullinger as mine author. If it please you to apply it unto yourself, or to some of your company which be more pure, I cannot let[3] you. But this I say, that this word " conventicle" is soft enough for such meeting in corners: and I further add, that such schismatical assemblies be not tolerable in a church reformed, and that these persons which so separate themselves from the church, if they be not anabaptists, they be of some other such like sect[4]. Well saith Augustine, in his book *De Unitate Ecclesiæ*, that, "although a man agree with the scriptures in the chief and principal points of doctrine, yet, if he divide himself from the unity of the church, he is not a member of the same[5]." Schismatical assemblies not tolerable.

August. de Unitate Ecclesiæ.

The word of God is oftentimes preached, or the sacraments administered, in the conventicles of the anabaptists and other heretics; and yet, as Augustine saith, *Qui unitati*[6] *ecclesiæ non communicant non sunt in ecclesia*[5]: " Those Ibidem.

[³ Let: hinder.]

[⁴ Cartwright observes on this: "I grant the corruptions of the church of England to be such that man in abstaining from the pollutions thereof ought not so [to?] sever himself from those open assemblies wherein the eternal word of the Lord God is preached and the sacraments administered, although not in that purity which they ought to be." He goes on to object to the name of "conventicles" as "too light and contemptuous."—Sec. Repl. p. 38.]

[⁵ Et rursus quicumque de ipso capite scripturis sanctis consentiunt, et unitati ecclesiæ non communicant, non sunt in ecclesia....Item quicumque credunt quidem quod Christus Jesus, ita ut dictum est, in carne venerit, &c.; sed tamen ab ejus corpore, quod est ecclesia, ita dissentiunt, ut eorum communio non sit cum toto quacumque diffunditur, sed in aliqua parte separata inveniatur; manifestum est eos non esse in catholica ecclesia.—August. Op. Par. 1679—1700. Contr. Donat. Epist. seu Lib. de Unit. Eccles. cap. iv. 7. Tom. IX. col. 342.]

[⁶ Unitate, Def. B.]

that break the unity and peace of the church are not in the church."

If there were either so many "free-will men, or maintainers of the consubstantiation," as there be of the sect of the puritans, or if they were maintained and justified by us, as the other be by you, then surely you might justly charge us with their errors; else the reason is not like. Your Admonition, to use soft words, would have become any man rather than you, who so uncivilly and roughly abuse both your terms and words.

Jo. Whitgift.

The Fifth Article, Page 3, Sect. 2.

Bull. fol. 1.

Fifthly, "they counted all them as wicked and reprobate which were not of their sect[1]."

T. C. Page 5, Sect. 2.

I answer as unto the last clause of the third article.

Jo. Whitgift.

And I refer myself to that which I have answered there, and to the whole discourse of both the Admonitions, and also to this your book, but especially to the 35. page of the Second Admonition.

Jo. Whitgift.

The Sixth Article, Page 3, Sect. 3.

Bull. fol. 10.

Sixthly, "they pretended in all their doings the glory of God, the edifying of the church, and the purity of the gospel[2]."

T. C. Page 5, Sect. 3.

We pretend it not, but we propound it, and herein we call God to witness against our own souls.

Jo. Whitgift.

I cannot let you to apply things to your ownselves at your pleasure. *Volenti non fit injuria.* I set that of the anabap-

[1 Impios vero nominabant omnes qui non essent suæ sectæ homines.—H. Bullinger. adv. Anabapt. Libri vi. Tigur. 1560. Lib. i. cap. i. fol. 1, 2.]

[2 Veruntamen in omnibus his rebus semper gloria Dei, recta ædificatio ecclesiæ et regni Christi, prætexebatur.—Id. ibid. cap. iv. fol. 10.]

tists down to this end, that men may understand not all those to seek "the glory of God, &c." which pretend the same; because the anabaptists have those pretences, and yet they seek nothing less. That the anabaptists, and such like disturbers of the church, have those pretences, not only M. Bullinger in those places by me quoted, but other godly and learned men also, do testify. Zuinglius, in his *Ecclesiast.* saith that "they boast that, whatsoever they speak, they speak it of zeal, being moved with the Spirit[3]." Gastius saith in his book, *De Exordio et Erroribus Catabap.*, that "under the pretence of zeal they subvert whatsoever other men have builded[4]." Bucer, in iv. *ad Ephes.*, saith, that "Satan covereth and cloketh arrogancy, self-love, envy, and hatred, with a false pretence of godly zeal for the purity of faith, for the sincerity of Christ's doctrine, and for the salvation of the church[5]." It is expedient for men to know this; else might they through simplicity easily be deceived.

All seek not the glory of God, that pretend so to do.

Ecclesiast.

Gastius.

Bucer.

Jo. WHITGIFT.

The Seventh Article, Page 3, Sect. 3.

"They earnestly cried out against pride, gluttony, &c. They spake much of mortification; they pretended great gravity; they sighed much; they seldom or never laughed; they were very austere in reprehending; they spake gloriously. To be short, *Magna et varia erat ipsorum hypocrisis:* They were great hypocrites; thereby to win authority to their heresy among the simple and ignorant people[6]."

Bull. fol. 11, 17.

T. C. Page 5, Sect. 4.

If you do not[7] these things (which we say not), we will rather do them

[3 H. Zvingl. Op. Tigur. 1581. Ecclesiast. Pars II. fol. 49. See below, page 128, note 2.]

[4 J. Gast. De Anabapt. Exord. Error. &c. Basil. 1544. Lib. I. p. 302. See below, page 136, note 1.]

[5 M. Bucer. Prælect. in Epist. ad Ephes. Basil. 1562. cap. iv. See below, page 138, note 4.]

[6 Clamabant strenue contra superbiam, contra crapulam et ebrietatem, contra blasphemias et alia scelera. Vitam in speciem spiritualem agebant: erant graves, multum suspirabant, non ridebant: vehementes erant in correptionibus, magnifice loquebantur: ut his rebus sibi admirationem et auctoritatem apud simplices et pios homines compararent.—H. Bullinger. adv. Anabapt. Libri VI. Lib. I. cap. iv. fol. 11. In summa magna et varia erat ipsorum hypocrisis.—Id. ibid. cap. viii. fol. 17. 2.]

[7 Note, Def. A. & B.]

[WHITGIFT.]

with the anabaptists, than leave them undone with you. *Of our simple heart and meaning in them we have before protested.* In the mean season we will patiently abide, until the Lord bring our righteousness in this behalf unto light, and our just dealing as the noon-day. Touching our sighing, and seldom or never laughing, you give occasion after to speak of it, unto the which place I reserve the answer.

Psal. xxxvii. 6.

Jo. Whitgift.

I do not write this of them, because I would have men abstain from reproving vice, and exhorting to godliness, but to let it be understood that these be no certain proofs of the verity of the doctrine, being commonly used in most vehement sort of the heretics and sectaries, to allure the people unto them, and to win credit unto their opinions.

Jo. Whitgift.

The Eighth Article, Page 3, Sect. 5.

Bull. fol. 11. "If they were at any time punished for their errors, they greatly complained that nothing was used but violence, that the truth was oppressed, that innocent and godly men, which would have all things reformed according to the word of God, could not be heard, nor have liberty to speak: that Zuinglius stopped their mouths, and defended his cause, not by the word of God, but by the authority of the magistrate[1]."

T. C. Page 5, Sect. 5.

We are no stoics, that we should not be touched with the feeling of our griefs: if our complaints be excessive, shew them; and we will abridge them. What errors we defend, and how you maintain your part by the word of God, it will appear in the discourse of your book.

Jo. Whitgift.

And yet your complaint in this point, as it is without just cause, so is it common to you with the anabaptists, and

[1 Hinc autem factum est, ut anabaptistæ et ipsorum fautores cum in agro tum in urbe graviter conquererentur, vi omnia agi, veritatem opprimi, ac innocentes et pios homines, qui nihil aliud conentur quam quod verbo Dei contineatur, non audiri, neque illis pro ipsorum necessitate liberam dicendi facultatem dari....Simul etiam Zuinglius graviter accusabatur, quod nemini loqui permitteret, et veritatem in adversariorum suorum ore et quasi gutture opprimere conaretur: item quod hac ratione, causam suam non verbo Dei, sed clamoribus et magistratus imperio tueretur.—Id. ibid. cap. iv. fol. 11. 2.]

therefore no true note of the verity of your doctrine, nor any sufficient cause why you should therefore be more gracious unto the people. The chiefest thing that the common sort have to say in your defence is, that you be persecuted, put from your livings, &c.: which if it were altogether true, as it is reported, yet your complaint is no other than the anabaptists' is, and therefore no more to be alleged for the justifying of you, than the like is for the justifying of them.

Jo. Whitgift.

The Ninth Article, Page 3, Sect. 6.

"They found great fault with the baptizing of chil- dren, and ceremonies used in the same; but afterward did utterly condemn it[2]."

<small>Bull. fol. 10, 214.</small>

T. C. Page 5, Sect. 6.

Their finding fault without cause in the ceremonies of baptism cannot bar us from finding fault where there is cause. We allow of the baptism of children, and hope, through the goodness of God, that it shall be far from us ever to condemn it. But to let your slanderous tongue go (all the strings whereof ye seem to have loosed, that it may the more freely be thrown out and walk against the innocent), where[3] is the modesty you require in other, of not entering to judge of things unknown, which dare insinuate to the magistrate, that it is like they will condemn children's baptism, which do baptize them, preach they should be baptized, and which did never, by syllable, letter, or countenance, mislike of their baptism?

<small>Mark the modesty of the man.</small>

Jo. Whitgift.

Can you deny anything to be true that I have spoken of the anabaptists in this article? or can you deny but that yourselves also mislike the ceremonies used in baptism in this church? yea, and the same that they did? What followed in them is manifest: what will follow in you, God knoweth; I judge not. What be my suspicions, is declared in my Answer to the Admonition, which if you have truly taken away, I am satisfied; but I am afraid the contrary will appear in your book.

[² Incipiunt ergo pædobaptismum damnare, clamant baptismum infantum non a Deo institutum, sed a Nicolao pontifice inventum esse, ideoque iniquum et ex diabolo esse.—Id. ibid. fol. 10. 2. Conf. Lib. VI. cap. iii. foll. 213, 4.]

[³ Repl. 1, 2, and Def. A. repeat *where*.]

Jo. Whitgift.

The Tenth, Eleventh, Twelfth, Page 3, Sect. 7.

Bull. fol. 19.
"They taught that the civil magistrate hath no authority in ecclesiastical matters, and that he ought not to meddle in causes of religion and faith.

Page 4, Sect. 1.

Bull. fol. 19, 95, 242.
Fol. 178.
"That no man ought to be compelled to faith and to religion.

"That Christians ought to punish faults, not with imprisonment, not with the sword, or corporal punishment, but only with excommunication[1]."

T. C. Page 5, Sect. 7.

I answer as unto the fifth, and for further answer I will refer the reader to those places, where occasion shall be given to speak of those[2] things again.

Jo. Whitgift.

And I refer myself also to the Admonitions, and to your own book, and to my several answers which shall be made touching these matters.

Jo. Whitgift.

The Thirteenth Article, Page 4, Sect. 3.

Fol. 11, 242.
"They complained much of persecution[3]."

T. C. Page 5, Sect. 8.

This is a branch of the eighth, and added for nothing else but to make up the tale.

Jo. Whitgift.

And yet a worthy note; else should it not have been so often repeated, not only of Bullinger, but of other godly men also, as of Zuinglius, Gastius, and others.

[1 Magistratum non debere curare causas religionis aut fidei....Christianos non occidere, neque carcere neque gladio punire; sed tantum excommunicatione. Neminem ad fidem vi et imperio cogendum esse.—Id. ibid. cap. viii. fol. 19. Conf. Lib. III. cap. vi.; Lib. v. cap. vi. foll. 95, 178; Apolog. Anabapt. Sec. Caus. fol. 242.]

[2 These, Repl. 1 and 2.]

[3 Id. ibid. Lib. I. cap. iv. fol. 11. 2. See above, page 98, note 1. Conf. Apolog. Anabapt. Sec. Caus. fol. 242.]

Jo. Whitgift.

The Fourteenth Article, Page 4, Sect. 4.

"They bragged that they would defend their cause, not only with words, but with the shedding of their blood also[4]." Fol. 11.

T. C. Page 5, Sect. ult.

We fear no shedding of blood in her majesty's days, for maintaining that which we hope we shall be able to prove out of the word of God, and wherein we agree with the best-reformed churches; but certain of the things which we stand upon are such as that, if every hair of our head were a life, we ought to afford them for the defence of them. We brag not of any the least ability of suffering, but in the fear of God we hope of the assistance of God his holy Spirit to abide whatsoever he shall think good to try us with, either for profession of this or any other his truth whatsoever.

Jo. Whitgift.

Thanks be unto God, there is no cause why you should fear. But wherefore do you then beat any such suspicion into the people's heads? or why do you boast of that that you know is nothing near you, and which no man once goeth about to offer unto you? What mean you, in the 59. page of the Second Admonition, to say that there is "a persecution of poor Christians and the professors of the gospel suffered, not far unlike to the six articles, which crafty heads devised, and brought the king her noble father unto, as they would do her majesty now?" Can anything be spoken more untruly, more suspiciously, nay, I may rightly say, more seditiously? Second Admonition, fol. 59.

If there be such things in controversy betwixt us that require defence even unto death, "yea, and that, if every hair of our head were a life, we ought to afford them for the defence of the same;" then truly is there greater matters in hand than everybody doth consider of. Hitherto it hath been the common opinion, that our contention was but about trifles, about external things, such as might admit alteration, and were not of the substance of religion; but, if this be true that you here set down, belike a great sort have been hitherto deceived. Truly, if the matters be of such weight that they The state of the contention altered by T. C.

[4 ...palam et diserte præ se ferebant, se causam suam non modo verbis, verum etiam sanguine proprio velle testari.—Id. ibid. fol. 11.]

require defence of life, you are much to blame that have not hitherto made them better known. I trust we shall in this book understand what they are. In the mean time the stout brags that are used by some might well be spared: but we have oftentimes seen great clouds and small rain, and heard great cracks of thunder and (thanks be unto God!) small harm done. Neither are you more to be credited for these boastings than were the anabaptists for using the like.

Jo. Whitgift.

The Fifteenth Article, Page 4, Sect. 5.

Fol. 17, 77.

"Their whole intent was to make a separation and a schism, and to withdraw men from their ordinary churches and pastors, and therefore most odiously they inveighed against such pastors, and sought by all means to discredit them[1]."

T. C. Page 6, Sect. 1.

We make no separation from the church; we go about to separate all those things that offend in the church, to the end that we, being all knit to the sincere truth of the gospel, might afterwards in the same bond of truth be more nearly and closely joined together. We endeavour that, every church having a lawful pastor which is able to instruct, all might be ranged to their proper churches, whereas divers, unless they go to other than their own parishes, are like to hear few sermons in the year; so far are we from withdrawing men from their ordinary churches and pastors. Let him that inveigheth against any pastor without good cause bear the punishment: as for inveighing against heaping of living upon living, and joining steeple to steeple, and non-residence, and such ambition and tyranny, as beareth the sway in divers ecclesiastical persons, if the price of the pacification be the offending of the Lord, it is better you be displeased than God be offended.

Jo. Whitgift.

Whether you make a separation or no, and a schism in the church, let all men judge; and whether you "draw the people from their ordinary pastors," or no, let the secret con-

[1 Initio separationem præcipue spectabant, ut ecclesiam separatam haberent.—Id. ibid. cap. viii. fol. 17. 2. ...omnia sua dicta, consilia et facta, huc dirigunt, ut separationem et schisma faciant; nempe ut homines avellant aut fraudulenter abducant ab ordinariis suis ecclesiis et pastoribus....Quo autem facilius possint efficere, splendide loquuntur, ecclesiis et ipsarum ministris horribiliter conviciantur, et illis odium quod possunt maximum conflant.—Id. ibid. Lib. III. cap. i. fol. 77.]

venticles (for I can call them no better), used, not only in the city, but in other places of the country also, testify: whether justly, and as it becometh you, you "inveigh against such pastors" and preachers as mislike your opinion, and seek their discredit, let the bitter invectives in sermons before the people, when none of them is present, the common table-talk, both your Admonitions, the first and the second, yea, and this your passing modest book, declare. Truly this article, and every content in it, was never more truly verified of the anabaptists, than it is, and may be, of you.

What you have to say against the "ambition and tyranny" of any such as you especially shoot at, we shall see in your particulars: I trust you will speak all you know, and more too; else you do degenerate.

Jo. WHITGIFT.

The Sixteenth Article, Page 4, Sect. 6.

"There was no stay in them, but daily they invented new opinions, and did run from error to error[2]." Fol. 18.

T. C. Page 6, Sect. 2.

We stay ourselves within the bonds of the word of God: we profess of ourselves[3] to be of the number of those which should grow in know-
Eph. iv. 13. *ledge as we do in age, and which labour that the image of God may be daily renewed in us, not only in holiness of life, but*
Col. iii. 10. *also in knowledge of the truth of God; and yet I know no question moved, which hath not been many years before in other churches reformed holden as truth, and therefore practised, and in our church also have been some years debated.*

Jo. WHITGIFT.

Thus much might they allege for themselves also, and apply those texts of scripture to as good purpose as you do. For that place of the fourth to the Ephesians doth teach that Eph. iv. God hath therefore appointed his ministry in the church, that it might be a means to bring us to a perfect knewledge of Christ. The meaning is not that we should be daily altering our judgment, and broaching new opinions; for against such unconstancy the same apostle speaketh in the 14. verse of Eph. iv. 14.

[2 ...quotidie multa mutata et novata sunt a fratribus, quæ passim stulti homines, tanquam articulos cœlitus demissos, recipiebant...quo longius progrediuntur et plus ambulant, eo magis et longius aberrant.—Id. ibid. Lib. I. cap. viii. fol. 18.]

[3 Profess ourselves, Repl. 1, 2, and Def. A.]

the same chapter. True it is that we must daily grow in faith and love, to the full perfection whereof we cannot attain in this life; but it doth not therefore follow that we like children must be carried about with every wind of doctrine, and never remain constant in one religion. To the same end are the words of the apostle in the iii. to the Colossians to be referred[1].

I believe it will fall out, that in this your Reply there will be found sundry articles, neither allowed nor "practised in any church reformed," nor "in our church debated" at any time heretofore.

Jo. Whitgift.
The Seventeenth Article, Page 4, Sect. 7.

Bull. fol. 78, 244.

"They were very stubborn and wilful, which they[2] called constancy: they were wayward and froward, without all humanity, they judged and condemned all other men[3]."

T. C. Page 6, Sect. 3.

If we defend no falsehood or inconvenient thing, we cannot be counted stubborn or wilful; whereof we offer to be tried by the indifferent reader. For waywardness and inhumanity, we think it a fault, as we esteem godly society and affability to be commendable; and what is our behaviour herein, we likewise refer to their judgments with whom we are conversant and have to do with: being misjudged and untruly condemned of you, we judge nor condemn no man; their vices we condemn, so far forth as the lists of our vocation doth[4] permit us.

Jo. Whitgift.

Because the answer to this article consisteth of "If," and dependeth especially of the testimony of such as have been a convenient time "conversant" with you, I refer the judgment hereof to their experience and indifferent considerations.

[1 Cartwright rejoins that "the church of England changed the book of common prayer twice or thrice after it had received the knowledge of the gospel," and hence argues that alterations may be lawfully made.—Sec. Repl. pp. 41, 2.]

[2 Which stubbornness and wilfulness they, Answ. 2.]

[3 Sequitur etiam invicta pertinacia, quam constantiam nominant, et omnis benignitas et lenitas in asperitatem acerbitatemque mutatur. Nihil ab illis auditur quam querelæ, judicia et condemnationes aliorum omnium, tum hominum tum negotiorum.—H. Bullinger. adv. Anabapt. Libri vi. Tigur. 1560. Lib. iii. cap. i. fol. 78. 2. Conf. Apolog. Anabapt. Tert. Caus. foll. 243, 4.]

[4 Do, Repl. 1 and 2.]

Jo. Whitgift.

The Eighteenth Article, Page 4, Sect. 8.

"They sought to overthrow commonweals, and states of government[5]." Fol. 78.

T. C. Page 6, Sect. 4.

We allow of commonweals, as without which the church cannot long continue; we speak not against civil government, nor yet against ecclesiastical, further than the same is an enemy to the government that God hath instituted. This seemeth to be contrary to that which he hath[6], page 35.[7]

Jo. Whitgift.

So do the anabaptists in words protest, as it appeareth by these words of Zuinglius in his *Eccles.*: "Though they protest, and by oath deny, that they take any authority from magistrates, yet shortly after we should have seen it come to pass that they would have been disobedient to all laws of magistrates, if once they had increased to that number, that they might have trusted to their own strength[8]." But what your doctrine tendeth to (though peradventure you mean not so), it will, I think, appear when it is examined. Zuingl. in Ecclesiast.

Jo. Whitgift.

The Nineteenth Article, Page 4, Sect. 9.

"They gave honour and reverence to none, and they used to speak to such as were in authority without any signification of honour, neither would they call men by their titles, and they answered churlishly[9]." Fol. 79.

T. C. Page 6, Sect. 5.

If we give honour and reverence to none, let us not only have none again, but let us be had as those that are unworthy to live amongst men.

[5 ...politias quoque, quantum in ipsis est, lacerant et dissipant.—Id. ibid. Lib. III. cap. i. fol. 78. 2.]

[6 Cartwright denies this, and says: "If I had said that the church might be established without a magistrate, then there had been some likelihood of the contrariety he surmiseth."—Sec. Repl. p. 42.]

[7 See below, Tract. III. chap. VI. div. 5.]

[8 H. Zvingl. Op. Tigur. 1581. Ecclesiast. Pars II. fol. 54. See below, pages 128, 9, note 3.]

[9 Nemini præterea ullum honorem exhibent, et quosvis absque ulla honoris significatione alloquuntur, ac cunctis illiberaliter respondent.—H. Bullinger. adv. Anabapt. Libri VI. Lib. III. cap. i. fol. 79.]

I fear there be, of those which are your favourers, ecclesiastical persons, that, if they should meet with my lord mayor of London, would strain courtesy, whether he or they should put off the cap first. We give the titles of majesty to the queen our sovereign, of grace to duke and duchess, of honour to those which are in honour, and so to every one according to their estate. If we miss, it is not because we are not willing, but because we know not always what pertaineth unto them; and then our fault is pardonable. For answering churlishly, it is answered before in the seventh article[1]*.*

<small>Where nothing is mentioned of it, but it is referred (by like) to this place, and from hence posted over thither again.</small>

Jo. Whitgift.

Indeed the anabaptists in the end rejected all authority of superiors, and refused to give unto them their due titles and reverence; yet, when they had for a time obtained their own desire, they took that to themselves most ambitiously, which they refused to give to other. You are not so far gone as yet in all states, but in the contempt of the state ecclesiastical you may compare with them to the uttermost: what you will do in the end touching the civil magistrate (if you obtain your desire), I will not determine, but leave it to the discretion of such as shall peruse these our books of such controversies.

Jo. Whitgift.

The Twentieth Article, Page 4, Sect. 10.

<small>Bull. fol. 85.</small> " They attributed much unto themselves, and pleased themselves very well, other men they contemned; and therefore their minds were full of pride and contempt[2]."

T. C. Page 6, Sect. 6.

With acknowledging of our manifold wants and ignorances, we doubt not also to take upon us, with thanksgiving, that knowledge which God hath given to every of us according to the measure of faith: we seek not to please ourselves, but the Lord and our brethren, yea, all men in that which is good. We reverence other men's gifts, so as we think the contempt of them redoundeth to the giver. Therefore, although the common infection be in us, yet we hope pride doth not reign in our mortal bodies. <small>Psal. xix. 13.[3]
Rom. vi. 12.[3]</small>

[1 See before, page 97.]

[2 Quin potius videte ne a vobis ipsis polluamini, propterea quod multum vobis tribuitis, judicatis omnes, et plurimum vobis placetis, itaque spiritualis superbia et contemptus nimium vestris animis insidet. — Id. ibid. cap. iii. fol. 85. 2.]

[3 These references are inserted from Repl. 2.]

Jo. Whitgift.

Well, for the right application of this article, I will go no further than to this your own book. Surely, if the rest of your fellows have the same spirit, there was never anabaptists in these qualities to be compared unto you. But I think better of some of them; so would I have done of you also, if I had not seen the contrary in you, even sithence our first acquaintance, but especially sithence the time wherein, upon just occasions, I began to stir you, and now most evidently in your Reply; yea, this very answer of yours to this article verifieth the same to have place in you, which in this 20. article is ascribed to the anabaptists.

Jo. Whitgift.

The Twenty-first Article, Page 4, Sect. 11.

"They went not to preach in such places where the gospel was not planted, but only they insinuated themselves into those places wherein the gospel had been diligently preached; and, where there were godly and quiet men, there they made a stir, they raised up factions and bred discord[5]."

_{Fol. 88. Preaching where least need is[4].}

T. C. Page 6, Sect. ult.

We hold that it is no minister's part to choose his own place where he will preach, but to tarry until he be chosen of others; likewise, that he insinuate not himself, but abide a lawful calling: and therefore this cannot agree to us, but to those rather which content themselves with a roving and wandering ministry, and defend the minister's own presenting and offering himself or ever he be called.

_{How happeneth it then that so many of you flock together at London? who calleth you?}

Jo. Whitgift.

And why have you then hitherto chosen such places to remain and preach in as London, &c. where the gospel without you, and before your time, was planted? Why have you there, and in such like places, disquieted the church and

[4 This marginal note is inserted from Answ. 2.]

[5 ...qui fit quod non se conferunt aut mittuntur in illa loca in quibus evangelium hactenus non est annunciatum? Tantum illis in locis se insinuant, in quibus ante multo labore et opera evangelium populo est annunciatum, et ecclesiæ reformatæ sunt. Atque ubi pii homines, pacati, et sedato animo sunt, illic anabaptistæ turbas movent, dissidia atque factiones excitant.—Id. ibid. cap. iv. fol. 88. 2.]

sown the seed of contention? What calling have you had in those places, which you might not have by the self-same means in other places also, where the gospel is not so well planted? Truly this note is so common to all anabaptists, and so notorious, that I know very few writing against the anabaptists which do omit it. Zuinglius reporteth it of them in his *Elench. contra Anabapt.*, in his *Ecclesiastes* divers times, and in his book *De Baptismo*[1]; Gastius likewise, in his book, *De Exordio et Erroribus Catabaptist.*[2]: which they would not do, if it were not a note worthy to be noted. Surely I think that I am able to prove divers of you to have insinuated yourselves to places (which pleased you) before you were called thereunto. And I am of that judgment, that a man may lawfully so do, if he desire to do good and to profit. For St Paul saith, 1 Tim. iii. *Qui episcopatum &c.*: "If a man desire the office of a bishop," &c.: which place, by the judgment of all the interpreters that I have read, doth signify that a man may offer himself with a mind to do good, so that he do not intrude himself, or seek by unlawful means to obtain that which he desireth; for then it is like that he seeketh not to profit other, but to profit himself[3].

If there be any "roving" or "wandering" ministers, it is amongst yourselves, which wander up and down, from place to place, to sow contention, and to deface by slanderous reports such as mislike your proceedings. Any other that may so truly and aptly be called "rovers" and "wanderers" I know none.

Jo. Whitgift.

The Twenty-second and Twenty-third Articles, Page 5,

Sect. 1, 2.

"They sought to be free from all laws, and to do what they list.

[1 H. Zvingl. Op. Tigur. 1581. Elench. contr. Catabapt. Pars II. fol. 8. 2; Id. Epist. præf. Ecclesiast. fol. 41. 2; Id. de Bapt. Lib. Tract. I. fol. 72. 2. See below, pages 125, 6, note 6; page 127, note 7; page 130, note 2.]

[2 J. Gast. De Anabapt. Exord. Error. &c. Basil. 1544. Lib. I. p. 11. See below, pages 133, 4, note 1.]

[3 Cartwright refers for answer touching the place of Timothy "to the treatise of the discipline of the church lately set forth."—Sec. Repl. p. 42. The title of it was "A full and plaine declaration of Ecclesiasticall Discipline owt off the word

"They were animated by crafty and subtle papists, Fol. 11. which did seek the overthrow of the gospel, and the restoring of papism[4]."

T. C. Page 7, Sect. 1.

I answer as to the fifth, and touching the 23. refer the reader to a further answer in that place, where occasion is offered to speak of it again.

Jo. Whitgift.

And for just application of the 22. article I refer you to the 60. and 61. page of the Second Admonition, where I would have you consider what their meaning is by that proviso that they would have for themselves, and by that exemption that they require to have from the jurisdiction of the bishops, justices of peace, &c. It is not amiss also to weigh what the equality meaneth that they seek for among the clergy, and the state of the seigniory, where the pastor must be the chief, of what degree soever the rest of the seniors be, whether earls, barons, &c.

Jo. Whitgift.

The Twenty-fourth Article, Page 5, Sect. 3.

"To be short, the people had them in great admi- Fol. 11. ration, because of their hypocrisy and straitness of life; and such as were of contentious natures joined with them, and commended their doings[5]."

T. C. Page 7, Sect. 2.

So far forth as we may (for the infirmities wherewith we are inclosed), we endeavour to adorn the doctrine of the gospel which we profess; we seek not the admiration of men: if God do give that we have honest report, we think we ought to maintain that, to the glory of God, and

off God, and off the declininge off the churche off England from the same. Imprinted M.D.LXXIIII." This was, it seems, a translation, by Cartwright himself, of a work written by Walter Travers. For the place referred to, see pp 33, 4.]

[4 ...quoniam huc spectant ipsorum verba, ut libertatem christianam æstiment positam, ut non subjecti sint bonis legibus, sed ut liberi possint credere et facere quicquid libuerit.—H. Bullinger. adv. Anabapt. Libri vi. Tigur. 1560. Lib. iii. cap. vi. fol. 95. ...cum tamen nihilominus a quibusdam confirmarentur, qui evangelii oppressionem et papatus incrementa sperabant.—Id. ibid. Lib. i. cap. iv. fol. 11.]

[5 ...cum tamen...a quibusdam confirmarentur, qui evangelii oppressionem et papatus incrementa sperabant, ad quod præsens contentio inserviebat, &c.—Id. ibid. See also before, page 97, note 6.]

advancement of the gospel. What is our "straitness of life" any other than is required in all Christians? We bring in, I am sure, no monachism or anchorism, we eat and drink as other men, we live as other men, we are apparelled as other men, we lie as other men, we use those honest recreations that other men do; and we think there is no good thing or commodity of life in the world, but that in sobriety we may be partakers of, so far as our degree and calling will suffer us, and as God maketh us able to have it. For the hypocrisy that you so often charge us with, the day shall try it. If any man join with us with mind to contend, it is against our will; notwithstanding we know none; and what great stirrers and contenders they be which favour this cause, let all men judge.

Who is so blind as he that will not see?

Jo. WHITGIFT.

These be fair speeches, sooner said than proved: I accuse you not of these matters; I do but report the qualities of the anabaptists: if your own consciences accuse you, or if you will needs apply these things unto yourselves (as I have said before), I cannot let you.

Jo. WHITGIFT.

An Exhortation, &c. Page 5, Sect. 4, 5.

These were the manners, conditions, practices, and proceedings of the anabaptists in Germany, before they uttered their seditious and monstrous heresies.

I leave the application hereof to your wisdoms, who easily can conjecture what kind of men they be that come nearest to these steps. Only I desire you to be circumspect, and to understand that anabaptism (which usually followeth the preaching of the gospel) is greatly to be feared in this church of England, and almost plainly professed in this Admonition, the authors whereof agree with them in these forenamed practices and qualities.

T. C. Page 7, Sect. 3.

Do you think to mock the world so that, when you have so unjustly and so heinously accused, you may wipe your mouth, and say, as you did before, that you will not " accuse " any ; and as now, that you "leave[1] *the application?" is not this to accuse, to say that the authors of the Admonition do almost plainly profess anabaptism? is not this to apply, to say that they agree with the anabaptists in all the forenamed practices and qualities? You would fain strike us, but you would do it in the night, when*

A falsification; for he addeth this word, "all."

[[1] You will leave, Repl. 1 and 2.]

no man should see you; and yet, if you have to do against anabaptists, you need not fear to proclaim your war against them: you have a glorious cause, you shall have a certain victory. I dare promise you that you shall have all the estates and orders of the [2] *realm to clap their hands and sing your* ἐπινίκια *and triumphant songs. But that you would convey your sting so privily and hissingly, as the adder doth, it carrieth with it a suspicion of an evil conscience, and of a worse cause than you make the world believe you have.*

Jo. Whitgift.

Truly I am in good earnest: I mock not: I greatly fear anabaptism, which is an heresy that hath many branches, and creepeth in secretly under notable pretences; and therefore I thought it convenient to gather these notes together out of such learned and godly writers as have had experience of them; the which also I have more at large set out in the second edition of my book[3]. If this offend you, the offence is taken and not given: you are not able to accuse me justly hitherto of any untruth. I accuse none, because I know none that will openly profess himself to be one, or plainly affirm any article which is of the substance of their heresy. But I see divers walking in the same steps that the anabaptists did towards their heresies; and therefore I thought it my duty to admonish those that be in authority to take heed of them (let men apply them as they see cause, and have experience); there can be no hurt in that: it shall make them the more circumspect, and arm them against the hypocrisy of divers. How "the authors" of both the Admonitions do "agree with the anabaptists in these forenamed practices," I have declared in my Answer to your Reply.

You falsify my words, when you affirm that I say, "they agree with the anabaptists in *all* the forenamed practices and qualities;" for I have not this universal sign "all :" if they agree with them in many, they are to be suspected. I think the anabaptists themselves, as they have divers and several opinions in doctrine, so had they also sundry qualities concerning life and conversation; and yet some there are which be common to them all. I know that "all the estates and orders of this realm" hate anabaptism: I require not your "promise" for that matter, which you offer unto me *satis*

Page 19, &c.

[² This, Repl. 1, 2, and Def. A.]   [³ See below, pages 125, &c.]

pro imperio. I know their detestation of that heresy, and therefore I am bold to open these practices and qualities unto them, lest they may by some men's hypocrisy and close dealing be deceived. My words and writings be public, my speeches plain; and therefore if I "sting," it is openly enough. The "privy hissers" and "stingers" be those that secretly smite their neighbour, and "hiss" at them in their absence, at tables, and in corners, and "sting" them behind their backs, when they are not present to answer for themselves: such "adders" and scorpions swarm among you.

Jo. Whitgift.

An Exhortation, &c. Page 5, Sect. 6.

Donatists.

Moreover, it may please[1] you to consider the conditions and practices of the Donatists, who divided themselves from the congregation, and had their peculiar churches, or rather conventicles, in Africa. They taught also that all other churches were spotted and impure, because of their ministers: finally, that there ought to be no compulsion used in matters of religion and faith, and that none should be punished for their conscience.

T. C. Page 7, Sect. 4.

Now you carry us from the anabaptists in Europe to[2] the Donatists in Afric, and you will paint us with their colours; but you want the oil of truth, or likelihood of truth, to cause your colours to cleave and to endure. The Lord be praised that your breath, although it be very rank, yet it is not so strong that it is able either to turn us, or change us into what forms it pleaseth you. I shall desire the reader to look Theodoret. lib. 4. de Fabulis Hœreticorum, *and* Augustin. ad Quod-vult-Deum, *and in his first and second books against Petilian's Letters*, where he shall find of these heretics, that by comparing them with these, to whom M. Doctor likeneth them, the smoke of this accusation might the better appear; for these slanders are not worth the answering. To this division from the churches, and to your supposed conventicles, I have answered. They taught that there were no true churches but in Africa; we teach nothing less than that there is no true church but in England. If the churches be considered in the parts, whether minister or people, there is none pure and unspotted; and this is the faith of the true church, and not of the Donatists: if it be considered in the whole and general government, and outward policy of it, it may be pure and unspotted, for any thing I know, if men would labour to purge

[1 May also please, Answ.]   [2 Unto, Repl. 1 and 2.]

it. The Donatists vaunted themselves to be exempted from sin; and what likelihood is there between any assertion of the authors of the Admonition and this fancy of the Donatists? To the last point of no compulsion to be used in matters of religion, denying it to be true, I refer[3] the further answer to another place.

Jo. Whitgift.

This that I have set down of the Donatists is all true; neither can you disprove one word of it. I write so much of their practices as be correspondent to the doings of the authors of the Admonition. The Donatists divided themselves from the congregation, and had peculiar churches, or rather conventicles, in Africa: these also divide themselves from the church; and although they tie not the church of Christ to any one corner, yet have they their several churches and secret meetings. The Donatists made this their excuse why they departed from other churches, because they were not pure and unspotted, and their ministers of evil life: these men for the like causes separate themselves from the church also. The Donatists would have no compulsion used in matters of religion and faith: these men in effect be likewise minded; for they would have no corporal punishment used; which may appear by that which is written in the Second Admonition, fol. 57, where they say that "it availeth not to make any laws but mere civil, because the government of the church is already perfit in the word;" and, fol. 56[4], and in divers places else, they speak to the like purpose, whereof occasion will be given hereafter better to consider.

The Admonitors compared with the Donatists.

Second Admonition, fol. 57.

Augustine, in his book *De Hæresibus ad Quod-vult-Deum,* sheweth that some of the Donatists were also Arians, but not all; and some of them were Circumcellions[5], of which sect

Aug. de hæresib. ad Quodvult.

Lib.iv.deFab. Hæret.

[3 Reserve, Repl. 1 and 2.]

[4 And thus I say, that neither they, nor any order we have in England this day, doth or can do that, which only God his order can do, and was appointed to do....And therefore to make laws it availeth not, save mere civil.—Sec. Adm. p. 57. Conf. ibid. p. 56; where there is a complaint of the variety of causes which come before the ecclesiastical courts.]

[5 Exstant scripta ejus [Donati], ubi apparet eum etiam non catholicam de Trinitate habuisse sententiam, sed quamvis ejusdem substantiæ, minorem tamen Patre Filium, et minorem Filio putasse Spiritum sanctum. Verum in hunc, quem de Trinitate habuit, ejus errorem Donatistarum multitudo intenta non fuit;...Ad hanc hæresim in Africa et illi pertinent, qui appellantur Circumcelliones, &c.—August. Op. Par. 1679-1700. Lib. de Hæres. Hær. lxix. Tom. VIII. cols. 21, 2. Conf. Contr. Litt. Petil. Libb. I. II. Tom. IX. cols. 205, &c.]

Theodoretus speaketh in the place by you cited[1]. But what is all this to the purpose? I speak not of all their opinions, nor of all their conditions, but of such only wherein these that separate themselves in our days seem to agree with them. *Similia* (as you know) agree not in all points: it is sufficient if they do in those things *in quibus comparantur.* Neither do I any otherwise report of them, than M. Calvin himself doth in his book against the anabaptists, and Augustine, with others that write of them.

Surely neither in the "whole," nor "in part," can "the church be unspotted" in this world, no, not "in the outward policy" and government of it; neither do I think that you are able to shew any examples of such purity: we have to the contrary even in the apostolical churches in the apostles' time, as the church of Corinth, and of the Galatians[2]. M. Calvin in his book *Adversus Anabaptistas*[3] is directly against you: and indeed I think that you are not able to shew one learned writer of your opinion in this point.

Jo. Whitgift.

An Exhortation, &c. Page 5, Sect. 7.

Comparison between these libellers and papists.[4] To conclude, these men flatly join with the papists, and by the self-same assertions bend their force against this church of England.

T. C. Page 7, Sect. ult.

Salomon saith that "the beginning of the words of an unwise man is foolishness; but the latter[5] end of them is mere madness:" Eccles. x. 13. *even so it falleth out by you; for, whilst you suffer yourself to be carried*

[1 Οὗτοι δὲ, κατὰ μὲν τὴν αἵρεσιν, τοῖς Ἀρείου συμφέρονται, καινὸν δὲ μανίας ἐπενόησαν εἶδος. τὸν γὰρ βίαιον θάνατον μαρτύριον ὀνομάζουσι...σφᾶς αὐτοὺς τοίνυν κορυβαντιῶντες ῥίπτουσιν ἀφ' ὕψους κατὰ κρημνῶν, κ.τ.λ.— Theodor. Op. Lut. Par. 1642-84. Hæret. Fab. Lib. iv. cap. vi. Tom. IV. p. 239.]

[2 Cartwright declares that Whitgift "hath untruly said of Master Calvin;" and that "the examples of the churches of Corinth and Galatia...rather make against him."—Sec. Repl. pp. 42, 3.]

[3 Olim duæ fuerunt hæreticorum sectæ, quæ ecclesiam vehementer turbarunt: quorum alteri Græco nomine Cathari, id est, Puri; alteri Donatistæ ex primi auctoris et magistri nomine appellabantur. Utrique in eodem errore fuerunt quo isti somniatores: ecclesiam quærentes, in qua nihil posset desiderari. &c.—Calvin. Op. Amst. 1667-71. Instr. adv. Anabapt. Tom. VIII. p. 363.]

[4 This marginal note is inserted from Answ. 2.]

[5 Later, Repl. 1 and 2.]

headlong of your affections, you hurl, you know not what, nor at whom, whatsoever cometh first to hand, and speak things that the eyes and ears of all men see and hear [6] *to be otherwise. Whilst you compare them to the anabaptists* [7] *and Donatists, some friend of yours might think you said truly, because such, always seeking dark and solitary places, might happily have some favourers, which are not known: but, when you join them with the papists, which are commonly known to all men, whose doctrine they impugn as well as you, whose marks and badges they can less away with than you, whose company they fly more than you, whose punishment they have called for more than you for your part have done, and therefore are condemned of them as cruel, when you oftentimes carry away the name of mildness and moderation, which forsooth know (as you have professed) no commandment in the scripture to put heretics to death; when, I say, you join them thus with the papists* [8]*, you do not only leese your credit in these untrue surmises (wherein I trust with the indifferent reader you never had any), but you make all other things suspected which you affirm, so that you give men occasion to take up the common proverb against you, I will trust you no farther* [9] *than I see you. After you have thus yoked them with the papists, you go about to shew wherein they draw with them. Wherein I first* [10] *ask of you, if all they, that affirm or do anything that the enemies of the church do, are forthwith joined and conspired with them against the church, what say you to St Paul, that joined with the Pharisees in the resurrection, with the false apostles in taking no wages of the Corinthians; our* [11] *Saviour Christ, which spake against the Jews, which were then the only people of God, as the gentiles did which were their enemies; will you say therefore that either St Paul joined with the Pharisees or false apostles against the church, or that our Saviour Christ joined against the Jews with the gentiles? But let us see your slanders particularly.*

And yet in facing and depraving this church of England they fully join with them; and so do not I.

Acts xxiii. 6.
2 Cor. xi. 12.
1 Cor. ix. 6.[12]

I say, that neither Christ nor Paul joined either with gentiles, Pharisees, or false apostles against the church.

Jo. Whitgift.

The same Salomon saith, that "in the mouth of the foolish is the root of pride, &c." Even so it falleth out with you; for, whilst with such proud words you seek to drive at me, you do but condemn yourself of folly. Pilate and Herod were at enmity betwixt themselves, and yet they joined together against Christ: the Pharisees and Sadducees were of contrary opinions, yet were they both enemies to the doctrine of Christ. The Turk and the pope be of contrary religions, yet do they both conspire against the gospel: papists and anabaptists agree not either in opinion or in society, yet do they both seek to

Prov. xiv.

Men of contrary judgments join together against the truth.

[[6] Hear and see, Repl. 1 and 2.]   [[7] To anabaptists, Repl. 1 and 2.]
[[8] With papists, Repl. 1 and 2.]   [[9] Further, Repl. 1 and 2.]
[[10] First I, Repl. 1 and 2.]   [[11] Corinthians to our, Repl. 2.]
[[12] This verse is added from Repl. 2.]

8—2

deface the church of Christ. Even so they, though they "impugn the doctrine of" the papists never so stoutly, and cast away their "marks and badges" never so far from them, though they cannot abide their "company," yet do they with them, by the same assertions (though not by the same arguments), assault this church of England, and bend their force against it. Did not the seditious Jews within Jerusalem join with the Romans, being their enemies, in procuring the destruction of that city? You are not so ignorant as you would seem to be; I am sure you understand my meaning.

How or where have you called for the "punishment of the papists more than I have done," and therefore you counted "cruel," and I "mild and moderate?" Certainly I know not; I hear only yourself say so. What I have done, and where, I mind not to brag of at this time, I leave that for you.

What I "have professed" concerning the "putting to death of heretics," the same do I profess still, and am ready thereof to give an account at all times, as I shall be required: although neither you, nor any man else, have heard me teach that doctrine, or "profess it;" but this is one of your glances by the way: when occasion is given me to speak of that matter, I will plainly utter my conscience by the grace of God. In the meantime, it is no cause why I should be better thought of among the papists; for both their practice and their doctrine is clean contrary[1].

To your question I answer that, if they do that against the church which the enemies do against the same, then do they in that conspire with them against the church; and therefore all your examples here used are to no purpose at all. For "St Paul joined with the Pharisees and with the false prophets" in those things which were allowed of the church, and for the commodity of the church, and therefore in no respect "against the church:" the same answer I make to the example of Christ justly reproving the Jews. If you would have used apt examples for your purpose, then should you

[1 Cartwright insists that Whitgift "hath taught that there is no commandment in the scripture to put heretics to death," and declares "there be more witnesses of this than his bare denial is able to bear down;" adding that, "although the papists abuse this doctrine to the horrible murder of the church, yet the doctrine is the doctrine of God, and not the papists'; and you by staying the course of it nourish them to the day of slaughter and shedding of the blood of the saints of God."—Sec. Repl. pp. 43, 4.]

have brought in such as, being of contrary judgments, have notwithstanding sought to overthrow one and the self-same thing, although by diverse means. But then should you have concluded against yourself, as you must of necessity do. So that here, where you would seem to say much, you have said nothing at all.

Jo. Whitgift.

An Exhortation, &c. Page 5, Sect. ult.

First[2], the papists affirm that we are not the true church, no, that we have not so much as the outward face and shew of the true church; and so do these men almost in flat and plain terms.

T. C. Page 8, Sect. 1.

They do not deny but there is a visible church of God in England; and therefore your sayings[3] of them, that they do "almost in plain and flat terms" say that we have not so much as any "outward face and shew of the true church," argueth that you have almost no love in you, which, upon one word once uttered, contrary to the tenor of their book and course of their whole life, surmise this of them; and how truly you conclude of that word "scarce," it shall appear when we come to that place.

Jo. Whitgift.

They do in plain and flat terms write as much as I do report of them in this article: for a manifest proof thereof I refer the reader to the 6. page of the Second Admonition, and the 33. of the first Admonition[4], and to the whole discourse of both. My "almost" is equivalent to their "scarce." But whosoever shall well consider "the tenor of their books," and the course of their life, may easily understand that both I might have left out my "almost," and they their "scarce," likewise.

Jo. Whitgift.

An Exhortation, &c. Page 6, Sect. 1.

Secondly, the papists say that we have no ministry, no bishops, no pastors, because they be not rightly and

[2 For first, Answ.]
[3 Saying, Repl. 1 and 2.]
[4 ...I say that we are so scarce come to the outward face of a church rightly reformed, &c.—Sec. Adm. p. 6. ...we...are so far off, from having a church rightly reformed,...that as yet we are scarce come to the outward face of the same.—Adm. to Parl. fol. A. ii. 2.]

canonically called to these functions: the self-same do these men affirm.

T. C. Page 8, Sect. 2.

I have answered this in the second article of anabaptism, that you charge us with[1].

Jo. Whitgift.

Then have I answered the same there also.

Jo. Whitgift.

An Exhortation, &c. Page 6, Sect. 2.

Thirdly, the papists say that our sacraments be not rightly ministered; and so say they likewise.

T. C. Page 8, Sect. 3.

This is also[2] *answered in the third*[3].

Jo. Whitgift.

That is, you have there closely confessed this to be true. But, that the reader may understand that it is most truly verified of them, let him peruse that which is written in the Second Admonition, fol. 43, where they say, "The sacraments be wickedly ministered[4];" and in the first Admonition, fol. 89; and that also that followeth in this book.

2. Admonition, fol. 43.

Jo. Whitgift.

An Exhortation, &c. Page 6, Sect. 3.

Fourthly, the papists wholly condemn our book of common prayers, set out by public authority, and the whole order of our service: in that point do these men[5] fully join with them also; for they condemn it wholly, and that with most bitterness.

T. C. Page 8, Sect. 4.

I answer, that they do not condemn it wholly, but find fault with it, as in some points disagreeing with the word of God.

[1 See before, pages 83, &c.]
[2 Also is, Repl. 1 and 2.]   [3 See before, pages 92, &c.]
[4 Would...the sacraments be so wickedly, without examination at the supper, or sincerity at baptism, be so (I say) wickedly ministered?—Sec. Adm. p. 43. Conf. Adm. to Parl. fol. A. iiii.]
[5 These men do. Answ.]

Jo. Whitgift.

For the proof of this article, read the first Admonition, fol. 85, 86, &c.; 148, &c.; the Second Admonition, fol. 9, 10, 38, 39, &c.[6]

Jo. Whitgift.

An Exhortation, &c. Page 6, Sect. 4.

Fifthly, the papists would not have the scriptures read in the church to the people: no more would they; for they say, reading is not feeding, but as evil as playing on[7] a stage, and worse too.

T. C. Page 8, Sect. 5.

All men shall perceive, when I come to that place, how you have racked their words to another sense than they spake them; in the mean season it is enough that they confess that reading in the church is godly.

Jo. Whitgift.

It is well that you confess it to be "godly:" it will appear, when I come to that place, that the authors of the Admonition both write and think far otherwise, except they write one thing and think another.

Jo. Whitgift.

An Exhortation, &c. Page 6, Sect. 5.

Sixthly, the papists deny the civil magistrate to have any authority in ecclesiastical matters; and so do they.

T. C. Page 8, Sect. 6.

I have answered in the tenth article of anabaptism[8]

Jo. Whitgift.

Your answer is there very confused and uncertain; but for the proof of this article, I refer the reader to certain notes which I have collected out of your book, touching this matter, in this my Defence.

> Where you have not spoken one word of it.

[6 Remove homilies, articles, injunctions, and that prescript order of service made out of the mass-book.—Adm. to Parl. fol. A. iiii. We must needs say as followeth, that this book is an unperfect book, culled and picked out of that popish dunghill, the portuise and mass-book full of all abominations.—Ibid. fol. A. viii. 2. ...it is wicked, to say no worse of it, so to attribute to a book, indeed culled out of the vile popish service-book, with some certain rubrics and gloses of their own device, such authority as only is due to God his book.—Sec. Admon. pp. 9, 10. Again, where learned they to multiply up many prayers of one effect, so many times Glory be to the Father, so many times The Lord be with you, so many times Let us pray? Whence learned they all those needless repetitions? is it not the popish Gloria Patri? &c.—Ibid. pp. 38, 9.]

[7 Upon, Answ.]   [8 See before, page 100.]

Jo. Whitgift.
An Exhortation, &c. Page 6, Sect. 6.

To be short, the papists refuse to come to our church, to communicate with us in the Lord's supper; and these men would not have them by laws and punishment compelled thereunto.

T. C. Page 8, Sect. ult.

I answer, that Doeg, when he said that David came to Abimelech, said nothing but truth; and when they that witnessed against Christ that he said, "Destroy the temple, and in three days I will build it up again," said nothing but that our Saviour Christ said: but yet Doeg was a slanderer, and the other, false witnesses; because the one spake of[2] mind to hurt, and the other understood it of another temple than our Saviour Christ meant it. So, although you do in part rehearse their words, yet, taking them contrary to their meaning (which might easily appear by the circumstances), I see not how you can be free from these faults, unless it be done ignorantly, which I wish were true for your own sake. And here I will desire thee, gentle reader, to mark with what conscience this man saith, that they are joined and confederate with the papists[3] against the church. The papists mislike of the book of common prayers[4] for nothing else, but because it swerveth from their mass-book, and is not in all points like unto it. And these men mislike it for nothing else, but that it[5] hath too much likelihood unto it. And judge whether they be more joined with the papists, which would have no communion or[6] fellowship with them, neither in ceremonies, nor doctrine, nor government; or they which, forsaking their doctrine, retain part of their ceremonies, and almost their whole government: that is, they that separate themselves by three walls, or by one; they that would be parted by the broad sea from them, or which would be divided by narrow water, where they may make a bridge to come again[7], and displace the truth of the gospel, as they have done in times past; they that would not only unhorse the pope, but also take away the stirrups, whereby he should never get into the saddle again; or they that[8], being content with that that he is unhorsed, leave his ceremonies, and his government especially, as stirrups whereby he may leap up again, when as occasion serveth; they that are content only to have cut the arms and body of antichristianity[9], or they which would have stump and root all up.

Psal. lii. 1.[1]
Matt. xxvi. 61.[1]

Jo. Whitgift.

Better it is to have a bad excuse than none at all. Their words and meaning is plain, as shall appear when I come to them. I think indeed their meaning is, that they would

[1 These references are inserted from Repl. 2.]
[2 Spake it of, Repl. 1 and 2.]   [3 With papists, Repl. 1 and 2.]
[4 Common prayer, Repl. 1 and 2.]   [5 But because it, Repl. 1 and 2.]
[6 Nor, Repl. 1 and 2.]   [7 Come in again, Repl. 1 and 2.]
[8 Which, Repl. 1 and 2.]   [9 Body of the tree of antichristianity, Repl. 1 and 2.]

not have them compelled to come to our churches, and to communicate in the Lord's supper with us, as it is now ministered. For it is well known, how they themselves refuse to do the same, and how they have defaced both this church, and the manner and form of administering the sacrament: what they would do, if they might have their own devised reformation, and have the law in their own hands, I cannot tell; but it is very like that they would be sharp and severe enough in compelling men to come. I speak of their opinion touching the compelling of men to come to our church, unto the which they come not themselves.

That which followeth in your Reply I have sufficiently answered before[10], where I have declared how that it is no strange thing for men of clean contrary judgments and opinions to join together in oppugning one and the self-same truth. The papists pretend one cause of misliking the book of common prayers; and they pretend another cause of misliking the same: do they not now both join in defacing and overthrowing it? That which followeth is but words: those things which they reprove in that book be godly, and most of them not to be bettered. The persons that stand in the defence of that book have all points of papistry in as great detestation as they, and, peradventure, greater; for they so occupy themselves in these external things, which be of small importance, that in the meantime they slip over matters of weight and substance, even the principal points wherein we differ from them. Wherefore this comparison of yours standeth upon a false ground. For I am fully persuaded, that you and they do the pope great good service, and that he would not miss you for anything. For what is his desire but to have this church of England (which he hath accursed) utterly defaced and discredited, to have it by any means overthrown, if not by foreign enemies, yet by domestical dissension? And what fitter and apter instruments could he have had for that purpose than you, who under pretence of zeal overthrow that which other men have builded; under colour of purity seek to bring in deformity; and under the cloke of equality and humility would usurp as great tyranny and lofty lord-likeness over your parishes as ever the pope did over the whole church? For who should be the chief man of the seigniory but the pastor, what state and degree of men

Page 51.

The admonitors gratify the papists.

Equality made a cloke for ambition.

[[10] See before, page 115.]

soever else were in that parish, yea, the prince herself? Look their Admonitions, and especially the Second, and this book also, and tell me whether it be so or no. Wherefore these glorious words of yours be but mists to blind the eyes of the simple, in like manner, and to the like purpose, used of the anabaptists against Zuinglius, Œcolampadius, Bucer, and such like sincere professors of the word of God. Peruse the notes that I have collected, not only out of Bullinger, but out of Zuinglius, and Gastius also[1], and you shall see them in all points to use these plausible pretences, and to accuse their adversaries after the like manner.

In the second edition of the Answer to the Admonition.

Jo. WHITGIFT.
An Exhortation, &c. Page 6, Sect. ult.

Hereby it is manifest, that the papists and they jointly do[2] seek to shake, nay to overthrow, the self-same foundations, grounds, and pillars of our church, although not by the self-same instruments and engines. Wherefore it is time to awake out of sleep, and to draw out the sword of discipline, to provide that laws, which be general, and made for uniformity as well of doctrine as ceremonies, be generally and universally observed, that those, which according to their consciences[3] and duty execute them, be maintained and not discouraged. Either boldly defend the religion and kind of government in this realm established, or else (if you can) reform and better the same: for it cannot be but that this freedom given to[4] men to obey and disobey what they list, to speak what they list, against whom they list, and where they list, to broach what opinions and doctrine they list, must in the end burst out into some strange and dangerous effect. The Lord both grant unto you that be magistrates the spirit of government, and to all other that be subjects the spirit of true obedience. Amen.

T. C. Page 9, Sect. 1.

Note the mildness of the man in this section.

After you have all-to[5] be-blacked and grimed with the ink of anabaptism, Donatism, and papism, those whom you found clear from the least spot or speck of any of them, you whet the sword, and blow the fire, and you will have the godly magistrate minister of your choler; and therefore,

A charitable surmise.

instead of fear of leesing the multitude of your livings, foregoing your

[¹ See below, pages 125, &c.]   [² *Do* is not in Answ.]
[³ Conscience, Answ.]   [⁴ Unto, Answ.]   [⁵ All-to: altogether.]

pomp and pride of men, and delicacy of fare, unlawful jurisdiction, which you have, and hereafter look for, conscience, religion, and establishment of the commonwealth must be pretended. What! have you forgotten that which you said in the beginning, that you accused none, but suspected certain? would you have the sword to be drawn upon your suspicions? But now you see that they whom you have accused are nothing like either anabaptists, Donatists, or papists, and yourself most unlike to[6] *him that you profess to be, and that*[7] *you see that all your slanders are quenched by the innocency (as it were by water) of those men whom you so heinously accuse,* Deut. xix.18, *you are to be put in mind of the law of God, which decreeth that* 19.8 *he which accuseth another, if he prove it not, shall suffer the punishment which he should have done, against whom the accusation had been justly proved. The Romans did nourish in Capitolio certain dogs and geese, which by their barking and gagling should give warning in the night of thieves that entered in; but, if they cried in the day-time, when there was no suspicion, and when men came in to worship, then their legs were broken, because they cried when there was no cause. If therefore he have accused justly, then is he*[9] *worthy to have his diet allowed him of the common charges: but if otherwise, we desire not that his legs may be broken, as theirs were; but this we humbly crave, that, if this our answer do not sufficiently purge us, that we may be sifted and searched nearer, that if we nourish any such monstrous opinions as are surmised, we may have the reward of them; if we do not, then, at the least, we may have the good abearing against such slanderous tongues, seeing that God hath not only committed unto the magistrate the safety of our goods and life, but also the preservation of our honest report.*

Other similitudes might have beseemed you better.

JO. WHITGIFT.

Convicta impietas, dum non habet quod respondeat, convertit se ad convitia: "Ungodliness being convicted, when she is destitute of a good answer, turneth herself to reproachful words:" but your heat of words and forgetfulness of duty and reverence I pass over with silence. "The multitude of livings" which I have I do enjoy by law, and may retain (I thank God) with a far better conscience than T. C. did one living for the space of certain years, and would have done still with all his heart if he might have been winked at, though it were expressly against his oath[10]. My "pomp" is very small: my "pride of men" is but according to my calling; it were more for my profit if I had fewer. My "delicate fare"

[6 Unto, Repl. 1 and 2.]   [7 Now, Repl. 2.]
[8 This reference is inserted from Repl. 2.]   [9 He is, Repl. 1 and 2.]
[10 Reference, it would seem, is made to Cartwright's having continued to hold his fellowship at Trinity College without being ordained priest: he himself maintained that it was sufficient to be a deacon. But the language of the Statute is, "ut socii qui magistri artium sunt, post septem annos in eo gradu plene confectos *presbyteri* ordinentur." See Stat. Trin. Coll. Cant. cap. xix.]

is very simple: I have witnesses enow of it: peradventure, if you were kept to that diet, it would not be with you as it is. If my "jurisdiction" be "unlawful," I am content it be reformed; it is according to the statutes of the college where I am (to the which T. C. hath been sworn), and to the laws of the realm. What I "hereafter look for," it is hard for you to judge: but I most humbly thank my heavenly Father, that in all this storming of yours, wherein you have blown out against me what you could possibly imagine, you have only uttered your boiling stomach, and not touched me in anything whereof I need to be ashamed; which surely you would have done if you could.

The sword of discipline necessarily called for.

I "whet the sword" no otherwise against you than christian charity and the state of the church requireth. It is neither the sword that taketh away life, nor fire that consumeth the body, which I move unto; but it is the "sword of correction and discipline," which may by sundry other means be drawn out than by shedding of blood. That sword of discipline I call for still, and say with Zuinglius: "If it be permitted that every man may freely defend his errors, and spread abroad in the church false doctrine, there will be more contentions, sects, and discord among christian churches, than ever there was among infidels[1]." And again: "If every man may, without controlment, preach among the people his own private fancy and opinion, contrary to the determination and authority of the church, it will shortly come to pass that we shall have more errors than Christians[2]."

In his epistle before his book called Ecclesiastes.

If I have accused any man unjustly, there is a law whereunto I am subject; but your words are not of that weight, neither your defence such, that therefore they please or satisfy wise men, because you speak them. If they can say no more for themselves than you have said for them, then they must remain still in the same suspicion.

If there be any just cause why ye should "have the good abearing against" any man, if you will come forth and orderly require it, I am sure you may have it. But, O the mildness, the patience, and the quietness of this spirit of yours!

[1 Si enim hoc impune fieri permiserimus, ut qui erroris et mendacii convictus est, nihilominus errorem suum aliis quoque ingerere possit et doctrinam manifeste falsam in ecclesia seminare: plus equidem contentionum, dissidiorum et sectarum inter christiani nominis ecclesias quam apud infideles oboriri videbimus.—H. Zvingl. Op. Tigur. 1581. Epist. præf. Ecclesiast. Pars II. fol. 40. 2.]

[2 Id. Epist. præf. de Bapt. Libr. fol. 57. See before, page 8.]

CERTAIN NOTES[3]
and properties of anabaptists, and other perturbers of the church, collected out of Zuinglius and others: not thereby meaning to condemn any, but to admonish all to take heed of such in whom these notes or many of them do concur; and also to let all men understand, that the before-mentioned qualities and properties be not devised by some one man, but agreed and consented upon by all such learned, zealous, and godly writers, as had to do with that sort of men, I mean anabaptists.

Zuinglius, in his book intituled *Elenchus contra Anabaptistas*, writeth thus of them:

"If a man modestly and justly reprove their manners Fol. 5. and enterprises, yea, if he humbly desire them that they do nothing rashly, by and by they pour out in speech against him whatsoever they can imagine against the enemies of the gospel; neither do they omit any reproach[4]."

"They do much more bitterly inveigh against those that do profess the gospel, than they do against papists[5]."

"They bitterly inveigh against the magistrate. They con- Fol. 8. demn the ministers of the word. They speak evil both of the civil magistrate and of the ministers of the church; that, if at any time either of them according to their office withstand or reprove them, they may straightway say that therefore they be enemies unto them, because they tell them of their faults.

"They be altogether like unto Ate; wheresoever they come, πάντας ἀᾶνται, they trouble all, and pervert the state.

"If any city have begun to embrace the gospel, thither they resort, there they make contention; neither will they teach in those places where the gospel is not planted.

"They seek confusion of all things[6]."

[[3] These Notes are inserted from the second edition of Whitgift's Answer.]
[[4] Si vero mores atque instituta ipsorum et jure et modeste censeas, imo si supplex preceris, ut nihil temere, jam nihil est conviciorum apud evangelii hostes, quod in te non regerant; nihil dirarum apud furias, quod in te non jactitent.— H. Zvingl. Op. Epist. ad Lect. præf. Elench. contr. Catabapt. Pars II. fol. 5. 2.]
[[5] Id. ibid. fol. 6. 2. See before, page 47, note 1.]
[[6] Magistratum diris oppugnant modis: evangelii ministros devovent...Utrosque

126   THE DEFENCE OF THE ANSWER

Fol. 21.

"The papists call us heretics; and the anabaptists call us half papists.

"Whom they have drawn to their factions, him they forbid to come to any sermon made by any that is an adversary unto their sect.

"They condemn going to churches[1]."

Fol. 23.

"They be full of melancholy; for it is anger and wrath, not zeal or the Spirit, whereof they glory, and whereby they set forth themselves[2]."

"They be clothed and armed with hypocrisy, cursed speaking, discord, and false reporting of others[3]."

Fol. 37.

"They glory that the multitude followeth them[4]."

The same Zuinglius, in an epistle prefixed before his book called *Ecclesiastes*, and in the same book, speaking of the anabaptists, saith as followeth:

Fol. 40.

"They so slander, revile, and backbite the ministers of the word and of the church, that they ought of all godly men to be suspected and hated, even for their slanderous and cursed speaking. But their end and purpose is by this means to win credit unto themselves, and to discredit such as set themselves against them and detect their errors[5]."

ministros et ecclesiæ et reipublicæ in primis proscindunt, ut si unquam pro officio contra mutiant, protinus dicere possint: Ideo sibi esse infestos, quod eorum vitia contrectaverint.—Id. Elench. contr. Catabapt. fol. 8.

Ac in universum talem speciem præbent qualem Ate; quocunque diverterint πάντας ἀάνται, omnia turbant inque pessimum statum commutant. Cœpit urbs aliqua paulo sanius de cœlesti doctrina sentire? illo properant ac turbant; nec enim eas Domino initiant, quæ verbum non recipiunt...videtis...nihil quam turbas rerumque omnium tam divinarum quam humanarum confusionem ac perniciem quærere.—Id. ibid. fol. 8. 2.]

[1 Adpellamur ergo a pontificiis hæretici, a catabaptistis autem secundo-papistæ...Ut primum aliquem ad factionem suam pertraxerunt, ante omnia vetant ne...ad nullam concionem conveniat, ubi is doceat qui sectæ suæ adversetur... Ad ecclesias item profectiones damnant.—Id. ibid. fol. 21. 2.]

[2 ...melancholici homines: bilis enim est, non spiritus, quo se venditant.—Id. ibid. fol. 23.]

[3 Mundani ergo magistratus, !inquiunt, armantur ære atque ferro: catabaptistæ hypocrisi et maledicentia, mendaciis, injuria, dissidio, perfidia, &c.—Id. ibid. fol. 25. 2.]

[4 ...isti gloriantur de turbis et seditiosa, imo hæretica ecclesia.—Id. ibid. fol. 37. 2.]

[5 ...eos vero qui verbi et ecclesiæ ministri sunt, in primis autem me, contumeliis tam impuris et impudenti conviciorum rabie proscindunt, ut non immerito omnibus piis ob maledicentiam suam suspecti et exosi esse debeant. Sed illud unum hæc agendo spectant, ut suam auctoritatem omnibus aliis commendabiliorem reddant; iis vero qui illorum artibus dolisque sese opponunt, eosdem detegunt et convellunt, omnem fidem derogent.—Id. Epist. præf. Ecclesiast. fol. 40. 2.]

"They teach that such cannot preach the gospel sincerely Fol. 41. which have benefices; but their hope is to have the true pastors expelled, that they may succeed in their places: and yet they publicly protest that they seek for no living[6]."

"They never sow the pestiferous seed of their doctrine anywhere but in such places where the gospel hath been truly taught: there they go about to subvert whatsoever hath been builded with their frivolous contentions about external things[7]."

"They take upon them to teach other, but they cannot Fol. 44. suffer themselves either to be taught or admonished; although in words they pretend the contrary. They sow discord and contention wheresoever they come; but we mean in those churches only where the gospel hath been truly preached: for these churches only do they trouble; in them they sow discord; neither do they ever join themselves to those churches where the gospel hath not been planted: wherefore, seeing they be authors of contentions, and troublers of those churches (and that about external matters), which before enjoyed peace and were in great quietness, they have not the God of peace, but of tumult, contention, and envy[8]."

"They be burdensome to poor simple men whom they Fol. 47. have deluded by their doctrine, whose labours they consume.

"They seem to be very humble, and to contemn riches;

[[6] Quod ut facilius efficerent falso affirmabant, neminem, qui stipendium vel sacerdotium aliquod sibi collatum usurparet, evangelium sincere pureque prædicare posse. Sic enim fore sperabant, ut expulsis omnibus ecclesiarum ministris, ipsi in eorum locum surrogati omnium stipendia et sacerdotiorum bona occuparent. Interim tamen in publico nunquam non vociferabantur, se non aliqua stipendia ambire.—Id. ibid. fol. 41.]

[[7] Qui nusquam alibi quam in iis locis, in quibus jam ante sincera veritatis doctrina annuntiari cœpit, doctrinæ suæ pestiferum semen spargunt. Tunc enim externis quibusdam rebus et nihili omne illud, quod per evangelii doctrinam bene et feliciter ædificatum est, subvertere conantur.—Id. ibid. fol. 41. 2.]

[[8] Ecclesias ergo, non ut discant, sed ut alios doceant, ingredi solent: nec enim quenquam alium vel doctorem vel monitorem ferre possunt, etiamsi splendidis verbis multum de sese polliceantur et sese institui postulent...Ceterum cum dissidiorum studiosissimi ubique locorum discordiam seminent,...De illis enim ecclesiis tantummodo, in quibus evangelii veritas prædicari consuevit, hoc loco dicimus. Has enim isti turbant, in hisce solis lites et dissidia seminant, nec unquam infidelium cœtibus vel ecclesiis sese admiscent. Quapropter cum dissidiorum auctores et ecclesiarum turbatores sint, earum nimirum quæ firmo pacis vinculo prius coagmentatæ fuerunt, interim vero hæc agendo non aliud quam externa quædam spectent et carnalia; nemini obscurum esse potest, hujusmodi homines Deum pacis nequaquam habere, sed deum tumultus, contentionum et simultatis.—Id. Ecclesiast. fol. 44. 2.]

but in the mean while they thrust themselves into other men's families, and live at other men's tables¹."

Fol. 49.

" If they were sent of God, and endued with the spirit of love, they would have construed in the best part those external things which be not as yet rightly reformed; they would have become all things to all men, that they might have won all to Christ. But, when they challenge unto themselves such purity and holiness that no man may touch or reprove them, and do boast that, whatsoever they speak, they speak it of zeal, being moved with the Spirit; for their arrogancy and rashness they deserve the same discipline that the bishop of Rome doth.

" Their contention cometh not of zeal, as they pretend, but of envy and bitterness of heart ²."

Fol. 45.

" Christ never made any contention for temporal and external things; and therefore, seeing they contend for such things, it is manifest that they are not sent of God.

" Though they protest, and by oath deny that they take any authority from magistrates, yet shortly after we should have seen it come to pass that they would have been disobedient to all laws of magistrates, if once they had increased to that number, that they might have trusted to their own strength.

" Their doctrine bringeth forth nothing but contentions and tumults, in the defence whereof they allege that Christ said, ' I came not to send peace, but the sword.' To whom we answer, that this sword hath no place among the faithful; for it divideth the faithful from infidels: but they make contention and brawling among the faithful, and that for external things³."

[¹ ...miseris et simplicibus quibusdam agricolis oneri fuerunt, quorum laboribus sese sustentarunt, cum ipsi penes se aurum et argentum in marsupiis suis circumferrent...magna quadam humilitatis specie amicti eos sese simulant, qui non aliqua opum terrenarum cupidine teneantur, cum interim non alium sibi finem praescriptum habeant, quod ex illorum artibus et insidiis, quibus sese omnium familiis ingerere solent, facile deprehenditur.—Id. ibid. fol. 47.]

[² ...qui si a Deo missi venissent, caritatis spiritu donati omnia ea, quae in externis minus probe adhuc administrantur, commode interpretari possent, et omnibus fierent omnia, ut omnes Christo lucrifacerent. Cum vero eam sibi puritatem et sanctimoniam vendicent, ut nemo illos contingere aut perstringere audeat, quicquid vero loquantur Spiritus nomine venditent, sua illa arrogantia et temeritate eandem, quam Romanus pontifex, disciplinam merentur...Quando autem intelligetis...hoc altercandi studium, quo tenemini, non spiritum, sed invidam et rabidam esse invidi pectoris amarulentiam ?—Id. ibid. fol. 49. 2.]

[³ Si ergo Christus ob res temporarias et terrenas tumultus movit et seditiones,

"They have their secret conventicles in corners, without Fol. 55. the consent and determination of the church, whereunto they and their doctrine ought to be subject[4]."

"Those that before were gentle of nature and lowly, religious also, and lovers of peace, as soon as they embrace their doctrine, and be allured to their sect, become contentious, lovers of discord, seekers of themselves, and most desirous of revengement[5]."

In his epistle set before his book *De Baptismo*, and in the same book, writing also against the anabaptists, among many other things, he hath these:

"The anabaptists pretend great humility, which was always a ready way for Satan to deceive the simple and ignorant people, and whereby he hath brought in such a number of monks. This hypocritical humility of theirs (that is, of the anabaptists) is well known to those that have had conference with them: *quam sit illorum oratio omni felle amarulentior.*

"Their manner is in their secret meetings to pour out their opprobrious and slanderous speeches against magistrates and the ministers of the church[6]."

jam et illos decet...Sed cum Christum hæc alia hujusmodi fecisse nusquam legatur, certo constat, eos a Deo missos nequaquam esse...Constat ergo tam doctrinam quam anabaptismum illorum et Deo et paci christianæ ex diametro esse contrarium. Licet enim jurejurando quoque hoc pertinacissime negent, brevi tamen hoc eventurum videremus, ut omnibus magistratuum decretis immorigeri, omne quoque debitum negarent, si quando ad tantam multitudinem augerentur, ut propriis viribus nonnihil possent confidere...Cum ergo tam baptismum quam doctrinam ipsorum, præter turbas et tumultus, nihil aliud parere cernamus...Sed objiciunt hic id quod Christus dixit, Non veni ut pacem mittam, sed gladium. Quibus respondemus: gladium hunc, cujus Christus meminit, inter fideles locum non habere aliquem. Hunc enim fideles ab infidelibus separaturum esse Christus prædicat. Hi vero non nisi inter fideles propter externa quædam et inania turbas et rixas seminant.—Id. ibid. fol. 54.]

[4 Interim vero clancularios cœtus in angulis et tenebris congregare citra totius ecclesiæ, cujus judicio omnes et doctrinæ omnium subjectæ sunt, consensum et decretum.—Id. ibid. fol. 55.]

[5 Quandoquidem eos, qui natura mites erant et humiles, religiosi et pacis amantes, ut primum horum doctrinam auribus et animis perceperunt, contentiosos, dissidiorum studiosos, sua quærentes et vindictæ amantissimos videre licet.—Id. ibid. fol. 55. 2.]

[6 ...miram quandam humilitatis speciem præ se ferre et simulare noverunt, quæ semper decipiendi rudes et simplices via Satanæ fuit omnium expeditissima; quæ denique omnem hanc infaustam monachorum sobolem nobis peperit...Hypocritica illorum humilitas illis satis nota et perspecta est, qui cum his aliquando sermones contulerunt: quam scilicet sit illorum &c...Omitto hic sermones ipsorum omnis honestatis expertes, quos non sine impudentissima mentiendi libidine

[WHITGIFT.]

Fol. 58.   "They wander up and down, and haunt the houses of such as be simple and unlearned; they love to have their meat and drink of other men's provision, like unto minstrels[1]."

Fol. 72.   "They go about innovations of their own private authority in those churches where the gospel is truly and diligently taught, and that in external things, which they ought not to do without the consent and determination of the church[2]."

Fol. 83.   "Whosoever doth withstand them, him they account wicked and an atheist: they think all men to be blind and ignorant but themselves; neither do they think any man worthy the name and title of a Christian, that doth not in all things frame himself to their deeds[3]."

Fol. 97.   "They cry out against witnesses (that is, godfathers and godmothers) in baptism, saying that the scripture doth nowhere appoint them[4]."

The same Zuinglius, in his book intituled *Ad Libellum Baltazaris Responsio*, speaking unto Baltazar, an anabaptist, saith on this sort:

"Wherefore we will also call thee an heretic and an author of factions in the church. For thou, without the advice of the church wherein thou teachest, hast begun to ordain re-baptization. What! that which is commonly said of all, that thou hast secluded from the supper of the Lord all those that were not re-baptized? to pass over that wicked subtilty and craft in giving over thy bishoprick for this cause only, that thou mightest again be chosen to the same by thine own faction; whereby thou hast divided the faithful people com-

in conventiculis suis clanculariis evomere consueverunt : in quibus tanta et tam mordax est omnium verborum protervia, &c.—Id. Epist. præf. de Bapt. Libr. foll. 57. 2, 58.]

[1 Ut interim de erronibus illis nihil dicam, qui cum incertis sedibus vagentur, apud simplices quosdam et rerum imperitos locum sibi quærunt, et securum victum instar tibicinis ambiunt.—Id. ibid. fol. 58. 2.]

[2 Qua fronte enim, inconsulta prius ecclesia, innovandis rebus studentes tam audacibus cœptis privata auctoritate talia conamini? De his ecclesiis duntaxat loquor, in quibus Dei verbum publice summa cum fide et studio indesinenti prædicatur.—Id. de Bapt. Lib. Tract. I. fol. 72. 2.]

[3 Cum itaque alibi quoque idem ab illis factum sit, ut...quemlibet illorum somniis et erroribus sese opponentem impium, $\ddot{a}\theta\epsilon o\nu$, et dæmoniacum temere vocitent,...Interim tamen illorum judicio omnes nos cæci dicimur....Illorum judicio nemo hominum Christiani titulum meretur, nisi qui illorum factis sese per omnia accommodat.—Id. ibid. Tract. II. fol. 83.]

[4 Ceterum de testibus quoque baptizatorum catabaptistæ novos clamores suscitant. Ubi enim locorum (inquiunt) institutum est, ut testes baptismo adhibeantur?—Id. ibid.Tract. III. fol. 97. 2.]

mitted to thy charge into contrary factions, and made them subject to great dangers. Now, therefore, I would have thee to consider who they be that deal more violently and abuse their authority; whether we, the ministers of the church of Tigurine, which have attempted nothing of our private authority, but have submitted ourselves to the judgment of the whole church, or, at least, of the magistrates; or rather thou, which so arrogantly dost command what thou list, not requiring the judgment of the church, which thou shouldest have tarried for[5]."

"These men (meaning anabaptists) with their factions and Fol. 113. opinions divide the unity of the church, trouble the state, and adnihilate all laws and decrees of magistrates[6]."

Zuinglius, in his book entitled *De Seditionum Auctoribus*, writeth thus:

"The fourth kind of men which maketh the doctrine of Fol. 132. the gospel hateful and contemptible to the world is of those which are rather puffed up with knowledge than kindled with the fire of charity. For they rather seek curiosity and ostentation than to follow the christian meekness of life. They take upon them to teach all men, and challenge unto themselves liberty to judge all other; but they themselves will not be taught. In all other men they find something that displeaseth them, something that they may reprehend as contrary to christian laws; but in themselves they can find nothing worthy of reprehension, no, not the least blot or spot. Whatsoever they do, that (in their own judgment) is holy, just, and right: whatsoever they do determine or appoint

[5 Quapropter te quoque hæreticum te factionum in ecclesia auctorem esse dicemus. Nam et tu inconsulta ecclesia, in qua doces, rebaptismum instituere cœpisti. Quid quod publice ab omnibus affirmatur, te quoque omnes illos a cœna Domini repellere voluisse, quotquot rebaptizati nondum essent? Ut interim dolum illum nefandum et perniciosum transeam, quo episcopatu tuo hanc unam ob causam temetipsum abdicavisti, ut a rebaptizatorum turba denuo eligereris. Quo facto pium et fidelem populum tuæ commissum fidei in partes scidisti contrarias, et gravissimis periculis involvere non es veritus. Hic ergo expendas velim, utrinam violenter res agant et sua abutantur potentia: nosne, qui Tigurinæ ecclesiæ præfecti nihil privato consilio tentamus, sed vel totius ecclesiæ vel saltem Diacosiorum judicio omnia nostra subjicimus; an tu potius, qui tanto cum fastu pro tua libidine quævis imperas, nec interim ecclesiæ tuæ judicium, quod te exspectare oportebat, requiris?—Id. ad Libell. Baltaz. Hvebm. Resp. fol. 100. 2.]

[6 Horum enim factionem et dogmata ecclesiarum unitatem scindere, rerum ordinem interturbare, et omnes magistratus sanctiones annihilare constat.—Id. ibid. fol. 113.]

deserveth (as they think) praise: whatsoever they tread upon they believe to be either violets or roses, &c. They contend about external things. Sometime they would have no magistrate at all, and sometime they say that magistrates be necessary, but yet not to be lawful for Christians to be magistrates. By and by they dream of a peculiar and new church, &c. As Africa was always wont to bring forth some news, so they daily coin new toys, new dreams, and stir up new contentions. In the mean time they cease not from railing, backbiting, slandering, envy, hatred, and the most pernicious affections of contending. But yet those men extol them, and say that they be endued with the Spirit of God, which in backbiting, slandering, and contending be most like unto them. Furthermore, they arrogate unto themselves such innocency and holiness, that they will not vouchsafe to salute such as do in any point displease them. Everywhere, in marketplaces, and other common assemblies, in the streets, in taverns, in shops, to be short, in all public places, where any little occasion is given, they fill all with most bitter disputations, nay, brawlings and contentions. When they perceive that these their quarrellings in such places be misliked, they have their secret places to meet in, where they being gathered together, as judges sitting in their thrones, do examine all other men's lives and manners, and give their censure upon them: at the length they fall out among themselves, and this miserable, confused, troublesome, cankered and bitter stomach they call zeal, or the Spirit[1]."

[[1] Nunc vero quartum hominum genus sese profert, qui evangelii doctrinam mundo exosam et invisam reddunt. Sunt autem hi, qui scientia potius inflati quam caritatis igne incensi sunt. Hi enim curiositati potius student et ostentationi, quam ut christianam vitæ suæ mansuetudinem sectentur. Omnes homines docere instituunt, et in omnes judicandi arbitrium sibi vendicant, seipsos vero doceri nolunt. In omnibus inveniunt quod displiceat, quod ceu christianis legibus contrarium carpere possint; in seipsis vero ne minimam labem quidem et maculam deprehendere possunt. Quicquid ab ipsis fit, illud suo judicio sanctum, justum et æquum est: quicquid instituunt, laudem meretur: quicquid calcant, vel violas vel rosas esse sentiunt...ob res externas nunquam non digladiantur. Nunc enim magistratum omnem abolere volunt et tollere; nunc vero magistratu opus esse clamitant, interim tamen Christianum esse negant, qui magistratum gerit aliquem. Mox novam quandam et peculiarem ecclesiam somniant...Ut Africa semper novi aliquid parere consuevit, ita hi quoque indies novas nugas, nova somnia, et lites novas texere solent. Interim vero, ne semel quidem a convitiandi libidine, ab obtrectationibus, ab invidiæ, iræ, odii, et litigandi affectibus perniciosissimis sibi temperant: sed eos demum vere christiano spiritu præditos

Gastius, in his books *De Exordio et Erroribus Catabaptistarum*, painteth them out in this manner:
"They promise to prove their doctrine by shedding of Lib.1. page 7. their blood, when they perceive that they cannot defend the same by the scriptures².''

"Their knowledge is without love, joined with hypocrisy, Page 9. which maketh them more bold than a man would think, and more subtile than wise men at all times perceive³."

"They rail and speak evil of magistrates, and of the Page 9 and 10. ministers of the gospel; and if at any time they be by them reproved or punished, they say it is done because they reprove them for their sins: the people easily believe whatsoever they speak against magistrates and the ministers of the church, and be greatly delighted with such schoolmasters; yea, they so profit in boldness and impudency, that such as were yesterday simple hearers are ready to-day to revile the magistrate, even to his face⁴."

"They trouble all places where they come, neither will Page 11. they continue but in such cities and places where the gospel is already planted.

esse dicunt, qui conviciandi rixandique libidine ipsis quam simillimi sunt. Quin eam sanctimoniæ et innocentiæ laudem sibi vendicant, ut neminem, qui ipsis aliqua ex parte displicet, salutationibus suis dignentur...passim in foro, vicis, plateis, tabernis, officinis, tonstrinis, balneis, in omnibus denique locis publicis, ubicunque levis quædam occasio datur, imo rixis et contentionibus omnia miscent. Ubi vero se deprehendi et ab hujusmodi rixis sibi interdici sentiunt, mox palæstras proprias habent et conciliabula peculiaria, in quibus congregati, ceu judices quidam pro tribunali sedentes, omnium vitas et mores examinant, de iisdem suas ferunt sententias. His autem peractis, ipsi quoque inter se dissidentes, mutuis jurgiis et conviciis tanta cum animorum acerbitate sese laniant et polluunt....Hunc vero animum plus quam miserum, turbulentum, confusum et amarum ipsi Spiritum nominare consueverunt.—Id. De Sedit. Auctor. Pars II. fol. 132.]

[² Promittunt ergo se sanguine probaturos, quod scripturis non possent.— J. Gast. De Anabapt. Exord. Error. &c. Basil. 1544. Lib. I. p. 7.]

[³ Ut enim scientia sine caritate inflat, ita cum hypocrisi conjuncta et audacior est, quam ille de plebe putet, et callidior quam nasutus etiam deprehendere possit.—Id. ibid. p. 9.]

[⁴ Magistratum diris oppugnant modis, evangelii ministros devovent...Utrosque ministros et ecclesiæ et reipublicæ in primis proscindunt; ut si unquam pro officio contra mutiant, protinus dicere possint, ideo sibi esse infestos, quod eorum vitia contrectaverint. Jam quisque de plebe auditor quicquam prius suspicatur et de magistratu et de ecclesiarum ministris, quam de versipellibus istis præstigiatoribus. Procedunt furioso impetu concitati ad istorum magisterium....Crescit audacia et impudentia, ut qui heri simplex auditor adstiterat, hodie magistratum in faciem contumelietur.—Id. ibid. pp. 9, 10.]

"Their hypocrisy is much greater than the bishops of Rome[1]."

Page 33. "There is none of them but they have some one or more of these crimes, lying, unfaithfulness, perjury, disobedience, contention, idleness, dividing themselves from others: as for heresies, sects, stubbornness, and erroneous doctrine, they be common to them all[2]."

Page 40. "The world loveth such prophets, and heareth them, only to disturb the public peace and quietness[3]."

Page 41. "They fare daintily every day, and at tables and meals they jest upon the ministers of the gospel, and pour out their poison against them; for this is their usual manner, to bring the preachers of the gospel (that be not of their sect) in contempt with their hearers[4]."

Page 59 and 60. "The effects that their doctrine worketh in the hearers be these: *Odisse ecclesias, ministros convitiis incessere, magistratus damnare, negare census et decimas, pueros ad baptismum non admittere, disputationem instituere, quomodo omnium facultates sint omnibus communes, &c.*[5]"

Page 101. "The end of anabaptism is to have no order in the church, no consent and agreement among the godly[6]."

Page 102. "They much offend the weak by their continual barking against the ministers and preachers of the word.

"They craftily insinuate themselves into the company and

[1 Ac in universum talem speciem præbent, qualem Atæ: quocunque diverterint, πάντας ἅαντι, omnia turbant, inque pessimum statum commutant. Cœpit urbs aliqua paulo sanius de cœlesti doctrina sentire, illo properant ac turbant: nec enim eas Domino initiant, quæ verbum non recipiunt....Romani pontificis hypocrisis in lucem est producta; nunc res cum ipsa est hypocrisi nobis gerenda.—Id. ibid. p. 11.]

[2 Nec tu quenquam ex illis mihi ostendes, qui non aliquo prædictorum flagitiorum commaculatus sit: mendacium dico, perfidiam, perjurium, inobedientiam, seditionem, otium, desertionem, turpitudinem. Ex his licet non omnia omnibus, singula tamen singulis adhærent: ut interim taceam hæresim et sectas, pertinaciam, et eorum falsam ac erroneam doctrinam.—Id. ibid. p. 33.]

[3 Tales prophetas amat mundus iste perversus, iisque aures præbet et credit, solummodo ut publicam pacem et tranquillitatem perturbent et evertant.—Id. ibid. p. 40.]

[4 Epulabantur quotidie splendide idque summa alacritate, et inter epulandum contra evangelii ministros virus effundebant. Morem enim illum perpetuo servant, ut evangelii ministros apud suos auditores odiosos reddant.—Id. ibid. p. 41.]

[5 Id. ibid. pp. 59, 60.]

[6 Agitur enim nihil aliud in hac hæresi, quam ut nullus sit posthac in ecclesia ordo, nulla bonorum consensio contra improborum furorem et audaciam.—Id. ibid. p. 101.]

friendship of rich and wealthy men, especially such as mean simply, that they may allure them to their sect[7]."

"Craftsmen, inn-keepers, and vintners, the common people, women, and such like, follow them and believe them.

"They are desirous of innovations, and in matters of religion they will have some singular device of their own, that they may be therefore commended[8]."

"*Sermo eorum nihil aliud crepat, quam reprehensionem ministrorum verbi, libertatem in externis[9].*"

"They depend upon popular fame, and seek to be commended of the people for their constancy; and therefore, if they be convicted of any error, they will not publicly acknowledge the same, lest they should leese their credit[10]."

"They say that those pastors which have ecclesiastical livings be of the devil; for the apostles had propriety in nothing, but went from house to house to seek their dinner and supper[11]."

"In Germany they creep into the houses of noblemen; and therefore it is to be feared lest thereby some great detriment happen to the gospel, unless in time it be foreseen. For who be greater enemies unto the gospel than these kind of men, which spread abroad foolish opinions, renew old heresies, and trouble all churches, whom also the papists undesired do aid and help forwards? To be short, all their doctrine tendeth to discord and contention[12]."

[7 Concionatoribus piis oblatrant, non sine maxima offensione infirmorum. Insinuant se mirabili astutia in amicitiam et divitum et simplicium, quo rete extenso avicularum instar pios capiant, perfida secta polluant, ad interitum ducant.—Id. ibid. pp. 101, 2.]

[8 Quos enim solent commovere...? Opifices et tabernarios, rusticum et simplicem populum, fœmellas quarum aures pruriunt....Cupidi sunt rerum novarum, proprium quid volunt in religionis negotio habere, quo laudentur ab aliis.—Id. ibid. pp. 102, 3.]

[9 Et catabaptistarum sermo nihil &c.—Id. ibid. p. 143.]

[10 ...id quod fere solent, qui a populari aura pendentes hoc solum agunt, populo ut ob constantiam placeant. Sic enim judicant, satius esse agnitum etiam errorem non fateri, quam cum nominis per scelus quæsiti jactura, si quid deliquerunt, agnoscere.—Ant. Corvin. ad Georg. Spalat. in eod. ibid. p. 163.]

[11 Item illud, Pastores qui beneficia ecclesiastica habent, ex diabolo esse. Apostolos nihil habuisse proprii, de domo ad domum ivisse, si prandendum aut cœnandum.—J. Gast. ibid. p. 211.]

[12 Passim in Germania catabaptistæ in domum divitum et potentum irrepunt; eam ob rem timendum periculum ingens ab illorum veneno, et maximum evangelio detrimentum, nisi mox remedium adponatur, sentiet. Quis enim æque contra renatum evangelium pugnat, stolidas opiniones spargit, quam hoc

Page 302.

"They acknowledge no church of Christ but that which is without all spot, and under the pretence of zeal they subvert whatsoever other men have builded. 'Such kind of men (saith Augustine), not for the hatred of other men's iniquity, but for the desire of contention, seek to draw the people (entangled with an opinion of them) either wholly after them, or at the least to divide them: they be proud, perverse, quarrellous, contentious, troublesome; and, lest they should seem to be void of the truth, they pretend great severity. Those faults which in the scriptures are commanded modestly to be reproved in brethren, and without the breach of unity and peace, they abuse to make schisms, and make them an occasion of division. So doth Satan transform himself into an angel of light, whilst by the occasion of just severity he persuadeth great cruelty, seeking nothing else but to corrupt and break the bond of peace and unity, which being whole among Christians, his strength is weakened and his devices overthrown[1].'"

Lib. ii. Page 373.

"They have a several ministry and congregation, and divide themselves from those churches where the gospel is truly preached, and where idolatry and other abuses are removed[2]."

hominum genus, quod omnium hæreticorum dogmata renovat, omnia turbat, quibus auxiliares copias adversarii evangelio mittunt, non rogati...Quid multis? omnis illorum doctrina ad discordiam, ad seditionem, ad intestina bella spectat.—Id. ibid. pp. 268, 9.]

[1 Qualiter hodie faciunt anabaptistæ, qui nullum cœtum Christi agnoscunt, nisi angelica perfectione omni ex parte conspicuum; sub prætextu sui zeli, quicquid est ædificationis, subvertunt. Tales, inquit Augustinus, non odio iniquitatis alienæ, sed studio suarum contentionum, infirmas plebes, jactantia sui nominis irretitas, vel totas trahere, vel certe dividere affectant. Superbia tumidi, pervicatia vesani, calumniis insidiosi, seditionibus turbulenti, ne luce veritatis carere eos pateat, umbra rigidæ se veritatis obtendunt. Et quæ in scripturis, salva dilectionis sinceritate, et custodita pacis unitate, ad corrigenda fraterna vitia, moderatiori curatione fieri jubentur, ad sacrilegium schismatis et occasionem præcisionis usurpant. Ita se transfigurat Satan in angelum lucis, dum per occasionem quasi justæ severitatis crudelem sævitiam persuadet, nihil aliud appetens, nisi ut corrumpat atque dirumpat vinculum pacis et unitatis, quo firmo inter Christianos, vires ejus omnes invalidæ fiunt ad nocendum, muscipulæ insidiarum comminuuntur, et consilia eversionis evanescunt, &c.—Id. ibid. pp. 302, 3. Conf. August. Op. Par. 1679-1700. Contr. Epist. Parmen. Lib. III. cap. i. 1, 3. Tom. IX. cols. 55, 8. The passage is not quite accurately quoted.]

[2 Præterea anabaptistæ a consortio ecclesiæ sese separant, et etiam in his locis, ubi pura evangelii doctrina ebuccinatur, et ubi offendicula, abusus, et idololatriæ remota ab oculis sunt. Proprium ministerium et congregationem instituunt, quod similiter contra Dei mandatum est.—Delib. Quorund. Doct. Vir. ap. eund. Lib. II. pp. 372, 3.]

I might recite other learned men's writings, which also set down either all or many of these notes; but these may suffice all such as hate contention, and love the peace of the church.

CERTAIN NOTES collected out of learned and godly writers of our time, whereby we may know who they be that may aptly be called schismatics and disturbers of the church.

Zuinglius, in his book, intituled *Ad Libellum Baltazaris Responsio*, saith, that " those be schismatics and sectaries, who without the ordinance and authority of the church (whereunto they ought to submit themselves) do conspire among themselves in some new opinion[3]." And in his epistle prefixed before his book, *De Baptismo*, he saith thus: *Hæretici sunt qui factionibus student, et novis quibusdam dogmatibus sectas instituunt et discipulos colligunt*[4]; " Those be heretics that give themselves to factions, and through new opinions make sects in the church, and gather disciples after them."

Bullinger and Gastius say that those be anabaptists which trouble and divide the church for external things[5].

Œcolampadius in a certain epistle writeth thus: " To contemn the custom of the church, which is neither forbidden in the manifest words of the scripture, nor derogateth anything from faith and love, which also hath been observed without any contradiction, argueth a proud and a foolish man[6]."

Divers learned men, in a conference against the anabaptists (which Gastius reporteth in his second book *De Erroribus Catabaptistarum*), make this determination: "That, where the doctrine is true, and idolatry hath no place, there to make

[3 Sectas autem et partes sequuntur, qui neglecta ecclesiarum ordinatione et constitutione publica, cui jure obedire debebant, inter sese in novo quodam dogmate conspirant.—H. Zvingl. Op. Tigur. 1581. Ad Libell. Baltaz. Huemb. Respons. Pars II. fol. 100.]

[4 Id Epist. præf. de Bapt. Libr. fol. 57.]

[5 Si interrogas, Quare separationem facitis, et ab iis ecclesiis, quarum doctrinam et Dei cultum reprehendere non potestis? Respondent, Male vivitis, avaritiæ vitio laboratis, &c. Sic persuasi de nova ecclesia instituenda.—Delib. Quorund. Doct. Vir. ap. J. Gast. De Anabapt. Exord. Error. &c. Lib. II. pp. 373, 4. Conf. H. Bullinger. adv. Anabapt. Libri VI. Tigur. 1560. Lib. I. cap. iv. fol. 10.]

[6 Frivole consuetudinem ecclesiæ contemnere, quæ nec prohibita apertis verbis in scripturis, nec fidei aut caritati aliquid detrahentem, quæque etiam sine ulla unquam contradictione religiose observata, superbum et stolidum hominem arguit.—Jo. Œcolamp. Epist. ap. J. Gast. De Anabapt. Exord. Error. &c. Lib. II. p. 328.]

a separation or invent a new ministry, is to do against God, and to be like unto the Donatists, who divided themselves from the church under these pretences, that the ministers were ungodly, and that the church was not perfect[1]."

Calvin, in his book *Adversus Anabaptistas*, saith that "when, under the colour of a zeal of perfection, we can bear no imperfection, either in the body or in the members of the church, it is the devil which puffeth us up with pride, and seduceth us with hypocrisy to make us forsake Christ's flock[2]."

Musculus, in his Common-places, saith that "the root of all heresy is to hate and contemn the communion of the church:" and he addeth that "such they are whom no church nor reformation can please, having always something to reprove in others, nothing in themselves; which is a manifest token of singularity[3]."

Bucer, *in iv. ad Ephes.* saith that "arrogancy, self-love, envy, and hatred, be the instruments whereby Satan useth to stir men up to make contention in the church: *Quas pestes* (saith he) *convestit et tegit Satan ementito amiculo zeli divini pro puritate fidei, pro doctrinæ Christi sinceritate, pro ecclesiæ salute*[4]*:* The which vices Satan doth cloak and cover with a false pretence of godly zeal for the purity of faith, for the sincerity of Christ's doctrine, and for the salvation or safety of the church."

[1] Ubi enim doctrina vera regnat, et nullæ idololatriæ in ecclesiis locum habent, ibi omnes homines coram Deo, ut constituto et manifesto ministerio se subjiciant, et separationem nullam instituant. Qui in hac re separationem et nova ministeria excogitat, verissimum illum contra Deum agere. Ut olim Donatistæ anabaptismum et separationem instituebant, nullam causam prætendentes, nisi illam, esse sacerdotes et homines in altera ecclesia, qui probitati non studerent, se velle ecclesiam, quæ tota immaculata esset, erigere.—Delib. Quorund. Doct. Vir. ap. eund. Lib. II. p. 373.]

[2 Hinc ergo moneamur quum sub specie studii perfectionis imperfectionem nullam tolerare possumus aut in corpore aut in membris ecclesiæ, tunc diabolum nos tumefacere superbia et hypocrisi seducere, ut ad deserendum Christi gregem nos instiget: certo sciens se victoriam obtinere, quum nos inde abduxit.— Calvin. Op. Amst. 1667-71. Instr. adv. Anabapt. Tom. VIII. p. 363.]

[3 This passage has not been found in the Common-Places of Musculus: but see before, page 42, note 4.]

[4 Utitur autem ille maxime ad divellendum animos eorum, qui religionem Christi, atque ideo verissimam animorum pacem et consensionem, docere ac provehere debent, dissimulata inflatione φιλαυτίας καὶ φιλαρχίας fastidiis, si non etiam invidentiæ donorum Dei in fratribus, quas pestes convestit tegitque ementito &c.—M. Bucer. Prælect. in Epist. ad Ephes. Basil. 1562. cap. iv. p. 152.]

And hereunto it shall not be unmeet to add the opinion of Origen, who, describing the manners of heretics in his Commentaries upon the sixteenth of Ezekiel, saith thus: "In my opinion, an heretic of good life is much more hurtful, and hath more authority in his words, than he that doth discredit his doctrine with his life: therefore we must take heed of heretics which seem to be of godly conversation, &c.[5]"

The anabaptists pretend pureness of life, contempt of the world, perfection in external things, fervent zeal, &c. *Hi sunt veri hæreticorum mores, et hæc est via seducendi commodissima.* But this hypocrisy may easily be espied, if the former notes be well marked.

By the judgment of these learned and godly men it may now appear, who they be that may truly be called disturbers of the peace of the church, and authors of contentions.

The Lord grant that, all affection set aside, we may seek in time to suppress contentions, and provide for the peace of the church.

[5 Ac juxta mei quidem animi sensum multo nocentior est hæreticus bonæ vitæ, et plus in doctrina sua habet auctoritatis eo qui doctrinam conversatione maculet....Idcirco sollicite caveamus hæreticos, qui conversationis optimæ sunt, quorum forte vitam non tam Deus quam diabolus instruxit.—Orig. Op. Par. 1733-59. In Ezech. Hom. vii. 3. Tom. III. p. 382.]

⁋ The Preface of the Admonition.

To the godly Readers, grace and peace from God, &c.

Two treatises ye have here ensuing, beloved in Christ, which ye must read without ªpartiality or blind affection: for otherwise you ªshall neither see their meaning, nor refrain yourselves from rashly condemning of them without just cause. For certain men there are of great countenance, which will not lightly like of them, because they principally concern their persons and unjust dealings, whose credit is great, and whose friends are many; we mean the lordly lords, archbishops, bishops, suffragans, deans, doctors[1], archdeacons, chancellors, and the rest of that proud generation, whose kingdom must down, hold they never so hard, because their tyrannous lordship cannot stand ᵇwith Christ's kingdom. And it is the special mischief of our English church, and the chief cause of backwardness, and of all breach and dissension. For they whose authority is ᶜforbidden by Christ will have their stroke without their fellow-servants, yea, though ungraciously, cruelly, and pope-like, they take upon them to ᵈ beat them, and that for their own childish articles, being for the most part against the manifest truth of God. First, by experience their rigour hath too plainly appeared ever since their wicked reign, and specially for the space of these five or six years last past together. Of the enormities, which with such rigour they maintain, these treatises do in part make mention, justly craving redress thereof. But the matters do require a larger discourse. Only the authors of these thought it their parts to admonish you at this time of those inconveniences, which men seem not to think upon, and which without reformation cannot but increase further dissension; the one part being proud, pontifical, and tyrannous; and the word of God for the other part express and manifest, as, if it pleased the state to examine the matters, it would be evident. And would to God that free conference in these matters might be had! For, howsoever learned and many they seem to be, they should and may in this realm find enow to match them and shame them too, if they hold on as they have begun. And out of this realm they have all the best-reformed churches throughout Christendom against them[3]. But in a few words to say what we mean. Either must we have a right ᵉministry of God, and a right ᶠgovernment of his church, according to the scriptures set up (both which we lack); or else there can be no right religion, nor

ª 1 Thess. v. 21, James i. 19, 20. James ii. 1.

ᵇ Matt. xv. 23. 2 Luke xvi. 15.

ᶜ Matt. xx. 25, 26. Matt. xxiii. 8, 9, 10. Mark x. 42, 43. Luke xxii. 15, &c.
ᵈ Matt. xxiv. 48, 49.

ᵉ Matt. ix. 37, 38. Eph. iv. 11, 12.
ᶠ Matt. xviii. 15, 16, 17.

[1 University doctors and bachelors of divinity, Adm. Whitgift printed the Admonition as it originally appeared. Additions and alterations were subsequently made. See below, page 147.]

[2 Adm. has *Matt. xv.* 13; and at reference (¹) 1 *Cor.* v. 7. 1 *Cor.* vii. 20; it also omits &c. after Luke xxii. 15. in reference (ᶜ). At reference (ᵍ) Answ. 1. substitutes 1 *Tim.* iii. 8. for *Prov. xxix.* 18.]

[3 Here Adm. introduces, *They were once of our mind, but since their consecration they be so transubstantiated, that they are become such as you see.*]

yet for contempt thereof can ᵍ*God's plagues be from us any while deferred. And therefore though they link in together, and slanderously charge poor men (whom they have made poor) with grievous faults, calling them Puritans, worse than the Donatists, exasperating and setting on such as be in authority against them, having hitherto miserably handled them with revilings, deprivations, imprisonments, banishments, and such like extremities, yet is these poor men's cause never the* ʰ*worse; nor these challengers the better; nor God his* ⁱ*hand the further off, to link in with his against them; nor you, christian brethren, must never the rather without examination* ᵏ*condemn them. But thankfully take this taste which God by these treatises offereth you, and weigh them by the word of God, and do your endeavour, every man*⁴ *in his* ˡ*calling, to promote his cause. And let us all, with more*ᵐ *earnest prayer than we are wont, earnestly commend it to God his blessing; and namely that it will please him by his Spirit to lighten the heart of our most gracious sovereign, and the rest in authority, to the benefit of his small flock, and the overthrow of their proud enemies, that godliness may by them proceed in peace, and God his glory through Jesus Christ be throughly advanced; which we call God to witness is our only labour and suit. And so presently we leave you, heartily beseeching God to grant it. Amen.*

ᵍ Prov. xxix. 18.
Amos viii. 11, 12, &c.
Matt. xxi. 23, &c.
1 Cor. xi. 30.

ʰ Matt. x. 16.
ⁱ Isai. lix. 1.

ᵏ Exod. xxiii. 1, 2.
Matt. vii. 1, 2.
James iv. 11, 12.
ˡ 1 Cor. v. 20.
1 Cor. vii. 27.
ᵐ Psalm l. 15.
Matt. vii. 7.
1 Tim. ii. 1, 2.

⦗ An Answer to the Preface of the Admonition.

These two treatises contained in this Admonition, as they be void of sound learning, so are they full of blind affection, and stuffed with uncharitable and unchristian terms and phrases. Wherefore it is to be feared that they proceed not of love, but of hatred; not of zeal, but of malice; not of humility, but of arrogancy; not of minds desirous to reform, but of stomachs seeking to deform and confound that which is in due form and order by lawful authority established. For what charitable, zealous, and humble spirit would so spitefully and slanderously speak of their brethren, whose doctrine is pure, whose zeal is fervent, whose suffering for the gospel hath been in time of trial comparable with any man's that now liveth; who have also painfully taught the word of God in this realm, and do at this day, and by whose ministry the gospel hath taken

Arrogancy and unchristian speeches of the libellers.⁵

[⁴ One, Adm. and Answ.]
[⁵ This and the four succeeding marginal notes are not in Answ. 1.]

root, and is come to that increase that now (God be thanked) appeareth. Surely these opprobrious terms, "proud generation," "tyrannous lordships," "ungracious," "cruel," "pope-like," "wicked reign," "proud enemies," &c., applied to brethren, proceed not from the humble and mild Spirit of God, but from the proud and arrogant spirit of Satan. Therefore by this unseemly preface it may appear from what spirit the rest of this Admonition springeth. Touching the cruelty and rigour these men complain of, I shall need to speak little, being manifest to all that be not with sinister affection[1] blinded, that lack of severity is the principal cause of their licentious liberty. But who seeth not their hypocrisy, which would make the world believe that they are persecuted, when they be with too much lenity punished for their untolerable contempt of good laws, and other disordered dealings? Nay, such is their perverseness, or rather arrogancy, that, if they be debarred but from[2] the least part of their will and desire, by and by they cry out of cruelty and persecution: it is to be doubted what these men will do when persecution cometh indeed, which now make so much of a little, or rather of nothing. As for this great brag, "For, howsoever learned and many they seem to be, they should and may in this realm find enow to match them, and shame them too, if they hold on as they have begun," *satis arroganter dictum est*, and verifieth that to be true, that is commonly spoken of these kind of men, that is, that they contemn all other in comparison of themselves, that they think themselves only zealous, only learned, &c. But it is possible that they[3] may be matched; and I know no man of learning afraid to encounter with them, either by word or writing. Touching the ministry and government of the church, what faults there is to be therein found we shall understand, when we come to their reasons. God grant us humble and meek spirits, that godly unity may be maintained in the church.

Pretended persecution.

Stout brags.

Scriptures abused in the Admonition.

One thing I must desire thee to note, gentle reader, (wherein the folly of these men marvellously appeareth,) how they have painted the margent of their book with quoting of scriptures, as though all were scripture they

[1 Affections, Answ.]   [2 Of, Answ.]   [3 Possible they, Answ.]

write, when as indeed they abuse the[4] scripture and thee. For what one place of scripture is in all this preface alleged to any purpose? and yet how many is there quoted! [They may very aptly be compared to furious or mad men, who in the vehemency of their anger rashly smite their enemy, and throw at him whatsoever is next them, as tables, stools, tongs, pots, or anything else: even so these men apply to their purpose *quicquid in buccam venerit*, although it be never so far fetched[5].]

To prove that we must read these two treatises without partiality or blind affection, here is noted in the margent 1 Thess. v., ver. 21, Jam. i., Jam. ii. The place to the Thessalonians is this: "Try all things, and keep that which is good." The place of the first of James is this: "Wherefore, my dear brethren, let every man be swift to hear, slow to speak, and slow to wrath." And the second place of James is this: "My brethren, have not the faith of our Lord Jesus Christ in respect of persons." And to what purpose are these places alleged? what prove they? or what need is there to allege them? These apostles in these places speak not of railing libels, but of hearing the word of God, and judging of matters of faith according to the truth, and not to the persons.

Scriptures wrested.

To prove that tyrannous lordship cannot stand with Christ's kingdom, they allege the xv. of Matthew, and Luke xvi. The place in the xv. of Matthew, ver. 23, is this: "But he answered her not a word: then came to him his disciples, and besought him, saying, Send her away; for she crieth after us." In the sixteenth of Luke it is thus: "Then he said unto them, Ye are they which justify yourselves before men; but God knoweth your hearts: for that which is highly esteemed among men is abomination in the sight of God." I would gladly know how their assertion and these two texts hang together. I allow not tyrannous lordship to stand with Christ's kingdom; but it may well enough, for anything in these two places to the contrary. Tyrannous lordship is not esteemed among men, but hated.

[[4] Abuse both the, Answ.]   [[5] This sentence is inserted from Answ. 2.]

❡ The Reply unto the Answer of the Preface.

It may be said unto you, that which Aristotle said of a certain philosopher, that he knew not his own voice. For, if that you had remembered that which you do so often promise, that you will not answer words but matter, the printer should not have gained so much, men should not have bestowed so much money of a thing not of so great value, nor that (which is more) the world should not be burdened with unprofitable writings. For how often runnings out have you, to draw the authors of the Admonition into hatred, by inveighing bitterly against their unlearnedness, maliciousness, &c. (as it pleaseth you to term it); so that, if there were any excess of speech in them, you have paid it again with measure pressed down, and running over. How often charge you them with pride and arrogancy; men that confess once or twice of themselves their want of skill, and which profess nothing of themselves, but only a bare and naked knowledge of the truth; which may be done with modesty, even of them which have no learning. And yet those that know them know that they are neither void of the knowledge of the tongues, nor of the liberal arts, albeit they do not make so many words of it as you. Salomon saith, that "he that is despised, and hath but one servant, is better than he which magnifieth and setteth out himself, and yet wanteth bread;" whereby he meaneth, that the man that hath but a little, and carrieth his countenance accordingly, is much more to be esteemed than he which beareth a great port, and hath not to support it. These brethren have not undertaken the knowledge of logic, philosophy, and other school-learning, whereof notwithstanding they are not destitute: you, in so often reproaching them with the ignorance of them, would make us believe that you are so notable a logician and philosopher, as if logic and philosophy had been born with you, and should die with you; when as it may appear, partly by that which hath been spoken, and partly by those things which will fall out hereafter, that you are better acquainted with the names of logic and philosophy, than with any sound or substantial knowledge of them. But let that be the university's judgment, where you have been brought up, and are best known. To return to your unprofitable excursions, how oftentimes in your book do you pull at the magistrate's sword; and what sword you would have, I leave to the consideration of all men, seeing you are not satisfied with their imprisonment; whereupon also doth ensue the expense of that which they have. What matter is in all these that bringeth any help to the decision of these[1] causes that are in question between us? How many leaves have you wasted in confuting of the quotations, which, you say, are vain, foolish, unlearned, and to no purpose of that for which they are alleged? And, if they be so, where learned you to spend so much time about them? Did you never learn that σπουδῇ τὰ μὴ σπουδῆς ἄξια ἐλέγχειν τῶν ἀτόπων ἐστὶ,

Prov. xii. 9.

Though they be vain, yet were they alleged of them for sound proofs, and therefore necessarily confuted.

[¹ The, Def. B.]

"*to confute trifling things seriously is a point of those which have no judgment to know what is meet for the time and place, and other such circumstances?" If I should, of the other side, now go about to maintain every place to be not unfitly quoted unto that end wherefore it is alleged, and shew how unjust your*[2] *reprehensions are, and how small cause you have to lead them oftentimes so gloriously in triumph as you do, which I assure you I could do in the most places—as what could be more fitly* 1 Thess. v. 21.[3] *alleged to induce to read the book, than that they should "try all things?" what more fitly to hold men from rash condemn-* James i. 19, 20.[3] *ing of things, than that they should be "slow to speak?" what more fitly to move that they should not mislike of the goodness of the cause for the simplicity or base degree of them that defend it, than that* James ii. 1.[3] *we should "not have the faith of our Lord Jesus Christ in respect of persons?" and what more unjustly done, than that you should whip them for the printer's fault, in putting one place for another?—if, I say, I should thus go about to make good every place, how evil should I deserve either of learning, or of the truth itself, in blotting of much paper, whereby no profit would come to the reader! And if the days of a man were as many as the days of an oak, I would neither willingly trouble, nor be troubled, with such strife of words. Seeing therefore God hath shut us in so narrow terms, methink men should have conscience of pestering the world with such unprofitable treatises.*

Marginal notes: It is no trifling thing to abuse the scripture. You would if you could, seeing they are the foundation and grounds of that book. What meant you then to pester the world with yours?

Page 10, Sect. 1.

Therefore all these, and whatever else wandering words I shall meet with in this book, I mean (by God's grace[4]*) as dead things and nothing worth to bury with silence, and will answer to those things which touch the matters that lie in controversy between us. And, as for the unlearnedness, blind zeal, malice, intolerable pride, contempt of all good orders, and twenty such more things, wherewith M. Doctor chargeth us, if our life and conversation doth not confute them sufficiently, our words and profession of ourselves will not do it. And therefore we will first stay ourselves with the testimony of our own consciences, and then in the equity of the judgment of all those which shall indifferently consider these things that we are charged with. And as for the sword that is so hotly and hastily called for, we hope it be in their hands which will use it better than they are by you directed.*

Jo. Whitgift.

I think those that shall read my book with indifferent judgment will say that I have performed my promise, and am as spare in words without matter as conveniently I could be, and much more sparing than you are, either in this place where you have nothing but words, or in the rest of your

[2 You, Def. B.]   [3 These references are inserted from Repl. 2.]
[4 By God his grace, Repl. 1 and 2.]

book. The "value" of my book, and the "unprofitableness" of it, I refer to the judgment of others. I have done my duty in it (as I am persuaded), and satisfied my conscience.

I do "inveigh against the authors of the Admonition" in no other wise and sort than modesty and the cause itself requireth. If I have, shew the particulars, note the places. I speak not of their knowledge and learning otherwise than it is uttered in their book. I neither despise them in such sort, nor magnify myself: I leave that to you and yours, and therefore I require the testimony of this your own book.

I boast not of any profound skill "in school-learning" (I thank God for that which I have), I refuse not the "university's judgment" of me, from the time of my first being sophister unto this day. I think it hath been, and is, better persuaded of me than I am worthy; which appeareth in that it hath laid upon me (as much as upon any one man) from time to time, from my first peeping out unto this day, all the public exercises in all sciences that I have professed, without my seeking, nay, against my will; and I trust that I neither have in doing of them disgraced her, nor shamed myself. But surely I am ashamed thus to burst[1] out to the defence of myself, if I were nor thereunto compelled by your uncivil and opprobrious speeches.

My "excursions" be necessary. I "pull" no oftener, nor in any other manner, nor at any other "sword of the magistrate," than the state of the church, my office and vocation, and charity itself, requireth; neither do I mean the authors of the Admonition only, but their adherents also. Surely I believe that by that means these controversies would shortly be ended, and the church kept in great quietness and good order.

The vain quotations were necessarily confuted.

The "confutation of the quotations" was most necessary, and it is that that doth pinch you most sharply. True it is, that they be "vain, unlearned, and to no purpose," and yet used as grounds of that Admonition, and the doctrine therein contained. Wherefore the opening of the vanity and unaptness of them is the overthrow of that book, which the common sort thought to be all scripture, and nothing else but scripture, and therefore the doctrine therein contained to be most true; when as in deed the scriptures be there as manifestly wrested,

[1 Editt. *brust*.]

and unfitly used, as they be of the papists and anabaptists. And therefore, though they were vainly alleged of them, yet were they necessarily confuted by me. M. Calvin, in his book against the anabaptists, saith that "they win credit with those that be zealous, because they pretend the word of God, and have it always in their mouth[2]." And therefore, though their allegations be frivolous, yet doth he spend much labour in detecting them. Even so say I, you pretend the word of God in all things, and thereby you do deceive the godly and zealous people; wherefore it is expedient that your grounds be laid open, to the intent it may be known how crookedly and evil-favouredly you build upon them.   *Calv. advers. Anabap.*

If you could "maintain every place," or many of the places, I dare say you would; but surely I commend your rhetoric. Those places that you would seem to give some countenance unto bewray your lack of ability to defend either them or the rest. For you answer not one word to the reasons for the which I disallow them, nor to the true sense and meaning which I give of them. Truly, if you should thus "go about to make them good," in so doing you should do your cause no great good. But here you have wholly omitted the xv. of Matthew and the xvi. of Luke: the one whereof, though it be corrected, yet it is in a manner as far from the purpose as it was before, as it may appear in the "Additions and alterations, &c." at the end of the first book[3]. Your words of pleasure which follow, because they be but words, I wholly omit them, as I will also do in many other places where I shall find nothing else, lest I make this book longer than is convenient.

[[2] Quia vero nulla specie illustriore seduci possunt miseri Christiani, qui zelo aliquo Deum sectantur, quam dum prætenditur verbum Dei; anabaptistæ, adversus quos nunc scribimus, ipsum perpetuo in ore habent, idque semper præfantur.—Calvin. Op. Amst. 1667-71. Instr. adv. Anabapt. Tom. VIII. p. 356.]

[[3] The variations from the first of the subsequent editions of the Admonition are meant. Whitgift, it will be seen, hereafter examines these.]

¶ **Whether Christ forbiddeth rule and superiority unto the Ministers. Tractat. I.**

The true interpretation of the twentieth of Matthew, &c. *Reges gentium, &c.*

Chapter i. The First Division.
Answer to the Admonition, Page 13, Sect. 3.

Scriptures wrested.

To prove that they whose authority is forbidden by Christ will have their stroke without their fellow-servants, &c. is quoted Matt. xx. Matt. xxiii., Mark x., Luke xxii. In the xx. Matthew[2] it is thus written: "Ye know that the lords of the gentiles have domination over them, &c." In the xxiii. of Matthew: "Be[3] ye not called Rabbi; for one is your doctor or teacher, to wit, Christ." The places in Mark and Luke be all one with that in the xx. of Matthew. The conclusion that is gathered of these places is very dark and general: they should have declared who they be that have this authority forbidden, and what the authority is. Touching these places alleged in the xx. of Matthew, x. of Mark, xxii. of Luke, Musculus[4] and divers other learned men think that they extend, not only to the apostles, and men of the clergy, as we call them, but to all Christians, of what state soever they be. And it is the common opinion of all writers, that these words of Christ do not condemn superiority, lordship, or any such like authority, but the ambitious desire of the same, and the tyrannical usage thereof.

The true exposition of the xx. of Matt. &c.[1]

The places of scripture, Matt. xx., Mark x., Luke xxii., expounded.[5]

T. C. Page 10, Sect. 2 and 3.

To come therefore unto the matter out of the places of the xx. of Matthew, and the xxii. of Luke, where our Saviour Christ, upon occasion of the inordinate request of the sons of Zebedee, putteth a difference between the civil and ecclesiastical function, he placeth the distinction of them in two points, whereof the one is in their office, the other is in their names and titles.

This is a note of your own devising.

[1 True exposition of Matt. xx., Answ. 2.]   [2 xx. of Matt., Answ.]
[3 But be, Answ.]   [4 See below, page 158.]
[5 This marginal note is inserted from Answ. 2.]

The distinction of the office he noteth in these words, "The kings of the gentiles have dominion over them, and the princes exercise authority over them; but it shall not be so with you." Whereupon the argument may be thus gathered, That wherein the civil magistrate is severed from the ecclesiastical officer doth not agree to one minister over another. But the civil magistrate is severed from the ecclesiastical officer by bearing dominion. Therefore bearing dominion doth not agree to one minister over another. Petitio principii. Æquivocatio.

Page 11, Sect. 1 and 2.

Touching their names and titles, he putteth a difference in these words: "And they are called gracious lords; but it shall not be so with you." And so the argument may be framed as before, that, forasmuch as they are severed in titles, and that to the civil minister doth agree the title of gracious lords, therefore to the ecclesiastical minister the same doth not agree. For, as it is fit that they whose offices carry an outward majesty and pomp should have names agreeable to their magnificence, so is it meet that those that God hath removed from that pomp and outward shew should likewise be removed from such swelling and lofty titles, as do not agree with the simplicity of the ministry which they exercise. And, whereas it might seem somewhat unjust that he that hath the greater gifts should not be preferred to those which have less, our Saviour Christ sheweth that the matter is far otherwise. For, by how much every man doth excel his fellow in the gifts of the Holy Ghost, by so much more he ought to employ himself to the benefit of others; so that in a manner he should become (as it were) their servant to do them good, which although it be in part common to the civil magistrate with the minister of the word, yet he doth never let down himself so low, nor giveth his service either to the church or commonwealth, but that he doth and ought, in that service, to retain that dignity and countenance, with the marks and notes thereof, which his princely estate doth require.

In the end he propoundeth himself for example, in whom he setteth before their eyes a perfect pattern of the ministry. For seeing he, being Lord, took upon him to be a servant, and, being Emperor and King of heaven and earth, was content to want all the glory and shew of the world (his ministry so requiring), it should be great shame for them which were his disciples, chosen out for the ministry, not to content themselves, but to aspire unto such offices and dignities as they dreamed of.

Jo. Whitgift.

You say that Christ in that place "putteth a difference between the civil and ecclesiastical functions," and that "in two points, in their office, and in their names and titles: the distinction of the office" (you say) "he noteth in these words: 'The kings of the gentiles, &c.', of their names and titles in[6] these: 'And they are called gracious lords, &c.'" Whereupon you conclude as though all were cock sure.

[6 This is inserted from the table of errata.]

But, I pray you, tell me whereupon do you gather that Christ maketh any such "distinction" here, either "of offices" or "titles?" Indeed he would have a difference both betwixt the authority of his disciples and other Christians, and the dominion of heathenish princes; and also betwixt their affections in desiring the same; and therefore doth he expressly say, "The kings of the gentiles, &c." If he had meant any such "distinction of offices or titles," as you would make us believe, he would have said, "The kings and princes of the Jews, &c." or rather, "kings and princes," without any further addition: but, seeing that he saith, "the kings and princes of the gentiles," it is manifest that he forbiddeth, not only to his disciples, but to all Christians, such tyrannical kind of government as the gentiles used, and that ambitious desire and affection of the same which ruled in them. For Christ useth to call back those that be his from errors and corrupt affections by the example of the gentiles, as he doth in the vi. of Matthew from too much carefulness for meat and drink, and such like: *Nam omnia ista gentes exquirunt:* "For after all these things do the gentiles seek;" where he doth not forbid them to seek for meat, drink, and clothing, but to seek for it too carefully, and with mistrust of God's providence, as the gentiles did. In like manner, here he forbiddeth not government, either in the civil or ecclesiastical state; but he forbiddeth such government as the gentiles used, and such corrupt affections as they had in desiring the same.

Government not forbidden of Christ, but the kind of government.

Two faults in the argument of T. C.

The civil magistrate doth not simply differ from the ecclesiastical by bearing dominion.

Touching your argument, I say it hath two faults. First, it is a fallation, *a petitione principii;* for you take it as granted, that "the civil magistrate is severed from the ecclesiastical officer by bearing dominion;" which I will not simply grant unto you, for that is partly our question. Secondly, your *minor* is ambiguous, and therefore, in that respect, your argument may also be placed in the fallation of "equivocation;" for the word "dominion" may have divers significations. It may signify such dominion as Christ speaketh of in this place, that is, rule with oppression. It may also signify the absolute authority of a prince, such as is mentioned 1 Samuel viii. Thirdly, it may signify any peculiar office of superiority and government under the prince, at the appointment of the prince, as the authority of a judge, justice, mayor, &c. Last of all, it may signify any jurisdiction or kind of govern-

Divers significations of the word dominion.

ment. If you take it in either of the two first significations, your *minor* is true; if in either of the two latter significations, it is false. For we grant that there is great difference betwixt the dominion of kings and princes, and betwixt the jurisdiction and authority of bishops. Kings have power over life and goods, &c.; so have not bishops. Kings have authority in all causes, and over all persons within their dominions, without any limitation: if bishops have any such dominion, especially in civil causes, it is not in the respect they be bishops, but it is from the prince, and limited unto them.

Touching "their names and titles," you say, "he putteth a difference in these words, 'And they are called gracious lords; but it shall not be so with you, &c.'" The words of the twentieth of Matthew be these: "And they that are great exercise authority over them." In the x. of Mark the same words be used. In the xxii. of Luke the Greek word is εὐεργέται καλοῦνται, *benefici vocantur*, "they are called bountiful," or "beneficial;" which I see not how you can by any means apply to your purpose: for Matthew and Mark refer this clause, "It shall not be so among you," not to any name, but to the ambition and tyrannical kind of dominion, which our Saviour Christ there reproveth, as it is most manifest. And therefore this place of Luke must also be expounded by them. Neither is this word εὐεργέται of any such imperiousness, that Christ should forbid his disciples the name. Master Calvin, in his commentaries interpreting these words of St Luke, saith thus: "As touching the words, where Matthew hath, that 'kings exercise authority over them,' in Luke we read that 'they are called bountiful,' in the same sense; as though he should say, kings have plenty of all things, and are very rich, so that they may be bountiful and liberal[1]." And a little after he saith, that they do *appetere laudem munificentiæ*[2], "desire the commendation of bountifulness." I know that certain of the kings of Egypt were called εὐεργέται, *munifici et benefactores*, "bountiful and benefactors;" and that they were delighted to be so called. I

Calvinus.

[1 Quod ad verba spectat, ubi Matthæus habet, *Reges exercere potestatem in eas,* apud Lucam legitur, *vocari beneficos,* eodem sensu. ac si diceret, rerum copiam affluere regibus, eosque magnis opibus pollere, ut munifici et liberales esse possint.—Calvin. Op. Amst. 1667-71. Comm. in Harm. Euang. Tom. VI. p. 230.]

[2 ...laudem tamen munificentiæ appetunt.—Id. ibid.]

know also that among the Hebrews their princes were called *munifici et liberales, per antonomasian;* but what then? If either they vain-gloriously desired that name, or were so called, when they deserved rather the names of tyrants and oppressors, doth it therefore follow that they be unlawful names for such as may deserve them? The most that can be gathered of this place (for anything that I perceive) is, that the kings of the gentiles had vain and flattering titles given them, being nothing less indeed than that which their names did signify; and so may it be a good admonition for men to learn to answer to their names and titles, and to do indeed that which by such names and titles is signified. Now then, if you will have *vos autem non sic,* "but it shall not be so with you," to be a prohibition to all Christians, and especially to bishops, that they shall not ambitiously seek dominion, as the gentiles did; unjustly and tyrannously use their authority, as they also did; nor have names and titles to the which they do not accordingly answer, no more than the gentiles did; then I agree with you. But, if you will have *vos autem non sic* to restrain them from being called εὐεργέται, that is, "liberal benefactors," &c.; as your interpretation agreeth not with the words of the other two evangelists, so doth it not with any learned interpreter that I have read.

<small>How the words, *Vos autem non sic*, may be referred to names.</small>

To your argument concerning "names and titles" I answer as I did to the former. Some names and titles are proper to the civil magistrate only, as the names of emperor, king, prince, duke, earl, &c.: these names are not given to any of the clergy in this church to my knowledge. Some names are common to the civil magistrate with ecclesiastical persons, as certain names of reverence, of superiority, and of office. The name of "gracious lord" is a name of superiority and of reverence, according to the manner of the country where it is used, and therefore may well agree either to the civil or ecclesiastical persons; and in many places divers are called by this name "lord" (which is in Latin *dominus*) for reverence and civility, which have very small dominion. As for the name of archbishop, or metropolitan, that is not proper to any civil magistrate, and therefore without the compass of your argument. Thus then you see that some titles are proper to the civil magistrate, some to the ecclesiastical, and some common to both; whereby your *major* is utterly overthrown.

<small>Divers kinds of names.</small>

<small>Names common to civil and ecclesiastical persons.</small>

As for this word εὐεργέται, upon the which you seem to ground your argument, I see not why it may not be common to all men that shew themselves liberal and beneficial.

There is no man denieth but that there is, and must be, great difference betwixt "the pomp and outward shew" of a prince, and the state of an ecclesiastical person, both in titles and other majesty; and I think that he is very blind, that seeth it not so to be in this church of England: yet may the ecclesiastical person shew forth the countenance of his degree, whereunto he is called of God, by his prince, and by the laws of that realm wherein he is a subject.

It is true that an ecclesiastical minister doth much differ from a civil magistrate, touching his ministry and spiritual calling; yet is he not so distinct, that he may exercise no such civil office wherein he may do good, and which is an help to his ecclesiastical function. As the civil magistrate may in some things exercise jurisdiction ecclesiastical, and meddle in matters of the church; so may the ecclesiastical person in some causes use civil jurisdiction, and deal in matters of the commonwealth, if it shall be thought expedient or necessary by the chief magistrates. M. Calvin, in his commentaries upon this text, though in some points he agree with you, yet hath he these words: "Add hereunto, that Christ did not so much respect the persons of men as the state of his church; for it may so be, that he which is lord of a village or city do also (necessity constraining) exercise the office of teaching[1]." Whereby it is plain, that a temporal lord (if necessity require) may together with his lordship become a preacher of the gospel. M. Brentius, in his 48. homily upon Luke, speaking of this matter, saith, that "bishops, which glory themselves to be the successors of the apostles, may not, under the pretence of their ecclesiastical office, usurp external dominion over kings and princes, to make kings whom they list, and to displace whom they list[2]." And by and by he objecteth and

Ministers may execute some kind of civil jurisdiction.

Calvin.

A temporal lord may be a preacher.

Brentius.

What kind of external dominion is denied to ministers.

[1 Adde quod non tam hominum personas respexit Christus quam ecclesiæ suæ statum. Fieri enim posset ut qui pagi vel urbis erit dominus, simul docendi quoque munus, urgente necessitate, obeat.—Id. ibid. p. 229.]

[2 Deinde docet pontifices et episcopos, qui gloriantur se esse apostolorum successores, quod non liceat ipsis prætextu ecclesiastici sui officii usurpare externam potestatem super reges et principes, ut quos velint in reges instituant, et quos velint dejiciant, sed quod debeant ministerio suo ecclesiæ servire.—J. Brent. In Evang. sec. Luc. Hom. Franc. 1563. In post. capp. Hom. xlviii. p. 1118.]

answereth as followeth: "Therefore thou wilt say, it is not lawful for a minister of the church (whether thou callest him a bishop or a preacher) to have temporal dominion, and to govern the people committed unto him by civil policy? I answer, that it is not lawful for a minister of the church to usurp such rule and dominion under the pretence of the gospel and of his ecclesiastical ministry: Peter must not therefore have dominion over Antioch or Rome, because he is an apostle, &c. But, if temporal dominion or possession happen to the minister of the gospel, either by inheritance or ordinary election, or any other civil or lawful contract, &c., then may he enjoy these external things, &c.[1]" And in his 52. homily, upon these words of Christ now in question, he writeth thus: "What shall we then say to these things? because Christ saith, 'The kings of the nations bear rule over them, and are called bountiful; but it must not be so among you,' shall it not be lawful for a christian man to bear rule in a temporal kingdom, and acknowledge the titles of honour, as of bountifulness and clemency, which are given unto princes? Is it not lawful also for a bishop to have temporal dominion? Christ in this place doth not think it unlawful for Christians to be magistrates, neither doth he forbid bishops to have external dominion; but he sheweth a difference between the kingdom of this world and his kingdom. He teacheth that the kingdom of this world and his kingdom are so distinct, that he which is a minister of his kingdom must not, in that respect, usurp the kingdom of this world: for the apostles thought that, because they were apostles, therefore they should possess the kingdoms of the world; and therefore Christ in this place condemneth their false opinion, &c. Christ doth not condemn magistracy among Christians, &c. No, he doth not forbid bishops to have external dominion, if they come unto it by inheritance or by lawful election. It is

What kind of temporal dominion a minister may exercise.

Idem.

Christ forbiddeth not temporal dominion, either to Christians in general, or particularly to bishops.

[1 Ergo, inquis, non licet ministro ecclesiæ, sive illum episcopum sive ecclesiasten voces, habere externum principatum, et populum externa politia sibi subjectum? Non licet, inquam, ministro ecclesiæ talem principatum usurpare prætextu evangelii et ecclesiastici ministerii. Petrus non idcirco debet Antiochiæ aut Romæ dominari, quia apostolus est....Quod si vero externus principatus aut externorum bonorum possessio contigerit ministro ecclesiæ vel legitima hæreditate, vel ordinaria electione, aliove civili et legitimo contractu, ibi tum, etsi difficillimum sit, una externas opes administrare, et prædicando evangelio servire, &c.— Id. ibid. pp. 1118, 9.]

a very hard matter both to preach the gospel and to exercise temporal dominion; and yet it is not of itself unlawful together with the ministry to keep and use temporal dominion, if it come ordinarily and lawfully. For Christ came not to trouble civil laws, and the ordinary governments of the kingdoms of this world, but rather that, these being preserved, his gospel might be preached quietly[2]." *Hæc Brentius.* But of civil authority in ecclesiastical persons, occasion will be given to speak more at large hereafter.

That which Christ said, *Quicunque major erit inter vos,* &c.; "Whosoever will be great among you, let him be your minister;" though it may especially appertain to the apostles, yet it is also a general rule for all Christians, and so is the example of him also, which he propoundeth unto them. And so doth Musculus very truly interpret this place; to whom M. Bucer agreeth, whose words be these: "The anabaptists think here that they are able to prove that it pertaineth not to a Christian to bear rule, and that no man can be together a magistrate and a Christian, because Christ said here to his disciples, *Vos autem non sic;* not considering that those, which godlily and according to the will of the Lord bear rule, *nihil minus quam dominari, imo maxime servire, et tanto pluribus, quanto pluribus præfuerint;* do nothing less than bear rule indeed, yea verily, do most of all serve,

Quicunque major erit inter vos, &c. expounded.

Bucer in xx. Matt.

They which bear rule godlily serve.

[2 Quid ergo ad hæc dicemus? Num quia Christus dicit, Reges gentium dominantur eis, et vocantur benefici, inter vos autem non sic, non licebit homini christiano in externo regno dominari, nec agnoscere honoris epitheta, nimirum, beneficentiæ aut clementiæ, quæ principes audiunt? non licebit etiam episcopo ecclesiæ externum administrare principatum?...Christus enim hoc loco non sentit, Christianis suis non licere magistratus gerere, et in hoc seculo regnare, nec vetat episcopum ecclesiæ habere externam dominationem; sed docet discrimen inter regna hujus seculi, et suum regnum: docet regnum hujus mundi et suum regnum ita inter se distincta esse, ut qui sit minister sui regni, non debeat ideo usurpare regnum hujus seculi. Existimabant enim apostoli quod, quia essent apostoli Christi, idcirco deberent invadere regna hujus mundi, et in hoc mundo dominari. Christus autem damnat hoc loco falsam apostolorum opinionem....Non damnat Christus inter Christianos magistratum et externa imperia...Ad hæc Christus nec ipsos quidem ecclesiæ episcopos vetat habere externam dominationem, videlicet, si ad hanc vel hæreditaria successione vel legitima electione pervenerint. Difficillimum quidem est simul ministerium prædicandi evangelii in ecclesia recte perficere, et externum regnum administrare; per se tamen non est impium retinere una cum ministerio ecclesiastico externam dominationem, si ea legitime et ordinarie obvenerit. Christus enim non venit, ut turbet civiles leges et ordinarias regnorum hujus mundi administrationes; sed potius, ut his conservatis, euangelion suum tranquille adnuncietur.—Id. ibid. Hom. lii. pp. 1151, 2.]

and even unto so many do they serve, over how many soever they bear rule. Surely Christ would have his apostles to have their authority in churches, and they themselves did greatly require to be obeyed: but, because in that they sought nothing unto themselves, but only salvation and the glory of God in those whom they ruled, they did govern the churches; they had everywhere the superiority; they ruled such as believed; they would have the godly to be obedient unto them; *interim nihilominus servierunt omnibus, dominati sunt nemini:* and yet in the meantime served all, and had dominion over none. So also in the civil government, who was ever in greater dignity than Moses, or more to be feared for his authority and power? and yet who ever served more, more diligently, and more humbly, which never sought anything for himself, or took anything unto himself, &c.; but day and night, to the uttermost of his power, sought for the safety of the people, &c.? If any now so bear office, and rule the works of the hands of the Lord, and govern the sheep of his pasture according to his will, what doth he else but serve all those whom he governeth? And therefore Christ doth not here dehort from bearing rule, and being a magistrate, but from seeking rule and dominion: for I had rather take this saying of the Lord in this generality, than to restrain it to the apostles only; *eo quod omnino pius magistratus serviat, non dominetur, habeatque per se omnia secundum præsentem Domini cohortationem;* because a godly magistrate doth altogether serve, and not bear rule, and hath by himself all things agreeable to this present exhortation of the Lord[1]."

<small>The place of Matt. xx. general.</small>

[1 Porro hic putant anabaptistæ sese posse probare, alienum esse a Christiano, ut magistratu fungatur, neque posse quenquam simul et magistratu fungi et Christianum esse, eo quod hic discipulis Dominus dixerit, Vos autem non sic: non animadvertentes, eos qui pie et ex voluntate Domini magistratum gerunt, nihil minus quam dominari, imo servire maxime, et tanto pluribus, quanto pluribus præfuerint. Certe et apostolos Christus suam auctoritatem in ecclesiis habere voluit, et ipsi, ut sibi obediretur, magnopere requisierunt. Verum quia eo nihil sibi, sed iis tantum, quos regebant, salutem quærebant, ac Dei gloriam, præfuerunt quidem ecclesiis, primas ubique habuerunt, credentes gubernarunt, dicto audire sibi sanctos volebant; interim nihilominus servierunt omnibus, dominati sunt nemini. Sic etiam in externarum administratione rerum, quis Moscheh unquam dignitate præstantior et auctoritate potestateque formidabilior fuit; at quis simul unquam pluribus, magis sedulo et summisse servivit, qui nihil scilicet omnino sibi vel quæsierit vel acceperit unquam, ut de se apud Dominum gloriabatur 3. Moscheh 16. sed dies noctesque ut populi salutem promoveret, fere supra vires desudaverit? Si quis jam sic magistratum gerat, et opera manuum Domini,

Thus you see Bucer's judgment upon these words of Christ.

Chapter i. The Second Division.

Answer to the Admonition, Page 14, line 11.

And it is the common opinion of all writers, that these words of Christ do not condemn superiority, lordship, or any such like authority, but the ambitious desire of the same, and the tyrannical usage thereof[2].

T. C. Page 11, Sect. 3 and 4.

Against this is said, that the places do nothing else but condemn ambitious desire and tyrannical usage of authority, and doth not bar the ministers of these things.

Then belike all those godly and learned men, which have used these places to prove that the pope, which professeth himself to be an ecclesiastical person, ought not to have the civil sword, nor to usurp unto himself such glorious pomp, have abused them. For you teach him how he should answer, that there is nothing forbidden but ambition and tyranny; and indeed this is the answer of all the papists to that objection.

The bishop of Salisbury so allegeth this place in his Defence of the Apology against M. Harding, p. 653.[3]

Jo. Whitgift.

Those godly and learned men, which have used these places against the pope, have rightly used them: and, if it had pleased you, you might have understood that in the very next leaf following I say, that "these places may be aptly alleged against the pride, tyranny, and ambition of the bishop of Rome, which seeketh tyrannically to rule and not to profit; but not against the lawful authority in any state of men[4]." They therefore allege it truly; and yet you untruly expound it: for the pope's dominion is such as is in this place forbidden, that is, usurped and tyrannical, because he hath not only

These places are rightly used against the pope, notwithstanding this interpretation.

The pope's dominion such as Christ here forbiddeth.

ovesque pascuæ ejus, ad ipsius voluntatem gubernet, quid quæso aliud quam serviat omnibus quos gubernat? Non igitur regere et magistratu fungi, sed sibi quærere præcellentiam et potestatem, id demum est, a quo hic Christus dehortatus est. Nam placet magis in hac generalitate hoc Domini dictum accipere, quam ad solos apostolos id contrahere, eo quod omnino plus [pius?] magistratus serviat, non dominetur, habeatque se per omnia secundum præsentem Domini cohortationem.—M. Bucer. Enarr. Perp. in Quat. Evang. Argent. 1530. In Evang. Matt. cap. xx. fol. 159. 2.]

[2 This sentence is repeated from page 148.]

[3 See Bishop Jewel's Works, Park. Soc. Edit. Vol. IV. pp. 984, 5.]

[4 See below, page 169.]

entered into the spiritual kingdom of Christ, and sought to reign in men's consciences, but also pulleth from princes the power of earthly dominion, saying that he hath that immediately from God, and the emperors and princes immediately from him. And so do the learned expound this place, and it is their answer to the objection of the anabaptists. I fully agree with my lord of Salisbury his allegation of this place; for bishops may not be kings, nor have any such civil dominion as the pope claimeth and usurpeth.

Chapter i. The Third Division.
Answer to the Admonition, Page 14, Sect. 1; and Page 15, Sect. 1 and 2.

Musculus[1]. Musculus, expounding these places, saith in this sort: "'Whosoever will be great among you, &c.' He saith not, no man ought to be chief among you; which he should have said, if it had not been lawful in the kingdom of God for some to be great and chief, or if it had been necessary that all should have been in all things equal. The celestial spirits are not equal: the stars be not equal: the apostles themselves were not equal: Peter is found in many places to have been chief among the rest, which we do not deny. Therefore this is not Christ's meaning to have none great or chief among Christians, seeing the very necessity of our state requireth that some be superiors and betters; so far is it from being repugnant to charity. In a commonweal it is necessary that some should excel other; so is it in a well-ordered family. In like manner there must be in the church governors, presidents, rulers, of whom Paul maketh mention Rom. xii., 1 Cor. xii., Heb. xiii., as there is also in the body some principal members, some inferior, &c. Therefore Christ doth not require that in his kingdom all should be equal, but this he doth require, that none should desire to be great, or to be thought and counted chief[2]." Hitherto Musculus.

[1 This word is not in Answ. 1.]
[2 *Quicunque voluerit*, inquit, *inter vos magnus esse, primus esse, &c.* Non dicit, Nemo debet inter vos magnus esse, nemo primus: quod tamen dicere deberet, si omnino non liceret in regno Dei primos esse et magnos, et necesse esset omnes in omnibus prorsus esse æquales: stellæ non sunt æquales: spiritus cœlestes

Which interpretation must needs be true: else we may say that Christ in this place rejecteth and disalloweth the princes and magistrates of the gentiles, and also forbiddeth the same among Christians; which is false and anabaptistical.

Likewise the same Musculus saith that Christ teacheth in this place what he ought to be indeed that desireth to bear rule over other; to wit, " that he ought to be a servant to other, that is (as he doth interpret it) to profit other, and to serve for the commodity of other[3]:" for, though the name of a prince and of a lord be a name of honour and dignity, yet is it the office of a prince and lord to serve those which be under them, in governing of them carefully, and in providing for their wealth and peace.

T. C. Page 11, Sect. 5 and 6.

But Musculus a learned man is of that judgment. And M. Calvin, as learned as he, and[4] divers other, are of that judgment that I have alleged[5]: this is no great proof on[6] your side, nor reproof of ours: let us therefore see the reasons wherewith this exposition is warranted. [a]*Musculus' reason is this, that, if he should have meant that the apostles should have been equal, and none greater than another, then there should be equality of all, and none should have authority over other. And so there should be* This is a simple answer to oppose one man's authority against another.

[a] A false collection upon M. Musculus his words.

non sunt æquales. Apostoli ipsi non erant æquales omnino. Deprehenditur Petrus multis locis primus fuisse inter reliquos; quod nos non negamus. Ergo non hoc agit hic Christus, ut nolit aliquem esse primum vel magnum inter Christianos, cum ipsa status nostri necessitas exigat, ut aliqui sint potiores et majores; tam abest ut illud repugnet caritati. In republica necesse est esse, qui aliis præcellant, ita et in domo bene constituta; ita et in ecclesia debent esse gubernatores, præsides, præpositi, quorum Paulus meminit Rom. 12. 1 Cor. 12. Ebr. 13. ut in corpore sunt quædam principaliora membra, quædam minus principalia. &c.... Itaque non exigit hoc Christus, ut prorsus in regno suo sint omnes æquales: sed hoc exigit, ne quisquam cupiat magnus et primus haberi et videri. Non dicit, *Qui vult inter vos magnus videri, in honore præcipuo esse:* sed, *Qui vult magnus esse.*—Wolfg. Muscul. Comm. in Matt. Evang. Basil. 1611. cap. xx. Tom. II. p. 442.]

[3 Quid illi faciendum est? *Sit omnium minister et servus,* inquit....Quid est autem servire omnibus? Est omnibus prodesse, servire ad aliorum utilitatem, salutem ac necessitatem.—Id. ibid.]

[4 With, Repl. 1 and 2.]

[5 Sic David, Ezekias, et alii similes, quum voluntarii essent omnium servi, sceptro tamen, diademate et solio, aliisque insignibus fuerunt ornati. Ecclesiæ autem gubernatio nihil tale admittit, quia pastoribus nihil plus Christus detulit quam ut ministri sint, a dominio autem prorsus abstineant.—Calvin. Op. Amst. 1667-71. Comm. in Harm. Euang. Tom. VI. p. 229.]

[6 Of, Repl. 1 and 2.]

no degrees of the prince and subject in the commonwealth, of master and servant in a family, of people and minister in the church. But it is no good reason to say, there is nor ought to be any inequality amongst the apostles; therefore there is none, nor ought to be none at all: or to say, there is no inequality amongst the pastors; therefore there is no inequality between the pastors and the people. For, as the commonwealths[1], and[2] families, and churches are preserved by inequality, and in that some are higher, and some are lower, some rule, and some obey; so are the same likewise preserved by equality of certain amongst themselves; as, albeit[3] the consuls in Rome were above other officers[4] and the people, yet were they equal between themselves. And, although it be the preservation of the family, that the master should be above the servant, and the father above the son; yet it tendeth also to the quiet of the house, that the servants amongst themselves, and the brethren amongst themselves, should be equal. And so we grant that, for the preservation of the church, it is necessary that there be some should bear rule, and other should be under their rule; but I deny that thereof followeth that one minister should bear rule over another. Whereas M. Musculus saith, that "Peter was found in many places chief among[5] the rest," if he mean as Eusebius, cap. 14. lib. II. doth, which saith that he was τῆς ἀρετῆς ἕνεκα τῶν λοιπῶν ἀποστόλων προήγορον[6], "for his virtues and gifts he had one that spake before the rest, and in the name of the rest" (which he seemeth to do in that he doth not absolutely give any chiefty unto him, but only in certain places), I agree with him, and do not deny but such chiefty may be amongst the ministers; as shall appear more at large hereafter.

This interpretation of M. Musculus (Master Doctor saith) "must needs be true; or else Christ should reject princes and magistrates, amongst both Christians and other." I have shewed that it doth not follow, because[7] he forbiddeth that rule unto ministers[8], therefore he forbiddeth it simply and altogether; no more than the law, which forbiddeth that any stranger should be king of the realm, forbiddeth therefore that there should be no king of the realm. Whereas you say, M. Musculus teacheth how he ought to rule which ruleth, and what he ought to be, I have told you before, other think otherwise; and therefore you, having set down his judgment before, needed not to have repeated it here again.

Jo. Whitgift.

Not only M. Musculus doth so expound this place, but also Bucer and sundry others, both old and new writers: as Chry-

[1 As commonwealths, Repl. 1 and 2.] [2 Repl. 2 omits *and*.]
[3 As for example albeit, Repl. 2.] [4 Offices, Repl. 2.]
[5 Amongst, Repl. 1 and 2.]
[6 ...τὸν καρτερὸν καὶ μέγαν τῶν ἀποστόλων, τὸν ἀρετῆς ἕνεκα τῶν λοιπῶν ἁπάντων προήγορον Πετρὸν, κ.τ.λ.—Euseb. in Hist. Eccles. Script. Amst. 1695-1700. Lib. II. cap. xiv. p. 41.]
[7 How it doth not follow that because, Repl. 2.]
[8 Unto the ministers, Repl. 1, 2, and Def. A.]

sostom, Theophylact, &c.[9] I know that M. Calvin doth otherwise think of it; but that is no sufficient answer to Musculus his reasons. The first reason of Musculus you collect on this sort: "If Christ should have meant that the apostles should have been equal, &c., then there should be equality of all:" wherein you deal with Musculus as you deal with me; that is, you make his arguments against his express words; for where doth Musculus reason in that manner?

The first reason of Musculus is this: "If Christ had meant that it should not be lawful in the kingdom of God for some to be great and chief, then would he have said, No man ought to be great among you; but he said not so, for his words be, 'Whosoever will be great among you, &c.'; therefore, &c." And this is a better reason than you can well answer. If you could have done it, you would not have shifted it off with a vain confutation, not of Musculus, but of your own devised argument. *Musculus his reasons upon the xx. of Matt.*

Musculus his second reason is this: " There is superiority in the kingdom of God, and one above another, as there is in the celestial spirits, in the stars, and in other states. For Peter is found in many places to have been chief among the rest; and therefore this is not the meaning of Christ, that none should be great or chief among Christians."

His third reason may be thus gathered: " The very necessity of our state requireth that some should be superiors and betters, as well in the church as in the commonwealth, &c.; therefore it is not Christ's meaning to have no superiors, &c."

In like manner doth he reason out of the xii. to[10] the Romans; 1 Cor. xii.; Heb. xiii., and of the parts and members of man's body: and in the end thus he concludeth: "Therefore Christ doth not require that in his kingdom all should be equal, but this he doth require, that none should desire to be great, &c."

To these reasons you answer not one word, but shift them off by telling us, that " as commonweals, and families, and churches are preserved by inequality, &c., and as albeit the consuls of Rome, &c.;" which be to no purpose, and make directly against you. For not only in a family the master is *Musculus his reasons not answered, but shifted off by T. C.* *The examples of T. C. against himself.*

[9 Chrysost. Op. Par. 1718-38. In Matt. Hom. lxv. Tom. VII. pp. 649, &c. Conf. Op. Imperf. in Matt. Hom. xxxv. ex cap. xx. Tom. VI. pp. cliii. &c.; Theophyl. Op. Venet. 1754-63. In Matt. Comm. cap. xx. Tom. I. pp. 107, 8.]

[10 Of, Def. A.]

above the servant, but one servant also above another; whereunto Christ himself alludeth Matt. xxiv., when he saith, "Who is a faithful servant whom his master hath made ruler over his household, &c." In like manner, not only the father is above the son, but also in the same family one brother is above another; and even in the scripture, Gen. xlix., and other places, it may be seen that pre-eminence of dignity hath been always (for the most part) given to the eldest: wherefore these similitudes help you not.

And, whereas you seem to grant that the pastor must be superior to the people, and yet one pastor not to be above another, the words of Christ rather import the contrary: for the dominion that is here forbidden is not of one minister over another, but over the people of God; as the similitude of them that sit at the table and of them that serve doth evidently declare; for who are they that sit at the table to be served but the people (which is the church), in respect of whom the ministers are servants? Therefore this place is very unfitly alleged to prove that there should be no superiority between ministers; for such superiority in government, as by your own confession may be in ministers over the people, may also be in one minister over another, for anything that this place hath to the contrary.

But whether one minister ought to be above another, or no, shall be discussed in his proper place.

What superiority soever M. Musculus giveth unto Peter over the rest, that example is aptly applied to the justifying of his exposition upon this place that we have now in hand. But I must tell you that you do not truly translate the words of Eusebius concerning Peter. For this word προήγορος signifieth not only to "speak before the rest, and in the name of the rest" (as you translate it), but it signifieth also *principem in omni re gerenda*: "a chief ruler or guide in every matter or business." Wherefore I say still that "this interpretation of M. Musculus must needs be true;" and that it may as well be alleged to take away superiority from christian princes, as it may from ecclesiastical ministers.

This of M. Musculus that he saith, that "Christ here teacheth what he ought to be indeed that beareth rule over other," neither have I before rehearsed, nor you hitherto answered.

Chapter i. The Fourth Division.

Answer to the Admonition, Page 15, Sect. 3 and 4.

Moreover the Greek words that Christ useth in all these places, as κατακυριεύουσιν and[1] κατεξουσιάζουσιν, do signify to rule with oppression, and to rule as a man list.

Furthermore, Christ doth not say, that no man shall be great among them, or bear rule, but he saith,: *Quicunque voluerit inter vos magnus fieri, &c.*: "He that desireth to be great among you, &c."

T. C. Page 12, Line 8.

But "the Greek words (you say) κατακυριεύουσιν καὶ κατεξουσιάζουσιν do signify to rule with oppression." And why may not I say that this preposition κατὰ doth not signify here a perverseness of rule, but an absoluteness, and a full power, and jurisdiction; as καταμαθεῖν, καταλαμβάνειν, is not to learn, or to perceive, evilly and perversely, but to learn exactly, and to perceive throughly and perfectly? But what need we to follow conjectures in so plain a matter, when as St Luke useth the simple words, without any composition, of ἐξουσιάζειν καὶ κυριεύειν? do you not perceive that the preposition wherein you put so great confidence deceiveth you? besides the manifest untruth you commit in saying that all three evangelists have κατεξουσιάζουσιν καὶ[2] κατακυριεύουσιν. Furthermore, you say that our "Saviour Christ saith not, that no man shall be great among[3] them, but he that desireth to be great among[3] them." He had said so before, when he had said, "It shall not be so amongst you," and therefore needed not to repeat it. And yet another evangelist saith not, he that desireth to be great, but, "let the greatest among you be as the least;" whereby he doth not reprehend only the desire of being great, but will not have them to be one above another.

Side-notes: Because then you should say contrary to the judgment of all learned men. Untruth; for I name not three evangelists. Luke xxii. 26.

Jo. Whitgift.

You ask me, "why you may not say that this preposition κατὰ doth not signify here a perverseness of rule, but an absoluteness and a full power of[4] jurisdiction?" I answer that, if you should so say, you should say otherwise than the truth is, and contrary to the judgment of the best interpreters. Erasmus, expounding that place of Matthew, saith thus: *Nec est simpliciter dominantur, sed κατακυριεύουσι, dominantur in eas, sive adversus eas; frequenter enim ea præpositio in*

Side-note: The true interpretation of κατακυριεύουσιν and κατεξουσιάζουσιν. Eras. in Annot.

[1 *And* is not in Answ. 2.] [2 And, Repl. 1 and 2.]
[3 Amongst, Repl. 1, 2, and Def. A.] [4 And, Def. A.]

malum sonat, quod tyranni populi male gerant principatum[1]*:* "Neither is it simply, they have dominion, but they have dominion over them, or against them; for that preposition (κατά) doth oftentimes sound in evil part, because the tyrants of the people do rule evil." And, expounding the other word κατεξουσιάζουσιν, he saith: *Et præpositio similiter in partem malam sonat, judicans eam potestatem esse tyrannicam et cum malo parentium esse conjunctam*[2]*:* "And the preposition (κατά) likewise soundeth in the evil part, declaring that power to be tyrannical, and joined with the hurt of the subjects." M. Beza, in his notes upon the same place, well alloweth this interpretation. "But this also," saith he, "is to be understood (which Erasmus did not let pass), *hoc vocabulo, et eo quod proxime sequitur, non quamvis dominationem significari, sed cum imperiosa quadam acerbitate conjunctam, quam prohibet Paulus Eph. vi.* &c.[3]: that by this word, and that which next followeth, all kind of domination is not signified, but that which is joined with a certain imperious cruelty, which Paul forbiddeth, Eph. vi.: so it is taken Acts xix. and 1 Pet. v. For otherwise the faithful ministers of the word of God do exercise an authority not at all to be contemned: and therefore also I have interpreted κατεξουσιάζουσιν αὐτῶν, *licentia utuntur adversus eas:* ' They use licence or unlawful liberty against them.'" That place of the xix. of the Acts, verse 16. doth manifestly declare the true meaning and signification of this word κατακυριεύουσιν, both in this place and in the 1 Peter v. verse 3; for there it is manifest that it signifieth a violent kind of dominion.

The place of St Luke must be interpreted by these places of Matthew and Mark. It is sufficient that these two evangelists have these words, and a manifest declaration how that place of St Luke is to be understood.

My words be not as you report them; I do not say, "in

[1] Erasm. Op. L. Bat. 1703-6. Annot. in Evang. cap. xx. sec. Matt. Tom. VI. col. 105; where *malo gerant*.]

[2] Id. ibid.; where *indicans*.]

[3] Sed hoc quoque observandum est quod Erasmus non præteriit, hoc &c. consequitur, non quamvis &c. Ephes. 6. b. 9. Sic accipitur Act. 19. c. 16, & 1 Pet. 5. a. 3. Nam alioquin fideles verbi Dei ministri auctoritate funguntur minime omnium contemnenda, quam paucis explicat Paulus 2. Corinth. 10. a. 4, & deinceps. Ideo etiam interpretatus sum κατεξουσιάζουσιν αὐτῶν, licentia utuntur adversus eas, quum alioquin soleamus ἐξουσίαν interpretari auctoritatem.— Nov. Test. cum Th. Bezæ Annot. H. Steph. 1565. Evang. sec. Matt. cap. xx. p. 92.]

all three evangelists," but " in all these places," meaning of Matthew and Mark. This is but a shift to dally off a matter which you cannot answer; and the untruth returned upon yourself.

When I say that " Christ doth not say, that no man shall be great among them, but he that doth desire to be great, &c.", I say as the words be, and as Musculus himself noteth[4]. That place of Luke which you recite is so far from answering this, that it doth confirm it rather: for in that that Christ there saith, " he that is great among you, &c.", he insinuateth that there must be some great among them, whom he there teacheth how to use himself; as I have before declared out of M. Bucer; and as Musculus doth likewise note.

The place of Luke insinuateth a majority among the apostles. Luke xxii.

Chapter i. The Fifth Division.

Answer to the Admonition. Page 15, Sect. 5 & 6.

To conclude, it is manifest, that in Matthew and Mark he reproveth the ambition of the sons of Zebedee, who ambitiously desired the one to sit on his right hand, the other on his left; and in Luke, the ambition of the rest of the apostles, who contended among themselves which of them should be greatest.

So that it is plain that these places suppress ambition and desire of rule in all kind of men; and not superiority, not magistracy, not jurisdiction in any kind of persons.

T. C. Page 12, Sect. 1.

Last of all you conclude that our Saviour Christ, in the xx. of Matthew, reproveth the ambition of the sons of Zebedee, and, in the xxii. of St Luke, all the rest of the apostles. I grant you he doth so; and that could not be done better than in telling them, that they desired things not meet for them, and which would not stand with their calling. And if, as you say, the ambition only was reprehended, and the desire of rule to oppress others with, the answer you attribute to our Saviour is not so fit; for they might have replied and said, that he forbade tyrannical rule and oppression of their inferiors, but they desired that which was a moderate and well-ruled government. And seemeth it unto you a probable thing that St Luke meaneth tyrants and oppressors, when as he saith they " are called beneficial and[5] gracious lords?" Men do not use to call oppressors liberal or bountiful lords; neither is it to be thought of all the apostles,

Untruth; for I say not only.

That is not so.

[4 See before, page 158, 9, note 1.]   [5 Or, Repl. 1 and 2.]

that they desired rule one over another, to the end that they would use cruelty, or tyranny, or oppression, one over another; for that were to do them great injury: besides that it is said that the rest of the disciples disdained at the two brethren, which they would not have done, if they had had any purpose or mind to have oppressed them; then[1] they would have contemned them rather than have disdained them, if they had broken out into such gross faults. For Aristotle teacheth that νέμεσις (which *In his Rhet.* is the same that ἀγανάκτησις is, the verb whereof the evangelist *ad Theod.* useth) is against those that are supposed of them that bear the disdain to be lifted up higher and into better estate than they are worthy of[2]; which agreeth with that interpretation which I have alleged, and cannot agree with the other which you set down. For who (speaking properly) would speak after this sort: The rest[3] of the apostles disdained at the two brethren, or thought them unworthy that they should bear tyrannical rule over them?

It is not the same; for one is more general than the other.

Jo. Whitgift.

I have declared both my authors and their reasons concerning the exposition of these places, which may satisfy any man that is not wilful. Your reasons to the contrary have no ground, but only used, that it may be thought that you have said something. Be it that Christ told the sons of Zebedee, that "they desired things not meet for them," what is that to the purpose to prove that he did not reprove their ambition? as though there may not be ambition both in desiring that which is unlawful, and that also which is lawful.

I do not say that their ambition "only" was reprehended (I marvel what you mean so to falsify my words); for I think also that he reproveth the tyrannical rule of the kings of the gentiles. But this I, with Musculus, Bucer, and other learned men, constantly affirm, that he condemneth not rule, but violent and heathenish rule; not superiority or government, but the ambitious and greedy desire of the same.

If it so displease you that I interpret the Greek words to signify "a tyrannical rule, and a government by oppression," blame Erasmus, Musculus, and Beza, who so interpret them; nay, blame St Luke, who doth most evidently in the xix. of the Acts, verse 16. use one of these words in the same signification. Why they were called "liberal" and "bountiful," notwithstanding they be tyrants and oppressors, I have before declared: they desired the commendation of bountiful-

[1 For then, Repl. 2.]
[2 ...εἰ γάρ ἐστι τὸ νεμεσᾶν λυπεῖσθαι ἐπὶ τῷ φαινομένῳ ἀναξίως εὐπραγεῖν, κ.τ.λ.—Arist. Op. Lut. Par. 1629. Rhet. Lib. II. cap. ix. Tom. II. p. 560.]
[3 Residue, Repl. 1 and 2.]

ness and liberality, though they did not deserve it. It is no strange matter for men of great authority to be called by such titles as they do not deserve. The pope is called *sanctissimus*, and *servus servorum Dei;* and yet is he far from doing anything by these names signified. Men use to call their rulers and governors by their accustomed titles, howsoever they deserve them, though it be "gracious or bountiful lords," when they have no spark of grace or bountifulness. What rule or superiority soever it was that the apostles desired, they desired it ambitiously and out of time, and therefore were justly reproved for their ambition.

_{Men called by titles not deserved.}

I told you before that Christ in those places condemneth not ambition "only," but unlawful government also, even such as the gentiles used, of whom Christ in those places speaketh. And, whereas you say, that "the rest of the disciples disdained the two brethren, &c." you do but spend ink and paper in dallying. The disciples heard by their request that they desired promotion and preferment above the rest, and therefore they disdained them: what opinion they had of their usage in their offices, that is unknown either to you or to me, because the scripture hath not expressed it; but this I think, that they were as ambitious in disdaining as the other were in desiring. Your definition of νέμεσις out of Aristotle is needless (but only that thereby we may know you be an Aristotelian); for the apostles disdained them because they desired rule and dominion, not because they desired to rule well or to rule evil. And surely an envious person, and a disdainful, hath not so much respect to the lawfulness or unlawfulness of the preferment and promotion of him whom he doth envy and disdain, as he hath to the party that is preferred, and to the preferment itself; as it is not unlike that there are some of you that disdain such as be in place above you, be they deans, bishops, or archbishops, although you say that their offices be unlawful and tyrannical. And this vice is too common among you; for you think some of us to be lifted up higher and to better estate, that be not so worthy as yourselves; *et hinc illæ lacrymæ:* if I judge amiss, let the modesty of your book reprove me.

In that you say νέμεσις and ἀγανάκτησις be all one, you are much deceived; for νέμεσις is *indignatio ob res prosperas alicujus seu felicitatem, qua indignus est,* "a disdain for the

_{Νέμεσις and ἀγανάκτησις not one.}

prosperity or felicity of some man, which he is unworthy of:" ἀγανάκτησις est indignatio seu stomachatio quælibet et de qualibet causa, " is any kind of indignation or stomaching, and for any cause;" so that ἀγανάκτησις doth contain νέμεσιν, and is as it were *genus* unto it.

The Exposition of the place Matt. xxiii.
Chapter ii.
Answer to the Admonition, Page 15. Sect. ult. and Page 16. Sect. 1 and 2.

<small>Rabbi Ma. &c.[1]
The place of Matt. xxiii. expounded.</small>

Touching the place in the xxiii. of Matthew, where Christ said unto his disciples, "Be not you called Rabbi; Call no man father; Be not called masters:" who is so ignorant to think that Christ forbiddeth by these words one christian man to call another lord, master, father? Shall not children call their parents father? Shall not scholars call their teacher master? And shall not servants call him master under whose government they are? Is it not lawful for one to call another master, doctor, father, lord, &c.? Paul (notwithstanding these words of Christ) 1 Cor. iv. calleth himself their "father;" and 1 Tim. ii. he calleth himself the "doctor of the gentiles." Wherefore it is manifest that these names be not here prohibited, much less the offices; but only the pharisaical, ambitious, and arrogant affection of superiority; as it is also manifest by this that followeth: "Whosoever exalteth himself, &c." And surely, as Christ condemneth here the ambitious affection of such as ambitiously desire these names of superiority, so doth he in like manner condemn those who be so puffed up with pride and arrogancy, that they contemn and disdain to call men in authority by the titles of their offices. For pride, contempt, and arrogancy, is as well in refusing to give honour and reverence, as it is in ambitiously desiring the same.

But the chief purpose of Christ in this place is to teach us not so to depend upon men, as though it were

[1 Answ. 2 has *Rabbi, master*. It may be stated here, once for all, that none of the marginal notes, except those belonging to the portions of the Admonition quoted, are found in Answ. 1.]

not lawful to break their decrees, or to decline from their authority; for there is one only Father, Lord, and Master, to whom we are so bound, that by no means we may decline at any time from his precepts.

These places therefore may be aptly alleged against the pride, tyranny, and ambition of the bishop of Rome, which seeketh tyrannically to rule, and not to profit; but it maketh nothing at all against the lawful authority of any other in any state or condition of men.

T. C. Page 12. Sect. ult.

Concerning the exposition and sense of that place I agree with you, and suppose that it is quoted of the authors of the Admonition, rather to note Belike it was fondly *the ambition of certain which gape greedily at these bishopricks which we* alleged, when *have, to the end they might be saluted by the name of lords and honours,* you do but suppose their *than to prove that one minister should not have dominion over another.* meaning. *And therefore, although these places be against no lawful authority of any estate or condition of men; yet, as they are aptly alleged against the bishop of Rome, the one against his estate and authority simply, the other against his tyranny and evil usage of himself in that authority, so it may be aptly alleged against any other which shall fall into the like fault of the bishop of Rome.*

Jo. WHITGIFT.

It is manifest that they quote this same place to the selfsame purpose that they do the other: there can be no mist so thick that may darken the eyes of men from seeing it, except they seeing will not see, as you do at this time.

I am glad that you "agree with" me in the exposition of this place: surely in so doing you must also agree with me in the exposition of the other. For, as Christ here doth not forbid the names, but the arrogant and ambitious desire of them; so doth he not there forbid authority and superiority, but the coveting of it, and ambitious and inordinate desire of the same. And, if you well mark the words, Christ doth here much more plainly forbid these names, than he doth there those offices of superiority.

If any man doth imitate the bishop of Rome's ambition, either in office or in name, he hath me as great an enemy as he hath you. But, in that you pass over with silence these words of mine, " these places therefore may be aptly alleged, &c.," you seem either to allow my expositions of the other places also, or else you are ashamed of your own unfaithful and subtle dealing, which before would have made your reader believe that I had misliked "all those godly and learned men's" judgments, which use these places against the bishop of Rome. It had been plain dealing to have set down my words in order, as I have done yours.

Answer to the Admonition, Page 17. Sect. 1, 2, 3.

<small>Unapt allegations of scripture used in the Admonition[1].</small> How aptly that place of the xxiv. of Matthew, "But if the evil servant shall say in his heart, &c." is alleged, let all men judge. I think it forbiddeth not to punish such as break good laws. But, Lord, how these men[2] are beaten, which do as they list, say what they list, and that with rejoicing thereto! that is[3], if they be no otherwise beaten than hitherto they have been, they will not only with schisms and factions tear in sunder this church of England, but in time overthrow the whole state of the commonwealth.

To prove that either we must have "a right ministry of God, and a right government of his church, according to the scriptures[4], set up, &c. or else there can be no right religion, &c." is alleged the ninth of Matthew, the fourth to the Ephesians, and the eighteenth of Matthew. In the ninth of Matthew the place they allege is this: "Surely the harvest is great; but the labourers be[5] few; wherefore &c." In the fourth to the Ephesians: "He therefore gave some to be apostles, &c." In the eighteenth of Matthew: "If thy brother trespass against thee, &c." The first place declareth that ministers of the word are necessary in Christ's church: the second, that there is divers kinds and[6] degrees of them: and the third sheweth an order of correcting secret sins and private offences, and meddleth not with those that be open and known to other. Now therefore consider to what purpose those places be noted in the margent, and how little they prove that which is concluded.

As for all the rest of the places of scripture[7] that

[1 Superfluous allegations. Lack of discipline. Answ. 2.]
[2 *Men* is not in Answ. 2.] [3 Answ. 2 has not *that is.*]
[4 Scripture, Answ. 2.] [5 Are, Answ. 2.]
[6 Of, Answ. 2.] [7 Of the scripture, Answ. 2.]

followeth noted in the margent of this preface, I know not to what purpose they be alleged, but only for vainglory, to blear the eyes of the ignorant people, and to make them believe that all that which is written in this book is nothing else but scripture itself. They have dealt very subtilly to quote the places only, and not to set them down in plain words; for by this means they think that of the most part it shall never be understanded, how unaptly and to what small purpose they be alleged. Subtlety in quoting places only.

Jo. Whitgift.

All this T. C. passeth over in silence, thereby (as I think) acknowledging it to be true.

Answer to the Admonition, Page 18.

This name Puritan is very aptly given to these men; not because they be pure, no more than were the heretics called Cathari[9]; but because they think themselves to be *mundiores ceteris*, "more pure than others," as Cathari did, and separate themselves from all other churches and congregations, as spotted and defiled: because also they suppose the church which they have devised to be without all impurity. The name of Puritans.

T. C. Page 13. Line 1. Sect. 1.

The pureness that we boast of is the innocency of our Saviour Christ, who shall cover all our unpureness, and not impute it unto us. And, Acts xv. 9.[10] *forsomuch as faith purifieth the heart, we doubt not but God of his goodness hath begun our sanctification, and hope that he will make an end of it even until the day of our Lord Jesus. Albeit we hold divers points more purely than they do which impugn them, yet I know none that by comparison hath either said or written that all those that think as we do in those points are more holy and more unblameable in life than any of those that think otherwise. If we say that in those points which we hold from them that*[11] *we think soundlier than they do, we are ready to prove it; if we say also that we live not so offensively to the world commonly, by getting so many livings into our hands as would find four or five good learned able ministers, all the world will bear us* And yet some of you have a competent number, without doing any duty at them.

[8 This marginal note is not in Answ. 2.]
[9 Here Answ. 2 inserts *that is, puritans.*]
[10 This marginal reference is inserted from Repl. 2.]
[11 *That* is not in Repl. 2.]

witness. Other *pureness we take not upon us. And therefore, as the name was first by the papists maliciously invented, so is it of you very unbrotherly confirmed. Whereas you say that they are puritans which "suppose the church which they have devised to be without all impurity," if you mean without sin, you do notably slander them, and it is already answered. If you mean that those are puritans, or Catharans, which do set forth a true and perfect pattern or platform of reforming the church; then the mark of this heresy reacheth unto those which made the book of common prayer, which you say is a perfect and absolute rule to govern this church, wherein nothing is wanting, or too little, nor nothing running over, nor too much. As for the Catharans (which were the same that are otherwise called Novatians), I know no such opinion they had, and they whom you charge are as far from their corruption as you be.*

<small>An untruth; for I do not say so in any place.</small>

Jo. Whitgift.

You have said unto me in one place of your book, *Quid verba audiam cum facta videam?* even so I say to you. For why will they not come to our sermons or to our churches? Why will they not communicate with us in our sacraments, not salute us in the streets, nay, spit in our faces, and openly revile us? why have they their secret conventicles? You know all this to be true in a number of them. I know not why they should do so, except they think themselves to be contaminated by hearing us preach, or by coming to our churches, or by communicating otherwise with us: which if they do, it argueth that they persuade themselves not only of such an outward perfection, but of such an inward purity also, that they may as justly for the same be called Puritans, as the Novatians were. You know that the first occasion why Novatus did separate himself from the church was because he could not obtain the bishoprick of Rome, which he ambitiously desired. You know also that his pretence was because the bishops did receive those into the church which had fallen in the time of persecution. Afterwards he fell into greater and more absurdities; for commonly such as once divide themselves from the church fall from error to error, without stay. This Novatus, though he seemed to condemn ambition in all other men, yet was he most ambitious himself; though he by vehement oaths denied himself to desire a bishoprick, yet did he most greedily seek for it; though he boasted of more perfection in life, and of a more perfect platform of a church than

<small>The qualities of Novatus, and cause of his heresy.</small>

he thought others had, yet was it nothing so. He was the first that I read of that forsook his ministry, and that said, *Se nolle amplius presbyterum esse, sed alterius philosophiæ studiosum:* "That he would no longer be a minister, but a student in other philosophy." Read Eusebius in his sixth book of his Ecclesiastical History, *cap.* 43, and Nicephorus in his sixth book also, and third chapter[1]. Surely the story of Novatus is worthy to be noted; because there be so many at these days, which do not so much differ from him in opinions, as they agree with him in conditions.

Novatus the first that forsook his ministry.

You affirm that I say, "The book of common prayer to be a perfect and absolute rule to govern this church, wherein nothing is wanting, or too little, nor nothing running over, or too much." If I have said any such thing, quote the place, that the reader may consider of it, and know that you speak the truth. But, if I never either spake or writ any such thing, then are you a false witness, and I have to desire the reader to consider of the rest of your slanderous reports according to the truth of this. I have learned with St Augustine to give this reverence only to the writers of canonical scriptures, that I think none of them to have erred in writing[2]. And I do firmly believe that only the books of the canonical scripture are of that absoluteness and perfection that nothing may be taken away from them, nothing added to them. I do not think the communion-book to be such but that it may admit alteration. I do not believe it to be so perfect but that there may be both added to it, and taken from it. But this I say, that it is a godly book, without any error in substance of doctrine, and nothing in it (that I know) against the word of God; and those imperfections, or rather motes, that you say to be in it, not to be such that any godly man ought to stir up any contention in the church for them, much less to make a schism, and least of all to divide himself from the church. This is my opinion of that book, which

The canonical scriptures are only absolute and perfect.

[1 Euseb. in Hist. Eccles. Script. Amst. 1695-1700. Lib. vi. cap. xliii. pp. 197, &c. See particularly p. 199. Conf. Niceph. Call. Eccles. Hist. Lut. Par. 1630. Lib. vi. cap. iii. Tom. I. pp. 391, 2.]

[2 Ego enim fateor caritati tuæ, solis eis scripturarum libris, qui jam canonici appellantur, didici hunc timorem honoremque deferre, ut nullum eorum auctorem scribendo aliquid errasse firmissime credam.—August. Op. Par. 1679-1700. Ad Hieron. Epist. lxxxii. cap. i. 3. Tom. II. col. 190.]

unless by learning and good authority I justify, let me have the blame and shame of it. I will not enter into your hearts, to judge what you think of your inward purity (which notwithstanding in comparison you have in this present place arrogated unto yourselves): that very perfection of an outward platform of a church, which you challenge unto yourselves, is one step to Novatianism, and well deserveth the name of Catharism.

¶ Of the Authority of the Church in things indifferent. Tract. II.

Some things may be tolerated in the church touching order, ceremonies, discipline, and kind of government, not expressed in the word of God.

Chapter i. The First Division.

Admonition[1].

Seeing that nothing in this mortal life is more diligently to be sought for, and carefully to be looked unto, [a]than the restitution of true religion and reformation of God's church, it shall be your parts, dearly beloved, in this present parliament assembled, as much as in you lieth to promote the same, and to employ your whole labour and study, not only in abandoning all popish remnants both in ceremonies and regiment, but also in bringing in and placing in God's church those things only which the Lord himself [b]in his word commandeth; because it is not enough to take pains in taking away evil, [c]but also to be occupied in placing good in the stead thereof. Now, because many men see not all things, and the [d]world in this respect is marvellously blinded, it hath been thought good to proffer to your godly considerations a true platform of a church reformed, to the end that, it being laid before your eyes to behold the great unlikeness between[3] it and this our English church, you may learn, either with perfect [e]hatred to detest the one, and with singular love to embrace, and careful endeavour to plant, the other; or else to be without excuse before [f]the majesty of our God, who (for the discharge[5] of our conscience, and manifestation of his truth) hath by us revealed unto you at this present the sincerity and simplicity of his gospel. Not that you should either [g]wilfully withstand, or ungraciously tread [h]the same under your feet, (for God doth not disclose his will to any such end,) but that you should yet now at the length with all your main and might endeavour that Christ (whose [i]easy yoke and light burden we have of long time cast off from us) might rule and reign in his church by the sceptre of his word only.

- [a] 2 Reg. xxiii.
- 2 Chron. xvii.
- 2 Chron. xxix. 30, 31.
- Psal. cxxxii. 2, 3, 4.
- Matt. xxi. 12.
- John ii. 15.
- [b] Deut. iv. 2. Deut. xii. 32.
- [c] Psal. xxxvii. 27. Rom. xii. 9.
- [d] 1 Cor. ii. 14.
- [e] Psal. xxxi. 6.
- Psal. cxxxix. 22.
- [f] John xv. 21.[4]
- [g] 1 Tim. iii. 8.[4]
- [h] Matt. vii.
- [i] Matt. xi. 31.

¶ Answer to the Admonition[6].

Page 20. Sect. 1 and 2.

I will not answer words, but matter, nor bare affirmations or negations, but reasons; and therefore in as few words as I can I will comprehend many lines.

[[1] Before the following paragraph there is a notice in the first edition of the Admonition of some typographical faults. This notice will be introduced in the place where the faults occurred.]

[[2] 3, Def. A. and B.]   [[3] Betwixt, Adm.]
[[4] Adm. has *John* xv. 22, and 2 *Tim. iii.* 8.]   [[5] For discharge, Answ. 2.]
[[6] Answ. 2 has as a running title in the margin, *Arguments* negative a scriptura. Frequent instances occur, which will not be hereafter noticed, of a running title in Answ. 1, not transferred to the Defence.]

But, before I enter into their reasons, I think it not amiss to examine that assertion which is the chief and principal ground (so far as I can gather) of their book; that is, that "those things only are to be placed in the church which the Lord himself in his word commandeth." As though they should say, nothing is to be tolerated in the church of Christ, touching either doctrine, order, ceremonies, discipline, or government, except it be expressed in the word of God. And therefore the most of their arguments in this book be taken *ab auctoritate negativa*, which by the rules of logic prove nothing at all.

<small>The ground of the Admonition.</small>

T. C. Page 13. Sect. 2.

You give occasion of suspicion that your end will be scarce good, which have made so evil a beginning. For, whereas you had gathered out of the Admonition, that nothing should be placed in the church, but that God hath in his word commanded; as though the words were not plain enough, you will give them some light by your exposition. And what is that? You answer that it is as much "as though they would say, nothing is to be tolerated in the church of Christ, touching either doctrine, order, ceremonies, discipline, or government, except it be expressed in the word of God." Is this to interpret? is it all one to say, nothing must be placed in the church, and nothing must be tolerated in the church? He hath but small judgment that cannot tell that certain things may be tolerated and borne with for a time; which, if they were to be set in and placed, could not be done without the great fault of them that should place them. Again, are these of like weight, except it be commanded in the word of God, and except it be expressed in the word of God? Many things are both commanded and forbidden, for[2] *which there is no express mention in the word, which are as necessarily to be followed or avoided as those whereof express mention is made. Therefore unless your weights be truer, if I could let it, you should weigh none of my words. Hereupon you conclude, that their arguments, taken* ab auctoritate negative, *prove nothing. When the question is of the authority of a man, indeed it neither holdeth affirmatively nor negatively. For, as it is no good argument to say, it is not true because Aristotle or Plato said it not; so is it not to say, it is true because they said so. The reason whereof is, because the infirmity of man can neither attain to the perfection of any thing whereby he might speak all things that are to be spoken of it, neither yet be free from error in those things which he speaketh or giveth out; and therefore this argument neither affirmatively nor negatively compelleth the hearer, but only induceth him to some liking or misliking of that for which it is brought, and is rather for an orator to persuade the simpler*

<small>Deut. iv. 2.[1]
Deut. xii. 32.[1]</small>

<small>But their quarrel is in tolerating, not in placing.</small>

<small>A papistical assertion.</small>

<small>Untrue.</small>

[1] These references are inserted from Repl. 2.]
[2] Of, Repl. 1, 2, and Def. A.]

TO THE ADMONITION.

sort, than for a disputer to enforce him that is learned. But, forsomuch as the Lord God, determining to set before our eyes a perfect form of his church, is both able to do it, and hath done it, a man may reason both ways necessarily: The Lord hath commanded it should be in his church; therefore it must: and of the other side: He hath not commanded; therefore it must not be. And it is not hard to shew that the prophets have so reasoned negatively. As when in the person of the Lord the prophet saith: "Whereof I have not spoken, and which never entered into my heart;" and as where he condemneth them because "they have not asked counsel at the mouth of the Lord."

<small>Jer. vii. 31, 32. Isai. xxx. 2.</small>

JO. WHITGIFT.

This my interpretation of their words is grounded upon the whole discourse and drift of their book, as it may evidently appear to be true to any that hath eyes to see, and ears to hear; and shew you, if you can, any one place in their book which doth overthrow this my interpretation of their words. I know it is one thing to say that "nothing must be placed in the church," and another thing to say that "nothing must be tolerated;" but I see that they make no difference between them, neither in their writing nor yet in their practice. And I think also that there is some difference betwixt these two manner of speeches, "except it be commanded in the word of God," and "except it be expressed in the word of God." For I know sundry things to be expressed in the word of God, which are not commanded; as Christ his fasting forty days, and his other miracles: and therefore by that interpretation I have given unto them a larger scope than they themselves require; which if it be an injury, it is to myself, and not to them.

But I think you were not well advised when you said, that "many things are both commanded and forbidden, of which there is no express mention in the word of God, which are as necessarily to be followed or avoided as those whereof express mention is made." If you mean that "many things are commanded or forbidden" in the word, which are not expressed in the word, in my opinion you speak contraries; for how can it be commanded or forbidden in the word, except it be also expressed in the same? If you mean, that "many things are commanded or forbidden to be done," necessary unto salvation, which notwithstanding are not expressed in the word of God, then I see not how you differ from that opinion, which

<small>An unadvised assertion of T. C. tending to papistry.</small>

is the ground of all papistry, that is, "that all things necessary unto salvation are not expressed in the scriptures[1]." Howsoever you mean it, it cannot be true; for there is nothing necessary to eternal life which is not both "commanded" and "expressed" in the scripture. I count it "expressed," when it is either in manifest words contained in scripture, or thereof gathered by necessary collection[2]. If I had to do with a papist, I could prove this to be true by the manifest testimonies of the scripture itself, and also by sundry other, both ancient and late writers; but, because I think it hath but overslipped you, and that upon better advice you will reform it, therefore I will cease to deal further in it, until I understand more of your meaning.

What is said to be expressed in the scripture.

My conclusion touching "arguments negative *ab auctoritate*" (as I understand it, and have expounded it in the words following) is very true, and must of necessity be so. You say that, "when the question is of the authority of a man, it holdeth neither affirmatively nor negatively[3]." Wherein you shew yourself not to be so skilful in that, the ignorance whereof you do so often in your book object unto me: for not in Aristotle only, *Lib. iii. Top.* and *Lib. ii. Rhet. ad Theod.*, but in every "half-penny logic" (as you term them) the place *ab auctoritate* is expressed, and the arguments taken out of the same said to hold affirmatively, and not otherwise; the rule whereof is this, *Unicuique in sua arte perito credendum est*[4]. It is a good argument to say that it is true, because Aristotle or Plato said it, if it be of anything pertaining to that art wherein Aristotle or Plato were cunning and expert.

Arguments ab auctoritate negative.

An argument ab auctoritate abideth affirmatively.

1. Top. cap. 8.

[1 Cartwright rejoins: "He needed not to have travelled far to have seen how far I am from popery...And as for that which I set down, I did it upon good grounds. For who is there which knoweth not that these things, that there is one essence and three Persons in the Godhead, that there is in our Saviour Christ one Person and two natures, are not expressed, but only contained in the word of God?"—Sec. Repl. p. 45.]

[2 Cartwright to this says: "I answer that I suppose that there was never writer, holy nor profane, that ever spake so; and that it biddeth defiance both to divinity and humanity."—Ibid. p. 46.]

[3 "That which I said of the argument of authority of a man to be neither good affirmatively nor negatively, farther than to induce the reader into some liking or misliking, and not to have force to compel, is apparent unto all which have any spark of judgment."—Ibid. p. 47.]

[4 Aristot. Op. Lut. Par. 1629. Top. Lib. III. cap. i. Tom. I. p. 205; Rhet. Lib. II. cap. xx. Tom. II. pp. 569, 70; Top. Lib. I. cap. x. Tom. I. p. 186.]

Whether all things pertaining to the outward form of the church be particularly expressed, or commanded in the scripture, or no, is the question that we have now in controversy: that God could do it, and therefore "hath done it," is no good reason, no more than it is for the real presence in the sacrament.

Affirmatively the argument is always good of the authority of the scripture; as, God hath there commanded it to be done; therefore it must be done: or, The scripture affirmeth it to be so; ergo, it is so. But negatively it holdeth not, except in matters of salvation and damnation: which is not my opinion only, but the opinion of the best interpreters. Zuinglius *in Elencho contra Catabaptist.* reproveth them for reasoning on this sort: his words be these: "You shall find no way to escape; for fondly you reason *a factis et exemplis* negatively; yea, *a non factis et non exemplis;* for what other reason use you than this, We read not that the apostles baptized infants; *ergo*, they are not to be [5]baptized[6]?" *Zuinglius in Elench.*

The examples that you use in the vii. of Jerem. ver. 31, 32, and xxx. of Esay, ver. 2, to prove that in external and indifferent matters we may reason negatively of the authority of the scriptures, are far-fetched, and nothing to your purpose. For that which the prophet Jeremy speaketh of is a matter of great importance, even most horrible and cruel sacrifices, wherein they burnt their sons and daughters: which they were not only not commanded to do, but expressly forbidden; as it appeareth in the xviii. of Levit. ver. 21, and the xx. of Levit. ver. 3, and the xviii. of Deuter. ver. 10. Now to reason thus, God hath commanded that you shall not give your children to be offered to Moloch, and he hath not given you any commandment to the contrary; therefore you ought not to have offered them, is affirmative, not negative; although in this case, being a matter of substance, and of salvation or damnation (for to kill and murder is of that nature), a negative argument is very strong. The prophet Esay reproveth the *The places which T. C. quoteth prove not his purpose.* *Jer. vii. 31.* *Isai. xxx. 2.*

[5 Non invenietis rimam ullam qua possitis elabi. Factis enim atque exemplis stulte ad negativam argumentamini. Imo a non factis, et non exemplis: quid enim aliud agitis, quam, Apostoli non leguntur baptizavisse infantes; ergo baptizandi non sunt?—H. Zvingl. Op. Tigur. 1581. Elench. contr. Catabapt. Pars II. fol. 13.]

[6 " ...Zuinglius reproveth the anabaptists not for reasoning negatively of the authority of the scripture, but that they reasoned negatively of an act or an example."—Sec. Repl. p. 50.]

Jews for using their own advice, and seeking help of the Egyptians in the time of their adversity, and not of the Lord: which they did both contrary to their own promise, and also contrary to the commandment of God, Deuter. xvii. ver. 16. But what is this to prove that we may reason negatively of the authority of the scriptures in matters of rites and ceremonies, and other indifferent things? You accuse me for not alleging of scriptures: better it were to allege none, than thus to allege them to no purpose, or rather to abuse them.

Chapter i. The Second Division.

Answer to the Admonition. Page 21. Sect. 1, 2, 3.

Wherein the scripture is sufficient. It is most true, that nothing ought to be tolerated in the church as necessary unto salvation, or as an article of faith, except it be expressly contained in the word of God, or may manifestly thereof be gathered; and therefore we utterly condemn and reject transubstantiation, the sacrifice of the mass, the authority of the bishop of Rome, worshipping of images, &c.

When an argument a scriptura negative is good 2. And in this case an argument taken *ab auctoritate scripturæ negative* is most strong; as for example: It is not to be found in scripture that the bishop of Rome ought to be the head of the church; and therefore it is not necessary to salvation to believe that he ought to be the head of the church, &c.

It is also true, that nothing in ceremonies, order, discipline, or government in the church, is to be suffered, being against the word of God: and therefore we reject all ceremonies wherein there is any opinion to salvation, worshipping of God, or merit; as creeping to the cross, holy bread, holy water, holy candle, &c.

T. C. Page 14. line 3.

But you say that in matters of faith and necessary to salvation it holdeth: which things you oppose after[3] *and set against matters of cere-*

[1 Cartwright refers here to bishop Jewel as using the argument of authority negatively, and saying that it "is taken to be good, whatsoever proof is taken of God's word, and is used not only by us but also by many of the catholic fathers." —Ibid. p. 50. Conf. Bp. Jewel's Works, Park. Soc. Edit. Vol. I. p. 175.]

[2 This marginal note is inserted from Answ. 2.]   [3 Afterwards, Repl. 2.]

monies, orders, discipline, and government; as though matters of discipline and kind of government were not matters necessary to salvation, and of faith. The case which you put, whether the bishop of Rome be head of the church, is a matter that concerneth the government, and the kind of government of the church, and the same is a matter that toucheth faith, and that standeth upon our salvation. Excommunication, and other censures of the church, which are forerunners unto excommunication, are matters of discipline; and the same are also of faith and of salvation. The sacraments of the Lord's[4] *supper and of baptism are ceremonies, and are matters of faith, and necessary to salvation. And therefore you, which distinguish between these, and say that the former, that is, matters of faith, and necessary to salvation, may not be tolerated in the church, unless they be expressly contained in the word of God, or manifestly gathered; but that this*[5] *later, which are ceremonies, order, discipline, government in the church, may not be received against the word of God, and consequently received if there be no word against them, although there be none for them—you, I say, distinguishing or dividing after this sort, do prove yourself to be as evil a divider as you shewed yourself before an expounder; for this is to break in pieces, and not to divide.*

As though it were enough for you to say so, upon such silly proofs. *Arg. ex solis particularibus.*

Jo. Whitgift.

That "matters of ceremonies, discipline, and kind of government, be matters necessary unto salvation," is a doctrine strange and unheard of to me; whereof I will by and by speak more at large, after I have in a word or two answered your objections of "the bishop of Rome," and of "the sacraments of baptism, and the Lord's supper:" for you say, "The case which" I "put, whether the bishop of Rome be head of the church, is a matter that concerneth the government, and the kind of government of the church; and the same is a matter that toucheth faith, and that standeth upon salvation." Whereupon belike you would conclude, that "matters of government, and kind of government," are "matters necessary to salvation." Surely I put no such case; but I put such an example to prove, that we may reason *ab auctoritate scripturæ negative.* For this is a good argument: We find it not in the scripture that the bishop of Rome ought to be the head of the church; *ergo,* it is not necessary to salvation to believe that the bishop of Rome is the head of the church: the which thing notwithstanding the papists do affirm; for they say thus: *Subesse Romano pontifici omni animæ est de necessitate salutis:* [6] " To be subject to the bishop of Rome is

[[4] The Lord his, Repl. 1 and 2.]   [[5] These, Repl. 2.]
[[6] Porro subesse Romano pontifici omni humanæ creaturæ declaramus, dici-

of necessity of salvation to all men." Now, sir, my reason is framed thus against them: Whatsoever is necessary to salvation is contained in the scriptures : but that the pope should be the head of the church is not contained in the scriptures; therefore it is not necessary to salvation. But you reason clean contrary; for you conclude thus: Whether the pope be the head of the church is a matter of government, and of the kind of government; but the papists say (for that I take to be your meaning) that it is a matter necessary unto salvation, that the pope should be the head of the church; *ergo*, matters of government, and kind of government, are necessary unto salvation. Thus you see how popishly, with a popish reason, you make a very popish conclusion. Certainly no government is to be brought into the church that is directly against the word of God, as the pope's is, which doth not only usurp the office and authority of kings and princes, but of Christ also, and commandeth things contrary to faith and to the manifest word of God; wherefore his authority is wicked and damnable: but it doth not therefore follow to make this a general rule, that " the government of the church, or kind of government, is necessary to salvation." Do you not know of what force an argument is *ex solis particularibus?*

To prove that ceremonies are necessary to salvation you reason thus: "The sacraments of the Lord's supper and of baptism are ceremonies, and are matters of faith, and necessary to salvation; *ergo*, &c."

Undoubtedly you are as evil a reasoner, as I am either "an expounder" or "divider :" because "the supper of the Lord and baptism be matters of salvation," therefore are all ceremonies " matters of salvation?" Will you *ex solis particularibus* conclude an universal proposition? Furthermore, you know that the supper and baptism be not only " ceremonies," but also sacraments, instituted and commanded by Christ, having promises of salvation annexed unto them ; and so have not other ceremonies. And you speak too basely of them when you call them " ceremonies," not shewing how or in what sort they may be so called. It is the next way to bring the sacraments into contempt, and it argueth that you have

mus, diffinimus, et pronunciamus omnino esse de necessitate salutis.—Bonifac. VIII. in Corp. Jur. Canon. Lugd. 1624. Extrav. Comm. Lib. I. De Major. et Obed. cap. 2. col. 212.]

not so reverent an opinion of them as you ought to have. Therefore the reader must understand that there be two kinds of ceremonies, the one substantial, the other accidental. Substantial ceremonies I call those which be *de substantia religionis*, "of the substance of religion," and commanded in the word of God as necessary, and have promises annexed unto them, as the supper of the Lord, and baptism. Accidental I call such as may be done or undone as order requireth, and altered according to time, place, person, and other circumstances, without any opinion of justification, necessity, or worship in the same, pertaining only to external comeliness, order, decency, &c.; of the which kind these be that the apostle St Paul mentioneth 1 Cor. xi. that "men should pray bare-headed, and not women," and such like; as I have in my answer to the Admonition more particularly declared. Such "ceremonies" I deny to be "matters of salvation;" and in such I say (as you also afterwards confess[1]) the church hath authority to appoint from time to time, as shall be thought expedient, though the same ceremonies be not expressed in the word of God: so that my division holdeth, and is stronger than you shall be able to overthrow with all the force you have.

Two kinds of ceremonies.

Substantial ceremonies.

Accidental ceremonies.

1 Cor. xi.

Fol. 15, sect. 5.

But now to your paradox: you say that "matters of discipline and kind of government are matters necessary to salvation, and of faith." And you add that "excommunication, and other censures of the church, which are forerunners unto excommunication, are matters of discipline; and the same are also of faith and of salvation." There are two kinds of government in the church, the one invisible, the other visible; the one spiritual, the other external. The invisible and spiritual government of the church is, when God by his Spirit, gifts, and ministry of his word, doth govern it, by ruling in the hearts and consciences of men, and directing them in all things necessary to everlasting life: this kind of government indeed is necessary to salvation, and it is in the church of the elect only. The visible and external government is that which is executed by man, and consisteth of external discipline, and visible ceremonies practised in that church, and over that church, that containeth in it both good and evil, which is usually called the visible church of Christ,

Matters of the kind of government and discipline are not necessary to salvation.

Two kinds of government of the church.

[[1] See below, page 195.]

Matt. xiii. and compared by Christ to "a field" wherein both "good seeds" and "tares were sown," and to "a net that gathered of all kind of fishes." If you mean this kind of government, then must I ask you this question, whether your meaning is that to have a government is necessary to salvation; or to have some one certain form and kind of government, not to be altered in respect of time, persons, or place? Likewise would I know of you what you mean by "necessary unto salvation;" whether you mean such things without the which we cannot be saved, or such things only as be necessary or ordinary helps unto salvation: for you know that this word "necessary" signifieth, either that without the which a thing cannot be, or that without the which it cannot so well and conveniently be[1].

Diverse signification of the word "necessary."

But, forsomuch as you afterward make mention of "excommunication, and other censures of the church, which are forerunners unto excommunication," I take it that you mean the external "government" of the church, and that "kind of government." And yet must I ask you another question, that is, whether you mean that this "government" and "kind of government" is "necessary" at all times, or then when the church is collected together, and in such place where it may have government. For you know that the church is sometimes by persecution so dispersed that it appeareth not, as we read Apocal. vi., nor hath any certain place to remain in; so that it cannot have any external government, or exercise of any discipline. But to be short, I confess that in a church collected together in one place, and at liberty, government is necessary in the second kind of necessity; but that any one kind of government is so necessary that without it the church cannot be saved, or that it may not be altered into some other kind thought to be more expedient, I utterly deny; and the reasons that move me so to do be these:

In what respect government is necessary.

Reasons why the church is not tied to any one certain kind of external government.

The first is, because I find no one certain and perfect kind of government prescribed or commanded in the scriptures to the church of Christ; which no doubt should have been done, if it had been a matter necessary unto the salvation of the church.

[1 Cartwright accuses Whitgift throughout this division of "unskilfulness," "ridiculous" assertion, "ignorance," "childishness," &c.—Sec. Repl. pp. 51, &c.]

Secondly, because the essential notes of the church be these only; the true preaching of the word of God, and the right administration of the sacraments: for, as Master Calvin saith in his book against the anabaptists, "This honour is meet to be given to the word of God and to his sacraments, that, wheresoever we see the word of God truly preached, and God according to the same truly worshipped, and the sacraments without superstition administered, there we may without all controversy conclude the church of God to be[2];" and a little after: "So much we must esteem the word of God and his sacraments, that, wheresoever we find them to be, there we may certainly know the church of God to be, although in the common life of men many faults and errors be found[3]." The same is the opinion of other godly and learned writers, and the judgment of the reformed churches, as appeareth by their confessions[4]. So that, notwithstanding government, or some kind of government, may be a part of the church, touching the outward form and perfection of it, yet is it not such a part of the essence and being, but that it may be the church of Christ without this or that kind of government; and therefore the "kind of government" of the church is not "necessary unto salvation."

The church of Corinth, when Paul did write unto it, was the church of Christ; for so doth he call it, 1 Cor. i., where also he doth give unto it a singular commendation: and yet it had not at that time, when he so commendeth it, that "kind of government and discipline" that you mean of, that is, "excommunication," as appeareth 1 Cor. v.

My third reason is this. If "excommunication" (which is a kind of government) "be necessary to salvation," then any man may separate himself from every church wherein is no excommunication; but no man may separate himself from every church wherein is no excommunication; therefore excommuni-

[2 Id enim honoris nos sacrosancto Dei verbo sanctisque ejus sacramentis deferre par est, ut ubicunque annunciari hoc verbum videmus, atque ex regula, quam nobis præscribit, pure Deum adorari, rejecta omni superstitione administrari sacramenta, illic sine ulla controversia ecclesiam Dei esse concludamus.— Calvin. Op. Amst. 1667-71. Instr. adv. Anabapt. Art. ii. Tom. VIII. p. 360.]

[3 Tanti enim facere debemus verbum Dei et sacramenta, ut ubicunque viderimus ea, ibi ecclesiam Dei esse certo sciamus, quamvis errores et vitia in communi hominum vita reperiantur.—Id. ibid.]

[4 Confess. et Expos. Fid. Christ. cap. xvii. in Corp. et Syntagm. Confess. Fid. Genev. 1654. pp. 33, 4.]

cation (which is a kind of government) is not necessary to salvation. The first proposition is evident; for no man is bound to remain in that church where anything is wanting without the which he cannot be saved. As for the second proposition, that is to say, that no man ought to separate himself from every church where excommunication is not; because it is learnedly proved by such as have written against the anabaptists, who both did teach and practise the contrary, it shall be sufficient to refer you unto them[1]. Master Calvin, in his book against the anabaptists, saith thus: "Herein is the controversy betwixt the anabaptists and us, that they think there is no church where this government" (meaning excommunication) "is not appointed, or not used and exercised as it ought to be, nor that a christian man there ought to receive the supper; and under that pretence they separate themselves from the churches where the word of God is truly preached, &c.[2]" M. Bullinger also, in his sixth book against the anabaptists, saith: "This the anabaptists do urge, that there is no true church acceptable unto God where there is no excommunication, the which they use. To these therefore we answer, that the church of Corinth was a true church, and so acknowledged of Paul to be, 1 Cor. i., before there was any use of excommunication in it, &c.[3]" Of the same judgment is M. Gualter, writing upon the first to the Corinth. v.: "Whilst the anabaptists persuade themselves that there can be no discipline without excommunication, they trouble the churches

Want of excommunication is no just cause of separation from any church.

Calvin. adv. Anabap.

Bull. Lib. vi. adv. Anabap.

Gualter in 1 Cor. v.

[1 "...his authorities, drawn out of M. Calvin, the Helvetian Confession, Bullinger, are quite beside the cause. For they are to prove that there may be a church without excommunication. As though the question were, what things the church (of those which be prescribed by the word of God) may want, and yet be the church of God; and not, what things it ought to have by the prescript of the word of God. Or as though the question were, how sick the church might be, and yet live, how maimed and yet not slain; and not what are the means, which the Lord hath appointed, for a whole and wholesome constitution of the body of the church."—Sec. Repl. p. 52.]

[2 In hoc tota est controversia, quod putent nullam ibi ecclesiam esse, ubi hæc politia non est constituta, aut non eo quo decet modo exercetur; nec illic homini christiano licere cœnam recipere. Eoque prætextu sese ab ecclesiis segregant, in quibus verbum Dei pure annunciatur: &c.—Calvin. Op. Amst. 1667-71. Instr. adv. Anabapt. Art. ii. Tom. VIII. p. 359.]

[3 Et hoc urgent, non esse illic veram ecclesiam, Deo acceptam, ubi non sit excommunicatio qua ipsi utuntur. His igitur respondemus, Corinthiacam ecclesiam veram ecclesiam fuisse, et a Paulo talem agnitam fuisse, 1 Corinth. i., priusquam ullus excommunicationis usus apud eos esset.—H. Bullinger. adv. Anabapt. Libri VI. Tigur. 1560. Lib. VI. cap. x. fol. 234. 2.]

everywhere, &c.[4]" In the same chapter he saith that there is no one certain kind of government or discipline prescribed to the churches, but that the same may be altered as the profit of the churches shall require. His words among other be these: "Let every church follow that manner of discipline which doth most agree with the people with whom it abideth, and which seemeth to be most fit for the place and time. And let no man here rashly prescribe unto others, neither let him bind all churches to one and the same form[5]." But of this matter I shall have occasion to speak more hereafter; where it shall appear how far this learned man, M. Gualter, is from allowing that kind of government now in this state of the church, the which T. C. would make us to believe to be so necessary. This have I briefly set down, not to disallow "discipline or government" (for I think it very convenient in the church of Christ), nor yet to reject "excommunication," which also hath a necessary use in the government of the church; but to declare that this assertion cannot stand with the truth, and with learning, that "the kind of government" (meaning, as I think, some one certain kind of external government) "is necessary to salvation."

Ibidem.

Chapter i. The Third Division.

T. C. Page 14. Sect. 1 and 2.

And it is no small injury which you do unto the word of God, to pin it in so narrow room, as that it should be able to direct us but in the principal points of our religion; or as though the substance of religion, or some rude and unfashioned matter of building of the church, were uttered in them, and those things were left out that should pertain to the form and fashion of it; or as if there were in the scriptures only to cover her nakedness[6], and not also chains and bracelets and rings and other jewels to adorn her and set her out; that[7], to conclude, there were sufficient to quench her thirst and kill her hunger, but not to minister unto her a

T. C. accounteth external government more precious than the doctrine of faith.

[4 Ita anabaptistæ dum disciplinam absque excommunicatione consistere non posse sibi persuadent, ecclesias passim turbant, &c.—R. Gualther. In Prior. ad Corinth. Epist. Hom. Tigur. 1578. cap. v. Hom. xxiv. fol. 65. 2.]

[5 Eam vero disciplinæ rationem singulæ ecclesiæ sequantur, quæ genti in qua degunt quam maxime convenit, quæque pro locorum et temporum ratione omnium commodissima esse videtur. Neque hic quisquam aliis temere præscribat, neve ad eandem formam omnes astringat.—Id. ibid.]

[6 Cover the church's nakedness, Repl. 2.]

[7 Out or that, Repl. 1, 2, and Def. A.]

more liberal and (as it were) a more delicious and dainty diet. These things you seem to say, when you say that matters necessary to salvation and of faith are contained in the scripture, especially when you oppose these things to ceremonies, order, discipline, and government.

And, if you mean by matters of faith, and necessary to salvation, those without which a man cannot be saved, then the doctrine that teacheth there is no free-will, or prayer for the dead, is not within your compass. For I doubt not but divers of the fathers of the Greek church, which were great patrons of free-will[1], are saved, holding the foundation of the faith, which is Christ. The like might be said of a number of other, as necessary doctrines as that[2], wherein men being misled have notwithstanding been saved. Therefore, seeing that the point of the question lieth chiefly in this distinction, it had been good that you had spoken more certainly and properly of these things.

<small>Note this assertion.</small>
<small>He that dieth in the opinion of free-will holdeth not this foundation.</small>
<small>Why then have not you done it, speaking so dangerously?</small>

Jo. Whitgift.

When you say that "it is no small injury that" I "do unto the word of God, to pin it up in so narrow room, &c.," you do but enlarge the volume of your book with bare words that might well be spared. I give that perfection to the word of God which the word itself requireth, and all godly-learned men consent unto; and much more do I attribute unto it than you do in saying that " many things are both commanded and forbidden, of the which there is no express mention in the word, which are as necessary to be followed or avoided as those whereof express mention is made[3];" which I take to derogate much from the perfection of the scriptures, to be mere papistical, and quite contrary to that that you do pretend. I also confess that in all other things we must so be directed by the scriptures that we do nothing contrary to the true sense and meaning of them, no, not in external and in the least matters; neither do I otherwise write, teach, or speak, of the perfection and authority of the scriptures, than all other learned men, and the reformed churches, teach, write, and believe: wherefore I pass over your words, and come to your reasons.

<small>Page 13, Sect. 2.</small>

If I "mean," say you, " by matters of faith, and necessary to salvation, those without the which a man cannot be saved, &c.:" I cannot but muse what you mean willingly to pretend ignorance. Is this, think you, a sound argument: " Divers of the fathers of the Greek church, which were great patrons

[1 Here Repl. 2 inserts, in a parenthesis, *at lest as their words pretend.*]
[2 Repl. 2 omits *as that.*]   [3 See before, page 176.]

of free-will, are saved, holding the foundation of the faith, which is Christ; *ergo*, the doctrine of free-will is not a doctrine of salvation or damnation?" You might as well say, that many in the popish church, which believed that the pope was supreme head of the church, that the mass was a sacrifice for the quick and the dead, and such like points of papistical religion, be saved; *ergo*, these are no matters of salvation or damnation. Surely by the same reason all other kind of sins (almost) might be without this compass. But it may please you to understand, that the mercy of God in his Son Jesus Christ is infinite, and that he pardoneth at his good will and pleasure not only misbelief proceeding of ignorance, but wilful errors, and sins also, though they be of themselves damnable: he also altereth the mind of man even in a moment; and therefore, as his mercies be infinite, so be his judgments unsearchable. Wherefore this your reason is uttered without due consideration. The doctrine "of free-will," because it is an enemy to the grace of God, must needs be of itself a damnable doctrine; yet doth it not prejudice the mercy of God, nor finally shut out repentance, the gift of God. And full well do you know that he cannot hold the foundation of faith (that is Christ) perfectly, which is a maintainer of free-will.

The mercy of God infinite.

But, leaving the weight of such kind of arguments to the consideration of the reader, I come to the purpose. When I say that an argument holdeth negatively from the authority of the scripture in matters of faith and necessary to salvation, my meaning is manifest; which is this, that the scriptures do contain all things necessary to be believed, and to salvation; and therefore, whatsoever is taught unto us as an article of faith and necessary to salvation, not contained in the scriptures, that same to be false and untrue, and therefore to be rejected. As for example, the doctrine of free-will, of purgatory, of praying for the dead, of praying to saints, of the sacrifice of the mass, &c. are not contained in the scriptures, and therefore they be not doctrines to be believed, nor necessary to salvation, but damnable doctrines of themselves, and repugnant to salvation[4]. Surely

[4 Cartwright in answer accuses Whitgift of speaking very "confusedly," lays down certain rules for determining what error of doctrine rases the foundations of faith, and concludes from them that free-will does not; but that "believing

I think in this point that you neither understand me nor yourself: my meaning is plain, that nothing is necessary to salvation which is not plainly contained in the scriptures.

Chapter i. The Fourth Division.

Answer to the Admonition, Page 21, Sect. 4.

What things the scripture hath not expressed, but left to the ordering of the church.

But that no ceremony, order, discipline, or kind of government, may be in the church, except the same be expressed in the word of God, is a great absurdity, and breedeth many inconveniences.

T. C. Page 14, Sect. 3.

The scripture wrested by T. C.

But to the end it may appear that this speech of yours doth something take up and shrink the arms of the scripture, which otherwise are so long and large, I say that the word of God containeth the direction of all things pertaining to the church, yea, of whatsoever things can fall into any part of man's life. For so Salomon saith in the second chapter of the Proverbs, "My son, if thou receive my words, and hide my precepts in thee[2]*, &c. then thou shalt understand justice, and judgment, and equity, and every good way." St Paul saith that, "whether we eat or drink, or whatsoever we do, we must do it to the glory of God." But no man can glorify God in anything but by obedience; and there is no obedience but in respect of the commandment and word of God: therefore it followeth that the word of God directeth a man in all his actions; and that which St Paul said of meats and drinks, that they are "sanctified unto us by the word of God," the same is to be understood of all things else whatsoever we have the use of. But the place of St Paul in the xiv. to the Romans is of all other*[3] *most clear, where, speaking of those things which are called indifferent, in the end he concludeth that "whatsoever is not of faith is sin:" but faith is not but in respect of the word of God; therefore whatsoever is not done by the word of God is sin. And, if any will say that St Paul meaneth there a full persuasion and* πληροφορίαν[4], *that that which he doth is well done, I grant it. But from whence can that spring but from faith? and how can we persuade and assure ourselves that we do well but where as we have the word of God for our warrant? so that the apostle by a metonymy,* subjecti pro

Chap. ii. 9.[1]

1 Cor. x. 31.[1]

1 Tim. iv. 5.[1]

Rom. xiv. 23.[1]

that the mass is a sacrifice for the quick and the dead...turneth upside down the material cause of our salvation...And therefore that error cannot be in any in whom there is faith."—Sec. Repl. pp. 53, &c.]

[[1] The first and last of these references, and the verses of the others, are inserted from Repl. 2.]

[[2] Repl. 2 omits *in thee*.]   [[3] St Paul is of all other, Repl. 2.]

[[4] πληροφορίαν and persuasion, Repl. 2.]

adjuncto, *doth give to understand from whence the assured persuasion* ^{Scripture}
doth spring: whereupon it falleth out that, forasmuch as in all our ^{wrested by}
actions, even civil and private[5], *we ought to follow the direction of the* ^{T. C.}
*word of God, in matters of the church and which concern all there may
be nothing done but by the word of God. Not that we say as you* ^{Then have}
charge us in these words, when you say that we say that "no ceremony, &c. ^{you hitherto
strived in}
may be in the church, except the same be expressed in the word of God;" but ^{vain.
Hold you}
that[6] *in making orders and ceremonies of the church it is not lawful to* ^{here.}
*do what men list, but they are bound to follow the general rules of the
scripture, that are given to be the squire whereby those should be squared
out.*

Jo. Whitgift.

When I say that the scriptures contain all things neces- ^{How the}
sary unto salvation, I do not mean that it containeth those ^{scripture
containeth}
things only; neither do I deny but that "the word of God ^{the direction
of all things}
so containeth" generally "the direction of all things pertain- ^{belonging to
the life of}
ing to the church," or that "can fall into any part of man's ^{man.}
life," that nothing ought to be done in the church, or in the
life of man, contrary to the word of God, or not according to
the true intent and meaning of the same[7]. Yet do I deny
that the scriptures do express particularly everything that is
to be done in the church (which you yourself afterward con- ^{Page 15.}
fess[8]), or that it doth set down any one certain form and kind
of government of the church, to be perpetual for all times,
persons, and places, without alteration; as I shall hereafter
more particularly declare.

The place you do allege out of the ii. chapter of Salomon's Proverbs doth not prove your purpose; for Salomon
there teacheth the fruits and commodity of wisdom, and in the
person of her declareth what understanding he shall have in
"righteousness, judgment, equity, and every good path," that ^{Prov. ii.}
hearkeneth unto wisdom, obeyeth her commandments, and
giveth his heart to knowledge. But what is this to prove

[5 Actions both public and private, Repl. 2.]

[6 In these words (that no ceremony, &c. may be in the church except the same
be expressed in the word of God) but that, Repl. 2.]

[7 Cartwright accuses Whitgift of insinuating that "there is some star or light
of reason, or learning, or other help, whereby some act may be well done and
acceptably unto God, in which the word of God was shut out, and not called to
counsel: as that which either could not, or need not, give any direction in that
behalf;" and says that afterwards he "is constrained to yield himself to that,
which he hath before found fault with."—Sec. Repl. p. 56.]

[8 See below, page 195.]

that the scripture hath expressed every particular ceremony or kind of government in the church? How followeth this reason, If princes and such as be in authority "receive the words of wisdom, and hide her commandments within them, &c., they shall understand righteousness, judgment, and equity, and every good path, &c.;" therefore the scriptures do express every ceremony, order, discipline or kind of government that is to be used in the church? Surely, except you take heed, you will wander as far out of the way in alleging the scriptures, as the authors of the Admonition did in quoting them. I grant you that princes must give themselves to the understanding of wisdom, and especially of the wisdom of God contained in his word; for so shall they understand "righteousness, judgment, and equity, and every good path, &c." But what is this to our question? Magistrates must be directed by the word of God; *ergo*, they must make no civil or ecclesiastical law or order, which is not expressed in the word of God: I deny this argument[1]. Your other text is written in the 1 Cor. x. "Whether therefore we eat or drink, &c." Whereupon you frame this argument: "Whatsoever we do, we must do it to the glory of God; but no man can glorify God in anything but by obedience; and there is no obedience but in respect of the commandment and word of God; therefore it followeth that the word of God directeth a man in all his actions." To omit the undigested form of this argument, wherein the conclusion agreeth not with the premises, this text is as far from the purpose as is the other: for what sequel is this, We must do all to the glory of God, we must obey the commandment and words of God; *ergo*, we must do nothing in our whole life but that which is particularly expressed in the word of God? Or, therefore the scripture expresseth every particular ceremony, order, or kind of government, to be used in the church? You may as well by this place conclude that every civil action, every private action, every civil kind of government, is expressed in the word. For this rule of St Paul is general, and pertaineth to all Christians, of what state, condition, or degree soever they be. But the true meaning of St Paul in that place is, that we seek the glory of God in all things, and do nothing that is

[1 Cartwright says Whitgift's answer to the text alleged "is uttered without all judgment."—Ibid. p. 57.]

against his word and commandment. He glorifieth God in meat and drink, which acknowledgeth God to be the giver of them, and then is thankful for them, and useth them moderately, &c.: the like is to be said of all other actions[2]. {Scriptures wrested by T. C.}

"That which St Paul," you say, "said of meats and drinks, that they are sanctified unto us by the word of God, &c.," it is true; but to what purpose do you allege that place? The word of God pronounceth all God's creatures to be good, and the use of them to be lawful ("for all things are clean to those that be clean"): the same are to be desired by us of him, as the author and giver of them, and when we have them we must be thankful for them; but what is this to the proof of anything that we have now in controversy? {1 Tim. iv.} {Tit. i. 15.}

"But the place of St Paul in the xiv. to the Romans," you say, "is of all other most clear, &c." Whereupon you frame this argument: "Paul, speaking of things which are called indifferent, saith that 'whatsoever is not of faith is sin;' but faith is not but in respect of the word of God; therefore whatsoever is not done by the word of God is sin." Still I omit the evil framing of your arguments; for I respect not the defacing of your skill, but the grounds of your proofs. That sentence of St Paul is also general, and it is to be extended to all civil actions, as well as it is to ecclesiastical; and therefore, if it prove that all civil and politic actions and kinds of government must be particularly expressed in the scriptures, it proveth the same in ecclesiastical matters also; else not. But the meaning of the apostle is that we should do nothing against our conscience, nothing but that which we do believe not to displease God, not to be against his word or commandment. For "not to be of faith" hath divers significations: first, it signifieth that that is contrary to the persuasion of the faith and judgment of the conscience; secondly, it signifieth not to be taken as an article of faith. If it be taken in the first signification, then it is not true that whatsoever cannot be proved in the word of God is not of faith: for then to take up a straw, to observe many civil orders, and to do a number of particular actions, were against faith, and so deadly sin; because it is not found in the word of God that we should do them. Which doctrine must needs {The place in the xiv. to the Romans expounded.}

[2 Cartwright requires all men to judge "how absurd an answer" this is.—Ibid. p. 58.]

[WHITGIFT.]

bring a great servitude and bondage to the conscience, restrain or rather utterly overthrow that part of christian liberty which consisteth in the free use of indifferent things, neither commanded nor forbidden in the word of God, and throw men headlong into desperation. For what man is able to shew the word of God for all things he doth? If it be taken in the second signification, then it is true that that is not of faith which cannot be proved by the word: for nothing is to be believed as an article of faith which cannot be proved by the word of God. In this xiv. to the Romans, "not to be of faith" is taken in the first signification, that is, against the persuasion of the faith and judgment of the conscience; as though he should say, whatsoever a man doth against his conscience, that is sin. And this to be the true meaning of this place, the words going before do declare;

Rom. xiv. 22. where the apostle saith: "Blessed is he that condemneth not himself in the thing which he alloweth," that is, whose doings are not against his conscience[1].

This rule (I say) of St Paul extendeth as well to civil actions as it doth to ceremonies and orders of the church; and therefore, what you will conclude of the one, that must you also conclude of the other. But I think you will not say that every civil action must be expressed or commanded in the word of God: wherefore neither can you prove by these words of St Paul, that every ceremony, order, or kind of government in the church, must be commanded by the word of God[2].

The matter in controversy is by T. C. confessed.

But what need I labour so much in a matter at the length confessed by yourself? for you deny that you "say that no ceremony, &c., may be in the church, except the same be expressed in the word of God; but that in making orders

[1 Cartwright says that Whitgift's exposition is "very absurd, and overthroweth the sense of the apostle;" that "it is spoken without all consideration of the place;" that "the fault is in his want of understanding." He adds that, St Paul "having shewed that he which doth anything doubtingly is condemned, he assigneth immediately this to be the reason, because he doth it not of faith. So that the apostle calleth that done not of faith which is done doubtingly; but he is said to do against conscience, which, having his knowledge and persuasion settled, goeth against it."—Ibid. pp. 58, 9.]

[2 "And where in the end he saith that these places do prove as much for all civil actions as for ecclesiastical, and that I can no more prove by these that a certain form of discipline is appointed in the scripture than that every civil action is precisely commanded to be done without any change, I grant it."—Ibid. p. 61.]

and ceremonies of the church, it is not lawful to do what men list, &c."

Hold you here, and we shall soon agree. For neither doth that that I have hitherto spoken in this matter, nor that which I intend to speak hereafter, disagree from this: the which you might have seen, if it had pleased you, pages 22. and 28. of the Answer to the Admonition, and in my whole discourse of that matter³. Wherefore, if you were constant, and not contrary unto yourself, or at the least not desirous to have shewed yourself contrary to that which I have in this point written (though you here confess it to be true), you might have both eased yourself and me of this labour.

<small>Page 22, Sect. 2.
Page 28, Sect. 2.</small>

Chapter i. The Fifth Division.

T. C. Page 15, Line 8, and Sect. 1, 2, 3, 4, 5.

Which rules I will here set down, as those which I would have as well all orders and ceremonies of the church framed by, as by the which I will be content that all those orders and ceremonies which are now in question, whether they be good and convenient or no, should be tried and examined by. And they are those rules which St Paul⁴ gave in such cases as are not particularly mentioned of in the scripture⁵.

<small>1 Cor. x. 32.⁶</small>   *The first, that they offend not any, especially the church of God.* <small>You add "especially" to the text.</small>

<small>1 Cor. xiv. 40.⁶</small>   *The second is (that which you cite also out of Paul), that all be done in order and comeliness.*

<small>1 Cor. xiv. 26.⁶
Rom. xiv. 6, 7.⁶</small>   *The third, that all be done to edifying.*

The last, that they be done to the glory of God.

So that you see that those things which you reckon up of the hour, and time, and day of prayer, &c., albeit they be not specified in the scripture, yet they are not left to any to order at their pleasure, or so that they be not against the word of God; but even by and according to the word of God they must be established, and those alone to be taken which do agree best and nearest with these rules before recited. And so it is brought to pass (which you think a great absurdity), that all things in the church should be appointed according to the word of God: whereby it likewise appeareth that we deny not but certain things are left to the order of the church, because they are of that nature which are varied⁷ by times, places, persons, and other circumstances, and so could not at once be set down and established for ever; and yet so left to the order of the church, as that it do nothing against the rules aforesaid. But how doth this follow, that

<small>Here, in effect, T. C. confesseth the matter in question.
What is affirmed otherwise in the Answer to the Admonition?</small>

[³ See below, pages 201, and 246, 7.]   [⁴ Which Paul, Repl. 2.]
[⁵ In scripture, Repl. 2.]   [⁶ The verses are inserted from Repl. 2.]
[⁷ Of the nature of those which are varied, Repl. 2.]

certain things are left to the order of the church, therefore to make a new ministry by making an archbishop, to alter the ministry that is appointed by making a bishop or pastor without a church or flock, to make a deacon without appointing him his church whereof he is deacon[1], *and where he might exercise his charge of providing for the poor, to abrogate clean both the name*[2] *and office of the elder, with other more—how, I say, do these follow*[3] *that, because the church hath power to ordain*[4] *certain things, therefore it hath power to do so of these which God hath ordained and established; of the which there is no time, nor place, nor person, nor any other circumstance, which can cause any alteration or change? Which thing shall better appear both in the discourse of the whole book, and especially there, where you go about to shew certain reasons why there should be other government now than was in the time of the apostles.*

Jo. Whitgift.

<small>The first rule of T. C. concerning ceremonies examined.</small>
You set down four rules, which you would "have all orders and ceremonies of the church framed by, &c. The first is, 1 Cor. x., that they offend not any, especially the church of God;" which rule I think you take out of these words of <small>1 Cor. x. 32.</small> that chapter, *Tales estote, ut nullum præbeatis offendiculum, neque Judæis, &c.:* "Be such as you give no offence, neither to the Jews, nor to the Grecians, nor to the church of God." But truly they make little or nothing for your purpose, neither yet any other thing contained in that chapter. For the apostle there sheweth how one private man should behave himself towards another, yea, and towards the church in things that may be done, or not be done: he prescribeth no general rule for the church to make orders and appoint <small>The orders of the church depend not upon every man's liking or misliking.</small> ceremonies by. For what reason were it that the orders of the church should so depend upon one or two men's liking or misliking, that she should be compelled to alter the same so oft as any should therewith be offended? which must of necessity come to pass, if this your rule were general. For what church is void of some contentious persons, and quarrellers, whom no order, no reason, no reformation, can please[5]?
<small>Musculus.</small> It is true that Musculus saith: "There be some whom no church can please, having always something to reprove in

[¹ Is a deacon, Repl. 1 and 2.]   [² Both name, Repl. 1, 2, and Def. A.]
[³ Say doth it follow, Repl. 2.]   [⁴ Order, Repl. 1, 2, and Def. A.]
[⁵ Cartwright says this "answer proceedeth of too foul an oversight and want of understanding of the word 'offence.' For St Paul by offence doth not mean displeasure or discontentment, but that whereby occasion is given to any of sin and transgression of the law of God."—Sec. Repl. p. 62.]

other men, and nothing in themselves[6]." The anabaptists, the libertines, the papists, and other unquiet minds and contentious persons, are offended with such rites and ceremonies as the reformed churches use; neither is there (as I suppose) any reformed church void of some of these kind of persons: shall they therefore by and by alter the form and state? St Paul in this place would have no just offence given to any, either faithful or infidel: for Christians ought to be such at whose examples, doctrine, and life, no man might justly take any offence. True it is, that in all orders and ceremonies the church must take heed that there be no just offence given; but she hath not to depend upon every private man's judgment.

Whereas you say, "especially the church of God," you add to the words of the apostle; for he saith not "especially[7]:" and, if you mark his meaning well, you shall rather find that he would have "especial" care taken that there be no offence given to such as are not yet come to the church (which some understand by the Jews and Grecians), lest they should still be withdrawn from the church, when as there is no such fear to be had of those that be already members of the same. *T. C. addeth to the text to make it serve his turn.*

Your second rule, 1 Cor. xiv., is a good and necessary rule, not only alleged by me, but allowed and embraced as most convenient; but who shall judge what is most comely, and the best order? shall every private man, or rather such as have the chief care and government of the church? This is a rule prescribed by the apostle to the church, whereby she must direct her orders and government; not to every private person, to pick a quarrel to disquiet the church. *The second rule of T. C. allowed. The judgment of comeliness and order resteth not in every private person.*

The third, 1 Cor. xiv., "that all be done to edifying." This sentence cannot be applied generally to all things used in the church, if we truly interpret the meaning of the apostle, but to the gift "of tongues, to prayers, and to prophecies," whereof he hath made mention before. Neither can I perceive that any learned interpreter doth take it as a general rule for all rites and ceremonies, but only for the exercises of "praying, singing of psalms, interpreting, and prophesying." For of things used in the church, some pertain to instruction, *The third rule examined.*

[6 Wolfg. Muscul. in Evang. Matt. Comm. Basil. 1611. cap. xvi. Tom. II. p. 385. See before, p. 42, note 4.]
[7 "...a mere cavil."—Sec. Repl. p. 62.]

and some to order and comeliness. For the first he giveth this rule, "Let all things be done to edifying." For both the first and the second he giveth this, *Omnia decenter &c.:* "Let all things be done decently and in order:" although those ceremonies and rites, which are appointed by the church for order and comeliness, do edify as ceremonies, that is, not of themselves, but *per accidens,* "accidentally," as I have in another place declared. It is sufficient if the governors of the church, and such as have authority to ordain such rites, do think them to be profitable in the respect of the time, person, and place; neither must every private man's judgment in this case be respected, as it is well set down by the Articles agreed upon by the Dutch church in London, allowed by M. Beza, and by divers other reformed churches. It is the third article: *Quid porro ad ædificationem faciat,* &c.[1]: "Moreover, what is profitable to edify, and what is not, is not to be determined by the judgment of the common people, nor of some one man, nor yet by the issue of men's actions, &c."

I cannot understand out of what part of the xiv. to the Romans your last rule is taken, except it be the sixth, seventh, or eighth verses, out of the which I would gladly know how you can derive any rule to frame ceremonies by, rather than all other actions of man whatsoever[2].

These be your rules to square by; and truly we refuse them not, though some of them pertain nothing to your purpose. The Dutch church and the other churches, in the 11. of those articles before mentioned, touching commanding or forbidding indifferent things, determine thus: *Qui propter aliam rationem* &c.[3]: "They, which for any other cause either command or forbid at their pleasure the free use of in-

In the treatise of apparel, Tract. vii.

Theses Ecclesiæ Belgio-Germanicæ, Art. iii.

The last rule pertaineth no more to ceremonies than to other actions.

Theses Eccles. Belg. Art. xi.

[1 Quid porro ad ædificationem faciat, quid minus, non est ex vulgi aut denique simplici cujusquam hominis judicio, neque etiam ex actionum eventu æstimandum, &c.—Th. Bezæ Lib. Epist. Theolog. Genev. 1575. Ad Peregr. in Angl. Eccles. Fratr. Epist. xxiv. Ad Art. iii. 3. p. 140. Conf. Strype, Life of Grindal, Book I. chap. xiii. and Append. No. xviii. This is the article (so also that in note 3) as corrected by Beza and the Genevan church.]

[2 "...a very strange argument, that, because it is a rule to guide all actions, therefore it is no rule to direct the churches."—Sec. Repl. p. 64.]

[3 Qui propter aliam rationem quam illam triplicem, id est, nec propter ædificationem, nec propter politicam aut ecclesiasticam constitutionem, liberum rerum mediarum usum pro libito vel præcipiunt vel interdicunt; ac præsertim qui alienas conscientias temere in his rebus judicant, graviter et in Deum et in proximum peccant.—Th. Bezæ Lib. Epist. Theolog. ubi supr. Ad Art. v. vi. vii. viii. 11. pp. 143, 4.]

different things, than for one of these three, that is, neither for edifying, nor for policy, nor ecclesiastical order, and especially those which do rashly judge other men's consciences in these matters, offend heinously against God, and against their neighbours." Whereby they seem to allow any order taken in indifferent things, if it tend either to edifying, or policy, or ecclesiastical order. But to return to your Reply: that which you speak of "hour, time, and day of prayer, &c.," justify my saying; for they be not expressed in the scripture, as you also now affirm, but left to the ordering, not of every private man, but of the church, or such as have the chief care and government of the same, to appoint as they shall think most convenient and agreeable to the general rules given in the scripture for that purpose. Neither is this contrary to anything that I have written. But both in this, and that also which immediately followeth, you are contrary to yourself[4], and directly *ad oppositum* to the Admonition, as by conference may appear; for these be your own words: "Whereby it likewise appeareth that we deny not but certain things are left to the order of the church, because they are of that nature which are varied by times, places, persons, and other circumstances, and so could not at once be set down and established for ever; and yet so left to the order of the church, as that it do nothing against the rules aforesaid." What doth this differ from these words of mine: "It is also true that nothing in ceremonies, order, discipline, or government of the church, is to be suffered against the word of God?" And to this end do all those authorities and places tend, that I have alleged for this matter. So that either you understand not me, or not yourself; or else your quarrel is against the person, not the cause. The Admonition in this point you defend not; for it saith directly that "those things only are to be placed in God's church which the Lord himself in his word commandeth[5]." And, although peradventure you will shift this off, by saying that they mean such things only as be commanded either generally or specially, yet the whole discourse of their book declareth that their meaning is, that nothing ought to be placed in the church which is not specially commanded in the word of God.

T. C. is contrary to himself, and to the Admonition, and agreeth with the answer.

Fol. 19.

[4 Cartwright denies that he is contrary to himself.—Sec. Repl. p. 64.]
[5 See before, page 175.]

But seeing you and I agree in this, that the church hath authority to ordain ceremonies and make orders which are not expressed in the word of God, it remaineth to be considered wherein we differ: which is (as I think) in this, that I say, "the church of England hath lawfully used her authority in such ceremonies and orders as she hath appointed, and now retaineth," and you deny the same; so that your controversy is against the church of England, and the ceremonies and orders used therein. And therefore you add and say, " but how doth this follow, that certain things are left to the order of the church, therefore to make a new ministry, &c.?" Whereby you give us to understand that the things you mislike in this church are the office and name of an archbishop, which you untruly call "a new ministry" (as it is by me declared in my Answer to the Admonition), our ministry, the government of our church, and (as you say) " other more," that is, all things at your pleasure. But how justly and truly this is spoken, shall appear in their proper places. In the mean time it is sufficient to tell you, that you are an unworthy member of this church, which so unjustly report of it, so unchristianly slander it, and so without grounds and sound proofs condemn it. There is nothing by it or in it altered, which God hath ordained and established not to be altered.

Chapter i. The Sixth Division.

Answer to the Admonition, Page 21, Sect. 5, 6, and Page 22, Sect. 1, 2.

The scripture hath not prescribed any place or time wherein or when the Lord's supper should be celebrated, neither yet in what manner. The scripture hath not appointed what time or where the congregation shall meet for common prayer, and for the hearing of the word of God, neither yet any discipline for the correcting of such as shall contemn the same.

The scripture hath not appointed what day in the week should be most meet for the sabbath-day, whether Saturday, which is the Jews' sabbath, or the day now observed, which was appointed by the church.

The scripture hath not determined what form is to

be used in matrimony, what words, what prayers, what exhortations.

The scripture speaketh not one word of standing, sitting, or kneeling at the communion; of meeting in churches, fields, or houses, to hear the word of God; of preaching in pulpits, chairs, or otherwise; of baptizing in fonts, in basons, or rivers, openly or privately, at home, or in the church, every day in the week, or on the sabbath-day only. And yet no man (as I suppose) is so simple to think that the church hath no authority to take order in these matters.

T. C. Page 15, Sect. ult. and Page 16, Sect. 1.

But, while you go about to seem to say much, and rake up a great number of things, you have made very evil meslin[1], and you have put in one things which are not pairs nor matches. Because I will not draw the reader willingly into more questions than are already put up, I will not stand to dispute whether the Lord's day (which we call Sunday), being the day of the resurrection of our Saviour Christ, and so the day wherein the world was renewed, as the Jews' sabbath was the day wherein the world was finished, and being in all the churches in the apostles' times (as it seemeth) used for the day of the rest and serving of God, ought or may be changed, or no. This one thing I may say, that there was no great judgment to make it as arbitrary and changeable as the hour and the place of prayer. It is less true dealing for But where was your judgment when you wrote that the scripture hath you to charge men appointed no discipline nor correction for such as shall contemn the com- with that which they mon prayers and hearing the word of God? What church-discipline have not affirmed. would you have other than admonitions, reprehensions, and, if these will not profit, excommunications[2]? and are they not appointed of our
_{Matt. xviii.} Saviour Christ, Matt. xviii.? There are also civil punishments,
_{15, 16, 17.³} and punishments of the body, likewise appointed by the word
_{Chap. xxii.} of God in divers places; in the xxii. of Exodus: "He that
_{20.³} sacrificeth to other gods, and not to the Lord alone, shall die Scriptures unskilfully
_{Chap.xix.19.³} the death." And in the xix. of Deuteronomy, "Thou shalt turn[4] alleged.
out the evil out of the midst of thee, that the rest may hear and fear[5], and not dare do the like." The execution of this law
_{2 Chron. xv.} appeareth in the xv. chap. 2 Chron. by king Aza, who made
_{13.³} a law that all those that did not seek the Lord should be killed.
And thus you see the civil punishment of contemners of the word and prayers.

[¹ Meslin: mixture, or medley.]
[² Excommunication, Repl. 1, 2, and Def. A.]
[³ These marginal references are inserted from Repl. 2, which does not name the chapters in the text.]
[⁴ Burn, Repl. 2; and so it is noted that it should be in errata of Repl. 1.]
[⁵ Learn, Repl. 2.]

There are other for such as neglect the word, which are according to the quantity of the fault; so that, whether you mean civil or ecclesiastical correction, the scripture hath defined of them both.

Or else you are deceived.

JO. WHITGIFT.

T. C. seeketh quarrels where none are offered.

Out of all these things, which I say the scripture hath not prescribed or appointed, you choose to carp at, first, "the Lord's day, which we call Sunday;" and you say, that you "will not dispute whether it ought or may be changed, or no:" when as you should rather have proved it to be appointed by the scriptures (which no doubt you would have done if you could); for that is it which I deny. Where have you heard me say that it may or ought to be altered? If you will confute, confute that which I have set down and affirm, not that which it pleaseth you to imagine.

The determination of the church ought not lightly to be altered.

In good sooth, this is no true dealing. No marvel it is that you have not set down my book, seeing you deal thus corruptly with it. I do not think that that which the church hath once determined, and by long continuance proved to be necessary, ought to be altered, without great and especial consideration. I say with St Augustine, *Epist.* 118. *ad*

Aug. Ep. 118.

Januar.: "If any thing be universally observed of the whole church, not to observe that, or to call it into question, is mere madness[1];" therefore, seeing that it hath had such time of continuance, that it was for so good and just causes appointed, and is so generally observed of the church, I do not think it now arbitrary, nor to be changed: much less do I make it as "arbitrary or changeable as the place and hour of prayer," which may be divers in divers churches; and it is among those rites and orders that be diversly observed in divers places; whereof also Augustine maketh mention in that epistle. Surely, as there had been little judgment in me, if I had "made it changeable," so is there small honesty in you to alter my words, and to falsify my meaning[2].

[1 Ad hæc itaque ita respondeo, ut quid horum sit faciendum, si divinæ scripturæ præscribit auctoritas, non sit dubitandum quin ita facere debeamus ut legimus....Similiter etiam si quid horum tota per orbem frequentat ecclesia. Nam et hinc quin ita faciendum sit disputare insolentissimæ insaniæ est.—August. Op. Par. 1679-1700. Ad Inq. Januar. Lib. I. seu Epist. liv. cap. v. 6. Tom. II. col. 126.]

[2 Cartwright charges Whitgift with writing "senseless speeches" here, and says that he contradicts himself. For, he says, "if it be mere madness for the church not to observe the Lord's day, how hath the church authority in that case?"—Sec. Repl. pp. 65, 6.]

Secondly, you mislike that I should say "the scripture not to have appointed discipline or correction for such as shall contemn the common prayers, and hearing the word of God." And you ask me where my "judgment was?" but I have more cause to demand of you, where that learning and skill is which you so much brag of, seeing that you so unskilfully allege the scriptures against their true meaning and sense? For where have you learned that Christ in the xviii. of Matthew doth appoint any general rule for public offences, such as negligence and contempt in frequenting public prayers, and hearing of the word of God is? The very words of Christ, "If thy brother trespass against thee, &c.," do teach that he meaneth not there of open and known, but of secret and particular sins: the which thing also the note that is in the margent of the bible printed at Geneva[3] might have taught you, if you had been as well disposed to have followed the same in this place, as you seem to have done in other places. M. Calvin, in his book against the anabaptists, reproving them for using this place to the establishing of their kind of discipline by excommunication, saith on this sort: "They are again deceived, in that they consider not that the Lord speaketh in that place of secret faults; for, as for those which are manifest, and give unto the people cause of offence, they are to be corrected by other means than by secret admonitions[4]." You must therefore seek for some other place than this, if you will prove that the scripture hath appointed any discipline and correction for such as shall contemn the common prayers and hearing of the word[5].

To prove that "there are also civil punishments, and punishments of the body, for contemning common prayers and hearing of the word," appointed by the word of God, you

Scriptures unskilfully alleged by T. C.

Matt. xviii.

Calvin. adv. Anabap.

[[3] Wherewith thou mayest be offended: he speaketh of secret or particular sins, and not of open or known to others.—The Bible, transl. according to the Ebrew and Greeke. Lond. 1578. Not. in Matt. xviii. 15. p. 9.]

[[4] Falluntur iterum in eo, quod non considerant Dominum eo in loco de secretis delictis verba facere. Manifesta enim, quæ populo offensionis causam præbent, alia ratione corrigenda sunt quam secreta monitione.—Calvin. Op. Amst. 1667-71. Instr. adv. Anabapt. Art. ii. Tom. VIII. p. 362.]

[[5] Cartwright insists that, if the scripture here "giveth authority to reprehend private faults, it doth much more authorise to rebuke public faults." He goes on to argue that, if this doctrine of Christ "touching excommunication may be carried no farther than to that case of private and secret injuries, then St Paul drew the sword and taught to draw it where it ought not."—Sec. Repl. pp. 66, 7.]

cite xxii. of Exodus, xix. of Deuteronomy, &c. But before I come to the answering of these places, I pray you, let me ask of you these questions.

First, whether you would have both ecclesiastical and civil punishment for the self-same fault?

Secondly, whether you would have negligence or contempt in frequenting of "common prayers and hearing of the word" punished with death, or no? for that punishment is appointed in those places by you alleged.

The unaptness of the proofs of T. C. Last of all, whether you think the judicial laws to be perpetual, and to bind the civil magistrate to the observing of them, and to restrain him from making any other, as shall be thought to him most convenient? for, except you will have two kinds of punishments for one and the self-same offence, except you will punish with death such as be negligent in coming to public prayers, to be short, except you will have the civil magistrate bound of necessity to practise these judicial laws of Moses (which indeed you affirm afterwards in your book), those places make nothing for your purpose. So that you are yet as far to seek for scripture that appointeth any certain kind of discipline for these matters as ever you were[1].

But, that it may be understood how unreasonably you wring and wrest the scriptures to make them serve your turn, I will in one word or two declare the meaning of those places, and set open the might of your arguments.

Exod. xxii. In the xxii. of Exodus, the place by you alleged, the punishment of death is appointed for idolaters; whereupon you would ground this argument: God in the xxii. of Exodus appointeth death as a punishment for idolaters; *ergo*, the word of God appointeth a certain kind of punishment for such as be negligent in frequenting public prayers, and contemn the hearing of the word. I say there is no sequel in this argument,

[[1] "...before he can give one answer he must ask three questions: the first is answered before in the beginning; the last is handled afterward in the 6. ch. and 5. division. And as for that part of the second question which with other his sayings following surmise that I would have the neglect of the word punished by death, it is directly against my express words, which (having shewed the punishments that should be executed upon contemners) add that 'there are other punishments for those that neglect the word, &c.' And as to that part of his question, which is whether contemners of the word ought to be put to death, it is, as his other questions be, of things not only affirmed and set down, but disputed of both parts. For this is that which we plainly affirm, and bring arguments to prove."—Ibid. p. 68.]

unless you will make all those that be negligent in coming to public prayers, and contemn to hear the word, idolaters, and this to be a perpetual law.

In the xix. of Deuteronomy there is nothing tending to any such purpose; only in the latter end of the chapter there is a punishment appointed for him that beareth false witness, whereupon these words, "So thou shalt take evil away from the midst of thee, &c.," by you here alleged, do follow. Now, if you will thus conclude: God in the xix. of Deuteronomy appointeth a punishment for a false witness; *ergo*, the scripture hath appointed discipline for such as neglect to come to public prayers, &c., then indeed you may prove anything; and it is but in vain to strive with you. But, Lord, what gibing and flouting would there be, if I should happen to fall into so manifest and open absurdities! *Deut. xix.*

In the 2. Chron. xv. Aza made the same punishment for idolatry that is mentioned in the xxii. of Exodus; and therefore the same answer serveth that place. Truly I think you take yourself to have free liberty to apply the scriptures at your pleasure; else would you never thus abuse them without all judgment or reason[2]. *2 Chron. xv.*

What I think of the necessity or continuance of these laws, I will declare in a more special place: in the mean-time, you blow the triumph before the victory; for as yet you have not proved that the scripture doth appoint any certain kind, either of "civil punishment" or "church-discipline, for such as contemn" or neglect the coming to "public prayers and hearing of the word" of God. *T. C. triumpheth before the victory.*

You say that "there are other punishments for such as neglect the word of God, &c."; but you neither tell us what they be, nor where to find them.

Chapter i. The Seventh Division.

T. C. Page 16, Sect. 1, line 3.

Chap. viii. 4.[3]   *I omit that there be examples of pulpits in Esdras; of*

[2 Cartwright insists upon his interpretation of the passages referred to, and accuses Whitgift of "his ordinary fault, that he cannot understand."—Ibid. pp. 68, &c.]

[3 This reference is inserted from Repl. 2.]

chairs in the xxiii. of Matthew[1], *whereby "the chair of Moses"* Chap. xxiii. *our Saviour Christ, meaning the doctrine of Moses, doth also* 2.[2] *declare the manner which they used in teaching; of sitting at the communion (which the evangelist noteth to have been* Matt. xxvi. *done of our Saviour Christ with his disciples); which ex-* 20.[2] *amples are not to be lightly changed, and upon many occasions.*

Jo. Whitgift.

"Examples of pulpits," you say, "we find in Esdras." True it is that in the viii. of Nehem. we read "Esdras stood upon a pulpit of wood," which he had made for the preaching: but the same was placed in the open street; neither did Esdras any thing but read. The other persons, with the Levites mentioned ver. 7. of that chapter, did cause the people to understand the law, that is, made them give diligent ear to the reading of the law. And, although there be words in the 8. verse, which (as they be translated) seem to insinuate some kind of interpretation, yet the meaning is nothing so; for these be the words: *Et apposuerunt intellectum, et intellexerunt scripturam illam,* that is (as learned men do interpret it) *adverterunt animum:* "they were attentive to the reading;" or, as some translate it: *Et legerunt in libro legis Dei distincte et apposite ad intelligendum; et intellexerunt cum legeretur:* "And they read in the book of the law of God, distinctly and in such sort as they might easily understand." Hereof may I much better gather that reading is preaching, than you can do that the scripture appointeth "pulpits." For, though Esdras did so, is it therefore by and by a rule to be followed? You read not of any of the apostles that did in like manner; neither is there any mention made of "pulpits" from the beginning of the new testament to the end of the same. And this place maketh rather for "pulpits" to read in, than for "pulpits" to preach in[3].

Neh. viii.

It is most certain that by "the chair of Moses" in that place is meant the doctrine of Moses; whether it declare any place or no made for Moses to teach the people in, that is but conjectural; neither have we any example expressed

[[1] In Nehemias, which the common translation calleth Ezra, of chairs in St Matthew, Repl. 2.]

[[2] These references are inserted from Repl. 2.]

[[3] Cartwright declares that Whitgift has "shamefully corrupted the place of Nehemias."—Ibid. p. 71.]

TRACT. II.]   TO THE ADMONITION.   207

either in Moses himself, or in any other that may resolve that doubt. Howsoever it is, the matter is not great. For things used in the old church do not prescribe any rule to the church of Christ, unless it can be shewed Christ himself and his apostles to have used the same.

My meaning is, that in the whole scripture there is neither "pulpit" nor "chair" prescribed to be used in the church of Christ, but that and such other like things left to the disposition of the church, as shall be thought most convenient from time to time.

What though Christ sat at his last supper, doth it therefore follow that of necessity we must needs sit? Why must we not then as well be bound to receive the same after supper? I say again, that the scripture doth nowhere prescribe whether we shall sit, stand, or kneel, at the communion: if it do prescribe sitting, why do some of you use walking, other some standing, which both do more differ from sitting than kneeling doth?

Chapter i.   The Eighth Division.

T. C. Page 16, Sect. 2 and 3.

But this I cannot omit, that you make it an indifferent thing to preach the word of God in churches or in houses, that is to say, privately or publicly. For what better interpretation can I have than of your own words, which saith[4] *by and by after of baptism, that it is at the order of* An untruth; for there is *the church to make it private or public. For, if it be in the power of the* no such thing said. *church to order that baptism may be ministered at the house of every private person, it is also in her power to ordain that the word be preached*
Prov. viii. 2, *also privately.   And then where is that which Salomon saith,*
3.[5]   *that "Wisdom crieth openly and in the streets, and at the* A place of scripture *corners of the streets where many meet?" and where be the examples of the* strangely *old church, which had, besides the temple at Jerusalem, erected up syna-* applied. *gogues in every town to hear the word of God, and minister the circumcision? what is become of the commandment of our Saviour Christ,* These places prove that
Matt. x. 27.[5] *which willed his disciples that they should preach openly, and* the word ought to be *upon the house-tops, that which they heard in the ear of him* preached *and secretly? and how do we observe the example of our Saviour Christ,* publicly, but not only *who, to deliver his doctrine from all suspicion of tumults and other* publicly.
John xviii. *disorders, said that he preached openly in the temple and in*
20.[5]   *the synagogues, albeit the same were very dangerous unto him? and the example of the apostles that did the same? for, as for the time of*

[4 Say, Repl. 2.]
[5 The verses of the first reference, and the others altogether, are inserted from Repl. 2: *Prov. viii.* is in Repl. 1.]

persecution, when the church dare not, nor it is[1] *not meet that it should shew itself to the enemy, no, not then is the word of God, nor the sacraments, privately preached or ministered, nor*[3] *ought to be.*   Acts iii. 1.[2] Acts iv. 1.[2]

For, although they be done in the house of a private man, yet, because they are and ought to be ministered in the presence of the congregation, there is neither private preaching, nor private baptism. For, like as wheresoever the queen's majesty lieth there is the court, although it be in a gentleman his house; so wheresoever the church meeteth, it is[4] *not to be holden private as touching the prayers, preachings, and sacraments, that shall be there ministered: so that I deny unto you that the church hath power to ordain at her pleasure whether preaching or ministering of sacraments should be private or public, when they ought not be but where the church is, and the church ought not to assemble (if it be not letted by persecution) but in open places; and, when it is driven from them, those places where it gathereth itself together, although they be otherwise private, yet are they, for the time that the churches do there assemble, and for respect of the word and sacraments that are there ministered in the presence of the church, public places. And so you see those (whom you charge slanderously with conventicles) are fain to glaze up the windows that you open to secret and private conventicles.*

<small>This is only said, but not proved.</small>

Jo. Whitgift.

But this you "cannot omit, that" I "make it an indifferent thing to preach the word of God in churches or in houses, &c." It is an argument that you lack good matter, when you make such excursions from the purpose. My words be, that "the scriptures speak not one word of meeting in churches, fields, or houses, to hear the word of God; of baptizing in fonts, in basons, or rivers, openly or privately, at home or in the church, &c." If I have said untruly, convince me with scripture, and shew me those places where these things be determined. Where do I say that these things be now indifferent? To have the word preached is not indifferent, but necessary; to have it preached in this place or in that place, in churches, in fields, or in houses, is indifferent, until such time as the church hath otherwise determined. So is it likewise in baptism: the sacrament is necessary, the circumstances of time and place, &c. be committed to the disposition of the church, and remain so long indifferent, until the church hath taken order in them; which being done, then they be no

<small>Things indifferent lose the nature of indifferency when they are commanded.</small>

[1 Nor is, Repl. 2.]   [2 These references are inserted from Repl. 2.]
[3 Neither yet, Repl. 2.]   [4 Meeteth that place is, Repl. 2.]

more indifferent. Do you not know that whereunto so many churches reformed, and learned men, have of late subscribed? It is the 6. assertion: *Res alioqui per se mediæ mutant quodammodo naturam, &c.*[5] : "Things otherwise indifferent of themselves after a sort change their nature, when by some lawful commandment they are either commanded or forbidden; because neither then can be omitted contrary to the commandment, if they are once commanded, neither done contrary to prohibition, if they be prohibited, as it appeareth in the ceremonial law." The place is not of the substance either of the word or of the sacraments; but yet to contemn or willingly to break the order appointed by the church in such matters is sin.

<small>Theses Eccles. Belg. Art. vi.</small>

You say that I affirm it "to be at the order of the church to make baptism private or public." Surely you do me great injury, and win yourself small credit, by this kind of dealing. Is it all one to say, that the scripture hath not determined whether baptism should be ministered "openly or privately, at home or in the church," and to say, that "the church may make baptism private or public?" For hereby you would give your readers to understand that I think it in the power of the church to appoint that there should be no public baptism; wherein (as I said) you do me great injury. My words therefore and meaning tend to this end, that the scripture hath not anywhere expressed when baptism should be celebrated publicly, when privately; but hath left that to the determination of the church, to do therein according to the circumstances of time, person, &c. Neither do I call baptism private in any other respect than of the place; and therefore my meaning is, that the scripture hath not determined where or when we should baptize, at home in private families, or in public and open places, as fields, churches, &c. For we have examples in scripture both of baptizing in houses, and of baptizing in fields, Acts viii., ix., x., and xvi. Therefore touching the place the scripture hath not determined anything; and in the respect of the place I call it public or private: although

<small>T. C. perverteth the words of the Answer.</small>

<small>Baptism is called private in respect of the place.</small>

[5 Res alioqui per se mediæ mutant quodammodo naturam, quum aliquo legitimo mandato vel præcipiuntur vel prohibentur; quia neque contra justum præceptum omitti possunt, si præcipiantur, neque contra interdictum fieri, si prohibeantur, sicut ex lege ceremoniali apparet.—Th. Bezæ Lib. Epist. Theolog. Genev. 1575. Ad Peregrin. in Angl. Fratr. Epist. xxiv. Ad Artt. v. vi. vii. viii. 6. pp. 142, 3. See before, page 198, note 1.]

I see nothing in the scripture to the contrary, but upon necessary occasion, and other circumstances, it may be private in the respect of persons that be present at the celebrating of baptism; for the number of standers by, or of such as are to be baptized, is not of the substance of the sacrament: therefore in that also the church may take order, and hath therein to deal.

And, as I think that in such respects baptism may be privately administered, so think I also that in the like respects the word may be privately preached. Neither did the apostles only preach in the synagogues, and in open places, but in private families and houses also; as it is manifest, Acts v., where it is said that "the apostles did not cease daily to teach and to preach Jesus Christ in the temple, and house by house." Acts x., Peter preached in Cornelius his house. And Acts xvi., Paul preached in prison. And not only was the word preached privately in respect of the place, but sometimes also in the respect of the persons; as Christ preached to the woman of Samaria alone, Joh. iv.; and Philip in the chariot to the eunuch, Acts viii.[1]

The word may be preached privately, both in respect of the place and persons.
Acts v.
Acts x.
Acts xvi.
John iv.
Acts viii.

Your scriptures brought in to prove that there may be "no private preaching" are very far-fetched, and some of them very strangely applied. That which Salomon saith, Prov. viii., proveth that God calleth all men by his word and by his works to follow that which is good, and fly from that which is evil: and I think that the meaning of Salomon in that place is, that God doth offer his word to all persons, in all places, so that there can be no ignorance pretended. But, I pray you, how doth this argument follow: The word of God is offered to all, and openly proclaimed; *ergo*, it may not be also privately taught? All your proofs and examples that follow be of like effect: they prove that the word of God ought publicly to be preached, but they do not take away

[[1] Cartwright persists that he has rightly taken Whitgift's assertions, and goes on: "If you had said that it had been in the church's power, according to the former rules prescribed, to have ordered whether preaching and administering the sacraments should be in the town or in the field, in a church (as they call it) or in some one man's house or other, I would have moved no question against you. But, when you say that it is in the power of the church to ordain whether it should be public or private, I cannot abide you. For even in the time of persecution, when it is preached in the house of a private man, I have shewed that, the church assembling there, the meeting is public; whereunto you answer not a word."— Sec. Repl. pp. 72, 3.]

private exhortations and preachings. It is true that both Christ and his apostles taught in synagogues, so it is true also that they taught in private families, as I have declared; but yet I say, the scripture hath not appointed any certain place of preaching. For Esdras read the law in the streets, Nehem. viii. "Wisdom crieth in the tops of the high places, by the way-side, in the paths, in the gates before the city," Prov. viii. Christ preached in the mountain, Matt. v., in the synagogue, Matt. iv.; the apostles in the temple, and in private families: do not you therefore see that there is no determination of any place? Wherefore the aptness of the place, and the convenience of it, likewise when the word is to be preached publicly, when privately, is left to the judgment and ordering of the church. And therefore it is true that I have set down, that the scripture hath not determined anything "of meeting in churches, fields, or houses to hear the word of God; or of preaching in pulpits, chairs, or otherwise." *Neh. viii. Prov. viii. Matt. v. Matt. iv. Acts v.*

There are and may be occasions, even in the time of prosperity, when both the word may be preached and the sacraments administered in private families, so that they be done according to the order of the church, and not in the contempt of common and public assemblies. And I think that such noblemen and gentlemen as upon occasion either of infirmity of body, or of distance of place, or some other urgent cause, have the word of God preached in their private families, and the sacraments ministered according to the order of the church, are greatly to be commended[2]. Neither doth this open any window to secret and schismatical "conventicles" (such I mean as seek corners), because they will not keep the orders and laws of the church, but contemn the same, and conspire in some new and erroneous opinions: in the which number those be whom I have truly charged with "conventicles;" for they, despising the order of the church, have wickedly separated themselves from the same: whose opinions notwithstanding you maintain, although you would seem to condemn their "conventicles." But it may be that you count

[2 "And, where he saith that the word of God 'may be taught privately,' and that 'a man may exhort privately;' that is nothing to the purpose. For we speak of the order which ought to be kept in the exercises that concern the body of the church, and not of the private exhortations...that...the minister ought to use towards the several persons of his flock, &c."—Ibid. p. 74.]

this time to be a "time of persecution," and so excuse their doings.

To be short, when I speak either of private preaching or of private ministering the sacraments, I mean it especially in respect of the place, and not in the respect of any schismatical separation; so that hitherto you have said nothing that impugneth anything that I have written. Neither have I spoken any otherwise in all these things than other learned and godly men have done; as it is to be seen by all their several authorities, which I have in their places set down.

Chapter i. The Ninth Division.

Answer to the Admonition, Page 22, Sect. 2.

I pray you what meant St Paul in 1[1] Cor. xiv. after he had prescribed certain orders unto them to be observed in the church, thus generally to conclude, *Omnia decenter et ordine fiant;* "Let all things be done decently and in order?" Doth he not there give unto them authority to make orders in the church; so that all things be done in order and decently? The best interpreters do understand this as a general rule, given unto the church to examine her traditions and constitutions by; and therefore without all doubt their judgment is, that the church hath authority in external things to make orders, and appoint laws, not expressed in the word of God; so that this rule of the apostle be observed.

Jo. Whitgift.

The ground of the assertion unanswered by T. C.

Here have you not answered one word to that which I have alleged out of the 1 Cor. xiv. for the justifying of my general assertion in this point, nor to the interpretation of it: that therefore being granted, the rest must needs stand in full force, that is, that the scripture hath left many things to the discretion of the church.

[1 In the 1, Answ.]

The opinion of ancient fathers and councils
of things indifferent.

Chapter ii. The First Division.

Answer to the Admonition, Page 22, Sect. 3, 4.

Now, if either godly councils, or ancient fathers, were anything at all regarded of these men (as they be not, such is their arrogancy), this controversy might soon be decided. For the most ancient fathers and best-learned, as Justinus Martyr, Irenæus, Tertullian, Cyprian, and other, do expressly declare that even from the apostles' time the church hath always had authority in such matters, and hath observed divers orders and ceremonies not once mentioned in the word of God[2]. *Ancient fathers of things indifferent.*

T. C. Page 16, Sect. 3, and Page 17, Sect. 1, 2.

Here are brought in Justin Martyr, Irenæus, Tertullian, Cyprian, and councils, as dumb persons in the stage, only to make a shew, and so they go out of the stage without saying anything. And, if they had had anything to say in this cause for these matters in controversy, there is no doubt but M. Doctor would have made them speak. For, when he placeth the greatest strength of his cause in antiquity, he would not have passed by Justin, Irenæus, Tertullian, Cyprian, being so ancient, and taken Augustine, which was a great time after them. And, if the godly councils could have helped here, it is small wisdom to take Augustine, and leave them. For I think he might have learned that, amongst the authorities of men, the credit of many be[3] better than of one; and that this is a general rule, that, as the judgment of some notable personage is looked unto in a matter that is debated[4] more than theirs of the common sort, so the judgment of a council, where many learned men be gathered together, carrieth more likelihood of truth with it than the judgment of one man, although it be but a provincial council, much more then if it be general[5]; and therefore you do your cause great injury, if you could allege them, and do not. This is once to be observed of the reader throughout your whole book, that you have well provided that you should[6] not be taken in the trip for misalleging the scriptures; for Wilful ignorance; for you know that every one of them greatly favoureth this cause.

[2 Here Answ. 2 goes on: Tertullian, *Li. De virginibus velandis,* saith thus: *Regula &c.* See below, page 217. The whole of the passage is given in Answ. 2, together with a translation verbally differing from that in the page just referred to.]
[3 Is, Repl. 2.] [4 Matter of debate, Repl. 2.]
[5 Be a general, Repl. 1 and 2.] [6 Would, Repl. 2.]

More scriptures than you, and something better applied.

that, unless it be in one or two points, we hear continually (instead of Esay, and Jeremy, St Paul, and St Peter, and the rest of the prophets and apostles) St Augustine, and St Ambrose, καὶ τὸ ἐν τῇ φάκῃ μύρον, Dionysius Areopagita, Clement, &c. And therefore I cannot tell with what face we can call the papists from their antiquity, councils, and fathers, to the trial of the scriptures, which[1], in the controversies which rise amongst ourselves, fly so far from them, that it wanteth not much that they are not banished of your part from the deciding of all these controversies.

And, as we say in our tongue, nettles among roses.

A better proof than to say, I say so, as you commonly use to do.

And, if this be a sufficient proof of things to say, such a doctor said so, such a council decreed so, there is almost nothing so true but I can impugn, nothing so false but I can make true. And well assured I am that by their means the principal grounds of our faith may be shaken.

Petitio principii.

And therefore, because you have no proof in the word of God, we comfort ourselves, assured that, forsomuch as the foundations of the archbishop, and lordship of bishops, and of other things which are in question, be not in heaven, that they will fall and come to the ground, from whence they were taken. Now it is known that they are from beneath, and of the earth, and that they are of men, and not of God.

Jo. Whitgift.

Sect. 1.

Here are many words which might well have been spared, but that you are desirous to have your modest speeches known to the world. In the 25. page I have told you where some of these "dumb persons" speak their parts[2]; but you are blind when you should see, and deaf when you should hear, that which you would not gladly see or hear[3]. I told you there, that Justinus Martyr speaketh of this matter "in his second Apology, and in his Book of Questions;" and that Tertullian speaketh of the same in his book *De Corona Militis*. It hath pleased you in that which followeth to

[1 Who, Repl. 2.]   [2 See below, page 237.]

[3 Cartwright says: "If he would have proved that which I deny, he should have shewed that these authorities affirmed that the church, in making laws of things whereof the scripture hath not precisely determined, need not to have respect to the general commandments of the scripture before received." He then goes on to accuse Whitgift of making an "unproper" and "ungodly choice" of the testimonies he has produced out of the ancient writers. "The first sort," he says, are "of those which are in controversy, as whether bishops may have suffringans, &c." "The second sort are of those things which being determined by the word of God, off or on, are out of the church's compass to take order in." "There is a third sort...whereof beside that divers of them were never convenient, some of them unlawful, they are all such as the authors do not permit to the order of the church, but under a false cloke of tradition put the church's neck under a servile yoke of them." "There are a fourth sort of places...wherein he putteth the greatest confidence, and upon which he hath laid greatest weight; and therefore by hands set over against them moveth the reader to lay sure hold on

reprove me for translating into my book other men's opinions *Ancient* *fathers of* and authorities; and here, though I have quoted the places *things in-* where you may find them, yet is it also your pleasure to *different.* spend your gibing and jesting eloquence upon me for not *Neither* translating them. Well, I will deceive your expectation, and *dumb nor* *speaking* make them speak. Justinus Martyr, in his second Apology, *persons can please T. C.* saith that "they used in baptizing to call upon the name of *Justin.* *Apol. 2.* God for such as were baptized, and after baptism to carry him that was baptized to the place where the brethren be gathered together, to pray both for themselves and for him also that is baptized; and in the end of their prayers that they salute one another with a kiss." Likewise he there saith that "when they celebrated the Lord's supper, there *Ibidem.* was used certain prayers and thanksgiving, to the which the people said Amen. Also that the deacons did give to the people the bread and the cup, and carry them likewise to such as were absent[4]." In his Book of Questions he sheweth how that singing was used in the church, and commendeth *Justin. Lib.* *Quæst.* it, and that they used not to kneel at prayers on the Sunday in token of the resurrection[5]. Divers other such ceremonies and orders doth he recite, used in his time, not prescribed by the word of God, but appointed by the church, whereof some

them." Of these are the quotations from Ambrose and Tertullian, to which he objects that the first is counterfeit, and that Tertullian was a Montanist. He afterwards cites several passages from various fathers, which maintain the paramount authority of scripture, to shew, he says, that there can be "fitter places brought for the maintenance of the Admonition," than Whitgift has alleged on his side.—Sec. Repl. pp. 76, &c.]

[4 'Ημεῖς δὲ μετὰ τὸ οὕτως λοῦσαι τὸν πεπεισμένον καὶ συγκατατεθειμένον, ἐπὶ τοὺς λεγομένους ἀδελφοὺς ἄγομεν, ἔνθα συνηγμένοι εἰσί, κοινὰς εὐχὰς ποιησόμενοι ὑπέρ τε ἑαυτῶν καὶ τοῦ φωτισθέντος, καὶ ἄλλων πανταχοῦ πάντων εὐτόνως, ὅπως καταξιωθῶμεν τὰ ἀληθῆ μαθόντες, καὶ δι' ἔργων ἀγαθοὶ πολιτευταί καὶ φύλακες τῶν ἐντεταλμένων εὑρεθῆναι, ὅπως τὴν αἰώνιον σωτηρίαν σωθῶμεν. ἀλλήλους φιλήματι ἀσπαζόμεθα παυσάμενοι τῶν εὐχῶν· ἔπειτα προσφέρεται τῷ προεστῶτι τῶν ἀδελφῶν ἄρτος, καὶ ποτήριον ὕδατος καὶ κράματος. καὶ οὗτος λαβὼν αἶνον καὶ δόξαν τῷ Πατρὶ τῶν ὅλων διὰ τοῦ ὀνόματος τοῦ Υἱοῦ καὶ τοῦ Πνεύματος τοῦ ἁγίου ἀναπέμπει· καὶ εὐχαριστίαν ὑπὲρ τοῦ κατηξιῶσθαι τούτων παρ' αὐτοῦ ἐπὶ πολὺ ποιεῖται· οὗ συντελέσαντος τὰς εὐχὰς καὶ τὴν εὐχαριστίαν, πᾶς ὁ παρὼν λαὸς ἐπευφημεῖ λέγων, ἀμήν.....οἱ καλούμενοι παρ' ἡμῖν διάκονοι διδοάσιν ἑκάστῳ τῶν παρόντων μεταλαβεῖν ἀπὸ τοῦ εὐχαριστηθέντος ἄρτου καὶ οἴνου καὶ ὕδατος, καὶ τοῖς οὐ παροῦσιν ἀποφέρουσι.—Just. Mart. Op. Par. 1742, Apol. I. 65, pp. 82, 3.]

[5 Ἡδύνει γὰρ τὴν ψυχὴν πρὸς ζέοντα πόθον τοῦ ἐν τοῖς ᾄσμασιν ἡδομένου· κ.τ.λ.—Id. Quæst. et Resp. ad Orthod. Quæst. cvii. p. 486. Τὸ δὲ ἐν τῇ κυριακῇ μὴ κλίνειν γόνυ, συμβολόν ἐστι τῆς ἀναστάσεως, κ.τ.λ.—Quæst. cxv. p. 490. These Questions and Answers are spurious.]

Ancient fathers of things indifferent.
Irenæus.

now be abrogated, because they be not so fit for this time as they were for that time.

Irenæus speaketh very plainly in that epistle which he writ to Victor, bishop of Rome, whereof also Eusebius maketh mention, *Lib. v. cap.* 25 and 26. In that epistle he declareth the diversity of divers churches for the day of Easter, the time of fasting, and such like[1]: which plainly argueth that the scripture hath not determined all things, but left much to the disposition of the church.

Tertull.

Tertullian, in his book *Adversus Praxean*, saith that the church then used *terna mersione in baptismo*, "thrice dipping in baptism[2]."

Idem.

And in his book *De Corona Militis*, although he recite some things which in time grew to be superstitious, yet doth he there plainly declare what his opinion is in this matter: he reciteth divers customs of the church then used, whereof there is no mention in the scriptures: he declareth that "those which were to be baptized must first profess that they renounced the devil, his pomp, and his angels, and that then they were thrice dipped in the water, *amplius aliquid respondentes quam Dominus in evangelio determinavit:* answering somewhat more than the Lord hath determined in the gospel[3]." Likewise he sheweth that "the sacrament of the supper, which the Lord celebrated at supper, and commanded to all, was then celebrated in the morning, and ministered only by those that be the chief[4]." And in the end he saith: *Harum et aliarum hujusmodi disciplinarum si legem expostules scripturarum, nullam invenies, &c.*[5]: "Of these and such like orders, if thou shouldest require a law out of the scriptures, thou shalt find none;" and a little after he addeth: *Annon putas omni fideli licere concipere et constituere duntaxat quod Deo congruat,*

[1 Οὐδὲ γὰρ μόνον περὶ τῆς ἡμέρας ἐστὶν ἡ ἀμφισβήτησις, ἀλλὰ καὶ περὶ τοῦ εἴδους αὐτοῦ τῆς νηστείας.—Euseb. in Hist. Eccles. Script. Amst. 1695-1700. Lib. v. cap. xxiv. p. 156. Conf. capp. xxv. xxvi. pp. 157, 8.]

[2 Nam nec semel, sed ter, ad singula nomina in personas singulas tinguimur. —Tertull. Op. Lut. 1641. Adv. Prax. 26. p. 659.]

[3 Aquam adituri, ibidem, sed et aliquanto prius in ecclesia sub antistitis manu contestamur nos renuntiare diabolo, et pompæ, et angelis ejus; dehinc ter mergitamur, amplius aliquid respondentes &c.—Id. de Coron. Mil. 3. p. 121.]

[4 Eucharistiæ sacramentum, et in tempore victus et omnibus mandatum a Domino, etiam antelucanis cœtibus, nec de aliorum manu quam præsidentium sumimus.—Id. ibid.]

[5 Id. ibid. 4. p. 122; where *ejusmodi*.]

quod disciplinæ conducat, quod saluti proficiat, dicente Ancient fathers of *Domino, Cur autem non et a vobis ipsis quod justum est* things in-*judicatis*[6]*?* "Dost thou not think that it is lawful for every different. faithful man to conceive and appoint at the least that which agreeth to God, which is convenient for discipline, which is profitable unto salvation; seeing the Lord saith, Why do you not of yourselves judge that that is right?" And, in his book *De Virginibus Veland.*, he hath these manifest words: *Re-* Idem. *gula quidem fidei una omnino est, sola immobilis et irreformabilis, credendi scilicet in Deum unicum omnipotentem, &c. Hac lege fidei manente, cetera jam disciplinæ et conversationis admittunt novitatem correctionis, operante scilicet et proficiente usque in finem gratia Dei*[7]: "There is only one rule of faith, which alone is immoveable, and not to be altered, to wit, to believe in one God the omnipotent Creator of the world, and in his Son Jesus Christ, born of the virgin Mary, crucified under Pontius Pilate, risen the third day from the dead, received into heaven, sitting now at the right hand of the Father, and shall come to judge the quick and the dead, by the resurrection of the flesh: this law of faith remaining, the other things of discipline, and trade of life, do admit alteration of amendment, the grace of God working and profiting to the end."

Cyprian, *Lib. i. Epist.* 12, mentioneth certain rites about Cyprian. baptism no where spoken of in the scriptures[8]; and, *Lib. iv.* Idem. *Epist.* 6, he sheweth it to have been the manner of the church then to receive the communion every day; which the scripture doth not command[9].

Thus you see that these doctors be not dumb, but can

[[6] Id. ibid.]

[[7] Regula &c. in unicum Deum omnipotentem, mundi conditorem, et Filium ejus Jesum Christum, natum ex virgine Maria, crucifixum sub Pontio Pilato, tertia die resuscitatum a mortuis, receptum in cœlis, sedentem nunc ad dexteram Patris, venturum judicare vivos et mortuos per carnis etiam resurrectionem. Hac &c.—Id. De Virg. Vel. l. p. 192.]

[[8] Sed et ipsa interrogatio quæ fit in baptismo testis est veritatis. Nam cum dicimus, Credis in vitam æternam, et remissionem peccatorum per sanctam ecclesiam? intelligimus remissionem peccatorum non nisi in ecclesia dari; &c. Ungi quoque necesse est eum, qui baptizatus sit, ut accepto chrismate, id est, unctione, esse unctus Dei...possit. &c.—Cypr. Op. Oxon. 1682. Ad Episc. Num. Epist. lxx. p. 190.]

[[9] ...considerantes iccirco se quotidie calicem sanguinis Christi bibere, ut possint et ipsi propter Christum sanguinem fundere.—Id. ad Pleb. Thibar. Epist. lviii. p. 120.]

speak sufficiently in that matter for the which they are alleged. And, lest you should cavil because I say that others also be of the same judgment, reciting only St Augustine, I have caused Ambrose, Jerome, and Basil, to bear witness in the same matter. The words of Ambrose be these: "After that churches were appointed in every place, and offices ordained, the matter began otherwise to be ordered, &c." And, after that he had declared the difference betwixt the apostolical church, and the church in his time, touching ceremonies and government, he concludeth thus: "Therefore do not the writings of the apostles in all respects agree with the order which is now in the church, because these were written in the first beginnings[1]." Jerome, writing *ad Lucinium*, and answering his questions touching fasting on the sabbath-day, and daily receiving the communion, saith on this sort: *Sed ego illud te breviter admonendum puto, traditiones ecclesiasticas (præsertim quæ fidei non officiant) ita observandas, ut a majoribus traditæ sunt; nec aliorum consuetudinem aliorum contrario modo subverti*[2]: "But this thing I think meet briefly to admonish thee of, that the ecclesiastical traditions (namely, such as do not hinder faith) are so to be observed as they are delivered of our elders; neither is the custom of one to be overthrown with the contrary custom of others."

Basil, in his 63. Epistle, written to the ministers of Neocæsaria, reciteth the manners and customs about public prayers and singing of psalms then used in the church, and there plainly declareth what his judgment is touching this question[3]. I omit that which he speaketh of this matter in his book *De Sancto Spiritu*, where although he giveth too much authority to unwritten traditions, yet doth it there appear that many things were then used in the church of

[1 Tamen postquam in omnibus locis ecclesiæ sunt constitutæ, et officia ordinata, aliter composita res est quam cœperat. Primum enim omnes docebant, et omnes baptizabant, &c. Ideo non per omnia conveniunt scripta apostoli ordinationi, quæ nunc in ecclesia est; quia hæc inter ipsa primordia sunt scripta. —Ambros. Op. Par. 1686-90. Comm. in Epist. ad Ephes. cap. iv. vv. 11, 12. Tom. II. Append. col. 241. These commentaries are not really by Ambrose.]

[2 Hieron. Op. Par. 1693-1706. Ad Lucin. Epist. lii. Tom. IV. Pars II. col. 579; where *breviter te*, and *nec aliarum consuetudinem aliarum contrario more subverti*.]

[3 Basil. Op. Par. 1721-30. Ad Cler. Neoc. Epist. ccvii. 2, 3, 4. Tom. III. pp. 310, &c.]

Christ which were not expressed in the word of God[4]. I might here allege Socrates, who in his fifth book and 22. chapter of his Ecclesiastical History handleth this matter at large; and speaking of Easter he saith: "The apostle and the gospel do in no place lay a bond of servitude upon them which come to the preaching; but men themselves have every one, according as they thought meet, in their countries celebrated of custom the feast of Easter, and other feasts for the resting from labour, and the remembrance of the healthful passion, &c." And in the same chapter: "No religion observeth the same rites, although it embrace the same doctrine of them; for they do differ among themselves in rites which are of the same faith[5]." And so he proceedeth in declaring the variety of ceremonies and other observances and rites in the churches; whereby it is manifest that (by his judgment) many things are committed to the disposition of the church, which are not expressed in the word of God. And that the church hath used this liberty from time to time, to the same effect speaketh Sozomen, *Lib. vii. cap.* 19: "They (he meaneth Polycarpus and Victor) thought it folly (and not without cause) to be separated one from another for ceremonies or customs, which did agree in the principal points of religion; for you cannot find the same rites and altogether like in all churches, no, though they do agree together[6]." I might pester this book (and that you know well enough) with the judgment of all the ancient fathers that have any occasion to speak of this matter; but these may suffice to declare that I have not vainly used their names for mutes "on the stage."

Socrates

Sozomen.

Touching councils, I marvel you will make any doubt of them: whereunto tend the most of their canons, in matters of ceremonies, and government of the church, but to teach that

Councils of things indifferent.

[4 Id. Lib. de Spir. Sanct. cap. xxvii. Tom. III. pp. 54, &c.]

[5 ...οὐδαμοῦ τοίνυν ὁ ἀπόστολος, οὐδὲ τὰ εὐαγγέλια, ζυγὸν δουλείας τοῖς τῷ κηρύγματι προσελθοῦσιν ἐπέθηκαν...ὅθεν ἐπειδὴ φιλοῦσι τὰς ἑορτὰς οἱ ἄνθρωποι, διὰ τὸ ἀνίεσθαι τῶν πόνων ἐν αὐταῖς, ἕκαστοι κατὰ χώρας ὡς ἐβουλήθησαν, τὴν μνήμην τοῦ σωτηριώδους πάθους ἐξ ἔθους τινὸς ἐπετέλεσαν...οὐδεμία τῶν θρησκειῶν τὰ αὐτὰ ἔθη φυλάττει, κἂν τὴν αὐτοῦ περὶ τούτων δόξαν ἀσπάζηται· καὶ γὰρ οἱ τῆς αὐτῆς πίστεως ὄντες διαφωνοῦσι περὶ τὰ ἔθη πρὸς ἑαυτούς· κ. τ. λ.—Socr. in Hist. Eccles. Script. Amst. 1695-1700. Lib. v. cap. xxii. pp. 232, 4.]

[6 ...εὔηθες γὰρ καὶ μάλα δικαίως ὑπέλαβον ἐθῶν ἕνεκεν ἀλλήλων χωρίζεσθαι, περὶ τὰ καίρια τῆς θρησκείας συμφωνοῦντες· οὐ γὰρ δὴ τὰς αὐτὰς παραδόσεις περὶ πάντα ὁμοίας, κἂν ὁμόδοξοι εἶεν, ἐν πάσαις ταῖς ἐκκλησίαις εὑρεῖν ἐστιν.—Soz. in eod. Lib. VII. cap. xix. p. 595.]

the scriptures have not expressed all things concerning the same, but left them to the order and appointment of the church? I pray you, where shall you find in the scripture the 13. Canon *Ancyrani Conc., De vicariis episcoporum et eorum potestate*[1]? or the 15., *Non debere presbyteros ecclesiastica jura vendere*[2]; and divers others in the same council? or the 11. Canon *Concil. Neocæsari.*, of the certain age of him that ought to be minister[3]? or the 1. Canon *Concil. Nicæni*, of eunuchs? the fourth, of ordering bishops? the sixth, of metropolitans? the seventh, of the bishop of Jerusalem? the twentieth, of standing in the time of prayer[4]? or the 7. *Canon Concil. Gangren.*, or the 18. or 20.[5]? or the 11. 15. 18. 19. &c. *Concil. Arelatens.*[6]? But what should I trouble the reader with such particular rehearsals of so many councils, which have made such a number of canons concerning such matters as must be ordered in the church, whereof the scripture hath particularly determined nothing? Is it not therefore manifest that councils, both general and provincial, by their acts declare that touching ceremonies, discipline, and government of the church, many things are left to the discretion of the church which be not expressed in the scriptures?

And, whereas you charge me for not alleging of scriptures, if I would without discretion cite places nothing pertaining to the purpose, as you hitherto have done, I could use a number; but I had rather have one text to my purpose than a hundred wrong and wrested, as yours be. How-

[1 Χωρεπισκόπους μὴ ἐξεῖναι πρεσβυτέρους ἢ διακόνους χειροτονεῖν, ἀλλὰ μηδὲ πρεσβυτέρους πόλεως, χωρὶς τοῦ ἐπιτραπῆναι ὑπὸ τοῦ ἐπισκόπου μετὰ γραμμάτων, ἐν ἑτέρᾳ παροικίᾳ.—Concil. Ancyr. can. 13. in Concil. Stud. Labb. et Cossart. Lut. Par. 1671-2. Tom. I. col. 1461.]

[2 Περὶ τῶν διαφερόντων τῷ κυριακῷ, ὅσα ἐπισκόπου μὴ ὄντος πρεσβύτεροι ἐπώλησαν, ἀναβαλεῖσθαι τὸ κυριακόν. ἐν δὲ τῇ κρίσει τοῦ ἐπισκόπου εἶναι, εἴπερ προσήκει ἀπολαβεῖν τὴν τιμὴν, εἴτε καὶ μή· διὰ τὸ πολλάκις τὴν εἴσοδον τῶν πεπραμένων ἀποδεδωκέναι αὐτοῖς τούτοις πλείονα τὴν τιμήν.—Can. 15. ibid.]

[3 Πρεσβύτερος πρὸ τῶν τριάκοντα ἐτῶν μὴ χειροτονείσθω, κ. τ. λ.—Concil. Neoc. can. 11. ibid. col. 1484.]

[4 Concil. Nicen. cans. 1, 4, 6, 7, 20. ibid. Tom. II. cols. 28, 9, 32, 7, 40.]

[5 Concil. Gangr. cans. 7. 18, 20. ibid. cols. 417, 20. These canons are respectively, De fructibus in ecclesiam, et non alibi, dandis: Non debere die dominico jejunare: Communicandum in basilicis martyrum.]

[6 Concil. Arelat. cans. 11, 15, 18, 19. ibid. Tom. I. cols. 1428, 9. The titles of these are, De puellis quæ gentilibus junguntur: Ut diacones non offerant De diaconibus urbicis, ut sine presbyterorum conscientia nihil agant: Ut peregrinis episcopis locus sacrificandi detur.]

beit, there is no cause why you should as yet complain; for hitherto I have alleged more than you have answered. To the 1 Cor. xiv. (as yet unanswered) I may join that which the apostle saith, 1 Cor. xi., *Quemadmodum tradidi vobis instituta tenetis:* "You keep the ordinances as I delivered them to you." The which words Master Calvin expounding saith on this sort: "I do not deny but that there were some traditions of the apostles not written, but I do not grant them to have been taken as parts of doctrine, or necessary unto salvation. What then? even such as did pertain to order and policy. For we know that every church hath liberty to ordain and appoint such a form of government as is apt and profitable for it; because the Lord therein hath prescribed no certainty. So Paul, the first founder of the church of Corinth, did also frame it with honest and godly institutions, that all things might there be done decently and in order[7]." And that also which is in the end of the chapter: "Other things will I set in order when I come." Whereupon the same Master Calvin saith: "But let such toys pass; seeing that it is certain that Paul speaketh but of external comeliness, the which as it is put in the liberty of the church, so it is to be appointed according to the time, places, and persons[8]."

Indeed I glory not in words so much of the scriptures as you do; but I trust that I have as sure ground there for anything that I have affirmed as you have, and much more, else would I be sorry. It is not boasting of the scriptures in words, and falsely applying of them, that can carry away the matter with those that be learned and wise. You know what Master Calvin saith of the anabaptists in his book written against them: *Quia vero nulla specie illustriore seduci possunt miseri Christiani, &c.:* "But, because the

[7 Ego autem non nego quin aliquæ fuerint apostolorum traditiones non scriptæ: sed non concedo fuisse doctrinæ partes, nec de rebus ad salutem necessariis. Quid igitur? Quæ pertinerent ad ordinem et politiam. Scimus enim unicuique ecclesiæ liberum esse politiæ formam instituere sibi aptam et utilem; quia Dominus nihil certi præscripserit. Ita Paulus ecclesiæ Corinthiacæ primus fundator institutis quoque piis et honestis eam formaverat, ut decenter et ordine illic agerentur omnia, sicut præcipiet cap. 14.—Calvin. Op. Amst. 1667-71. Comm. in Epist. I. ad Cor. cap. xi. Tom. VII. p. 177.]

[8 Sed facessant tales nugæ: quum certum sit, Paulum nonnisi de externo decoro loqui: quod ut in libertate ecclesiæ positum est, ita pro temporum, locorum, hominum conditione constitui debet.—Id. ibid. p. 185.]

woful Christians, which with a zeal do follow God, cannot by any other more notable shew be seduced, than when the word of God is pretended; the anabaptists (against whom we write) have that evermore in their mouth, and always talk of it[1]." And yet in lawful matters, not expressed in the scriptures, I know not to whom we should resort, to know the use and antiquity of them, but to the councils, stories and doctors.

Why the anabaptists always pretended the word of God.

Augustine of things indifferent[2].

The opinion of St Augustine of things indifferent.

Chapter iii. The First Division.

Answer to the Admonition, Page 23, Sect. 1.

Augustine.

That notable learned father Augustine hath divers sayings touching this matter worthy to be noted. In his epistle *Ad Casulanum* lxxxvi. he saith thus: *In his ...rebus, de quibus nihil certi statuit scriptura divina, mos populi Dei, vel instituta majorum, pro lege tenenda sunt*[3] : "In those things wherein the holy scripture hath determined no certainty, the custom of the people of God, and the traditions or decrees of our forefathers, are to be holden for a law." Whereby it is manifest that those things may be retained in the church, which are not expressed in the scripture. In the same epistle he reporteth the answer that Ambrose made unto him, being demanded whether it were lawful to fast on the sabbath-day, or not to fast, seeing that among the churches there was some diversity in this point. *Quando hic sum,* saith he, *non jejuno sabbato; quando Romæ sum, jejuno sabbato: et ad quamcunque ecclesiam veneritis,...ejus morem servate, si pati scandalum non vultis aut facere*[5] : "When

Idem.[4]

[1 Quia &c. Christiani, qui zelo aliquo Deum sectantur, quam dum prætenditur verbum Dei: anabaptistæ, adversus quos nunc scribimus, ipsum perpetuo in ore habent, idque semper præfantur.—Id. Instr. adv. Anabapt. Tom. VIII. p. 356.]

[2 Ancient fathers of things indifferent, Answ. 2.]

[3 August. Op. Par. 1679-1700. Ad Casulan. Epist. xxxvi. cap. i. 2. Tom. II. col. 68.]

[4 This word is not in Answ. 2.]   [5 Id. ibid. cap. xiv. 32. col. 81.]

I am here, I fast not on the sabbath; when I am at Rome, I do fast on the sabbath; and, to what church soever you come, keep the custom thereof, if you will neither suffer offence nor give offence." The whole epistle is worthy of reading.

Augustine of things indifferent.

T. C. Page 17, Sect. 3, 4, 5, 6.

The answerer goeth about to prove that they came yet out of good earth, and from good men; which if he had obtained, yet he may well know that it is no good argument to prove that they are good. For, as the best earth bringeth forth weeds, so do the best men bring forth lies and errors. But let us hear what is brought, that, if this visard and shew of truth be taken away, all men may perceive how good occasion we have to complain, and how just cause there is of reformation. In the first place of St Augustine there is nothing against anything which we hold; for that[6], that the church may have things not expressed in the scripture, is not against, that it ought to have nothing but that may be warranted by the scripture: for they may be according to the scripture, and by the scripture, which are not by plain terms expressed in the scripture. But against you it maketh much, and overturneth all your building in this book. For, if in those things which are not expressed in the scripture they are to be observed of the church, which are the customs of the people of God and the decrees of[7] our forefathers; then how can these things be varied according to time, place, and persons (which you say should be), when as that is to be retained which the people of God hath used, and the decrees of the forefathers have ordained? And then also, how can we do safelier than to follow the apostles' customs, and the churches in their time, which we are sure are our forefathers and the people of God?

Besides that, how can we retain the customs and constitutions of the papists in such things, which were neither the people of God nor our forefathers?

I will not enter now to discuss, whether it were well done to fast in all places according to the custom of the place. You oppose Ambrose and Augustine: I could oppose Ignatius and Tertullian; whereof the one saith it is (nefas) *a detestable thing to fast upon the Lord's day[10]; the other that it is to kill the Lord[11]; and this is the inconvenience that cometh of such unlearned kind of reasoning: St Ambrose saith so; and therefore it is true.*

A true saying, but not truly applied.

But it is against that, that nothing should be placed in the church which God in his word hath not commanded; and therefore you do here but shift off the controversies[8].

Tertull. de Cor. Milit.[9] Ignat. ad Phi. Epist. v.[9]

Untruth, proceeding of ignorance.

[6 This, Repl. 2.]
[7 Scripture that is to be observed of the church which is the custom of the people of God and decree of, Repl. 2.]
[8 Controversy, Def. A.]
[9 These marginal references are not printed in Repl. 1.]
[10 Die Dominico jejunium nefas ducimus, vel de geniculis adorare.—Tertull. Op. Lut. 1641. De Coron. Mil. 3. p. 121.]
[11 Εἴ τις κυριακὴν ἢ σάββατον νηστεύει, πλὴν ἑνὸς σαββάτου τοῦ πάσχα, οὗτος χριστοκτόνος ἐστίν.—Ignat. Epist. ad Philip. 13. in Coteler. Patr. Apostol. Amst. 1724. Vol. II. p. 119. This epistle is spurious.]

Augustine of things indifferent.

And, although Ambrose and Augustine, being strangers and private men at Rome, would have so done, yet it followeth not that if they had been citizens and ministers there, that they would have done it; and, if they had done so too, yet it followeth not but that they[1] would have spoken against that appointment of days and νομοθεσίαν of fasting; whereof Eusebius saith that Montanus was the first author[2]. I speak of that which they ought to have done: for otherwise I know they both thought corruptly of fasting, when as the one saith: "*it was remedy or reward to fast other days, but in Lent not to fast was sin*[4];" and the other asketh, "*what salvation we can obtain if we blot not our sins by fasting, seeing that the scripture saith that fasting and alms doth deliver from sin,*" and therefore calleth them "*new teachers that shut out the merit of fasting*[5]:" which I therefore recite, because you would seem by Augustine' and Ambrose' judgments to allow of the weekly and commanded fasts.

xvii. chap. of the v. book.[3]
Aug. de Temp. Serm. 62.
Ambros. 10 Lib. Epist.

Jo. Whitgift.

I have sufficiently proved that the scripture hath not expressed all things that may be used in the church touching ceremonies, order, and such matters; for that is the question we have now in handling; and for further proof and confirmation of the same, I do not disdain the authority of any man, especially of Augustine, a man for his excellent learning and sound judgment in most points of religion esteemed of all that have any shew of learning or sparkle of modesty: his opinion of the sufficiency of the scripture in matters of salvation, of the authority of it in judging matters of controversy, is perfect and sound; as may be seen, *Lib. ii. adversus Cresc. Gramm.; Lib. iii. contra Maxim.; Lib. de Unitate Ecclesiæ; Lib. ii. de Doct. Christ.; Cap. 16 & 20 Evang. Johannis; Epist. 112*[6]; and in a number of places else. He speaketh

Augustine delivered from untrue surmises.

[1 But they, Repl. 1 and 2.]

[2 Οὗτός ἐστιν ὁ διδάξας λύσεις γάμων· ὁ νηστείας νομοθετήσας.—Euseb. in Hist. Eccles. Script. Amst. 1695-1700. Lib. v. cap. xviii. p. 149.]

[3 This reference is supplied from Repl. 1 and 2.]

[4 ...aliis diebus jejunare aut remedium aut præmium est; in quadragesima non jejunare peccatum est.—August. Op. Par. 1679-1700. Serm. cxlii. In Quadrag. iii. 1. Tom. V. Append. col. 252. This sermon is not by Augustine: it is most probably the work of Cæsarius.]

[5 Aut quæ nobis salus esse potest, nisi jejunio eluerimus peccata nostra; cum scriptura dicat, Jejunium et eleemosyna a peccato liberat? Qui sunt ergo hi præceptores novi, qui meritum excludant jejunii?—Ambros. Op. Par. 168-690. Epist. Class. I. Ad Vercell. Eccles. Epist. lxiii. 16, 17. Tom. II. col. 1026.]

[6 Neque enim sine caussa tam salubri vigilantia canon ecclesiasticus constitutus est, ad quem certi prophetarum et apostolorum libri pertinent, quos

also of ceremonies and traditions as moderately, as divinely, and as warely as any man doth; as it appeareth evidently in these places that I have in my Answer alleged. And therefore he is not with such contempt to be rejected, nor yet defaced with untrue surmises.

Augustine of things indifferent.

That which cometh from so good and learned a man is the rather to be believed, so long as it is not repugnant to the word of God. And, although " the best earth bringeth forth some weeds," yet the good fruit must not for the weeds' sake be refused. This is a very mean reason: good men sometimes err and be deceived; therefore they must never in anything be believed.

But to come to the purpose. You say that "this first place of St Augustine is nothing against anything that you hold, &c." Surely, and it maketh wholly for that which I hold: for it proveth directly that there be some things wherein the scripture hath not determined any certainty, but left them to the disposition of others; for he saith, *In his rebus de quibus nihil certi statuit scriptura divina, &c.;* and that these things be not such as be repugnant, or against the word of God, but according to the rule of St Paul, 1 Cor. xiv. (if you were not of purpose disposed against your own conscience and knowledge to abuse the reader), you might easily understand by my expressed words, uttered in this portion of my Answer, and in all other places where I have occasion to speak of the like matters.

I would wish you to deal sincerely. The question that we have now in hand is, "Whether the scripture hath expressed all external things touching the orders, ceremonies, and government of the church." I prove it hath not, both by the scripture itself, and by manifest examples, and by the judgment of the best-learned: you, not being able to answer, and yet desirous to seem to say somewhat to shift off these examples and authorities, dally at the matter, and would

The subtle dealing of T. C. in altering the state of the controversy.

omnino judicare non audeamus, et secundum quos de ceteris litteris vel fidelium vel infidelium libere judicemus.—August. Op. Contr. Crescon. Donatist. Lib. II. cap. xxxi. 39. Tom. IX. col. 430. Conf. Contr. Maxim. Arian. Lib. II. cap. xiv. 3. Tom. VIII. col. 704; Contr. Donat. Epist. seu Lib. de Unit. Eccles. cap. iii. 5, 6. Tom. IX. cols. 340, 1; De Doctr. Christ. Lib. II. cap. ix. 14. Tom. III. Pars I. col. 24; In Johan. Evang. cap. xvi. Tractat. xcvi. 1, 2, 3. Tom. III. Pars II. cols. 733, 4; Lib. ad Paulin. seu Epist. cxlvii. cap. xxiii. 54. Tom. II. col. 496. In the reference to John xx. there seems to be a mistake.]

Augustine of things indifferent. make your reader believe that I would have things used in the church contrary, or not " according to the scriptures ;" from the which opinion I am as far off as you, and a great way farther, except you revoke some points of your book. You should, therefore, now have kept you to the improving[1] of this general proposition ; and if hereafter, in speaking of particular matters, I had approved anything against the word of God, you might have spent your wit and eloquence in confuting of that.

You say that "this place of St Augustine maketh much against me, &c.;" but you are greatly deceived: for St Augustine in that place doth not give a certain rule to the whole church, but to particular men; for it is his answer to Casulanus demanding of him, *Utrum liceat sabbato jejunare.* A private man may not take upon him to violate the particular orders of any particular church, much less such orders as be observed of the whole church, except they be against the scriptures; for both in this, and such other rules of Augustine, that is generally to be observed which the same Augustine doth add Aug. Ep. 118. in his 118. epistle *ad Januarium : Quod neque contra fidem neque bonos mores injungitur, &c.*[2] And that this rule, *In his rebus de quibus nihil certi &c.*, is given to particular men to drive them from schisms and contentions in the church, it is evident by that which the same Augustine writeth in the end Idem. of that epistle *ad Casulanum:* "Wherefore, if you will willingly content yourself with my counsel (namely, which have in this cause, being by you required and constrained, spoken peradventure more than enough), do not resist your bishop herein, and follow that which he doth, without any scruple or doubt[3]." Wherefore, when St Augustine saith, *Mos populi Dei, &c.*, his meaning is, that they are to be observed as rules to keep private and particular men in order, and in quiet obedience to the church[4]: although indeed the church itself may not

---

[1 Improving : disproving.]

[2 Quod enim neque &c. neque contra bonos mores esse convincitur.—August. Op. Par. 1679-1700. Ad Inq. Januar. Lib. I. seu Epist. liv. cap. ii. 2. Tom. II. col. 124.]

[3 Quapropter si consilio meo, præsertim quia in hac caussa plus forte quam satis fuit, te petente atque urgente, loquutus sum, libenter adquiescis ; episcopo tuo in hac re noli resistere, et quod facit ipse, sine ullo scrupulo vel disceptatione sectare.—Id. ad Casulan. Epist. xxxvi. cap. xiv. 32. Tom. II. col. 81.]

[4 Cartwright rejoins that Whitgift "condemneth himself of having alleged

without just cause change such things as have been generally observed, not being *contra fidem et bonos mores*, "against faith and good manners," "as the Lord's day, the day of the resurrection, ascension," and such like. And there may be just causes why things once determined by the church should not be changed afterwards, though before the same things were arbitrary, and might have been otherwise, and in some other manner decreed, as the church had thought most convenient. If no such causes be, it may alter any use, ceremony, or order, which it hath before determined; as St Augustine himself declareth, *Epist.* 118. *ad Januarium*: *His enim causis, id est, propter fidem aut propter mores, vel emendari oportet quod perperam fiebat, vel institui quod non fiebat. Ipsa quippe mutatio consuetudinis etiam, quæ adjuvat utilitate, novitate perturbat*[5]: "For these causes, that is to say, for faith and good manners, either that must be amended which was evil done, or appointed which was not done; for even that change of custom, which helpeth through profit, doth trouble through novelty."

{Augustine of things indifferent. The church may not alter any order generally observed, without just cause. Idem.}

Now how true this collection of yours is—Augustine prescribeth this rule to Casulanus, that, "in those things wherein the scripture hath determined no certainty, he should follow the custom of the people of God and the decrees of our forefathers," that is, that he should use himself in those things that be not against faith and good manners according to the order of the churches where he cometh; therefore these customs upon just cause may not be altered by the church— let the learned reader judge. A private man (as I said) may not break the lawful and good orders of the church, though they be not expressed in the word of God; yet may such as God hath given that authority unto in his church alter and change them as shall be most expedient, even according to this rule of Augustine (*his enim causis, id est, aut propter fidem aut propter mores, vel emendari oportet quod perperam fiebat, vel institui quod non fiebat, &c.*) before by me recited.

We must follow such "customs of the apostles" and ex- {What examples and}

that sentence clean beside the cause. For it is manifest by the words immediately going before that he alleged it to prove the authority of the church in things indifferent."—Sec. Repl. p. 82.]

[5 August. Op. Ad Inq. Januar. Lib. I. seu Epist. liv. cap. v. 6. Tom. II. col. 126; where *aut propter fidem.*]

Augustine of things indifferent.

customs of the apostles we must follow.

amples, as they have used and done for us to follow; but such customs or doings of the apostles as were either peculiar unto themselves, or convenient only for such times as they were in, we are not compelled to follow. For, as in the scriptures there be some precepts general, some only personal, so are there in the same of examples and orders some that for ever are to be observed, and some for a time only: and that there were such customs and orders among them, shall be declared in several places, as occasion is ministered.

Tract. vii.

Whether we have received, or may "retain, customs, &c. of the papists," or no, is partly to be discussed where I speak of apparel, and partly in other places, where more particular occasion is offered to speak of the same; and therefore I will pass it over until I come to those places. "Whether it were well done to[1] fast in all places according to the custom of the place," or no, is not the question.

I look to Augustine's meaning and purpose, not to every one of his examples: howbeit I think that there is a great difference betwixt the manner of fasting used then in the church, and the manner of fasting used now in some churches. I think that in Augustine's time a man might have observed this rule of fasting without any offence to God. But I do not think that he may do so in like manner now; because it is certain that in the church of Rome there are many wicked opinions, both of differences of meats, times, &c., and also of merit joined to their fasting, and therefore are *contra fidem et bonos mores,* and so not within the compass of this rule of St Augustine.

The replier setteth the fathers together by the ears, without cause.

I perceive no repugnancy at all betwixt Ambrose, Augustine, Ignatius, and Tertullian. For the sabbath-day mentioned by Ambrose and Augustine is not the "Lord's day," which we call the Sunday, and whereof both Ignatius and Tertullian speak; but it is the Saturday, which is called *Sabbatum.* And that this is true, you might have read in the same epistle of Augustine to Casulanus, where he saith

Ibidem.

thus: "Whereas you ask of me, whether it be lawful to fast on the sabbath-day, I answer, if it were by no means lawful, truly neither Moses, nor Helias, nor our Lord himself, would have fasted forty days together. But by this reason it is concluded that the fast on the Lord's day is lawful also:

[1 So, Def. B.]

notwithstanding, whosoever doth think that this day ought to be dedicated unto fasting, as some do observe the sabbath fasting, he shall give no small offence to the church[2]." And after in the same epistle: "And truly of the sabbath-day the case is more easy; because the church of Rome doth fast, and some other also, although but few either of those that be next, or far from it. But to fast on the Lord's day is a great offence, especially since that detestable heresy of the Manichees, which is much repugnant to the catholic faith, and most manifestly contrary to the scriptures of God, hath been openly known, which do appoint unto their hearers this day as lawful to be fasted; whereby it is come to pass that the fast on the Lord's day is accounted more horrible[3]." You see therefore how you may be deceived for all the great reading you would seem to be of: for these fathers agree among themselves; and you have faulted in "opposing them to Augustine and Ambrose:" so that, for anything that is yet proved against them, a man may well use their authority in such matters without that inconvenience that you suppose; for I know how far they themselves would be believed, and whereunto their authority extendeth[4].

It is like that both Ambrose and Augustine would have done that themselves, which they moved other men unto, and much more being "citizens," than "being strangers:" it is also like that, if they had been "ministers" there, they would have in time and place reproved such things as were amiss; for it had been their duty so to do: yet do I likewise think that they would have had great respect to that advertisement that Augustine gave to Casulanus in that epistle in these

Augustine of things indifferent.

[2 Quod ergo me consulis, utrum liceat sabbato jejunare: Respondeo, si nullo modo liceret, profecto quadraginta continuos dies nec Moyses, nec Elias, nec ipse Dominus jejunasset. Verum ista ratione concluditur, etiam Dominico die non illicitum esse jejunium. Et quisquis tamen hunc diem jejunio decernendum putaverit, sicut quidam jejunantes sabbatum observant, non parvo scandalo erit ecclesiæ; nec immerito.—Id. ad Casulan. Epist. xxxvi. cap. i. 2. Tom. II. col. 68.]

[3 Et de die quidem sabbati facilior caussa est, quia et Romana jejunat ecclesia, et aliæ nonnullæ, etiamsi paucæ, sive illi proximæ sive longinquæ: die autem Dominico jejunare scandalum est magnum, maxime posteaquam innotuit detestabilis multumque fidei catholicæ scripturisque divinis apertissime contraria hæresis Manichæorum, qui suis auditoribus ad jejunandum istum tanquam constituerunt legitimum diem; per quod factum est, ut jejunium diei Dominici horribilius haberetur.—Id. ibid. cap. xii. 27. col. 78.]

[4 Cartwright persists in his rejoinder that he is right in imputing repugnancy between the fathers.—Sec. Repl. pp. 82, 3.]

Augustine words: *Utique cavendum est, ne tempestate contentionis serenitas caritatis obnubiletur*[1]: "Verily we must take heed lest in the storm of contention the fairness of love be darkened."

Augustine of things indifferent. Ibidem.

The errors which Ambrose or Augustine had must not prejudice their authority in speaking truly. This is but a very simple kind of answering, to deny the author where he speaketh truly, because in some other place he hath erred and been deceived. I neither allege Ambrose nor Augustine, "to allow" or disallow "weekly and commanded fasts;" but to prove the matter that I have in hand, which is, that the scripture hath not expressed all things used in the church. Howbeit, I know nothing in this place affirmed either by Ambrose or Augustine touching fasting, which may not be observed without just offence[2].

Chapter iii. The Second Division.

Answer to the Admonition, Page 23, Sect. 2.

That which he writeth in his epistle *ad Januarium*, 118, is a most plain declaration of his judgment in this matter: *Illa autem quæ non scripta sed tradita custodimus, quæ quidem toto terrarum orbe observantur, dantur intelligi, vel ab ipsis apostolis, vel plenariis conciliis, quorum est in ecclesia saluberrima auctoritas, commendata atque statuta retineri, sicuti quod Domini passio, et resurrectio, et ascensio in cœlum, et adventus de cœlo Spiritus sancti anniversaria solemnitate celebrantur, et si quid aliud tale occurrerit, quod servatur ab universa quacunque se diffundit ecclesia*[4]: "Those things, which be not written, but kept by tradition, which are observed through the whole world, are to be understanded either to be delivered unto us from the apostles themselves, or else decreed by general councils, whose authority is great in the church; as that

Aug. Ep. 118.[3]

[1 August. Op. Par. 1679-1700. Ad Casulan. Epist. xxxvi. cap. i. 2. Tom. II. col. 68; where *serenitatem caritatis* [interminata luctatio] *obnubilet*.]

[2 Cartwright accuses Whitgift of misrepresenting him here: "Where he bringeth me in concluding that, because the ancient fathers erred in some things, therefore they said true in none; my words carry no such sense."—Sec. Repl. p. 84.]

[3 This marginal reference is not in Answ. 2.]

[4 August. Op. Ad Inq. Januar. Lib. i. seu Epist. liv. cap. i. 1. Tom. II. col. 124; where *orbe servantur datur intelligi*, and *tale occurrit*.]

we yearly with solemnity celebrate the passion of the Lord, and his resurrection, his ascension into heaven, and the coming of the Holy Ghost; and if there be any other thing that is observed of the whole church." *[margin: Augustine of things indifferent.]*

T. C. Page 18, Line 1, and Sect. 1, 2, 3, 4.

What you mean to cite this place ad Januarium, 118, I cannot tell. You charge the authors of the Admonition to be conspired with the papists: I will not charge you so, but will think better of you until the contrary do more appear.

But I appeal to the judgment of all men, if this be not to bring in popery again, to allow of St Augustine's saying, wherein he saith, that the celebrating of the day of the passion, &c., is either of some general council, or of the apostles commanded and decreed; whereby a gate is open unto the papists to bring in, under the colour of traditions, all their beggary whatsoever. For you plainly confirm that there is something necessary to be observed which is not contained any ways in the scripture. For to keep those holy days is not contained in the scripture, neither can be concluded of any part thereof; and yet they are necessary to be kept, if they be commanded of the apostles. Therefore in your opinion something is necessary to be kept which is not contained in the scriptures, nor cannot be concluded of them. And, if you say that St Augustine leaveth it in doubt whether it were the apostles' tradition and statute, or a general council's, then you bring us yet to a worse point, that we cannot be assured of that which is necessary for us to know, that is, whether the apostles did ordain that these days should be kept as holy days, or the councils. And that it is St Augustine's meaning to father such like things of apostles[5], it may appear by that which he writeth, saying: _{Sermo 7. de Baptis. cont. Donatist. lib. v. cap. 23.7} *"There are many things which the whole church holdeth, and therefore are well believed to be commanded of the apostles, although they be not found written[6]." If this judgment of St Augustine be a good judgment, and a sound, then there be some things commanded of God which are not in the scriptures; and therefore there is no sufficient doctrine contained in the scriptures, whereby we may be saved. For all the commandments of God, and of the apostles, are needful for our salvation.* *[margin: Not one whit, but the contrary shall be proved. A pretty and sound collection.[8] A great untruth and absurdity.]*

And mark, I pray you, whither your affections carry you. Before you said that the Lord's day, which was used for the day of rest in the apostles' *[margin: Nay, mark how your affections move you to speak untruly.]*

[5 Of the apostles, Repl. 2.]

[6 ...sicut sunt multa quæ universa tenet ecclesia, et ob hoc ab apostolis præcepta bene creduntur, quamquam scripta non reperiantur.—Id. de Bapt. contr. Donatist. Lib. v. cap. xxiii. 31. Tom. IX. col. 156.]

[7 This marginal reference is not printed in Repl. 1; Repl. 2 has *Tom.* 7.]

[8 Cartwright on this says: "...the soundness of the collection is apparent to all which will open their eyes. And because the answerer will yield no obedience unto the truth, unless she taking him by the collar have her hand upon his throat, &c."—Sec. Repl. pp. 84, 5.]

Augustine of things indifferent. time, *may be changed, as the place and hour of prayer; and*[1] *the day of the passion and resurrection, &c., you either thrust upon us as the decree of the apostles, or at least put upon us a necessity of keeping of them, lest happily*[2] *in breaking of them we might break the apostles' decree; for you make it to lie between the councils and the apostles, which of them decreed this.*

And do you not perceive how you still reason against yourself? For, if the church have had so great regard to that which the apostles did in their times, that they kept those things which are not written, and therefore are doubtful whether ever they used them or no; how much more should we hold ourselves to these things which are written that they did, and of the which we are assured!

As touching the observation of these holy days, I will refer the reader unto another place, where occasion is given again to speak of them.

Jo. Whitgift.

The rule of St Augustine doth not establish, but overthrow popery.

My meaning therein I have set down in my Answer. It is to let you understand St Augustine's judgment in the matter we have in hand. The rule is true and good, and so far from establishing any piece of popery, that it rather quite overthroweth the same.

By it we may prove the supremacy, which the bishop of Rome claimeth over all churches, neither to be written in the word, nor yet to be appointed by the apostles, nor yet determined by ancient general councils; for neither hath he been always, nor in all places, taken to be the head of the church. And it is manifest that Phocas, the traitor and murderer, gave first unto him and his church that prerogative[3], and therefore not left unto him by the apostles, nor given him by the general councils. The like may be said of all other things used in the church against the word of God. For it is certain that they have not been generally observed in all places, and at all times; and, if some of them have been so observed, yet not in that manner and form that the church of Rome doth now observe them. So that you find fault with this rule before you have cause. Master Zuinglius (who would have been loth one whit to strengthen the papists), speaking of the like place of St Augustine, in his book *de Baptismo*, saith thus: "But, leaving those things, let us return to the words of Augustine, who among other things addeth this: *Quanquam quod universa tenet ecclesia nec conciliis institutum, sed semper retentum*

Zuingl. de Baptis. of the rule of Aug.

[1 But, Repl. 2.] [2 Haply, Repl. 2.]
[3 See Plat. De Vit. Pont. Col. 1551. Bonifac. III. p. 75.]

est, non nisi auctoritate apostolica traditum rectissime cre- Augustine *ditur, &c.:* "Let these words," saith he, "prevail with other men as they may, yet no man can deny but that there lieth great weight of authority in them. For, if there be nothing in councils concluded of the baptizing of infants, and yet the same was universally of the whole church observed in Augustine's time; what other things can be gathered, but that it hath always been used without contradiction[4]?" Master Calvin also, *Lib. Insti. cap. xiii. sect.* 21, useth this rule of Augustine to the same purpose, where he, speaking of popish traditions, for the which they abuse the authority of Augustine, saith thus: *Ego vero non aliunde quam ex ipsius Augustini verbis solutionem afferam. Quæ toto, inquit, terrarum orbe servantur, vel ab ipsis apostolis, vel conciliis generalibus, quorum est in ecclesia saluberrima auctoritas, statuta esse intelligere licet*[5]: "Verily I will fetch a solution from no other place than from the very words of Augustine. 'Those things,' saith he, 'which are observed throughout the whole world are understood to have been instituted either of the apostles themselves, or of general councils, &c.';" as it is in the Answer to the Admonition.

I know no reason why the apostles may not be said to be the authors of "celebrating the day of the passion, &c." Neither yet do I understand any cause why the church may not still observe the same: sure I am that they were not the authors of the superstitions and errors used in them by the papists; neither doth Augustine say so; for this is no good argument to say, The apostles appointed these days to be celebrated; *ergo*, they appointed the manner of celebrating used by the papists. The days may be with more godliness and profit to the church observed (being cleansed from superstition and erroneous doctrine) than abrogated. Neither is this "to

[4 Ceterum omissis his ad Augustini verba revertamur, qui inter alia et hoc addit, Quanquam &c. creditur. Valeant verba hæc apud alios quantum possunt; magnum tamen in ipsis auctoritatis pondus latere nemo non animadvertit. Si enim in conciliis de parvulorum baptismo nihil unquam tractatum nihilque statutum est, interim vero Augustini seculo ab universa ecclesia receptus in usu fuit, non equidem aliud hinc colligi potest, quam eundem illum semper fuisse irrefragabilem.—H. Zvingl. Op. Tigur. 1581. De Bapt. Lib. Tract. III. Pars II. fol. 94.2. Conf. August. Op. Par. 1679-1700. De Bapt. contr. Donatist. Lib. IV. cap. xxiv. 31. Tom. IX. col. 140.]

[5 Calvin. Op. Amst. 1667-71. Inst. Lib. IV. cap. x. 19. Tom. IX. p. 320; where *saluberrima in ecclesia*.]

Augustine of things indifferent.
open a gate to papistical traditions," but to shut it close up[1], as I have said before. For let the papists (if they can) name any wicked thing used in their church, which either hath been generally observed, or whereof I am not able to shew the first author and inventor[2].

Neither Augustine in this place, nor I in any place, have said or "confirmed any thing not contained in the scripture, to be so necessary to be observed," that (upon just consideration) it may not be altered by such as have authority[3]. And therefore all that you do say, have said, or shall say to that effect, is forged, and untrue, devised only by you as a shift to flee[4] unto, when otherwise you are to seek for answer.

To these your words, "they are necessary to be kept if they be commanded by the apostles" (meaning such things as Augustine speaketh of), I answer with M. Calvin, who, as I told you before, writing upon these words, 1 Cor. xi. *Quemadmodum tradidi vobis*, &c., doth grant that "there were some traditions of the apostles not written," but he denieth them "to be taken as parts of doctrine, or necessary to salvation," saying that "they be only such as pertain to order and policy[5]."

The rest of this section of yours is nothing but *petitio principii*. For neither do I move any such doubt in Augustine's words; neither is it material whether I do, or no; neither yet is it true that there "is any thing commanded of God, or of the apostles," as necessary to salvation, which is not contained in the word of God; neither are these and such like traditions "parts of doctrine and of salvation" (as M. Calvin truly saith), but "of order and policy."

A gross error of T. C.
Who would think that any man (except he had hardened his face without blushing to affirm untruths) would have fallen into such gross absurdities, and uttered such strange assertions void of all truth? Have you ever read in scripture, or in the writings of any learned man, or can you by reason prove

[1 "...the door is not so close shut against corruptions as he pretendeth."—Sec. Repl. p. 87.]
[2 "...it is well the church standeth not in need of this defence of yours."—Ibid. p. 88.]
[3 Cartwright accuses Whitgift here of mocking the world "with fast and loose at his pleasure."—Ibid. p. 85.]
[4 Fly, Def. A.]
[5 Calvin. Op. Comm. in Epist. i. ad Cor. cap. xi. v. 2. Tom. VII. p. 177. See before, page 221, note 7.]

this paradox, that "all the commandments of God and of the apostles are needful for our salvation?" ^{Augustine of things indifferent.}
What is to lay an intolerable yoke and burden upon the necks of men, if this be not? or whereby could you more directly bring us into the bondage of the law, from the which "we are made free," than by this assertion? For, if "all the commandments of God, &c. are needful for our salvation," then must we be bound, upon necessity of salvation, to observe the whole ceremonial law, which was the commandment of God. What? was the commandment unto Abraham, to offer his son Isaac; unto the Israelites, to rob the Egyptians; unto Moses, to put off his shoes; unto Saul, to kill Amalech, and infinite other, "needful for our salvation?" is the commandment of the apostles, to "abstain from blood, and that which is strangled;" or of Paul unto Timothy, to drink wine, &c. "needful for our salvation?" What a torment is this doctrine able to bring unto a weak conscience, which hath not observed any one of these! You must therefore understand that there are divers kinds of "commandments of God, and of the apostles," some general, and given to all; other personal, and pertain only to one singular person, or to one nation and kind of people, &c. Again, there are some which are perpetual, and not to be omitted or altered; other which are temporal, and may be omitted or altered, as the circumstance of time, place, and persons doth require. Whereby it may appear how grossly you have erred in affirming that "all the commandments of God, and of the apostles, are needful for our salvation." I might in more ample manner prosecute this matter; but this that hath been spoken may suffice[6]. ^{Gal. v.} ^{Gen. xxii.} ^{Exod. xi. Exod. ii. 1 Sam. xv.} ^{Acts xv.} ^{1 Tim. v.} ^{Divers kinds of commandments.}

What I have said "of changing the Lord's day," and how you have satisfied my words, is declared before; and so is the answer made likewise unto this your feeble conclusion, grounded upon a false principle.

Which of us two is "carried" furthest by his "affections," let the indifferent reader judge by these and such other like dealings of yours.

[6 "...when I speak of all the commandments of God and of the apostles, neither by the deduction of that which I handled, nor by any judgment not altogether perverted, could I be thought to mean any other commandments than those which pertain unto us....For the ceremonial law, and personal laws given in times past (being now no commandments of God, and the apostles), cannot be comprehended under my words of 'the commandments of God &c.' "—Sec. Repl. p. 89.]

Augustine of things indifferent. I have told you before how much this and the other places of St Augustine maketh for my purpose[1]; which you cannot but understand, if you sought not corners to creep into, for the avoiding of such reasons and authorities as be most apt for my purpose.

"Things which the apostles have done," for us to follow, without any exception may not be violated: but the question is, whether these things, which they have done and written, be sufficient for the ordering and government of all churches, in all times and states, or no; and whether in all things that they have done we may or ought to follow them: both which you have hitherto very slenderly touched.

Chapter iii. The Third Division.

Answer to the Admonition, Page 24, Sect. 1, 2, 3, and Page 25, Sect. 1.

And again, *Quod...neque contra fidem neque contra bonos mores injungitur, indifferenter est habendum, et pro eorum inter quos vivitur societate servandum est*[2]: "That which is enjoined, being neither against faith nor good manners, is to be counted indifferent, and to be observed, as the society of those with whom we live requireth."

In the same epistle, answering this question (whether upon the Thursday before Easter the Lord's supper should be celebrated in the morning, or at night, because Christ did institute this sacrament, and deliver the same to his disciples after supper), he giveth these three rules worthy to be noted. The first is this: "If the holy scripture prescribe any thing to be done, there is no doubt but that must be observed as it is there prescribed." The second is this: "That, if any thing be universally observed of the whole church" (not repugnant to the scriptures), for so he meaneth, "not to keep that, or to reason of that, is madness." The third: "If it be not

[1] See before, page 225.]
[2] August. Op. Par. 1679-1700. Ad Inq. Januar. Lib. I. seu Epist. liv. cap. ii. 2. Tom. II. col. 124; where *mores esse convincitur, propter eorum*, and *societatem*.]

universally observed, but diversly in divers churches, *faciat quisque quod in ea ecclesia in quam venit invenerit:* Let every man do as he findeth in that church into the which he cometh; *modo non sit contra fidem aut contra mores:* so that it be not against faith or good manners³;" for so he addeth.

Augustine of things indifferent.

In the same epistle again he saith, that the Lord hath not in scripture declared in what order and manner his supper should be celebrated, but left that to his disciples⁴. And in his hundred and nineteenth *ad Januar.:* "In those things," saith he, "that be diversly observed in divers places, this rule as most profitable is to be kept, that those things which be not against faith neither good manners, and make something to exhort unto a better life, wheresoever they are instituted, we ought not only not to disallow them, but to praise them, and to follow them⁵." By all these places of this learned father it is evident that it hath been received from time to time as a certain truth, that the church of Christ hath authority to ordain and constitute, as shall be necessary, in those things before of me rehearsed.

For a further proof hereof I could allege that ancient and learned father, Justinus Martyr, in his second Apology *pro Christianis,* and in his Book of Questions; Tertullian, in his book *De Corona Militis;* Basil also in his 63. epistle, written to the ministers of⁷ Neocæsarea; Eusebius, *Lib. v. Ecclesiast. Hist. cap.* 25 and 26⁸; and divers other; but I omit them for brevity' sake:

Justinus Martyr.

Tertull.⁶
Basil.⁶

Euseb.⁶

[³ Ad hæc itaque ita respondeo, &c. See before, page 202, note 1...Restat igitur ut de illo tertio genere sit, quod per loca regionesque variatur. Faciat ergo quisque &c. invenerit. Non enim quidquam eorum contra fidem fit, aut contra mores, hinc vel inde meliores.—Id. ibid. cap. v. 6. col. 126.]

[⁴ Et ideo non præcepit quo deinceps ordine sumeretur, ut apostolis, per quos ecclesias dispositurus erat, servaret hunc locum.—Id. ibid. cap. vi. 8. col. 127.]

[⁵ Miror sane quid ita volueris, ut de iis, quæ varie per diversa loca observantur, tibi aliqua scriberem, cum et non sit necessarium, et una in his saluberrima regula retinenda sit, ut quæ non sunt contra fidem neque contra bonos mores, et habent aliquid ad exhortationem vitæ melioris, ubicumque institui videmus, vel instituta cognoscimus, non solum non improbemus, sed etiam laudando et imitando sectemur, si aliquorum infirmitas non ita impedit, ut amplius detrimentum sit.—Id. ibid. Lib. II. seu Epist. lv. cap. xviii. 34. cols. 141, 2.]

[⁶ The first and third of these marginal references are not in Answ. 2; which has *Basil. Epist.* 63. *ad &c.*]

[⁷ In, Answ.]   [⁸ See before, pages 215, 16, 18.]

Augustine of things indifferent. neither do I allege those[1] learned fathers because I think their authority any thing at all prevaileth with the authors of the libel, but for the wise, discreet, humble, and learned, whose humility and wisdom will not suffer them to despise the judgments of so learned and godly fathers.

T. C. Page 18, Sect. 5, 6, 7, 8, 9, and Page 19, Sect. 1.

As for that rule that he giveth when he saith, "Whatsoever is not, &c." and for the last of the three rules, I receive them with his own interpretation, which he hath afterward in 119. Epist. ad Januarium, *which is, that it be also profitable.*

And as for those three rules, which you say are worthy to be noted, I can see nothing that they help your cause one whit; for I know no man that ever denied but that the church may, in such things as are not specified and precisely determined, make orders, so they be grounded of those general rules which I have before alleged out of St Paul.

And as for the second of the three rules, I cannot at any hand allow it: for, when all Christianity was overrun with popery, things were universally observed which to keep were mere wickedness; and this strengtheneth the papists' universality.

Concerning your gloss ("if it be not repugnant to the scripture"), besides that it is not enough, because it must be grounded by the scripture, and that it is wicked to give such authority to any decree of men, that a man should not inquire of it or reason of it I have shewed that he meant nothing less. For, affirming that such things are the apostles' commandments, his meaning was, that they should be without all exception received, and absolutely. How much better is it that we take heed to the words of the apostle, than either to St Augustine's or yours, which saith that, "if

M. Doctor speaketh not of preaching another gospel, but of appointing other rites and orders.
Because it nothing pertaineth to my purpose. St Augustine mangled, and not truly reported.

he, or an angel from heaven, should preach any other gospel, Gal. i. 8.[2] *than that which he had preached, that they should hold him accursed!" he saith not any contrary or repugnant doctrine, but "any other gospel."*

But tell me, why passed you by that in Augustine which he writeth to January likewise[3]*, that "those things which are not contained* Epist. 119.[2] *in the scripture, nor decreed of councils, nor confirmed by general customs, but are varied by the manners of regions and of men, upon occasion offered ought to be cut off, although they seem not to be against faith, because they press with servile burdens the religion which Christ would have free*[4]*"? This sentence belike was too hot for you, you could not carry it. The rest whose names you recite (which you say you leave off for brevity' sake) I leave to the judgment of the reader to consider wherefore they be left out, seeing that Augustine, in whom you*

[1 These, Answ.]
[2 These references are inserted from Repl. 2.]
[3 *Likewise* is not in Repl. 2.]   [4 See below, page 241, note 2.]

put so great trust, answereth so little to your expectation. This is cer- Augustine
tain, that brevity (which you pretend) was in small commendations[5] of things
with you, which make so often repetitions, stuff in divers sentences of indifferent.
doctors and writers, to prove things that no man denieth, translate whole pleasure.
leaves to so small purpose, upon so light occasions make so often digres- Turpe est
sions, sometimes against the unlearnedness, sometimes against the malice, doctori, &c.
sometimes against the intemperancy of speech of the authors of the Admonition, and every hand while pulling out the sword upon them, and throughout the whole book sporting yourself with the quotations in the margent; so that, if all these were taken out of your book, as wind out of a bladder, we should have had it in a narrow room, which is thus swelled into such a volume; and, instead of a book of two shillings, we should have had a pamphlet of two pence.

And, whereas you say that you have not alleged " these learned fathers for the authors of the libel, but for the wise, discreet, humble, and learned;" to them also I leave it to consider upon that which is alleged by me: first, how like a divine it is to seek for rules in the doctors to measure the making of ceremonies by, which you might have had in the scriptures; there at the rivers, here at the fountain; uncertain there, which here are certain; there in part false, which are here altogether true; then to how little purpose they serve you; and last of all how they make against you.

Jo. Whitgift.

I take that which you grant: both the first rule, which is, Quod neque contra fidem, &c., and the last of the three, with what "interpretation" soever you admit them, serve my turn very well, and fully prove my present purpose. Wherefore in granting of them you have granted as much to me as hitherto I have desired. Of "the rules out of St Paul," I have spoken before: so have I likewise of the ends which the church must have a respect unto in her decrees of orders, ceremonies, and government; whereof also I shall have occasion to speak hereafter.

"The second of the three rules" you "cannot at any hand allow;" but there is no cause why you should mislike it. For Augustine did give it as a rule meet for his time, not for all times; although it may serve also for all times, if his meaning be joined with it, that is, " If that which is universally observed of the whole church be not repugnant to the word of God;" and so " it strengtheneth" not one whit " the papists'" pretended " universality."

In matters of order, ceremonies, and government, it is sufficient if they " be not repugnant to the scripture." Neither

[[5] Commendation, Repl. 2.]

<small>Augustine of things indifferent.</small> do I think any great difference to be betwixt "not repugnant to the word of God," and "according to the word."

That which is generally observed, and of that kind that the rule meaneth, is not only man's tradition and "decree," but God's also. M. Calvin teacheth you in his Institutions, <small>Decrees that pertain to order and comeliness are not only human.</small> *cap. xiii. sect.* 31[1], that such kind of "decrees" as pertain to order and comeliness, are not only human, but divine. And he bringeth in for an example kneeling at public prayers.

St Augustine's meaning is, that he would have no factions or contentions in the church, or any man to trouble the peace thereof, by setting himself against lawful orders and customs of the same: otherwise I think that he neither forbiddeth to "inquire or reason" of any such matter. But you think that Augustine was so addicted to such decrees of the apostles, "that his meaning was to have them received without all exception." Surely I think that he was so persuaded indeed of such decrees as he meaneth and speaketh of in that place: but, forasmuch as in such rules he hath sundry times made such exceptions, *Quod neque contra fidem*, &c., therefore this rule also is to be received of us according to his meaning in all such like rules.

God forbid that I should not "take heed to those words of the apostle, and hold him accursed which shall preach any other gospel than that which he had preached." For I take him that preacheth any other gospel to preach contrary and repugnant doctrine to the apostle; and undoubtedly he that teacheth any thing to be necessary to salvation, which is not comprehended in the scripture, teacheth a false doctrine, and clean contrary to the doctrine of the scripture. But you do not use this place (I am sure) against any thing that is here said. Our question is not of matters pertaining to salvation, but of ceremonies, of external orders, and discipline; whereof St Paul speaketh nothing in that place. I make them not matters of salvation; neither are they.

I will tell you why I "passed by that which St Augustine writeth to January," *Epist.* 119, and is now recited by you: because it nothing pertaineth to my purpose; and yet it is rather with me than against me.

<small>St Augustine mangled, and untruly reported by T. C.</small> But let me now ask you another question: Why do you not truly report St Augustine's words, but maim them

[1 See below, pages 244, &c. note 3.]

both before, behind, and in the midst? For Augustine, in the words that immediately go before, saith that he "was much grieved, because that many things which were more profitably commanded in the word of God were neglected by reason of so many presumptuous observations of outward ceremonies; the omitting whereof was more grievously punished than the breaking of God's commandments." And upon this occasion he concludeth thus: *Omnia itaque talia quæ neque sanctarum*, &c. : "All such ceremonies" (*scilicet*, as be impediments to the observing of the commandment of God, and are preferred before God's commandments), "being neither contained in the holy scriptures, nor found decreed in the councils of bishops, nor confirmed by the custom of the whole church, but are varied innumerably by the divers manners of divers regions, so that scarcely or never the causes can be found out which men followed in appointing of them; when occasion is offered, I think they ought to be cut off without any doubt[2]." Hitherto Augustine.

Augustine of things indifferent.

Therefore in reciting the words of St Augustine in this place, first, you have omitted the words going before, that express his mind, and declare that he meaneth such ceremonies as be impediments to the observing of God's commandments; for, having spoken of such before in manifest words, he concludeth (as I have said) on this sort: *Omnia itaque talia*, &c. : "All such ceremonies, &c.;" which words you have fraudulently kept back.

Secondly, where St Augustine speaketh of the unreasonable multitude of ceremonies, using these words, *innumerabiliter variantur*, "are varied innumerably," you have likewise left out this word "innumerably," which also expresseth Augustine's meaning.

Last of all, you have concealed a sentence in the midst,

[2 Sed hoc nimis doleo, quod multa quæ in divinis libris saluberrime præcepta sunt, minus curantur; et tam multis præsumptionibus sic plena sunt omnia, ut gravius corripiatur qui per octavas suas terram nudo pede tetigerit, quam qui mentem vinolentia sepelierit. Omnia itaque talia, quæ neque sanctarum scripturarum auctoritatibus continentur, nec in conciliis episcoporum statuta inveniuntur, nec consuetudine universæ ecclesiæ roborata sunt, sed pro diversorum locorum diversis moribus innumerabiliter variantur, ita ut vix aut omnino nunquam inveniri possint caussæ, quas in eis instituendis homines secuti sunt, ubi facultas tribuitur, sine ulla dubitatione resecanda existimo....Sed ecclesia Dei inter multam paleam multaque zizania constituta multa tolerat, &c.—August. Op. Par. 1679-1700. Ad Inq. Januar. Lib. II. seu Epist. lv. cap. xix. 35. Tom. II. col. 142.]

<small>Augustine of things indifferent.</small> which is very material to the declaring of Augustine his mind. The sentence is this: *Ita ut vix aut omnino nunquam inveniri possint causæ, quas in eis instituendis homines secuti sunt:* "So that scarcely or never the causes can be found out, which men followed in appointing of them." Whereby it is plain that he also meaneth such ceremonies as be appointed without reason or cause. And yet in the latter end he addeth: "But the church of God, being placed betwixt much chaff and darnel, doth tolerate many things, &c." But I am so far from defending the multitude or burdensomeness of ceremonies, that I consent in all points with that saying of Augustine: wherefore "this sentence is" nothing "too hot" for me, but pleaseth me right well; and it had been more for your commendation if you had not meddled withal[1].

They "whose names" I here "recite" (though I have not written their words), yet in the places which I have quoted do affirm as much as I recite them for: which you might have found, if you had taken pains to search for the same; as I think verily you have done, and found little for your purpose, and therefore are content to pass them over in silence.

If I "make so oft repetitions," I do but as I am occasioned by them whom I answer, and as you do yourself in this Reply, though it pleaseth you not to be acknown[2] of it. The "sentences of doctors and writers that" I "stuff in" argue that I have read them, and that I am not ashamed to lay them open, to the end my plain dealing may be seen in alleging of them. But what? did you before find fault with my "dumb doctors," and can you not now abide them speaking? Surely I intend not to be directed by so unconstant a guide.

If I "prove things that no man denieth," you had the less labour in replying: if I "translate whole leaves to so small

---

<small>[1 Cartwright rejoins: "As for that he chargeth me with leaving out of things before, in the midst, and after, and thereof hath almost filled a whole side; it is utterly unworthy any answer, considering that I have left nothing out which is in controversy, nothing which I do not willingly confess, nothing that he hath any advantage by: yea, I left that out whereby I could have taken advantage. For, beside that the ceremonies with us are in greater number than Augustine alloweth, all men see that they are more urged, and the omitting of them severelier punished, than the breach of the commandments of God: in which case he will have them abrogated. For he scapeth far better, which hath not preached a whole half year in his church, than which, preaching every week twice, leaveth off his surplice once, &c. All which things the place of Augustine giving me occasion of, I notwithstanding for shortness' sake passed by."—Sec. Repl. p. 91.]

[2 Acknown: known.]</small>

purpose," they be the sooner answered: if "upon so light occasions" I "have made so often digressions," you will take heed, I am well assured, that you offend not in the like; which truly you have forgotten in this place, for here is "a digression" without all reason. But I will let your reverend and modest speeches pass, and not recompense them with the like; for it neither savoureth the Spirit of God, neither yet any modest and good nature, but a stomach swelling rather against the person than against the cause.

Augustine of things indifferent.

My purpose is not in this place "to seek for rules to measure ceremonies by," but to prove that in ceremonies and other external things much is left to the discretion of the church, which is not to be found in scriptures; and yet I know none of these rules unmeet for "a divine" to search for, or to understand, unless it be such a one as contemneth all other men's learning but his own[3]. But how happeneth it that you have answered nothing to the last place that I have alleged out of Augustine? Or why say you nothing to my conclusion, which is, that "by all those places of this learned father it is evident, &c."?

In all this your reply you have greatly faulted in *ignorantia elenchi*; for you have not reasoned, nor answered *ad idem*, but spoken altogether from the purpose.

T. C. faulted in ignorantia elenchi.

The Opinion of M. Calvin of things
indifferent.

Chapter iv.

Answer to the Admonition, Page 25, Sect. 2, 3, and Page 26, 27, 28, and Page 29, Sect. 1, 2, 3, 4.

But I trust M. Calvin's judgment will weigh something with them, who in his Institutions, *cap. xiii. Sect.* 31 and 32, speaking of traditions, saith in[4] this sort:

"Because the Lord hath both faithfully and plainly comprehended and declared in the holy scriptures the whole sum of true righteousness, and all the parts of the true worshipping of him, and whatsoever is necessary unto

[3 "And where he saith 'they are meet for a divine to know;' it is no answer, considering that it may be profitable for a divine to know many things, which it is dangerous to propound unto the church, much more to propound them as rules to ground the church's laws upon."—Ibid. p. 92.]

[4 On, Answ.]

Calvin of things indifferent. salvation, therefore in those things he is only to be heard as a master, or teacher. But, because in external discipline and ceremonies he would not particularly prescribe what we ought to follow, because he foresaw that this depended upon the state and condition of the time, neither did judge one form or manner to be agreeable to all ages; here we must have a respect[1] to those general rules which he gave, that according to them might be examined such things as the necessity of the church requireth to be commanded for order and decency. Finally, because in these things he hath expressed nothing (for that they are neither necessary to salvation, and may be diversly applied to the edifying of the church, according to the manner and custom of every country and age), therefore, as the commodity of the church requireth, and as shall be thought convenient, both the old may be abrogated and new appointed. I grant that we must not rashly, nor often, nor for every light cause, make innovations: but what hurteth, and what edifieth, charity will best judge; which if we will suffer to be the moderatrix, all shall be safe and well. Now it is the office of christian people with a free conscience, without superstition, with a godly mind and ready and willing to obey, to observe those things which are appointed according to this rule, not to contemn them, nor negligently to omit them; so far off ought they to be from breaking them openly through disdain and contumacy.

"But thou wilt say, What liberty of conscience can there be in so precise and strait observing of them? Truly the liberty of conscience may well stand with it, if we shall consider that these laws and decrees, to the which we are bound, be not perpetual, or such as are not to be abrogated, but only external rudiments of man's infirmities; whereof notwithstanding we all stand not in need, yet we all use them, because one of us is mutually bound to another, to nourish love and charity among ourselves.

"This we may learn in the examples used before. What? doth religion consist in a woman's veil, that by

[1] Have respect, Answ.

no means she may go abroad bare-headed? or is the commandment touching her silence such as it may not be broken without wickedness? or is there any mystery in kneeling, or in burying the dead, that may not be omitted without great offence? No, truly; for, if such haste be required of a woman to help her neighbour, that she can have no leisure to cover her head, she doth not offend, though she run out bare-headed. And there is a time and place, when and where it is as meet for her to speak, as it is elsewhere to hold her peace. Him also to pray standing, which, being letted with some disease, cannot kneel, there is nothing forbiddeth. To be short, it is better in time to bury the dead, than to tarry for a winding-sheet, or some to carry him, until he stink above the ground. But there is somewhat even in those things which the custom of religion, laws, and decrees, humanity itself, and the rule of modesty, willeth us to do, and to take heed of, wherein if we shall through ignorance and forgetfulness offend, there is no sin committed; but if through contempt or contumacy, it is to be reproved. In like manner it skilleth not what days be appointed, what hours, what manner of places touching the building, what psalms are to be sung this day or that day; and yet there must certain days be appointed, and certain hours, and a place meet to receive all, if we have any respect to keep unity and peace. For what confusion were it, and of how great contentions and brawlings the seed and cause, if every man, as he listeth, might alter and change those things which pertain to the common state; seeing that it would never be brought to pass that one thing could please all men, if such matters were left indifferent, and committed to every man's arbitrement! Now, if any man repine or grudge, and will here seem wiser than it behoveth him, let him consider by what reason he can excuse his waywardness in[2] the Lord. Notwithstanding, that saying of St Paul must satisfy us: 'We have no custom to contend, neither the churches of God[3].'" Thus far Calvin.

Calvin of things indifferent.

1 Cor. xi.

[2 To, Answ.]

[3 ...nempe quia Dominus et totam veræ justitiæ summam, et omnes cultus numinis sui partes, et quicquid ad salutem necessarium erat, sacris suis oraculis

Calvin of things indifferent.

Collections out of Calvin.

In which words we have these things to consider: first, that God hath in the scripture[1] fully and plainly comprehended all those things that be necessary to salvation.

Secondly, that in ceremonies and external discipline he hath not in scripture particularly determined any

tum fideliter complexus est, tum perspicue enarravit; in his solus Magister est audiendus. Quia autem in externa disciplina et ceremoniis non voluit sigillatim præscribere quid sequi debeamus (quod istud pendere a temporum conditione prævideret, neque judicaret unam seculis omnibus formam convenire), confugere hic oportet ad generales quas dedit regulas, ut ad eas exigantur quæcunque ad ordinem et decorum præcipi necessitas ecclesiæ postulabit. Postremo quia ideo nihil expressum tradidit, quia nec ad salutem hæc necessaria sunt, et pro moribus uniuscujusque gentis ac seculi varie accommodari debent ad ecclesiæ ædificationem; prout ecclesiæ utilitas requiret, tam usitatas mutare et abrogare quam novas instituere conveniet. Fateor equidem, non temere, nec subinde, nec levibus de causis ad novationem esse decurrendum. Sed quid noceat vel ædificet, caritas optime judicabit: quam si moderatricem esse patiemur, salva erunt omnia. Jam vero christiani populi officium est, quæ secundum hunc canonem fuerint instituta, libera quidem conscientia, nullaque superstitione, pia tamen et facili ad obsequendum propensione servare, non contemptim habere, non supina negligentia præterire: tantum abest ut per fastum et contumaciam violare aperte debeat. Qualis (inquies) in tanta observantia et cautione conscientiæ libertas esse poterit? Imo vero præclare constabit ubi reputabimus, non fixas esse et perpetuas sanctiones quibus adstricti simus, sed externa humanæ infirmitatis rudimenta: quibus tametsi non indigemus omnes, tamen omnes utimur, quia alii aliis ad fovendam inter nos caritatem mutuo sumus obnoxii. Hoc in exemplis superius positis recognoscere licet. Quid? an in mulieris carbaso sita religio est, ut nudo capite egredi sit nefas? An sanctum de ejus silentio decretum, quod violari sine summo scelere non possit? An aliquod in genuflexione, in humando cadavere mysterium, quod præteriri sine piaculo non possit? Minime. Nam si tali festinatione opus sit mulieri in juvando proximo quæ velare caput non sinat, nihil delinquit si aperto capite accurrat. Et est ubi loqui non minus opportunum illi sit quam alibi tacere. Stantem quoque orare, qui morbo impeditus curvare genua nequit, nihil vetat. Denique satius est mature humare mortuum, quam ubi linteum deest, ubi non adsunt qui deducant, exspectare dum inhumatus putrescat. Sed est nihilominus in istis rebus quod agendum aut cavendum mos regionis, instituta, ipsa denique humanitas et modestiæ regula dictet: ubi si imprudentia et oblivione quid erratum fuerit, nullum admissum crimen est; sin contemptu, improbanda est contumacia. Similiter dies ipsi qui sint, et horæ, quæ locorum structura, qui quo die canantur psalmi, nihil interest. Verum et certos dies et statas esse horas convenit, et locum recipiendis omnibus idoneum, siqua servandæ pacis ratio habetur. Nam quantarum rixarum semen futura sit earum rerum confusio, si prout cuique libitum sit, mutare liceat quæ ad communem statum pertinent! quando nunquam futurum est ut omnibus idem placeat, si res, velut in medio positæ, singulorum arbitrio relictæ fuerint. Quod siquis obstrepat et plus sapere hic velit quam oportet, viderit ipse qua morositatem suam ratione Domino approbet. Nobis tamen istud Pauli satisfacere debet, *nos contendendi morem non habere, neque ecclesias Dei.*—Calvin. Op. Amst. 1667-71. Inst. Lib. IV. cap. x. 30, 31. Tom. IX. p. 323.]

[1 In scripture, Answ.]

thing, but left the same to his church, to make or abrogate, to alter or continue, to add or take away, as shall be thought from time to time most convenient for the present state of the church; so that nothing be done against that general rule of St Paul, 1 Cor. xiv.: "Let all things be done decently and in order."

Calvin of things indifferent.

Thirdly, that it is the duty of a christian man without superstition willingly to obey such constitutions, not to contemn them, not to neglect them, much less stubbornly and arrogantly to break them.

Fourthly, that the observing of them taketh not liberty from the conscience, because they be not made to be perpetual and inviolable, but to be altered as time, occasion, and necessity, requireth.

Fifthly, that all ought to obey such ordinances, for charity' sake, though all stand not in need of them.

Sixthly, that, if a man do violate them by ignorance or forgetfulness, he doth not offend; if by contempt or stubbornness, he doth greatly offend.

Seventhly, that confusion (which is to suffer every man to do what he list) is the seed of contention and brawling.

Last of all, that the true ministers of God be not contentious, neither yet the churches of God.

These things among other I thought good to note out of M. Calvin's words; which if they were diligently considered, such contentions might soon be ended.

T. C. Page 19, Sect. 2, 3, 4, 5, and Page 20, Sect. 1.

Why should you trust that M. Calvin's judgment will weigh with them, if they be anabaptists (as you accuse them), if they be Donatists, if Catharists, if conspired with the papists, how can you think that they will so easily rest in M. Calvin's judgment, which hated and confuted all anabaptism, Donatism, Catharism, and papism? But it is true which the proverb saith, Memorem, &c.: *"He that will speak an untruth had need have a good memory;" and this is the force of the truth in the conscience of man, that, although he suppress it, and pretend the contrary, yet at unwares it stealeth out. For what greater testimony could you have given of them, that they hate all those heresies, which you lay to their charge, than to say that you trust M. Calvin's judgment will weigh with them? Now indeed, that you be not deceived, we receive M. Calvin, and weigh of him, as of the notablest instrument that the Lord hath stirred up for the purging of his churches, and of the restoring of the plain*

Calvin of things indifferent.

and sincere interpretation of the scriptures, which hath been since the apostles' time[1]. And yet we do not so read his works, that we believe any thing to be true because he saith it, but so far as we can esteem that that which he saith doth agree with the canonical scriptures. But what gather you out of M. Calvin?

First, that all necessary things to salvation are contained in the scripture: who denieth it?

In the second collection, where you would give to understand that ceremonies and external discipline are not prescribed particularly by the word of God, and therefore left to the order of the church, you must understand that all external discipline is not left to the order of the

You say after that there are but these[2] two.

church, being particularly prescribed in the scriptures, no more than all ceremonies are left to the order of the church, as the sacraments of baptism, and the supper of the Lord: whereas, upon the indefinite speaking of M. Calvin, saying "ceremonies and external discipline," without adding

Untruth; for I have reported his words to no other end than he hath written them.

all, or some, you go about subtilly to make men believe that Calvin[3] had placed the whole external discipline in the power and arbitrement of the church. For, if all external discipline were arbitrary, and in the choice of the church, excommunication also (which is a part of it) might be cast away; which I think you will not say. But, if that M. Calvin were alive

You should have shewed wherein his words are racked and writhen.

to hear his sentences racked and writhen, to establish those things which he strove so mightily to overthrow, and to overthrow those things that he laboured so sore to establish, what might he say? And the injury which is done to him is nothing less because he is dead.

Concerning all the rest of your collections, I have not lightly known a man which taketh so much pain with so small gain, and which soweth his seed in the sea, whereof there will never rise increase. For I know none that ever denied those things, unless peradventure you would make the reader believe that all those be contentious which move any controversy of things which they judge to be amiss; and then it is answered before: and now I answer further, that they that move to reformation of things are no more to be blamed as authors of contention than the physician which giveth a purgation is to be blamed for the rumbling and stir in the belly, and other disquietness of the body; which should not have been, if the evil humours and naughty disposition of it had not caused or procured this purgation.

Whereas you conclude that these contentions would be soon ended if M. Calvin's words were noted, here we will join with you, and will not

In any place that maketh with you, but not otherwise.

refuse the judgment of M. Calvin in any matter that we have in controversy with you: which I speak not therefore, because I would call the decision of controversies to men and their words (which pertain only to God and to his word), but because I know his judgment in these things to be clean against you, and especially for that you would bear men in hand that M. Calvin is on your side, and against us.

[1 Times, Repl. 1, 2, and Def. A.]   [2 There, Def. B.]
[3 That M. Calvin, Repl. 2.]

Jo. Whitgift.

If you yourself will of necessity enforce these qualities and conditions of anabaptists (which I in the beginning rehearsed) upon the authors of the Admonition, who can let you? The most that I have said is, that "I suspect them," because they so "agree with them in certain qualities and practices." But, if they were bent that way, yet doth it not follow that they would by and by seem to contemn M. Calvin's, or any other famous and learned man's judgment. For you know that the chief captains of the anabaptists did not forthwith utter either all their contempt of learned men, or all their pestiferous opinions at the first; but used therein some policy, such as might most prevail to win credit unto their faction. You remember that Zuinglius, in his book called *Ecclesiastes*, saith of the anabaptists that, "though they protested, and by oath denied, that they meant to take any authority from the magistrate, yet shortly after it would appear that they would have been disobedient to all laws of magistrates, &c.[4];" as I have before rehearsed: the practice whereof is to be seen in Sleidan and other stories[5].

Calvin of things indifferent.

Zuinglius adversus Anab.

And, although in the beginning it was pretended that the contention was but in matters of no great importance, as "cap, surplice, tippet, &c.;" yet, in the additions to the first Admonition, fol. 9, it is protested that the strife is for greater matters, as "for a true ministry and government of the church[6];" and now you say that certain matters which be in controversy "are matters of life and death, of salvation and damnation," foll. 5, and 14. Besides all this, the additions that you make to the protestation of your obedience to the civil magistrate, fol. 6, &c.[7] is very suspicious; so is your doctrine touching the authority of the civil magistrate also; as I have in another place declared. Wherefore how far both they and you will as yet proceed, is not certainly known. In the mean time, if, by allowing such as M. Calvin is, some credit were not maintained, wise and learned men would the sooner espy their doing[8].

Fol. 5, sect. ult. Fol. 14, line 5. Fol. 6, sect. 4.

When I say that "I trust M. Calvin's judgment will weigh

[4 H. Zvingl. Op. Tigur. 1581. Ecclesiast. Pars II. fol. 54. See before, pages 128, 9, note 3.]
[5 J. Sleidan. Comm. de Stat. Relig. &c. Argent. 1572. Lib. x. foll. 104, &c.]
[6 Adm. to Parl. fol. B. viii. 2; where *regiment of the church*.]
[7 See before, pages 101, 5, 81.]   [8 Doings, Def. A.]

<small>Calvin of things indifferent.</small> something with them," I speak it but in comparison to the authority of such as I have before alleged. For I know they make small account of any author that writeth against them, but least of all of the old ancient fathers, whom some of them are not ashamed to call "pillory doctors." They may therefore bear a countenance to such as "hate and confute anabaptism, papism, &c.;" and yet both join with the papists and the anabaptists, &c. in disturbing the church.

As the words of M. Calvin be directly to my purpose, and my collections truly gathered out of them, so is your answer thereunto very weak, and indeed nothing. The words of M. Calvin whereupon my second collection is gathered be these: "But, because in external discipline and ceremonies he would not particularly prescribe what we ought to follow, because he foresaw that this depended upon the state and condition of the time, neither did judge one form or manner to be agreeable to all ages, here we must have respect, &c.[1]" Confer these words with my collection, and you shall see them agree in all points. And surely M. Calvin saith that fully and plainly in this place which I have taken in hand to prove. M. Calvin neither addeth "all," nor "some;" and therefore neither have I added them, lest I might seem to be a corrupter of his words.

Your objection "of the supper of the Lord, and of baptism," is altogether frivolous: for they be substantial ceremonies; and not ceremonies only, but sacraments also, and therefore must have of necessity an express commandment in the word of God.

Touching "excommunication" I shall speak hereafter: it is the matter that the anabaptists so greatly urged, and for the not using of the which they separated themselves from the churches where the gospel was preached; as appeareth in the books both of Calvin, Bullinger, and others, against them. I know that touching excommunication, whether the use of it be at all times so necessary or no that it may not be altered, learned men do vary in judgments; whose opinions in that matter I will defer, until I come where I have farther occasion to speak of it.

"If M. Calvin were alive," and understood the state of our church and controversy truly, I verily believe that he

[1 See before, page 244.]

would utterly condemn your doings; and I am the rather induced to think so, because I understand him to have allowed many things in the English church being at Geneva, which you altogether mislike, as funeral sermons, &c. And therefore he would not think his words racked one whit tò establish anything that he would have had overthrown.

Calvin of things indifferent.

"The rest of" my "collections" are most agreeable to M. Calvin's words, most necessary for this present time, and most apt for my purpose; and your passing them over so slightly doth argue your lack of ability to answer them. Indeed they flatly determine this controversy, and in effect overthrow your whole book.

Those that make contention in the church for such matters as you do, and in such sort and manner, cannot avoid the just accusations of being "contentious" persons; and, if "the physician giveth a purgation" where there is no need, or a more vehement "purgation" than is convenient for the disease, or minister it out of time, or give one "purgation" for another, &c.; what "rumbling and stir" soever follow in the body, he may be justly said to be the author and cause of them. Do you not know what Zuinglius saith in his *Ecclesiastes*, speaking of anabaptists? "If they were sent of God, and endued with the spirit of love, they would have construed in the best part those external things, &c.²" And again: "Christ never made any contention for external things³;" and in his book *De Baptismo:* "They go about innovations of their own private authority, &c.⁴"

Zuinglius in Ecclesiast.

Idem de Baptismo.

I use M. Calvin's judgment, as I use the judgment of other learned men; neither will I refuse any learned man's opinion in these controversies, that truly and wholly understandeth the state of this church, and the ground of all things used in it. But I doubt how you will hereafter stand to this offer.

[⁵ The same Master Calvin, writing upon these words, 1 Cor. xi. *Quemadmodum tradidi vobis instituta tenetis*,

[² H. Zvingl. Op. Tigur. 1581. Ecclesiast. fol. 49. 2. See before, page 128, note 2.]

[³ Id. ibid. fol. 54. See before, pages 128, 9, note 3.]

[⁴ ...proprio et privato temeritatis suæ consilio eam doctrinam reipsa obtrudere conantur, quæ &c.—Id. Epist. præf. de Baptism. Libr. fol. 57.]

[⁵ The paragraphs between brackets are inserted from Answ. 2.]

saith on this sort: "I do not deny but that there were some traditions of the apostles not written; but I do not grant them to have been taken as parts of doctrine or necessary unto salvation. What then? even such as did pertain to order and policy. For we know that every church hath liberty to ordain and appoint such a form of government as is apt and profitable for it; because the Lord therein hath prescribed no certainty. So Paul, the first founder of the church of Corinth, did also frame it with honest and godly institutions, that all things might there be done decently and in order[1]." And again, expounding these words in the latter end of that chapter, *Cetera cum venero disponam*, he writeth thus: "But let such toys pass, seeing that it is certain that Paul speaketh but of external comeliness, the which as it is put in the liberty of the church, so is it to be appointed according to the times, places, and persons[2]." To conclude, the same Calvin writing upon these words, 1 Cor. xiv. *Omnia decenter et ordine fiant*, he saith: "Hereof we gather a perpetual doctrine to what end the policy of the church must be directed. The Lord hath therefore left external rites to our liberty or discretion, that we should not think the worship of him to consist therein[3]."

Peter Martyr likewise upon 1 Cor. i. writeth thus:

Peter Martyr. "There be three kinds of traditions: some are expressed in the scriptures; and in this kind of traditions all men ought to communicate among themselves: other there be plain repugnant to the word of God; and all such are to be rejected, by what authority soever they be obtruded, &c.: there be other some traditions which we may call neuters; because they be neither contrary to the word of God, nor yet necessarily joined to the same; in which we must obey the church, these three cautions being observed: first, that they be not obtruded as worship of God or peculiar holiness, but as pertaining to order, and the civil commodity of the

[[1] Calvin. Op. Amst. 1667-71. Comm. in Epist. i. ad Cor. cap. xi. Tom. VII. p. 177. See before, page 221, note 7.]
[[2] Id. ibid. p. 185. See before, page 221, note 8.]
[[3] Hinc (ut dixi) colligimus perpetuam doctrinam, quem in finem dirigenda sit ecclesiæ politia. Dominus externos ritus in libertate nostra ideo reliquit, ne putaremus cultum ejus illic inclusum.—Id. ibid. cap. xiv. 40. p. 201.]

church, and to comeliness in divine actions; for all things be sufficiently contained in scripture that pertain to the worshipping of God and holiness. Secondly, that they be not counted so necessary, but that they may be altered if time require: let the church keep her interest and authority in these indifferent things, to appoint what shall be thought most meet to edifying. Last of all, that the people of God be not burdened with too great a multitude of them[4]." Whereby it is plain that the church of God hath authority to appoint rites not expressed in the word of God, these three cautions observed.

Beza, in his book called *Confessio Christianæ Fidei, cap. v.* saith that "one cause of councils and synods was to make rules of ecclesiastical discipline, and to appoint the government of the church according to the diversity of time, place, and persons. For it is necessary that in the house of God all things should be done in order: of the which order there is one general reason in the word of God, 1 Cor. xiv., but not one and the same form, agreeing to all circumstances[5]." And again in the same chapter he saith: " The rules or canons (of rites and orders in the church) have respect to comeliness in external things,

Beza.

[4 Quare haud nos latere oportet, traditiones ejus triplici differentia sejungi. Quædam earum omnino ex sacris literis consequuntur: et quoad hoc genus tenentur universi fideles inter sese communicare. Aliæ reperiuntur, quæ cum verbo Dei prorsus pugnant: omnes hujus generis rejiciendæ sunt, quacunque auctoritate obtrudantur....Sunt nonnullæ quoque traditiones, quas neutras appellare libuit, quod verbo Dei nec adversentur, nec illi necessario cohæreant; in quibus mos ecclesiæ gerendus est, tribus interpositis cautionibus. Primum videndum est, ne obtrudantur quasi Dei cultus et peculiaris quædam sanctimonia; quandoquidem potius recipiendæ sunt ad ordinem conservandum et civilem ecclesiæ commoditatem atque sacrarum actionum decorum: alioquin in sacris literis luculenter habemus descripta, quæ ad sanctitatem et cultum Dei conducunt. Præterea cavere oportet, ne quæ sic traduntur ita putemus necessaria, ut pro tempore amoveri non possint. Servetur ecclesiæ suum jus de his mediis, ut quoad illa statuat quicquid viderit magis ædificationem credentium promovere. Consideretur demum sæpius, nimiis traditionibus et ceremoniis in immensum auctis populum Christi sic gravari, ut tantum non obruatur.—P. Martyr. Comm. in D. Pauli prior. ad Corinth. Epist. Tigur. 1572. cap. i. 10. p. 8.]

[5 Altera causa fuit conventuum ecclesiasticorum, ut disciplinæ ecclesiasticæ canones, et, ut paucis omnia comprehendam, ut politiam ecclesiasticam pro diversa temporum, locorum, et personarum circunstantia constituerent. Necesse enim est ut in domo Dei omnia ordine fiant; cujus ordinis una quidem est universalis ratio ex verbo Dei petenda, sed non una et eadem forma quibusvis circunstantiis conveniens.—Th. Bezæ Confess. Christ. Fid. Genev. 1587. cap. v. 17. p. 128.]

and therefore they be neither general for the most part, nor perpetual: for that which is profitable to edifying in some place in other some places would rather hurt; and, moreover, the diverse respects of the time are such that that same thing, which for good considerations was ordained, must of necessity sometime be abrogated; whereof it comes to pass that there is not only so great variety in the old canons, but contrariety also[1]." Again in the same chapter: "We must not always look what the apostles did *in politia ecclesiastica*, in the government of the church, seeing there be most diverse circumstances, and therefore *absque κακοζηλία*, without preposterous zeal, all things cannot in all places and times be reduced to one and the same form, &c.[2]"

Zuinglius, in his book *De Baptismo*, doth in plain words determine this matter: "There be many things of this sort (saith he), whereof notwithstanding there is no express and manifest word of God; yet are they not repugnant to his will, but rather agree with the same: such is this, that we make women partakers of the Lord's supper, when as we read not that any woman was present in that supper which Christ did institute. I would not have any faithful man offended with this my saying, for I do not condemn women; but I am compelled to use this example, through the importunity of those that deny the baptism of infants. For thus they reason: We read not that infants were baptized of Christ; therefore it is wicked to baptize infants. If this be a good argument, then may we also reason thus: Christ when he celebrated his supper with his disciples had no women there present; *ergo*, women must be secluded from the Lord's table; the which how wicked and how ungodly a thing it is, there is none that doth not understand: and there be many other

[1] Regulæ autem illæ sive canones spectant potius τὸ πρέπον in rebus exterioribus, ideoque neque sunt universales, magna ex parte, neque perpetuæ. Quod enim alicubi prodest ad ædificationem, alibi potius noceret: et adeo quoque diversa est temporum ratio, ut quod optimis de causis aliquando fuit constitutum, necesse sit interdum abolere: quo fit ut magna in veteribus canonibus non tantum varietas, sed etiam repugnantia inveniatur.—Id. ibid. 18. p. 129.]

[2] Neque enim simpliciter spectandum quid sit ab apostolis factum in politia ecclesiastica, quum diversissimæ sint circumstantiæ, ac proinde absque κακοζηλίᾳ non possint omnia omnibus locis ac temporibus ad unam eandemque formam revocari, &c.—Id. ibid. 35. p. 152.]

things of this sort. But here I know they will quarrel and call heaven and earth against me, and say unto me, This was thy only and strongest buckler: by this instrument as a most sure help thou hast hitherto defended thyself against the munitions and fortresses of the papists, for thou saidest that they were of no force or authority, because they could not be proved and defended by any testimonies of the word of God: how darest thou therefore now (as unmindful hereof) say that many things are not contained in scriptures, which notwithstanding are not repugnant to God and his will? Where is that thy strong army? where is that thy sharp axe, wherewith thou hast cut in sunder all Faber's knots, oftentimes repeating this one thing, *Frustra me colunt decentes* [*docentes*] *doctrinas hominum*, Matt. xv., Esa. xxix.? But, I pray you, hear my answer: Whatsoever I then spake, the same do I speak now, neither will I ever so long as I live cease to speak them; neither shall you find me by any arguments to speak contrary things, if you understand me truly, and will hear a truth. Mark therefore diligently the meaning of these things which I have spoken; for I speak not as you feign me to speak. I speak this only of external and indifferent things; whereof there be many, which are neither commanded nor forbidden by any express word of God, and yet we may use them without all impiety and disobedience. But we shall better understand the matter by an example: The supper of our Lord, which other call a thanksgiving, if thou look upon the word of God, and the first institution thereof, it hath no other name than the name of a memorial, neither can any other name be applied unto it out of the holy scriptures, howsoever the whole multitude of papists storm and rage.

"This is an external thing and elemental, but not indifferent; so that to convert this action into a sacrifice, and to take it *pro hostia*, is wicked and unlawful; as the word of God declareth, and especially Paul in the epistle to the Hebrews, &c.[3]"

[3 Multa enim hujus generis invenire licet, quæ tametsi nullum de ipsis extet disertum minimeque ambiguum Dei pronunciatum, cum illius tamen voluntate non pugnant, quin potius eidem conveniunt. Tale enim est, quo mulieres quoque cœnæ dominicæ participes facimus, cum tamen mulieres in ea cœna, quam

These words be plain, that the scripture containeth all things necessary to salvation, and not all external and indifferent things, which notwithstanding may be well used.

And in the same book he addeth: " Yet, christian reader, thou must take heed lest, being deceived by occasion of this pestilent contention and discord, thou dost suffer thyself again to be enwrapped with the errors of the papists; for they say that many things necessary unto salvation are not contained in the scriptures, but afterwards set forth by the holy fathers, bishops, and popes. For this that we speak of is not necessary unto salvation, but it is external; of the which kind many things may be found omitted in the scriptures; for Christ did many

Christus instituit, nullæ accubuisse legantur. Nolim autem quenquam fidelium hoc meo sermone offendi : nec enim mulieres damno, sed eorum, qui infantibus baptismum negant, improbitate compulsus hoc exemplo uti cogor. Sic enim hi argumentantur, Infantes a Christo baptizatos esse nunquam legitur, ergo infantes baptizare nefas et impium est. Quod si sic argumentari licebit, jam et hoc dicemus, Cum Christus cœnam cum discipulis celebraret, mulieres nullas simul accubuisse videre licet : ergo fœmineus sexus a mensa Domini arceri debet. Quod quam impium, iniquum, et indignum facinus foret, nemo non intelligit. Atqui alia hujus generis quam plurima invenire licet. Quiritantur hic, scio, et cœlum, terras et maria contra me invocant. Unicum hoc, inquiunt, scutum tibi fuit validissimum, hoc uno præsidio longe tutissimo contra pontificiorum phalanges temetipsum hactenus tutatus es, quod ea nullius momenti et auctoritatis esse diceres, quæ nullis divini verbi testimoniis probari et defendi possunt. Qua fronte ergo nunc, quasi hujus oblitus, multa in sacris literis non contineri dicis, quæ tamen cum Deo et voluntate ipsius nullo modo pugnent? Ubi ergo cuneus ille tuus validissimus, ubi bipennis tua plus quam Tenedia, qua omnes Fabri nodos fortissime dissecasti ? hoc unum semper ingeminans, Frustra me colunt docentes doctrinas hominum, Matth. 15. Esaiæ 29. Sed audite quæso responsionem meam, O boni. Quæ olim locutus sum, ea et nunc loquor, nec unquam quoad vixero loqui desinam : nec ullis argumentis me diversa loqui deprehendetis, modo vobis quoque intellectus simplex sit, qui simplicem veritatis sermonem possit percipere. Diligentius ergo sensum eorum, quæ dixi, inspicite. Nec enim sic loquor, ut vos me loqui fingitis. De externis rebus et indifferentibus hæc dicimus, quales multæ sunt, quæ nullo quidem certo et expresso Dei oraculo vel jubentur vel prohibentur, iisdem tamen citra omnem impietatem et inobedientiam utimur. Sed exemplo rem clarius intelligemus. Cœna dominica, quam alii eucharistiam vocant, si Dei verbum et primam illius institutionem inspicias, non aliud quam commemorationis nomen meretur ; nec ullum nomen aliud ex sacris literis huic accommodari poterit, utcunque insaniat et tumultuetur universus pontificiorum cœtus. Est hæc quidem res externa et elementalis, non tamen indifferens, sic nimirum, ut eadem hæc actio in sacrificium converti, et pro hostia quadam haberi possit. Hoc enim nefas esse et illicitum divini verbi oracula, in primis vero Paulus in ea quam ad Hebræos scripsit epistola, copiose simul et perspicue tradiderunt.— H. Zvingl. Op. Tigur. 1581. De Bapt. Lib. Tract. III. Pars II. fol. 85.]

miracles which were unpossible to be contained in the scriptures, John xxi.; and yet we may say they were done, though the scriptures do not express them. But concerning doctrines of faith and those things which do inform our faith and the inward man, we must always use this as a present medicine: that which God hath not commanded us to believe, that is not necessary to salvation to be believed. God hath not commanded or appointed this worship; and therefore it cannot please and be accepted unto him. But there is a far other reason in ceremonies: for we cannot say, these ceremonies are not mentioned in scriptures; therefore they were not used, &c. But here may every man see the subtilty of contentious Satan, who through these brawlings for external things doth open wide windows to the purposes of the papists. In such things the rule of Paul ought to be followed, 1 Cor. xiv.; where he, speaking of the use of tongues, saith on this sort: 'Let all things be done decently and in order.' Likewise writing to the Philippians, chap. iii., he saith: 'If any man think otherwise, God will also reveal the same unto you; nevertheless in that whereunto we are come, let us proceed by one rule, that we may mind one thing, or agree among ourselves.' In the which place Paul disputeth of nothing else than of external ceremonies and rites (for those things that inform the soul and the inward man may not be otherwise used than the Lord hath appointed), the use and administration whereof he saith is in our will and power; so that we do nothing repugnant to the commandment of God, neither trouble the public peace (whereof we ought to have especial regard) for external things[1]." Hitherto Zuinglius.]

[1 Nunquam tamen admittes, christiane lector, ut pestiferæ contentionis et litis hujus occasione deceptus pontificiorum erroribus te denuo involvi patiaris. Dicunt enim hi, multa adhuc ad æternæ salutis acquisitionem restare, quæ sacris literis prodita non sint, sed a patribus sanctis, episcopis item et pontificibus postea demum exposita. Illud enim, de quo nobis hic sermo est, ad salutis substantiam nihil facit, sed externum est, cujus generis plura invenire licet omissa in scripturis. Plura enim miracula Christus edidit, quæ omnia literis complecti longum foret et impossibile, Joan. 21. De his ergo dicere licet, quod facta sint, licet scripturis sacris non exprimantur. Ceterum quod ad dogmata fidei spectat, et eas res quæ fidem nostram et internum hominem informant, perpetuo hoc ceu præsenti antidoto utendum est, Quod Deus non præcepit credere, ut credamus ad

The Opinion of Bucer of things indifferent.

Chap. v.

Answer to the Admonition, Page 29, Sect. 5 and 6.

Bucer of things indifferent[1].

Of the same judgment in this matter is M. Bucer, as it appeareth in his epistle to M. Alasco: these be his words: "If you will not admit such liberty, and use of vesture, to this pure and holy church, because they have no commandment of the Lord, nor example of it, I do not see how you can grant to any church that it may celebrate the Lord's supper in the morning, and in an open church, especially consecrated to the Lord; that the sacrament may be distributed to men kneeling or standing, yea, to women as well as to men. For we have received of these things neither commandment of the Lord, nor any example: yea, rather the Lord gave a contrary example. For in the evening, and in a private house, he did make his supper, and distributed the sacraments, and that to men only, and sitting at the table[2]." *Hæc Bucerus.*

But to end this matter, is it not as lawful for a godly prince, with the advice and consent of godly and learned bishops, and other of the wisest, to make orders in the

salutem necessarium non est. Cultum hunc non descripsit nec injunxit Dominus; ergo illi placere et acceptus esse non potest. Ceremoniarum autem ratio longe alia est. Nec enim dicere licebit, De ceremoniis istis in scriptura nihil proditum est: ergo ceremoniis istis usi non sunt: &c....Hic vero singulis videre licet, quænam sit contentiosi istius Satanæ calliditas, qui hujusmodi rixis propter externa quædam institutis papatui amplissimas fenestras denuo aperire voluit. In hujusmodi utique rebus Pauli apostoli regula nobis observanda est, quam 1 Corinth. 14. de linguarum usu disputans, sic tradidit, Omnia decenter et secundum ordinem fiant. Similiter Philippensibus suis scribens, cap. 3. inquit, Si quid aliter sentitis, hoc quoque vobis Deus revelabit: attamen ad id, quod assecuti sumus, eadem procedamus regula, ut simus concordes. Quo in loco non aliud equidem agit Paulus, quam quod de externis ceremoniis et ritibus disputat (quæ enim animam adeoque hominem internum informant, aliter quam Dominus instituit, usurpari non debent), quorum usum et administrationem in nostro arbitrio et potestate sitam esse ait, sic tamen ne quid cum Dei instituto pugnans committamus, et ne pacem publicam, cujus nobis præcipua cura esse debet, propter externa hæc interturbare libeat.—Id. ibid. fol. 87. 2.]

[1 Answ. 2. has not *of things indifferent.*]

[2 This letter was printed at the end of "A briefe examination for the tyme, of a certaine declaration, &c." Lond. Jugge. See fol. D 1.2; where *if therefore you, nor no example, especially consecrate,* and *that the sacraments.* Conf. Strype, Eccles. Memor. Vol. II. Book I. chap. xxviii., and Append. LL.]

church, and laws ecclesiastical, as it is for every private man to use what manner and form of service he list, and other order and discipline in his own parish, which these men seek and strive to do?

T. C. Page 20, Sect. 1, 2, 3, 4, 5, and Page 21, Sect. 1.

And as for Peter Martyr, and Bucer, and Musculus, and Bullinger, Gualter, and Hemingius, and the rest of the late writers, by citing of whom you would give to understand that they are against us in these matters, there is set down in the latter end of this book their several judgments of the most of these things which are in controversy: whereby it may appear that, if they have spoken one word against us, they have spoken two for us. And, whereas they have written (as it is said), and alleged in their private letters to their friends, against some of these causes, it may appear that they have in their works published to the whole world that they confirm the same causes. So that, if they wrote any such things, they shall be found not so much to have dissented from us as from themselves; and therefore we appeal from themselves unto themselves, and from their private notes and letters to their public writings, as more authentical. You labour still in the fire that is unprofitable[3], *to bring M. Bucer his epistle to prove that the church may order things whereof there is no particular and expressed commandment; for there is none denieth it: neither is this saying, that all things are to be done in the church according to the rule of the word of God, anything repugnant unto this, that the church may ordain certain things according to the word of God.*

But, if this epistle, and others of M. Bucer's, with his notes upon the book of common prayer[4], *which are so often cited, and certain epistles of M. Peter Martyr, were never printed (as I cannot understand they were); then, besides that you do us injury, which go about to prejudice our cause by the testimonies of them, which we can neither hear nor see, being kept close in your study, you also do your cause much more injury, whilst you betray the poverty and nakedness of it, being fain to ransack and ruffle*[5] *up every dark corner, to find something to cover it with.*

Therefore it were good, before you took any benefit of them, to let them come forth, and speak their own testimonies, in their own language, and full out. For now you give men occasion to think that there are some other things in their epistles which you would be loth the world should know, for fear of fall of that which you would gladly keep.

There is no man that saith that it ought to be permitted to every person in the church where he is minister, to have such order or discipline, or to use such service, as he listeth; no man seeketh for it: but to have the order which God hath left, in those things which the word precisely appointeth, and in other things to use that which shall be according to the

You do learned men great injury, in accusing them of contrariety.

You cannot but understand that they are printed.

What say you then to the 14. reason of the Admonition, "then ministers were not so tied to any form of prayers, &c."

[3 Unprofitably, Repl. 1 and 2.]
[4 For these see M. Bucer. Script. Anglic. Basil. 1577. Censur. Bucer. sup. Libr. Sacror. &c. pp. 456, &c.]   [5 Rifle, Repl. 2.]

rules of St Paul before recited, agreed by the church, and confirmed by the prince.

An untruth; for I give it not to the bishops only, but to a godly prince, with the advice and consent of godly and learned bishops, and other of the wisest.

And, whereas you have ever hitherto given the ordering of these things to the church, how come you now to ascribe it to the bishops? You mean, I am sure, the bishops, as we call bishops here in England, whereby you fall into the opinion of the papists unawares[1], which, when they have spoken many things of the church magnifically, at the last they bring it, now to the doctors of the church, now to bishops.

As for me, although I doubt not but there be many good men of the bishops, and very learned also, and therefore very meet to be admitted into that consultation wherein it shall be considered what things are good in the church; yet, in respect of that office and calling of a bishop which they now exercise, I think that every godly-learned minister and pastor of the church hath more interest and right, in respect of his office, to be at that consultation, than any bishop or archbishop in the realm, forasmuch as he hath an ordinary calling of God, and function appointed in the scriptures, which he exerciseth, and the other hath not.

But how this authority pertaining to the whole church, of making of such orders, may and ought to be called to a certain number, that confusion may be avoided, and with the consent also of the churches, to avoid tyranny, it shall appear in a more proper place, where we shall have occasion to speak of the eldership or government in every church, and of the communion and society, or participation and intercommuning of the churches together, by councils and assemblies, provincial[2] or national.

Jo. Whitgift.

The occasion of men's writings must be considered.

Divers of those learned men here named, being rightly informed of the state of this controversy, with all the circumstances pertaining thereunto, have set down their opinions in writing; and therefore, if it should so come to pass (which as yet is not proved, neither as I think will be) that in their public writings they should seem to affirm anything contrary to their private letters, it is because they, speaking generally of all, and having respect to the time and place wherein and when such things were abused, have generally spoken of them otherwise than they do, as they be now used in this church of England. And surely in my opinion these their epistles, wherein of purpose (being required) they give their sentence of such matters, ought to be more credited than their general writings, wherein they may seem otherwise to speak upon other occasions[3]. But I think that in the end it will fall out, that

[1 Unwares, Repl. 1 and 2.]   [2 Provintional, Def. B.]
[3 ..."where he saith that 'the private sentences of men in their epistles of these points are of more credit than that which they have published unto the whole

they have written nothing publicly against anything that is written by them privately; and of some of them I am sure that their public and private writings of these matters do fully agree. But where have you learned to answer on this sort to the authority of learned men? To accuse them of contrariety, before you have manifestly proved it, is to do unto them great injury.

The place of M. Bucer maketh directly for my purpose; and therefore, in giving place unto it, you grant as much as I hitherto have required. For M. Bucer used the example of apparel, which is one thing in controversy betwixt us, and saith plainly that the church hath authority to appoint such things, as have neither commandment nor example in the scripture.

These epistles of M. Bucer, and of M. Martyr, with the epistles of other learned men, be printed and published wholly and fully, and it cannot be that the same should be unknown unto you, the books being so common: your pleading of ignorance in this thing is but a colour.

When every minister must be chief of the seigniory, and have with some other of the parish the whole authority ecclesiastical; when they must "not be so tied to any form of prayers, but, as the Spirit moveth them, so to pour out supplications;" when the prince is secluded from authority in appointing of ceremonies and orders of discipline, that is, when in ecclesiastical matters you give to the civil magistrate no more than the papists do, to wit, *potestatem facti*, and not *potestatem juris*, as will afterwards more plainly appear— what is it else but for every minister to be pope in his own parish, and "to use such order, discipline, and service, as he himself listeth?" _{First Admon. the 14. reason.}

If you had been disposed to speak the truth, and to report my words as they be written, you would have eased your book of these lines which follow. For where do I give this authority to the bishops? or in what words do I restrain the church to them? My words be these: "Is it not as lawful for a godly prince, with the advice and consent of godly and learned bishops, and other of the wisest, to make

world;' it is a saying meet for such a cause as he defendeth. For all understand that men be more sudden in letters to their friends, than in their books: &c."—Sec. Repl. p. 92.]

orders in the church? &c." You see that I join the prince, the bishops, and other of the wisest together in making of orders, &c.; and, whensoever I name the church in such a case, I mean not the confused multitude of the church, but such as God hath called to govern his church in the external government; whom I take to be, in this church, the prince, the bishops, the council, and such other as, by the order of this church, have to do in such like matters.

Your falsifying hurteth not me, but discrediteth yourself, and your cause[1].

The bishops have much to thank you, that it would please you "to admit them into that consultation" of yours, if they would give over that "office and calling." But (thanks be unto God) you have as yet no such authority committed unto you. Wherefore this, and such like kind of speeches, do but declare how magnifically you think of yourself, &c.

If it pertain "to the whole church," that is (as I think you understand it) to the whole multitude of the church, to make such orders, how can you restrain it to a certain number? or why not as well to some one, if the multitude think it so convenient? But of this matter, when you come to your seigniory and kind of government.

Answer to the Admonition, Page 30, Sect. 1.

An examination of the places[2], &c.

To prove that nothing in this mortal life is more diligently to be sought for, and carefully to be looked unto, than the restitution of true religion, and reformation of God's church, there is noted 2 Kings xxiii.; 2 Chron. xvii.; 2 Chron. xxix., xxx., xxxi.; Psalm cxxxii.; Matt. xxi.; John ii. In the first place it is declared how Josiah, after he had found the book of the law, reformed the church. In the second place, Jehosaphat took away the high places and groves out of Juda, &c. In the xxix.,

[1 " Where I suppose him to attribute the order of church matters unto the bishops, which he parteth with the prince, and other wise men (albeit it will appear that he shutteth out divers, which have interest in that consultation), yet he might have some cause to complain in that behalf, and it was, I confess, my oversight."—Ibid. p. 92.]

[2 An examination of the places of scripture alleged in this portion of the Admonition, Answ.]

xxx., xxxi. of the 2 Chron., is described the doings of Ezechias, in repairing the temple and reforming religion, &c. In the cxxxii. Psalm it is declared with what care David went about to build the temple of God, after that he was once established in his kingdom. In the xxi.[3] of Matt., Jesus went into the temple, and cast out all them that bought and sold[4] in the temple, &c. The like he did in the second of John. All this is confessed to be true, and no man denieth it. And I pray God make us thankful for the queen's majesty, who hath not been slack in this point, but hath, like a virtuous, religious, and godly prince, in the very entering into her reign, notwithstanding the multitude of her adversaries, both at home and abroad, abolished all superstition, and restored the simplicity of the gospel. But these men allege these places to the discredit of this reformation, and of the whole government of this church. How aptly and how truly, let godly, wise, and learned men judge.

Jo. Whitgift.

All this is passed over with silence, and nothing said unto it, good or bad.

The exposition of the places, Deut. iv. and xii., quoted by the Admonition.

Chapter vi. The First Division.
Answer to the Admonition, Page 30, Sect. 2.

To prove that these things only are to be placed in God's church which God himself in his word commandeth, is noted the fourth and the twelfth of Deut. "Ye shall put nothing to the word that I command you, neither shall you take anything therefrom, &c." And in the other place: "Whatsoever I command you, take heed you do it; thou shalt put nothing thereto, nor take ought therefrom." God in the old law to his people prescribed perfect and absolute laws, not only moral and judicial, but ceremonial also; neither was there the least[6] *The places in the iv. and xii. of[5] Deut. expounded.*

[3 12, Def. A and B.]
[4 Sold and bought, Answ.]
[5 And 12 chapter of, Answ. 2.]
[6 Lest, Def. A. and B.]

The places of Deut. expounded. thing to be done in the church omitted in the law. And therefore for them at that time, and during that state, it was not lawful to add anything, nor to take anything away, no, not in ceremonies and[1] other civil laws. Now in the time of the gospel God hath left unto his church, expressed in his word, a perfect rule of faith and manners, and sufficient to salvation; and cursed is he that shall add anything to it, or take anything from it in that behalf; for therein it is perfect and absolute. But, as he hath left the judicial law to the discretion of the magistrate, to add thereunto or take therefrom, or alter and change the same, so that no law be made against the rule of faith and good manners expressed in the word of God, &c.[2]

T. C. Page 21, Sect. 2.

Unto the places of Deuteronomy, which prove that nothing ought to be done in the church but that which God commandeth, and that nothing should be added or[3] *diminished, first, you answer that that was a precept given to the Jews for that time, which had all things, even the least, prescribed unto them. I see it is true which is said, that, one absurdity granted, a hundred follow. For, to make good that things ought to be done besides the scripture and word of God, you are driven to run into part of the error of the Manichees, which say that the old testament pertaineth not unto us, nor bindeth not us. For what is it else than to say that these two places served for the Jews' time, and under the law? for surely, if these two places agree not unto us in time of the gospel, I know none in all the old testament which do agree. And, I pray you, what is here said which St John in the Apocalypse saith not, where he shutteth up the new testament on*[4] *this sort: "I protest unto every man which heareth the prophecy of this book, that, whosoever addeth anything to it, the* Rev. xxii. 18.[5] *Lord shall add unto him the plagues which are written in it; and, whosoever taketh away any thing from it, the Lord shall take away his portion out of the book of life, and out of the things that are written in it?" which admonition if you say pertaineth to that book of the Apocalypse only, yet you must remember that the same may be as truly said of any other book of the scripture.*

A wilful perverting of manifest and plain words.

Jo. Whitgift.

The first answer justified. My first answer to that place of Deuteronomy is true; neither can you disprove it by any sound reason or good

[1 Or, Answ.]
[2 Answ. has not &c. but proceeds with the sentence as it follows, page 279.]
[3 Nor, Repl. 1 and 2.]   [4 In, Repl. 1 and 2.]
[5 The verse of this reference is added from Repl. 2.]

authority: for, if you will have this precept now to be under- *The places of Deut. expounded.* standed of all the self-same ordinances and laws, of the which and for the which it was at that time given, then must we of necessity keep the ceremonial and judicial precepts of the law being at that time in force. The which thing, as I suppose, no learned man will once imagine; but yet, as this precept was then given to them, that they should add nothing to the laws of God then in force, or take any thing from them, so is it perpetual for us also, that we should add nothing to the law of faith and manners, which is likewise perfectly prescribed unto us in the book of God[6].

And thus you see how far I am from "the error of the *How far that precept in Deut. is extended.* Manichees," and from thinking "that the old testament doth not appertain unto us:" and yet I am not so Jewish to think that we are bound either to the ceremonial or judicial law; and therefore I say that that precept, applied unto us, doth not extend any further than to such things as God hath commanded or forbidden us that be Christians to do in his word. How unjustly therefore you charge me to say, that "these two places agree not unto us under the gospel," when as I have plainly declared how they agree to them under the law, and to us under the gospel, let any man judge.

The words in the last of the Apocalypse, although they be properly and namely spoken of that book, yet I am fully persuaded that they may also be affirmed of the whole testament. And I am so far from allowing either addition or detraction, to or from the word of God, that I utterly condemn as false that which you have set down before in your book, fol. 13.[7] that "many things are both commanded and forbid- *Fol. 13, Sect. 2.* den of which there is no express mention in the word, which are as necessarily to be followed or avoided as those whereof express mention is made."

Chapter vi. The Second Division.

T. C. Page 21, Sect. 3.

Then you are driven to say that the Jews under the law had a more certain direction, and consequently a readier way, than we have in the time

[6 "... he should have understood that in restraining the rule after that sort, thereby shutting out the laws of making orders and ceremonies of the church, he still falleth into that fault whereof he is accused."—Sec. Repl. p. 93.]

[7 See before, page 176.]

The places of the gospel; of the which time the prophet saith that then a
of Deut. man should not teach his neighbour, they shall be so taught of Jer. xxxi. 34.
expounded. God: as if he should say that they that live under the gospel should be all, in comparison of that which were under the law, doctors. And Esay saith that in the days of the gospel the people shall not Isai. lvi. 5.[1]
stand in the outward courts, but he will bring them into the sanctuary; that is to say, that they should be all, for their knowledge, as learned as the Levites and priests, which only had entrance into it.

Jo. Whitgift.

Wherein the Jews had a more certain direction than we.

In matters of ceremonies and judicials they had more particular rules prescribed unto them, and "a more certain direction." For we have very little in these matters particularly written in the new testament; but the moral law we have as perfect as they had, and in the law of faith, which is the law of the gospel and the rule of salvation, we do far exceed them. Other meaning than this there cannot (with all the violence that you have) be wrung out of my words.

Jer. xxxi.

Your places alleged out of the prophet Jeremy and Esay improve nothing that I have spoken; for the prophet Jeremy speaketh of the elect of God, whom he doth teach and illuminate, not only with the outward preaching of his word, but by the marvellous operation of his Spirit also. The words of

Isai. lvi.

the prophet Esay (if you mean the 7. ver. of the lvi. chapter; for else there is no such words there) do signify that God will gather the gentiles and strangers into his church, and make no distinction betwixt them and the Jews, in the time of the gospel; but how you should gather of that place that the people "should be as learned as the priests and Levites," I cannot conjecture. Neither truly do I know to what purpose this text is alleged, except it be a little by the way to flatter the people and to claw them.

Chapter vi. The Third Division.

T. C. Page 21, Sect. 4, 5.

Now, if the Jews had precepts of every the least action, which told them precisely how they should walk, how is not their case in that point better than ours, which, because we have in many things but general rules, are to seek oftentimes what is the will of God which we should follow? But let

[1 The verse of this reference is added from Repl. 2: it is not printed at all in Repl. 1.]

us examine their laws, and compare them with ours in the matters per- {The places of Deut. expounded.} taining to the church; for, whereas the question is of the government of the church, it is very impertinent that you speak of the judicials, as though you had not yet learned to distinguish between the church and commonwealth.

To the ordering and governing of the church they had only the moral and ceremonial law: we have the same moral that they had: what special direction therefore they enjoy by the benefit of that, we have.

Jo. Whitgift.

The Jews, as it is confessed by learned men, had their laws more particularly prescribed unto them, and especially touching ceremonies, not only because they were prone to idolatry, but also oftentimes in subjection to idolatrous princes, where they had occasion offered unto them to worship their false gods. Therefore a learned interpreter saith: *Fateor.... in multis ceremoniis divinitus mandatis fuisse occupatos, ne alias appeterent*[2]: "I confess that they were occupied in many ceremonies commanded of God, lest they should desire other." This then was one, though not the only cause of their ceremonial laws; and in this respect their case was not better, but indeed much more servile and worse than ours, who are delivered from that yoke of ceremonies, and bound only to two, as Augustine, *Epist.* 118. *ad Januar.*, saith, "most easily to be observed, and most excellent in signification, that is, the supper of the Lord and baptism[3]." So that you are much deceived if you think us to be in worse case than they were, because we have not so many particular rules for ceremonies as they had; for we are delivered from the bondage of ceremonies, as the apostle declareth to the Galat. v.: and therefore M. Calvin, in his book against the Anabaptists, answering this reason of theirs ("There is more perfection required in the church of Christ than there was among the Jews; and therefore Christians may not use the sword or be magistrates") saith on this sort: *Hoc quidem verum est, quod ad ceremo-*

{Why the Jews had their ceremonies particularly prescribed. Calvin. in Harm. in Pentateuc. Aug. Epist. 118. Gal. v. Calvin. adv. Anabap.}

[2 Calvin. Op. Amst. 1667-71. Harm. in Quat. Libr. Mos. Sec. Præcept. Tom. I. p. 410; where *ne alienas*.]

[3 Primo itaque tenere te volo....Dominum nostrum Jesum Christum....leni jugo suo nos subdidisse et sarcinæ levi: unde sacramentis numero paucissimis, observatione facillimis, significatione præstantissimis, societatem novi populi colligavit, sicuti est baptismus Trinitatis nomine consecratus, communicatio corporis et sanguinis ipsius, &c.—August. Op. Par. 1679—1700. Ad Inq. Januar. Lib. I. seu Epist. liv. cap. i. 1. Tom. II. col. 124.]

nias attinet[1]: "This is true as touching ceremonies;" meaning that we are not now bound to so many laws of ceremonies, but have freedom and liberty therein. I speak of accidental ceremonies as well as of sacraments.

You say that, "whereas the question is of the government of the church, &c."; wherein *antiquum obtines*. For our present question is, whether all things to be used in the church are prescribed in the scripture. And that which I speak of "the judicial law," I speak it by occasion of the interpretation of these places of Deuteronomy. Howbeit I see no such distance betwixt "the church and the commonwealth," but the laws of the one doth and ought to pertain to the other; except you will do as the papists did, that is, seclude the civil magistrate altogether from meddling in any ecclesiastical matter. And I am well assured that not only the ceremonial and moral law, but the judicial also, pertained to the government of the church of the Israelites, and that these precepts, of "not adding to or taking from," pertained to that law also. M. Musculus, in his Common-places, *cap. de Legibus*, divideth the judicial law into two parts, into ecclesiastical and civil: his words be these: "Wherefore these precepts may not unfitly (he meaneth judicial) be divided into two kinds, whereof some are ecclesiastical and other civil[2]." M. Beza, in like manner, in his book *De Hæreticis a Magist. puniend.*, saith that "the judicial law doth partly consist in the external manner of worshipping God, partly in the civil affairs of this life[3]." And M. Calvin, in his *Harmo.* upon the five books of Moses, expounding this in the xxiii. of Exodus, "Thou shalt utterly overthrow them and break in pieces their images," calleth it a politic law, and yet notwithstanding an appendix to the first precept, and added to confirm that which he had spoken before against idolatry[4]. Therefore "to the ordering

[1 Nullum igitur superest istis omnis ordinis hostibus subterfugium, quam ut dicant majorem a Domino perfectionem in ecclesia christiana, quam olim in populo Judaico requiri. Hoc &c.—Calvin. Op. Amst. 1667-71. Instr. adv. Anabapt. Art. vi. Tom. VIII. p. 364.]

[2 Quare non incommode possent hæc præcepta [judicialia] in duas classes dividi, ut alia sint ecclesiastica, alia forensia.—Wolfg. Muscul. Loc. Comm. Theol. Basil. 1599. De Leg. p. 131.]

[3 Rursum judicialis a ceremoniali differt, primum in eo quod ista externum religionis cultum tradit, illa partim quidem in divini cultus externa conservatione, ...partim vero in civilibus hujus vitæ negotiis versatur.—Th. Bezæ De Hæret. a civil. Magistrat. pun. Libell. Par. 1554. p. 221.]

[4 Postquam autem docuit Moses quod observatu necessarium erat, quo dili-

and governing of the church" the Jews had not only "the moral and ceremonial," but the judicial law also.

The places of Deut. expounded.

Chapter vi. The Fourth Division.

T. C. Page 21, Sect. ult.

We have no ceremonies but two, the ceremonies or sacraments of baptism and of the Lord's supper; and we have as certain a direction to celebrate them, as they had to celebrate their ceremonies, and fewer and less difficulties can rise of ours than of theirs; and we have more plain and express doctrine to decide our controversies than they had for theirs. What hour had they for their ordinary and daily sacrifices? was it not left to the order of the church? what places were appointed in their several dwellings to hear the word of God preached continually, when they came not to Jerusalem? The word was commanded to be preached, but no mention made what manner of place they should have. Where was pulpits commanded or chairs? and yet they had both. Where any form of burial in the law? and yet it is a thing pertaining to the church, that the dead be after a comely sort buried. Where any order or form of marriage? and yet it is known they had. It was (which is more) in the discretion of that church, upon occasion of dearth, or war, plagues, or any other common calamity, to proclaim a fast.

Jo. Whitgift.

"We have no ceremonies," which be sacraments, "but two," and in them, and for all things pertaining to their substance, "we have as certain direction as they had" for any of their sacraments. But yet is not every circumstance to be used about the celebrating of them so particularly, nor so certainly prescribed unto us, as was to them in their ceremonies, sacraments, and sacrifices; for they had every particular circumstance to be used about their sacrifices, sacraments, and ceremonies, set down unto them, as it is evident Exod. xii. xxv. xxvi., &c., and in Leviticus. We are not bound to any such prescript form of outward ceremonies and circumstances, but have free liberty, not only to appoint, but also to alter and change the same, as shall be thought most convenient; so that nothing be done against the word of God, and that the general rule be observed, 1 Cor. xiv., "That all things be done decently and in order." All this therefore that you speak of "hour," "place," and of "the form of burial," and of "marriage," &c. infirmeth nothing that I have said: for these

How we have but two ceremonies.

1 Cor. xiv

gentius sibi populus caveat, politicam legem addit de frangendis statuis et diruendis altaribus.—Calvin. Op. Harm. in Quat. Libr. Mos. Sec. Præcept. Tom. I. p. 472.]

The places of Deut. expounded.

be circumstances not used in the service of God, but in other actions; and I speak of such ceremonies and circumstances as are used in the church, about the service and worshipping of God, which were to the Jews particularly prescribed (as appeareth in the places before alleged), but be not so to us[1].

Chapter vi. The Fifth Division.
T. C. Page 22, Sect. 1, 2.

A large offer, but not so soon performed.

I will not be long, whereas you say that they had nothing but was determined by the law, and we have many things undetermined, and left to the order of the church; I will offer, for one that you shall bring that we have left to the order of the church, to shew you that they had twenty which were undecided of by the express word of God. For, as their ceremonies and sacraments are multiplied above ours, so grew the number of those cases which were not determined by any express word; and therefore I will conclude that, forsomuch as we have the same laws to direct us in the service of God which they had, besides[2] that, a noble addition of the new testament to make things more manifest, and to bring greater light unto the old testament, we have also precise direction of our religion as they had; and therefore those places of Deuteronomy stand in as great force now, touching the government of the church, as they did then.

And, as for the judicial law, forasmuch as there are some of them made in regard of the region where they were given, and of the people to whom they were given, the prince and magistrate, keeping the substance and equity of them (as it were the marrow), may change the circumstances of them, as the times and places and manners of the people shall require. But to say that any magistrate can save the life of blasphemers, contemptuous and stubborn idolaters, murderers, adulterers, incestuous persons, and such like, which God by his judicial law hath commanded to be put to death, I do utterly deny, and am ready to prove, if that pertained to this question. And therefore, although the judicial laws are permitted to the discretion of the prince and magistrate, yet not so generally as you seem to affirm, and, as I have oftentimes said, that not only it must not be done against the word, but according to the word, and by it.

Jo. Whitgift.

Surely, if you can " shew me twenty things" to be done of them in the service of God, or discipline of the church, "left to the order of the church, and undetermined" in the law, " for one that I can shew left to the order of our church," you

[1 Cartwright says that in this and the former division Whitgift "answereth not to the matter."—Sec. Repl. p. 93.]

[2 Beside, Repl. 1 and 2.]

can do more than any man that I know hath either spoken or written. Musculus, *Loc. Com.*, after that he hath made a particular recital of the ceremonial laws, saith that " God did therefore appoint unto them such a number of ceremonies, because they should not invent any other, seeing they had ceremonies enow whereby they might be exercised, and as it were by a certain kind of schooling might be instructed in the spiritual sense[3]." To our discretion is left, as I have said, the most of the circumstances pertaining to both the sacraments, most of all external rites, ceremonies, and other things that pertain to comeliness and order, yea, and the disposition of many things also which appertain to the external discipline and government of the church; which are to be varied according to time, persons, and place, as shall hereafter be proved. If you be able to shew that the same liberty was left unto them in so many things, you shall do more than I can conceive.

But admit all this to be true that you say, there can be nothing spoken more directly for the justifying of my cause. For, if the Israelites, notwithstanding these places of Deuteronomy, had liberty to order things in the church, not commanded or prescribed unto them in the word of God, then do the authors of the Admonition unaptly use these places of Deuteronomy to prove that those things "only are to be used and placed in the church which God himself in his word hath commanded." For, if the Jews (notwithstanding these precepts) did lawfully use those things that were not in the word commanded, without adding to the word, or taking from it, surely we may do so in like manner. And thus have you taken much pains in justifying that cause, which you would so gladly overthrow.

Where you say that "we have the same laws to direct us in the service of God that they had," if you mean the same moral laws, you say truly, but nothing to the purpose: if you mean the same ceremonial laws (which properly are said to be "laws directing them in the service of God"), then do you *Judaizare*, "play the Jew." And certainly I

[3 Has ceremonias populo suo Israeli ac sacerdotibus illius præscripsit Deus,... ne ipse [populus] sibi proprio arbitratu cultus fingeret et institueret,...sed in obedientia verbi sui persisteret, et interea abunde satis haberet sacrorum rituum, quibus exerceretur, et quasi pædagogia quadam ad sensus spirituales instituere‑ tur.—Wolfg. Muscul. Loc. Comm. Theol. Basil. 1599. De Leg. pp. 133, 4.]

The places of Deut. expounded. marvel what you mean by this saying, seeing that you know our external manner and kind of worshipping of God to be far distant from theirs; and our sacraments, though spiritually the same, yet both in number, form, matter, observation, and kind of signification, much differing from them, and especially seeing that their ceremonial law is utterly abolished. Neither do I well understand what your meaning is when you add, "Besides that, a noble addition of the new testament, to make things more manifest, and to bring a greater light unto the old testament[1]." For, if you mean that the new testament is added to the ceremonial law, that cannot be so, for it is the end of the ceremonial law, and doth *Rom. x.* utterly abrogate it. *Nam finis legis Christus, &c.:* "Christ is the end of the law." For as well the figures, as the promises contained in the law and the prophets, are fulfilled in the new testament by the coming of Christ; as he himself *Luke xxiv.* saith, Luke xxiv. If you mean that it is added to the moral law, that is also untrue; for it only explaineth it, it addeth nothing unto it. Indeed it bringeth "a great light to the old testament," because all things are there fulfilled which were prophesied of, and prefigured, in the old testament. *Calvin. Inst.* M. Calvin, *Institu. cap. iii. sect.* 9, saith that to think Christ to have added anything to the law is "most pernicious[2]."

I must crave pardon of the reader for making such excursions out of the way; for I am compelled to follow you, which interlace your book with such by-matters, and those so suspicious and dangerous, that I cannot safely pass them over *Whether the magistrate be bound to observe the judicial law of Moses.* with silence. And even now again do you enter into a strange and dangerous opinion in my judgment; for you would have the civil magistrate bound to observe all the judicial laws of Moses, "except such as were made in respect of the region where they were given, and of the people to whom they were given." Of the which laws the magistrates, you say, "may

[1 Cartwright rejoins that he had sufficiently explained his meaning in calling the new testament "a noble addition to the law," and asserts that Calvin had used the same manner of speech.—Sec. Repl. p. 95.]

[2 Hæc qui non viderunt, finxerunt Christum alterum Mosen, legis euangelicæ latorem, quæ defectum Mosaicæ illius suppleverit. Unde illud vulgatum axioma de perfectione legis euangelicæ, quæ legem veterem longo intervallo superet: quod multis modis est perniciosissimum.—Calvin. Op. Amst. 1667-71. Inst. Lib. II. cap. viii. 7. Tom. IX. p. 93.]

only change the circumstances, as the times, and places, and manners of the people shall require." But you "utterly deny, and are ready to prove, if that pertained to this question, that any magistrate can save the life of blasphemers, contemptuous and stubborn idolaters, murderers, adulterous persons, and such like, which God by his judicial law hath commanded to be put to death." *The places of Deut. expounded.*

Howsoever you pass this matter over "as impertinent to this question," yet, forasmuch as you have here set it down (and I am fully persuaded that it is untrue), I mind to touch it something, and to utter the reasons of my persuasions. I leave it to the consideration of those that know the laws and state of the realm, and especially such as have the chief government and care of the same, what lieth hid under this your opinion. First, all the laws of this land, that be contrary to these judicial laws of Moses, must be abrogated: the prince must be abridged of that prerogative which she hath in pardoning such as by the law be condemned to die: the punishments of death for felony must be mitigated according to Moses' law, which doth by other means punish the same, Exod. xxii. To be short, all things must be transformed: lawyers must cast away their huge volumes and multitude of cases, and content themselves with the books of Moses: we of the clergy would be the best judges; and they must require the law at our hands, Deuter. xvii. verse 8. And so, while we make them believe that we seek for equality among ourselves, we seek indeed regal dominion over them. Look Deuter. xvii. verse 12. But, to omit all these considerations, which I leave to those to whom they do especially pertain, I will shew, as briefly as I can, how far this opinion is from true divinity. *The inconveniences joined with the assertion of T. C.* *Exod. xxii.* *Deut. xvii.*

First, besides all those places of scripture which make generally for the abrogation of the whole law, we have especial places for the judicial law, and namely those where Christ maketh laws of divorcement for adultery, Matt. v. and xix.; which were altogether needless, if she that is taken in adultery should of necessity be stoned to death, according to the law of Moses. Augustine, *ad Pollentium de Adult. Conjug. Lib. ii.* *capp.* 6, 7, 8, and 14, proveth by that which is written of Christ, John viii., touching the woman deprehended in adultery, and brought unto him by the scribes and Pharisees, *The judicial law abrogated.* *Matt. v. & xix.* *Augustine.* *Joh. viii.*

[WHITGIFT.] 18

The judicial law of Moses.

Cyril.

Muscul.

Hemingius.

that the wife taken in adultery ought not to be punished with death, but suffered to live, that she might be reconciled to her husband, or at the least repent[1]. Cyril also, upon the xi. of Leviticus, saith that, "though the punishment of death was according to the law of Moses appointed for adultery, and certain other crimes, yet among Christians there is no such commandment in force[2]." Musculus, in his Common-places, *Tit. de Legib.*, speaking of the law, saith thus : " They ask the question whether the whole law be abrogated : we answer, if whole Moses gave place to Christ, then hath his whole law given place to the law of Christ[3]." And a little after: " The commandments of the law are moral, judicial, ceremonial. That the ceremonial commandments have ceased it is evident; forsomuch as the priesthood of the law, to the which the ceremonies were annexed, is abrogated by the priesthood of Christ, according to the order of Melchizedech ; and that the judicials also are ceased it doth herein appear, for that the whole order of government of Israel, which was requisite unto the inhabiting of the land of promise, hath from that time ceased, when as they, being expelled, began to dwell amongst the gentiles without a king, without governors, without a priest, and without a law[4]."

Hemingius, in his *Enchir.*, is of the same judgment: his words be these : " There is also the judicial law, which expired with the commonwealth of Moses ; so that it doth not bind any man of necessity, but so far only as some portion of it doth pertain to the law of nature (as the law against incestuous

[1 August. Op. Par. 1679-1700. De Conj. Adult. Lib. II. capp. vi. vii. viii. xiv. 5, 6, 7, 14, 15. Tom. VI. cols. 407, 8, 12, 13.]

[2 Secundum legem adulter et adultera morte moriebantur....Hoc autem servabatur et in singulis quibusque criminibus quibus erat poena mortis adscripta. Apud Christianos vero si adulterium fuerit admissum, non est præceptum ut adulter vel adultera corporali interitu puniantur.—Orig. Op. Par. 1733-59. In Levit. Hom. xi. 2. Tom. II. p. 248. These homilies were formerly ascribed to Cyril.]

[3 Quærunt an tota [lex] sit abrogata ? *Respondemus :* Si totus Moses cessit Christo, utique tota illius lex cessit legi Christi.—Wolfg. Muscul. Loc. Comm. Theol. Basil. 1599. De Leg. p. 141.]

[4 Mandata legis sunt moralia, judicialia, ceremonialia. Ceremonialia cessasse ex eo patet, quod ipsum sacerdotium legis, cui annexæ fuerunt ceremoniæ, per sacerdotium Christi secundum ordinem Melchizedek est abrogatum, et jam olim reipsa cessavit. Judicialia quoque cessasse in eo declaratur, quod tota Israëlis œconomia, qualem terræ promissæ inhabitatio requirebat, ab eo tempore cessavit, quo expulsi inter gentes sine rege, sine ducibus, sine sacerdote, et sine lege habitare cœperunt.—Id. ibid.]

marriages, Levit. xviii.), and so much of it likewise as the civil magistrate shall admit for policy⁵." *The judicial law of Moses.*

I omit that place of M. Calvin, which is written in his Harmony upon the 5. books of Moses, where he, speaking of these laws, Exod. xxiii., Deut. xii., Numb. xxxiii., which were given for the breaking of images, destroying of places where idolatry was committed, &c. saith that they were but temporal exercises, to keep the people in obedience, &c.⁶ And in the same book, speaking of the vii. of Deuteronomy, "The graven images of their gods shall ye burn with fire, and covet not the silver and gold that is on them, &c.;" saith, "Although this was a politic law, and given only to the ancient people for a time, yet hereby we may gather how detestable idolatry is, &c.⁷" But of all other places that is most evident which he hath in his *Institu. cap. xx. sect.* 13, 14, 15; and therefore I will rehearse it more at large: *Sunt qui recte compositam rempub. negent, &c.*⁸*:* "There are certain which deny that commonwealth to be well ordered, which, omitting the politic laws of Moses, is ruled by the common laws of the gentiles. The which opinion how dangerous and seditious it is, let other men consider; it is enough for me to have declared that it is both false and foolish. *Calvin.* *Deut. vii.* *Calvinus.*

[⁵ Est et lex judicialis, quæ cessante republica Mosis expiravit, ita ut non necessario ullum hominem obliget in specie, nisi quatenus portio ejus aliqua aut pars est legis naturæ, ut lex contra incestas nuptias Levi. 18. aut a magistratu proponitur politico fine.—N. Hemming. Opusc. Theol. 1586. Enchir. Theol. Class. II. cap. i. col. 378.]

[⁶ Nunc temporalibus exercitiis confirmat doctrinam illam, ut populum veterem in officio contineat.—Calvin. Op. Amst. 1667-71. Harm. in Quat. Libr. Mos. Sec. Præcept. Tom. I. p. 472.]

[⁷ Quamvis autem politicum hoc fuerit præceptum, et tantum veteri populo ad tempus datum, ex eo tamen colligimus quam detestabilis sit idololatria, quæ ipsa etiam Dei opera sua fœditate inficit.—Id. ibid. p. 475.]

[⁸ Sunt enim qui recte compositam esse rempublicam negent, quæ, neglectis Mose politicis, communibus gentium legibus regitur. Quæ sententia quam periculosa sit et turbulenta, viderint alii: mihi falsam esse ac stolidam demonstrasse satis erit. Est autem observanda vulgata illa partitio, quæ universam Dei legem per Mosen promulgatam in mores, ceremonias, judicia distribuit: ac dispiciendæ singulæ partes, ut habeamus quid ex iis ad nos pertineat, quid minus. Nec interim quempiam moretur hic scrupulus, quod ad mores etiam judicia et ceremoniæ pertinent. Veteres enim qui partitionem hanc tradiderunt, tametsi duas istas posteriores partes non ignorabant circa mores versari, quia tamen salvis moribus mutari et abrogari poterant, morales non dixerunt. Primam illam partem peculiariter appellarunt eo nomine, citra quam non constet vera morum sanctitas et immutabilis recte vivendi norma.—Id. Inst. Lib. IV. cap. xx. 14. Tom. IX. p. 402.]

The judicial law of Moses.

But that usual division is to be observed, which divideth the whole law of God delivered by Moses into manners, ceremonies, and judgments; and every part thereof is diligently to be considered, that we may understand what pertaineth unto us thereof, and what doth not. In the meantime, let no man be troubled with this, that both the judicials and ceremonies did appertain unto manners; for the ancient fathers, the inventors of this division, although they were not ignorant that these two latter parts were occupied about manners, yet (because they might be altered and abrogated without any prejudice unto manners) they called them not moral. They called that first part properly by that name moral, without the which the true holiness of manners, and the immutable rule of living, could not well consist." And again: "The law of God forbiddeth to steal: what punishment was appointed for theft in the policy of the Jews, appeareth in Exodus. The most ancient laws of other nations punished theft with double: they which followed afterward made a difference betwixt open theft and that which was secret: others condemned the thieves with exile and banishment: others adjudged them to be whipped; and, last of all, others, to be put to death. False witness amongst the Jews was punished with equal pain in respect of the hurt; in other places only with infamy; in other places with hanging, &c. All laws jointly do revenge murder with blood, but yet with divers kinds of death. In some places there are grievouser pains appointed for adulterers, in other places those which are more easy: yet we see how they all, by this diversity of punishment, tend to one end; for they all with one consent do give sentence of punishment against those offences which are condemned by the eternal law of God, to wit, murder, theft, adultery, false witness; but they agree not all in the manner of the punishment. Neither truly is it necessary or expedient that they should agree herein. There is a country which should out of hand be destroyed with thieves and slaughter, if it did not with horrible example deal very sharply with murderers. There is also some time which requireth the augmentation of the sharpness of punishment, and some people very prone unto some certain sin, except they be with great rigour kept in awe. He is then very evil affected, and envieth the public commodity, that is offended with this diversity, which is most

Exod. xxii.

meet to retain the observation of the law of God. For that which some men object, that by this means injury is done to the law of God, whiles, it being abrogated, other laws are preferred before it, is most vain. For other laws are not preferred before it, but allowed, not by any simple comparison in respect of God's law, but according to the condition of time, place, and nation; neither can that be said to be abrogated which was never prescribed unto us; for God delivered it by the hands of Moses, not for all nations, but particularly for the Jews, &c.[1]" M. Beza likewise, in his book *De Hær. a Magist. puniend.*, of this matter writeth thus: " We acknowledge those politic laws to be prescribed only to the country of the Jews; neither are we so unskilful that we would have Moses' commonwealth or government called back again, as though it were not lawful for every magistrate within his own dominion to make laws in civil matters[2]." And a little after: "The judicial

The judicial law of Moses.

Beza.

[1 Lex Dei furari prohibet. Quæ furtis constituta fuerit pœna in politia Judæorum, videre est in Exodo. Aliarum gentium vetustissimæ leges furtum duplo puniebant: quæ postea sequutæ sunt, discreverunt inter manifestum et non manifestum. Aliæ ad exilium progressæ sunt, aliæ ad flagrum, aliæ denique ad capitis supplicium. Falsum testimonium talionis pœna inter Judæos plectebatur: alibi gravi tantum ignominia, alibi suspendio, alibi cruce. Homicidium omnes pariter leges sanguine ulciscuntur, diversis tamen mortis generibus. In adulteros alibi severiores, alibi leviores edictæ sunt pœnæ. Videmus tamen ut ejusmodi diversitate in eundem omnes finem tendant. Nam uno simul ore pœnam pronunciant in ea quæ æterna Dei lege damnata sunt facinora; nempe homicidia, furta, adulteria, falsa testimonia: sed in pœnæ modo non coveniunt. neque vero id necesse est, neque etiam expedit. Est regio, quæ nisi horrendis exemplis in homicidas sæviat, cædibus statim et latrociniis perdenda sit. Est seculum, quod pœnarum acerbitatem augeri postulet. Siquid turbatum sit in statu publico, novis edictis corrigenda sunt quæ inde nasci solent mala. Belli tempore in armorum strepitu concideret omnis humanitas, nisi insolito pœnarum metu injecto. In sterilitate, in pestilentia, nisi adhibeatur major severitas, pessum ibunt omnia. Est gens in vitium quoddam propensior nisi acerrime compescatur. Quam malignus fuerit, ac publico bono invidus, qui tali diversitate offendetur, ad retinendam legis Dei observationem accommodatissima! Nam quod jactatur a quibusdam, fieri contumeliam legi Dei per Mosem latæ, quum, abrogata illa, novæ aliæ illi præferuntur, vanissimum est: neque enim aliæ illi præferuntur dum magis probantur, non simplici collatione, sed temporum, loci, gentis conditione; aut illa abrogator quæ nobis lata nunquam fuit: siquidem non eam Dominus per manum Mosis tradidit quæ in gentes omnes promulgaretur, et ubique vigeret; sed quum Judaicam gentem in fidem, patrocinium, clientelam suam suscepisset, illi etiam peculiariter legislator esse voluit, &c.—Id. ibid. 16. ibid.]

[2 Agnoscimus enim...politicas esse istas leges, et uni tantum Judæorum genti perscriptas. Neque sumus tam imperiti ut politiam Mosaicam velimus revocare, quasi peculiares de negotiis civilibus leges sancire cuique magistratui in sua ditione non liceat.—Th. Bezæ De Hæret. a civil. Magistrat. pun. Libell. Par. 1554. p. 219.]

The judicial law of Moses.

laws were framed only for one nation. Therefore, seeing they were never written for us, they cannot be said to be abrogated[1]." And again: "Only the Israelites were bound to the judicial laws, that is, those that dwell in Jewry, because they were made fit for that commonwealth only[2]." And, after that he hath shewed by an example of the law for theft, that that manner and kind of punishment did only bind the Israelites, and that other magistrates in their countries for good causes may appoint a sharper kind of punishment for the same, he concludeth thus: *Lex enim illa Mosis, quatenus pœnæ modum præscribit, aliis gentibus neque unquam fuit posita, neque nunc est proprie abrogata*[3]: "That law of Moses, insomuch as it prescribeth the manner of punishment, was neither at any time given to other nations, neither is it now properly abrogated." So that now they that be disposed may perceive how this doctrine of yours not only tendeth to the overthrowing of states of commonwealths, but is contrary also to the truth, and opinion of learned men, and those especially of whom you yourself make greatest account. Therefore it is true that I have said in my Answer to the Admonition, that is, "The judicial law to be left to the discretion of the magistrate, to add to it or to take from it, or to alter and change it," as shall be thought most fit for the time, manner of the country, and condition of the people; as M. Calvin also very aptly noteth in the very end of that fifteenth section before rehearsed[4].

Idem.

[1 ...Leges autem judiciales ad unius reipublicæ rationem fuerunt accommodatæ. Itaque quum nobis nunquam scriptæ fuerint, ne abrogatæ quidem dici possunt.—Id. ibid. p. 221.]

[2 Contra vero judicialibus legibus soli Israelitæ tenebantur, id est qui in Judæa habitabant: quia scilicet huic uni reipublicæ erant accommodatæ.—Id. ibid. p. 222.]

[3 Id. ibid. p. 223.]

[4 Cartwright in his Second Reply argues at great length against Whitgift's assertions on the subject of the law: "It is not," he says, "that the magistrate is simply bound unto the judicial laws of Moses, but that he is bound to the equity, which I also called the substance and marrow of them. In regard of which equity I affirmed that there are certain laws amongst the judicials which cannot be changed." He admits that the ceremonial law was to be taken away, but considers that Whitgift "hath very dangerously set down that the whole law of God generally is abrogated." For the moral law is in full strength; and "those judicial laws of Moses, which are merely politic, and without all mixture of ceremonies, must remain." He urges for proof that St Paul unhesitatingly quoted it, 1 Cor. ix. 9. Of the judicial laws which cannot be changed are those, he says, "that a blasphemer, contemptuous, and stubborn idolater, &c.

Chapter vi.   The Sixth Division. *The judicial law*
Answer to the Admonition, Page 31, line 21. *of Moses.*

So hath he left authority unto his church to make laws, and appoint orders and ceremonies, as shall from time to time be thought most expedient and profitable for the same; so that nothing be done contrary to his word, or repugnant to the same.   And this authority hath the church used, even from the apostles' time, as it is manifest, both by the scriptures, Acts vi., Acts xv., 1 Cor. xi., and other ecclesiastical stories, and ancient fathers, as is before by me proved.

Jo. Whitgift.

To this nothing is answered.

Chapter vi.   The Seventh Division.
Answer to the Admonition, Page 31, Sect. 1.

But to come to the words of Deuteronomy themselves, what is it to add to the word of God, or to take from it? Truly to think otherwise, or teach otherwise of God than he hath in his word revealed : those take from the word, that believe less than in the word is expressed : those add to the word, first, which teach or decree anything, either in matters of faith or ceremonies, contrary to the word; secondly, those that make anything necessary unto salvation not contained in the word; thirdly, such as make any religion or opinion of merit in anything that they themselves have invented besides the word of God; last of all, they add to the word, which forbid that for a thing of itself unlawful which God's word doth not forbid, and make that sin which God's word doth not make sin.

[Zuinglius, in his book *De Baptismo*, speaking of the weak reasons that the anabaptists use against the baptizing of infants, saith thus : " I cannot keep secret their lies, and other things which may be hurtful to christian people; as that argument which they take out of the fourth and

ought to be put to death ;" and calls " the exceptions against this doctrine " " of no value." He disallows all the authorities cited, that ascribed to Cyril in particular, which alleged more fully in another place he altogether rejects, and declares that some of the authors referred to were of his opinion.—Sec. Repl. pp. 95, &c.]

The places of Deut. expounded. twelfth chapters of Deuteronomy: 'Thou shalt add nothing to my word nor take any thing therefrom.' But God hath no where commanded that infants should be baptized; *ergo*, infants are not to be baptized. To this foolish argument I answer after two sorts. First, I ask of them whether God any where in the scriptures hath forbidden infants to be baptized: they must, whether they will or no, confess that it is no where forbidden; except therefore they can shew certain places of the scripture which forbiddeth infants to be baptized, it is certain that they add that unto the scriptures of their own, which is no where contained in them. My other answer is this: It is not sufficient in those things which you say to be unlawful oftentimes to repeat this, *Nihil addes verbo meo, &c.* But, if you will prove anything to be sin, you must bring forth a manifest law and prohibition out of the word of God. For as Paul saith, Rom. iv. 'Where there is no law, there is no transgression[1].'"][2]

But such as truly and sincerely embrace the word of God, and admit nothing contrary unto it, if in government and ceremonies, without any wicked and[3] superstitious opinion, they appoint or[4] retain such as they know not to be against the word of God, and profitable for the present state of the church, cannot truly be said to add anything to the word of God, or take anything from it though the same be not expressed in the word.

[[1] Interim tamen mendacia illorum, tum et alia quam plurima, quæ christianæ plebi damno esse possunt, silentio præterire nequaquam convenit. Quale illud est, cum ex verbis Dei, quæ Deut. 4. et 12. cap. extant, coram rudi plebecula sic argumentantur, Non addes verbo meo, nec quicquam etiam illi demas, dicit Dominus. Pueros autem vel infantes baptizare nusquam præcepit Deus. Ergo infantes baptizandi non sunt. Huic vero argumentationi ipsorum ineptissimæ bifariam responderi potest...Primum ergo quærimus ab illis, num alicubi in scripturis Deus, ne infantes baptizentur, prohibuerit? Nusquam hoc prohibitum esse vel inviti fatebuntur....Nisi ergo ostenderint certos scripturæ locos, quibus infantium baptismus prohibetur, certo constabit illos ipsos scripturis vim facere, et quod in illis nusquam continetur, de suo addere...Altera responsio, qua objectionem illorum retundimus, talis est: Nequaquam sufficit, O boni, ut de iis rebus, quas vos illicitas esse contenditis, illud unum subinde non sine clamoribus summis ingeminetur, Nihil addes verbo meo &c. verum si quid peccatum esse demonstrare volueritis, manifestam legem et prohibitionem e verbo Dei afferatis, necesse est. Nam (ut Paulus ad Romanos cap. 4. tradit,) Ubi non est lex, ibi non est transgressio.—H. Zvingl. Op. Tigur. 1581. Epist. præf. de Bapt. Libr. Pars II. fol. 58.]

[[2] This is inserted from Answ. 2; which proceeds *Such therefore as &c*]
[[3] Or, Answ.]   [[4] To, Def. B.]

T. C. Page 22, Sect. 3.

After you define what it is[5] *to take from and put to the word of God,* **The places of Deut. expounded.** *wherein, not to speak of your wonderful dexterity in defining, which can define two things, and those contrary (putting to, and taking fro), with one difference, which Zeno himself could never do, you leave out that which* **There is no great dexterity required to perform this.** *Moses especially meant to comprehend, which is, not to do more, nor to do less, than he hath commanded. And as for your division, it hath as evil success here, as in other places: for, when it is a great fault in dividing to have either too much or too little, you fault in both; for, whereas you say, "they add, which teach or decree, &c.," besides that you leave out [that] which Moses meant, you forget also that which yourself had said, which had placed adding to not only in teaching and decreeing, but in thinking or believing.*

And, whereas you make four parts of your division, the three last are found to be all under the first member, which is to make things of faith and ceremonies contrary to the word; and so your division is not only faulty, but no division at all. The which thing I could have easily forgiven you, and passed by as a thing not very commendable, to travail to shew the poverty of those things which do sufficiently of themselves (as it were) proclaim their own shame; but that it grieved me to see a book **All this is spoken in contempt of the person, not in defence of the cause.** *lengthened with first, second, third, last, as though every one of them contained some notable new matter, which needed an "O yes" before it, to stir up the attention of the reader; when there is nothing but a many of words without matter, as it*[6] *were a sort of fair empty apothecary's boxes without any stuff in them. And, for that you are so hard with other men for their logic, I will desire the reader to pardon me if I pursue these things more narrowlier than some peradventure will like of, or I myself delight in. And so, for any definition or division that I can perceive, it standeth fast, that nothing is to be done in the church of God but by his commandment and word directing the same. It is true indeed, if they be not against the word of God, and profitable*[7] *for the church, they are to be received as those things which God by his*[8] *church doth command, and as grounded of the word of God. But there is the question; and therefore you, taking this as a thing granted always, do always fall into that which you charge other with, of the fallation of* Petitio principii.

Jo. Whitgift.

There is neither definition nor division here that can please you; but what remedy? When your jests be uttered, and you a little sported yourself, and the matter cometh to trial, there appeareth very slender corrections. I have, after my rude and simple manner, declared what it is "to add to the word of God, or to take from it," and have not sought for

[[5] Is it, Repl. 1 and 2. The former, however, corrects to *it is* in the list of errata.]
[[6] *It* is repeated, Repl. 1.] [[7] And be profitable, Repl. 2.]
[[8] The, Repl. 1, 2, and Def. A.]

The places of Deut. expounded.

Two contraries may be defined with one difference.

any exact definition. But yet (by your leave) "two contraries may be defined by one" general "difference," when we talk of those things which be common to them both, and do not seek to separate them from among themselves, but from all other things that be not of the same kind. So is "virtue" and "vice" by this difference, *sensim acquiri et sensim amitti*, separated from all other that be not *sub habitu;* as *homo* and *brutum* by this difference, *sensibile*, be separated from all other creatures that be not under *animal*. It is a common rule, that the definition of that which is called *genus* doth agree to every part and member under it, which we call *species*, be they contrary, repugnant, or otherwise disagreeing the one from the other, howsoever. Therefore, declaring generally what it is "to add to the word, or to take from the word," I say it is "to think otherwise or to teach otherwise of God than he hath in his word revealed:" which in *genere* doth aptly expound them both. For as well he that addeth to the word, as he that taketh from the word, doth think or teach of God otherwise than he hath in his word revealed. So you see that a man of small "dexterity in defining" may do that which you thought "Zeno himself" could not perform[1].

But what needed all this pastime of yours? do I not immediately after severally declare both what it is "to add to the word," and what also "to take from" it? Are you able to prove that the expositions which I set down be not true? can you better them? Will you still more and more declare your quarrel to be rather against the person than the cause? You say I "leave out that which Moses especially meant to comprehend, which is, not to do more, nor to do less, than he hath commanded." Surely, if you were disposed to deal modestly and sincerely, as it behoveth you in so weighty a matter, you would not thus wittingly and willingly seek occasion of quarrelling. Whether that which you say is left out must not of necessity be included in those words that I have spoken of adding to the word, and taking from it, or no, I leave to the indifferent reader to consider.

Touching my "division," I say as I did of the "definition." I am not curious in dividing, but I plainly and after my rude manner tell how many ways a man may add to the word of God. Neither doth he always divide, that sheweth how

[[1] Cartwright calls all this "absurd," and says, "he maketh himself pitiful to all that ever saluted that school."—Sec. Repl. p. 119.]

many ways a thing may be done; and yet is there nothing left out necessary to be expressed. For this that you speak of "thinking and believing" is included in the third kind of adding to the word. "The three last kinds are" not "found to be under the first:" for it is not all one "to teach or decree anything contrary to the word;" "to make anything necessary to salvation not contained in the word;" "to put any religion or opinion of merit in anything that men themselves have invented besides the word;" and "to forbid that as unlawful which God doth not forbid."

The places of Deut. expounded

In the first kind is invocation of saints, worshipping of images, &c.; which be directly contrary to the express word of God. In the second is that decree of pope Boniface, which maketh it necessary to salvation to be subject to the bishop of Rome[2], and such like, whereof there is no mention in the scriptures. In the third kind are all outward ceremonies invented by man, wherein any opinion of worshipping or merit is put, as holy bread, holy water, and other ceremonies of that sort. In the last part is the decree of pope Nicholas, *Dist. xxii. Omnes;* where it is decreed that he which infringeth the privileges of the church of Rome is an heretic[3]. And in this sort do those add also to the word, which condemn the use of things indifferent as unlawful; for in so doing they make that sin which the word of God doth not make sin.

Again, that there is a great difference in the parts of my division, and that they are not confounded, you might have perceived, if it had pleased you with better advice to have weighed them. For things may be decreed contrary to the word, and yet not made necessary unto salvation. Things may be made as necessary to salvation, which of themselves are not contrary to the word, and yet not contained in the word: men may have an opinion of religion and merit in such things as they think not to be of necessity to salvation. To be short, men may make that sin, which the word of God maketh not sin; as all those do which forbid the use of indifferent things, and make the same unlawful, as I have said before. You see now that there is no one part of this "division" (as you call

[2 Bonifac. VIII. in Corp. Jur. Canon. Lugd. 1624. Extrav. Comm. Lib. I. De Major. et Obed. cap. 1. col. 212. See before, pages 181, 2, note 6.]

[3 Qui autem Romanæ ecclesiæ privilegium ab ipso summo omnium ecclesiarum capite traditum auferre conatur, hic proculdubio in hæresim labitur.— Nicol. II. in eod. Decret. Gratian. Decr. Prim. Pars, Dist. xxii. can. 1. col. 100.]

it) which doth not include something not contained in the other parts; and therefore all those unseemly and immodest taunts and words might have been forborne.

The places of Deut. expounded.

I ask no forgiveness of you for anything that I have written; but I beseech God forgive you your outrageous contempts, and unchristian flouts and jests, wherewith your book is more pestered than any of Harding's is, where he sheweth himself most scurrilous. But I will omit them all, and only desire the reader to consider of what spirit they come, and in both our writings to respect the matter, not the person.

Touching the exposition of the places of Deuteronomy, let the learned reader compare it with the expositions of the learned interpreters, and then judge of my unskilful "dividing" and "defining."

Here now I would gladly know what T. C. hath proved against the thing that I have here written, or how he hath justified the proposition of the Admonition which I have refelled. For the sum of all is this: the authors of the Admonition say that "those things only are to be placed in the church which God himself in his word commandeth." This I confess to be true in "matters of salvation and damnation." But I say it is untrue in matters of "ceremonies, rites, orders, discipline, and kind of government;" which, being external matters and alterable, are to be altered and changed, appointed and abrogated, according to time, place, and person; "so that nothing be done against the word of God." And T. C. confesseth, page 15, that "certain things are left to the order of the church, because they are of that nature which are varied by times, places, persons, and other circumstances, and so could not at once be set down and established for ever; and yet so left to the order of the church, as that it do nothing against the rules aforesaid[1]." The same doth he affirm in effect in this place. Now, I pray you, tell me what difference is there in our words? He saith that "certain things are left to the order of the church, &c.; so that nothing be done against the rules aforesaid:" and I say that "the church hath authority to appoint orders, rites, ceremonies, &c.; so that nothing be done against the word of God." Indeed he goeth much further in this matter than I do; for, where I say, "the scripture expresseth all things necessary to salvation," he affirmeth

The replier hath spent many words in confuting that which he himself confesseth.

Page 15, Sect. 5.

[1 See before, page 195.]

that "many things are both commanded and forbidden, &c.;" as I have before noted, and is to be seen page 13. of his book[2]. But, to end this matter, I have justified my assertion by the scriptures, 1 Cor. xiv., Acts vi. and xv., 1 Cor. xi.; also by the testimonies of Justinus Martyr, Irenæus, Tertullian, Cyprian, Ambrose, Basil, Augustine, &c.; likewise by the practices of councils, the report of historiographers, as Socrates and Sozomenus; finally, by the judgment of late writers, M. Calvin and Bucer. Now will I also add a few words for the further confirmation of the same, and so end this question.

Other late writers of things indifferent. Page 13, Sect. 2.

The opinion of other late writers concerning things indifferent.

The Seventeenth Chapter.

Zuinglius, in his book *De Baptis.*, after that he had declared how the scripture contained all things necessary unto salvation, he sheweth that "in external things and matters of ceremonies many things are to be used in the church which be not contained in the [3]scriptures[4];" and speaking of this place, Phil. iii. ("If any think otherwise, God will also reveal the same unto you: nevertheless, in that whereunto we are come, let us proceed by one rule, or agree among ourselves"), saith that "the apostle there speaketh of nothing else than of external ceremonies and rites, the use and administration whereof the same apostle in that place affirmeth to be in our will and power, so that we do nothing repugnant to the commandment of God, neither trouble the public peace (whereof we ought to have especial regard) for external things[5]." These be the very words of Zuinglius; in the which there is first to be noted the interpretation of the words of the apostle, Phil. iii.; secondly, that he useth this exception, "so that we do nothing repugnant to the commandment of God," which T. C. so much misliketh[6]. The same Zuinglius, in the same book, verifieth in plain words that which I before have, touching a negative argument from the authority of the scriptures.

Zuinglius.

Collections out of Zuinglius.

[2 See before, page 176.]
[3 H. Zvingl. Op. Tigur. 1581. De Bapt. Lib. Tract. III. Pars II. fol. 85. See before, pages 254, 5, note 3.]
[4 Cartwright says that Whitgift "untruly fathereth" this sentence "of Zuinglius."—Sec. Repl. p. 119.]
[5 H. Zvingl. Op. ubi supra, fol. 87. 2. See before, page 257, note 1.]
[6 "... I never found fault with that."—Sec. Repl. p. 119.]

Other late writers of things indifferent. P. Martyr.

Peter Martyr upon the 1 Corinth. i. writeth that "there be three kinds of traditions, one expressed in the scriptures; another plain repugnant to the word of God; the third neither contrary to the word of God, nor yet necessarily joined to the same; in the which we must obey the church, these three cautions being observed: first, that they be not obtruded as worship of God, or peculiar holiness, but as pertaining to order, and the civil commodity of the church, and to comeliness in divine actions; for all things be sufficiently contained in scriptures that pertain to the worshipping of God and holiness. Secondly, that they be not counted so necessary, but that they may be altered, if time require. Let the church keep her interest and authority in these indifferent things, to appoint what shall be thought most necessary and meet to edifying. Last of all, that the people of God be not burdened with too great a multitude of them.[1]" Thus far Martyr.

Gualter.

Gualter, in his preface to the first epistle to the Corinthians, after that he hath declared the diversity of rites used in divers churches, concludeth on this sort: "Wherefore St Augustine writing to Januarius, after that he had laid forth divers ceremonies of churches observed in his time, did very well think that this should be the most safe rule unto christian men, if they did frame themselves unto those churches whereunto they should come, in those things which might be done without any prejudice unto faith and godliness: his words are these: 'There is in these things (meaning customs and rites) no better rule or instruction for a grave and wise Christian, than that he do after that manner the which he seeth used of the church unto the which he shall peradventure come, &c.' The which moderation if all men would use at this day, there would be less contention in the church, neither should christian liberty be abridged by the superstitious traditions of men. But why do they condemn whole churches for indifferent things, which, if they would obey St Paul, ought to apply themselves to the weakness of every one[2]?"

[1 P. Martyr. Comm. in D. Paul. prior. ad Corinth. Epist. Tigur. 1572. cap. i. 10. p. 8. See before, pages 252, 3, note 4.]

[2 Recte ergo divus Augustinus ad Januarium scribens, cum diversos, qui suo tempore observabantur, ecclesiarum ritus exposuisset, hanc regulam christianis hominibus tutissimam fore putavit, si in iis quæ salva fide et pietate fieri possunt, sese ecclesiis ad quas venerint accommodent. Ejus verba sunt hæc: Nulla disciplina in his est melior gravi prudentique Christiano, quam ut eo modo agat, quo agere viderit ecclesiam, ad quamcunque forte devenerit. Quod enim

Beza, in an epistle of his prefixed before the Confession of the churches in Helvetia, saith that "all rites and ceremonies are not to be received without exception, which the apostolic church itself hath used, either as profitable or necessary for their times[3];" and, in his book called *Confessio Christ. Fidei, cap. v.*, he writeth that "one cause of councils and synods was, to make rules of ecclesiastical discipline, and to appoint the government of the church according to the diversity of time, place, and persons. For it is necessary that in the house of the Lord all things should be done in order; of the which order there is one general reason in the word of God, 1 Cor. xiv., but not one and the same form, agreeing to all circumstances[4]." And again in the same chapter he saith: "The rules or canons (of rites and orders in the church) have respect to comeliness in external things, and therefore they be neither general, for the most part, nor perpetual: for that which is profitable in some place in other some places would rather hurt; and, moreover, the diverse respects of the time are such, that the same thing which for good considerations was ordained must of necessity sometime be abrogated; whereof it comes to pass, that there is not only so great variety in the old canons, but contrariety also[5]." Again in the same chapter: "We must not always look what the apostles did in *politia ecclesiastica*, in the government of the church; seeing there be most diverse circumstances, and therefore *absque κακοζηλίᾳ*, without preposterous zeal, all things cannot in all places and times be reduced to one and the same form, [6] &c.[7]"

Other late writers of things indifferent. Beza. Idem.

Idem.

Idem.

neque contra fidem, neque contra bonos mores injungitur, indifferenter est habendum, et pro eorum inter quos vivitur societate servandum.........Qua moderatione si hodie omnes uterentur, minus contentionum esset in ecclesia, neque superstitiosis hominum traditionibus libertas christiana circumscriberetur. Cur vero totas ecclesias damnant propter res indifferentes et medias, qui (si Paulo obedire velint) singulorum infirmitati sese accommodare debent?—R.Gualther. in Prior. ad Corinth. Epist. Hom. Tigur. 1578. Præf. fol. *a.* 5. 2. Conf. August. Op. Par. 1679-1700. Ad Inq. Januar. Lib. I. seu Epist. liv. cap. ii. 2. Tom. II. col. 124.]

[3 Itaque quicquid ab apostolis factitatum est, quod ad ritus attinet, nec statim nec sine aliqua exceptione pro regula sequendum existimo.—Th. Bezæ Lib. Epist. Theolog. Genev. 1575. Ad Grindal. Episc. Lond. Epist. viii. p. 71. The editor has not found the epistle said to be prefixed to the Helvetian Confession.]

[4 Id. Confess. Christ. Fid. Genev. 1587. cap. v. 17. p. 128. See before, page 253, note 5.]

[5 Id. ibid. 18. p. 129. See before, page 254, note 1.]

[6 Id. ibid. 35. p. 152. See before, page 254, note 2.]

[7 "...he ought to have understood that those things which M. Beza noteth

In the Confession of the churches in Helvetia, &c., it is thus written: "Men shall easily gather this also, that we do not by any wicked schism sever or cut off ourselves from Christ's holy churches of Germany, France, England, and other christian nations, but that we well agree with all and every one of them in the truth of Christ, which here we have acknowledged. For, albeit there is some variety in divers churches, about the uttering and setting forth of their doctrine, and about rites and ceremonies, which they receive as a mean to edify their churches, yet that variety never seemed to minister cause of dissension and schism in the church; for in such matters the churches of Christ have always used their liberty; as we may read in the ecclesiastical history[1]."

Confess. Ecclesiarum Helvet.

I omit here the Confession of the church of Wirtenberg[2], and the testimonies of sundry other notable learned men. I know no learned writer that doth deny the church to have authority in appointing rites, ceremonies, discipline, and kind of government, according to the place, time, persons, and other circumstances, though the same be not expressed in the word of God; so that it do nothing repugnant to the same.

But what need I labour so much in a matter confessed by him that would seem to overthrow it? for, if "the Jews had twenty things left to their order in the church for our one[3]" (as T. C. hath affirmed), and yet this commandment not broken, Deut. iv. and xii. *Nihil addes verbo, &c.*, then may the church of Christ use her liberty in like manner, without any breach of the same. Wherefore, to conclude, I now refer it to

Page 21, Sect. 1.

under the name of 'discipline left at the order of the church' are nothing less than these which he would insinuate. Which he might yet easilier have understanded by the place which he allegeth out of the Corinths, that leaveth it not in the church's power, either who shall govern, or what they ought to do which must govern; but how that government which is prescribed may be used most decently in regard of circumstance of time, &c."—Sec. Repl. p. 120.]

[1 Colligent itaque et illud, nos a sanctis Christi ecclesiis Germaniæ, Galliæ, Angliæ, aliarumque in orbe christiano nationum, nefario schismate nos non sejungere atque abrumpere: sed cum ipsis omnibus et singulis in hac confessa veritate christiana probe consentire, ipsasque caritate sincera complecti. Tametsi vero in diversis ecclesiis quædam deprehenditur varietas, in loquutionibus et modo expositionis doctrinæ, in ritibus item vel ceremoniis, eaque recepta pro ecclesiarum quarumlibet ratione, opportunitate et ædificatione, nunquam tamen ea ullis in ecclesia temporibus materiam dissentionibus et schismatibus visa est suppeditare. Semper enim hac in re Christi ecclesiæ usæ sunt libertate. Id quod in historia ecclesiastica videre licet.—Præf. Confess. et Expos. Fid. Christ. in Corp. et Syntagm. Confess. Fid. Genev. 1654. fol. a. 2. 2.]

[2 Wirtemb. Confess. in eod. De Cær. Eccles. pp. 136, 7.]

[3 See before, page 270.]

the judgment of the reader, whether it be true or not that I have affirmed against the authors of the Admonition; to wit, that "those things only are" not "to be brought in, or used in the church, which the Lord himself in his word hath commanded," but that of necessity in external things and outward government the church hath authority to determine according to time, place, person, &c., though the same be not commanded or expressed in scripture; so that it be not repugnant to the word.

Answer to the Admonition, Page 32, Sect. 1, 2; and Page 33, Sect. 1.

The other places noted in this margent, as Psalm xxvii., Rom. xii., 1 Cor. ii., and the rest, are not alleged to prove anything in controversy, but only without judgment placed in the margent to make a shew: how aptly they be applied, I leave to the consideration of the diligent reader. *Scriptures unchristianly abused by the Admonition[4].*

This one thing I cannot but marvel at, that these fellows so please themselves in the platform of their church, and attribute so much thereunto, that they exhort, nay, rather charge the court of parliament "with perfect hatred to detest" the present state of the church, and "with singular love to embrace" that which they prescribe in this book; and, to move them rather to this perfect hatred of us and singular love of themselves, they use the authority of the xxxi. and cxxxix. Psalm. In the one David saith that "he hath hated them that give themselves to deceitful vanities, because he trusteth in the Lord." In the other, speaking of the contemners of God, of wicked and bloody men, and of such as blaspheme God, and be his enemies, he saith, "I hate them with an unfeigned hatred, &c." *Mark this spirit.*

As though all such as like or allow of the present state of the church of this realm of England gave themselves to deceitful vanities, were contemners of God, wicked and bloody men, blasphemers of God, and his enemies. I will not aggravate this blasphemy of theirs: let prince, nobles, and all other lovers of God and his word, consider diligently this spirit, and in time prevent

[4 This marginal note is not in Answ. 2.]

the burning malice of the same. No Turk, no Jew, no papist, could possibly have spoken more spitefully of this church and state: but such is the spirit of arrogancy. To the like effect they allege the xv. of John, 1 Tim. iii., Matt. vii. and xi., as though they only had the word of God, and were of the church, and we contemners and rejecters of the same. Oh, where is humility? Truly, if these men be not by discipline bridled, they will work more harm to this church than ever the papist did.

Jo. WHITGIFT.

To this there is not one word spoken.

Admonition.

May it therefore please your wisdoms to understand, we[1] in England are so far off from having a church rightly reformed, according to the prescript of God's word, that as yet we are not come[2] to the outward face of the same. For, to speak of that wherein all consent[3], and whereupon all writers[4] accord, the outward marks, whereby a true christian church is known, are preaching of the word purely, ministering of the sacraments sincerely, and ecclesiastical discipline, which consisteth in admonition and correcting[5] of faults severely. Touching the first, namely, the ministry of the word, although it must be confessed that the substance of doctrine by many delivered is sound and good, yet herein it faileth, that neither the ministers thereof are according to God's word proved, elected, called, or ordained; nor the function in such sort so narrowly looked unto, as of right it ought, and is of necessity required.

Answer to the Admonition, Page 34, and 35.

The proposition that these libellers would prove is, that "we in England are so far from having a church rightly reformed according to the prescript of God's word, that as yet we are not come[7] to the outward face of the same." For proof hereof they use this argument: there be three "outward marks whereby a true christian church is known"—"preaching of the word purely, ministering of the sacraments sincerely, and ecclesiastical discipline, which consisteth in admonition and correction of faults severely." But this church of England (for so in

The proposition that these men would prove, and how they prove it[6].

[1 Understand that we, Adm.]
[2 We are scarce come, Adm.; we are not scarce come, Answ.]
[3 The best consent, Adm.]   [4 All good writers, Adm.]
[5 Correction, Adm.]   [6 This marginal note is added from Answ. 2.]
[7 Not scarce come, Answ. 2.]

effect they say) is void of all these; *ergo,* it hath not so much as the external face of a church. To prove that the word of God is not preached truly, they reason on this sort: "the ministers of the word are not according to God's word proved, elected, called, or ordained; nor the function in such sort so narrowly looked unto, as of right it ought, and is of necessity required;" and therefore the word of God not truly preached. Here (thanks be to God) they allege not one article of faith, or point of doctrine, nor one piece of any substance, to be otherwise taught and allowed of in this church (for not every man's folly is to be ascribed to the whole church) than by the prescript word of God may be justified; neither can they. Now, how this conclusion followeth (though the antecedent were true), let those judge that be learned. The ministers are not rightly proved and elected, &c.; *ergo,* the word of God is not truly preached. How wicked soever the man is, howsoever he intrude himself into the ministry, yet may he preach the true word of God: for the truth of the doctrine doth not in any respect depend upon the goodness or evilness of the man. I pray you, how were you and some other of your adherents called, elected, &c.? But to come to the purpose: they would prove that the ministers of the word in this church of England are not "according to God's word proved, elected, called, or ordained."

All points of doctrine pure in this church.

An unapt reason.

What force and pith is in their arguments, shall appear in the several answers to every one of them. This one thing I must let you understand, that these men seek to deface this church of England by the selfsame grounds that the papists do, although by another kind of proof. For what have the papists else to say but that we have no ministers, because they be not rightly called, and so consequently no word, no sacraments, no discipline, no church? And certainly, if it were well examined, I believe it would fall out, that the authors of this book have conspired with the papists to overthrow (if they could) the state both of this church and realm, howsoever subtilly they seem to detest papistry[9].

Agreeing with papists[8].

[[8] This marginal note is inserted from Answ. 2.]
[[9] Answ. here adds, *But now to their reasons.*]

T. C. Page 23, Sect. 1, 2, 3.

<small>Where do I affirm that they say so?</small>

Where in effect do they say that the church of England is void of preaching and ministering of the sacraments? is it all one to say that the word in the church of England is not purely preached, and the sacraments sincerely, and discipline severely administered, with this, that the church of England is void of all these? Again, where do they reason thus, that the word of God is not truly preached, because the ministers are not rightly proved, and elected, when as they have not one word of true preaching?

<small>A cavil.</small>

Is it all one to say it is not purely preached, and to say, it is not truly preached? St Paul to the Philippians is glad[1] that the gospel be preached, although it be not purely; but he would never have been glad that it should have been preached falsely, or not truly. <small>Phil. i. 16, 18.[2]</small> Again, he inveigheth not against the false apostles in the church of Corinth, because they preached the word untruly; but because they, using painted words and affected eloquence, and making a great shew of learning and tongues, did not preach the gospel sincerely: so that you see that it is one thing not to preach truly, and another thing[3] not to preach purely; and so you see their reason is not so evil; for the want of a good calling may give occasion to say that the word of God is not sincerely taught, because there is not a lawful and ordinary calling. For although, for the substance of doctrine and the manner of handling of it, they that St Paul speaketh to of[4] the Philippians did not[5] fault, yet St Paul saith that they did not preach purely, because they did it of contention, or of envy; which was no fault in the doctrine, but in him that taught. Therefore let men judge how just your weights are that expound "not purely," "not truly," and whether this be to confute other men's arguments rather than to skirmish with your own shadows.

I know no papists reason thus, that, "because we have no ministers, therefore no word, no sacrament[6], no discipline, no church." For they deny that we[7] have the word or sacraments, because we hold not their word and sacrifice; but, if there be that so reason, yet these men that you charge have neither any such antecedent, or such a consequent. For they never said that there is no ministry in England, nor yet do ever conclude that there is "no word, no sacraments, no discipline, nor church."

For, in saying that the face of the church doth not so much appear (for so the whole process of their book doth declare that they mean, when they say that we have not scarce the face of the church), they grant that we have the church of God; but that, for want of those ornaments which it should have, and through certain the deformed rags of popery which it should not have, the church doth not appear in her native colours, and so beautiful as it is meet she should be prepared to so glorious a husband as is the Son of God. Say you certainly, and do you believe, that "the authors of this

---

[[1] St Paul is glad, Repl. 2.]
[[2] These references are inserted from Repl. 2.]
[[3] *Thing* is not in Repl. 1 or 2.] [[4] *Of* to, Repl. 2.]
[[5] No, Repl. 2.] [[6] Sacraments, Repl. 1 and 2.]
[[7] Deny we, Repl. 1 and 2.]

book are conspired with the papists to overthrow this church and realm?"
Now certainly I will never do that injury unto them, as once to go about
to purge them of so manifest slanders, nor never be brought by the outrage
of your speeches to prove that noonday is not midnight; and therefore, as
for you, I will set your conscience and you together. The reader I will
desire not to think it a strange thing; for it is no other than hath happened to the servants of God, even from those which have professed the same
religion which they did; as it appeareth in the xxxvii. of
Jeremy [8], which was accused of certain of the Israelites that he
had conspired with the Babylonians their mortal enemies, and laid to his
charge that he was going to them, when he was going to Benjamin.

<sub>Chap.xxxvii.
12, 13.²</sub>

Jo. Whitgift.

Who is so blind as he that will not see? Do they not in plain words say that "the outward marks, whereby a true christian church is known, are preaching of the word purely, ministering the sacraments sincerely, and ecclesiastical discipline, &c.?" Is not their whole drift in the Admonition to prove that neither the word is preached purely, nor the sacraments sincerely ministered, &c. in this church of England? and what do I otherwise report of them? Be not my words plain? Where do I affirm that they should "say that the church of England is void of preaching and ministering the sacraments?" But let the reader consider my words, and accordingly judge of your plain dealing. Where I write that "they in effect say the church of England is void of these," I am sure you will refer "these" to that which went before, that is, "preaching of the word purely, ministering of the sacraments sincerely, and ecclesiastical discipline, &c.;" neither can you otherwise do, though you would wrest my words never so violently: and therefore that which I report of them is, that "they say this church of England neither hath the word purely preached, nor the sacraments sincerely ministered, &c."

T. C. willingly perverteth the words of the Answer.

I make no great difference betwixt "purely" and "truly;" neither doth it follow that the word of God is truly preached always when the truth is preached. For, as a man may do *justa*, not *juste*, "just things," and yet not "justly;" so may the truth be preached, and yet not "truly." A man may do that which is just unwittingly, or for gain, or for pleasure, or for malice; but then he doth it not justly, *quia non ex habitu et animo*: even so a man may preach the true word of God of

Purely and truly.

[⁸ In Jeremy, Repl. 2.]

affection, of contention, ambition, for profit, &c.; but then he doth not preach it "truly." So that your distinction betwixt "purely" and "truly" is to no purpose.

Neither doth St Paul help you anything at all, but is clean contrary unto you; for in the 18. verse of the first chapter to the Philippians these be his words: τί γάρ; πλὴν παντὶ τρόπῳ, εἴτε προφάσει εἴτε ἀληθείᾳ, Χριστὸς καταγγέλλεται, &c., which in the bible printed at Geneva is thus translated: " What then? yet Christ is preached all manner ways, whether it be under a pretence, or sincerely[1]." So you see that there is no difference made betwixt " sincerely " and " truly ;" for the Greek word signifieth " truly." And Master Beza, in his notes upon the same chapter and 16. verse, expounding οὐχ ἁγνῶς, " not purely," saith thus: *Non puro scilicet animo, quum alioqui pura esset doctrina*[2]*;* " to wit, not with a pure mind, seeing that otherwise the doctrine is pure :" so that these adverbs " purely " and " truly " in this place are referred, not to the doctrine, but to mind of him that teacheth. I would wish that both you and others would cease from drawing the scriptures to your phantasies and affections[3].

That this is one reason of the papists to prove that we are not the church, because we have no true ministry, I marvel you can be ignorant; seeing there is nothing oftener in their mouths.

Whether the authors of the Admonition reason in like manner or no, tell me, when you have well considered these words of theirs in the epistle to the reader: " Either must we have a right ministry of God, and a right government of his church, according to the scriptures set up (both which we lack); or else there can be no right religion[4]." Likewise when you have without partiality viewed the rest of their book. Truly I think him to be more than blind, that seeth not this to be their kind of reasoning. Their meaning is plain; and the Second Admonition maketh it plainer; howsoever you

[1 The Bible, transl. according to the Ebrew and Greeke.—Lond. 1578. Phil. i. 18. fol. 86.]

[2 Non puro videlicet animo, &c.—Nov. Test. cum Th. Bezæ Annot. 1565. Epist. ad Phil. cap. i. 16. p. 407.]

[3 Cartwright in reply urges that the reasons are futile "for the defence he maketh to prove truly and purely all one."—Sec. Repl. pp. 120, 1.]

[4 See before, page 140.]

would seem to colour and cloak the matter : for what other meaning can it have to say that we have " no right religion," and to speak so bitterly against the whole form of the church, and the most of such things as be in the same?

I do believe "certainly" that there is some papistical practitioners among you: neither is it strange; for so conspired they with the anabaptists also, as I have declared; and the anabaptists hated them as much as you, and pretended the simplicity of the word of God as much as you; and, both in pretence of zeal, of purity of life, and other qualities, for the most part were equal unto you. And, though the prophet Jeremy were unjustly accused, yet doth not that improve anything that I have said : for they are not the prophet Jeremy, neither in person, office, or cause; neither yet have I accused them unjustly in anything.

¶ Of the Election of Ministers.
Tract. III.
Of the trial of Ministers both in learning and conversation.

Chapter i. The First Division.
Admonition.
The first is this:

For, whereas in the old church a trial was had [1] both of their ability to instruct, and of their godly conversation also; now by the letters commendatory of some one man, noble or other, tag and rag, learned and unlearned, of the basest [m] sort of the people (to the slander of the gospel in the [n] mouths of the adversaries) are freely received.

[1] Acts i. 12. [l] Acts vi. 3. [l] 1 Tim. iii. 2. 7, 8, 2. Tit. i. 6. [m] 1 Re. xii. 31. [n] Rom. ii. 14. 3

Answer to the Admonition, Page 36.

It is true that in the old church trial was had of their ability to instruct, and of their godly conversation. But the place in the margent alleged out of the first chapter of the Acts of the Apostles maketh nothing for that purpose; being therein no mention at all of any trial made either of learning or manners, but only of presenting two, and of praying and casting of lots. And M. Calvin in his Institutions saith plainly, that out of this place of the Acts and example there can be no certain rule gathered of electing and choosing ministers; for, as that ministry was extraordinary, so was the calling also [4]. Read M. Calvin, and you shall soon see how little this place, so oft in the [5] margent quoted, maketh for that purpose for the which it is quoted.

T. C. Page 23, Sect. 4, 5, and Page 24, Sect. 1, 2, 3, 4.

It maketh for the purpose which is alleged out of the first of the Acts, to prove that there ought to be trial of those which are chosen to the ministry; for, when St Peter saith that such a one must be chosen as hath been continually conversant with our Saviour Christ, and from the beginning

---

[1 Acts i. 21, Adm.]   [2 Adm. has not 8.]   [3 Rom. ii. 24, Adm.]

[4 Hujus autem rei certa regula ex apostolorum institutione peti non potest, quæ nonnihil habuit a communi reliquorum vocatione dissimile. Quia enim extraordinarium ministerium erat, &c.—Calvin. Op. Amst. 1667-71. Inst. Lib. IV. cap. iii. 13. Tom. IX. p. 284.]

[5 This, Answ.]

of his preaching until the day wherein he ascended into heaven, he meant Surely that *nothing else but that such a one should be chosen which was sufficiently* much meant, *instructed, and had been continually a scholar of our Saviour Christ, and* as that he might be a *therefore fit to teach and to witness that which they had seen, and whose* the doings of *godly conversation was notoriously known.* Christ and of his resur-

Besides that, albeit those two Matthias and Barsabas were therefore set rection. up in the midst, that the church, in the prayer that was made for their election, might by seeing them pray the earnestlier for them; yet it was also as much to say that, if any could object any thing against them, that he should prefer his objection.

And whether they were examined or no, the matter is not great; neither, when it is said that a trial should be had, it is meant that, when the parties are famously known to those which have the right of election, that[6] there should be always necessarily an apposing and examining: so that the sufficiency of doctrine and holiness of life (for the which cause the trial and examination is commanded) be known and agreed upon by them that chose[7], it is enough.

And so these two, being notoriously known and consented of by the church to be fit men, might happily not be examined; but yet the words of St Peter declare plainly, that in the choice of them there was regard had to both their ability to teach and honesty of conversation.

And, although there be certain things extraordinary in this election, as If all these *that such a one must be chosen which had been conversant with our Saviour* ordinary, *Christ, and that there were two put up for one place, and that it was per-* you left in *mitted to lots, to cast the apostleship upon one of them two, as if the Lord* as ordinary? *should by the lots from heaven tell who should have it; yet it followeth not* or how prove *to say that the rest of the things that are there used should not be practised* to be ordi- *in ordinary callings, forasmuch they will well agree with them.* than some of these?

And Master Calvin in the place you allege saith that the ordinary callings somewhat differ from the calling of the apostles, and after sheweth wherein; that is, in that they were appointed immediately of God, and by his mouth; whereby it appeareth that, for the residue of those things which are there mentioned, he holdeth that they may well stand with the ordinary elections.

Jo. Whitgift.

This reply standeth all by conjectures: it is certain that there was no trial had of them, because they were sufficiently known; and therefore the text without discretion alleged, to prove that there ought "to be a trial of their ability to instruct, &c." If it had been quoted to prove that such as were admitted into the function were meet for the same, both for their life and doctrine, it had been to some purpose. I think it necessary that such as be admitted into the ministry (unless they be very well known) should be tried, both in

[6 Right of trying as that, Repl. 2.] [7 Choose, Repl. 1 and 2.]

learning and life: but this place maketh nothing at all for that purpose, but rather contrary, for it speaketh of such two as were well known, and therefore needed no "trial;" so that, if we conclude anything of that place, it must be this, that none ought to be admitted into the ministry but such as be well known, and need no trial.

There was no other cause of presenting them than that which is expressed in the text; and it is presumption to make the scripture serve to maintain our contentions, against the express words and plain meaning.

If this be a rule to be followed, it must be followed wholly; for where have you learned to add, or take from any law or rule prescribed in God's word? or how do ye know that this example must be followed in one thing, and not in another? what special revelation have you to make any such dismembering of this action? No doubt this example is extraordinary, and not of necessity to be followed.

The words of M. Calvin are plain, that "there can be no certain rule gathered of this example for the electing of ministers; because the calling of the apostles doth something differ from the calling of other ministers[1]."

Chapter i. The Second Division.

Answer to the Admonition, Page 36.

In the sixth of the Acts mention is made of deacons only, whom you will not allow to be ministers of the word; and therefore this place serveth not your turn: neither is there anything spoken of any trial, but only they are willed to look out among them seven men of honest report, and full of the Holy Ghost and wisdom, to be appointed deacons.

T. C. Page 24, Sect. 5.

And, where you say that the sixth of the Acts, because it speaketh of deacons, is nothing to the matter, methink you should have easily understanded that, if a trial be necessary in deacons (which is an under office in the church, and hath regard but to one part of the church, which is the poor, and is occupied in the distribution of money), much more it ought to

[1 Cartwright in reply contradicts severally Whitgift's assertions; maintains that on the occasion in question there was "a proffer of trial," even though no "trial" followed; and claims Calvin's judgment as being on his side.—Sec. Repl. pp. 121, &c.]

be in an office of greater charge, which hath respect to the whole church, and is occupied in the dispensing of the holy word of God.

Jo. WHITGIFT.

That there should " be a trial" of such as are to be admitted to the ministry, I think it most convenient (as I told you before), except the parties be sufficiently known to such as have authority to admit them; but I say that this place of the Acts doth not prove it, both because the office of a deacon (by their opinion) is altogether distinct from the office of a minister of the word, the one pertaining to the body, the other to the soul, the one occupied about money, the other in the word, and also for that there is in that place no mention made of any trial. That place rather proveth that which before was noted Acts i., that such only should be appointed to that office as be known by good experience to be fit for such a function.

Tell me one word in that text that signifieth any such "trial" as the Admonition speaketh of. Therefore I say again, as I said before, that such as be well known need no farther "trial;" as both that example Acts i., and this also Acts vi., manifestly declareth[2].

Chapter i. The Third Division.

Answer to the Admonition, Page 36, Sect. 1.

The rule of St Paul in the 1 Tim. iii. and Tit. i. is to be followed. And the book of ordering ministers and deacons, set forth and allowed by this church of England, requireth that whosoever is to be admitted into the[4] order of the ministry should so be tried, examined, and proved, both for learning and life, as St Paul there requireth. Read the book with indifferency and judgment, and thou canst not but greatly commend it. If

_{The book of ordering ministers justified concerning examination[3].}

[2 Cartwright rejoins "that, albeit there be not this word 'try,' yet there is that which weigheth as much; for the Greek word (ἐπισκέψασθε) 'look out,' cannot be severed from a trial. And, if St Luke had but used the simple verb, which in our tongue signifieth 'consider,' yet that of itself had force to have led the choosers to a trial of them which were to be chosen: now using the compound thereby he laid upon them a greater necessity and a more careful diligence of trial of them."—Ibid. p. 127.]

[3 Answ. 2 has instead of this note: *True examination in England appointed.*]
[4 Any, Answ.]

any man neglect his duty in that point, his fault must not be ascribed to the rule appointed, neither yet to the whole church. Is the law evil because some lawyers in their office swerve from it? This is a fallation *a non causa ad causam.*

<small>The book of ordering ministers.</small>
<small>Wickedness of men causeth not laws to be evil.</small>

T. C. Page 24, Sect. 6.

But in the end you agree that they should be tried; so that now the question standeth only how and by what means; wherein you, for your part, say that the book of ordering ministers is a sufficient and good rule. I have read it, and yet I cannot commend it greatly. But you will say, not with judgment, or indifferency. I will promise you with this indifferency, that I wished that all that is there were good and convenient, and such as I might say unto, So be it. With what judgment I do disallow it, I leave it to all men to esteem upon these reasons.

Jo. Whitgift.

The question is not whether you allow or disallow that book; neither is it material whether you do or not. Your reasons used against it I will severally, for memory' sake, examine.

Chapter i. The Fourth Division.

T. C. Page 24, Sect. 7, 8, 9.

<small>The reasons of T. C. against the book of ordering ministers.</small>

First, that the examination of his doctrine wholly, and partly of his life, is permitted to one man. For, considering of the one part the greatness of the charge that is committed unto the ministers, and the horrible peril that cometh unto the church by the want of those things that are required in them; and of the other part weighing the weakness of the nature of man, which, although he seeth many things, yet is he[1] *blind also in many, and that even in those things which he seeth he suffereth himself to be carried away by his affection of love, or of envy, &c.—I say, considering these things, it is very dangerous to commit that to the view and search of one man, which may with less danger and more safety be referred unto divers. For herein the proverb is true:* Plus vident oculi quam oculus. <small>Many eyes see more than one.</small>
And almost there is no office of charge in this realm, which lieth in election, committed so slightly to any, as that, upon one man's report of his ability, all the rest which have interest in the election will give their voices: so that, if we were destitute of authority of the scripture, the very light of reason would shew us a more safe and warier way.

But there is greater authority: for St Luke, in the first of the Acts, sheweth that St Peter would not take upon him to present two, as fit for the place which was void, but saith "they did present or set up;" whereby

[1] He is, Repl. 2.

appeareth that the examination of their ability was committed to many. The same appeareth also in the 6. of the Acts, when as the apostles will the church, wherein there were so excellent personages, to "look out seven full of the Holy Ghost and wisdom, &c." They do not there permit the discerning of their wisdom and other gifts to one, but to many. The book of ordering ministers.

JO. WHITGIFT.

Your first reason is partly grounded upon bare conjectures, or rather common suppositions, that may be supposed in the most perfect government, partly upon the place, Acts i., either not understood or willingly misconstrued, nothing pertaining to the purpose. But first it is untrue that "the examination either of doctrine or life is in this church wholly committed to one man:" for the book committeth the examination of such as are to be admitted into the ministry, not only to the bishop, but to the archdeacon also; to the bishop in the beginning of the book by plain and express words; to the archdeacon, because he must present them unto the bishop of his knowledge, which he cannot do truly without diligent examination[2]. But admit it be so, that the examination is committed to one man only: what then? Forsooth, "considering on the one part the greatness of the charge, &c., and of the other part the weakness of the nature of man, &c., it is more dangerous to commit that to the view of one man, &c." If you respect "the greatness of the charge that is committed to ministers, &c.," who is better able to consider thereof than the bishop, which both knoweth what such a charge meaneth, and hath had himself long experience thereof; to whom also divers several charges do appertain, for the which it behoveth him to foresee that there be meet ministers? If you speak of blind affections, as love, envy, &c., who may be supposed to be more void of them, than he that is called to such an high office in the church, that is so well instructed in the scriptures, of so long time known both for his life, learning, religion, and wisdom, meet to have that credit committed unto him? Surely if any one man, or more, be void of such affections, and be thought meet to have such matters committed unto him, it is the bishop; and, if he be meet and worthy for that place and office, then may he also be safely credited with all things incident unto the same.

The first reason of T. C. hath either a weak, or a false ground.

The bishop most meet to have the examination.

[² Cartwright confesses that he has not the book; and so he leaves this point. —Sec. Repl. p. 128.]

<small>The book of ordering ministers.</small>

But what have you here said against one man, in this case, that may not be likewise said of another man in all other like cases? against one king, one judge; yea, against many, even the whole multitude, in whom not only lack of knowledge and discretion in such matters, but great abundance of affections, of wrath, of hatred, of love, of fear, of contention, &c., for the most part reigneth; as experience of all times and places declareth? But of this matter occasion will be ministered to speak more hereafter.

The proverb, *Plus vident oculi quam oculus,* "Many eyes see more than one," is not always, nor in all cases, true: one man of wisdom, experience, learning, and discretion, may see more, know more, and judge better in those things that he can skill of, than ten thousand other that be ignorant, or that in such matters be far inferior unto him.

You say that "almost there is no office of charge in this realm, &c.:" which is not so; for the offices of greatest importance and charge in the whole realm, both in the ecclesiastical and civil state, are in the only election of the prince; and they be best bestowed and upon the meetest and worthiest persons. Those offices that be committed to the voices of many either are bestowed of custom, or at the entreaty of some in authority, or by extreme suit and labour made by some parties; or else is there great contention stirred up about them by some busy-bodies. And indeed when are there more unworthy men chosen to offices, when is there more strife and contention about elections, when do partial and sinister affections more utter themselves, than when an election is committed to many?

And, whereas you say that "upon one man's report all the rest which have interest in the election would not give their voices so slightly to any," experience teacheth you clean contrary; for do you not see that in all such elections, for the most part, some one man ruleth the rest? Moreover, where is the request of such as be in authority for any denied in such elections? I could bring you a number of examples.

If the election of the minister should be committed to every several parish, do you think that they would choose the meetest? Should not the lord of the town, or some other among them of countenance, lead them as he list? Would they have no respect to their neighbours' children, though not the meetest? Would there be no contention among them? Would they not have like people, like pastor? But of this also more must be spoken in another place. *The book of ordering ministers.*

That in the first of the Acts is nothing for your purpose: for there is no order of election prescribed, but an extraordinary calling to an extraordinary office, as I have said before. Neither did the multitude present them, but only the apostles, as M. Beza saith, *Lib. Conf. cap. v. titu.* 35[1]. Neither were they examined, as is also declared; and therefore that place altogether impertinent.

To that in the sixth of the Acts I have answered sufficiently: it proveth not examination. And M. Beza, in the aforenamed book and chapter, saith plainly that "Luke hath not set down what the church did observe in the election of deacons;" and shortly after concludeth thus: *Certam igitur regulam non est quod nimium curiose quisquam hic præscribat; sed si recta fuerit conscientia, facile fuerit pro temporum et locorum circumstantia definire quid expediat*[2]: "Therefore there is no cause why any man should here over curiously prescribe any certain rule; but, if the conscience be upright, it may be easy to determine what is convenient for the circumstance of time and place." And these words he speaketh of that place of the Acts. But, I pray you, answer me this one question: if you will make these two places, Acts i. and Acts vi., rules which we must of necessity follow in electing of ministers, how will you join them together, being in nothing like? for, Acts i., the apostles presented two to the people; Acts vi., the whole multitude did present seven to the apostles: Acts i., they cast lots; Acts vi., they laid on hands: Acts i., they prayed to God to shew whether of the two he had chosen; Acts vi., there is no such thing: Acts i. of two that were presented one was chosen; Acts vi., all were chosen that were presented: so that there is great difference in the two places, and therefore no prescript rules for us to follow[3]. *Beza, Lib. Conf. cap. v.*

The elections Acts 1 and Acts 6, do nothing agree.

[1 Apparet enim....fuisse multitudini propositos ab apostolis eos quos maxime idoneos censebant.—Th. Bezæ Confess. Christ. Fid. Genev. 1587. cap. v. 35. pp. 152, 3.]

[2 In diaconorum electione non adscripsit Lucas quid ecclesia observarit...Certam &c.—Id. ibid. 37. p. 154.]

[3 Cartwright replies at great length to this division, urging that "it maketh no great matter how many examine, seeing the election and ordination hangeth only upon the bishop's pleasure;" that the question is not whether the bishop "be of others most fit, but whether it be fit that he alone should do it;" and objecting strongly to such authority being lodged in his hands. And he goes on

The book of ordering ministers.

Chap. i. Fifth Division.

T. C. Page 24, Sect. ult.

Secondarily, I cannot commend it for that, that one man is the archdeacon, which must examine the pastors and judge of their sufficiency. For what is the archdeacon? is he not a deacon? for he, being the chief deacon, must needs be also a deacon himself; and therefore, although the chief deacon, yet inferior to any of the pastors, and the gifts which are required in him inferior to those which are required in the pastor: and so to make[1] *him judge of the aptness and ableness of the pastor is to make the inferior in gifts judge of the superior; he that hath by his calling less gifts, judge of his which hath by his calling greater gifts; which is nothing else than to appoint him that hath but one eye to oversee his sight that hath two.*

1 Tim. iii.

Jo. Whitgift.

T. C. reasoneth against himself.

You will not stand in this reason, I think, when you have something better remembered yourself: will you not have "the archdeacon, because he is but a deacon, examine the pastors, and judge of their sufficiency?" Do you think that, because he is "inferior to the pastors, and the gifts required in him inferior to those which are required of the pastors," therefore he is not meet to examine the pastor, and to judge of his aptness? What greater argument can be used against yourself? for, if this be true, how can the people examine the pastors, or judge of their aptness, being far inferior to deacons, in respect of their office, and in gifts not like unto them? or how can you admit your seniors to the examination or allowing of them, not only being inferior in office and calling, but in gifts also? yea, the most of them rude and ignorant; for such seniors you must of necessity have, if you will have any. Surely I marvel that you have so much forgotten yourself. A deacon is superior to the people, yea, to your seniors (though you deny it), and more gifts required in him than in both the other, 1 Tim. iii. Wherefore, if he be not meet "to examine pastors, and judge of their sufficiency, because that were to make the inferior in gifts to judge of the

to say: "And set me all the boroughs and cities together in the whole realm where elections pass by voice, you shall find they cannot all afford so many unworthy officers, as have swarmed ministers from the sole election of the most part of the bishops of England." He considers it "great presumption" so "to judge the church of God," as to anticipate abuses if elections were committed to the several parishes.—Sec. Repl. pp. 129, &c.]

[1 And to make, Repl. 2.]

superior, &c." much less are the people and your seniors able to be examiners and judges in that matter.

The book of ordering ministers.

Furthermore, if none must examine and judge of the pastor but such as be superior, or at the least equal unto him, and such in whom more or as many gifts are required, then truly I see not to whom this office may more orderly or safely be committed than to the bishop, who is superior to the pastor, both in office and also in gifts.

It is not true that the book committeth the examination of ministers only to the archdeacons, or especially: it is otherwise in the beginning of the book in plain words. Your reason whereby you would prove an archdeacon to be only a deacon is no reason at all; for what sequel is there in this argument, An "archdeacon is the chief deacon;" *ergo,* he is only a deacon? as though you were ignorant of the state of our church, and knew not that archdeacons may be also ministers of the word[2].

Chapter i. The Sixth Division.

T. C. Page 25, Sect. 1.

Thirdly, I mislike the book, because it permitteth that the bishop may admit the minister upon the credit and report of the archdeacon, and upon his examination, if there be no opposition of the people; which appeareth by these words in the book, where as to the archdeacon, saying thus, "Reverend father in God, I present unto you these persons to be admitted to be priests, &c.[3]*", the bishop answereth, "Take heed that the persons whom you present unto us be apt and meet, for their godly conversation, to exercise their ministry duly to the honour of God, and edifying of his church*[4]*." And thereupon I think it cometh that the archdeacon is called the eye of the bishop. But why doth not he himself take heed unto it? With what conscience can he admit a minister, of whose fitness he knoweth not*

[2 Cartwright rejoins that "it followeth not, because one deacon is inferior to the pastor, therefore the whole church is inferior to either the pastor or the deacon:" he censures Whitgift as more cruel than Nahash, who would have deprived the people of Jabesh-gilead of their right eyes. Whitgift, he says, "is not content with that," he would put out both the eyes of the people, "and leave them as blind and ignorant buzzards." He goes on to complain of a contradiction, for that elsewhere "a bishop is avowed to be a pastor," whereas here he is said to be "superior to a pastor;" and asserts that no man may be a deacon and a pastor at the same time; and that, if the archdeacons be pastors, they "do not examine by that they are pastors, but only in respect that they be archdeacons."—Ibid. pp. 139, &c.]

[3 Persons to be made priests, Repl. 2.]

[4 See Liturgical Services, Q. Eliz. Park. Soc. Edit. pp. 274, 5, 87.]

The book of ordering ministers. but upon the credit of another, although he were otherwise very fit? Where can he have that full persuasion that he doth well, upon the report of others, when the report of his life and learning is made but of one? And therefore St Paul ordained that the same should be the ordainers and the examiners, and not to hang upon the faith or report of another man in things that are so weighty, and whereof he may himself take notice.

1 Tim. iii.

Jo. Whitgift.

This reason, though it differ in some circumstances, yet in effect it is all one with the second; for it is against the examination of the archdeacon; and so was that. But your argument is not sound; for doth the bishop therefore admit ministers only "upon the credit, and at the report of the archdeacon," because the archdeacon presenteth them unto him? You know that none is admitted to any degree here in Cambridge, but the same is first presented to the vice-chancellor, and to the university, by some one of that faculty, who giveth his fidelity for them: doth the university therefore admit them only upon the credit and report of that one man? You know the contrary: even so it is here: the archdeacon presenteth to the bishop: the bishop doth inquire if he hath diligently examined them, &c.; doth he therefore, think you, not examine them himself? I have known bishops reject those whom their archdeacons have allowed.

If any bishop do give that credit to his archdeacon, he doth more than I would wish he should do, and otherwise than the book requireth of him; neither must his example, done without the book, prejudice that which is well appointed in the book.

Paul, 1 Tim. iii., declareth what qualities and conditions a bishop ought to have; but can you gather of anything there written that "the same should be the ordainers and examiners?" It is most meet it should so be, I grant; but yet would I not have the scriptures made shipmen's hose, to serve our turns as it pleaseth us to turn them, lest we fall into that fault ourselves which we justly reprove in the papists.

T. C. contrary to himself. But still you are contrary to yourself: for, if "the same must be the ordainers and the examiners," then must the bishops of necessity be "the examiners;" for you cannot deny but that the bishops must be "the ordainers." And, if you will have 1 Tim. iii. to serve your purpose, then must you of force confess it; for there St Paul writeth to Timothy, being a bishop, and but one man: so that this reason is directly against the first[1]. *The book of ordering ministers.*

Chap. i. The Seventh Division.

T. C. Page 25, Sect. 2.

Fourthly, for that, albeit the church is demanded whether they[2] have any thing to object, yet that church whereof he is to be pastor, and which it skilleth especially that he be fit, is not demanded, and which would (because it standeth them upon) inquire diligently of him.

Jo. Whitgift.

And how would you have "that church whereof he is to be pastor demanded whether they have anything to object against him?" would you have every one that is to be minister first go and dwell among them, that they might have trial of him? Indeed so did Matthias and Barsabas among the apostles, and the seven among them by whom they were chosen deacons. But how long shall he then remain among them? for it had need be a good time; else shall they not throughly know him, nor then neither; for he may play the hypocrite. But who shall in the mean time bear his charges there and find him? for a number of parishes in England be not able sufficiently to find one, much less more. Or how shall they have any trial of his doctrine, learning, and ability to preach, seeing that he may not publicly either teach or exhort, because he is not yet called to the ministry? *The absurdities that of necessity follow the assertion of T. C.*

Surely I understand not how your device could be well brought to pass, except you will make in every parish an university, or some school of divinity or college of learning; as indeed they had in most great cities of the old church, where the election of ministers was committed to many; or except you imagine that some such may be dwelling and continuing in every parish, as by inspiration, or some other extraordinary means, may be made able to be their pastor when the place shall be void.

[1 Cartwright maintains his own view, and charges Whitgift with not dealing truly in this division.—Sec. Repl. pp. 143, 4.]
[2 It, Repl. 2.]

The book of ordering ministers. But tell me this one thing: Would you have him that is to be chosen their pastor remain among them, they having yet a pastor? or come unto them after the death or departure of their pastor, as the Second Admonition would have it, fol. 14.[1]? If the first, then must the parish be double burdened, that is, they must find both him that is, and him also that shall be, their pastor: moreover, it is uncertain how long he must remain with them, expecting the death or departure of the other; likewise how he shall in the mean time occupy himself, &c. If the second, then must they of long time be destitute of a pastor: for they cannot have sufficient trial of him, except also sufficient time be granted unto them to try him in; which cannot be less than one whole year at the least.

But admit all these impossibilities and great absurdities to be possible and convenient, yet are there further doubts. What if the parish be wholly, or the most part, simple, ignorant, and unlearned men, not able to judge? what if they be all or the most part corrupt in religion? what if they be such as can be better content with one that will wink at their faults, than with him that will reprove them? what if they be such as will be overruled with some one whom they dare not displease? To be short, what if they cannot agree among themselves upon some one, but be divided into factions, &c.? All these things being considered, you shall find it the fittest and best way that the bishop, even according to the form prescribed in the book, have authority to admit and allow of such as are to be ministers. Would you have him that is brought up in the university, and well known in all respects to be meet for the ministry, to whom also a cure in some place of Westmoreland is to be committed, to be kept from the same because he is unknown unto them? Let other men think of your devices as they list; in my judgment they be mere fancies and fond dreams, grounded neither upon the

---

[1 When any parish is destitute of a pastor, or of a teacher, the same parish may have recourse to the next conference, and to them make it known that they may procure, chiefly from the one of the universities, or if otherwise, a man learned and of good report, whom after trial of his gifts had in their conference, they may present unto the parish which before had been with them about that matter; but yet so, that the same parish have him a certain time amongst them, that they may be acquainted with his gifts and behaviour, and give their consents for his stay amongst them, if they can allege no just cause to the contrary.—Sec. Adm. p. 14.]

word of God, neither yet of any other good consideration[2]. Sure I am that they are contrary to the practice of reformed churches, and namely the churches of Berne and Tigure: as M. Musculus reporteth in his Common-places, *Tit. de Ministris verbi*[3]; and M. Bullinger, 1 Tim. iv.[4] Touching this supposition of yours, that "none should be admitted into the ministry, except the same have some certain cure committed unto him," occasion will be given to speak in another place.

The book of ordering ministers.

Tract. iv. cap. 1.

Chapter i. The Eighth Division.

T. C. Page 25, Sect. 3, 4.

Again, they are demanded which can object nothing of his insufficiency,

[2 Cartwright makes light of the difficulties urged by Whitgift, considers that the church can better judge of the fitness of a candidate than a single bishop, and asserts that there have not been "so many unworthy ministers chosen by all the churches throughout the world" since the apostles' times, as within a few years by the English bishops.—Sec. Repl. pp. 145, &c.]

[3 ...arbitror haud fore ingratum lectori, si commemorem, quomodo in celebri hac Bernensi ecclesia eligantur et confirmentur verbi ministri. Ubi necessitas ecclesiæ hoc requirit, ut minister eligatur, denunciatur ministris verbi a senatu, ut circumspiciant de aliquo, quem idoneum fore judicent, et hunc communibus suffragiis eligant, deque eo ad senatum referant. Si talem ab illis eligi contigerit, cujus fides, eruditio et doctrina non sit satis conspicua, remittitur a senatu ad ministros, ut examinetur, et facto examine referatur denuo ad senatum, qualis esse videatur, idoneusne, vel secus. Si idoneus, confirmatur a senatu illius electio, si mittendus sit ad ecclesiam aliquam in agro: si vero in ipsa est civitate ministraturus Domino, defertur illius electio ad majorem senatum, qui consuetis senatoribus et numero aliquo civium ex plebe constat. Hic colliguntur suffragia per χειροτονίαν, quibus is qui electus est vel confirmatur vel repudiatur. Sic electio quidem penes ministros verbi est, confirmatio vero penes senatum....Præsentatur autem non sine auctoritate senatus et ecclesiastici ordinis. Mittuntur enim ad eam præsentationem senator aliquis et verbi minister, qui pro concione publica electum pastorem plebi præsenti deputat et commendat; idque non sine precibus ad Dominum, &c.—Wolfg. Muscul. Loc. Comm. Theol. Basil. 1599. De Ministr. Verb. p. 200.]

[4 Hinc Tigurina ecclesia, posteaquam quæstuosæ et inordinatæ episcopi pontificii valedixisset ordinationi, viros e doctis et verbi ministris, e senatoribus item et diacosiis, hoc est e plebe aliquot delegit, qui ex optimis, hoc est honestissimis atque doctissimis diaconis (quoties ecclesiæ alicui sanctus præficiendus est episcopus) certos senatui et plebi statuant. Ex his vero unum aliquem libera electione designant, quem protinus ecclesiæ cui præficiendus est mittunt et commendant per legatum ac senatorem honestissimum. Atque hic quidem præstantissimus ejus ditionis loci aut urbis antistes pro publica concione perorat, fiunt ab ecclesia ad Deum preces publicæ, interque precandum in ipso in conspectu totius populi imponit antistes ille sacrorum manus futuro illi episcopo, cui et ecclesiam commendat fideliter. Hæc vero plurimum momenti habere et episcopo plurimum auctoritatis conciliare nemo est qui nesciat.—H. Bullinger. in Omn. Apostol. Epist. Comm. Tigur. 1558. In 1 Epist. ad Tim. cap. iv. p. 585.]

The book of ordering ministers. *whom for the most part they never see nor heard of before, as one that came of one day unto the town, and goeth away the next.*

Further, they have no reasonable space given them wherein they may inquire and[1] *hearken out of his honest conversation, and have some experience of his soundness in teaching, and discretion and judgment to rule his flock. But if, as soon as ever it be said that those that are strangers to them should object against them*[2], *no man stand forth to oppose against them, forthwith*[3] *he is made a minister. And these are those things wherein I think the book of ordering ministers faulty, touching the trial and examination of the ministers; which self-same things are likewise of the trial of the deacon. And so you see, that besides the faults of those that execute the law, that there be faults in the laws themselves; and therefore the cause is truly assigned, although you see it not.*

Jo. Whitgift.

There is none that ought to be admitted by any bishop but such as have dwelt and remained in his diocese a convenient time. No time of admitting (except it be of some singular person whose ability is not doubted of) is appointed, but the same is before a sufficient time notified in the notablest places of the whole diocese, chiefly to this end and purpose, that there may be resort thither by such as have anything to object against any that is to be admitted at that time into the ministry; neither ought any to be admitted, except he bring a sufficient testimonial of his good behaviour from that place where he hath had his abode: and therefore, if they come not, it is a token that they have nothing to say; or, if they have to object, and do not, the fault is in themselves: they may if they will[4].

I told you before, that he may not teach before he be thereunto admitted, nor rule a flock before he have one committed unto him; and therefore of necessity he must at the least be admitted into the ministry of the word before they can give any judgment of him. So that indeed, though you

[1 Or, Repl. 1, 2, and Def. A.]
[2 Said to those that are strangers that they should object against him, Repl. 2.]
[3 To object anything forthwith, Repl. 2.]
[4 Cartwright rejoins that "the scholars of Cambridge go indifferently for orders (as they call them) either to Ely, or Bugden, or Peterborough, and sometimes to London," and argues that archbishops ordain throughout their provinces, inferring that, if there be any rule that a man should be ordained only in the diocese in which he lives, "it is evil kept." He adds that "the notifying the day of orders" is useless, and goes on to charge Whitgift with contradicting himself.—Sec. Repl. pp. 148, &c.]

have used many words, yet have you in effect said little or nothing; and the slenderness of your reasons against the book, together with the inconveniences that must of necessity follow, hath procured a great credit unto it; and it still remaineth true that I have answered to the Admonition, that is, that the faults that be are in the persons, not in the law. *The book of ordering ministers.*

Chapter i. The Ninth Division.

Answer to the Admonition, Page 37, line 1.

Again, if some be admitted into the ministry, either void of learning, or lewd in life, are all the rest for their sake to be condemned? Or is this a good argument, Some be admitted into the ministry without trial; therefore none is lawfully admitted into the ministry? or, Some ministers be unlearned and evil; *ergo*, there is none good? I think you will not deny but that there is now within this church of England as many learned, godly, grave, wise, and worthy ministers of the word, as there is in any one realm or particular church in all christendom, or ever hath been heretofore. *Weak arguments[5]. Worthy ministers in England.*

T. C. Page 25, Sect. 5, 6, 7.

And what mean you still to use this fighting with your own shadow? For where are the words, or what be they, that condemn all the ministers for some? that say all the ministers are unlawfully admitted for some? or that there is none good, because some are bad? If there be no such words as carry with them any such sense, then you do wrong to your brethren. If there be words that declare the clean contrary, then all men see what you be, which, although you often fault in, yet I am loth so often to name and charge you with it. When it is said that "learned and unlearned are received," it is evident that they condemn not all.

The Lord bless and increase an hundred-fold the godly, wise, learned, grave ministers of this church: and, because these words seem to rock us asleep, and to bring us into forgetfulness of the great ruins and desolations of the church, I must tell you that two thousand able and sufficient ministers, which preach and feed diligently and carefully the flock of Christ, were hard to be found in this church; which have been notwithstanding found in the church of France, by the estimation of those which know the estate, even under the time of the cross, where there were no such helps of magistrates and appointed stipends, as, God be praised, we have.

And again, you are to be put in mind, that a great number of those

[[5] This marginal note is inserted from Answ. 2.]

were bred in king Edward's days; so that I fear me a man need no great arithmetic to count the numbers of such able ministers as the late years have brought forth. And yet I am well assured that, if the ministry were reformed, and worthy men were sought for, there are great numbers of zealous and learned men that would lay their hands to serve this kind of building by the ministry. For, besides numbers that the universities would yield, which sigh for the repairing of the decays of the church, to help forward so great a work, the inns of court, and other the gentry of the realm, Galen and Justinian would bring their tenths, and (as it were) pay their shot in this reckoning.

Jo. Whitgift.

Their words be plain; for they say, " whereas in the old church a trial was had, &c; now by the letters commendatory of some one man, &c.:" whereby they set this time as contrary unto that, because some have been admitted without trial, and therefore make that fault general which is particular, and in very deed condemn all for some. If it were not so, why should either they or you condemn the rule, and not the persons only? Why should they say that we have "no right ministry?" Why should the Second Admonition from the beginning to the end so rail upon all the states and degrees of ministers and preachers in this church which do not consent with them in disturbing the church and opposing themselves against lawful orders and laws? Look fol. 32. of the 2. Admonition especially [1], and so forth, where they speak in most unchristian manner. And, though these men in this place say "learned and unlearned," yet doth it not follow "that they condemn not all" of an unlawful calling, and of not being tried and examined as well in life as learning. But what need you make such ado in cloaking a matter too notorious? for what do either they or you but deface even the best-learned and wisest of such as withstand you, thinking none sufficiently learned but yourselves and your adherents?

For the number of "sufficient ministers in France" able to preach " in the time of the cross," I will not take upon me to define anything; yet have I talked with some wise, godly, and learned preachers of that country, such as had good cause

[1 ...let us a little consider of this order of the election of the ministers,...whether the bishops' course be better, or this be the best....This alloweth only painful and true preachers, theirs ignorant asses, loitering and idle-bellied epicures, or profane and heathenish orators, that think all the grace of preaching lieth in affected eloquence, in fond fables to make their hearers laugh, &c.—Sec. Adm. p. 32.]

to know the state of that church, touching that matter; and truly, for anything that I can learn of them, you have overshot yourself in reckoning at the least 14. hundred. But I am not curious in matters not pertaining unto me, and I write but of credible report. God be thanked for the number that they had, or have, how many or how few soever they are.

Touching the number of preachers throughout England, I cannot write any certainty; but of this university, because I have some experience, you shall give me leave to speak as earnestly in truly commending of it, as you have done in untruly and unkindly defacing aud slandering it. The number of known preachers, which this university hath bred since the beginning of the queen's majesty's reign to this time of the year of our Lord, *anno* 1573, are at the least 450., besides those that have been called to that office after their departure from hence, and are not yet known to me. The number of preachers that be now in this university remaining is 102.; and no doubt but God will increase the number of them daily more and more: although it must be confessed that the factions and tumults, which you and some others have made in the church, do discourage a great number from the ministry, causeth many to contemn it, and think the calling to be unlawful, and therefore to abstain from it. Moreover, I know by experience, that some of you devise and practise, by all means possible, to stir up contention in this university, to dissuade men from the ministry, to bring such as be sober, wise, learned, and godly preachers, into contempt, and to make a confusion, and divide every college within itself. But, howsoever hitherto you have prevailed (as you have prevailed too much), yet I trust you shall never throughly bring to pass that which you desire. And I doubt not but that your undutiful, uncivil, and uncharitable dealing in this your book, your many errors and foul absurdities contained in the same, hath so detected you, that honest, discreet, quiet, and godly-learned men will no more be withdrawn by you, and such as you are, to any such schism or contention in the church; but rather bend themselves against the common adversary, and seek with heart and mouth to build up the walls of Jerusalem, which you have broken down, and to fill up the mines that you have digged, by craft and subtlety to overthrow the same. And, howsoever some will

_{The contentions in the church is an hinderance to the profession of divinity in the universities.}

still be waywardly disposed, yet I doubt not but that, if such as be in authority will do their duties, they may by convenient discipline either be kept within the bonds of modesty, or else removed from this place, wherein of all other places they may do most harm.

For "the inns of court," what they would do I know not; howbeit I think very few have gone from this place thither, which had ever any purpose in them to enter into the ministry. And surely from that place where I am, I have not known any go to the inns of court, in whom there hath appeared any kind of inclination to the ministry. What store of fit preachers those "inns" would yield, if your church were framed, I know not, but I think that some of them would not refuse the spoil of this. I doubt not but that there are many in the inns of court well affected in religion: God continue them, and increase the number of them, and give them grace to take heed that they be not seduced by overmuch credulity in themselves, and pretensed zeal in others.

What "Galen and Justinian" would do may be doubted; for, though both "Galen and Justinian" have forsaken our ministry[1], yet do they keep such livings as they had in the respect of the same, and are so far from yielding of "tenths," that they can be well content to receive "tenths[2]."

Chap. i. The Tenth Division.
Answer to the Admonition, Page 37, Sect. 1.

Letters commendatory of wise and godly men[3].

Touching letters commendatory of some one man noble or other, it may be that the parties which give

[1 For some of the persons alluded to, see abp. Grindal's Works, Park. Soc. Edit. Lett. lxxiii. p. 348.]

[2 Cartwright in his Reply says: "Take you good leave to speak all good of the university: it shall be my recreation after your importunate barkings: it is my daily prayer it may go well with her; and, although I be from her, yet I carried some of her bowels with me; so that whether there be in her either just cause of joy or sorrow, I have them in common with her. I can take no exception unto your 450. university preachers, not having the register of the university. But you did warely say 'known preachers,' and not godly preachers; for some of those have troubled the university and other places with popish leaven, &c."..."I fear me that I may cut off from the number of 2000. able ministers in the whole church of England, which I assigned before, as many as you take from that number which I reported to be in France." He then reproaches Whitgift for being suspicious of "the inns of court, which of their yearly exhibitions given to maintain their studies have erected up three divinity lectures; more for any thing I know than all the bishops have done."—Sec. Repl. pp. 152, &c.]

[3 Of wise men, Answ. 2.]

these letters be of that zeal, learning, and godliness, that their particular testimony ought to be better credited than some other subscribed with an hundred hands. And I think there is both noblemen and other who may better be trusted in that point than a great number of parishes in England which consist of rude and ignorant men, easily moved to testify anything, and in many places, for the most part, or altogether, drowned in papistry. I know no reason to the contrary, and I see no scripture alleged why one learned, godly, and wise man's testimony may not be received in such a case; and yet the book expresseth no such thing, but requireth due examination of learning, and sufficient testimonial of conversation, and giveth liberty to any one particular man to object any crime against any such as are to be ordered, and willeth that the party accused be kept from the ministry until he have cleared himself of the crimes objected. If "tag and rag" be admitted, "learned and unlearned," it is the fault of some, not of all, nor of the law; and, if they were called and elected according to your fantasy, there would some creep in as evil as any be now, and worse too. *The book requireth due examination of life and learning[4].*

T. C. Page 26, line 8.

It is not denied but the testimony that a nobleman which professeth the truth doth give ought to be weighed according to his degree and place which he hath in the commonwealth; but, where you think that the testimony of one wise man, learned, and godly, is sufficient warrant to proceed to an election of a minister, you considered not well the circumspection which St Paul used, who, when he admitted Timothy into his company to be a companion in his journey, to cut off all occasion of evil speech, received him not but upon commendation of the brethren both in Lystra and Iconium. Acts xvi.2,3.[5]

Jo. Whitgift.

I know that the testimony of many godly and wise men is of more weight than the testimony of one only; but this is no answer to that which I have said. The place of Paul and Timothy, Acts xvi., declareth how well Timothy was thought of and commended unto Paul; but it followeth not

[4 Examination of ministers, Answ. 2.]
[5 The verses are added from Repl. 2.]

Zuinglius.

that Paul would not also have received him, if he had been commended unto him but by some one. Howsoever it is, this your argument is nothing worth: *Nunquam licet* (saith Zuinglius), *neque in divinis neque in profanis, a facto ad jus argumentari*[1]: "It is never lawful, neither in divine nor in profane matters, to argue *a facto ad jus.*" Neither is the text as you report it: for the words do not signify that Paul would not have taken him with him, unless they had all given such testimony of him; neither can there be any such sense truly gathered out of that place. And it is manifest that the apostles received Paul into their company at the testimony and commendation of Barnabas only[2].

Of a deed or example to make a law.

Acts ix.

Chap. i. The Eleventh Division.

Answer to the Admonition, Page 38, Sect. 1.

You say that there be admitted into the ministry of "the basest sort of the people." I know not what you mean by "the basest sort:" this I am sure of, that the ministry is not now bound to any one tribe, as it was to the tribe of Levi in Jeroboam's time. Now none is secluded from that function of any degree, state, or calling; so that those qualities be found in him which in that office are to be required.

T. C. Page 26, line 14.

You know they meant by "the basest of the people" such as gave but one leap out of the shop into the church, as suddenly are changed out of a serving-man's coat into a minister's cloak, making for the most part the ministry their last refuge, &c. And seeing that, besides the words be plain, the daily experience teacheth it, you need not make it so strange, as though you knew not what they meant.

Jo. Whitgift.

I hear you say so; but why did they then quote the 1 *Reg.* xii. vers. 31, that manifestly proveth the same sense

[1 Nunquam enim licet &c.—H. Zvingl. Op. Tigur. 1581. Elench. contr. Catabapt. Pars II. fol. 9. 2.]

[2 Cartwright makes a long answer to this division, insisting that, "if the most part had misliked of" Timothy, St Paul "would not have taken him;" censuring Whitgift for disallowing an argument "drawn of an act of the apostle," and contending that the example of Paul's being brought to the apostles by Barnabas is not apposite.—Sec. Repl. pp. 154, &c.]

that I have gathered of their words? and that text only occasioned me so to do.

Chap. i. The Twelfth Division.

Answer to the Admonition, Page 38, Sect. 2, 3, 4.

I marvel to what purpose the twelfth chapter of the first book of Kings is here quoted; for Jeroboam is there reproved because he took the priesthood from the tribe of Levi, to the which only it did appertain.

The papists never took so great occasion of slan- *Offences given to the papists by their contentions.* dering the gospel at the ignorance of the ministers (for they have of themselves those that be as ignorant and more), as they do at your schisms and fond opinions, wherewith you disquiet the peace of the church, and lay stumbling-blocks before the weak; for the which God will surely call you to account.

The second chapter to the Romans is here quoted only to paint the margent.

Jo. Whitgift.

All this is passed over in silence.

Whether idolatrous sacrificers and mass-mongers may afterward be ministers of the gospel.

Chap. ii. The First Division.

Admonition.

The Second:

In those days ° no idolatrous sacrificers of⁴ heathenish priests were appointed to be preachers of the gospel; but we allow and like well of popish mass-mongers, men for all seasons, king Henry's priests, king Edward's priests⁵, queen Mary's priests, who of a truth, if God's word were precisely followed, should from the same be utterly removed. ° Heb. v. 4. *Ezek. xliv.* 10, 12, 13. *Jer. xxiii.*

Answer to the Admonition, Page 38, Sect. ult.

The place in the fifth chapter of the Hebrews⁶, quoted in the margent, speaketh nothing of idolatrous

[³ Your, Answ. 2.] [⁴ Or, Adm.]
[⁵ The last three words are not in Adm.]
[⁶ Of the epistle to the Hebrews, Answ.]

Idolatrous sacrificers and mass-mongers. sacrificers or heathenish priests, but only by the example of Aaron proveth that no man ought to intrude himself into the office of a bishop or priest except he be called of God. Lord, how dare these men thus wring the scriptures? In the xxiii. of the prophet Jeremy there is much spoken against false prophets, but not one word (for anything that I see) to prove that idolatrous sacrificers may not be admitted to preach the gospel.

Jo. Whitgift.

To this is nothing answered.

Chap. ii. The Second Division.
Answer to the Admonition, Page 39, Sect. 1, 2, 3, 4.
and Page 40, Sect. 1.

Ezek. xliv. 10.[1] The places of the xliv. of Ezechiel have some shew in them; for there the Lord commandeth the Levites which had committed idolatry to be put from their dignity, and not to be received into the priests' office, but to serve in inferior ministries.

I think you will not make this a general rule, to debar such from preaching[2] of the gospel as have through infirmity fallen, and be now with hearty repentance returned. We have many examples to the contrary. *Peter's forswearing.* Peter forswore his Master Christ, which was as evil as sacrificing to idols; and yet he was not put from his apostleship. We have divers examples in the primitive church of such as by fear being compelled to sacrifice to strange gods after repented, and kept still the office of preaching the gospel, and did most constantly die in the same.

T. C. Page 26, Sect. 1.

What ought to be general if this ought not, to put the minister that hath been an idolater from his ministry? Is it not a commandment of God, and given, not of one Levite or two, but of all those that went back, not at one time, but at others also, when the like occasion was given; as appeareth in the book of the Kings[3], when[4] all the priests of the Lord, that had sacrificed in the high places, were not suffered to come to the [2 Chap. xxiii. 9.[5]]

[1 This marginal reference is inserted from Answ. 2.]
[2 From the preaching, Answ. 2.] [3 Of Kings, Repl. 2.]
[4 Where, Repl. 1, 2, and Def. A.]
[5 The verse is added from Repl. 2.]

TRACT. III.]   TO THE ADMONITION.   319

altar in Jerusalem? Doth not St Paul make smaller causes of deposing Idolatrous
from the ministry than idolatry? For, after he hath described what sacrificers
  manner of men the ministers should be, and deacons, he addeth: and mass-mongers.
1 Tim. iii. "*And, being tried, let them execute their functions as long as* St Paul his
they remain blameless." I think, if so be a man had been known to be an meaning
adulterer, although he repented him, yet none that is well advised would falsified.
*take him into the ministry. For, if St Paul reject him that had two wives
at once (which was a thing that the Jews and gentiles thought lawful, and
that was common amongst them, and had prevailed throughout all the
world), how much less would he suffer any to be admitted to the ministry
which should be an adulterer, and have another man's wife, which is condemned of all that profess the name of Christ, and which is not so general
a mischief as that was, and suffer*[6] *him to abide in the ministry which
should commit such wickedness during his function; and*[7] *likewise of a
murderer! Now the sin of idolatry is greater and more detestable than
any of them, inasmuch as, pertaining to the first table, it immediately
staineth God's honour, and breaketh duty to him unto whom we more owe
it (without all comparison) than to any mortal man. And, if St Paul, in
the choice of the widow to attend upon the sick of the church, which was the
lowest office in the church, requireth not only such a one as is at the time of
the choice honest and holy, but such a one as had*[8] *led her whole life in all
good works and with commendation; how much more is that to be observed
in the minister or bishop of the church, that he be not only at the time of
his choice, but all other times before, such a one as had*[8] *lived without any
notable and open offence of those amongst whom he had his conversation!*

Jo. Whitgift.

It is not such a commandment as must of necessity be The place,
perpetually kept, and made a general rule for ever; for it touching
pertaineth to the judicial law which is not perpetual, as I sacrificers
have before proved[9]. Moreover, why should this precept Tract. II.
rather be perpetual than that which goeth before, that "no Ezek. xliv.
stranger uncircumcised in heart, and uncircumcised in flesh,
should enter into the sanctuary?" or than that which followeth, that "the priests, when they enter in at the gates,
must be clothed with white linen, &c.?" Do not the circumstances of the place best declare the meaning of it? The
like also is to be said to that example, 2 *Regum* xxiii.[10]

The place of St Paul, 1 Tim. iii., is untruly by you The corrupt
                   dealing of
                   T. C.
                   1 Tim. iii.

[6 Or would he suffer, Repl. 2.]   [7 *And* is not in Repl. 2.]
[8 Hath, Repl. 1 and 2.]   [9 See before, pages 271, &c.]
[10 Cartwright observes that "it doth not follow that because the ceremonial
law is abrogated, therefore the judicial is also," and declares that Whitgift's
"pen is a pen-knife to cut asunder all the scriptures."—Sec. Repl. pp. 162, 3.]

Idolatrous sacrificers and massmongers.

alleged and corruptly translated; for the words of the apostle be not as you report them: "and, being tried, let them execute their functions as long as they remain blameless." But thus the apostle saith: "and let them first be proved, then let them minister being blameless:" the Greek word is ἀνέγκλητοι ὄντες, that is, "if in trial they be found blameless, then let them minister." For trial may be had whether they be blameless, or no, but not whether they will so "remain." Moreover, the apostle in that place speaketh of deacons, and not of ministers. I marvel what you mean so manifestly to falsify the words of the scripture, or to what purpose you have invented this new translation, except it be to justify that error of the anabaptists, that the virtue of the word and of the sacraments doth depend upon the good life of the minister. Certain it is that you have neither Greek, Latin, nor English text that doth so translate it[1]. Neither doth the apostle St Paul there speak of deposing ministers, or deacons, but of electing them, as it is manifest. I doubt not but that a whoremonger, after he hath repented him (if other things be correspondent), may be admitted to the ministry, even as well as Peter, after his denial, was admitted to be an apostle, or Paul after that he had been a persecutor. St Paul would not that a bishop should have two wives at once, but he doth not seclude him from being a bishop that hath had two wives; except you will establish in this place the popish bigamy. In like manner he would not have an whoremonger, a drunkard, a covetous person, to be chosen a bishop; yet doth he not seclude from that function such as have been guilty of these crimes (and now of godly conversation) for their former offences: for then should he deal otherwise with them than he himself was dealt with; neither have you any example in the new testament of any deposed from their ministry, though they were found in many things guilty. Christ knew that Judas was a traitor, yet did he not depose him from his apostleship: he knew that the scribes and Pharisees were criminous in divers points, yet did he will them to be taken and heard as God's ministers, when he said: *In cathedra Mosis sedent scribæ, &c.:* "The scribes and Pharisees sit in

[1 Cartwright replies, "I took the sense which was fit for my cause, and neither against the scope of the apostle nor any grammar construction."—Ibid. p. 163.]

Moses' seat, &c." Matt. xxiii. And St Paul knew of divers wicked and ungodly preachers in the church of Philippi; yet did he not will their ministry to be taken from them, but shewed himself to be very glad for their labour and travail taken in preaching the gospel. Phil. i.

Idolatrous sacrificers and mass-mongers. Matt. xxiii.

Phil. i.

True it is that idolatry is an horrible and great sin; yet doth repentance stretch unto it, which so altereth and changeth a man through the mercy of God, be he never so defiled, that it maketh him pure and clean: and shall we seclude him from ministering unto God that is pure in the sight of God? or shall we not think him to be a meet minister in the visible church, that is a member of the unvisible and elect church? In the old law there were many things that defiled the body, and made the man for a time unclean; but now all such things "are clean to those that be clean." In like manner there were then certain crimes pertaining to the mind which could not be expiated but by corporal punishment; but repentance is a medicine for all; and the greatest idolater, truly repenting, may become a more zealous preacher than he that in the sight of the world never committed the least offence.

Repentance stretcheth to idolatry.

Tit. i.

St Paul "in the choice of widows" doth not require such a one "as hath led her whole life in all good works;" for how could that be at that time, when they had but in one part of their life known Christ and professed the gospel, being thereunto converted by the apostles? But his meaning is, that such be chosen as were known to have been diligent in all good works, that is, to have been liberal and beneficial towards the poor; for so doth M. Calvin interpret it[2]. If you would have none chosen to be ministers but such as have all their life-time been blameless, I think you are like to have but a few, and more like to refuse such as be very meet and fit for that function. But, as the apostle would not have any admitted to the ministry upon a sudden trial or conversion, so doth he not appoint for the same the whole former time of man's life, but a reasonable and sufficient time, such as may suffice for the trial of a man in such matters[3].

[2 ...in officiis omnibus, quæ sunt illius [functionis] propria, longo usu exercitatas esse vult : qualia sunt labor et sedulitas in liberis educandis, hospitalitas, ministeria erga pauperes, et reliqua beneficentiæ opera.—Calvin. Op. Amst. 1667-71. Comm. in Epist. I. ad Tim. cap. v. Tom. VII. p. 461.]

[3 Cartwright reproaches Whitgift for alleging the examples of St Peter and St Paul out of place, and goes on at great length to maintain that a person guilty

<small>Idolatrous sacrificers and mass-mongers.</small>

Chapter ii. The Third Division.

T. C. Page 26, Sect. 2, 3; and Page 27, Sect. 1.

If I should stand with you, whether Peter his forswearing that he knew not Christ were a greater fault than to go from the gospel to idolatry, and therein for some long space to continue, as the Levites did, I should trouble you. For, if a man suddenly and at a push for fear, and to save his life, say and swear he is no Christian, and the same day repent him of his fault; although it be a great and heinous crime, yet it seemeth not to be so great as his is, which not only denieth Christ in words, but doth it also in deeds, and worshippeth antichrist, and continueth in that worship, not a day, but months and years.

But I will answer you that, even as our Saviour Christ called St Paul in the heat of his persecution, and when he was a blasphemer, unto the apostleship, so he, having the law in his own hands, and making no laws for himself, but for us, might call St Peter also to that function, which had thrice denied him.

But, as it is not lawful for us to follow the example of Christ in calling of Paul, by admitting those which are new converted, having a contrary precept given, that no new plant, or green Christian, should be taken to the ministry; so is it not lawful also[2] *to follow that example of our Saviour Christ, the contrary being commanded, as I have before alleged. For, albeit the examples of our Saviour Christ be to be followed of us, yet, if there be commandments general to the contrary, then we must know that it is our parts to walk in the broad and beaten way, as it were the common causey*[3] *of the commandment, rather than an outpath of the example.* <small>1 Tim. iii.6.[1]</small>

Jo. Whitgift.

Peter, having before bragged of his constancy, lately admonished by his Master Christ, almost even in the presence of his Master, wittingly and willingly denied, not once, but thrice, yea, bitterly forswore him; which fault no doubt was as grievous as any kind of idolatry: and therefore, if "you stand with" me in that matter never so long, you cannot greatly "trouble" me; for, the circumstances being considered, there is nothing to excuse Peter's denial.

As "Christ in the heat of Paul's persecution" did choose him to be an apostle, and called Peter also to that function, after he had thrice denied him, even so doth he still continue of some notorious sins should never after be admitted into the ministry, or if admitted should be deposed; arguing that the example of Christ is not always to be followed by us, and denying all Whitgift's reasons as of little weight.— Sec. Repl. pp. 166-177.]

[1 The verse is supplied from Repl. 2.]   [2 *Also* is not in Repl. 2.]
[3 Causey: causeway.]

his mercy; neither is it one whit straitened; and these Idolatrous examples hath he set before us, that we should at no time sacrificers and massdespair of his mercy and goodness. So saith St Paul, 1 Tim. i.: mongers. *Verum ideo misericordiam consecutus sum, &c.:* "Notwithstanding, for this cause was I received to mercy, that Jesus Christ should first shew on me all long-suffering, unto the example of them which shall in time to come believe in him unto eternal life."

Although these examples of our Saviour Christ are not at all times, and in all points, to be followed, yet do they sufficiently declare that no man for any crime is to be secluded from any lawful vocation, if he repent him and become a new man. And there be "no general commandments contrary hereunto;" but this doctrine is consonant to the whole course of the gospel[4].

Chapter ii. The Fourth Division.
T. C. Page 27, Sect. 2.

I know Ambrose was taken newly from paganism to be bishop of Mi- T. C. picketh *lan, for the great estimation and credit he had amongst the people: but,* a quarrel to deprave *besides that I have shewed that such things are unlawful, being forbidden,* Ambrose, out of place and *the errors and corrupt expounding of scriptures, which are found in his* unjustly. *works, declare that it had been more safe for the church, if by study of the scriptures he had first been a scholar of divinity or ever he had been made doctor.*

Jo. WHITGIFT.

You needed not to have wiped away the example of Ambrose with so much disgracing of him, being so worthy a man and so learned a father: though[5] he were not christened when he was chosen bishop, yet had he long before that time professed the name of Christ, and was soundly grounded in religion; for in those days many did long defer the time of baptism after the time of their conversion. And St Paul (1 Tim. iii.) by his "green Christian," as you term him, doth understand such as be newly converted. Ambrose was a man of notable learning, and singularly commended in all histories that make any mention of him: his "errors" be not

[4 Cartwright rejoins: "...you do him open injury, when you say that 'his fault was as grievous as any kind of idolatry;'" and goes on to compare the circumstances of his denial with those of the sin committed by " a great number of idolaters."—Sec. Repl. pp. 178, 9.]

[5 For though, Def. A.]

Idolatrous sacrificers and mass-mongers. so many, nor his expositions so simple, that you should so contemptuously write of him[1].

Chapter ii. The Fifth Division.

T. C. Page 27, Sect. 2.

There may be more examples shewed out of that which you call the primitive church to the contrary of that which you say. For, when they used oftentimes against those that had so fallen such severity (indeed extreme and excessive), that they were never after until their deaths admitted to the Lord's table, I leave to you to think whether they would then suffer any such to execute the function of the ministry. Besides that St Cyprian hath also a special treatise of this, that those that have sacrificed to idols should not be permitted any more to minister in the church[2], *i. Lib. Epist. in the first book of his Epist. Epistle vii.*[4] *Epist. 7.*[3]

Jo. Whitgift.

It appeareth in that 7. epistle of Cyprian that he meant of such as, after they had sacrificed to idols, took their ministry again upon them, without any signification or shew of repentance, but rather justifying, or at the least excusing, their former fact. And that this was Cyprian's meaning, it may be gathered by these words in the same epistle, which he speaketh to the people to whom he writ touching Fortunatianus, who, having sacrificed to idols, would have again resumed his ministry: *Ergo contumaces, et Deum non timentes, et ab ecclesia in totum recedentes, nemo comitetur. Quod si quis impatiens fuerit ad deprecandum Dominum qui offensus est, et nobis obtemperare noluerit, sed desperatos et perditos secutus fuerit, sibi imputabit cum judicii dies venerit*[5]: " Wherefore let no man keep company with those which are stubborn, not fearing God, and wholly depart from the church. But, if any will not ask forgiveness at the Lord which is offended, and will not obey us, but will needs follow them which are desperate and past hope, he shall lay the blame on none but on himself at the day of judgment." Whereby it is plain that Cyprian meant such as had wholly departed from the church, and were desperate in wickedness. It is manifest

Cypr. Lib. i. Epist. 7.

[1 "...I gave him indeed the wipe, but it was with the sword of God....I know Ambrose was a notable man, and learned in human knowledge; yet I might without either great disgrace or any contempt say that which I said."—Ibid. pp. 180, 1.]

[2 Cypr. Op. Oxon. 1682. Ad Epictet. Epist. lxv. pp. 162, &c.]

[3 This reference is inserted from Repl. 2.]

[4 The clause from *in the first* is not in Repl. 2.] [5 Id. ibid. p. 164.]

that in Cyprian's time those that did offend in such crimes, and afterwards repented, were appointed a time of public repentance, according to the quality of the fault committed, and until that time was expired they were not admitted unto the Lord's table, except only at the point of death. Idolatrous sacrificers and mass-mongers.

But I grant that there was "extreme severity" in Cyprian's time shewed to such as "had fallen in the time of persecution," and that it evidently appeareth in other of his epistles that such were no more admitted to the ministry. But this law was made by Cyprian and others, as it is evident, *Lib. ii. Epist. i.*[6], in that council of Carthage, where it was also concluded that such as were baptized of heretics should be re-baptized, and therefore of the less force, seeing that that whole council is for just cause rejected[7].

Chapter ii. The Sixth Division.
Answer to the Admonition, Page 39, Sect. 2, 3.

I pray you, what say you to M. Luther, Bucer, Cranmer, Latimer, Ridley, &c.? were not all these sometimes mass-mongers, and yet singular and notable instruments of promoting the gospel and preaching the same? whereof many have given testimony by shedding their blood. Luther, Cranmer, Latimer[8].

And by whose ministry especially hath the gospel been published, and is as yet in this church of England, but by such as have been mass-mongers, and now zealous, godly, and learned preachers?

T. C. Page 27, Sect. 2, 3.

But you ask what they say to M. Luther, Bucer, Cranmer, Latimer, Ridley? I pray you, when did these excellent personages ever slide from the gospel unto idolatry? which of them did ever say mass after God had opened them the truth? what hath so blinded you, that you cannot distinguish and put a difference between one that, having been nousled from his youth up in idolatry, cometh afterwards out of it, and between him which, having knowledge of the gospel, afterward departeth from it? And of such is the place of Ezechiel; of such, I say, as have gone back and fallen away. Even the Admonition which I confute; for it speaketh generally, and maketh no such distinction.

[6 Addimus plane et adjungimus,...consensu et auctoritate communi, ut etiam si qui presbyteri aut diaconi,...sacrificia foris falsa ac sacrilega offerre conati sint, eos quoque hac conditione suscipi cum revertuntur, ut communicent laici, &c.— Id. ad Stephan. Epist. lxxii. p. 197.]

[7 Cartwright rejoins that Cyprian makes for him, and declares that another of his epistles (Conf. ad Cler. et Pleb. Hisp. Epist. lxvii. p. 174) proves that the council which decreed for re-baptizing was not the same with that which concluded "against restoring of ministers fallen into idolatry."—Sec. Repl. pp. 181-3.]

[8 This marginal note is inserted from Answ. 2.]

Idolatrous sacrificers and mass-mongers.

I know none that have been preachers of the gospel, and after in the time of queen Mary " mass-mongers, which now are zealous, godly, and learned preachers;" and, if there be any such, I think, for offence' sake, the church might better be without them than have them. You say " God in that place sheweth how grievous a sin idolatry is, in the priests especially." And is it not now more grievous in the minister of the gospel, whose function is more precious, and knowledge greater? and, if the sin be greater, should it have now a less punishment than it had then? How shall the fault be esteemed great or little, but by the greatness or smallness of the punishment? You said before, the places of Deuteronomy, touching adding and diminishing nothing from that which the Lord commandeth, were for the Jews, and are not for our times. And this commandment of God in Ezechiel you say served for that time, and not for ours.

Jo. Whitgift.

The examples of Luther, &c. are directly against the Admonition.

The examples of M. Luther, Bucer, Cranmer, &c., do sufficiently confute the Admonition; the words whereof be these: "In those days no idolatrous sacrificers or heathenish priests were appointed to be preachers of the gospel; but we allow and like well of popish mass-mongers, men for all seasons, king Henry's priests, &c." Here you see that they do not only condemn such as once "knowing the truth have afterwards departed from it," but such also as have at any time sacrificed: why should they else name "king Henry's priests," seeing it is evident that the mass was not abolished in king Henry's time? so that I have better cause to ask, "what hath so blinded you" that you could not understand their meaning, the words being so plain? or rather, that you would in that point wilfully blind yourself and others also? I know some that being "preachers of the gospel, and after in the time of queen Mary mass-mongers, which now are zealous, godly, and learned preachers," and of as good fame and credit with godly men as any be in this land (without offence be it spoken); neither be the quiet and humble members of the church offended with them, but rejoice at their conversion, and praise God for them.

Doctrine framed according to men's persons.

But you frame your doctrine according to your affection towards certain persons, as the manner now-a-days of some is: for this doctrine hath been taught generally, that "no idolatrous priest should remain in the ministry;" and these examples of Luther, Bucer, &c., have been lightly rejected as repugnant to the commandment of God: but now, being better advised, and remembering that some in that case be great promoters of your opinions, this mitigation forsooth must be made, "that such as were preachers in king Edward's time, &c.:" they (I mean your fautors) were professors, though they were no preachers, they were also in queen Mary's time mass-mongers, and now they be preachers, and yet all is well; for you have the law in your hands to coin what opinions you list, to add to them or to take from them what you list, to apply and not apply them, to whom and when you list, even pope-like[1].

Idolatrous sacrificers and mass-mongers.

The sin of idolatry is now as great an offence as it was then; but the external and civil punishment for the same is in the power of the magistrate, being a portion of the judicial law; the necessity whereof is wholly abrogated, as I have proved before[2].

Tract II. cap. 6. The Fifth Division.

Those precepts in Deuteronomy were given to the Jews, both for the judicial and ceremonial law also: they be given to us for the law of faith and good manners only; for we are clearly delivered from the ceremonies of the law; and the judicials (whereof this in Ezechiel is a portion) are not enjoined to Christians upon any necessity, but left to the discretion of the civil magistrate. And therefore I have said nothing either of those places of Deuteronomy, or of this of Ezechiel, which I will not by learning and good authority justify.

Chapter ii. The Seventh Division.

Answer to the Admonition. Page 39, Sect. ult.

God in that place of the prophet Ezechiel sheweth how grievous a sin idolatry is, especially in the priests; but he prescribeth no general rule of secluding them from their ministry, if they falling afterward repent.

[If you will have this a perpetual rule and general, then must those precepts also be perpetual and general that follow in the same chapter, *scil.*, that the priests when they enter in at the gates must be clothed with white linen garments, and have no wool upon them; that they must have linen bonnets upon their heads,

[1 "The slanderous untruths that are here uttered I will not defile my pen with."—Sec. Repl. p. 184.]
[2 See before, pages 271, &c.]

Idolatrous sacrificers and mass-mongers. linen breeches upon their loins; that they shall marry no widows, or such as have been divorced, but maidens or the widow of a priest. If you will make these precepts ceremonial or judicial, and so temporal (as I am sure you will), then must you make the other so in like manner; for, as they be all in one chapter, and of the same spirit, so be they also of one nature. The like may be also said of that which goeth before in the same chapter, which of necessity you must confess to be either ceremonial or judicial, and therefore not perpetual[1].]

T. C. Page 27, Sect. 4.

You work a sure way which, to maintain your corruptions, deny the scripture which speaketh against them, to be understanded of those which be in our time, and that to be understanded of our ministers which was of theirs, or of our faults which was of theirs. This is not the way to anabaptism, but to all heresies and schisms, that ever have been or shall be. For, if you go forward in clipping the scripture as you begin, you will leave us nothing in the end, wherewith we may either defend ourselves against heretics, or be able to strike at them.

Jo. Whitgift.

I neither "deny the scriptures nor clip them;" neither can my doctrine open "the way to any heresy:" but I speak of them in this point as all learned and sound writers do, old or new; if I do not, disprove me, not by words, but reasons[2] and authorities.

Chapter ii. The Eighth Division.

Answer to the Admonition, Page 40, Sect. 1.

Besides this, there is a great difference betwixt the severity of the law and the lenity of the gospel, betwixt the external regiment of the church before Christ and the church after Christ; neither can you make the one in all points correspondent to the other; likewise betwixt the declining of those priests, which was wholly from God to gentility, and the falling of ours to papistry, which confesseth the same articles of faith that we do, although not sincerely. It is one thing wholly to worship false gods, another thing to worship the true God falsely and superstitiously. But among all other things

[1 This paragraph is inserted from Answ. 2.]   [2 But by reasons, Def. A.]

I would gladly know wherein king Edward's priests have offended you. It is happy you let queen Elizabeth's priests alone. I marvel whose priests you are. *Idolatrous sacrificers and mass-mongers.*

T. C. Page 27, Sect. 5, 6.

Whereas you say "there is a great difference between the severity of the law and lenity of the gospel," methinks I smell a spice of the error of the Manichees, which were also scholars in that behalf of the old heretic Cerdon, that there is a good and an evil, a gentle and a severe God, one under the law, and another under the gospel. For to say that God was then a severe punisher of sin, and that now he is not at so great hatred with it, but that he will have it gentlier and softlier dealt with, is even all one in effect with that which supposeth two Gods. I will join with you in it, that the transgressions of the law in the time of the gospel ought rather to be severelier punished than they were under the law; forasmuch as the knowledge is greater, and the abundance of the Spirit of God, whereby the laws are kept, is more plentiful than under the law.

Chap. xiii. 3.3 *At this time I will content me with the place of Zachary, which, prophesying of the kingdom of Christ and of the time of the gospel, saith that then the father and mother of the false prophet shall cause their own son to be put to death.* *The place of Zech. misunderstand⁴.*

Jo. Whitgift.

My opinion touching "the severity of the law and lenity of the gospel" is farther from "the error of the Manichees," than yours is from the Turks or Jews. I know God is as "severe a punisher of sin now as he was then;" but the manner and kind of corporally punishing it is not the same now that it was then. Neither will I refuse to join with you in this, that christian magistrates are not bound to the judicial laws of Moses, touching the kind and manner of punishing sin; and yet is not this to extenuate sin one whit, but the contrary rather; as Cyril doth note in his xi. book upon Leviticus, where he sheweth a reason why adultery and other crimes were commanded in the law to be punished with corporal death, and not in the gospel; which reason fully answereth your objection, *Quid igitur? dicemus quod lex Mosi crudelis est, &c.*[5]: *"What then? shall we say that* *Difference betwixt the severity of the law and the lenity of the gospel.*

[3 The verse is added from Repl. 2.]   [4 Misunderstood, Def. A.]
[5 Quid igitur? dicemus quod lex Moysi crudelis sit, quæ jubet puniri adulterum, vel adulteram; et evangelium Christi per indulgentiam resolvit auditores in deterius? Non ita est. Propterea enim sermonem Pauli protulimus in superioribus dicentis: *Quanto magis deterioribus suppliciis dignus est qui Filium Dei conculcaverit, &c.* Audi ergo quomodo neque tunc crudelis fuerit lex, neque

Idolatrous sacrificers and mass-mongers. the law of Moses is cruel, which commandeth that the adulterer and adulteress should be punished; and that the gospel of Christ, through indulgence and pardon, maketh the hearers the worse? It is not so; for to this purpose did we bring in that saying of Paul before: 'How much more is he worthy of more grievous punishment, which treadeth under feet the Son of God, &c.' Hear therefore how neither the law was then cruel, neither yet the gospel is now dissolute for the greatness of forgiveness; but in both, though diversely, the loving-kindness of God remaineth. This that is according to the law (as for example, that the adulterer and the adulteress were punished with present death), forsomuch as both of them have suffered punishment for their sin, and have received due reward for the wickedness which they committed; what revengement shall afterward hang over their souls, if they have committed no other fault, if there is no other sin which may condemn them, but only have committed this fact, and for the same have received the punishment due by the law? The Lord will not punish one thing twice; for they have received the reward for their sin, and the pain for their offence is finished. And for this cause is not this kind of commandment cruel (as the heretics affirm, accusing the law of God, and denying that there is any kind of humanity in it), but it is full of mercy; because hereby the people should rather be purged from their sins than condemned. But now there is no punishment laid upon the body, nor any purging of sin through corporal punishment, but through repentance; which if a man do worthily work, so that he may seem worthy to have the punishment withdrawn, he may find

nunc dissolutum videatur evangelium propter veniæ largitatem, sed in utroque Dei benignitas diversa dispensatione teneatur : hoc quod secundum legem (verbi causa) adulter vel adultera præsenti morte puniebatur, propter hoc ipsum quod peccati sui pertulit pœnam, et commissi sceleris exsolvit digna supplicia. Quid erit post hæc, quod animabus eorum ultionis immineat, si nihil aliud deliquerunt? si aliud peccatum non est quod condemnet eos, sed hoc solum commiserunt, et tunc tantum cum puniti sunt, et legis pro hoc supplicium pertulerunt? Non vindicabit Dominus bis in idipsum ; receperunt enim peccatum suum, et consumta est criminis pœna. Et ideo invenitur hoc genus præcepti non crudele, sicut hæretici asserunt accusantes legem Dei, et negantes in ea humanitatis aliquid contineri; sed plenum misericordia, idcirco quod per hoc purgaretur ex peccatis populus magis, quam condemnaretur. Nunc vero non infertur pœna corpori, nec purgatio peccati per corporale supplicium constat, sed per pœnitentiam : quam utrum quis digne gerat, ita ut mereri pro ea veniam possit, videto.—Orig. Op. Par. 1733-59. In Levit. Hom. xi. 2. Tom. II. p. 248. See before, page 274, note 2.]

forgiveness." But, howsoever this answer of Cyril may in some points minister occasion of quarrelling to such as be disposed; yet this is evident, that the quantity of sin, and the heinousness of it, is not to be esteemed according to the corporal and external punishment, but according to the commandment of God to the which it is repugnant, and according to the threatenings of God in the scriptures pronounced against the same; for we see that lesser faults are by man punished with greater torments, even according to the state of every country. And this "smelleth" not one whit " of the Manichees' heresy," but the clean contrary. Neither do I make this difference " betwixt the severity of the law and lenity of the gospel," in any other respect than of temporal punishment appointed in the law.

Idolatrous sacrificers and mass-mongers.

The place of Zachary doth not make for your purpose, except you will give to the parents power of life and death over their sons and daughters, and give liberty for one private man to kill another. The prophet in that place declareth what zeal shall be in the people against false prophets, and how much they shall prefer the true religion of God before their own natural affection, and rather forsake their children, yea, hate them, and kill them, than by their means they should be withdrawn from God: this is the true meaning of that place, if you will refer it to the time of the gospel. But, if you will apply it to the Israelites, to whom this prophet now preacheth and prophesieth, then doth he declare unto them what zeal and fervency God requireth in them, if they truly repent them of their former idolatry; even that they shall not spare their own children, but deal with them according to the law, Deut. xiii., ver. 6, &c. M. Luther, expounding this place and referring it to the time of the gospel, saith thus: *Et est hæc sententiæ summa,* &c.[1]: "The sum hereof is, that Christians shall retain and defend true and pure doctrine, without respect of any person, whether it be his kinsman or friend: for it is necessary that there should be false doctrine and heresies, that the truth might be tried; but yet they shall not have the upper hand, or prevail." And, in-

The true meaning of Zech. xiii.

Luther.

[1 Et est hæc sententiæ summa: Christiani retinebunt et propugnabunt veram et puram doctrinam, citra ullius respectum, quantumvis cognatus aut amicus sit: necesse enim est falsas doctrinas et hæreses esse, ut probetur vera doctrina, non tamen vincent nec superabunt.—M. Luther. Op. Witeb. 1552, &c. Enarr. in cap. xiii. Proph. Zach. Tom. V. fol. 567. 2.]

Idolatrous sacrificers and mass-mongers.

terpreting these words, "His father and his mother that begat him shall thrust him through when he prophesieth," he saith: *Id est, non ferreis aut æreis armis et gladiis ipsum conficient, sed verbo Dei; erit enim spirituale et suave certamen, quale est parentum cum suis liberis; sicut et divus Paulus Corinthios confodit, et ipsorum errores verbo Dei reprehendit*[1]: "That is to say, they shall destroy him, not with iron or brasen armour and weapons, but with the word of God; for the strife shall be spiritual and pleasant, such as is between parents and their children; like as St Paul doth pierce through the Corinthians, and reprehendeth their errors by the word of God."

The bloody assertion of T. C.

But would you indeed conclude of this place, that those which have taught false doctrine must of necessity "be put to death," though they repent? yea, that their own parents and friends must kill them, or cause them to be killed, and not rather receive them willingly, if they will convert, and embrace them most joyfully? Undoubtedly the prophet hath no such meaning; neither have you any example of such extremity committed by a true Christian towards a repentant idolater, from the nativity of Christ unto this hour: neither is there anything in the whole new testament whereby any such fact can be warranted. And, howsoever this place may make for the severe punishing of stubborn and perverse idolaters, it maketh nothing at all for such as repent and be converted: and therefore it may be, that this place of scripture doth "content" you; but surely it cannot persuade any that duly considereth it that idolaters, though they repent, may not be received both to mercy, and also into the ministry.

And, if any man shall think that I wring his words against his meaning, let him consider against whom he bendeth his force, and urgeth this place of Zachary (that is, against them which have fallen, and have been mass-mongers, and now are none, but preachers of the gospel), and he shall easily perceive both the bloodiness of his opinion, and also that I have not herein dealt unfaithfully. Surely, all circumstances considered, it is not unlike that this hath been some occasion of the mischievous attempt which of late hath been put in practice[2].

[1 Id. ibid.]
[2 It is not clear to what attempt allusion is here made.]

Chap. ii. The Ninth Division.

T. C. Page 28, line 2, and Sect. 1.

Idolatrous sacrificers and mass-mongers.

It is as absurd which is brought to prove that the papists, which worship God falsely, do not fault so heinously as the Israelites did, which worshipped the idols. *As who should say, the Jews, or any other the grossest idolaters that ever were, did ever take those things which they worshipped, serpents, oxen, fire, water, &c. to be God, or knew not the images, before which they fell down, were wood or stone, silver and gold. And who knoweth not that they thought that they worshipped, by them and in them, the God which made heaven and earth? The Jews, when they molted a golden calf, and fell down before it,* Exod. xxxii. *did never think that to be God, but said that they would keep holy day to the Lord Jehovah. Wherein I will put you over to the learned treatises of the godly new writers, which do refute this distinction, being brought of the papists as a shift to prove that the idolatry which is forbidden in the old testament toucheth not them, because they worship God by these things, and the idolatrous Jews and infidels worshipped nothing else, nor looked at nothing else than the bare things before which they fell down: which self-same distinction you bring to prove that papistry is not so detestable as the idolatry of the Jews. It may be that certain of the gentiles worshipped by their images Jupiter and Juno, &c. But you cannot shew that the Israelites ever worshipped any other god than the true God; so that their fault was only in that they worshipped him otherwise than he had appointed. And the gentiles, that worshipped many gods, worshipped one as the head and chief, and the rest as small companions, and, as they termed them,* minorum gentium deos, *as the papists do God as the chief, and the saints as other petty gods.*

And here all men may see what a good proctor you be for the papists, both in lessening their faults, and abating their punishments; and yet will not I say that you are conspired with them, or have received your fee of them. But, if you can shew where, or in what one point, those that you charge with confederacy have laid so soft pillows under their heads as these are, they refuse not to be called confederate and conspired with the papists.

As who should say, that any man can doubt of this.

A gross error; for most of the wisest gentiles thought that the heavens and earth were never created.

A manifest untruth, as shall appear.

An untruth; for they said not so.

This is contrary to that which you spake immediately before.

Jo. Whitgift.

The distinction betwixt the worshipping of the false gods wholly, and the worshipping of the true God falsely and superstitiously, is not yet by you proved to have any "absurdity" in it. But it is great boldness for you to affirm, that "the gentiles and the most gross idolaters never took those which they did worship for gods, but that in them and by them they thought they worshipped the God that made heaven and earth." For what profane philosopher, what drunken poet, what boy in the grammar-school knoweth not the contrary? Was Jupiter, Apollo, Venus, Diana, &c., gods or goddesses "that created heaven and earth?" or thought to have "made heaven and earth?" And yet these and such like they were whom the gentiles did worship even in their images. Nay they took the very images themselves sometimes to be their gods. Doth not the cxv. Psalm, Esay xliv., Jer. x., Baruch vi., the story of Bel and the Dragon, and the scripture in sundry places else, manifestly declare it? And did not the Jews oftentimes sin in this point as grossly as the gentiles did? Look Judg. ii. ver. 10, 11, 12, &c., 1 *Reg.* xviii.; wherein it is plain that the Jews were as gross in taking those things to be gods indeed as were the gentiles. And surely I think the places in the scripture before alleged so manifest for the proof hereof, that no man reading the same can anything doubt of this matter.

The words of the text do expressly signify unto us that the Israelites took the golden calf to be God; but be it that they may be taken there metonymically (which is but a conjecture), that cannot excuse their grossness at other times, when they were conversant among the gentiles, and allured to worship their gods. But this example serveth very well for my purpose: for Aaron did not only make this calf, but also sacrificed unto it, and caused the people to worship it; and yet notwithstanding he was not deposed from his priesthood, although his case was all one with theirs against whom you now speak.

You say the people "said, that they would keep holy day to the Lord Jehovah," and therefore did not take the calf to be God: wherein you say not truly; for those were the words, not of the people, but of Aaron: the people said, "These be thy gods, O Israel, which brought thee out of the land of Egypt;" so that that reason may shew what Aaron thought of it; and this, what was the opinion of the people. I would have you to deal sincerely in alleging of the scriptures.

You "put" me "over to the treatises of godly new writers, which do refuse this distinction, &c." But you neither name those writers unto me, nor let me understand where to find those treatises; which maketh me suspect that you neither know whose, nor where they be: but the matter is not great.

I do as much mislike that distinction of the papists, and the intent of it, as any man doth, neither do I go about to excuse them from wicked and (without repentance and God's singular mercy) damnable idolatry; but yet do I say the idolatry both of the Jews and of the gentiles (for the causes by me alleged) to be much greater. For there are three kinds of idolatry. One is, when the true God is worshipped by other means and ways than he hath prescribed, or would be worshipped. The other is, when the true God is worshipped together with false gods, 2 *Regum* xvii. The third is, when we worship false gods either in heart and mind, or in external creatures, living or dead, and altogether forget the worship of the true God[1]. All these three kinds are detestable; but the first is the least, and the last is the worst; in the which kind the Israelites sundry times offended, as is manifest in the places before mentioned.

Idolatrous sacrificers and mass-mongers.

Three kinds of idolatry. Martyr in Jud. ii. Musculus in Loc. Com. in expla. 1. præcept.

The papists worship God otherwise than his will is, and otherwise than he hath prescribed, almost in all points of their worship: they also give to the creature that which is due to the Creator, and sin against the first table: yet are they not, for ought that I can see or learn, in the third kind of idolatry; and therefore, if they repent unfeignedly, they are not to be cast either out of the church, or out of the ministry.

The papists have little cause to thank me, or to fee me, for anything that I have spoken in their behalf as yet: you see that I place them among wicked and damnable idolaters. My defence is of those that have been papists, and be not, and for no other: for them I speak my conscience according to my poor knowledge, take it as you please[2].

[1 In cultu Dei trifariam peccari potest. 1. Primum, quando pro vero et unico Deo coluntur, qui dii non sunt. Sic communiter peccarunt ethnici...2. Deinde, quando verus quidem et unicus Deus colitur, verum non rite secundum illius voluntatem, sed per superstitionem, et cultus humanitus institutos : quos Christus reprobos esse admonet,...3. Tertio, quando verus quidem Deus, sed non solus et unice colitur: quod ab illis fit, qui juxta verum Deum simul et alios colunt.— Wolfg. Muscul. Loc. Comm. Theol. Basil. 1599. Explan. Præcept. i. pp. 46, 7. Conf. P. Martyr. in Libr. Jud. Comm. Heid. 1609. cap. ii. foll. 41, &c.]

[2 Cartwright accuses Whitgift of "shameful and foreheadless dealing," and proceeds, at great length and with many quotations, to maintain his view of the heathen idolatry: he excuses his representation of Exod. xxxii. by alleging that he had not the text before him when he wrote, but still persists that he "altered nothing of the meaning of the place ;" and concludes that the case of

Of ministers learning of Catechisms.

Chapter iii.

Admonition.

The Third:

Then ᵖ*they taught others; now they must be instructed themselves, and therefore like young children they* ᑫ*must learn catechisms*[1].   ᵖ 1 Tim. iv. 11.
ᑫ *Ministers of London enjoined to learn M. Nowel's Catechism.*

Answer to the Admonition, Page 40, Sect. 3, 4, 5, and Page 41, Sect. 1, 2.

God be thanked, there is a great number of ministers that can teach others, and may be your schoolmasters in all kind of learning; except you have more than you utter in these treatises.

If they that find some want of learning in themselves, or that be crept into the ministry unlearned, either of their own accord, or by commandment of their ordinary, read and learn godly and learned catechisms, they are to be commended; and so is he that provoketh them thereunto.

That catechism, which you in derision quote in the margent, is a book fit for you to learn also; and I know no man so well learned but it may become him to read and learn that learned and necessary book. But some arrogant spirits there be that think themselves of all men best learned, and disdain to learn of any.

That place of the fourth chapter of the first to Timothy doth not forbid a man to learn.

A sign of a modest preacher[2].   He that is a good and modest preacher will not disdain as well to be taught as to teach.

T. C. Page 28, Sect. 2, 3.

What should become of the people in the mean season, whilst they learn their catechism? and when they have learned it, they are no more fit to be ministers, and to teach other, than he that hath learned his accidence is meet to set up a school. And it cannot be defended, but it was a gross

Aaron's not being deposed from his priesthood " is a singular example and may not be drawn into imitation."—Sec. Repl. pp. 184, &c.]

[¹ Here Adm. adds, *And so first they consecrate them and make them ministers, and then they set them to school.*]

[² This marginal note is inserted from Answ. 2.]

oversight to enjoin ministers to learn a catechism. It were much to compel them to read it. And, if a man would have declaimed against the ignorance of the most part of the ministers three whole days together, he could not have said more against them than that canon which sendeth them to their A. B. C, and principles of their religion. How know you that they quote the catechism in the margent in derision? is there any syllable or letter that soundeth that ways? If you conjecture it because they have set it in the margent, you may as well say that they likewise quote the scriptures in derision, being also placed there.

But how followeth this: It is meet that ministers should learn every day; therefore it is meet they be enjoined to learn catechisms? it is meet they should read catechisms; therefore meet to learn them, and be enjoined to learn them? Is there nothing worthier the learning and profession of the minister than to learn catechisms? or doth a man learn those things always which he readeth? Doth he not read things sometime to record the things that he hath learned? For, because they say it is not meet that ministers should be enjoined to learn a catechism, you conclude of their words, that they would not have a minister to learn or to read anything: which is as far from their meaning, or words either, as you are from the reasonable and upright expounding of them.

It followeth even as the rest of your arguments do; for it is your own, and no man's else.

Jo. Whitgift.

God be thanked, the people need not pine away for lack of food: they have the scriptures read unto them, they have also profitable and fruitful homilies, they have the sacraments rightly ministered, and public prayers in a known tongue; and sometime God sendeth unto them some well-disposed preacher further to instruct them; and the curate is not so slothful and careless but that he will also communicate with them that which he himself hath by diligent reading learned.

Catechisms (and that especially) do contain the grounds of religion, and the principal points of faith and good life, and therefore not unfit or unprofitable for any man to read. I know not what weightier matters they can learn than those that be contained in that book; except you think nothing weighty but such matters as you now contend for, and for the which you so much disturb the peace of the church. It is well done " to enjoin them to learn" it, and it shall be no disgracing, no, not to yourself, to read it.

We do not deny but that there be unlearned ministers in England, and we think it no discredit at all " to enjoin them to learn" such things as are most profitable both for them to know, and to teach unto other. To read and to learn such an A. B. C. is not unprofitable for any; but you will still shew that good opinion that you have of yourself, and how greatly you disdain all other men's labours.

Whether I have truly said that note to be placed in the margent "in derision," or no, let the reader judge; to whom also I do refer the consideration of your modesty touching that matter. He that indifferently considereth their quotations of scriptures, will think that the most of them were not placed there in good earnest.

The argument which it hath pleased you to frame of my words (I grant) "followeth" not: but this followeth right well, It is fit that ignorant ministers should be enjoined to learn such things as be meet and profitable for them; *ergo*, they may be enjoined to learn catechisms. And in like manner, It is meet they should read such books as may instruct them; *ergo*, they may read catechisms. I think a man by reading learneth; and I suppose that to read those things again which a man hath forgotten, is to learn them again, if to learn be "to understand," and "to remember."

But all this your dallying about this matter is to bring discredit unto this state of the church, because there be many ignorant ministers. Wherefore I will answer you with the very words in the confession of the churches in Helvetia: "We condemn all unmeet ministers not endued with gifts necessary for a shepherd that should feed his flock. Howbeit we acknowledge that the harmless simplicity of some shepherds in the old church did sometimes more profit the church, than the great, exquisite, and fine or delicate, but a little too proud, learning of some others: wherefore we reject not now-a-days the good simplicity of certain; so that they be not altogether unskilful of God and his word[1]."

Confess. Eccles. Helvetic.

[1 Damnamus ministros ineptos et non instructos donis pastori necessariis. Interim agnoscimus quorundam in veteri ecclesia pastorum simplicitatem innocuam plus aliquando profuisse ecclesiæ, quam quorundam eruditionem variam, exquisitam, delicatamque, sed paulo fastuosiorem. Unde ne hodie quidem rejicimus simplicitatem quorundam probam, nec tamen omnino imperitam.—Confess. et Expos. Fid. Christ. cap. xviii. in Corp. et Syntagm. Confess. Fid. Genev. 1654. p. 38.]

Of election[2] of Ministers by the voices and consent of the people.
Chapter iv. The First Division.
Admonition.
The Fourth:

Acts i. 26. *Then election was made by the common*[3] *consent of the whole church: now every one picketh out for himself some notable good benefice, he obtaineth the next advowson by money or by favour, and so thinketh himself sufficiently*[4] *chosen.*

Answer to the Admonition, Page 42, Sect. 4, 5, 6.

To prove that the election was then made by the common consent of the whole church, you quote the first of the Acts. I told you before Master Calvin's judgment of that place[5]: there is no mention of electing by any common consent. And in the place by you quoted, which is the 26. verse, it is declared how they gave forth their lots, and that the lot fell on Matthias, and that he was by a common consent counted with the eleven apostles: here is no mention of any election. But, when he was extraordinarily, through God's providence, by lot appointed, then they all counted him and esteemed him as one of the apostles; whereas before some of them would have had Barsabas. *(Matthias elected extraordinarily.)*

I think your meaning is not to have always two at once to be presented to the ministry, and then one of them to be chosen by lot. I know none of that opinion. Wherefore this example is singular and extraordinary, and therefore no general rule to be followed.

[☞Furthermore, you must needs confess that there is great difference betwixt the manner and form of calling an apostle, and of electing a pastor; as all writers do testify[6].☜]

If any man seeketh a benefice extraordinarily, or unlawfully; if any man desire *honorem*, "the honour," not *onus*, "the burden;" *opes*, "the riches," not *opus*, "the work;" he hath to answer for it: but I trust you will not accuse all, though perhaps you know some, I mean of yourselves, and peradventure your own self.

[[2] Of the election, Def. A.] [[3] Made by the elders with the common, Adm.]
[[4] Himself to be sufficiently, Adm.] [[5] See before, page 296, note 4.]
[[6] This sentence is inserted from Answ. 2.]

Admonition.

The Fifth :

Then the congregation [3]*had authority to call ministers: instead thereof now they run, they ride, and by unlawful suit and buying prevent other suitors also.* ᵃ *Acts vi. 2, 3.*

Answer to the Admonition. Page 42, Sect. 2, 3.

To prove that the congregation had then authority to call ministers, you allege the sixth of the Acts; which place of the Acts I touched before[1]. It speaketh not of ministers of the word, but of deacons, which were appointed to make provision for the poor only (as you say); neither did the multitude of the disciples (for so they be called) elect them, before they were willed so to do by the twelve apostles.

<small>A good rule may be broken by some, and yet good still.</small>   It may be that some use to "run and ride, and by unlawful suit and buying prevent others," and it may be that you have experience hereof; but all do not so. This is the fault of the man, not of the calling: you may not ascribe men's infirmities to a lawful order. The rule may be good, though it be by some broken.

T. C. Page 28, Sect. 4.

It hath been likewise shewed what was in that election extraordinary, and what pertaineth to the ordinary callings. And in the sixth of the Acts it was shewed, if[2] *the deacons should not be thrust upon the congregation against the will of it, much less ought the minister. And if that congregation had, by the commandment of the apostles, an interest in the choice of their governors, I see not why the same commandment remaineth not to be followed of other churches. Your reasons, wherewith you would make difference, shall be after considered.*

Jo. Whitgift.

And I have likewise answered to whatsoever you have said there; but you tell us neither there nor here how aptly this part of the text, *scilicet*, verse 26, is in this place quoted. To your reason also, gathered out of the sixth of the Acts in the electing of deacons, I have there answered; only I thought good in this place to set down the judgment of Chrysostom, <small>Chrysost. Hom. 14. in Act.</small> *Hom.* 14. *in Act.: Ideo hoc non permiserunt sorti, neque, cum possent ipsi Spiritu moti eligere, hoc faciunt ; sed magis statuunt quod multorum testimoniis approbatur. Nam defi-*

[¹ See before, pages 298, 9.]   [² Shewed that if, Repl. 2.]

*nire numerum, et ordinare, et in talem usum, hoc sibi vendicant; eligere autem viros illis permittunt, ut ne videantur ipsi in gratiam quorundam agere*³: " The apostles did not commit the election of deacons to lot, neither they, being moved with the Spirit, did choose them, though they might have so done; for to appoint the number, to ordain them, and to such an use, they challenged as due unto themselves. And yet do they permit the election of them to the people, lest they should be thought to be partial, or to do anything for favour." Your reasons to prove that to be a perpetual rule shall not (God willing) be passed over in their place⁴.

Chapter iv. The Sixth Division.

Admonition.

The Sixth:

*Acts xiv.13.*⁵   Then no ᵗminister placed in any congregation, but by the
2 Cor. viii.
19.   consent of the people⁶.

Answer to the Admonition. Page 42, Sect. ult.

To prove that no minister was placed in any congregation, but by the consent⁷ of the people, you allege the xiv. of the Acts, and of the 2. to the Corinthians, the eighth chapter. In the xiv. of the Acts, verse 23 (for the which you have quoted the 13), it is thus written: "When they (that is, Paul and Barnabas) had ordained them elders by election (for so is some translation) in every church, and prayed and fasted, &c." The text is plain that Paul and Barnabas did ordain them elders⁸.

T. C. Page 29, Sect. 1, 2, 3, 4, 5.

Unto these places of the first and sixth of the Acts is added, first, the

[³ Chrysost. Op. Par. 1718-38. In Act. Apost. Hom. xiv. Tom. IX. p. 114.]

[⁴ Cartwright admits " that Chrysostom might have here the meaning the D. supposeth," but adds that " so the D. is not helped."—Sec. Repl. p. 193.]

[⁵ Acts xiv. 23, Adm.]

[⁶ The remainder of the sentence which appears below, is placed here in Answ.]

[⁷ By consent, Answ.]

[⁸ Cartwright says that all Whitgift's " principal both arguments and solutions have been word for word ministered unto him out of the books of the rankest enemies of the truth;" and refers to several places of Pighius, and Hosius.—Sec. Repl. p. 194.]

place of the fourteenth of the Acts; where the authors of the Admonition do prove that the election ought not to be in one man his hand, but ought to be made by the church: against which Master Doctor taketh three exceptions. The first is, for that it is said that Paul and Barnabas ordained elders; whereby he would conclude that the congregations had nothing to do. But how slender a reason that is, it may be considered of infinite places in the scripture, whereof I will recite two or three.

In the fifth chapter of Josua it is said that "Josua made him sharp knives for the circumcising of the children of Israel," and a little afterwards[2], that "Josua circumcised them." Shall we now upon these words conclude that Josua did make the knives himself, or was a cutler, or, being made to his hand, did whet them and sharpen them; or shall we say that he did circumcise the children of Israel in his own person, and himself alone, when as that was done by many, and by the Levites to whom that office appertained? No, but the scripture declareth that Josua procured sharp knives to be made, and exhorted and commanded the people to be circumcised. Josh. v. 3.[1]

In the eighteenth of Exodus[3] it is said that "Moses did appoint unto the people princes, captains over thousands and hundreds, &c." And, if any conclude thereupon that he did it himself alone, he is by and by confuted by that which is written in Deuteronomy, where it appeareth that the people did choose them, and presented them to Moses. What is it then that is said in Exodus, that Moses appointed them, but that Moses assembled the people, and exhorted them to appoint rulers, and told them what manner of men they should be, and, in a word, sat as it were moderator in that election? Exod. xviii. 25.[1]
Chap. i. 15.[4]

To come to the new testament. In the Acts it is said that Paul and Timothy delivered unto the churches the orders and decrees of the apostles and elders; and yet it appeareth in another place that the church had also to do, and gave their consent unto the making of those decrees: so that the former place meaneth that the apostles and elders did go before, and were the chief and directors of that action. Acts xvi. 4.[4]
Acts xv. 23.

<small>You say so, but you shew not one.</small> *The same manner of speech is used of the Roman stories; wherein it is said that the consul did make magistrates, for because that he gathered the assembly and voices whereby they were made: and so St Luke saith here that Paul and Barnabas ordained, because they, being the moderators of the election, caused it to be made, assembled the churches, told them of the necessity of having good pastors and governors, gathered the voices, took heed that nothing should be done lightly, nothing tumultuously or out of order. And so, to conclude, it is an evil reason to say, as M. Doctor doth, that, because St Luke hath that Paul and Barnabas ordained, therefore the people were excluded.*

[[1] These references are inserted from Repl. 2.]
[[2] Afterward, Repl. 1; after, Repl. 2.]   [[3] In Exodus, Repl. 2.]
[[4] In the first of these references, Repl. 1 gives no verse, Repl. 2 has 13; in the other the verse is inserted from Repl. 2.]

Jo. Whitgift.

If the reason grounded upon the plain words of the scripture be but "a slender reason," then do I confess that to be so likewise. Howbeit very godly and learned men think it a reason sufficient. Zuinglius, in his *Ecclesiastes*, saith that some were called and elected to the ministry of the word by the apostles only[5]. Bullinger, in his third book *Advers. Anabap.*, cap. iv., saith thus: *Paulus et Barnabas presbyteros seu ministros elegerunt in ecclesiis Asiæ*[6] : "Paul and Barnabas did choose elders or ministers in the churches of Asia[7]."

Zuinglius.

Bullinger.

Those places of scripture that you recite may prove that there are such manner of speeches in the scripture, but they prove not that this is such; and therefore you have in vain rehearsed them.

The example of Josua is far from proving this phrase to be such; for you affirm that Josua "is said to make sharp knives and to circumcide, only because he procured sharp knives to be made, and commanded the people to be circumcided, and not because he himself did sharpen the knives, or circumcide in his own person." But it is certain that Paul and Barnabas had to do in this action, and did themselves, in their own persons, ordain ministers, and not command others to ordain them. Wherefore the manner of speech cannot be like; except you will expound this place thus: Paul and Barnabas ordained them elders, that is, commanded the people to choose them elders; which interpretation were strange for this place, and unheard of before.

That in the first of Deuteronomy doth not directly prove that Moses alone did not appoint those magistrates: for, although he willed the people to bring unto him "men of

[5 Electionem vero triplicem apud veteres fuisse legimus. Quidam enim communi omnium fidelium in unum congregatorum et unanimi consensu electi sunt, ut...in Matthiæ exemplo demonstratum est. Alii rursus a solis apostolis electi munus hoc aggressi sunt, ut cum apostolorum decreto in Samariam ablegantur Petrus et Joannes, Act. 8. Tertios autem invenire licet, quos unicus aliquis apostolus et elegit et misit, qualis Titus est, &c.—H. Zvingl. Op. Tigur. 1581. Ecclesiast. Pars II. fol. 53. 2.]

[6 H. Bullinger. Adv. Anabapt. Libri vi. Tigur. 1560. Lib. iii. cap. iv. fol. 90. 2.]

[7 Cartwright accuses Whitgift of "unfaithful dealing" and "shameful boldness," and cites other passages of Zuinglius and Bullinger to shew that those authors rather agreed with him.—Sec. Repl. pp. 194, &c.]

wisdom and of understanding, &c.;" yet it followeth not that they did so, but it rather appeareth that they committed the choice of them wholly to him; for after, in the fifteenth verse of the same chapter, he saith, "So I took the chief of your tribes, wise and known men, and made them rulers, &c." Manifest it is that, whether the people named any unto him or no, he appointed them, and gave them their authority: so that the manner of speech is proper, and without any trope or figure.

<small>Deut. i. 15.</small>

<small>T. C. under another pretence pusheth at the civil magistrate.</small>
But do you not still secretly push at the authority of the civil magistrate under the pretence of speaking against the state ecclesiastical? For, howsoever you would seem to bring in the place in the eighteenth of Exodus, to prove the phrase and manner of speaking, yet may you be thought secretly to insinuate that princes may not appoint under-officers without the election of the people. And surely, if your dealing in this place be well marked, it may easily be seen that in reasoning against the government of the church you lay the grounds of confounding, or, at the least, of changing the state of the commonwealth.

In the fifteenth of the Acts, verse 22. and 23, there appeareth that the whole church, together with the apostles and elders, did send certain chosen men of their own company to Antiochia with Paul and Barnabas, &c., and wrote letters by them containing these decrees; whereunto though the people subscribed "and gave their consent," yet it followeth not but that the apostles and elders made them; as it also appeareth, verse 2. and 6. of the same chapter. Every one that consenteth to orders and subscribeth unto them doth not therefore make them. Wherefore they may properly be said to be made by the apostles and elders only; though the people allowed well of them, and consented to them. And therefore saith M. Calvin: "The modesty of the people herein doth appear, that, after they had committed the deciding of the controversies to the apostles and other doctors, they were also content to subscribe to their decree[1]." Whether there be any such "manner of speech" or no "in the Roman stories," it is not material; neither is there anything here spoken which

<small>Calv. in xv. Act.</small>

[1 Plebis etiam modestia hinc colligitur, quod postquam apostolis et reliquis doctoribus judicium permisit, nunc quoque subscribit eorum decreto.—Calvin. Op. Amst. 1667-71. Comm. in Act. Apost. cap. xv. 22. Tom. VI. p. 143.]

proveth that this is such a manner of speech: wherefore it χειροτο-
must remain as proper and literally true, until there be νία.
stronger reasons brought to prove as plainly that the people
ordained ministers, as it is here written that Paul and Barnabas did[2].

Chapter iv. The Third Division.
Answer to the Admonition. Page 43, line 8.

And the Greek word χειροτονεῖν, although it signify
to elect by putting up of hands, yet it is the common
opinion almost of all ecclesiastical writers, that this
word in scripture is used for the solemn manner of ordering ministers by the imposition of hands.

T. C. Page 29, Sect. 6, and Page 30, Sect. 1, 2, 3, 4.

*And I marvel with what conscience he could answer so in this place;
especially where it is forthwith added, that they ordained them by the
suffrages and voices of the church. But you say that "the Greek word
χειροτονεῖν is, by the common opinion of almost all ecclesiastical writers,
used in the scripture for the solemn manner of ordaining of ministers
by the imposition of hands;" which is the second exception you take to
this reason. Wherein, but that I have promised to hold myself to the
matter, and that these bold asseverances in matters most untrue are so
common that, if I should every foot pursue them, I should weary myself
and all others, I could not keep myself from running out to marvel at
such high speeches void of truth. First, where you say that some translation hath that they ordained ministers without making mention of election, what have you gained thereby, when I can shew more that translate it
otherwise, and say it is, that they ordained by election, or voices, or suffrages? I had not the commodity of books, whereby I could see the judgment of all ecclesiastical writers: but, of those which I had, I find that
there was but one, only M. Gualter, of that mind; and yet he doth not
shut out the people's consent in the election; neither[3] M. Calvin, M. Beza,* An untruth,
M. Bullinger, M. Musculus, M. Brentius, he that translated Chrysostom as will
upon that place, Erasmus in his Paraphrases upon that place[4], are of

[2 Cartwright stoutly maintains his view of the passages of scripture in question, and refers to Livy, Libb. II. and III. for proof of what he had alleged respect-
ing the Roman consul appointing magistrates.—Sec. Repl. pp. 198, &c. Conf.
Calvin. Op. Inst. Lib. IV. cap. iii. 15. Tom. IX. p. 285.]

[3 Repl. 2 has not *neither*.]

[4 Quumque ipsis per suffragia creassent per singulas ecclesias presbyteros,
&c.—Nov. Test. cum Th. Bezæ Interp. &c. H. Steph. 1565. Act. Apost. cap.
xiv. 23. p. 70.
....ordinarunt presbyteros, a fidelibus electos.—Wolfg. Muscul. Loc. Comm.
Theol. Basil. 1599. De Ministr. Verb. p. 198.
Et cum suffragiis creassent illis per singulas ecclesias presbyteros, &c.—J.
Brent. Op. Tubing. 1576-90. In cap. xiv. Act. Apost. Hom. lxv. Tom. VII.
p. 272.

χειροτο- the contrary judgment: *of whose judgment I would not have spoken, if
νία.   you would not have gone about thus to abuse your reader with such
manifest untruths to overthrow the order which God hath established.*
    But let all authorities of men go, and let us examine the thing itself[1].
*If so be that the Holy Ghost had meant the solemn putting on of the hands
upon the head[2] of him that was created elder and minister, had he not
words enow[3] to utter this his meaning? would he have for laying on of
hands used a word that signifieth lifting up of hands? would he have used
a word signifying holding up for laying down? for, when the hands are
laid of the head of another, they are laid down, and not holden up. There
are words in the old testament, and in the new, before Luke wrote and
after he wrote, to express this ceremony of laying on of hands; and yet
none have ever expressed this.*

St Paul speaketh thrice of it in his epistles to Timothy, 1 Tim. iv. 14.[4]
and always he useth ἐπίθεσις τῶν χειρῶν. *In the old testament,* 1 Tim. v. 22.[4] 2 Tim. i. 6.[4]
*where this ceremony is used and spoken of, the Septuaginta did
never translate* χειροτονεῖν, *but, as the writers of the new testament,* ἐπίθεσις χειρῶν. *And what should I stand in this, when as St Luke himself,
both before and after, speaking of that ceremony of laying on* Acts viii. 17.[4]
of hands, doth never use this word χειροτονεῖν, *but the same* Acts ix. 17.[4]
word which St Paul useth, and the Septuaginta? And, al- Acts xix. 6.[4]
*though the Holy Ghost speak properly and well, by whomsoever he speaketh,
yet it could have been worst of all said by St Luke, of all the canonical
writers, that he should speak thus unproperly, who of them all writeth most
purely and elegantly, according to the phrase of the most eloquent Grecians;
and therefore he borrowed this speech of the ancient Greek writers, which
did use to express their elections by this word, because they were made and
voices given by this ceremony of lifting up of hands.*

*But what if St Luke have used this word before, and in this[5] book, in
the signification of choosing by voice? dare you then say that he useth it
here for putting on of hands?*

In the x. of the Acts[6] St Peter saith that Christ, after his
resurrection, appeared not unto the whole people, but unto those Chap. x. 41.[7]

If you will *whom he had before chosen by his voice to be his witnesses: he useth this*[8]
grant that
this word is προκεχειροτονημένους. *Now, if you will say here that it is to be turned,*
taken for
electing by *those of whom he laid his hands, I will ask you where you read that ever*
one voice, we
shall soon
agree.

    Cum autem suffragiis delegissent illis seniores per ecclesias, &c.—Chrysost.
Op. Lat. Basil. 1547. In Act. Apost. cap. xiv. Hom. xxxi. Tom. III. col. 653.
Conf. Op. Par. 1718-38. In Act. Apost. Hom. xxxi. Tom. IX. p. 242.
...delectos populi suffragiis per singulas civitates presbyteros præfecerunt illis,
&c.—Erasm. Op. Lugd. Bat. 1703-6. Paraphr. in Act. Apost. cap. xiv. 22.
Tom. VII. col. 725.
    See also below, page 346, notes 10, 11.]
    [1 Thing in itself, Repl. 1, 2, and Def. A.]
    [2 Heads, Repl. 2.]   [3 Enough, Repl. 1 and 2.]
    [4 The verses are added from Repl. 2.]
    [5 His, Def. B.]   [6 In the Acts, Repl. 2.]
    [7 These references are inserted from Repl. 2.]
    [8 Repl. 1 and 2 here insert *word*.]

Matt. xxviii. 19.[7] he laid his hands of their heads. *I will shew you where he did* χειροτο-*via. by his heavenly voice appoint them. And I think you are not* able to shew in any Greek author ancient, and which men do take to be authentical to teach the property or eloquence of the Greek tongue, (I mean which were before St Luke his time,) where the word χειροτονεῖν is taken for the laying on of hands of the head of any.

This I confess, that the Greek ecclesiastical writers have sometimes used it so: but you must remember that St Luke could not learn to speak of them that came two or three hundred years after him; but he borrowed this phrase of speech of those that were before him, and therefore speaketh of elections as they did. So that you see this shift will not serve.

Jo. Whitgift.

There is nothing to prove that they ordained them by the suffrages of the church, but this word, χειροτονήσαντες, the acceptation whereof in this place is now in question. I say still that, "although it" properly "signify to elect by putting up of hands, yet is it the common opinion almost of all ecclesiastical writers, that it is used in scripture for the solemn manner of ordering ministers by the imposition of hands." And that this is neither so strange nor so untrue as you would seem to make the reader believe, I have set down these authors which have taught me so to say.

The signification of the word χειροτονήσαντες.

Bullinger, upon the same place, saith thus: *Ceterum dictio* χειροτονήσαντες *ita ponitur, ut vel suffragiis populi delectos esse, vel manuum impositione inauguratos, intelligere* [9]*possimus*[10]: "But the word χειροτονήσαντες is so placed that we may understand either that they were chosen by the voices of the people, or ordained by the laying on of hands."

M. Calvin upon the same place hath these words: *Verbum Græcum* χειροτονεῖν *significat aliquid manibus sublatis decernere, qualiter in comitiis populi fieri solet. Scriptores tamen ecclesiastici nomen* χειροτονίας *alio sensu usurpant, nempe pro solenni ordinationis ritu, qui in scripturis vocatur manuum impositio*[11]: "The Greek word χειροτονεῖν signifieth to determine something by holding up of hands, according as it was usual in the assemblies and elections of the people: notwithstanding the ecclesiastical writers use this word χει-

Calvin.

[[9] *Possumus*, Def. B.]
[[10] H. Bullinger. in Act. Apost. Comm. Libri VI. Tigur. 1540. In cap. xiv. Lib. III. p. 117.]
[[11] Calvin. Op. Amst. 1667-71. Comm. in Act. Apost. cap. xiv. 23. Tom. VI. p. 132.]

ροτονία in another sense, for the solemn manner of ordering, which in the scriptures is called the laying on of hands." And this saying of M. Calvin hath Marlorat also written in his collections, as allowing the same[1]. The same M. Calvin, *Instit. cap. viii. sect.* 65: *Sequitur jam ut tractemus &c.*[2]: "It followeth now that we should entreat of the manner whereby the ministers of the primitive church were placed in their office. This the Latinists call ordering or consecration, the Grecians χειροτονίαν, and sometimes also χειροθεσίαν; although χειροτονία is properly called that kind of election wherein the voices are signified by lifting up of hands."

Gualter.

Likewise Gualter upon the fourteenth of the Acts: *Deinde χειροτονίας mentionem facit Lucas, &c.*[3]: "Furthermore Luke maketh mention of χειροτονία; by the which not only the gathering of voices, but also the laying on of hands, which was a sign of consecration, may be signified; and surely the latter seemeth most convenient. For it is not likely that the apostles would depart from that order, which we see to have been observed in the election of Matthias, and permit anything to the judgment of man (which in voices oftentimes cometh to pass), seeing that they stirred up the whole church to prayer and fasting."

Thus then you see that the matter is nothing so strange as you make it; for all these learned writers affirm as much touching the acceptation of this word, as I have done: and, if you will give me leave to allege the canons attributed to the apostles, as you do, I will find it there taken in the same signification also; for in the first canon it is thus written:

Can. Apost. 1 & 2.

Ἐπίσκοπος χειροτονείσθω ὑπὸ ἐπισκόπων δύο ἢ τριῶν: "Let a bishop be ordained of two or three bishops." And in the second canon: Πρεσβύτερος ὑπὸ ἑνὸς ἐπισκόπου χειροτο-

[¹ A. Marlorat. Nov. Test. Cathol. Expos. H. Steph. 1570. In Act. Apost. cap. xiv. p. 716.]

[² Sequitur jam ut tractemus quo ritu post electionem initiarentur veteris ecclesiæ ministri in suum officium. Hanc Latini ordinationem vel consecrationem, Græci χειροτονίαν, interdum etiam χειροθεσίαν vocarunt: licet χειροτονία id genus electionis proprie dicatur, ubi declarantur suffragia manuum elevatione. —Calvin. Op. Amst. 1667-71. Inst. Lib. IV. cap. iv. 14. Tom. IX. p. 289.]

[³ Deinde χειροτονίας mentionem facit Lucas, per quam non modo suffragiorum collectio, verum etiam manuum impositio, quæ consecrationis symbolum erat, intelligi potest. Et posterius quidem magis convenire videtur. Nec enim verisimile est, apostolos a primo ritu, quem in Matthiæ electione observatum fuisse vidimus, recedere, et quicquam humano judicio (ut in suffragiis fieri consuevit) permittere voluisse, cum ad preces et jejunia ecclesiam universam excitarint.—R. Gualther. in Act. Apost. Hom. Tigur. 1586. cap. xiv. Hom. c. fol. 189.]

νείσθω⁴: "Let a minister be ordained of one bishop." You cannot deny but that the old translations and commentaries also make only mention of electing and ordaining, and not of electing or ordaining by voices.

Œcumenius, in his commentaries upon this place, doth affirm that Paul and Barnabas did create and ordain them⁵: so do other likewise; and, howsoever the word in Chrysostom is "translated," yet Chrysostom giveth no signification in his commentaries that his meaning was so. But *Hom. xiv. in Act.* he writeth thus: *Vide quomodo scriptor, &c.*⁶: "Mark how the writer is not superfluous, for he doth not declare how, but he simply declareth that they were ordained by prayers; for this is χειροτονία, i. *ordinatio*, that is to say, ordaining: the hands are laid upon the man; but God worketh the whole, and it is his hand that toucheth the head of him that is ordained, if he be ordained as he ought to be." Hierome also, writing upon the lviii. of Esay, saith that "χειροτονία is usually taken for the ordaining of clerks, by prayer and laying on of hands⁷."

Chrysost. in xiv. in Act.

Hierome.

I deny not but that many do translate it as you say; yet is it doubtful in divers of them whether they meant the voices of the whole church, or of the ministers, or of Paul and Barnabas only. M. Bullinger saith that "he is elected by the common suffrages of the people, *qui optimorum testimonio probatus est;* which is approved by the testimony of the best⁸." And the law saith: *In publico negotio qui se non opponit, cum possit, consentire intelligitur*⁹: "He is thought

Bullinger.

[⁴ Canon. Apost. 1, 2. in Concil. Stud. Labb. et Cossart. Lut. Par. 1671-2. Tom. I. col. 25.]

[⁵ Σημειωτέον δὲ ὅτι οἱ περὶ Παῦλον καὶ Βαρνάβαν ἐπισκόπων εἶχον ἀξίαν, ἐξ ὧν ἐχειροτόνουν οὐ μόνον διακόνους, ἀλλὰ καὶ πρεσβυτέρους.—Œcumen. Op. Lut. Par. 1631. Enarr. cap. xxii. in Act. Apost. Tom. I. p. 119.]

[⁶ Ὅρα πῶς οὐκ ἔστι περιττὸς ὁ συγγραφεύς. οὐ γὰρ λέγει πῶς· ἀλλ' ἁπλῶς ὅτι ἐχειροτονήθησαν διὰ προσευχῆς. τοῦτο γὰρ ἡ χειροτονία ἐστίν. ἡ χεὶρ ἐπίκειται τοῦ ἀνδρός· τὸ δὲ πᾶν ὁ Θεὸς ἐργάζεται, καὶ ἡ αὐτοῦ χείρ ἐστιν ἡ ἁπτομένη τῆς κεφαλῆς τοῦ χειροτονουμένου, ἐὰν ὡς δεῖ χειροτονῆται.—Chrysost. Op. Par. 1718-38. In Act. Apost. Hom. xiv. Tom. IX. p. 114.]

[⁷ Plerique nostrorum χειροτονίαν, id est, *ordinationem clericorum,* quæ non solum ad imprecationem vocis, sed ad impositionem impletur manus, (ne scilicet, ut in quibusdam risimus, vocis imprecatio clandestina clericos ordinet nescientes,) sic intelligunt, ut assumant testimonium Pauli scribentis ad Timotheum: &c.—Hieron. Op. Par. 1693-1706. Comm. Lib. XVI. in Isai. Proph. cap. lviii. Tom. III. col. 432.]

[⁸ Eligitur enim communibus populi suffragiis, qui &c.—H. Bullinger. in Act. Apost. Comm. Libri VI. Tigur. 1540. In cap. xiv. Lib. III. p. 117.]

[⁹ Scientiam hic pro patientia accipimus, ut qui prohibere potuit, teneatur, si

*χειροτο-
νία.*

to consent in a public business which doth not withstand when he may."

I think your complaint for lack of books is without cause, and very unlikely it is to be true, all things considered. Howsoever M. Calvin or M. Bullinger do take that word themselves, yet have they affirmed as much of the other signification as I have done, and therefore the more like to be true. Neither have you as yet alleged anything that can prove the contrary.

You may not teach "the Holy Ghost" how to speak, neither must you in such matters use so light and vain reasons. Neither M. Bullinger nor M. Calvin disalloweth that signification, or goeth about to confute it; and you yourself "confess that the Greek ecclesiastical writers have sometime used it so;" as indeed they commonly do, which may easily be understanded by that that I have hitherto spoken.

He that layeth his hands upon a man's head doth lift them up before he can lay them on; and therefore you do but trifle in making so much ado about "holding up and laying down." There be other words (I grant) to express this ceremony of laying on of hands; and I know that Luke and Paul do use another word for the same, and the Septuagint in like manner: but what is all this to the purpose? What can you conclude hereof? Is this sufficient to prove, that this word therefore in this place may not signify the same? Are these bare conjectures sufficient to improve so many learned men's judgments?

I do not say that χειροτονία doth signify only the bare ceremony of laying on of hands, but the whole solemnity of creating ministers, which is also sometimes signified by ἐπίθεσις τῶν χειρῶν, as namely, 1 Tim. v. But St Luke, when he useth in other places ἐπίθεσις τῶν χειρῶν, he doth use it in the bare signification of laying on of hands, and not for any other rite or solemnity, as he doth this word χειροτονία in this place; and therefore you do *petere principium*, when you frame your proofs as though it were affirmed or granted that St Luke by this word should mean only the bare "ceremony of imposition of hands."

T. C. bringeth a place against himself.

The place that you allege out of the tenth of the Acts

non fecerit.—Corp. Jur. Civil. Amst. 1663. Digest. Lib. ix. Tit. ii. 45. Tom. I. p. 176. Conf. Lib. xxxix. Tit. ii. 24. § 6. p. 564; Lib. l. Tit. xvii. 50. p. 790, and not. in loc.]

maketh most against yourself, and overthroweth your whole building: first, because χειροτονεῖν is not there taken for lifting up of hands, but for appointing or ordaining only; for Christ did not appoint his disciples by lifting up of hands: secondly, it signifieth not to appoint or to ordain by the suffrages and consent of other; for Christ required no man's consent in the choice of his apostles: so that you have lost and not gained by alleging of that place; for, as this word προκεχειροτονημένοις in the tenth of the Acts doth not signify that the apostles were chosen by the consent or voice of any other than of Christ only, so doth χειροτονήσαντες also in this fourteenth of the Acts signify that Paul and Barnabas did appoint and ordain them ministers by their own voices only, and not by the suffrages of the people. Certainly that place of the tenth of the Acts manifestly declareth that this word in scripture doth not signify any common election by the voices of the people; as you would have it to do. Wherefore I think that their judgment cannot justly be misliked, which say this word, in this fourteenth of the Acts, to signify the solemn manner of ordaining ministers by the imposition of hands; not meaning thereby the bare ceremony, but the whole action of ordaining. To conclude, I will desire no other interpretation of this word in the xiv. of the Acts, than that same place which you have alleged, Acts x.: which also answereth whatsoever you have here spoken of St Luke's skill in the Greek tongue, or of the use of this word in the scriptures; so that I shall not need any other author before St Luke's time to prove the same[1].

Chapter iv.   The Fourth Division.

Answer to the Admonition, Page 43, line 12.

Surely, howsoever the word is taken, yet here is no general rule prescribed of electing ministers. You may as well conclude that all things ought to be common among Christians, because we read, Acts ii., that "all those *No good argument facto ad jus*[2].

[[1] Cartwright rejoins at great length, saying, "how idle for the most part this talk is. And verily all these authorities here brought are either vain, or directly against himself, or insufficient to prove that which he undertaketh." He also argues that, "if this word which noteth the choice by voices should be restrained unto Paul and Barnabas; then also the word which declareth that they prayed should only be restrained unto them; for, as that is given unto them, so is this."
—Sec. Repl. pp. 199, &c.]

[[2] This marginal note is inserted from Answ. 2.]

which believed had all things common among them;" and that those which be converted to the gospel ought to sell their goods and lands, to be distributed at the discretion of the ministers, because they did so, Acts ii. and iii.

T. C. Page 30, Sect. 5, 6; and Page 31, Sect. 1, 2, 3, 4.

Let us therefore see your third, which is that, although the church's consent was then required, yet it is not[1] *now; and that it is no general rule, no more than (say you) that all things should be therefore common now, because they were in the apostles' time.*

The authors of the Admonition, with their favourers, must be counted anabaptists, no one word being shewed which tendeth thereunto; you must accuse them which confirm that foundation whereof they build their community of all things, which is one of their chief heresies. If I should say now that you are like to those that row in a boat, which, although they look backwards, yet they thrust another way, I should speak with more likelihood than you have done. For, although you make a countenance, and speak hotly against anabaptists, yet indeed you strengthen their hands with reasons. But I will not say so, neither do I think that you favour that sect; but only the whirlwind and tempest of your affection, bent to maintain this estate whereby you have so great honour and wealth, driveth you upon these rocks, to wrack yourself on and others.

For, I pray you, what community is spoken of either in the two, or three, or[2] *fourth of the Acts, which ought not to be in the church as long as the world standeth? Was there any community but as touching the use, and so far forth as the poor brethren had need of, and not to take every man alike? Was it not in any man his power to sell his houses, or lands, or not to sell them? When he had sold them, were they not*[4] *in every man his liberty to keep the money to himself at his pleasure? And all they that were of the church did not sell their possessions, but those whose hearts the Lord touched singularly with the compassion of the need of others, and whom God had blessed with abundance, that they had to serve themselves, and help others; and therefore it is reckoned as a rare example that Barnabas the Cyprian and Levite did sell his possession*[6]*, and brought the price to the feet of the apostles.*

Acts ii. 45.[3]
Acts v. 4.[3]

The text saith plainly, that "as many as were possessors of lands, &c., sold them."

Acts iv. 36.[5]

And as for Ananias and Saphira, they were not punished for because they brought not the price of their possessions to the apostles, but because they lied, saying that they had brought the whole when they had brought but part. And to be short, is there any more done there than St Paul prescribeth to the Corinthians, and in them to all churches to the world's end? After he had exhorted to liberality towards the poor church in Hierusalem, "not," saith he, "that other should be relieved, and you oppressed, but upon like condition at this time your abund-

2 Cor. viii. 13, 14.[3]

[1] Is it not, Repl. 1 and 2.]   [2] The second, third, or, Repl. 2.]
[3] The verses are added from Repl. 2.]   [4] Was it not, Repl. 2.]
[5] This reference is inserted from Repl. 2.]   [6] Possessions, Repl. 1 and 2.]

ance supplieth their lack, that also their abundance may be for your lack, that there might be equality; as it is written, He that gathered much had nothing over, and he that gathered little had not the less."

Surely it were better you were no doctor in the church, than that the anabaptists should have such hold to bring in their community as you give them.

In sum, the apostolic community, or the churches in their time, was not anabaptistical.

Jo. Whitgift.

I have shewed before in the beginning of my Answer to the Admonition, not only how weak, but also how dangerous a kind of reasoning it is to say that the apostles did it; *ergo*, we must do it; or, the apostles did it not; *ergo*, we must not do it. Zuinglius, a notable learned man, doth especially reprove the anabaptists for this kind of reason, and saith that an argument *a facto ad jus*, or *a non facto ad non jus*, is never good, except those examples be grounded upon some law or rule[7]. Wherefore, when I thus labour to overthrow the vicious manner and kind of the anabaptistical argument, I trust no indifferent man will suspect me of their errors: when I say that this is no good argument, In the apostles' time those that believed had all things common among them; therefore Christians must have all things common; do I confirm their heresy of having all things common? I know not why you should so charge me "with the whirlwind and tempest of" my "affection bent to maintain this estate, &c.," except you be offended because I shew the weakness of the anabaptists' reasons for their community.

My "honour and wealth" is not so much; but yet I would be loth to have it common; and you may not blame me though I maintain that state where all men may quietly enjoy their own without confusion.

I know the anabaptists do not only err in their kind of reasoning, but in the right understanding of the scriptures also, even of those places whereupon they frame their argument. But the text saith plainly, *Omnes qui credebant, &c.*: "All which believed were in one place, and had all things common." Acts ii. and iv. *Quotquot enim possessores præ-*

No good argument a facto ad jus.

Acts ii.

Acts iv.

[7 Nunquam enim licet neque in divinis neque in profanis a facto ad jus argumentari, sed tunc solummodo licet factum pro lege adducere, quum factum jure factum esse probatum est.—H. Zvingl. Op. Tigur. 1581. Elench. contr. Catabapt. Pars II. fol. 9. 2.]

diorum aut domorum erant, &c.: "For as many as were possessors of lands or houses sold them, &c." And, though they were greatly to be commended in selling their lands and possessions, and in so lightly esteeming the riches of this world, yet it followeth not that no man can be a good Christian, unless he follow that example. There are sundry places of the scripture that overthrow the anabaptistical community; and therefore, howsoever they understand these examples, yet can they not prove their error; for it is true that Zuinglius saith: *Nullius facta juri præjudicant*[1]: "Examples must give place when they be against a general law, commandment, or right."

I have not spoken one word of "Ananias and Saphira," and therefore I muse to what purpose you bring them in; neither am I against the interpretation of those places of the Acts: yet do I say that no man is bound of necessity to follow those examples, except it were in the like time and state. So that, if the anabaptists both err in the understanding of those places, and in their kind of reasoning also, as they do in both, M. Doctor may keep his doctorship still, and they be far enough from their community. The community that was in the apostles' time was christian, and most fit for that time; but the same may not now be urged in the self-same manner and form without suspicion of anabaptism. And it is a very good argument against you; for, as the community used amongst the Christians, Acts ii. and iv., was godly, and yet not necessary nor meet for all states of the church, even so the election then used was also godly, and yet not at all times to be practised, but only in the like state of time[2].

Chapter iv. The Fifth Division.

Answer to the Admonition, Page 43, line 20, and Sect. 1.

In the second to the Corinthians, viii. the apostle declareth how the churches had chosen Luke (or, as some think, Barnabas) to be his companion in his journey; but what maketh[3] this for electing of ministers?

[1 Id. ibid.]

[2 "Therefore you cannot escape with this circuit of words: for either that community in the Acts was such as ought to be amongst us, which you deny, and propound as an absurd thing; or else it was anabaptistical, which is blasphemous against the Spirit of God."—Sec. Repl. p. 208.]

[3 Makes, Answ.]

How followeth this argument: The churches had chosen Luke or Barnabas to be Paul's companion in his journey; therefore ministers of the word must be elected by the people?

These three last reasons are all one, and the places of scripture, which I have set down and answered, be alleged of you to prove that the election of ministers was then made by the common consent of the people, and that every congregation had authority to call their ministers.

T. C. Page 31, Sect. 4.

Unto the place of the 2. Epistle to the Corinthians and viii. chapter, you ask, "what maketh that to the election of the ministers?" But why do not you say here, as you did in the other place, that the apostle meaneth nothing else but the putting on of the hands of them which ordained? For the same word χειροτονηθείς is here used that was there; and this place doth manifestly, and without all contradiction, convince your vain signification that you make of it in the other place, and the untruth wherein you say that[4] *the scripture useth this word for a solemn manner of ordering ministers by putting on of hands. For here it is said that he that was joined with Paul was χειροτονηθείς by the church; and it is manifest that the im-* 1 Tim. iv.14.[5] *position of hands was not by the church and people, but by the* 2 Tim. i. 6.[5] *elders and ministers; as it appeareth in St Paul to Timothy.*

Now to come to that which you make so light of; for, say you, "how followeth this: The church chose Luke or Barnabas to be companion of Paul's journey[6]*; ergo, the churches must choose their ministers?" It followeth very well; for, if it were thought meet that St Paul should not choose himself, of his own authority, a companion to help him, being an apostle, is there any archbishop that shall dare take upon him to make a minister of the gospel, being so many degrees (both in authority and in all gifts needful to discern, and try out, or take knowledge of, a sufficient minister of the gospel) inferior to St Paul?*

And, if St Paul would have the authority of the church to ordain the minister that should aid him in other places to the building and gathering of other churches[7]*, how much more did he think it meet that the churches should choose their own minister which should govern them; and*[8] *which things may be also said of the election in the first of the Acts! For there the church first chose two, whereof one should be an apostle, which should* Untruth. *not be minister of that church, but should be sent into all*[9] *the world: so that always*[10] *the apostles have shunned to do anything of their own wills,*

[4 Untruth saying that, Repl. 2.]   [5 The verses are added from Repl. 2.]
[6 Paul his journey, Repl. 1 and 2.]
[7 Places for the gathering of relief of the poor churches, Repl. 2.]
[8 Repl. 2 has not *and*.]
[9 Always, Def. B.]   [10 All, Def. B.]

without the knowledge, either of those churches where they instituted any governors, or, if it were for the behoof of those places where there were no churches gathered, yet would they ordain none but by the consent of some other church which was already established.

Jo. Whitgift.

Of the acceptation of this word in the xiv. of the Acts I have spoken sufficiently. This place is not one whit contrary to anything that is said in that matter; for in the xiv. of the Acts it is referred to the appointing of ministers of the word, and in this place of the second Cor. viii. it is applied to the sending of some with Paul to gather the benevolence of the churches, and to carry the same to the poor saints. Now, though χειροτονία may signify the imposition of hands, or the whole action of ordering ministers when it is referred to that matter, yet doth it not follow that it should always signify so, to whatsoever it is applied. But take it as you list, it is as well spoken of one alone as of many; as the place, Acts x., manifestly declareth; and therefore doth not of necessity signify an election made by the people, except some other word be joined with it to express the same; as there is in this 2 Cor. viii. For thus the apostle saith, χειροτονηθεὶς ὑπὸ τῶν ἐκκλησιῶν; which addition should not have needed, if this word alone had of necessity signified in the scripture any such election as you would have it to do.

[Acts x. 41.]

2 Cor. viii.

Why the companions of Paul were chosen by consent.

In the argument there is no sequel at all: for it was very convenient and meet, for the avoiding of suspicion of private gain or corrupt dealing, that such as should have to do in gathering and distributing alms should be chosen by a common consent; and it is manifest that it was Paul's own request to have them in this business by the consent of the churches joined with him, for the stopping of the mouths of such as would otherwise have been ready to suspect Paul's integrity in that money-matter: and that this is true, these words declare: *Declinantes hoc, ne quis nos carpat in hac exuberantia quæ administratur a nobis, procurantes honesta,*

2 Cor. viii. &c.: "Avoiding this, that no man should blame us in this abundance that is ministered by us, providing for honest things, not only before the Lord, but also before men;" as though he would say, Therefore have I procured that by the consent of the churches some might be joined with me in this collec-

tion, lest any man should take occasion to suspect me of corrupt dealing, or to report that in this business I robbed the church to enrich myself.

Now therefore, how anything can be gathered of this place to prove that ministers of the word ought to be chosen by a common consent of the people, let the reader judge. Paul might have chosen them himself if he would, but he desired the churches to choose them, that his upright dealing in collecting and distributing of the alms might not be brought into suspicion; as I have said before. And therefore an "archbishop may dare take upon him to make a minister of the gospel, &c." for anything that is in this place to the contrary. Indeed, if an archbishop should be appointed to collect and to distribute alms, then were it fit (for his own credit' sake, and to avoid the slanderous speeches of those that be quarrelous) that he should desire some to be joined with him, by the common consent of those of whom he should collect. And this is the only thing that may be gathered of this place touching any election[1].

It is untrue that in the first of the Acts "the church did first choose" those "two" that stood in the election for the apostleship: the apostles only did propound them to the church; as M. Beza truly saith in these words: *Apparet,...cum eligendus esset qui in Judæ proditoris locum succederet, fuisse multitudini propositos ab apostolis eos, quos maxime idoneos censebant*[2]: "It appeareth, when he was to be chosen which should succeed in the room of Judas the traitor, that they were propounded unto the multitude by the apostles whom they thought most meet." Neither were the apostles chosen by men, but immediately by God, as all writers confess; which was the cause why Matthias was there chosen by lot, and not by the voices of men. Beza, Lib. Conf. cap. v.

Why in the apostles' time it was convenient to require the consent of the people in some things, and yet not convenient now so to do, is declared afterwards.

[1 Cartwright rejoins that the case referred to is in favour of his argument: "If therefore for the avoiding of suspicion of corruption by money it was needful for St Paul to communicate the election of such ministers with the church; how much more was it needful, for the avoiding of both the suspicion of that vice and divers others, he should do the like in the ordinary ministers!" He also denies that "St Paul might have chosen them himself."—Sec. Repl. pp. 209, &c.]

[2 Th. Bezæ Confess. Christ. Fid. Genev. 1587. cap. v. 35. pp. 152, 3.]

Chapter iv. The Sixth Division.
Answer to the Admonition, Page 43, Sect. ult.

The consent of the people unto Cyprian's time.

I do not deny but in the apostles' time, and after even to Cyprian's time, the people's consent was in many places required in the appointing of ministers.

T. C. Page 31, Sect. ult., and Page 32, Sect. 1.

You will "not deny but that in the apostles' time, and St Cyprian's time, in many places the consent of the people was required:" shew any one place where it was not.

Doth not St Luke say that it was done church by church, that is in every church? And, where you say it endured but to St Cyprian's time, it shall appear to all men that it endured in the church a thousand years[1] and more after his time; and it appeareth in the 4. epistle of *Cypr. i. Lib.* his first book that[2] he used it not as a thing indifferent, but *Epi. 4. ep.*[3] necessary, and argueth the necessity of it of the place of the first of the Acts, which is alleged by the authors of the Admonition[4]. And so they are not their arguments that you throw up so scornfully, saying, how followeth this, and this, what proveth it? but Cyprian's, whom by their sides you thrust through, and so unreverently handle.

An untruth; for I say not but to Cyprian's time.

Jo. Whitgift.

You bid me "shew any one place where the consent of the people was not required" in electing of ministers in the apostles' or in Cyprian's time. I might rather ask you this question, especially of the apostles' time, and bid you shew unto me any one place that directly proveth the consent of the people to have been required in the election of the ministers of the word. In the first of the Acts the apostles propounded two; and the election was not by voice, but by lot. In the xiv. of the Acts it is plain that Paul and Barnabas did choose the ministers of the word. St Paul saith to Timothy, 1 Tim. v., *Manus cito ne cui imponas:* "Lay hands on no man suddenly." And to Titus, chap. i., that "for this cause he left him at Creta, &c. that he should ordain elders in every city." To be short, Christ himself alone, without the consent of any other, appointed his apostles. Shew you me the like evident places for your purpose, if you can.

Election of ministers by the people not general in the apostles' time.

1 Tim. v.
Tit. i.

[¹ Year, Repl. 1 and 2.]   [² And it appeareth in that, Repl. 2.]
[³ This reference is inserted from Repl. 2.]
[⁴ See before, page 339; also below, page 361, note 2.]

The vi. of the Acts is but of deacons, who because they were occupied about money-matters, and collecting and distributing of alms, it was meet that they should be chosen by a common consent, to avoid the grudging of the people that gave alms, and the suspicion of others; as the place itself doth manifestly declare: Acts vi.: "There arose a murmuring of the Grecians towards the Hebrews, because their widows were neglected in the daily ministering, &c." The 2 Cor. viii. is to the like effect; whereof I have spoken sufficiently. There only remaineth to help you this word χειροτονεῖν, which I have proved not of necessity to signify in the scripture any election by the people, except there be some other word added unto it to express the same, as there is 2 Cor. viii.; and therefore my assertion is grounded upon the plain and evident places of the scriptures, yours upon likelihoods and conjectures only. And, if it were as lawful for me to allege the canons attributed to the apostles as it is for you (who have alleged them in sundry places), then could I tell you out of them also that the electing of ministers by the people was not general at that time; as it may be gathered out of the 36. canon[5].

Why deacons were chosen by common consent.

Acts vi.

2 Cor. viii.

Can. Apost. 36.

If you will believe Eusebius, *Lib. ii. Eccles. Hist. cap.* 23[6], or Zuinglius in his *Ecclesiastes*[7], you shall find that the apostles did appoint and ordain James to be bishop of Hierusalem. But I will not now stand upon this matter, I shall have more occasion to speak of it hereafter: in the mean time, this which I have said is sufficient to satisfy your request for the apostles' time. Touching that of Luke, "that it was done church by church," if you mean the ordering of ministers by Paul and Barnabas, it is answered before, where I have shewed that it maketh against you: if you understand by "every church," those churches where Paul and Barnabas were together, then do you expound "church by church" well; else not. But this is not material[8].

Euseb.

Zuinglius.

Now, that the electing of ministers by the people was not

Election of ministers by the people not general in the time of Cyprian.

[5 Can. Apost. 35. in Concil. Stud. Labb. et Cossart. Lut. Par. 1671-2. Tom. I. col. 33. See below, page 366, note 3.]

[6 Euseb. in Hist. Eccles. Script. Amst. 1695-1700. Lib. II. cap. xxiii. p. 50.]

[7 H. Zvingl. Op. Tigur. 1581. Ecclesiast. Pars II. fol. 48. 2.]

[8 "In the 1. 2. 3. sections of this division he hath filled up almost a whole side, wherein there is nothing at all which either is not gone before or cometh not after, and so grossly repeated without either new coat or new colour, that I marvel he is not ashamed."—Sec. Repl. p. 211.]

general in Cyprian's time, I prove by Cyprian's own words, *Lib. i. Epist.* 4; where he, speaking of electing by the people, saith: *Quod apud nos quoque, et fere per provincias universas, tenetur:* "Which also is observed with us, and almost throughout all provinces, &c." In that he saith, "it was almost in every province," he plainly signifieth that there were some provinces wherein this manner and form of electing was not used.

Cyprian. Lib. i. Epist. 4.

When I say that "the consent of the people was required in many places even to Cyprian's time," I do not deny but that it was also required after Cyprian's time; neither do I speak any otherwise in that point than Musculus hath spoken in his Common-places, *Tit. de Verbi Ministris,* where he saith thus: *Hæc forma electionis ad Cypriani usque tempora in ecclesiis duravit, &c.*[1]: "This form of election remained in the churches until Cyprian's time." I know it was both before and after Cyprian's time in many places; but that is not the question (for it partly is, and shall more at large hereafter be declared, that it was also otherwise both before and after Cyprian's time); but our question is, whether it ought to be so at all times or no, and at this time especially in this church of England.

Musculus.

You say "it appeareth that Cyprian in his 4. epist. of his i. book useth it not as a thing indifferent, &c." Surely, if Cyprian's words be well considered, you will be found not to have reported truly of him; for he with other bishops, answering the question that was demanded of them touching Martialis and Basilides, whether (seeing they were convicted of heinous crimes) they might still enjoy their office, and minister unto the Lord, first, declareth out of Exod. xix., Levit. xxi., &c. of what integrity and holiness those ought to be that serve the altar, and celebrate divine sacrifices. Likewise, they shew that such precepts must be obeyed, and heed taken that none be chosen into the ministry but such as be blameless; signifying by the way, how greatly that people doth offend that doth communicate with a sinful priest, and consenteth to the unjust and unlawful office of him that is placed over them; shewing out of the prophet Osee and the book of Numbers, what punishment is due unto them that be

The place of Cyprian examined.

[1 Wolfg. Muscul. Loc. Comm. Theol. Basil. 1599. Tit. de Minist. Verb. Dei, p. 198.]

contaminated with the sacrifice of a profane and unlawful
priest; whereupon he bringeth in these words: *Propter quod
plebs obsequens præceptis Dominicis, et Deum metuens, a
peccatore præposito separare se debet, nec se ad sacrilegi
sacerdotis sacrificia miscere, cum ipsa maxime habeat potestatem vel eligendi dignos sacerdotes, vel indignos recusandi.
Quod et ipsum videmus de divina auctoritate descendere, ut
sacerdos plebe præsente sub omnium oculis deligatur, et
dignus atque idoneus publico judicio ac testimonio comprobetur, &c.*[2]: " For which cause the people, obeying the commandments of the Lord, and fearing God, ought to separate
themselves from a wicked governor, and not to communicate
in the sacrifices of a wicked priest; forsomuch as they especially have authority either to choose those priests which be
worthy, or else to refuse them which are unworthy. The
which thing also we see to proceed of the authority of God,
that the priest should be chosen before the face of all, the
people being present, and that he which is fit and worthy
should by the public judgment and testimony be approved;
as the Lord commanded Moses in the book of Numbers, saying, ' Take Aaron thy brother, and Eleazar his son; for Aaron
shall be gathered to his fathers, and shall die there.' God
commanded the priest to be appointed before the whole synagogue; that is, he declareth that the ordering of priests ought
not to be but (*sub populi assistentis conscientia*) by the
knowledge of the people standing by; that, the people being
present, *vel detegantur malorum crimina, vel bonorum merita
prædicentur, &c.*, either the faults of evil men might be be-
wrayed, or the deserts of those which are good might be
commended; and that that ordering might be just and lawful,
which shall be examined by the voices and judgment of all.
Which thing was afterward observed according to the rule of

[[2] Propter quod &c. quando ipsa maxime &c. comprobetur, sicut in Numeris
Dominus Moysi præcepit, dicens: Apprehende Aaron fratrem tuum, et Eleazarum filium ejus, et impones eos in montem coram omni synagoga, et exue Aaron
stolam ejus, et indue Eleazarum filium ejus, èt Aaron appositus moriatur illic.
Coram omni synagoga jubet Deus constitui sacerdotem, id est instruit et ostendit
ordinationes sacerdotales non nisi sub populi assistentia conscientia fieri oportere,
ut plebe præsente vel &c. prædicentur, et sit ordinatio justa et legitima; quæ
omnium suffragio et judicio fuerit examinata. Quod postea secundum divina
magisteria observatur in Actis Apostolorum; quando de ordinando in locum
Judæ apostolo Petrus ad plebem loquitur.—Cypr. Op. Oxon. 1682. Ad Pleb. et
Cler. Hisp. Epist. lxvii. pp. 171, 2.]

God, when as Peter spake unto the people concerning the choosing of a bishop into the place of Judas."

Where the words of Cyprian and the other bishops be plain, that the ordering of ministers ought to be in the presence of the people, to the intent they may object anything against them if they can, but not that it ought to be by their voices and election: the which the example that he useth of Eleazar, Num. xx., and the words that he reciteth out of the first of the Acts, plainly declare; for, though Eleazar was placed in Aaron's room in the presence of the people, yet had they no voices in his election. No more had they in the election of Matthias, though it were in their presence.

That also which followeth in the same epistle doth prove this to be their true meaning; for a little after it is said: *Propter quod diligenter de traditione divina, &c.*[1]: "Wherefore it ought diligently to be observed and holden, as proceeding from the tradition of God and the observation of the apostles (the which also is retained almost throughout all provinces), that, to the intent orders should be rightly celebrated, all the next bishops of the same province should assemble unto that people to whom a governor is to be appointed, and that the bishop should be chosen in the presence of the people, which doth fully know the life of every one, &c.:" so that Cyprian's meaning is to have the people present at the ordering of ministers, that if they know any crime in them they may object it; if not, with their silence allow of the parties: for, as the law saith, *Taciturnitas pro consensu habetur*[2]: "Silence is taken for a consent." And to this purpose serve the places that he useth Num. xx., Acts i., and to no other; as the diligent reader may easily perceive. But, howsoever the words of Cyprian sound, certain it is that neither that in the xx. of *Numeri*, nor this in the i. of the Acts, can prove any election made by the people[3].

[1] Propter quod diligenter de traditione divina et apostolica observatione servandum est et tenendum, quod apud nos quoque et fere per provincias universas tenetur, ut ad ordinationes rite celebrandas, ad eam plebem, cui præpositus ordinatur, episcopi ejusdem provinciæ proximi quique conveniant, et episcopus deligatur plebe præsente, quæ singulorum vitam plenissime novit, et uniuscujusque actum de ejus conversatione perspexit.—Id. ibid. p. 172.]

[2] Qui tacet, consentire videtur.—Corp. Jur. Canon. Lugd. 1624. De Reg. Jur. ad calc. Sext. Decretal. Reg. xliii. col. 825.]

[3] Cartwright rejoins at considerable length, accuses Whitgift of "most gross ignorance," of misrepresenting Musculus, of repeating what he had said before, of employing "popish shifts," and concludes that "it is manifest both by the

Chapter iv. The Seventh Division.

Answer to the Admonition, Page 44, line 1.

But I say that in the whole scripture there is no commandment that it should so be, nor any example that maketh therein any necessary or general rule, but that it may be altered as time and occasion serveth. For in such matters not commanded or prohibited in scripture, touching ceremonies, discipline, and government, the church hath authority from time to time to appoint that which is most convenient for the present state; as I have before declared.

No certain form of calling and[4] electing ministers commanded in the scriptures.

T. C. Page 32, Sect. 1, 2, 3, 4, 5, 6.

But you say these examples are no general rules. Examples of all the apostles, in all churches, and in all purer times, uncontrolled and unretracted, either by any the primitive and purer churches, or by the[5] rule of the scripture, I think ought to stand. If it were a private example of one, or in one place alone, or if it were countermanded by any other rule of the scripture, then the example were not always safe to follow. But what if there be commandment also?

It will fall out that you have neither examples of all apostles, nor of all churches, nor of all purer times.

Chap. viii. 10.[6]   In the eighth of the book[7] of Numbers the Lord commandeth that the Levites, which preached the word of God to the people in their several congregations, should be brought before the Lord and before the people, and the people should lay their hands upon the Levites' heads; which what other thing is it than to declare their liking of them, and by that ceremony to consecrate them, and set them apart for that use of their ministry? And, if you say that it were a disorder that all should lay on their hands, I grant you; but so he speaketh, because the approbation was by all, and some in the name of the rest declared that by their laying on of hands.

You are driven to a strait, when you are glad to fetch a mandatum out of the ceremonial law.

But methinketh I hear your old answer, that this pertaineth not unto us, being a thing done under the law: but take heed what you say; for, if you will admit neither the general examples of the new testament, nor the commandments and examples of the old, take heed that you do not, or ever you be aware, spoil us of the chief and principal pillars and buttresses of our religion, and bring us to plain catabaptistry, which you say you are so afraid of.

For, to prove the baptism of children and young infants, what stronger words and whole drift of Cyprian that his judgment was, that by the ordinance of God in ecclesiastical elections the consent and judgment of the church is necessary."—Sec. Repl. pp. 211, &c.]

Not so, but you seem to bring us to plain Judaism.

[4 These two words are inserted from Answ. 2.]
[5 Any, Repl. 1, 2, and Def. A.]
[6 This reference is inserted from Repl. 2.]   [7 In the book, Repl. 2.]

hold have we than that God commanded in the old testament that they should be circumcised, and examples thereof in the new testament, for that the apostles baptized whole families, where by all likelihood there were children? Now we say that there is this commandment in the old testament of the ministers, and there are examples in the new testament general and throughout: why should it not then be necessary in this as well as in the other? Besides that in the vi. of the Acts the apostles command that the church should seek them out deacons, whom they might appoint over the poor.

<small>This is a silly place to prove a general commandment.</small>

Touching certain ceremonies, I have shewed that they are necessary, as namely the sacraments.

And, as for discipline and government, I have shewed partly, and more hereafter will be shewed, that they are of the substance of the gospel, if to have excommunication be to have discipline, or if to have pastors, or bishops, and doctors, and deacons, be government of the church.

Jo. Whitgift.

You do still *petere principium*, and build upon a false ground: for I deny that you have "examples" either "of all" or of any "of the apostles," or that this kind of election hath been in "all churches," and in "all purer times, &c.;" and, albeit for the proof of this sufficient is said before, yet will I add something now also. All the places of scriptures that you have hitherto alleged are Acts i., Acts vi., Acts xiv., and 2 Cor. viii.; which places neither agree in persons that were to be chosen, nor in the manner and form of choosing. For the first of the Acts is of an apostle, the vi. of deacons, the xiv. of bishops, and the 2 Cor. viii. of such as were joined with Paul for the collecting and distributing of alms. All men do grant that the calling and electing of an apostle is immediately from God, and therefore doth differ from all other elections of pastors, deacons, &c. But to let this pass, I pray you, consider the divers manner and form used in all these places. In the first of the Acts, Peter made an exhortation to the disciples, he appointed out of what company the new apostle should be taken: the apostles presented two: after prayers made lots were given forth; and the apostle was chosen by lot, and not by voice, but immediately taken and reputed with the eleven apostles.

<small>The diversity of elections in the apostles' time.</small>

In the vi. of the Acts, the twelve apostles willed the whole multitude to "look out seven men of honest report, &c." to be deacons; and the whole multitude did choose seven, and presented them to the apostles; and the apostles prayed and laid their hands on them.

In the xiv. of the Acts, Paul and Barnabas ordained ministers in every church with praying and fasting.

In the second Corinth. eight, at Paul's request the churches appoint certain to be collectors for the poor saints with him.

Which of all these examples would you follow? Will you name them to the people; or shall the people name them to you? Will you have two put up together, and one of them chosen by lot? or will you have the whole people for to choose, and you to lay on hands; or will you only have the bishops to choose? To be short, will you pray only at the election, or will you both pray and fast? Or have you any commission to make a mixture of all those examples, and so to make one rule whereunto all churches at all times must of necessity be bound?

I told you before that M. Calvin saith plainly, that out of that example in the first of the Acts no certain rule can be gathered of electing and choosing of ministers[1]; and M. Beza, *Lib. Confess. cap.* 5, is as plain, that there can be no certain rule gathered out of the vi. of the Acts, or out of that in the first: his words be these: "In the election of Matthias lots were cast, but for a peculiar cause; for it behoved the apostles to be chosen immediately of God: in the election of deacons Luke hath not set down what the church did observe; but in another place we may gather by Paul, that they of Asia used the holding up of hands; which manner was usual with the most of the Grecians: wherefore there is no cause why any man should over curiously prescribe here any certain rule,[2] &c.[3]" *Beza.*

Now to rehearse what variety hath been used in the churches touching this election were needless: it shall be sufficient only to set down that which M. Calvin speaketh of it in his *Instit. cap. viii. sect.* 60, &c.; where first he declareth that the rule of St Paul touching the qualities of a minister *Variety used in the elections in the primitive churches. Calvin.*

[1 See before, page 296.]

[2 In Matthiæ electione sortitio intervenit, sed peculiarem ob causam, quoniam videlicet apostolos oportebat ἀμέσως a Domino designari. In diaconorum electione non adscripsit Lucas quid ecclesia observarit. Alicubi colligere licet ex Paulo usos fuisse Asiaticos protensione manuum, qui mos in plerisque negotiis a Græcis observabatur. Certam &c.—Th. Bezæ Confess. Christ. Fid. Genev. 1587. cap. v. 37. p. 154. See before, page 303.]

[3 Cartwright reviles Whitgift as a "cuckoo," as only repeating what he had said before, and says that he must " imagine a great famine of learned writings, that dare thus abuse the ears and leisure of his reader."—Sec. Repl. p. 216.]

is to be observed, and that he is to be examined according to the same. Then doth he shew, how that there hath not always one order been observed touching the electors and appointers; for sometimes none was chosen without the consent of the whole people; and other sometimes the people committed the choice to the bishop and ministers or seniors, except it were in the election of the bishop; and sometimes only the ministers did first choose, and then offer those whom they had chosen to the magistrate, or to the senate, or to the chief rulers, who ratified the election if they liked it; if not, then did they choose out other, &c.[1] This variety of electing ministers doth M. Calvin declare in that place[2].

<small>Can. Apost. 36.</small> It appeareth in the 35. or, as some counteth, 36. of the canons attributed to the apostles, that bishops were not then chosen by the consent of the people; for that canon speaketh of such bishops as, being appointed to some church, were not received by the people, and yet remained bishops still[3]. To <small>Conc. Ancyr. can. 18. Conc. Antioch. can. 17, 18. Conc. Laodic. can. 12.</small> the like effect is the 18. can. *Con. Ancyra.*[4], and the 17. and 18. of the council of Antioch[5]. In the 12. canon of the council of Laodicea it is decreed, that the metropolitan with other bishops adjoining should have the election of bishops, <small>Can. 13.</small> and of such as are to be preferred to a cure. And the 13. can. of the same council doth forbid that the elections of ministers should be committed to the people[6]. So that you see your manner of electing by the people not to have been "in all churches in all purer times[7]."

It appeareth that you were put to a pinch for a com-

[1 Calvin. Op. Amst. 1667-71. Inst. Lib. IV. cap. iv. 10, &c. Tom. IX. pp. 288, 9.]

[2 "Touching the variety of elections which he citeth out of M. Calvin, unless, as unnatural women do their children conceived in adultery, he purpose to make away with his cause, I know not what he should mean to offer it thus into the hands of her enemies."—Sec. Repl. p. 216.]

[3 Εἰ καὶ μὴ δεχθείη, οὐ παρὰ τὴν ἑαυτοῦ γνώμην, ἀλλὰ παρὰ τὴν τοῦ λαοῦ μοχθηρίαν, αὐτὸς μενέτω ἐπίσκοπος, κ.τ.λ.—Canon. Apost. 35. in Concil. Stud. Labb. et Cossart. Lut. Par. 1671-2. Tom. I. col. 33.]

[4 Concil. Ancyr. can. 18. ibid. cols. 1461, 4.]

[5 Concil. Antioch. cans. 17, 18. ibid. Tom. II. col. 569.]

[6 Περὶ τοῦ τοὺς ἐπισκόπους κρίσει τῶν μητροπολιτῶν, καὶ τῶν πέριξ ἐπισκόπων, καθίστασθαι εἰς τὴν ἐκκλησιαστικὴν ἀρχὴν, ὄντας ἐκ πολλοῦ δεδοκιμασμένους, ἔν τε τῷ λόγῳ τῆς πίστεως καὶ τῇ τοῦ εὐθέος λόγου πολιτείᾳ.
Περὶ τοῦ, μὴ τοῖς ὄχλοις ἐπιτρέπειν τὰς ἐκλογὰς ποιεῖσθαι τῶν μελλόντων καθίστασθαι εἰς ἱερατεῖον.—Concil. Laod. cans. 12, 13. ibid. Tom. I. col. 1497.]

[7 Cartwright says: "Of your canons here alleged, one only excepted which maketh nothing for you, the rest make directly against you."—Sec. Repl. p. 218.]

mandment to establish your manner and kind of electing ministers, when you are constrained to fetch one out of the book of Numbers, and that nothing at all pertaining to your purpose. For what one word is there in that place that hath any shadow of your election? First, the people there did not elect the Levites: secondly, they laid their hands upon them, which I am sure you will not have the people to do in the ordaining of bishops; for you say that "only elders and ministers used to lay on their hands." So that this place of the book of Numbers doth command that which you will not admit, and speaketh not one word of that for the which you do allege it.

<small>T. C. seeketh a commandment in the ceremonial law for the election of the ministers of the gospel. The place, Numbers viii. proveth not his purpose.</small>

But tell me in good earnest, will you bind us to the observation of the ceremonial law also, as you have done before to the judicial? For what else is there in that whole chapter but laws touching ceremonies, and in that place by you alleged especially? For there he speaketh of the manner of purifying of the Levites and of their offering: he speaketh not of any election. For God himself had chosen the Levites before, for the first-born of the children of Israel, *cap. iii.*

I would to God men would but indifferently consider how undiscreetly you allege the scriptures, lest you should seem to be void of scripture. You say "the people by laying on their hands did by that ceremony consecrate them." Would you have the people to consecrate ministers by laying on of hands? Do you not care what absurdities and contrarieties you speak? You make a distinction in that which followeth betwixt "ordaining and electing," and you say that "election pertaineth to the people and ordaining to the bishop [8];" and in another place, "that the imposition of hands was not by the church and people, but by the elders and ministers [9]." But, if this be a "commandment" for us now to observe, then must you recant that saying.

<small>Pag. 40, lin. ult. &c.</small>
<small>Pag. 31, sect. 4.</small>

I do admit this scripture as a portion of the ceremonial law, but I do not admit it as a perpetual commandment, because I know the ceremonial law is abrogated; except you will have all those ceremonies which were used in that place, and are contained in the same commandment, as of "sprinkling them with water," of "shaving their bodies," of "washing their clothes," of "laying their hands on the heads of bullocks,

<small>The dealings of T. C. tend to Judaism.</small>

[8 See below, page 439.]   [9 See before, page 355.]

&c." practised in ordering ministers of the gospel. Neither is this any title of "catabaptistry:" but yours smelleth of Judaism; for you bound us before to the judicial law, and now you will bind us to the ceremonial also. What remaineth but to say that Christ is not yet come?

Circumcision is a figure of baptism; but the Levitical priesthood is no figure of the ministry of the gospel: therefore we may well prove the baptizing of infants by circumcision, but we cannot prove the ordering of ministers of the gospel by the ceremonies used about the Levites.

Those examples of the apostles do well prove the baptizing of children, because they be grounded upon these general places of the scriptures: *Ego sum Deus tuus, &c.*: "I am thy God, and the God of thy seed, &c.;" and Matt. xxviii. *Baptizantes omnes gentes*: "Baptizing all nations."

<small>Gen. xvii.</small>

<small>Matt. xxviii.</small>

Of "discipline" also "and government" I have something spoken before, and mind to speak hereafter, when further occasion is offered: in this place it is answer sufficient to say that the contention is not whether "discipline or government" be necessary in the church or no, but whether this or that kind of "discipline and government" be necessary, and whether there be one certain kind and form of "discipline and government" to be used in the church at all times and in all places. As for "pastors, bishops, doctors, deacons, &c.," they be necessary ministers in the church; but it doth not therefore follow that there must be always one kind and form of government[1].

<small>The contention is not whether discipline, &c. be necessary, but whether one kind be necessary.</small>

Chapter iv. The Eighth Division.

Answer to the Admonition, Page 44, Sect. 1.

And I add that, howsoever in the apostles' time that kind of electing and calling ministers was convenient and profitable, now in this state of the church it were most pernicious and hurtful.

<small>Diversity betwixt the time of the apostles and our time[2].</small>

[1 Cartwright maintains that he was justified in fetching a commandment out of the book of Numbers, accuses Whitgift of jesting, and warns him that by the exceptions he takes he is like "to wrest out of the hands of the church all the moral laws that ever were written."—Sec. Repl. pp. 220, &c.]

[2 This marginal note is inserted from Answ. 2.]

T. C. Page 32, Sect. 6, 7.

You say that, " howsoever in the apostles' time this use was of having the consent of the church in the choice of their pastor or bishop, now in this state³ it were most pernicious and hurtful." Wherein see how unadvisedly you condemn the churches of Geneva, of all France, of certain of the German churches, which keep this order. But you allege your reasons; therefore those are to be considered, because they come so rare. For your manner is that, if you can have but one writer, new or old, of your side, or which seemeth to be of your side, you run away with the matter, as though you had scripture, reason, doctors, and all.

I will therefore then take a view of your reasons, when as I shall have briefly set down those reasons whereby the perpetual equity, reasonableness, and conveniency of this order, that the church should have a stroke in her ministers' election, may appear.

_{This is an unadvised collection.}

Jo. WHITGIFT.

I "condemn" no "churches" that have appointed any order for the electing of their pastors which they think to be agreeable to their state, and most profitable for them; for therefore I say that no certain manner or form of electing ministers is prescribed in the scripture, because every church may do therein as it shall seem to be most expedient for the same. That may be profitable for "the churches of Geneva and France, &c.," which would be most hurtful to this church of England. And therefore I say that, "howsoever this popular kind of electing was convenient or profitable in the apostles' time, yet in this state of the church" of England it would be "pernicious and hurtful⁴."

You say, my "manner is that, if" I "can have but one writer, &c." Truly I do not stand so much in my own conceit, neither am I so well persuaded of my own wit and understanding, but that I greatly esteem the opinions of learned men; and I think myself to have reason sufficient, when I have good and learned authority, which is grounded both upon scripture and reason. And, to put you out of doubt, if you be offended because I so do, you must be offended still: for I had rather allege the authority of learned men, which is grounded both upon the scriptures and reason, than to stick to mine own fancy, both without authority and reason; as

[³ Estate, Repl. 1 and 2.]

[⁴ Cartwright declares that Whitgift can shew no reason why in other countries "this order of election by the consent of the people should be good, and pernicious in England."—Ibid. p. 224.]

those commonly do which are desirous of innovations, and have their heads filled with new devices.

But you "will take a view of" my "reasons, &c.;" and I will first examine your reasons severally, and then answer for my own.

An examination of the reasons which T. C. useth to prove the perpetual equity, &c. of elections by the people.

Chapter v. The First Division.

T. C. Page 32, Sect. 8.

It is said amongst the lawyers, and indeed reason, which is the law of all nations, confirmeth it, Quod omnium interest ab omnibus approbari debet[1]: *" That which standeth all men upon should be approved of all men." Which law hath this sense, that, if it may be, it were good that those things which shall bind all men, and which require the obedience of all, should be concluded, as far as may be, by the consent of all, or at least by the consent of as many as may be gotten. And therefore it draweth much the obedience of the subjects of this realm, that the statutes, whereby the realm is governed, pass by the consent of the most part of it, whilst they be made by them whom the rest put in trust, and choose for that purpose, being as it were all their acts.*

Jo. Whitgift.

<small>The first reason examined.</small>

You use for your purpose a rule of the law, which you do not understand, nor rightly interpret: for, whereas this word *debet* importeth a necessity, you expound it as a word of courtesy, saying, "if it may be," and "it were good to be concluded;" when as the law saith, *debet approbari*, "it ought to be allowed." And reason will the same, that, where many men have interest in anything, or have anything in common, whereof every of them hath a private interest, right, or property, there every man's consent should be had; as if a house, or any other thing, be common among half-a-dozen men by purchase, descent, or gift, and five of them would burden that thing with any charge, or do any act to prejudice the sixth man, it shall not bind him without his consent; for there this rule is true. Furthermore, a thing is said *omnes tangere,* "to pertain to all," which is common either

[1 Quod omnes tangit, debet ab omnibus approbari.—Corp. Jur. Canon. Lugd. 1624. De Reg. Jur. ad calc. Sext. Decretal. Reg. xxix. col. 812.]

pluribus ut universis, or else *pluribus ut singulis*. In the first kind are those things that pertain to bodies politic, as the body of a whole commonwealth, city, borough, town, college, church, &c.; wherein (as the lawyers say) this rule hath no force. The reason of the law is because, it being almost an impossible thing for all men in such a body to agree in one, and there being amongst men for the most part (as it were) a natural inclination to dissent and disagree one from another, there should never any law or order be made, if every singular man's consent should of necessity be had. It is therefore sufficient in such places and matters, if the laws, statutes, and customs of the place be observed.

Wherefore the rule hath only place in the second, that is, in things that are common *pluribus ut singulis*, "to many severally;" that is, wherein every man hath a propriety and particular right; as it is properly in lands, possessions, &c., in the which the minister cannot be comprehended: for it were a great absurdity that in the election of the minister every singular man's consent should of necessity be required; for then, if any one froward man in the whole parish were disposed to withstand the election, it could never be ended; and this must necessarily come to pass if you will build upon this law. This law cannot take hold in the election of ministers.

And yet in such cases this law admitteth this general exception, if there be especial reason and cause why that thing which concerneth many should be done by some other way, rather than by the consent of them which have interest. And these are taken for good reasons in this case: first, if it be rather behoveful for the commonwealth and church of God, to do that which concerneth a number some other way rather than by the consent of every particular man: secondly, if it be for the more quiet estate of the commonwealth not to have their consent: thirdly, if it be better for the parties themselves to have it otherwise provided: last of all, if it be against the laws of God, or of the customs and laws of any country. The law admitteth exceptions.

If I were a lawyer, I could tell you that this law admitteth many exceptions. What is more expedient for all men than to have a good prince, good councillors, good judges, &c.? and yet I think it were most pernicious to have those offices committed to the election of the people.

But what need I strive with you in this matter? For, if those things that be concluded by parliament be " by the consent of the most part of the realm," because the people's consent is there in their knights of their shires and other burgesses (as indeed it is, which you also confess), then have you no more to say in this matter: for the book of ordering ministers and deacons, &c. is allowed and granted by parliament; and therefore the bishops and ministers of this church of England are chosen by the consent of the people, nay (which is more) of the whole realm, because they are ordained and chosen according to that order and rule which the whole realm in parliament hath made and bound themselves unto[1].

But by the way, if this ground of law be good in that sense that you allege it, and be transferred to the civil state, it will be found very dangerous, and too too much savouring of popularity; as indeed the whole course of your doctrine is.

Chapter v. The Second Division.
T. C. Page 33, Sect. 1.

So is it also when the question is to choose the magistrate, mayor, or bailiff, or constable of every town; which things if they have grounds[2] in civil affairs, they have much better in ecclesiastical. For it is much more unreasonable that there should be thrust upon me a governor, of whom the everlasting salvation or damnation both of my body and soul doth depend, than him of whom my wealth and commodity of this life doth hang; unless those upon whom he were thrust were fools, or madmen, or children, without all discretion of ordering themselves; which, as I will shew, cannot agree with those that are the church of God, and are to have a pastor. For they of the church of God, although they be called sheep in respect of their simplicity and harmlessness, yet are they also, for their circumspection, wise as serpents in the wisdom especially which is to salvation; and, how vile account soever you will make of them, they are the people of God, and therefore spiritual, and forthwith those of whom St Paul saith, "The spiritual man discerneth all things." 1 Cor. ii. 15.[3]

No man maketh vile account of the people of God; but you partly of malice, partly of popular affection, would have it seem so, thereby to stir hatred against us.

JO. WHITGIFT.

Elections by the multitude are for the most part tumultuous.

The disorder of such popular elections hath been such, the contentions moved in them so great, the ambition of the per-

[[1] Cartwright defends his interpretation of the law, ridicules Whitgift for saying that "every minister is chosen by the whole realm," and says that he has forgotten that it is the point of controversy, "whether the parliament have done well in establishing of such an order of making ministers."—Sec. Repl. p. 224,&c.]

[[2] Have good grounds, Repl. 1 and 2.]

[[3] The verse is inserted from Repl. 2.]

sons standing in election so notorious, the partial affection of the people inclining to their kinsfolks, friends, or landlords, &c., so untolerable, to be short, the lack of judgment and discretion in many of them so apparent, that that manner of electing upon great considerations hath been altered in divers places, and desired to be altered in others also by all those that are wise and discreet, and that wish for quietness and good government. Neither is it true that the election of those officers which you name is everywhere in the people. In the best-ordered cities and towns it is otherwise; and experience doth teach that those offices which are in the prince's bestowing, and some other to whom she committeth the same, are the best bestowed, and upon the most worthiest persons, as bishopricks, the offices of judges, justices, &c.

In ecclesiastical affairs it is much meeter that such as have knowledge, zeal, and care for the people, should place over them a meet and fit pastor, than that the choice of him should be committed to the multitude, which is not only for the most part ignorant, but careless in such matters, yea, and oftentimes evil disposed, and commonly led by affection, as friendship, hatred, fear, &c.

I know that christian men are not called "sheep," because they be void of reason; for, as Chrysostom saith, *Oves sunt, sed rationales*[4]: "They are sheep, but such as are endued with reason." And God doth at one time or other (if they be his) open his truth unto them, and endueth them with the spirit of discerning betwixt true and false doctrine, in those things that do pertain to their salvation. But, because God doth in his good time open his truth unto them, are they therefore always void of affection and error? or, because some have this spirit of discretion, is it therefore common to all, or to the most part? Indeed, if you speak of the invisible church, which is only of the elect, then is it something that you say; but, if you speak of the visible church, which is a mixture of good and evil, and wherein the evil are the greater number, then hath your saying no probability in it. And why may not the pope as well reason of this place, 1 Cor. ii., that he cannot err in matters of religion[5], as you may, that parishes

<small>Christian men sheep.</small>

<small>Scripture unaptly alleged by T. C.</small>

[4 Chrysost. Op. Par. 1718-38. In Epist. ad Coloss. cap. iii. Hom. ix. Tom. XI. p. 391.]

[5 Bonifac. VIII. in Corp. Jur. Canon. Lugd. 1624. Extrav. Comm. Lib. I. De Major. et Obed. cap. i. col. 211.]

cannot be deceived in electing their pastors? for he doth allege this text for himself to the same purpose: but the meaning of the apostle is this; that he only which is ruled and governed by the Spirit of God hath the true knowledge of the mysteries of God, and is able to discern the truth from falsehood. You can no more prove therefore by this sentence, that the parishes cannot err in choosing their pastors, than the pope may do that himself, general councils, and the church, cannot err: and surely, the more I consider the matter, the more I marvel what your meaning is in alleging this text[1].

Chapter v. The Third Division.
T. C. Page 33, Sect. 2.

Moreover, reason and experience teacheth that it maketh much to the profiting of the church under the hand of the pastor or bishop, that the church love him and reverence him. For the contempt and hatred of the minister, for the most part, standeth not in his own person, but reacheth even unto the doctrine which he teacheth. But the minister that the church desireth it commonly best loveth and most revenceth, and, of the other side, hateth and contemneth him that is thrust upon them; therefore it maketh much to the profiting of the people in the doctrine of the gospel, that the minister come in by their consent. Likewise the people must, by St Paul his rule, follow the good example of the minister. But men will not likely follow their examples whom they love not, nor love them which are thrust upon them against their wills. Therefore it standeth with the good conversation and godly following of the steps of the minister, that he be with the consent of the church. 1 Tim. iv. 12.[2]

Jo. Whitgift.

The second reason examined.

This reason is builded upon a false ground; for it is certain that many pastors are dearly beloved of their flocks, which neither were elected by them, desired of them, nor known unto them before. And I think verily that there is not one parish in England which doth the worse "love or reverence their pastors" in that respect, except such only as you and your adherents have inflamed, not only with the spirit

[1 Cartwright retorts by accusing "the bishops' elections of ministers" of much greater evils than Whitgift had noted in "popular elections," charges him with speaking "slanderously," and says that, "to keep the bishop in his throne, down must go all elections by many...and in a word the whole estate almost of our commonwealth must be removed."—Sec. Repl. pp. 227, &c.]

[2 The verse is inserted from Repl. 2.]

of discord, but of disdain and contempt also towards all laws, orders, and persons, that be not in all points framed according to their imaginations. But would you that a papistical parish (such as there may be divers in England) should choose their pastor, that they might "love him?" Surely then would they not choose a protestant. Or do men always continue in loving of those whom they have chosen? You know that experience teacheth the contrary: so long only do they love him as he pleaseth them, and serveth their affections; which because he neither can nor ought to do, therefore their affection of love is soon quenched, and they begin to hate and to contemn him, and the rather because they did choose him. For in that respect they think him more bound to please them[3].

Chapter v. The Fourth Division.

T. C. Page 33, Sect. 3.

And, if it should happen (which may come to pass) that any church should desire, or choose, or consent upon, by the most part, some that is unmeet, either for doctrine or manners, then the ministers and elders of the other churches round about should advertise first, and afterward, as occasion should serve, sharply and severely charge that they forbear such election, or, if it be made, that they confirm it not by suffering him to exercise any ministry. And, if either the churches round about do fail of this duty, or the church which is admonished rest not in their admonition, then to bring it to the next synod; and, if it rest not therein, then the prince or magistrate, which must see that nothing in the churches be disorderly and wickedly done, ought to drive that church from that election to another which is convenient. Now I will examine the reasons which you add to prove that, although in times past the church choosed their ministers, yet now it must be otherwise. _{Where find you this manner and form in the scripture?}

Jo. Whitgift.

What scripture have you to prove that, if the parishes should "choose an unmeet" minister, "then the ministers and elders of other churches" should take in hand the matter, &c., and, if they will not, "then to bring it to the next synod;" _{T. C., in pretending scripture, bringeth in that which hath no warrant in scripture.}

[3 Cartwright maintains that his "reasons stand still untouched," says "that the papists are not the church nor of the church of Christ, and therefore not to be suffered to have to do with the election of the ministers," and censures Whitgift for imagining "of the church as of dogs, and which receiving meat at the hand of their pastor turn again upon him and rent him, and not as sheep which hear the voice of their pastor."—Ibid. pp. 229, &c.]

if that will not serve, "then that the prince or magistrate must and ought to drive that church from that election to another more convenient?" Where have you, I say, either commandment or example of any such order in the whole scripture? Will you of your own head and brain take upon you to prescribe a rule besides all scripture? And dare you so boldly condemn an order taken by the common consent of so great a church as this of England is, because it is not in all points correspondent to some examples in the scripture? Men may see, if they be not blind, what your meaning is. You think, peradventure, that, if this were once brought to pass, it should not be long or you were placed somewhere, according to your desire[1]. The like policy and practice hath been used by others: look Zuinglius in his *Ecclesiastes*[2].

T. C. contrary to himself. Pag. 33, sect. 1.

But to come to a nearer examination of this your device. First, you have forgotten yourself; for a little before you proved by that which St Paul saith, 1 Cor. ii., *Spiritualis omnia dijudicat;* "He that is spiritual discerneth all things, &c.," that they were spiritual[3], and therefore could not be without discretion of ordering themselves in choosing their pastor: and now you say, "if any church should by the most part choose some unmeet man, &c." Whereby you confess that they may be deceived, contrary to your former words.

The order which T. C. prescribeth unperfect, and full of inconveniences.

Secondly, your order is most unperfite, and full of intolerable inconveniences; for who shall complain of this election to other churches? And, when complaint is made, who shall call them together? When they be called together, what order shall be taken for the avoiding of confusion and tumult? or

[¹ Cartwright rejoins: "The scripture I prove it by is that St Paul, when he teacheth that all the faithful are members of one mystical body of Christ, which ought to have a mutual care one of another, laid the foundations of this polity." He argues also from other passages, as from that in Matt. xviii., that, if in the case of an individual a matter must be referred to the church, "so it is meet that the church that maketh light of the judgment of two or three churches should be pressed with the judgments of the diocese or province." He goes on to say: " I have looked Master Zuinglius' Ecclesiast. over and over again. The sum whereof is, that none should take upon him any ministry which is not called of some church and of the ministers near about, contrary to the practice of the anabaptists."—Ibid. pp. 231, 2.]

[² Sic enim fore sperabant, ut, expulsis omnibus ecclesiarum ministris, ipsi in eorum locum surrogati omnium stipendia et sacerdotiorum bona occuparent.— H. Zvingl. Op. Tigur. 1581. Epist. præf. Ecclesiast. Pars II. fol. 41.]

[³ See before, page 372.]

who shall bear their charges? or in what place shall they meet, or how often? Likewise, "if the churches round about do fail in this duty, &c." who shall "bring it to the next synod?" or who shall summon the synod? or in what place shall it be kept? or at what stay shall the parishes be for a pastor, until the matter be determined? or who shall complain to the "prince or magistrate?" or what if the "prince" will not "drive them to a new election," but allow of the old? Do you not see of what disorder, contentions, tumults, and inconveniences, this your disordered order would be the cause? For how many meetings of churches should we have! how many synods! what parts-taking! what running up and down! what loss of time! what cause of offence! what quarrels! yea, what not?

But, amongst all other things you have here appointed to the prince or magistrate a good office, that he must stand and behold all this, and in the end only "drive the parish to a new election;" which also you say that "he must do." Throughout your whole book you take from the civil magistrate his whole authority in ecclesiastical matters, and give unto him no more (as I have before declared) than the very papists do, that is, *potestatem facti*, and not *potestatem juris:* for he must only at your commandment execute such laws and orders as you and your seniors have devised. Again, considering the great number of parishes in this realm, the variety of men's minds, the diversity of opinions in religion, and the general inclination in the hearts of men to dissent and disagree among themselves, it cannot be but that in short space the prince should be overpressed and surcharged with the composing and ordering of these confused and tumultuous elections; so that she must be constrained to let pass the care of the government of the commonwealth, and be wholly troubled with hearing and redressing these matters. Wherefore, to conclude, if you have no better reasons for your popular elections than these, I think it will be long before you can persuade any reasonable or wise man to subscribe unto it. But now to the defence of my own reasons[4].

The prince's authority diminished and her troubles increased.

[4 Cartwright says: "There is nothing so easy which is not hard to him that is unwilling;" and accuses Whitgift that he "maketh difficulties where none is. And, as this partly cometh of his unwillingness, so divers of these questions (if he do not dissemble) come of want of knowledge, not only of the government of the churches now, but of all ancient times, &c."—Sec. Repl. pp. 232, &c.]

The diversity betwixt the apostles' times and ours requireth a divers kind of government, and of ordaining ministers.

Chapter vi. The First Division.
Answer to the Admonition, Page 44, Sect. 2.

Causes[1].   First, because in the apostles' time the church was under the cross, and therefore very few in comparison was there that embraced the gospel, and commonly they kept together, or at the least met oftentimes; so that one of them was throughly known to another, and they themselves could best judge who among them was the fittest to teach and instruct, having always divers fit for that function. Now the church is in prosperity, and therefore the number that professeth great, and dispersed into divers places, and in most parishes not one fit for the ministry among them, or known unto them; so that they should call they know not whom.

T. C. Page 33, Sect. 4.

You say it was in the apostles' times under the cross, and therefore few, and so might easily know one another, who were fit for the ministry. But you forget yourself marvellously. For in the apostles' times the

It is not so much to have the gospel sown in many places, as to have it generally received in a few.

church (I mean visible and sensible, for else how could it be persecuted?) was sown not only throughout all Asia (which is the greatest part of the world), but through a great part of Africa, and no small portion of Europe; and now it is shut in a small corner of Europe, being altogether banished out of Asia and Africa. And therefore there are not the tithe

There be many more Christians in profession now, than were at that time. For, though the gospel was then dispersed in many places, yet was it professed but of few persons.

now of those that professed the gospel then: and what a conclusion is this, the church[2] were few in number because they were under the cross! For, to let pass both other scriptures and stories ecclesiastical, have you forgotten that which is said in the first of Exodus[3], that, the more the children of Israel were pressed and persecuted, the Chap. i. 12.[4] *more they multiplied? Then you say they kept together, and met often, and so, knowing one another, were best able to judge one of another. But herein you speak as one that hath small experience of persecuted churches; for in the time of persecution the Christians that were in one great city were fain to gather themselves, out of all the corners and from all the ends of the city, to one place, being not able to divide themselves into many parishes, both for other considerations, and because they were not able to maintain*

[1 This is inserted from Answ. 2.]
[2 Churches, Repl. 2.]   [3 In Exodus, Repl. 2.]
[4 This reference is inserted from Repl. 2.]

many ministers, and elders, and deacons; so that we read that the church which was at Antioch wrote unto the church at Jerusalem, and that of Jerusalem unto them of Antioch, and St Paul to the church at Rome, at Ephesus, and at Philippos, &c.: which speeches do declare that by all likelihood[5] in one great city they had but one congregation, and therefore that must needs be scattered here and there, and so could not have the commodity, either of often meeting, or of knowing one another, so well as where such a city is divided into many churches. Those that know the estate of France in the time of persecution do well understand that every church almost was gathered of towns, whereof some were six miles, some seven, some more, from the place of meeting and keeping their congregations; and therefore could not meet so often, nor know one another so well, as we by the grace of God may do, which meet oftener, and in less number than they do.

<small>This proveth that there were but few Christians in those cities, in respect of the rest that were not Christians.</small>

Jo. Whitgift.

I remember myself very well, and I also remember that no learned writer, old or new, denieth this to be true that I have said. You only say that "in the apostles' time the visible church of Christ was sown, not only throughout all Asia, which is the greatest part of the world, but a great part of Africa, and no small portion of Europe;" you prove it not either by scripture, story, or any good writer. The gospel, I grant, was preached in all these parts of the world; yet was it not generally received in any one part of the world, no, not in any city, not at Jerusalem, where all the apostles were, not in any the least town. There were Christians at "Jerusalem," at "Antioch," at "Ephesus," at "Rome, &c.;" but not the tenth part in any of these or other places, in comparison to the Jews and the gentiles that were there, and not Christians. In the apostles' time the visible church of Christ at Rome was but an handful, in comparison to the times that followed, when the whole city was christened and professed Christ, and had christian magistrates. I speak not of the dispersing of the gospel into divers places, which I know was in the apostles' time; for that commandment had they of Christ, that they should "go into the whole world, &c.;" but I speak of the multitude of Christians gathered together in one place. In the apostles' time (as I said before) no one country or kingdom, no one city, no one town, did wholly profess Christ, or for the most part: now whole kingdoms, whole countries, whole nations, profess him.

<small>The multitude of Christians is now greater.</small>

<small>Mark xvi.</small>

[[5] Deacons, whereby it may be understand that by all likelihood, Repl. 2.]

When Matthias was chosen, the whole church was gathered together in one place; and so was it when the deacons were chosen: which thing now is unpossible, because of the multitude; so that, though the election might be by the whole church in the apostles' time, when it was together in one place, yet can it not be so now, seeing it is unpossible for any one kingdom to contain it. It might well be that the people in every city might meet in one place without confusion or tumult in the apostles' time, when as scarce the xx. part of the city were Christians; but it cannot be so now, when whole cities profess Christ. Wherefore I speak of the multitude of Christians gathered together in one place, not of the multitude dispersed throughout the whole world; though it is not to be imagined that the number of the Christians then dispersed through the whole world is comparable to the number of Christians which at this day be in Europe.

Comparison made in respect of the multitude in one place not dispersed.

How few Christians was there at Jerusalem not long before it was destroyed, being above 40. years after Christ! Doth not Eusebius, *Lib. iii. cap.* 5, testify that they all were received into a little town called Pella[1]? and yet the apostles had spent much time and labour in preaching there: but the number of such as did not profess Christ was infinite in that city at that time, if we believe histories, and especially Josephus, *De Bello Juda. Lib. vii. cap.* 17[2]. Wherefore your opinion of the multitude of Christians in the apostles' time, in comparison to those that be now, is but a very dream.

Persecution doth both diminish and increase the number of professors.

It is a very good reason to say that, "because the church was then under the cross, therefore few in comparison embraced the gospel" (for so do I say); because, notwithstanding the number of true professors do increase rather than diminish in the time of persecution, yet is it not so with hypocrites and dissemblers who would seem to profess the gospel, and whom also we must count professors because we see not their hearts. This is manifest by this example. In the time of king Edward, when the gospel was in prosperity, how many was there in London that seemed to be earnest and zealous professors of the same! but, when the time of persecution came under queen Mary, what became of that number? How few

[1 Euseb. in Hist. Eccles. Script. Amst. 1695-1700. Lib. III. cap. v. pp. 59, 60.]

[2 Joseph. Op. Amst. &c. 1726. De Bell. Jud. Lib. VI. cap. ix. Tom. II. pp. 398, 9.]

was there then in comparison! Do you not think that, if God should send a trial, there would be found in that city many false brethren? Moreover, in the time of prosperity true Christians may without danger shew themselves, and remain in their cities, though the number be never so great; but in the time of persecution they are dispersed into sundry places.

We may learn in the viii. of the Acts, that the church wholly remained at Jerusalem until that persecution wherein Paul was a doer, and that then they were dispersed. Shall we not then say that at Jerusalem the number of Christians, by reason of persecution, were few in comparison? True it is that this dispersing was the cause why the church of Christ was more enlarged; yet in the mean time was the number of Christians at Jerusalem marvellously diminished. Thus then you may understand, if you please, that this is a good reason to say, "the church was then in persecution, and therefore very few in comparison that embraced the gospel," both in the respect of the visible church generally, and also in respect of the same church particularly in every country or city. And yet it is true, that *Sanguis martyrum est semen ecclesiæ*[3]*:* "The blood of martyrs is the seed of the church;" but that seed must have time to grow in; and I speak of the external professors of the gospel.

That which you write to overthrow my words, touching the keeping together and often meeting of such churches as be persecuted, confirmeth my meaning: for I say they kept together in the time of persecution; and you affirm the same; whereupon I also conclude that therefore one of them must of necessity be well known to another. And, although our assemblies in time of prosperity be, peradventure, as frequent as theirs is, or rather more frequent, yet have we not such occasion to confer one with another, or to consider one another, or to know one another as they have; for they then admit none into their society at their meetings but such as are known to be brethren, and of whose religion and zeal they have good trial. And I think that those which have been exercised either in France, or elsewhere, in any such time of persecution, know this to be true, that they know none so throughly, or are acquainted with none so entirely, as with

Conference in the time of persecution is a cause of better knowing one another.

[3 Plures efficimur, quoties metimur a vobis: semen est sanguis Christianorum.—Tertull. Op. Lut. Par. 1641. Apolog. adv. Gent. 50. p. 45.]

such who have been with them in the time of persecution. You would fain, if you could, confute a known truth and a manifest thing; for who would deny but that such as keep together in the time of persecution must of necessity be known among themselves, "and best judge who is fittest among them for any function[1]?"

Chapter vi. The Second Division.
Answer to the Admonition, Page 44, Sect. 3.

Secondly, in the apostles' time, all or the most that were Christians were virtuous and godly, and such as did sincerely profess the word; and therefore the election of their pastor might safely be committed to them: *The church now full of hypocrites, &c.[2]* now the church is full of hypocrites, dissemblers, drunkards, whoremongers, &c.; so that, if any election were committed to them, they would be sure to take one like to themselves.

T. C. Page 34, Sect. 1.

To your second difference I answer, that indeed there be hypocrites in our churches now, and so were there then; but more now than then: I grant you that also; but there is no great danger in them, as touching the election of the minister or bishop; for that in such open and public actions, that come into the eyes of all men, there is no good man will do so sincerely[3], so holily, as they will do, although it be fainedly. The hurt that they do is in closer and secreter matters. But, where you say our churches are full of drunkards and whoremongers, besides that you utter, or ever you be aware, how evil success the preaching of the gospel hath had here (for want of discipline and good ecclesiastical government), you bewray a great ignorance. For, although there be hypocrites, which bear the face of godly men in the church, whose wickedness is only known to God, and *A dangerous assertion tending to the doctrine of the anabaptists.* *therefore cannot be discovered by men; yet in the churches of Christ there be no drunkards nor whoremongers, at least which are known: for either upon admonition of the church they repent, and so are neither drunkards nor whoremongers; or else they are cut off by excommunication (if they continue stubborn in their sins), and so are none of the church, and therefore have nothing to do in the election of the minister of the church. And methinketh you should not have been ignorant of this, that, although there*

[1 Cartwright at great length endeavours to prove that there were more professors of the gospel in the apostles' times than in his own, and scoffs at Whitgift for his assertions to the contrary.—Sec. Repl. pp. 234, &c.]
[2 This marginal note is not in Answ. 2.]
[3 Repl. 2 omits *so sincerely*.]

Matt. xiii. 25.[4] *be tares in the flour of the church which are like the wheat, and therefore, being ground, easily meeteth*[5] *together in the loaf, yet there are no acorns which are bread for swine: and, although there be* *Matt. xxv. 32.*[4] *goats amongst the flock of the church, because they have some likelihood with the sheep, feeding as they do, giving milk as they do, yet in the church of Christ there are no swine, nor hogs. It pertaineth to God only to sever the tares from the wheat, and the goats from the sheep; but the churches can discern between wheat and acorns, between swine and sheep.*

Jo. Whitgift.

There be not only "hypocrites" (which deal "sincerely" in nothing, no, not "in public actions"); but there be such also as be corrupt both in religion and life, who would no doubt be as corrupt in elections (if they might have to do therein) as they are in other matters.

In saying that the church is now full of "hypocrites, drunkards, whoremongers, &c.," I derogate no more from "the good success that the preaching of the gospel hath had," than the like or greater faults did from the same in the church of Corinth and Galatia. The church is a net that gathereth together of all kind of fish, Matt. xiii.: it is a field wherein the devil soweth tares as fast as the husbandman good corn; and for one that profitably heareth the word of God three do the contrary; as the parable of the sower declareth: "There be many called, but few chosen;" "and the gate is wide that leadeth to perdition." Therefore it is no discredit to the gospel or to the preaching thereof, nor yet to the good government of the church, to have many wicked and ungodly persons which cannot possible be rooted out until the time of harvest. But this hath been always an anabaptistical cavil against the true church of Christ, and lawful government thereof; as Bullinger declareth, *Lib. i. Adversus Anabap.*[6] And undoubtedly, if this were a good argument to prove that the gospel is not preached sincerely, then Esay, Jeremy, and other of the prophets, which had preached among the people many years, and smally prevailed with them, either concerning doctrine or manners, preached not sincerely.

Drunkards and whoremongers in the visible church.

Matt. xiii.

Matt. xxii.
Matt. vii.

Bullinger.

[4 The verses are added from Repl. 2.]   [5 Meet, Repl. 2.]
[6 Insuper ut disertis verbis in evangelio docetur, zizania creverunt inter bonum semen, &c. Contra hanc sententiam Muncerus cum sua factione prorumpit in medium, &c.—H. Bullinger. adv. Anabapt. Libri vi. Tigur. 1560. Lib. i. cap. ii. fol. 4. 2.]

Whereas you say that "in the church of Christ there be no drunkards or whoremongers, at the least which are known, &c.;" either do you greatly overshoot yourself, and forget the great crimes that were known to be in the church of Corinth, or else would you secretly bring in the error of the anabaptists, which say that not to be the true church of Christ in the which there appeareth manifest crimes: for the declaration of the which error, and confutation also, I refer you to the third book of Bullinger *Adversus Anabap.*, and the ii. and iii. chapter[1]; where you may likewise learn what profit hath come to this and the like churches, where the gospel is professed, by the preaching of the word, though many wicked still remain in the same. I grant you that these vices when they be known ought to be punished; but if, either because those that be in authority do not their duty therein, or else those vices continue notwithstanding, therefore you will conclude that this is not "the church of Christ," I tell you plainly that you have already entered into one branch of anabaptism.

A branch of anabaptism.

It cannot be denied but that the evil are continually mixed with the good in this world, even in the most purest church; and that then they abound especially, when the gospel is in prosperity: so that this is a good cause why the election of ministers may not safely be committed to the common people[2].

Chapter vi.   The Third Division.
Answer to the Admonition, Page 44, Sect. 4.

Thirdly, in the apostles' time all that professed Christ had knowledge, and were able to judge who were meet to be their pastor. Now the most be ignorant and without judgment in such matters.

The people now ignorant and not able to judge[3].

T. C. Page 34, Sect. 2.

If they had knowledge then, it was because they were taught; and that they are ignorant now, it is because they have no good ministers to teach them; and, if the churches should choose their ministers, I am sure they

You make a digression, and answer not the reason.

[1 Id. ibid. Lib. III. capp. ii. iii. foll. 79, &c.]

[2 Cartwright accuses Whitgift of borrowing his argument from Hosius, and maintains that the passages of scripture he refers to are misrepresented.—Sec. Repl. pp. 241, &c.]

[3 This marginal note is not in Answ. 2.]

could not choose worse than, for the most part, they have now, being thrust upon them.

Jo. Whitgift.

They were then diligently "taught," and they gave themselves wholly to learn, because it was a time of persecution; in the which men be commonly best disposed, and sequestered (as it were) from all worldly cares, looking continually to fall into the hands of the persecutors. Now, though they be in divers places well taught, yet, because they have not such a sense and feeling of the word in the time of prosperity as they have under the cross (when the church of Christ is purest), the election of their ministers cannot be so safely committed unto them now as it might be then. But why have you not answered my reason? for as yet that is untouched[4].

Chapter vi. The Fourth Division.

Answer to the Admonition, Page 45, Sect. 1.

Fourthly, in the apostles' time there was in the church no idolaters, no superstitious persons, no papists: now[5] the church is full of papists, atheists, and such like: who seeth not therefore what strange ministers we should have, if the election of them were committed to their several parishes? *The church now full of papists and atheists, &c.*[6]

T. C. Page 34, Sect. 3.

I see that, when a man is out of his way, the further he goeth the worse. Before you placed in the church whoremongers and drunkards, as filthy swine in the Lord's courts; now you bring in papists, idolaters[7], and atheists, which are not only filthy, but also poisoned and venomed beasts. I am not ignorant of that distinction which saith, that there be in the church which are not of the church, and those are hypocrites, as is before said: but I would gladly learn of you what scripture there is to prove that idola-

[[4] Cartwright rejoins: "That which you call the 'prosperity' might well be called the cross and whip of the gospel, if it drew such a tail of sin as you suppose." He goes on to say that, if such evils result, "it is through the great and unexcusable fault of all, and governors especially," and that "peace of itself is an aid to godly increase."—Ibid. pp. 243, &c.]

[[5] Not many idolaters or superstitious persons, no papists, no common and general error: now, Answ. 2.]

[[6] This marginal note is not in Answ. 2.]

[[7] Papists and idolaters, Repl. 1 and 2.]

The place is not rightly understood. ters *and papists and atheists are in the church; when St Paul calleth all such without the church, and with whom the church hath² nothing to do, nor they with the church: you might as well have placed in the church wolves, tigers, lions, and bears, that is, tyrants and persecutors. For those ye speak of, and³ (in the judgment of men and of the church) as well shut out of it as they, in the eye of the Lord, they may be⁴ of the church, and so may and are sometimes the persecutors themselves; so that⁵ the election of the church is not, nor ought not to be, hindered by those that have nothing to do with it. But now I hear you ask me, what then shall become of the papists and atheists, if you will not have them be of the church?* 1 Cor. v. 12.¹

This is true in the commonwealth of the Turks, but not in this commonwealth. Where find you this 'ought'? *I answer, that they may be of and in the commonwealth, which neither may nor can be of nor in the church; and therefore, the church having nothing to do with such, the magistrate ought to see that they join to hear the sermons in the place where they are made, whether it be in those parishes where there is a church, and so preaching, or where else he shall think best, and cause them to be examined how they profit, and, if they profit not, to punish them; and, as their contempt groweth, so to increase the punishment, until such times as they declare manifest tokens of unrepentantness; and then, as rotten members that do not only no good nor service in the body, but also corrupt and infect others, cut them off: and, if they do profit in hearing, then to be adjoined unto that church which is next the place of their dwelling.*

Jo. Whitgift.

How papists, &c. be in the church. You must of necessity admit this distinction, "some be of the church," and "some be only in the church," else can you not make any visible church; for we only know who be "in the church," but who be "of the church" is known to him alone who knoweth those that be his. If they communicate with us in hearing the word and receiving the sacraments, though otherwise they be drunkards, superstitious, or infected with errors in doctrine, &c., yet must we count them in the church, until they be cut off from it by excommunication. Wherefore whoremongers, papists, idolatrous and superstitious persons, though they be known to be such, if they do communicate with us in the word and sacraments, are to be counted in the church until they be orderly secluded from the same. And yet there may be papists, atheists, and such like, though they be not commonly known to be such. And you know well enough, that they which indeed are papists in opinion, yet, if they be content to conform themselves to the outward orders

[¹ This verse is supplied from Repl. 2.]
[² Had, Repl. 2.]
[³ Are, Repl. 2.]
[⁴ May in time be, Repl. 2.]
[⁵ So it appeareth that, Repl. 2.]

of the church, would stand in their own defence against him that should accuse them.

Neither is it true that only hypocrites are such as " be in the church, and are not of the church." That chapter which you quote in your margent, and almost the whole epistle, doth declare the contrary. For the incestuous Corinthian was in the church, until he was excommunicated. And the apostle there, speaking of whoremongers, idolaters, &c., saith: *Si quis cum frater appelletur fuerit scortator, &c.* : " If any which is called a brother be a fornicator, or covetous, or an idolater, or a railer, or a drunkard, or an extortioner, with such one eat not." By the name of brethren were those only then called which did profess themselves to be Christians, and were so accounted to be. And Master Calvin, speaking against the like error of the anabaptists, after that he had spoken of hypocrites in the church, áddeth and saith : *Nonnunquam etiam admixti contemptores Dei, vitæ dissolutæ et flagitiosæ, aut qui sibi cavebunt ne reprehendantur ab hominibus, sed interim ostendunt se nullo Dei timore, nulla reverentia tangi*[6]: " Oftentimes also there are mingled contemners of God, men of dissolute and wicked life, or such as will be sure to keep themselves out of danger of men's reprehension, when as notwithstanding they shew themselves not to be touched with any fear or reverence of God."

If you mean that place, 1 Cor. v., where St Paul saith, *Si quis cum frater appelletur, &c.*: " If any man which is called a brother, &c.," and think that thereby they are secluded from the external society of the church, you take the words of St Paul amiss, as the anabaptists did; to whom (objecting that place) M. Calvin answered in his book written against them in this manner: *Quod autem vetat Paulus cum his cibum sumere qui sunt vitæ dissolutæ, id ad privatam consuetudinem pertinet, non ad publicam communionem*[7]: " Whereas Paul forbiddeth that we should eat with them which are of a dissolute life and behaviour, that pertaineth only to private familiarity, and not to the public communion." Now, if we ought to receive the communion with them, we ought also to account them in the external society of the

[6 Calvin. Op. Amst. 1667-71. Instr. adv. Anabapt. Art. i. Tom. VIII. p. 360; where *ostendent*.]
[7 Id. ibid. p. 362; where *cum iis cibum*, and *qui vitæ sunt*.]

church. But why do you thus seek to shift off those matters which you cannot answer? Is it not certain that there is in the external society of the church a far greater number of such than there was in the apostles' time? which if it be true (as it cannot be denied), then do I still affirm that the election of the minister cannot be safely committed to the people.

It is well that you take upon you to prescribe unto the magistrate how to deal with such as be not in the church. I pray you, where find you any such manner of dealing towards them appointed unto the civil magistrate? If you have any scripture for it, why do you not allege it? if you have none, what presumption is entered into you thus imperiously to prescribe laws unto magistrates! But what if there be plain scripture that they ought not to be admitted to the hearing of the word, if they be dogs and swine, what say you to this, " Give not that which is holy to dogs, neither cast ye your pearls to swine?"

<small>Matt. vii.</small>

Your distinction betwixt the church and the commonwealth, if it were in Nero's or Dioclesian's time, might be admitted without exception; but in my opinion it is not so fit in this time, and especially in this kingdom. May he be a member of a christian commonwealth, that is not in the church of Christ? If you had said that he may be in the power, and at the will and pleasure, of a christian magistrate, that is not in the church of Christ, I could well have liked of it; but it cannot yet sink into my head that he should be a member of a christian commonwealth, that is not also a member of the church of Christ, concerning the outward society. M. Musculus, in my judgment, speaketh truly against this distinction of yours betwixt the church and a christian commonwealth, in his Common-places, *Tit. de Magistr.:* " Let the ethnics and infidels, living not in the unity of truth but in the confusion of errors, have diverse magistrates and law-makers, some profane, and some holy, because their life is altogether profane, and their religion nothing else but superstition. Christian people are in every respect holy, and consecrated unto the name and glory of Christ not in temples only and ecclesiastical ceremonies, but in all their life, in every place, at all times, in all things, actions, and studies; that, according to the admonition of the apostle, 1 Cor. x., whether he eateth or drinketh, or whatsoever he doth, he doth it to the glory of God, &c.

<small>Musculus.</small>

Wherefore that distinction of ecclesiastical and profane laws can have no place in it; because there is nothing in it that is profane, seeing that it is a holy people unto the Lord God; and the magistrate is holy and not profane, his authority holy, his laws holy, &c. Be it therefore far from the church of Christ, that it should be partly holy, partly profane, &c.[1]" But all this is from the purpose; and you make too many frivolous digressions from the matter, which compelleth me also in following you to do the like[2].

Chapter vi. The Fifth Division.

Answer to the Admonition, Page 45, Sect. 2.

Fifthly, in the apostles' time there was no church established, being[3] then no christian magistrates, and therefore the state of the church was popular: now there is christian magistrates, and a church established, and subject to rulers, &c.

In the apostles' time no church established, and no christian magistrate[4].

T. C. Page 35, Sect. 1.

If there be no churches established, because there were[5] no christian magistrates, then the churches of the apostles were not established. And it is absurd to say that the ministers now, with the help of the magistrate, can lay surer foundations of the church, or build more cunningly or substantially than the apostles could, which were the master-builders of the church of God: and, as for the consummation of the body of the church, and the beauty of it, seeing it consisteth in Jesus Christ, which is the head, that is always joined unseparably in all times of the cross and not the

[1 Habeant ethnici et infideles, non in veritatis unitate sed mendaciorum confusione viventes, diversos legislatores et magistratus, alios profanos, alios sacros, quorum omnis vita profana est, et religio nihil aliud quam templaria et ecclesiastica superstitio. Christianus populus per omnia sanctus est, et non in templis tantum et ritibus ecclesiasticis, sed in omni vita, omni loco, omni tempore, omnibus in rebus, factis et studiis nomini et gloriæ Christi consecratus: ut juxta apostoli admonitionem 1 Corinth. 10. sive edat sive bibat, vel quid operetur, omnia in gloriam Dei faciat: &c. Quare distinctio illa legum ecclesiasticarum et profanarum, locum in illo habere non debet: quia nihil in eo est quod sit profanum, cum sit populus Domino Deo suo sanctus. Et ipse magistratus sanctus est, non profanus, sanctaque illius potestas, sanctæ leges, et sanctus gladius, &c. Absit igitur hoc ab ecclesia Christi ut sit partim sancta, partim profana, &c.—Wolfg. Muscul. Loc. Comm. Theol. Basil. 1599. De Magistr. pp. 631, 2.]

[2 Cartwright in reply maintains his own view at length, declares that papists cannot "come into any account of the church of God," and accuses Whitgift of unfaithfulness in reporting his words, and shamefully alleging Calvin.—Sec. Repl. pp. 245, &c.]

[3 Established in any civil government being, Answ. 2.]
[4 This marginal note is not in Answ. 2.]   [5 Are, Repl. 2.]

cross with his body, which is the church; I cannot see why the churches under persecution should not be established, having both the foundation and the nethermost parts, as also the top and highest part of the church, as well as those which have a christian magistrate. If indeed the magistrate, whom God hath sanctified to be a nurse unto his church, were also the head of the same, then the church could not be established without the magistrate; _{The magistrate is head of the commonwealth, and but a member of the church, by T. C. his judgment.} *but we learn that, although the godly magistrate be the head of the commonwealth, and a great ornament unto the church, yet he is but a member of the same. The church may be established without the magistrate, and so that all the world and all the devils of hell cannot shake it; but it cannot be in quiet, in peace, and in outward surety, without a godly magistrate. And therefore the church, in that respect and such like, praiseth God and prayeth for the magistrate, by the which it enjoyeth so singular benefits. Thereupon you conclude that the church was then "popular," which is as untrue as the former part. For the church is governed with that kind of government which the philosophers that write of the best commonwealths affirm to be the best. For, in respect of Christ the head, it is a monarchy; and, in respect of the ancients and pastors that govern in common and with like authority amongst themselves, it is an aristocraty, or the rule of the best men; and, in respect that the people are not secluded, but have their interest in church-matters, it is a democracy, or a popular estate. An image whereof appeareth also in the policy of this realm; for as, in respect of the queen her majesty, it is a monarchy, so, in respect of the most honourable council, it is an aristocraty, and, having regard to the parliament, which is assembled of all estates, it is a democracy. But you should have shewed how this difference of having a christian magistrate and having none ought to bring in a diversity in the choice of the pastor by their church. It were not hard, if one would spend his time so unprofitably, to find out an*[1] *hundred differences between a persecuted church and that which is in peace; but, seeing you can shew me no reason why the church may not choose her ministers*[2], *as well under a godly magistrate as under a tyrant, I will be bold to shew*[3] *you how that, if it were lawful to break the order of God, it were meeter in the time of persecution that the election should be in some others'*[4], *discreet and learned persons', hands, to be made without the consent of the church, than in that time when there is a godly magistrate, and that it is then most convenient to be chosen*[5] *by the church.*

Jo. Whitgift.

_{How the church was not established in the apostles' time.} There was then no church "established" in any civil government; because the magistrates did then persecute, and not defend the church. The church in the apostles' time was "established" in doctrine most perfectly; in discipline, go-

[1 A, Repl. 1 and 2.]   [2 Minister, Repl. 1 and 2.]
[3 I will shew, Repl. 2.]   [4 Other, Repl. 2.]
[5 Convenient that he should be chosen, Repl. 2.]

vernment, and ceremonies, as was convenient for that time, and as the church may be in time of persecution: but the time was not yet come whereof the prophet said, "Kings shall be thy nursing-fathers, and princes shall be thy nursing-mothers;" therefore it was not "established" in any civil government, neither did it so publicly and openly shew itself. The gospel and the church was in queen Mary's time here in England; but it was persecuted, not "established," not maintained, not allowed of, nor professed by the public magistrate, and the laws of the land; and therefore of necessity a great difference betwixt the government of it then, and the government of it now; the outward shew of it then, and the outward shew of it now; the placing of ministers then, and the placing of them now. My meaning and my words be plain; you needed not to have offended again (as almost continually you do) in the ignorance of the *Elench.*, whilst you do not reason nor answer *ad idem*. *Isai. xlix.*

T. C. often offendeth in ignorance of the Elench.

If you speak of the church, as it is a communion and society of the faithful and elect only, and of the government thereof, as it is only spiritual; then is it most certain that the church is as throughly established, as perfectly governed, as gloriously decked and beautified, in the time of persecution, as it is or can be under the civil magistrate. But, if you speak of the external society of the church, which comprehendeth both good and evil, and of the outward government of it, then neither it is nor can be in such perfect state, nor so thoroughly established, or outwardly adorned, in the time of the cross, as it is and may be under a christian prince. The ignorance of this distinction of the church, and of the government thereof (of the which I have spoken more at large in another place[6]) causeth you to fall into so many and so gross errors concerning the same.   *Tract. ii.*

You say that, "if the civil magistrate were the head of the church, &c." Christ only and properly is the head of the church, for it is his body; but yet, in the respect of the external society of the same, and the supreme authority that is given of God to the prince over his people in all causes, he may be also in that respect called the head of the church, &c.   *The prince head of the church.*

Chrysostom, *in Epistol. ad Philip. Homil.* 13., giveth this name to certain women, of whom he saith thus: *Viden-*   *Chrysost.*

[6 See before, pages 183, &c., 261, 2.]

tur mihi istæ mulieres caput fuisse ecclesiæ quæ illic erat[1]: "These women seem to me to have been the head of the church which was there." And therefore a learned man, answering Hosius, who reproved Vergerius for moving the king of Polonia to take upon him to be the head of that church, saith on this sort: "As the church of Christ in earth is but one body, so hath it but one head (as the apostle teacheth), which is Jesus Christ, who is always present with his church, and governeth it with his Holy Spirit, &c.; but, because this church, being visible, is not only ruled by the word, but by the sword of the magistrate also, appointed by God, therefore we say, there are so many heads of churches as there are governors of countries[2]." So that you see the magistrate to be the head and chief governor of a particular church in this respect, that it is a visible society, and must have, besides the spiritual, an external government also; whereof because the civil magistrate is the head and chief, therefore it cannot be therein "established without the civil magistrate." Your spare speeches for the authority of a[3] magistrate in the government of the church I will note in a several place by themselves, and therefore will I the lightlier pass them over in this place. In the mean time this is no good[4] argument to say, that the magistrate is "but a member of the church;" therefore he "is not the head" and chief governor thereof in earth: for the head, though it be the chief, yet is it a part of the body. But you still confound the visible and invisible church of Christ, the spiritual and external government of the same; which confusion may make you seem to say something to such as do not diligently consider it, when in very deed you say nothing to the overthrow of anything that I have answered.

How the church may be established without a magistrate. The church may be established without the magistrate, touching true faith, and the spiritual government of it by Christ in the heart and conscience of man, but not touching the visible society and the external government. Upon this confusion also is that grounded which followeth, that "the church in respect of Christ the head is a monarchy, &c." For, when I said that "the state of the church was popular"

Jaco. Andræas.

[1 Chrysost. Op. Par. 1718-38. In Epist. ad Philip. cap. iv. Hom. xiii. Tom. XI. p. 301.]
[2 The work intended of this author has not been met with.]
[3 The, Def. A.]   [4 Good no, Def. B.]

in the apostles' time, I spake of the outward form, shew, and government of it; which therefore I call "popular," because the church itself, that is the whole multitude, had interest almost in every thing, especially whilst the church yet remained at Jerusalem.

I know that all these three kinds of governments may be mixed together after divers sorts; yet still the state of government is named according to that which most ruleth, and beareth the greatest sway: as, when matters are most commonly governed by the consent of the more part of the people, the state is called popular; when by divers of the best and wisest, it is called *optimorum status;* when by one, it is called a monarchy. As in this realm in the court of parliament, although all the states be represented, yet, because the judgment, confirmation, and determination resteth in the prince, therefore the state is neither "aristocraty," nor "democraty," but a "monarchy;" even so in the apostles' time (especially, as I have said, whilst the church remained at Hierusalem), though they might be counted *optimates,* yet, because most things in government were done by the consent of the people, therefore the state for that time was "popular."

You say, that I "should have shewed how this difference, of having a christian magistrate and having none, ought to bring in a diversity in the choice of the pastor by the churches." I have shewed you before the reasons of it; and now I add this, that, forasmuch as the magistrate is the chief and principal governor of the churches under Christ, and ought to have a special care and regard to and for the same, it is not meet that any thing touching the government of the churches, or any public function pertaining thereunto, should be otherwise done, than he shall think convenient and profitable for the present state of it. And therefore well saith M. Musculus in his Common-places, *Tit. de Verbi Ministris:* "It is not convenient that those things which are publicly to be done, or which concern the people subject unto them, or, to be short, are such as concern religion, and in that respect pertain unto them (except we will say with the fantastical anabaptists, that Christians may not be magistrates), should be done without the consent and knowledge of the civil magistrate[5]." And again: "Wherefore, for the condition of time,

Musculus.

[5 Non enim convenit, ut quæ publice sunt agenda, deinde et plebem ipsis sub-

necessity required that the magistrates and princes, by the means of a few men which were of excellent judgment, and had a care that the church of Christ should be provided for, might hereunto be induced, that they might appoint faithful and learned pastors over their subjects[1]." And, *Titulo de Magistratibus,* speaking of the civil magistrate, he saith: "First, that he should place ministers of churches where they are wanting, whether he chooseth them himself, or confirmeth them which are chosen of others by his commandment; for it is not convenient that any man should take upon him any public offices in the church, without the authority of the public magistrate. But (you will say) it was otherwise in the primitive churches, in which the prelates of the churches were chosen of the ministers and the people. I answer: Such was then the state of the churches, that the ministers were not otherwise to be chosen, because they had not a christian magistrate: if you call back the manners of those times, first call back the conditions and state of them also[2]." The prince hath to see that all things be done in the church orderly and profitably, and therefore hath he the altering and changing of such elections.

Your offering of an "hundred differences between a persecuted church and that which is in peace" shall go with that brag which you used, fol. 22., where you offered "twenty to one, &c.[3]" But to what purpose make you this offer? The more differences there are between them, the more is my cause justified. But you "will be bold to shew" me, "how

jectam publice concernunt, denique talia sunt, ut etiam religionis gratia ad ipsos pertineant (nisi dicturi cum fanaticis anabaptis sumus, principes et magistratus christianos esse, et ad ecclesiam fidelium pertinere non posse) sine ipsorum conscientia et consensu perficiantur.—Wolfg. Muscul. Loc. Comm. Theol. Basil. 1599. De Ministr. Verb. Dei, p. 198.]

[1 Quapropter pro conditione temporum ipsa requirebat necessitas, ut paucorum hominum opera, qui judicio prævalerent, et ecclesiæ Christi consultum cuperent, magistratus et principes ad hoc inducerentur, ut subditis suis fideles ac doctos pastores præficerent, &c.—Id. ibid. p. 199.]

[2 Principio ut constituat ecclesiarum ministros, ubi illi desiderantur, sive eligat eos ipse, sive ab aliis jussu ipsius electos confirmet. Neque enim convenit, ut præter auctoritatem potestatis publicæ publica quisquam munera in ecclesia obeat. Dices: At secus factum est in primis ecclesiis, in quibus a ministris ac plebe eligebantur ecclesiarum antistites. *Respondeo:* Talis tum ecclesiarum erat status, ut aliter non essent eligendi ministri, propterea quod christiano magistratu destituebantur. Si revocas temporum illorum mores, primum conditiones ac statum quoque illorum revoca.—Id. ibid. De Magistr. pp. 632, 3.]

[3 See before, page 270.]

that, if it were lawful to break the order of God, &c.;" and I will also be as bold to answer your reasons severally[4].

Chapter vi.   The Sixth Division.
T. C. Page 36, Sect. 1.

In the time of persecution a church chooseth an unlearned minister, or one that is wicked in life, howsoever it be he is unfit: the churches round about by their ministers or elders admonish this church of her fault, and move to correct it: the church will not by[5] no means be admonished: what can now the other churches do in the time of persecution? If they excommunicate the whole church, it is a hard matter; and yet, if they may do that, there is all they can do: the evil is not remedied, which may be easily taken away where there is a godly magistrate, and the church (as is before said) compelled to a better choice. So you see that there are inconveniences in the choosing of the pastor, and other the governors of the church, by the church, in the time of persecution, which are not in the time of peace, under a christian magistrate. This is but one, and yet none indeed; for the case you put is very unlikely in the time you speak of.

Jo. Whitgift.

This is your only reason to prove that in[6] a church persecuted it is meeter for the minister to be chosen without the consent of the church, than in a church being in prosperity. And surely it is even like to your reasons in other matters: for, first, that which you say of the churches round about (for admonishing, correcting, or excommunicating that church that shall choose an unmeet minister) is not to be found in all the scripture, either in commandment or example, and it is a mere device of your own head.

Secondly, it is most unlike that the church in the time of persecution should choose an unmeet or a wicked minister; because those that be persecuted themselves be godly, and well disposed, and careful to have such a one as they may safely commit themselves unto. For, though in the time of persecution there may be some hypocrites, that will for a time join themselves with the godly, yet the most part do of a con-

[[4] Cartwright remarks on this division: "I took the likeliest signification of your word 'established;' which is surely grounded without remove, and which hath all the parts of a church: now I see that by 'established' you mean allowed by the magistrate." He goes on to accuse Whitgift of inconsistency and untruth: "That he saith that the 'state of the church was in the apostles' time popular,' by his own judgment (which giveth the name unto the form of government of that part which most ruleth) is untrue, &c."—Sec. Repl. pp. 248, &c.]

[[5] Will by, Repl. 2.]   [[6] *In* is not in Def. B.]

science that which they do; else would they not endure persecution: wherefore, if ever the election of their minister may safely be committed unto them, it may then so be especially. Lastly, in the time of persecution they have no magistrate, they be all equal, neither is one bound to obey another by any civil law; none hath chief and special care over the rest as magistrate to compel: wherefore it cannot be otherwise then, but that such offices and functions should be chosen by a common consent; neither can there be therein, in that time, the half part of "inconveniences" that are in the same in time of prosperity; as any man of any consideration may evidently perceive[1].

Chapter vi.   The Seventh Division.
T. C. Page 36, Sect. 2, 3.

Where find you that I think so?

The words of this constitution are craftily suppressed.

He was Francorum, non Germanorum, primus imperator; for Conradus his nephew and Otho did first translate the empire from France to Germany; as some think.

Now I will shew you, which think that the consent of the church in their minister cannot stand with the time of a christian magistrate, that it hath not only stood, but hath been confirmed in their times and by them. In Codice Justiniani it is thus written: "*Following the doctrine of the holy apostles, &c., we ordain that, as often as it shall fall out that the minister's place shall be void in any city, that voices be given of the inhabitants of that city, that he of three (which for their right faith, holiness of life, and other good things, are most approved) should be chosen to the bishoprick, which is the most meet of them*[2]." Also Carolus Magnus, which was the first German emperor, in 63. Distinct. Sacrorum canonum, saith: "*Being not ignorant of the holy canons, that the holy church in the name of God should use her honour the freelier, we assent unto the ecclesiastical order, that the bishop*[3] *be chosen by election of the clergy and people, according to the statutes of the canons of that diocese*[4]."

[1 Cartwright rejoins that many heretics have been under persecution; and therefore unmeet ministers might then be chosen; and accuses Whitgift of inconsistency in asserting that ministers were appointed without the consent of the people in the times of Timothy, Titus, and Cyprian, which were times of persecution.—Ibid. pp. 250, 1.]

[2 ...ἀκολουθοῦντες δὲ καὶ τῇ διδασκαλίᾳ τῶν ἁγίων ἀποστόλων, κ.λ. διὰ τοῦ παρόντος νόμου θεσπίζομεν, ὁσάκις ἂν ἐν οἰᾳδήποτε πόλει ἱερατικὸν θρόνον σχολάσαι συμβαίνῃ, ψήφισμα γίνεσθαι παρὰ τῶν οἰκούντων τὴν αὐτὴν πόλιν ἐπὶ τρισὶ τοῖς ἐπὶ ὀρθῇ πίστει καὶ βίου σεμνότητι καὶ τοῖς ἄλλοις ἀγαθοῖς μεμαρτυρημένοις, ὥστε ἐκ τούτων τὸν ἐπιτηδειότερον εἰς τὴν ἐπισκοπὴν προχειρίζεσθαι.—Corp. Jur. Civil. Amst. 1663. Cod. Lib. i. Tit. iii. 41. Tom. II. p. 16.]

[3 Bishops, Repl. 1, 2, and Def. A.]

[4 Sacrorum canonum non ignari, ut in Dei nomine sancta ecclesia suo liberius potiretur honore, assensum ordini ecclesiastico præbuimus, ut scilicet episcopi per electionem cleri et populi secundum statuta canonum de propria diœcesi...eligantur, &c.-Ex. i. Lib. Capit. Carol. et Ludov. in Corp. Jur. Canon. Lugd. 1624. Decret. Gratian. Decr. Prim. Pars, Dist. lxiii. can. 34. cols. 330, 1.]

In the 63. *Distinction it appeareth that Ludovicus, Carolus his son, decreed that he should be bishop of Rome whom all the people of Rome should consent to choose*[5].

Jo. WHITGIFT.

Where do I say that "the consent of the church in the choice of their minister cannot stand with the time of a christian magistrate?" I have said that, "howsoever in the apostles' time that kind of electing ministers was convenient, now in this state of the church it were pernicious and hurtful;" which to be most true the differences of the times before by me alleged do prove[6]. The civil magistrate may commit this election to such as he liketh best, and may use that manner and kind of choice which he thinketh to be most convenient for that church whereof he hath the chief care next unto God; and these proofs that you here bring in to justify your cause, in my opinion, do quite overthrow the same. For it appeareth to have been in the power of emperors and civil magistrates to appoint the manner and form of such elections: why else should they have needed to make any laws or constitutions for that matter[7]? It is true that Musculus, *Loc. Com. Tit. de Magistr.*, speaking of the civil magistrate, saith: *Prudenter autem et magna &c.*[8]: "But he must wisely and very warily order the election of ministers, seeking nothing else but that the flock of the Lord might be provided for. He shall choose not only such men as are holy, but such as are also able to teach. He shall flee simony more than a dog or snake. But

The proofs of T. C. improve his purpose.

Musculus.

[5 ...liceat Romanis...eum, quem..........omnes Romani uno consilio atque concordia sine qualibet promissione ad pontificatus ordinem elegerint,...consecrare, &c.—Pact. Const. Ludov. ibid. can. 30. col. 329.]

[6 Cartwright replies that, as that which is "pernicious and hurtful" ought not to be done, therefore Whitgift's assertion comes to this, that "the church's election cannot stand with the time of a christian magistrate."—Sec. Repl. p. 251.]

[7 Cartwright produces examples of the civil authority commanding that which had been commanded by God, and argues thence that the making of such laws does not shew that a matter is therefore dependent on such authority.—Ibid. pp. 251, 2.]

[8 Prudenter autem et magna circumspectione ministrorum electionem dispensabit, nihil quærens aliud quam ut gregi Dominico sit consultum. Viros eliget non solum pios, sed et ad docendum instructos. Simoniam cane pejus et angue fugiet. Eligendi modum usurpabit, qui quam maxime sit ecclesiis accommodus. Et quoniam per seipsum non poterit omnibus quæ huc pertinent sufficere, utetur opera et ministerio fidelium ac Dei timentium virorum, sive illi sint in ministerio verbi, sive alterius ordinis, quorum humeris hanc curam imponat: sic tamen ut electos ipse cognoscat, et si idonei videntur, auctoritate ac potestate sua confirmet.—Wolfg. Muscul. Loc. Comm. Theol. Basil. 1599. De Magistr. p. 633.]

he shall use that manner of election which may be most profitable for the churches. And, forsomuch as he is not able of himself to do all things which pertain hereunto, he shall use the help and aid of faithful men, and of those that fear God, upon whose shoulders he may lay the care or burden, whether they be within the order of the ministry of the word, or of another profession; but notwithstanding in such sort that he himself do know them which are chosen, and, if they seem meet, do by his authority and power confirm them."

The proofs of T. C. against himself.

But to come to your authorities. The words that you allege *in Codice Justiniani* must somewhere else be sought for. I think your author Illyricus is deceived in quoting that place; for surely I cannot understand that they are to be found in that book. But from what author soever they come, you have subtilly left out the words that expound his meaning, and make directly against you. Wherefore I will recite them word for word, as they are reported in Illyricus, the author out of whom you have borrowed them: *Sequentes igitur doctrinam, &c.*[1]: "Following the doctrine of the holy apostles in that, that most pure and uncorrupt priests ought to be chosen, which are appointed for that cause chiefly, that by their prayers they might obtain the favour of the most merciful God towards commonwealths; we do decree by this present constitution, that as oft as it shall happen the room of any priest to be void, the inhabitants of the same city shall give their voices of three, which in true faith, holiness of life, and in all other good things, are approved and allowed of; that of these he which shall be most meet might be chosen bishop." The emperor saith that he "followeth the doctrine of the apostles" in this, that they prescribe what manner of men are to be chosen (*sci. integerrimi et incorruptissimi*, "most pure and most uncorrupt"), not in the manner or kind of electing; as you would seem to make the reader believe in noting these words only ("following the doctrine of the holy apostles"),

T. C. subtilly concealeth the words of his author that make against him.

[1 Sequentes doctrinam sanctorum apostolorum, de eo quod debeant eligi integerrimi et incorruptissimi sacerdotes, qui quidem ea re maxime constituuntur, ut suis precibus benevolentiam Dei clementissimi rebuspub. acquirant, præsenti constitutione sancimus: Quoties sacerdotalem sedem in civitate quapiam vacare contigerit, ut suffragia ferantur ab incolentibus eam civitatem de tribus qui in recta fide, ac vitæ sanctimonia, aliisque optimis in rebus spectati et probati sunt, ut ex iis, qui maxime idoneus erit, in episcopatum cooptetur.—Lib. de Elect. Episc. Cattop. 1667. ad calc. Catalog. Test. Verit. Franc. 1666. p. 63.]

and leaving out that which followeth; and declareth wherein he meant to follow their doctrine, namely, *de eo quod debeant eligi integerrimi:* "in that that they which are most pure ought to be chosen, &c." For else why doth he add and say, *sancimus,* "we have decreed," and not rather, they have decreed? But the words that follow are most plain: *quoties sacerdotalem sedem, &c.*: "As oft as it shall happen that the room of a priest shall be void, the inhabitants of that city shall give their voices of three, &c.;" for where did the apostles ever appoint that three should stand in the election? or what example have you of it in the whole scripture? So that you see here no one prescript rule or example of the apostles in all points followed, but that order to be taken, and law made by the emperor, which he thought for that state and time of the church to be most convenient.

In Novellis he seemeth to declare what is meant by "the inhabiters of that city;" for thus it is written: *Sequentes igitur ea, &c.*[2]: "Following therefore those things which are decreed in the holy canons, we make this pragmatical law, by the which we decree that, as oft as it shall be necessary to ordain a bishop, the clergy and primates of the city for the which the bishop is to be ordained, shall assemble together, and, tho evangelios being laid before them, shall agree and determine upon three persons; and every one of them shall swear by the holy word of God (and that to be enrolled with their determination), that they have not chosen these men either for reward, or for promise, or for friendship, or favour, or for any other affection, but only because they know them to be of the true and catholic faith, and of honest conversation, and that they are above five-and-thirty years old." So that it is plain, that by the inhabitants of the city he meaneth the clergy and the chief persons of the city. It followeth in the same constitution: *Ut ex tribus illis personis, quæ decre-*

The proofs of T. C. against himself.

Constitutione 123.

[2 Τοῖς οὖν ὑπὸ τῶν θείων κανόνων ὁρισθεῖσιν ἀκολουθοῦντες, τὸν παρόντα ποιούμεθα νόμον, δι' οὗ θεσπίζομεν, ὁσάκις χρείᾳ ἐπίσκοπον χειροτονηθῆναι, συνιέναι τοὺς κληρικοὺς, καὶ τοὺς πρώτους τῆς πόλεως ἧς μέλλει ἐπίσκοπος χειροτονεῖσθαι· καὶ προκειμένων τῶν ἁγίων εὐαγγελίων, ἐπὶ τρισὶ προσώποις ψηφίσματα ποιεῖν, καὶ ἕκαστον αὐτῶν ὀμνύναι κατὰ τῶν θείων λογίων καὶ ἐγγράφειν ἐν αὐτοῖς ὅτι οὔτε διὰ δόσιν, οὔτε διὰ ὑπόσχεσιν, ἢ φιλίαν, ἢ χάριν, ἢ ἄλλην οἱανδήποτε προσπάθειαν, ἀλλ' εἰδότες αὐτοὺς τῆς ὀρθῆς καὶ καθολικῆς πίστεως, καὶ σεμνοῦ βίου, καὶ ὑπὲρ τὸ τριακοστὸν ἔτος εἶναι τούτους ἐπελέξαντο, κ.τ.λ. Ἵνα ἐκ τῶν οὕτως ψηφιζομένων τριῶν προσώπων ὁ βελτίων χειροτονηθῇ τῇ ἐπιλογῇ καὶ τῷ κρίματι τοῦ χειροτονοῦντος.—Corp. Jur. Civil. Amst. 1663. Auth. Coll. ix. Tit. xx. Novell. cxxxvii. 2. Tom. II. pp. 195, 6.]

tis hoc modo eliguntur, melior ordinetur, electione et judicio ejus qui ordinandi jus habet: "That of those three which are in this sort chosen, the best may be ordained by the election and judgment of him that hath the authority to ordain." And this last clause may be an interpretation also of the meaning of that constitution, *ex Codice:* that is, that the inhabitants choose three, of whom the metropolitan should choose one to be bishop; for it is evident that the metropolitan had *jus ordinandi;* and that law *in Codice* differeth not one whit from this constitution.

The words of Carolus Magnus make with me rather than against me; for, in that he saith, *secundum statuta canonum de propria diœcesi,* "according to the statutes of the canons of that diocese," he plainly signifieth that in sundry dioceses there be sundry kinds and manners of elections; else would he have said, *secundum statuta canonum apost.,* "according to the statutes of the canons of the apostles," or *sacræ scripturæ,* "of the holy scripture," or such like. But that which followeth in the same law maketh the matter manifest: *Præcipimus etiam omnibus, &c.*[1]: "We will also and command all those which are subject to our jurisdiction, that no man attempt to spoil the privileges of the churches, monasteries, or the churches themselves, &c.;" meaning, no doubt, touching elections.

That of Lodovic, *Dist.* 63. declareth also that it was in the emperor's power to alter the manner of elections, or to stablish[2], them; for else to what purpose were these laws and confirmations made? All this verifieth my assertion, and proveth plainly that the manner and form of calling and electing ministers is, and hath been, in the power of the civil magistrate, to order as shall be most expedient for the present state of the church: if the prince think it convenient that the people should have voices in such elections, they may so have; if not, there is no law of God doth bind them to it: and that do all those laws of emperors manifestly prove[3].

[1 Præcipimus etiam omnibus ditioni nostræ subjectis, ut nullus privilegia ecclesiarum, monasteriorum, aut ecclesias diripere prætentet.—Lib. de Elect. Episc. Cattop. 1667. ad calc. Catalog. Test. Verit. Franc. 1666. p. 63. This portion of the law is not cited in Gratian. See before, page 396, note 4.]

[2 Establish, Def. A.]

[3 Cartwright denies the charge of leaving out any thing "subtilly:" "he left out," he says, "that which made nothing for or against the purpose." He goes on at great length to maintain his own view, and concludes "that the emperor took it for a law of God, that the church should choose her minister."—Sec. Repl. pp. 252, &c.]

Chapter vi.   The Eighth Division.

T. C. Page 36, Sect. 4, 5.

The proofs of T. C. against himself.

Platina also, in the life of pope Adrian the second, writeth that Ludovic the second by his letters commanded the Romans that they should choose their own bishop, not looking for other men's voices, which being strangers could not so well tell what was done in the commonweal where they were strangers, and that it appertaineth[4] *to the citizens*[5]*. The same Platina witnesseth in the life of pope Leo the VIII. that, when the people of Rome were earnest with the emperor Otho the first, that he would take away one pope John that lived very licentiously and riotously, and place another, the same emperor answered that it pertained to the clergy and people to choose one, and willed them that they should choose, and he would approve it; and when they had chosen Leo, and after put him out without cause, and chose one pope Benet, he compelled them to take Leo again*[6]*. Whereby appeareth, that in those estates where magistrates were christian, and where the estate was most of all monarchical, that is, subject to one's government*[7]*, and also, when the church put out any without good cause, that then the magistrates should compel the churches to do their duty. Indeed, the bishop of Rome gave the election then into the emperor his hands, because of the lightness of the people; as Platina maketh mention: but that is not the matter; for I do nothing else here but shew that the elections of the ministers by the church were used in the times of the emperors, and by their consents. And, seeing that Otho confessed it pertained not unto him, it is to be doubted whether he took it at the bishop his hands.*

An untruth; for he only commendeth them for so doing, he doth not command them to do so.

JO. WHITGIFT.

You have not truly reported the words of Platina, in the first place; for he saith not that "the emperor Ludovic did command the Romans that they should choose their own bishop," but that he commended them for their godly and sound choice. His words be these: *Supervenere a Ludovico imperatore literæ, quibus Romanos admodum laudat, quod*

Platina falsified by T. C.

Platina in vita Adriani II.

[4 Appertained, Repl. 1 and 2.]   [5 See below, p. 402, note 1.]
[6 Nam cum Johannes flagitiose nimium et intemperanter viveret, instarentque Romani apud imperatorem, ut alterum pontificem abrogato Johanne crearet, respondit electionem ad populum et clerum pertinere: Eligerent quem maxime idoneum putarent, se eum statim approbaturum. Unde cum Leonem elegissent, quem ipse confirmaverat, deinde mutata sententia abrogato eodem Benedictum suffecissent, iratus Otho eos vi et armis compulit, dedito etiam Benedicto, Leonem suscipere, qui statim, Romanorum inconstantiam pertæsus, auctoritatem omnem eligendi pontificis a clero populoque Romano ad imperatorem transtulit.—Plat. De Vit. Pont. Col. 1551. Leo VIII. p. 134.]
[7 Here Repl. 1 and 2 introduce, *that this use of the church remained and was confirmed by the emperors.*]

[WHITGIFT.]   26

summum pontificem sancte et integre creassent[1]*:* "There came letters from Ludovic the emperor, wherein he praiseth the Romans very much, because they had holily and sincerely created the high priest, &c." But Platina declareth how tumultuous an election that was, and how injuriously the emperor's ambassadors were secluded from the same, having therein interest; and, although the emperor was content to put up that injury, and to commend that election (peradventure for some worldly respect), yet it is manifest that then the bishops of Rome began to usurp upon the authority of the emperor, and to seclude him from having any interest in their elections. M. Bale, speaking of this election, saith: *Vi enim eligendi pontificis potestatem ad se tunc rapiebant Romani*[2]*:* "For the Romans then took by force unto themselves power to choose their bishop."

The second place of Platina argueth the undiscreetness of the people both in placing and displacing their bishop, and the authority of the emperor in taking this authority of placing and displacing from them when they do abuse it; for here he put out Benet whom they had chosen, and placed Leo whom they had displaced: whereby it appeareth that there was not then any one such prescript form of electing the bishop of Rome, but that it was in the authority of the emperor to abrogate, alter, or change it. All this is nothing to the improving of my assertion: for I deny not but that the people had interest in elections of bishops in divers places, and especially in the church of Rome, a long time; but this doth not prove that there is any prescript rule in scripture for the election of ministers, which may not be altered and changed from time to time, as shall be most convenient for the present state of the church; nay, whatsoever ye have hitherto said proveth the contrary.

Platina doth not write that "Otho confessed that the election" of the bishop of Rome "did not pertain unto him:"

[1 Non est habita in tanto tumultu cujuspiam ratio. Hanc ob rem Lodovici legati, qui ejus rei causa aderant, indignati, quod nusquam (ut par erat), dum hæc agerentur, interesse potuissent, et auctoritatem imperatoris in creando pontifice interponere........Supervenere &c. creassent, non expectato aliorum voto, qui forte ea in re ob ignorationem personarum minus judicii habuissent. Qui enim fieri posse dicebat, ut peregrinus et hospes dignoscere possit in aliena republica quis potissimum ceteris præferendus sit? Id maxime ad cives pertinere, et ad eos præsertim qui cum inquilinis familiariter vixere.—Id. ibid. Hadr. II. p. 122.]

[2 J. Balæi Act. Rom. Pont. Franc. 1567. Lib. IV. Hadr. II. p. 105; where *vi etenim*.]

you should have a care to report the words of the author truly. It is one thing to say, that the election of the bishop "pertaineth to the clergy and people," another thing to say, that it "pertained not to him;" for it might pertain to them all. And the same Platina in the life of John XIII. saith that, after John was condemned by a council and therefore fled away, the emperor Otho, at the request of the clergy, did create Leo bishop of Rome: his words are these: *Hanc ob causam Otho, persuadente clero, Leonem, Romanum civem Lateranensis ecclesiæ scriniarium, pontificem creat*[3]: "For this cause Otho, by the persuasion of the clergy, chooseth Leo, a citizen of Rome and keeper of the monuments of the church of Lateran, to be bishop." He further in that place declareth how the people after the emperor's departure deposed Leo, and placed Benet, and how the emperor by force compelled them to place Leo [4]again[5].

{The proofs of T. C. against himself.}

{Platina in vita Joan. XIII.}

That Otho the emperor "did take this grant at the bishop's hands," that the election of the bishop should be in him, and not in the people, M. Bale testifieth in manifest words, in the life of Leo VIII. where he saith thus: "After, he took from the clergy and people of Rome the power of choosing their bishop, which Carolus Magnus had given unto them before, and by a synodal decree did commit the same to Otho the emperor, for the avoiding of seditions which were wont to be in these elections; and Otho, receiving this grant thankfully, that he might shew himself again beneficial towards the see of Rome, restored all things which Constantine is feigned to have given, &c.[6]" In the which words also it is to be noted, that this liberty of choosing their bishop was granted unto the people and clergy of Rome by Carolus Magnus; the which not only M. Bale testifieth in this place, but M. Barnes also, in these words: "Leo the VIII., understanding the

{Bale in vita Leon. VIII.}

[3 Hanc ob rem Otho &c. scrinierium &c.—Plat. De Vit. Pont. Col. 1551. Johan. XIII. p. 133.]

[4 Id. ibid. See also before, page 401, note 6.]

[5 Cartwright denies that he falsified Platina: it was, he says, "nothing but change of one word for another without any gain at all." He goes on to maintain that Platina's testimony is in his favour.—Sec. Repl. pp. 255, 6.]

[6 Postea omnem eligendi pontificis potestatem a Carolo magno datam, ut Gratianus refert, a clero et populo Romano abstulit, ac synodali decreto in illum Othonem transtulit; quo vitarentur seditiones, quæ in electionibus exoriri solebant. Otho autem hanc concessionem grato suscipiens animo, ut se vicissim erga sedem Romanam beneficum exhiberet, restituit omnia quæ vel Constantinus donasse fingitur: &c.—J. Balæi Act. Rom. Pont. Lib. IV. Leo VIII. p. 131.]

The proofs of T. C. against himself.

wickedness of the Romans in obtruding their friends to the church by bribes, threatenings, and other wicked devices, did restore the interest of choosing the bishop to Otho the emperor[1]." Whereof I also conclude, that it is in the power of the civil magistrate to take order for elections of ministers, and that the consent of the people is not of any necessity required thereunto.

Chapter vi. The Ninth Division.
T. C. Page 36, Sect. 6.

And, if the emperors permitted the election of the bishop to that city, where it made most for their surety to have one of their own appointment, as was Rome, which with their bishops did oftentimes put the good emperors to trouble; it is to be thought that in other places, both cities and towns, they did not deny the elections of ministers[2] to the people; besides that certain of those constitutions are not of Rome, but of any city whatsoever. And these emperors were and lived between 500. and odd years until the very point of a thousand years after Christ; so that hitherto this liberty was not gone out of the church, albeit the pope, which brought in all tyranny, and went about to take all liberty from the churches, was now on horseback, and had placed himself in that antichristian seat.

Jo. Whitgift.

In that the emperors did but "permit" such "elections to the people," it is manifest that the interest was in them; else why should they be said to have "permitted" it? Indeed true it is that the emperors so long did remit of their interest in such elections, that afterwards, when they would have claimed their right therein, they could not obtain it, but by violence were shut from all; as the histories manifestly declare[3].

T. C. hath not reasoned ad idem.

Hitherto you have proved nothing in question, neither have you reasoned *ad idem*; for you should either have proved that the election of ministers doth of necessity pertain to the people, or that the same manner of electing is convenient for this church of England in this time and state: both which I have improved, and do still utterly deny, neither doth anything that you have alleged prove either of them.

[1 Leo VIII. comperta Romanorum nequitia, qui suos in electione pontificis ecclesiæ obtrudere consueverunt largitionibus, minis, aut aliis malis artibus, jus eligendi pontificem olim Carolo magno datum consensu synodi Ottoni I. restituit.—R. Barns, Vit. Rom. Pont. Witeb. 1536. fol. N iiii. 2.]

[2 Of the ministers, Repl. 1 and 2.]

[3 Cartwright rejoins that he spoke of the emperor permitting elections, because he might by power and violence have taken the elections from the churches; but "it followeth not that he might without breach of God's law take them from the church."—Sec. Repl. p. 256.]

Chapter vi. The Tenth Division.
Answer to the Admonition, Page 45, Sect. 3.

Therefore this diversity of the state of the church requireth a diverse kind of government, and another kind of ordaining ministers. For this cause, *in Concilio Laodicensi*, which was anno 334, it was decreed that the election of ministers should not be permitted to the people[5].

Concil. Laod.[4]

T. C. Page 37, Sect. 1, 2.

Those that write the Centuries suspect this canon, and doubt whether it be a bastard or no, considering the practice of the church. But here, or ever you were aware, you have stricken at yourself. For before you said that this order of choosing the minister by voices of the church was but in the apostles' time, and during the time of persecution. And the first time you can allege this liberty to be taken away was in the 334. year of our Lord, which was at the least 31. years after that Constantine the great began to reign. I say, at the least, because there be good authors that say that this council of Laodicea was holden anno 338, after the death of Jovinian the emperor; and so there is 35. years between the beginning of Constantine's reign and this council. Now I think you will not say that the church was under persecution in Constantine's time. And therefore you see you are greatly deceived in your account.

Now[6], *if it be as lawful for us to use M. Calvin's authority, which both by example and writings hath always defended our cause, as it is for you to wring him and his words to things which he never meant, and the contrary whereof he continually practised, then this authority of yours is dashed. For M. Calvin saith, whereas it is said in that council that the election should not be permitted to the people, it meaneth nothing else but that they should make no election without having some ministers or men of judgment to direct them in their election, and to gather their voices, and provide that nothing be done tumultuously, even as Paul and Barnabas were chief in the election of the churches*[7]. *And even the same order would we have kept in elections continually for avoiding of confusion; for, as we would have the liberty of the church preserved, which*

This is untrue; as shall appear.

An untruth; for I said not so.

The church was under persecution in Constantine's time by the space of 13. years; for the Maxentius and Licinius did then persecute.

Upon the Acts xvi.

[4 Council of Laodicea, Answ. 2.]

[5 Concil. Laod. can. 13. in Concil. Stud. Labb. et Cossart. Lut. Par. 1671-2. Tom. I. col. 1497. See before, page 366, note 6. It is uncertain when this council was held. Labbe and Cossart place it A. D. 320; but they add that it is also ascribed to A. D. 364, 357, 367.]

[6 And, Repl. 2.]

[7 Ergo in pastoribus creandis libera fuit populi electio; sed ne quid tumultuose fieret, præsident Paulus et Barnabas, quasi moderatores. Sic intelligi debet Laodicensis concilii decretum, quod vetat plebi electionem permitti.— Calvin. Op. Amst. 1667-71. Comm. in Act. Apost. cap. xiv. 23. Tom. VI, p. 132.]

Christ hath bought so dearly, from all tyranny, so do we again condemn and utterly abhor the¹ barbarous confusion and disorder.

Jo. Whitgift.

Where do "those that write the Centuries suspect that canon?" Why note you not the place? There is not one word tending to that end in that place where they speak of this council. Neither, as I think, are you able to shew any such thing affirmed by them; and it is the first time that ever I either read or heard it doubted, whether this were a canon of that council or no. In the iv. Cent. col. 435. I find these words: *Variant ab hac consuetudine, mirum qua veritate, constitutiones concilii Laodiceni, quæ ordinationes judicio multitudinis fieri prohibuerunt*² : "The constitutions of the council of Laodicea, which forbad the ordaining (of ministers) to be done by the judgment of the multitude, do vary from this custom (of electing by the people), it is marvel by what truth." But no man can hereof gather that they "doubt whether this" canon "be a bastard or no:" only they doubt whether this decree was made according to the truth. The general council at Constantinople, which is called *Synodus* 6., did both allow this council and ratify it³.

It is not greatly material at what time this council was holden; neither doth it follow that, because this decree was now made against such elections of the people, therefore the people had before this time in all places interest in electing of ministers: for it may be that some claimed this interest, and moved the people to contend for it then, as you do now; and therefore the synod might upon that occasion make this determination; as the like might be made at this time in this church of England, against such parishes as take upon them the election of their pastors, as you before affirmed some to do⁴; and yet we could not thereupon truly conclude that before the time of this prohibition the election of ministers was either generally or orderly committed to the people in this church of England.

[¹ All, Repl. 1 and 2.]
[² Centur. Eccles. Hist. Basil. 1560, &c. Cent. iv. cap. vi. col. 435; where *quia veritate*.]
[³ Concil. Quinisext. can. 2. in Concil. Stud. Labb. et Cossart. Lut. Par. 1671-2. Tom. VI. col. 1139.]
[⁴ See before, page 84.]

I have not in any place said that "this order of choosing the minister by the voices of the church was but in the apostles' time, and during the time of persecution," neither yet that they could claim it of duty in either of these times, or that it was then general and in all places; for I have before shewed the contrary.

And, where you "think that" I "will not say the church was under persecution in Constantine's time" (though it be not material), yet must I tell you that I think it was: for even then Maxentius and Licinius did persecute, and continued in persecuting by the space of 13. years after Constantine began his reign; and it is said of Licinius that he killed many thousands of Christians.

The church in persecution in Constantine's time.

I have not at any time "wrung M. Calvin's words" to any other sense than he himself hath written them: if it be otherwise, make it known; for I have dealt plainly and set down his words; so have not you. In his Institutions, *cap. viii. sect.* 63. thus he writeth of this council: *Est quidem et illud fateor, &c.*[5]: "And surely I confess that it was upon great reason decreed in the council of Laodicea that the election should not be permitted to the multitude; for it scarcely at any time happeneth that so many heads should with one consent determine anything; and that saying is almost true, that the unstable multitude is divided into contrary factions, &c." Then doth he tell what order was observed in elections: first the clergy only did choose, then did they offer him whom they had chosen to the magistrate, or to the senate and chief rulers, who after deliberation did confirm the election, if they liked of it; if not, then did they choose another whom they thought to be more meet. In the end, the matter was propounded to the multitude, rather to know their desire, and require their testimony, than to give them any interest either of choosing or refusing: this is the sum of Calvin's meaning, and this, he saith, was the meaning of that council; which I say is, in effect, to take away the election from the people.

Calvin of the council of Laodicea.

Your note in the margent must be corrected; for Calvin

[5 Est quidem et illud, fateor, optima ratione sancitum in Laodicensi concilio, ne turbis electio permittatur. Vix enim unquam evenit ut tot capita uno sensu rem aliquam bene componant: et fere illud verum est, *Incertum scindi studia in contraria vulgus*, &c.—Calvin. Op. Amst. 1667-71. Inst. Lib. IV. cap. iv. 12. Tom. IX. p. 288.]

hath no such thing "upon the xvi. of the Acts;" but the like he hath upon the xiv.; howbeit the words of the council be plain: *Quod non sit permittendum turbis electiones eorum facere qui sunt ad sacerdotium provehendi*[1]: "That it ought not to be permitted unto the multitude to make elections of them which should be preferred to the ministry." And there can be no doubt of the meaning of the council; because it appeareth in the 12. canon, that they would have bishops preferred to ecclesiastical dignity by the judgment of the metropolitan and other bishops[2].

"Liberty" and "tyranny" be too common in your mouth. It is no "tyranny" to restrain the people from that liberty that is hurtful to themselves, and must of necessity engender contentions, tumults, and confusion[3].

Chapter vi. The Eleventh Division.

T. C. Page 37, Sect. 3.

But, if councils be of so great authority to decide this controversy, then the most famous council of Nice will strike a great stroke with you; which in an epistle that it writeth unto the church of Egypt (as Theodoret maketh mention) speaketh thus: " It is meet that you should have power both to choose any man, and to give their names which are worthy to be amongst the clergy, and to do all things absolutely according to the law and decrees of the church; and, if it happen any to die in the church, then that those[4] *which were last taken to*[5] *be promoted to the honour of him that is dead, with this condition, if they be worthy, and the people choose them, the bishop of the city of Alexandria together giving his consent and appointing him."*

Jo. Whitgift.

The council in that epistle first declareth what was done with Arius; then what became of Melitius, how he was deposed

[1 Concil. Laod. can. 13. in Concil. Stud. Labb. et Cossart. Lut. Par. 1671-2. Tom. I. col. 1497. See before, page 366, note 6.]

[2 Can. 12. ibid. See ibid.]

[3 Cartwright rejoins that he "might have used the authority of the Centuries to the utter rejection of the canon of the council of Laodicea:" he proceeds to insist that the canon "cannot be understood to seclude the people from the election," and charges Whitgift with "opposing the authors to themselves," and with "most unfaithful dealing," in citing Calvin's Institutions.—Sec. Repl. pp. 256, 7.]

[4 Then those, Repl. 2.]   [5 Taken are to, Repl. 2.]

from his bishoprick, and yet suffered to remain in his own city, but to have no authority of choosing or ordaining ministers, either in the province or in any other city. After it sheweth that such as were ordained and made ministers, or promoted by him, should keep their ministry and honour, but not have any authority in elections, or in preferring of any to any degree of ministry; whereupon it by and by followeth: *Qui* *vero Dei gratia, &c.*[6] : "But those that, by the grace of God and your prayers, have not been factious and schismatical, but kept themselves undefiled in the catholic and apostolic church, it is meet that they should have authority and power both to choose any man, and to give their names which are worthy to be of the clergy, and to do all things according to the laws and decrees of the church." Their meaning is evident, that such only of the clergy should have to do in electing or preferring any to the ministry, which have not been schismatical and factious in the time of heresy: for these words of the council are not spoken of the people, but of the clergy, as the circumstance of the place doth declare; which thing Jacobus Grinæus noteth in the margent, in these words: *Jura clericorum qui orthodoxi manserunt*[7]. That which followeth, "and if it happen any to die in the church, &c.," doth argue that the people had a consent in those churches, according to the orders whereof the council would have them to proceed; but it maketh no new law for it, neither doth it decree anything as concerning it. And it is evident that their order herein was not general, but particular to those churches; for it followeth after in the same epistle: *Hæc proprie et peculiariter ad Ægyptum atque sanctissimam Alexandrinam ecclesiam pertinent.* So that it is manifest

The Lib. i. cap. 9.

This order was peculiar to Egypt and Alexandria.

[6 Τοὺς δὲ χάριτι Θεοῦ καὶ εὐχαῖς ὑμετέραις ἐν μηδενὶ σχίσματι εὑρεθέντας, ἀλλ' ἀκηλιδώτους ἐν τῇ καθολικῇ καὶ ἀποστολικῇ ἐκκλησίᾳ ὄντας, ἐξουσίαν ἔχειν καὶ προχειρίζεσθαι, καὶ ὄνομα ἐπιλέγεσθαι τῶν ἀξίων τοῦ κλήρου, καὶ ὅλως πάντα ποιεῖν κατὰ νόμον καὶ θεσμὸν τὸν ἐκκλησιαστικόν. εἰ δέ τινα ποτὲ συμβαίη ἀναπαύσασθαι τῶν ἐν τῇ ἐκκλησίᾳ, τηνικαῦτα συναναβαίνειν εἰς τὴν τιμὴν τοῦ τετελευτηκότος τοὺς ἄρτι προσληφθέντας, μόνον εἰ ἄξιοι φαίνοιντο καὶ ὁ λαὸς αἱροῖτο, συνεπιψηφίζοντος αὐτοῖς καὶ ἐπισφραγίζοντος τοῦ τῆς καθολικῆς Ἀλεξανδρείας ἐπισκόπου...ταῦτά ἐστι τὰ ἐξαίρετα καὶ διαφέροντα Αἰγύπτῳ, καὶ τῇ ἁγιωτάτῃ ἐκκλησίᾳ Ἀλεξανδρέων.—Theod. in Hist. Eccles. Script. Amst. 1695-1700. Lib. I. cap. ix. p. 31.]

[7 Euseb. &c. Eccles. Hist. per Io. Iacob. Grynæum illustr. Basil. 1570. Theod. Lib. I. cap. ix. p. 361.]

that the meaning of the council was not to bind all churches to this order. But all this labour of yours is lost; for you go about to prove that which no man denieth[1].

Chapter vi. The Twelfth Division.
T. C. Page 37, Sect. 4.

Another of the famousest councils, called the council of Constantinople, which was gathered under Theodosius the great (as it is witnessed by the Tripartite story), in an epistle which it wrote to Damasus the pope, and Ambrose, and others, saith thus: "*We have ordained* Lib. ix. cap. 14. *Nectarius the bishop of Constantinople, with the whole consent of the council, in the sight of the emperor Theodosius beloved of God, the whole city together decreeing the same.*" *Likewise he saith that Flavian was appointed by that synod bishop of Antioch, the whole people appointing him*[2].

Jo. Whitgift.

The words in that epistle, both as the Tripartite history and as Theodoret himself reporteth them, *Lib. v. cap.* 9, signify that the whole city was well pleased that Nectarius was chosen to be their bishop, and consented unto it. But it doth not therefore follow that the whole city did choose him. In Theodoret I find these words: *Reverendissimum et Dei amantissimum Nectarium episcopum præposuimus in generali nostro concilio, et præsente amantissimo Dei imperatore Theodosio, cum omnium clericorum ac totius civitatis approbatione*[3]: "We have placed or ordained the most reverend and loving Nectarius in our general council, both Theodosius the emperor, most beloved of God, being present, and also with the approbation of all the clergy and the whole city."

Theod. lib. v. cap. ix.

They say, "we have placed or ordained Nectarius, &c." and they which say so were bishops. Moreover, Theodoret in the chapter that goeth before saith plainly that the pastors

[1 Cartwright maintains what he had alleged from the council of Nice, and says that Whitgift in his Answer "doth but as a man which hath made shipwreck, snatcheth at every thing he can lay hold of at all adventure."—Sec. Repl. pp. 257, 8.]

[2 Cassiod. Hist. Trip. Par. Lib. ix. cap. xiv. fol. S ii. 2.]

[3 Theod. in Hist. Eccles. Script. Amst. 1695-1700. Lib. v. cap. ix. p. 211. The Greek original of the last clause is: παντός τε τοῦ κλήρου καὶ πάσης ἐπιψηφιζομένης τῆς πόλεως.]

TO THE ADMONITION. 411

and ministers did choose him bishop[4]. But be it that the whole city did give their voices, that is no proof that at all times it must of necessity be so.

The same answer I make to your example of Flavianus.

Chapter vi. The Thirteenth Division.

T. C. Page 37, Sect. 5, 6, 7.

Likewise in the council of Carthage, where Augustine was, holden about anno Domini 400, in the first canon of the council it is said: "When he hath been examined in all these, and found fully instructed, then let him be ordained bishop by the common consent of the clerks, and the lay-people, and the bishops of the province, and especially either by the authority or presence of the metropolitan[5]." Needless proofs.

And in the Toletan council, as it appeareth in the 51. Distinction, it was thus ordained: "Let not him be counted a priest of the church (for so they speak), whom neither the clergy nor people of that city where he is a priest doth choose, nor the consent of the metropolitan and other priests in that province had[6] sought after[7]."

Moreover, concilium Cabilonense, which was holden anno Domini 650., in the tenth canon hath this: "If any bishop, after the death of his predecessor, be chosen of any but of the bishops in the same province, and of the clergy and citizens, let another be chosen; and, if it be otherwise, let that ordination be accounted of none effect.[8]" All which councils prove manifestly that, as the people in their elections had the ministers round about, or synods and councils, directing them, so there was none came to be over the people but by their voices and consents.

Jo. Whitgift.

This which is affirmed of these councils is confessed to be true, but not to the purpose; for the question is, not whether

[4] Ταύταις οἱ ἄριστοι ποιμένες ταῖς ὑποθήκαις πεισθέντες Νεκτάριον...ἐπίσκοπον τῆς μεγίστης ἐκείνης ἐχειροτόνησαν πόλεως.—Id. ibid. cap. viii. p. 207.]

[5 Cum in his omnibus examinatus inventus fuerit plene instructus, tunc cum consensu clericorum et laicorum, et conventu totius provinciæ episcoporum, maximeque metropolitani vel auctoritate vel præsentia, ordinetur episcopus.—Concil. Carthag. iv. cap. 1. in Concil. Stud. Labb. et Cossart. Lut. Par.1671-2. Tom. II col. 1199.]

[6 Hath, Repl. 1 and 2.]

[7 Sed nec ille deinceps sacerdos erit, quem nec clerus nec populus propriæ civitatis elegit, vel auctoritas metropolitani vel comprovincialium sacerdotum assensus non exquisivit.—Ex Concil. Tolet. 4. c. 18. in Corp. Jur. Canon. Lugd. 1624. Decret. Gratian. Decr. Prim. Pars, Dist. li. can. 5. col. 272.]

[8 Si quis episcopus de quacumque fuerit civitate defunctus, non ab alio nisi a comprovincialibus, clero, et civibus suis, alterius habeatur electio: sin aliter, hujusmodi ordinatio irrita habeatur.—Concil. Cabilon. can. 10. in Concil. Stud. Labb. et Cossart. Tom. VI. col. 389.]

the people's consent were required at any time or no, but whether it must be required at all times.

Chapter vi. The Fourteenth Division.
Answer to the Admonition, Page 45, Sect. 4.

This alteration of government and orders in the church of Christ is well set out by Ambrose in the iv. to the Ephesians, upon these words, *Et ipse dedit &c.;* where he saith on this sort: "That the number of Christians might increase and be multiplied, in the beginning it was permitted to every one to preach the gospel, to baptize, and to expound the scriptures; but when the church was enlarged, there were certain parishes appointed, and governors and other officers ordained in the church, &c. Therefore the writings of the apostles do not in all things agree with the orders that are now in the church[1]." Thus far Ambrose.

Ambrose.

T. C. Page 38, Sect. 1.

The anabaptists glory of the same calling that you contend for.

Indeed, if you put such dark colours upon the apostles' church as this is, it is no marvel if it ought not to be a patron[2] to us of framing and fashioning our church after it. But, O Lord, who can patiently hear this horrible disorder ascribed to the apostles' church, which here you attribute unto it, that every one hand over head preached, baptized, and expounded the scriptures? what a window, nay, what a gate is opened here to anabaptists to confirm their fantastical opinion, wherein they hold that every man whom the Spirit moveth may come, even from the plough-tail, to the pulpit, to preach the word of God! If you say it is Ambrose' saying, and not yours, I answer, unless you allow it, why bring you it, and that to prove the difference between the apostles' times and these? For, if it be false (as it is most false), then there is no difference here between the apostles' times and ours. Doth not the whole course of the scriptures declare, and hath it not been proved, that there was none that took upon him the ministry in the church but by lawful calling? What is this but to cast dust and dirt of the fairest and beautifullest image that ever was, to make a smoky, disfigured, evil-proportioned image to seem beautiful, to overthrow the apostles' buildings of gold and silver and precious stones, to make a cottage of wood, straw, and stubble to have some estimation, which could have none, the other standing? For in effect so you do, when, to uphold a corrupt use, that came in by the tyranny of the pope, you go about

[1 Ambros. Op. 1686-90. Comm. in Epist. ad Ephes. cap. iv. vv. 11, 12. Tom. II. Append. col. 241. See before, page 218, note 1.]

[2 Patron: pattern.]

to discredit the orders and institutions which were used in the apostles' times, and that with such manifest untruths.

Jo. Whitgift.

This is a very slender answer to Ambrose, whose autho- *Ambrose unworthily rejected by T. C.* rity, both for his excellent learning and virtue, and also for his antiquity, is not to be so contemptuously rejected. The self-same words, and to the same effect, doth Georgius Major in his commentaries upon the first to the Philippians recite out of one Rabanus bishop of Moguntia; who also borrowed them, as it should seem, of Ambrose[3]. Major alloweth well of them, and maketh no such exclamations as you do; and yet a man known to be learned and sound in religion, as his works declare. Likewise the authors of the Centuries, iv. Cent. *cap.* 7, allege this same place of Ambrose and allow of it[4]; and therefore the matter is not so heinous as you make it.

The anabaptists glory of the same calling that you now *Anabaptists pretend* contend for; as it appeareth in the iii. book of M. Bullinger, *a kind of calling by Adver. Anabap. cap. iv.*, whose words be these: *Suam vero* *the people.* *vocationem &c.*[5]: "They affirm that their calling is just, *Bullinger.* because they be called and sent of their churches, but our vocation to be unlawful, which is made of the magistrate; and therefore that they are sent of God, but we of the world and of men." You know that this was one of the first things that the rustical anabaptists moved sedition for, and that they required it of the magistrates; as Sleidan declareth, *Lib. v.:* *Ex his postulatis*, saith he, *primum erat, ut ipsis liceret* *Sleidan. ecclesiæ ministros eligere, qui verbum Dei pure doceant*[6]:

[3 Et Rabanus, qui ante annos septingentos Moguntiæ episcopus fuit, in quadam epistola sic refert: Primum &c. Ut ergo cresceret plebs et multiplicaretur, omnibus inter initia concessum est et evangelizare et baptizare, et scripturas in ecclesia explanare. At ubi omnia loca circumplexa est ecclesia, conventicula constituta sunt, et rectores et cetera officia in ecclesiis sunt ordinata, &c. Ideo non per omnia conveniunt scripta apostoli ordinationi quæ nunc est in ecclesia.— G. Major. Op. Witeb. 1569-70. Ad Philip. cap. prim. Tom. I. pp. 744, 5. Conf. Hraban. Maur. Op. Col. Agrip. 1626-7. Comm. in Epistt. Paul. Lib. xviii. cap. iv. Tom. V. p. 439.]

[4 Centur. Eccles. Hist. Basil. 1560, &c. Cent. iv. cap. vii. col. 491.]

[5 Suam vero vocationem justam esse anabaptistæ ostendunt ex eo, quod a suis ecclesiis vocati et missi sint; nostram vocationem, quæ a magistratu facta sit, illegitimam esse: itaque se a Deo, nos a mundo sive ab hominibus missos esse.—H. Bullinger. Adv. Anabapt. Libri vi. Tigur. 1560. Lib. iii. cap. iv. fol. 87. 2.]

[6 Ex iis postulatis &c.—J. Sleidan. Comm. Argent. 1572. Lib. v. fol. 50. 2.]

"Of those requests the first was, that they might choose ministers of the church, which might teach the word of God purely." You see therefore that the anabaptists, many of them, require a vocation, and one not much unlike that which you strive for in this place and at this time. When Ambrose saith that it was permitted to every man to "preach the gospel, &c.," he doth not say that it was permitted unto them without some kind of calling: if you will view the place well, and consider it at large, as it is in Ambrose, your heat will be something quenched, I doubt not.

It is no derogation at all from the apostolical church to have the orders of it in divers points altered: for, though such were most convenient then for that state, time, and persons, yet are they not so now in respect of this state, time, and persons; so that the form of the apostolical churches was then perfite and absolute, though now it admit (in the respect of divers circumstances) alteration[1].

Chapter vi. The Fifteenth Division.

Answer to the Admonition, Page 45, Sect. ult.

Musculus. Musculus also in his Common-places, answering to this question, why that ministers of the word are not chosen now by the ministers and the people, as they were in the primitive church, but appointed by the magistrate, saith thus: *Talis tum ecclesiarum erat status, ut aliter non essent eligendi ministri, quia christiano magistratu destituebantur. Si revocas temporum illorum mores, primum conditiones et statum quoque illorum revoca*[2]: "Such was then the state of churches that they could choose their ministers no otherwise, because they had no christian magistrates. If thou wouldest have the manners and customs of those times observed, then must thou call back their conditions and state."

Beza. [☞ Beza, *Lib. Confess. cap. v.*, speaking of this matter

[1 Cartwright rejoins: "If you would have done simply, you should have named Pighius, who proveth diversity of government of the church as you do by this counterfeit place of Ambrose;" and adds: "That which is brought out of Bullinger and Sleidan is but filling up of paper."—Sec. Repl. p. 259.]

[2 Wolfg. Muscul. Loc. Comm. Theol. Basil. 1599. De Magistr. p. 633. See before, page 394, note 2.]

writeth thus: "Because the multitude is for the most part ignorant and untractable, and oftentimes the greater part doth overcome the better, even in a popular state lawfully appointed, all things are not committed to the unruly people, but certain magistrates are appointed by consent of the people, to govern the common sort and multitude. Now, if this wisdom be required in worldly affairs, much more is a moderation necessary in those things wherein men oftentimes see but little. Neither is there any cause why any man of sound judgment should cry out and say that here is no place for wisdom or policy; except he can shew this wisdom or policy whereof I speak to be against the word of God; which truly I do not believe. For we must not simply look what was done of the apostles in *politia ecclesiastica*, in the government of the church, seeing there is most divers circumstances, and therefore without preposterous zeal all things in all places and at all times cannot be brought to one and the same form: but we must rather have respect unto their end and purpose; and that manner and form is to be used that may best bring that to pass. What then was their end and purpose, when they appointed pastors and deacons in those churches which were planted by them? Truly this, that those which were chosen might be (as near as they could) irreprehensible, and not obtruded violently unto their flock. As oft as they could bring that to pass by a general consent, they used it; but, when they could not so bring it to pass, as I think, they did never use it. For it appeareth that, when one was to be chosen into the place of Judas the traitor, there was propounded by the apostles to the multitude those whom they thought to be most meet. In the election of the deacons it was something otherwise done, lest the fidelity of the apostles might by any means be suspected. But, although we grant that in the apostles' time the whole church in such matters gave their voices, yet I think no man will bind all churches to this one form, if it be manifest that for the multitude and ignorance of the people and wickedness of many a door may be opened to wolves; for then in those churches that be builded or reformed all things must not be committed to the voices of the multitude; neither yet are the pastors to be chosen without the consent of the church, &c.¹"

In these words of Beza these things be plain:

1 First, that there is a discreet policy to be used in the church, the same not being repugnant to the word of God.

2 Secondly, that we cannot without preposterous zeal follow all things that the apostles did in the government of the church, because of the diversity of time, place, and other circumstances; but that it is sufficient, if we have respect to their end and purpose, that is, to appoint meet ministers.

3 Thirdly, that the apostles themselves in their elections did not always observe one manner and form.

4 Last of all, that all churches in electing ministers are not bound to follow the form used by the apostles, because of the multitude, ignorance, and wickedness of the people.

[¹ Quoniam enim plerumque multitudo imperita est et intractabilis, et major pars sæpe meliorem vincit, ne in democratia quidem legitime constituta omnia permissa sunt effræni vulgo, sed constituti sunt ex populi consensu certi magistratus qui plebi præeant, et inconditam multitudinem regant. Quod si hæc prudentia in negotiis humanis requiritur, multo sane magis opus est certa moderatione in iis rebus in quibus homines prorsus cæcutiunt. Neque causa est cur quisquam sani judicii homo clamitet nullum hic esse prudentiæ locum, nisi hanc prudentiam, de qua loquor, ostendat cum Dei verbo pugnare; quod sane non arbitror. Neque enim simpliciter spectandum quid sit ab apostolis factum in politia ecclesiastica, quum diversissimæ sint circumstantiæ, ac proinde absque κακοζηλίᾳ non possint omnia omnibus locis ac temporibus ad unam eandemque formam revocari: sed potius spectandus est eorum finis et scopus invariabilis, et ea deligenda forma ac ratio rerum agendarum, quæ recta eo deducat. Quid igitur spectarunt apostolici quum pastores et diaconos constituerent in ecclesiis quas ædificabant? Hoc nimirum, ut qui eligebantur, essent, quoad ejus fieri possent, ἀνεπίληπτοι, et invito gregi non obtruderentur. Id quoties fieri commode potuit missis in suffragium singulis, ea ratione factum est: quoties autem non potuit, nunquam, ut opinor, est factum. Apparet enim quum eligendus esset qui in Judæ proditoris locum succederet, fuisse multitudini propositos ab apostolis eos quos maxime idoneos censebant. In diaconorum electione videtur paulo aliter actum, ne ullo modo suspecta esset eo tempore apostolorum fides. Sed etiam si demus apostolorum temporibus totam ecclesiam, quum de his rebus ageretur, semper missam fuisse in suffragia, nemo tamen, opinor, ad hanc unam formam adstringet omnes ecclesias, si manifestum fuerit propter vulgi multitudinem, et imperitiam, et multorum etiam improbitatem ita fore ut lupis aditus patefiat. Tum ergo ne in ædificatis quidem ecclesiis erunt omnia suffragiis multitudinis committenda, neque tamen absque totius ecclesiæ consensu deligendi fuerint pastores, &c.—Th. Bezæ Confess. Christ. Fid. Genev. 1587. cap. v. 35. pp. 151, &c.]

TRACT. III.]   TO THE ADMONITION.   417

The same Beza in the same book and chapter saith that "in the election of deacons Luke hath not described what the church used; but in another place we may gather out of Paul, Acts xiv., that they of Asia used lifting up of hands: and therefore no man may here prescribe any certain rule; but, if the conscience be good, it is an easy matter to determine what is most expedient for time, place, and other circumstances[2]."

The words be plain, that the apostles have prescribed no certain form (at all times and in all places to be used) for the ordering of ministers, and that every church hath to respect the scope and purpose of the apostles (that meet ministers may be had), and not their manner of doing.

Zuinglius, in his book called *Ecclesiastes*, sheweth that there was three kinds of electing ministers used even in the apostles' time: his words be these: "Some were chosen by the whole consent of the faithful gathered together in one place: other some were chosen by the apostles only; and some we may find whom one only apostle did elect and send, as Titus, whom Paul left in Creta, committing unto him the cure of that church[3]."

Zuinglius.

Hereby it may appear, that there is no one certain form of calling and electing ministers prescribed and commanded in the scriptures at all times to be observed, but that the church hath liberty to ordain and appoint the same, as time and other circumstances require; so that the end and purpose of the apostles be observed, that is, that there be fit and meet ministers.   ][4]

T. C. Page 38, Sect. 2, 3, 4, 5, 6, 7, 8, ult.; and Page[5] 39, Sect. 1, 2.

The place is too common which you assign; you had I am sure the book before you; you might have told where the place was, and in what title. But that place of Musculus, in the title of the magistrate, is answered by himself in the same book, where he entreateth of the election of the ministers. For, going about (as it seemeth) to satisfy some of their ministers, which were brought in doubt of their calling because they were not chosen by their

[² Id. ibid. 37. p. 154. See before, page 365, note 2.]
[³ H. Zvingl. Op. Tigur. 1581. Ecclesiast. Pars II. fol. 53. 2. See before, page 343, note 5.]
[⁴ The passage between brackets is inserted from Answ. 2.]
[⁵ Sect., old editions.]

[WHITGIFT.]   27

churches, speaking of the use of the church in choosing their minister he saith thus:

First, it must be plainly confessed that the ministers were in times past chosen by consent of the people, and ordained and confirmed of the seniors.

Secondarily, that that form of election was apostolical and lawful.

Thirdly, that it was conformable to the liberty of the church, and that thrusting the pastor upon the church, not being chosen of it, doth agree to a church that is not free, but subject to bondage.

Fourthly, that this form of choice by the church maketh much, both to that that the minister may govern his flock with a good conscience, as also that the people may yield themselves to be easilier ruled than when one cometh against their wills unto them.

And, to conclude all these, he saith that they are altogether certain, and such as cannot be denied. After he saith that the corrupt estate of the church and religion driveth to alter this order, and to call the election to certain learned men, which should after be confirmed of the prince. And, that it may yet more clearly appear that his judgment is nothing less than to confirm this election, he setteth down their election in Bernland, which he approveth and laboureth to make good, as one which, although it doth not fully agree with the election of the primitive church, yet cometh very near unto it: as that not one man, but all the ministers in the city of Berne, do choose a pastor, when there is any place void.

Afterward he is sent to the senate, from the which, if he be doubted of, he is sent again to the ministers to be examined: and then, if they find him meet, he is confirmed of the senate (which standeth of some number of the people), and by the most part of their voices. By these things it appeareth that this election of the minister by the people is lawful and apostolic, and confessed also by him that those that are otherwise bring with them subjection unto the church and servitude, and carry a note and mark of corruption of religion.

Last of all, that he goeth about to defend the election used in the churches where he was minister by this, that it approached unto the election in the primitive church[1]. Now what cause there may be that we should bring the church into bondage, or take away the[2] order whereby both the minister may be better assured of his calling, and the people may the willinglier submit themselves unto their pastors and governors, or what cause to depart from the apostolic form of the choice of the pastor, being lawful, I confess I know not, and would be glad to learn.

To assign the cause hereof unto the christian magistrate, and to say that these things cannot be had under him (as you under Master Musculus' name do affirm), is to do great injury unto the office of the magistrate, which abridgeth not the liberty of the church, but defendeth it, diminisheth not the pastor his assurance of his calling, but rather increaseth it, by establishing the ordinary callings only, which in the time of persecution sometimes are not so ordinary, withdraweth not the obedience of the people from the pastor, but urgeth it where it is not, and constraineth it where it

[1 See below, page 421, note 1.] [2 That, Repl. 2.]

is not voluntary. And, seeing that also Musculus saith that these forced *Musculus' meaning per-* elections are remedies for corruption of religion and disordered states, *verted.* what greater dishonour can there be done unto the holy institution of God in the civil governor, than to say that these forced elections, without the consent of the people, must be where there is a christian magistrate? as though there could be no pure religion under him, when as indeed it may be easily under him pure, which can hardly, and with great danger, be pure without him. And, when as it is said that the church's consent should be had in the election of the minister, we do not deny the confirmation of *Here you are* the elections unto the godly civil magistrate, and the disannulling of them, *soon gone from your* if the church in choosing, and the ministers in directing, shall take any *apostolical form.* unfit man; so that yet he do not take away the liberty from the church of choosing a more convenient man.

So that you see that by Musculus' your witness' reasons this enforced election, without the consent of the people, is but corrupt, and so ought not to be in the church; and that, although it hath been borne withal, yet it must be spoken against, and the lawful form of election laboured for, of all those that love the truth and the sincerity thereof.

Jo. Whitgift.

Turpe est doctori, &c.: you have before told us what *T. C. tripped in that* Justinian saith *in Codice*; also of "an epistle sent from the *wherein he findeth fault* council of Nice unto the church of Egypt, as Theodoret maketh *with other.* mention;" of the "council of Carthage;" of "Toletane coun- *Pag. 36, sect. 2.* *Pag. 37,* Pag. 72, cil³;" and afterward you tell us what "Augustine and *sect. 3.* sect. 3. *Page 37,* Gratian say," and will that "the Centuries should be *Ibidem,* seen," &c.; and yet you neither tell us in what part of Justi- *sect. 6. Pag. 41,* nian's Code, in what book or chapter of Theodoret, in what *Pag. 71,* council of Carthage, or of Toledo, in what tome of Augustine, *sect. 6.* or part of Gratian, in what century or book of Centuries; which all require much more time to search out than this of Musculus, and especially your law, which (for any thing that I can perceive) asketh so long a search *in Codice Justiniani*, that I think it will never be found there. But it is no great marvel; for you report them as the author doth of whom you borrow them, without any further search or trial. But, to put you out of doubt, this place of Musculus is *Titulo de Magistratibus*.

Musculus indeed confesseth that in the apostles' time "ministers were chosen by the people, and ordained and confirmed by the elders." And, after that he hath shewed this manner of election to have been used in Cyprian's time, he addeth

[³ See before, pages 396, 408, 11, and below, page 443.]

<small>Tit. de Verbi Ministris.</small> and saith: *Ad hunc itaque modum eligebantur*[1], *&c.* : "After this manner in times past were ministers, bishops, and deacons elected; the which form also of electing churches retained unto the time of christian princes and magistrates, whose consent was required in the election of bishops, and that worthily; for it is not meet that those things, which are to be done publicly and concern the people which be their subjects, and pertain unto them in respect of religion (except we will say with the anabaptists, that Christians ought not to be magistrates), should be done without their consent."

After this, he declareth how the bishop of Rome, in the end, spoiled the magistrate and the people also of this liberty; and, when he hath spoken against the abuses of the Roman church in that matter, he maketh an objection of such churches as profess the gospel, saying: "But some peradventure will object that those churches, which in our time will seem to have reformed religion, receive their ministers of the magistrate, and not by any election of the people." To this objection he saith that he is compelled to answer for their sakes, " who, though they faithfully labour in the word of the Lord, yet do they doubt whether their vocation be lawful or no, because they were not elected and ordained according to the apostolical form." And, having confessed those points that you here set down, he maketh this resolution: *Verum si consideres diversum ecclesiæ statum, &c.*: "If thou shalt consider the divers state of the church, thou must confess that that, which in itself is apostolical, lawful, and usual, and convenient for the liberty of the churches, *primis quidem ecclesiæ temporibus prodesse potuisse, nostris vero non ita;* might well profit the church in the beginning, but not so in our time. For then there was not such a multitude of Christians, but that the minister without tumult might by common consent be chosen; which thing at this day were very hard to be done. Moreover, then the minds of the faithful were not so generally infected with common errors, nor so blinded with false worshippings, but they remained as yet in the doctrine and religion which they had received of the apostles: wherefore it might well

[[1] Ad hunc itaque modum eligebantur olim presbyteri, episcopi et diaconi, quem ecclesiæ in usu retinuerunt usque ad tempora christianorum principum et magistratuum, quorum consensus ad electionem episcoporum requirebatur, nec immerito. Non enim &c.—Wolfg. Muscul. Loc. Comm. Theol. Basil. 1599. De Ministr. Verb. Dei, p. 198. See before, page 393, note 5.]

be, that a true minister might be chosen by their common suffrages. But, after that the number of Christians was increased to an infinite multitude, and, first, schisms, then general ignorance, blindness, and sundry kinds of superstition, invaded the church, &c., there could no longer any true and sincere minister be elected by the general consent of the people, &c.: wherefore, for the condition of the time, necessity itself required that princes and magistrates should commit this matter to certain wise men careful for the church, by whose means meet pastors might be placed, &c." Then he addeth that "for the circumstances of time, as in all churches the apostolical form of electing and ordaining cannot be restored, so is there no cause why the minister of Christ, being called to preach the gospel by a godly prince and magistrate, should doubt of his calling, whether it be right and christian, or no. But he must remember that, where the state of the church and of religion is corrupt, another way must be found out to remedy the same than that which was used in the churches when all things was safe and sound[2]." In the end he declareth what

[2 Sed objecerit forsan ecclesias eas quisquam, quæ nostra ætate, cum quæ in doctrina et religione christiana desiderabantur reformasse videri velint, et ipsæ non adhibita plebe ministros verbi eligunt, sed a magistratu traditos accipiunt. Cogor hac de re quid sentiam dicere, haud propter eos qui hoc nobis objiciunt, sed propter rudiores et imbecilliores, qui licet in verbo Domini fideliter ministrent, de vocatione sua tamen subinde addubitare solent, sitne legitima vel secus, propterea quod non sunt electi et ordinati ad formam apostolicam, qua olim usæ sunt ecclesiæ. Plane fatendum est, fuisse olim ministros Christi præsente et consentiente plebe electos, et a senioribus per impositionem manuum ordinatos et confirmatos, quemadmodum supra ostendimus: deinde et eam eligendi formam esse apostolicam et legitimam: tertio, conformem esse libertati ac potestati ecclesiæ, cujus Cyprianus meminit: eam vero, qua plebi Christi cœperunt obtrudi homines non ab ipsa electi, convenire ecclesiæ non liberæ, sed servituti subjectæ: quarto pulchre ad hoc facere, ut et minister bona cum conscientia præsit gregi Dominico, a quo est in pastorem, doctorem et episcopum electus, et grex Domini vicissim illi sese facilius moderandum ac pascendum præbeat, quam ei qui præter ipsius est conscientiam, voluntatem, et electionem introductus. Hæc, inquam, omnino sunt certa et irrefragabilia. Verum si consideres diversum ecclesiæ statum, cogeris fateri id quod in se apostolicum, legitimum, usitatum, et liberæ est ecclesiæ conveniens, primis quidem ecclesiæ temporibus prodesse potuisse, nostris vero non ita. Tum enim non erat numerosa adeo plebs fidelium, ut citra tumultum in publicis conventibus omnium nequiret suffragiis eligi minister, id quod hodie fieret difficillime. Deinde non erant animi fidelium catholicis erroribus et falsis cultibus obcæcati, sed hærebant adhuc a doctrina et religione, quam acceperant ab apostolis. Quare commode fieri poterat, ut in medio plebis communibus suffragiis verus eligeretur Christi minister. Postquam vero aucta est in immensum credentium multitudo, et cœperunt obtinere in ecclesiis schismata, deinde passim invaluit catholica cæcitas et ignorantia, et amissa apostolicæ doctrinæ puritate regnarunt

manner of electing and ordaining ministers is used in the church of Berne[1]. Neither doth he in that place, or any other that I know, "go about to defend the election used in the church where he was minister by this, that it approached unto the election of the primitive church;" as you report him to do. Thus have I truly reported Musculus his words in that place, and his order; than the which what can be more directly spoken to my purpose? which is to prove that no one certain manner and form of electing ministers is anywhere appointed to be general and perpetual, but that the same may be altered according to place, time, and persons; and that the manner used in the apostles' time is not meet and convenient for this time. All this, I say, Musculus hath plainly and by good reasons here proved, which he doth also as manifestly confirm in the title *de Magistratibus*: for, after that he hath declared that it pertaineth to the magistrate to appoint church-ministers, he saith, *Dices, At secus factum est in primis ecclesiis, in quibus a ministris et plebe eligebantur ecclesiarum antistites: respondeo, Talis tum ecclesiarum erat status, &c.;* as it is in my Answer[2].

For the subjection and "bondage" of the church, which you so often talk of, this is my answer in few words; that subjection to lawful magistrates, in matters lawful, is no "bondage" to any, but to such as think dutiful obedience to be servitude and "bondage;" as the anabaptists do. Why the

falsa dogmata, et vera religio commutata est variis superstitionum generibus, non potuit amplius communi plebis assensu sincerus eligi Christi minister: ut non sit præter rationem, quod vetus eligendi forma dudum est in Romanis ecclesiis callido episcoporum studio repudiata, et ne in evangelicis quidem statim restitui potuit, propterea quod non potuit confestim haberi communis et catholicus plebis consensus ad eligendum evangelicæ doctrinæ ministrum. Quapropter pro conditione temporum ipsa requirebat necessitas, ut paucorum hominum opera, qui judicio prævalerent, et ecclesiæ Christi consultum cuperent, magistratus et principes ad hoc inducerentur, ut subditis suis fideles ac doctos pastores præficerent, qui illos verbo vitæ ad veram Christi cognitionem instruerent, quantumvis multi adhuc essent, qui doctrinam veritatis aversarentur. Propter hasce temporum circumstantias, ut non potest in omnibus statim ecclesiis apostolica electionis et ordinationis forma restitui; ita non est, cur minister Christi, a pio magistratu vel principe ad prædicandum evangelium vocatus, de vocatione sua, sitne recta et christiana vocatus, hæsitet ac fluctuet: sed cogitandum est, ubi corruptus est ecclesiæ ac religionis status, alium esse quærendum modum rebus corruptis consulendi, quam eum qui usitatus fuit in ecclesiis, quum omnia essent salva et integra.—Id. ibid. p. 199.]

[1 Id. ibid. p. 200. See before, page 309, note 3.]
[2 See before, page 414.]

people are debarred from electing (which you call "the apostolical form of the choice of the pastor"), you may learn by that which hath been hitherto spoken, if you be so desirous to learn as you would seem to be.

That the minister may be well assured of the lawfulness of his calling, though he be not called of the people, you have also heard of Musculus, who of purpose answereth that doubt. He that is sure of an inward calling need not to doubt of his outward calling, if it be according to the manner and form of that church wherein he is called. The minister may be assured of his calling, though he be not chosen by the people.

That the people do as willingly now submit themselves to their pastors and governors (though they have no interest in electing of them) as they did then, experience teacheth in all places where there be good and virtuous pastors, except only in such as you and yours have set on fire with contention and contempt. You say: "To assign the cause hereof to the christian magistrate, &c." We give unto the magistrate that which of duty belongeth unto him, in the respect that he is a christian magistrate, and hath the chief government of the church in all causes, and over all persons; and you, desirous of popularity, withdraw from the magistrate that which is due unto him, giving the same to the people and vulgar sort.

You count it an "abridging of the liberty of the church, a diminishing of the pastor's assurance of his calling, a withdrawing of the people from the pastor," to be short, "a bringing of the people into bondage," for the magistrate to maintain his right in using that kind of appointing ministers, which he thinketh to be most profitable for the church committed unto him; and is not this "to do great injury to the office of the magistrate?" Why do you not plainly say that the queen's majesty "abridgeth the liberty of the church, diminisheth the pastor's assurance of his calling, withdraweth the people from their pastor, urgeth and constraineth them to that which is voluntary, and bringeth them into bondage," because she will not suffer them to have freedom in the elections of their bishops and pastors? for this is your plain meaning. But temper your popular and undutiful speeches: the true liberty of the church, which is liberty of conscience, and freedom from false doctrine, errors, and superstitions, and not licence for every man to do what himself listeth, was never more in any church; pastors never had better cause to The true liberty of the church.

be assured of their calling; the people at no time more bound to cleave to their pastors; never less cause to complain of urging constraint, servitude, or bondage, than they have at this day under her majesty: but you go about to persuade them to the contrary, which whereunto it tendeth would be in time considered.

T. C. transferreth the corruptions of men's minds to the government.

Musculus saith that this manner of ordering ministers (for he doth not call it "forced elections") is a remedy against "corrupted states," not in respect of laws, government, magistrate, or religion by authority established, but of men's minds that are corrupted with errors, contentions, and sinister affections; and this is no "dishonour to the civil governor." For, if in a kingdom there be many wayward and disordered persons, the fault is in themselves, and not in the magistrate, nor in the kind of government, but a great commendation rather, when as by the diligence of the magistrate and profitable kind of government such disordered persons be corrected and reformed, or at the least kept under and restrained. Is it "a dishonour" to the prince, that, whereas she found the whole realm corrupted in doctrine, now it is otherwise, though not in the hearts of many, yet in external form and public regiment? Wherefore you do but subtilly (I will not say contemptuously) transfer that to the magistrate and kind of government, which Musculus meaneth of the corrupt minds and affections of the common sort of men.

T. C. urgeth the apostolical form, and yet bringeth in that which is not apostolical.

You add that, "when it is said that the church's consent should be had in the election of the minister, &c.;" but how shall we know that you mean as you speak? for you have no warrant so to do in any apostolical election, or in any form used in the apostles' time. Wherefore either you must break that rule which you would have both to be perfit, and perpetual for all times and states; or else do you but dissemble with the magistrate, and mind nothing less than that you say you would do.

The absurdities of the device of T. C.

But as good never a whit, as never a deal the better; for the magistrate must confirm them or reject them, "if he be godly, and take not from the church her liberty in choosing." First, what if the magistrate be ungodly? or who shall judge whether he be so or no? or how shall the magistrate know when the church in choosing, and the ministers in directing, shall take any unfit man? who shall complain to the prince of his unfitness, if both the ministers and people think him fit? or who shall judge of his fitness? or what privilege shall the magistrate have hereby, when he must have one of the people's electing, whether he will or no, or else must the church be destitute? Surely the magistrate should have a good office to be so troubled with such elections in this church of England. In good sadness tell me, do you not see the absurdities of these your fond and troublesome devices? or are you so blind, that you perceive not how far you would swerve from the form, which you say was used by the apostles, when you give to the civil magistrate the confirmation of ministers, which they in their time kept to themselves?

Musculus hath in most plain manner taught the self-same thing that I have done; as it may appear to all those that will understand; but you of purpose would blind both yourself and others[1].

¶ That bishops have authority to admit and ordain ministers.

Chapter vii. The First Division.

Admonition.

Now that authority is given into the hands of the bishop alone, who by his sole authority thrusteth upon them such as they many times, as well for unhonest life as also for lack of learning, may and do justly dislike[2].

Answer to the Admonition, Page 46, Sect. 1.

That bishops have authority to admit ministers (which is here denied), it is plain by that which is written, 1 Tim. v.: *Manus cito ne cui imponas:* "Lay thy

Bishops have authority to admit ministers[3].

[1 Cartwright answers: "I gave you as ready a way to find those testimonies as I had given me. If you took it out of Musculus yourself, then might have noted the place: if you had it of others, you should have named your collector, as I did mine. Here is occasion taken to repeat and translate a great deal out of Musculus, but nothing to purpose. For I deny not but that he is of judgment that a man constrained by corruption of times may depart from the apostolical election in shutting out the people; but I deny that that is warranted by substantial arguments. Beside I have shewed that here in words against us, in his reasons he standeth for us." He then goes on at great length to argue against Whitgift's deductions, and accuses him of begging the question.—Sec. Repl. pp. 259, &c.]

[2 This portion of the Admonition having appeared before (see page 341) is not inserted here in Answ.]

[3 This marginal note is inserted from Answ. 2.]

hands rashly on none." These words Ambrose[1], Chrysostom[2], and all learned writers, for the most part, do say to be an admonition to Timothy, that he ought to be circumspect in appointing of ministers. And to Titus, chap. i., Paul saith that he left him at Creta, *ut constituat oppidatim presbyteros;* "that he should appoint ministers in every town." This Hierome and others do expound of the authority that Titus had in placing ministers in every church[3].

T. C. Page 39, Sect. 3, 4, and Page 40, Sect. 1, 2.

A wilful depraving of the Answer.

Now you would prove that this election of ministers by one man was in the apostles' time. But you have forgotten yourself, which said a little before that this election by the church was not only in the apostles' times, but also in the time of Cyprian; now you say otherwise. And, if the election of the minister[4] by the church agree so well with the time of persecution, and when there is no christian magistrate; how cometh it to pass that in those days when persecution was so hot, and there were no such magistrates, that St Paul would have the election by one man, and not by the

Who hath said so?

church? Besides that, if this be St Paul his commandment, that the bishop should only choose the minister, why do you make it an indifferent thing, and a thing in the power of the church to be varied by times? for this is a flat commandment. Thus you see you throw down with one hand as fast as you build with the other. But to answer directly to the place of the fifth of the first to Timothy.

I say, first, that St Paul writeth to Timothy, and therefore instructeth him what he should do for his part in the appointing of the minister. If he had written to the whole church of Ephesus, he would likewise have instructed them how they should have behaved themselves in that business. If one do write unto his friend, that hath interest in any election, to take heed that he choose none but such as are meet, shall any man conclude thereupon that none hath to do in that election but he to whom that letter is written? Then I say, further, that St Paul attributeth that unto Timothy that was common to more with him, because he, being the director and moderator of the election, is said to do that which many do; which thing I have proved

[1 Sub testatione ergo ea, quæ ad ordinationem ecclesiæ mandat custodiri, præcipit nihil fieri sine præjudicio; ne facile aliquis accipiat ecclesiasticam dignitatem, nisi prius de vita ejus et moribus fuerit disputatum; ut dignus approbatus, minister aut sacerdos constituatur, &c.—Ambros. Op. Par. 1686-90. Comm. in Epist. ad Tim. prim. cap. v. vv. 21, 2. Tom. II. Append. col. 301.]

[2 Τί ἐστι ταχέως; μὴ ἐκ πρώτης δοκιμασίας, μηδὲ δευτέρας, μηδὲ τρίτης, ἀλλὰ πολλάκις περισκεψάμενος καὶ ἀκριβῶς ἐξετάσας, κ.τ.λ.—Chrysost. Op. Par. 1718-38. In I. Epist. ad Tim. cap. v. Hom. xvi. Tom. XI. p. 642.]

[3 Hieron. Op. Par. 1693-1706. Comm. in Epist. ad Tit. cap. i. Tom. IV. Pars I. col. 412. See below, page 433.]

[4 Ministry, Repl. 2.]

by *divers examples, both out of the scripture and otherwise, before. And even in this imposition of hands it is manifestly to be shewed: for that, whereas St Paul saith in the second epistle that Timothy was ordained by the putting on of his hands upon him, in the first epistle he saith that he was ordained by the putting on of the hands of the eldership. So that that, which he in one place taketh to himself alone, in the other he communicateth with more*[6]. *Again, it is a fault in you, that you cannot distinguish or put difference between the election and imposition of hands.*

2 Tim. i. 6.[5]
1 Tim. iv. 12.[5]

Last of all, I answer that, although this might agree to Timothy alone, as indeed it cannot, yet it followeth not that every bishop may do so. For Timothy was an evangelist, which was above a bishop; as hereafter shall better appear. And it is an evil argument to say, the greater may do it, therefore the less may do it; the superior, therefore the inferior. If you were at any cost with producing your witnesses, you should not be so wise[7] *to be so lavish of them as to cite Ambrose and Chrysostom to prove a thing that none hath ever denied; for who denieth that St Paul doth not give warning to Timothy to be circumspect? If you mean to use their testimony to prove that he only made the elections, they say never a word for you; if there be any thing, cite it. To the place of Titus I answer as to that of Timothy; for there is nothing there but agreeth also to this place. And as for Hierome, he hath nothing in that place, as he hath in no other, to prove that to the bishop only doth belong the right of the election*[8] *of the minister. I have shewed you reasons before, why it cannot be so taken of the sole election of the bishop, the church being shut out. If authority would do any good in this behalf, as it seemeth it ought, seeing that all your proof throughout the whole book is in the authorities of men (which Aristotle calleth* ἀτέχνας πείσεις, *"uncunning proofs"), I could send you to M. Calvin, which teacheth that it is not to be thought that St Paul would permit to Titus to ordain bishops and ministers by his own authority, when he himself would not take so much upon him, but joined his with the voices of the church*[9]. *But he peradventure savoureth not your taste; and yet you would make men believe sometimes that you make much of him, if you can get but one word unjointed, and racked in pieces from the rest, to make*

As if there were any such thing affirmed.

An untrue accusation.

[5 These verses are inserted from Repl. 2. The last, however, is a mistake for 14.]

[6 Repl. 2 here inserts: *And that he did it not himself alone, it may appear by those words which follow, " and communicate not with other men's sins;" as if he should say, if other will ordain insufficient ministers, yet be not thou carried away with their example. And further, that his authority was equal with other elders of that church, and that he had no superiority above his fellows, it may appear for that he saith, " Lay thy hands rashly of none;" where, if he had had authority over the rest, he would rather have said, Suffer none to lay his hands rashly.*]

[7 Unwise, Repl. 2.]

[8 Of election, Repl. 1 and 2.]

[9 Verum responsio facilis est, non permitti arbitrio Titi ut unus possit omnia, et quos voluerit episcopos ecclesiis imponat: sed tantum jubet ut electionibus præsit tanquam moderator, sicuti necesse est.—Calvin. Op. Amst. 1667-71. Comm. in Epist. ad Tit. cap. i. 5. Tom. VII. p. 497.]

good your part. If he weigh not with you, you have M. Musculus, whom you take to be a great patron of yours in this cause; which doth with greater vehemency affirm the same thing that M. Calvin saith, asking whether any man can believe that Paul permitted in this place to Titus, or in the place before alleged to Timothy, that they should ordain of their own authority, and by themselves, when as Paul would not do it but by the voices and election of the church[1].

Musculus in his Com. Pla. in his title of the election of ministers.

Jo. Whitgift.

Bishops may admit ministers.

The Admonition in the sixth article colourably, but in the 7. plainly, affirmeth that "the right of ordering ministers doth at no hand appertain to the bishop[2]." This do I improve in this place, and prove that the right of ordering and electing ministers doth appertain to the bishop: but I have contented myself with the fewer proofs; because their assertion is so absurd, that it cannot but discredit their learning with all learned men. And whatsoever T. C. hath hitherto said manifestly declareth it to be untrue; yet now it is his pleasure to gloss upon my words, and to say that I "would prove this election of ministers by one man to have been in the apostles' time, &c.:" whereas indeed my words be plain, and my meaning is to prove that the electing and ordering of ministers doth appertain to bishops; I do not say only to bishops.

When you say that the election of the pastor doth appertain to the people, do you mean that it only pertaineth to the people? But, because you think that to be so great a matter, to say that "in the apostles' time the election of ministers was by one man," seeing that I have said before that this election by the church was in the apostles' time and after, I will say now more than I said before, that they be both true; that is, that in the apostles' time there was divers manners of ordaining and electing ministers. For sometime one alone did choose and ordain, sometimes many, sometimes ministers only, and sometime the people also; as it may evidently be

Divers kinds of ordaining and electing ministers in the apostles' time.

[¹ Ergo jejunantes et orantes, quod in cœtu fidelium fieri solebat, ordinarunt presbyteros, a fidelibus electos:...Hanc formam eligendi et ordinandi presbyteros et episcopos commendavit etiam cooperariis suis apostolus, Tito ac Timotheo. Sic Tit. i. dicit: Hujus rei gratia reliqui te in Creta, ut ea quæ desunt corrigas, et constituas per civitates presbyteros, sicut ego disposui tibi. Quis enim credat aliter illum disposuisse Tito, quam ipse ac reliqui apostoli habebant in usu?—Wolfg. Muscul. Loc. Comm. Theol. Basil. 1599. De Ministr. Verb. Dei, p. 198.]

[² See below, page 485.]

gathered, both by that which is spoken before, and by this also that I do say in this place. Zuinglius in his book called *Ecclesiastes* saith thus: "We read in old time of three kinds of elections: some were chosen by the common and general consent of all the faithful gathered together in one place; other some were elected and sent by the apostles only; other some we may find, whom one only apostle did choose and send, as Titus whom Paul left at Creta, committing unto him the care of that church[3]." The like saith M. Bullinger, *Lib. iii. adversus Anabap. cap.* 4: "There is another calling of those, which are also called of God, but by men, which choose and send according to God's ordinance; as when Peter sent Mark, and Paul both called and sent Timothy, Titus, and Luke[4]." Thus you see that it is counted no strange matter to have divers kinds of calling and electing ministers, even in the apostles' time. And therefore, in saying now that "bishops have authority to admit ministers," I say nothing contrary to anything that I have said before, neither yet if I affirm that Timothy and Titus had this authority to themselves alone.

Zuinglius.

Bullinger.

The election of the minister by the church is fittest for the time of persecution; but that doth not seclude from the same time election and calling by one man: neither is this the question, whether choosing by the common consent of the people, or calling and sending by one man, be meetest for the time of persecution; but whether election made by the multitude is fitter for the time of persecution, and when there is no christian magistrate, than for the time of prosperity, and under a christian magistrate; and therefore you do but incumber the reader with false suppositions. Elections by the multitude, or by one only, may be used in the time of persecution, and at other times also, as shall be most expedient for the church.

Where do I say that it is "Paul's commandment that the bishop should only choose the minister"? Undoubtedly this is no true or divine dealing, willingly and wittingly to pervert a man's saying, neither can it come of a good con-

T. C. perverteth the sayings of the answerer.

[3 H. Zvingl. Op. Tigur. 1581. Ecclesiast. Pars II. fol. 53. 2. See before, page 343, note 5.]

[4 Altera vocatio eorum est, qui ipsi quoque a Deo vocantur, sed per homines intermedios, qui ex Dei instituto eligunt et mittunt, veluti cum Petrus Marcum, Paulus vero Timotheum, Titum, et Lucam vocavit et misit.—H. Bullinger. Adv. Anabapt. Libri vi. Tigur. 1560. Lib. iii. cap. iv. fol. 89. 2.]

science, and you have faulted in it very oft. I prove by that which St Paul said to Timothy, 1 Tim. v. ("Lay thy hands rashly on none"), "that a bishop hath authority to admit ministers;" because Timothy, to whom these words were spoken, was a bishop; and learned interpreters do say that St Paul by these words did admonish Timothy that he ought to be circumspect in appointing of ministers: therefore this is not "Paul's commandment," that a bishop only should ordain ministers, but this he giveth in charge to all bishops, in the name of Timothy, that they lay their hands rashly on none; whereby also he plainly signifieth that the ordering and electing of ministers doth appertain unto them; which is denied by the Admonition. Here is then nothing "thrown down that was before builded;" but you cast snow-balls at the windows of the building, which may for a time darken them, till your snow be melt away with the sun.

Touching your "direct answer" (as you call it) to the place, 1 Tim. v., thus I briefly reply, that it is but devised of your own head, not grounded upon any good authority, nor consonant to the circumstance of the place, or course of the epistle. Both Ambrose and Chrysostom and other learned writers (as I have said) do understand it to be meant of the authority that Timothy had in ordering bishops and ministers. The whole epistle and the circumstance of this place do plainly testify that this was spoken to Timothy only in the respect that he was a bishop. The precepts that be contained in this epistle, the most of them, and in this chapter especially, are such as properly pertain to Timothy in the respect that he was a bishop and a minister of the word. To conclude, if the election of a bishop had of necessity pertained to the people, Paul would not have written in this manner to Timothy as he hath done, describing unto him what qualities he that is to be elected bishop ought to have; but he would rather have written the same to the people, or willed Timothy to declare it unto them. Neither doth he anywhere in any of his epistles write to any church, to give them any instructions in this so necessary a matter, but only writeth of the same in those epistles to Timothy and Titus, being bishops; which may be an argument that the ordering of ministers doth properly appertain to a bishop, and that this also, *Manus cito, &c.* is spoken to Timothy in that respect.

"A man may write to his friend that hath interest in an election;" but Paul doth not only write unto Timothy as to one that hath interest, but as to one in whom the whole interest consisteth. When you say that "Paul attributeth that to Timothy that was common to him with more," if you mean more bishops, then it is true; for it is a rule for all bishops to follow: but, if you mean other of the people, then do you but shift off the matter with guessing.

To your proofs of that phrase and kind of speech I have answered before: it is but a starting-hole to fly unto, when you are foiled by the plain and evident words of the scripture. That which is by you alleged, 2 Tim. i. and 1 Tim. iv., maketh for my purpose: for you have before confessed that "imposition of hands was not by the church and people, but by the elders and ministers[1];" and you allege these places 1 Tim. iv. and 2 Tim. i. to prove the same. And therefore I much marvel to what end you now allege them, except it be to prove your phrase; for they cannot prove any election made by the people, unless you will say and unsay at your pleasure.

Fol. 31, sect. 4.

But, to put you out of doubt, *imponere manus*, "to lay on hands," sometimes signifieth the ceremony only of laying on of hands, and sometimes the whole manner and form of ordering. And in this second signification it is taken 1 Tim. v. and 2 Tim. i. Bullinger, expounding this place, 1 Tim. v., saith: *Manus enim imponere aliud non est quam ecclesiæ aliquem præficere et ordinare*[2]: "To lay on hands is nothing else but to ordain and appoint one over the church." And interpreting that also, 2 Tim. i., he saith: *Paulus in præsenti per donum Dei prophetiæ donum intellexit, et functionem episcopalem ad quam vocarat Timotheum Dominus, sed per ministerium Pauli, qui ideo nunc dicit donum illud in Timotheo esse per impositionem manuum suarum*[3]: "Paul doth here understand by the gift of God the gift of prophecy, and the office of a bishop, unto the which the Lord had called Timothy, but by the ministry of Paul; who for that cause now saith that that gift was in Timothy by the imposition of

To lay on hands, is diversly taken.

Bullinger.

[1 See before, page 355.]
[2 H. Bullinger. Comm. in Omn. Apost. Epist. Tigur. 1558. In 1 ad Tim. cap. v. p. 593.]
[3 Id. in 2 Epist. ad Tim. cap. i. p. 603; where *donum istud in Timotheo*.]

his hands." And M. Calvin, *Instit. cap.* 8, *sect.* 50, decideth this matter fully in these words: *Sed Paulus ipse alibi se, &c.*[1]: "But Paul himself in another place doth testify that he, and no more, did lay his hands upon Timothy: 'I admonish thee (saith he) that thou stir up the grace which is in thee by the imposition of my hands.' For, where it is said in the other epistle of the laying on of the hands of the eldership, I do not so take it as though Paul spake of the college of elders, but in this name (*videlicet presbyterii*) I understand the ordination itself; as if he should say, Endeavour thyself that the grace be not in vain, which thou hast received by the laying on of hands, when I ordained thee a minister." Again, upon this, 1 Tim. v., he saith thus: *Impositio manuum ordinationem significat; signum enim pro re ipsa capitur*[2]: "The imposition of hands signifieth the ordering; for the sign is taken for the thing itself." For what is it to appoint, but to call, elect, and ordain? Moreover, that which Paul saith to Titus, *Ut constituas, &c.*, doth expound this to Timothy, *Manus cito, &c.;* and therefore indeed I make no difference in this place betwixt election, ordaining, and imposition of hands.

"Last of all" you say that you "answer, though this might agree to Timothy alone, &c." If it agreed to Timothy alone, it must needs follow that it may agree to other bishops also; for Timothy was a bishop, as it shall be by better reason proved than you are able to shew any to the contrary. This that you speak of his evangelistship, and of his superiority in that respect, is only spoken without reason or authority; but you shall have store of both to the contrary (God willing), when I come to that place.

I am not so "lavish of my witnesses," as you are of scornful and unseemly taunts and speeches.

Both Ambrose and Chrysostom do not say that Paul here

[1 Sed Paulus ipse alibi se, non alios complures, Timotheo manus imposuisse commemorat. *Admoneo te* (inquit) *ut gratiam suscites quæ in te est per impositionem manuum mearum.* Nam quod in altera epistola de *impositione manuum presbyterii* dicitur, non ita accipio quasi Paulus de seniorum collegio loquatur: sed hoc nomine ordinationem ipsam intelligo: quasi diceret, Fac ut gratia quam per manuum impositionem recepisti, quum te presbyterum crearem, non sit irrita. —Calvin. Op. Amst. 1667-71. Inst. Lib. iv. cap. iii. 16. Tom. IX. p. 285.]

[2 Id. Comm. in Epist. I. ad Tim. cap. v. Tom. VII. p. 465; where *hoc est signum pro.*]

warneth Timothy only to be circumspect, but to be circumspect in appointing of ministers; and, if it were not so, I doubt not but that I should hear of it. The words are spoken to Timothy in respect that he was bishop; neither hath the apostle given any such like admonition to any church in any of his epistles, as I have before noted. And therefore Ambrose, in his exposition of this place to Timothy (after that he had shewed what circumspection the apostle would have to be used in ordaining of ministers), concludeth thus: *Hæc* Ambrose. *episcopus custodiens castum se exhibebit religioni*[3]: "A bishop observing these things shall shew himself pure in religion." Whereby he signifieth that this precept is properly pertaining to a bishop. Chrysostom also, in the 1 Tim. iv. upon these words, *cum impositione manuum presbyterii*, saith: *Non de* Chrysostom. *presbyteris hoc loco, sed de episcopis loquitur; non enim profecto presbyteri ipsum ordinarunt*[4]: "He speaketh not of priests in this place, but of bishops; for certainly priests did not ordain him." And Œcumenius upon the same words: *Presbyteros dicit episcopos; neque enim presbyteri episcopum* Œcumenius. *ordinabant*[5]: "He calleth bishops priests; for priests did not ordain a bishop." Whereby it plainly appeareth that these ancient fathers think this precept, *Manus cito ne cui imponas*, "Lay thy hands suddenly on no man," to be given only to Timothy in the respect that he was bishop, and therefore also to appertain unto bishops only to ordain ministers.

Hierome, upon that place to Titus, saith: *Audiant epi-* Hierome. *scopi, qui habent constituendi presbyteros per urbes singulas potestatem, sub quali lege ecclesiasticæ potestatis ordo teneatur*[6]: "Let bishops, which have authority to appoint ministers in every city, hear in what law the order of ecclesiastical authority doth consist." And a little after, speaking also of bishops: "Whereby it is manifest that those which, contemning the apostle's rule, will not bestow the ecclesiastical degree upon any for desert but for favour, to do against

[[3] Ambros. Op. Par. 1686-90. Comm. in Epist. ad Tim. prim. cap. v. vv. 21, 2. Tom. II. Append. col. 301.]
[[4] Chrysost. Op. Par. 1718-38. In I. Epist. ad Tim. cap. iv. Hom. xiii. Tom. XI. p. 618.]
[[5] Œcumen. Op. Lut. Par. 1631. Comm. cap. ix. in I. Epist. ad Tim. Tom. II. p. 234.]
[[6] Hieron. Op. Par. 1693-1706. Comm. in Epist. ad Tit. cap. i. Tom. IV. Pars I. col. 412; where *ecclesiasticæ constitutionis ordo*.]

Christ, &c.¹" Hierome here taketh the bishop only to have authority to ordain and appoint ministers. And Chrysostom upon the same place saith that "Paul did those things himself that required greater labour and travail, but left other things of honour and commendation to Titus, as ordaining of bishops²." So saith Theophylact likewise³. Thus then you see how evidently both those places of scripture, and also these ancient fathers, do overthrow that saying of the Admonition, that "the right of ordering ministers doth at no hand appertain to a bishop;" and how manifestly also the same have justified that which I have said, that is, "that bishops have authority to admit ministers;" for these be my very words.

The corrupt dealing of T. C.

Now how corruptly you have dealt with me here in this place, I would wish the indifferent reader to consider. Where I say, "that bishops have authority to admit ministers," you make me to say, "that the election of ministers by one man was in the apostles' time." And, where I say that these words of Paul to Timothy (*Manus cito ne cui imponas, &c.*) "be an admonition to Timothy that he ought to be circumspect in appointing of ministers," you make the reader believe that I say, that it is "a commandment given by Paul to Timothy, that the bishop only should choose the minister." And, where I say that "Hierome and others do expound" these words to Titus (*ut constituas oppidatim, &c.*) "of the authority that Titus had in placing ministers in every church," you report them as though I should say that "Hierome proveth the right of the election of the minister to belong to the bishop only." Where I have "ordaining," there you have "election;" and where I say, "belongeth to the bishop," there say you, "belongeth to the bishop only." Is this your sincerity? dare you accuse other men of corruption, being guilty of it yourself almost in every line? True it is that I am persuaded that both Timothy and Titus, and consequently

[¹ Ex quo manifestum est, eos qui, apostoli lege contemta, ecclesiasticum gradum non merito voluerint alicui deferre, sed gratia, contra Christum facere, &c.—Id. ibid.]

[² Ἔνθα μὲν γὰρ ἦν κίνδυνος καὶ πολλὴ δυσκολία, αὐτὸς κατώρθου παρών· ἃ δὲ τιμὴν μᾶλλον ἔφερεν, ἢ ἔπαινον εἶχε, ταῦτα ἐπιτρέπει τῷ μαθητῇ, τῶν ἐπισκόπων λέγω τὰς χειροτονίας, κ.τ.λ.—Chrysost. Op. Par. 1718-38. In Epist. ad Tit. cap. i. Hom. ii. Tom. XI. p. 737.]

[³ Theophyl. Op. Venet. 1754-63. Comm. in Epist. ad Tit. cap. i. Tom. II. pp. 625, 6.]

other bishops, have authority to ordain and appoint ministers alone; which I have also partly proved before, and shall do partly hereafter, as I have occasion: but yet all men that be not blind may see that I have affirmed no such thing in that part of my Answer to the Admonition.

I have always greatly esteemed the judgments and opinions of learned men; and, howsoever you are persuaded of your own excellency and dexterity of wit, yet am I content to submit myself to the opinions of other, to whom I am in no respect comparable; and then do I think myself to have reason sufficient, when I have good authority of the scriptures and of learned writers.

Aristotle spake as a heathenish philosopher of such profane sciences as be grounded, not upon authority, but upon natural and human reason; but that that we profess is of another nature, for it is grounded upon authority, and for the authority' sake to be believed, what reason soever there is to the contrary. And surely I marvel what you mean so often to quarrel with me for the alleging of the authority of learned writers, except it be because you have not read so many yourself, or else that you would seem yourself to be the author and inventor of those reasons, which you have borrowed of them: which indeed is to win the praise of a good wit unto yourself, and to rob the learned writers of their just commendation. Therefore, to answer you briefly in this matter, I think "authority" in divine matters to be the best reason, whether it be of the scriptures themselves, or of such learned men as do rightly interpret the same. And I deem it to be much more honesty in using their authorities to express their names (that they may have their just commendation, and the matter the more credit), than, using their authorities and suppressing their names, vainly and arrogantly to usurp as my own that which I have borrowed out of them. *Authority the best proof in divine matters.*

I know M. Calvin's interpretation upon that place, and likewise what Musculus saith of the same in his Commonplaces, *Tit. de Electione Ministrorum;* but the words of the text be plain. And, forasmuch as you make a distinction betwixt "electing" and "ordaining," and say that "electing pertaineth to the people, and ordaining to the bishop[4];" like- *Pag. 41, lin. 4.*

[4 See below, pages 438, 9.]

wise that the apostle in this place speaketh of ordaining, and not of electing, you must of necessity confess that, by saying, *sicut tibi ordinaram,* " as I appointed thee," he meaneth only imposition of hands and prayer; as though he should say, *Ut constituas oppidatim presbyteros, sicut tibi ordinaram, scil. per impositionem manuum et orationem:* "That thou shouldest ordain ministers in every city, as I appointed thee (that is to say), by laying on of hands and by prayer." And thus do learned interpreters also expound this place. Neither is Musculus his meaning much otherwise; as it may appear to those that well consider his words; especially if your distinction betwixt "electing and ordaining" hold, and if Paul speak here of "ordaining" only; for in "ordaining" of ministers the apostles used laying on of hands as a ceremony, they prayed also and fasted. But, if you will have the apostle here to speak of "electing" also, then doth he expound himself when he saith: *Si quis est inculpatus, &c.:* "If any be unreprovable, the husband of one wife, &c." For how can you otherwise make those words aptly to hang together? No doubt the apostle gave Titus an especial charge, in ordaining of ministers, to have respect unto these qualities: of which charge he putteth him in mind when he saith, that he "left him at Creta to ordain ministers in every city, as he appointed him," that is, such as be unreprovable, &c.

I know there be some that expound this place thus also: that, forasmuch as Paul, when he left Titus in Creta, did will him to ordain ministers in every city, now[1] he putteth him in mind of the same by his letters, and willeth him to do according to his appointment, that is, to place ministers in every city. And surely this interpretation hath good reason; for, being absent, we commonly use to put them in mind by letters, to whom we have committed anything to be done, of such things as we willed them to do when we were present with them.

I reverence M. Calvin as a singular man, and worthy instrument in Christ's church; but I am not so wholly addicted unto him, that I will contemn other men's judgments that in divers points agree not fully with him, especially in the interpretation of some places of the scripture, when as, in my opinion, they come nearer to the true meaning and sense of it in those points than he doth.

[1 How, Def. B.]

I did never cleave to Musculus, or any other man, so that for his or their sakes I derogate anything from such as be comparable to them, and have deserved singular commendation for their writings. If any one or more learned men be of my judgment, though all be not, I am not ashamed to use their testimony in that point, though in some other points I do not consent unto them.

If I either " unjoint, or rack in pieces from the rest," any word or sentence of M. Calvin's, make it known, set it open, that I may justly bear the blame of it: but, if I deal truly and faithfully with him, if I set down his own words, whole sentences, whole sections, and (as you say) whole leaves, without adding, altering, or diminishing, then how can you excuse your so untrue and unjust charging of me? which, if it were not so common and usual with you, might the better be tolerated[2].

Chapter vii. The Second Division.

Answer to the Admonition, Page 46, Sect. 1.

It is the general consent of all the learned fathers, that it pertaineth to the office of a bishop to order and elect ministers of the word. In this, saith Hierome *in Epist. ad Evagrium*, " a bishop doth excel all other[3] ministers, in that the ordering and appointing of ministers doth properly pertain unto him[4]." And yet these men say "that the right of ordering ministers doth at no hand appertain to a bishop." But for the order and

Hierome.

[2 Cartwright in his rejoinder to this division accuses Whitgift of desultoriness and repetition, and says that "it is hard to give answer with any convenient understanding of the reader." He then enters into a long examination of what Whitgift had said, and refers to a great many other parts of the Defence, and at length concludes: "And, where he saith that herein, although he hath left Calvin, yet he hath followed the judgment of other learned men, he may see that he hath not left Calvin only, but Musculus, Bullinger, and Zuinglius. As for his 'learned men,' I think verily that, Pighius, Hosius, and others of that stamp excepted, he is not able to allege one to confirm that Titus and Timothy had only the election of the ministers. For those alleged to prove that Timothy and Titus did ordain are nothing to the purpose; considering no man denieth that; but that they ordained alone, was to be shewed. And, if he had shewed that they alone ordained, which he shall never do, yet is not the election of the people thereby shut out; forsomuch as election and ordination are several things."—Sec. Repl. pp. 265, &c.]

[3 Others, Answ. 2.]

[4 Hieron. Op. Par. 1693-1706. Ad Evang. Epist. ci. Tom. IV. Pars II. col. 803. See below, page 439, note 5.]

manner of making ministers, peruse the book made for that purpose; and, as I said before so I say again, if thou hast any judgment, thou canst not but like it and allow of it.

T. C. Page 40, Sect. 3, 4, 5.

In the end you say, " It is the general consent of all the learned fathers that it belongeth to the bishop to choose the minister." Because you acquaint my ears with such bold and untrue affirmations, I can now the more patiently hear you thus vaunting yourself, as though you had all the fathers by heart, and carried them about with you wheresoever you went; whereas, if a man would measure you by the skill in them which you have shewed here, he would hardly believe that you had read the tenth part of them.

Are all the learned fathers of that mind? I think then you would have been better advised than to have set down but one, when as you know a matter in controversy will not be tried but by two or three witnesses, unless the Lord speak himself; and therefore you give me occasion to suspect that, because you cite but one, you know of no more. Now let us see what your one witness will depose in this matter.

<small>I had cited Ambrose and Chrysostom before.</small>

And, first of all, you have done more wisely than simply, in that you have altered Hierome's words. For, where he saith, " Wherein doth a bishop differ from an elder but only in ordaining?" you say, "A bishop doth excel all other ministers, &c." I report me here unto your conscience, whether you did not of purpose change Hierome[1] his sentence, because you would not let the reader understand what odds is between St Hierome's bishops in his days and between our lord bishops. For then the bishop had nothing above an elder, or other minister, but only the ordaining of the minister. Now he hath a thousand parishes, where the minister hath but one. For the matters also of the substance of the ministry, the bishop now excommunicateth, which the minister cannot[2] : besides divers other things, which are mere civil, which the bishop doth, and which neither bishop nor other minister ought to do. I say, I report me to your conscience whether you altered Hierome's words to this end, that you would keep this from the knowledge of your reader, or no. For answer to the place, it is an evil argument to say : The bishop had the ordaining of the minister; ergo, he had the election of him. The contrary rather is a good argument : The bishop had the ordaining of the minister; therefore he had not the election of him. For ordination and election are divers members of one whole, which is the placing of the pastor in his church; and one member cannot be verified of another, as you cannot say your foot is your hand. I will not deny but that sometimes these words may be found confounded in ecclesiastical writers; but I will shew you also that they are distinguished, and that the election pertaineth to the people, and ordaining unto the bishop.

<small>It is your argument, it is none of mine : my words import no such thing. Divers members of the whole may concur in one and the self-same persons, though one of them can not be verified of another. Then have you all this while strived in vain.</small>

[1 Jerome's, Repl. 1 and 2.]

[2 Here Repl. 1 and 2 add, *absolveth or receiveth into the church, which the minister cannot.*]

Jo. Whitgift.

Shew me one father that denieth that which I here affirm: if you neither do, nor can, then may my "skill in the fathers, and reading" also, be as much (for any thing here to the contrary) as you think I would have it seem to be. But I will not follow you in your vein of gibing. I had cited before Chrysostom and Ambrose for the same purpose; so that my witnesses be three, and therefore sufficient, except you will make some lawful exception against them: but, because you may understand that I have plenty and store sufficient, I will rehearse but one sentence unto you of M. Calvin's in his *Instit. cap.* 8 : *Ordinari episcopos a suis metropolitis* Calvin. *jubent omnes veteres synodi*[3]: "All ancient synods do command that bishops should be ordained of their metropolitans."

What cause should I have thus to report Hierome's words, to prove such difference betwixt the bishop and other ministers, seeing that doth not pertain to this place; and again, considering that I have at large proved the same in another place? Are you so dull of understanding as you would seem to be? do not both the words that go before, and those that follow also, declare my purpose in using that place? I do not translate Hierome's words, but I declare Hierome's meaning: and, if the offence be in this, that I say "a bishop doth excel all other ministers," then doth your own author Illyricus (out of whom you have *verbatim* borrowed so much), and the other writers of the Centuries, offend also; for thus he saith; *Ordinatio ministrorum propria erat episcopi, quo solo jure* Cent. iv. *ceteris sacerdotibus præstantiorem esse episcopum Hieronymus scripsit ad Evagrium*[4]*:* "The ordaining of ministers was proper unto the bishop; by the which (as Hierome wrote unto Evagrius) a bishop only excelleth other priests:" out of whom as I have borrowed this word "excel," so have you borrowed also this word "only;" for the words of Hierome be these: *Quid enim facit excepta ordinatione episcopus,* Hier. ad *quod presbyter non facit*[5]*?* "What doth a bishop which a Evang.

[³ Exstat autem decretum Niceni concilii, ut metropolites cum omnibus provinciæ episcopis conveniat ad eum qui ejectus [electus] fuerit ordinandum... Atque hic canon quum desuetudine obsolesceret, pluribus deinde synodis renovatus est.— Calvin. Op. Amst. 1667-71. Inst. Lib. iv. cap. iv. 14. Tom. IX. p. 289.]
[⁴ Centur. Eccles. Hist. Cent. Basil. 1560, &c. Cent. iv. cap. vii. cols. 489, 90.]
[⁵ Hieron. Op. Par. 1693-1706. Ad Evang. Epist. ci. Tom. IV. Pars ii. col. 803; where *non faciat.*]

minister doth not, except ordination?" Whereby he manifestly affirmeth as much as I in this place require, that is, "that the right of ordering ministers doth appertain to the bishop." The same also Chrysostom in the like words writeth in 1 Tim. iii[1].

Touching the difference betwixt a bishop and a common minister, of the superiority of bishops, and of their jurisdiction (for avoiding of confusion, whereunto you here provoke me), I will speak when I come to that part of this book.

Election and ordination may concur in one person.

You say that this is an evil argument: "The bishop hath the ordaining of the minister; *ergo*, he hath the election of him, &c." I think it is a very good argument, and that you are greatly deceived when you say, election and ordination cannot concur in one and the self-same person, although they may be distinguished the one from the other. Had not the master of the college interest in the electing of you when you were chosen to be fellow, and did he not also admit you? was there not then both election and admission in one man? And is not the like in other degrees of learning? Hath not he authority to elect that hath authority to admit, that is, to ordain? or have you an example of any lawfully placed in the ministry, without the election and admission of the bishop?

T. C. forgetteth himself.

Have you forgotten what you alleged before out of the council of Carthage, the council of Toledo, &c.[2]; where it is sufficiently expressed that the election of ministers doth as well pertain to the bishops as it doth to the people? and do not all the examples and places of scripture that you have alleged for your purpose verify the same? Wherefore, though "election and ordination" so differ the one from the other, that the one cannot be said to be the other; yet may they well be joined together in one subject, as prudence, justice, temperance, and fortitude are, being notwithstand-

An oversight of T. C.

ing "members of one whole." But this hath deceived you, that you think, because "divers members of one whole" cannot be confounded among themselves, and "one verified of another," therefore they may not meet together in one and the self-same person; which is a gross oversight of yours; for take

[1 Τῇ γὰρ χειροτονίᾳ μόνῃ ὑπερβεβήκασι [ἐπίσκοποι], καὶ τούτῳ μόνον δοκοῦσι πλεονεκτεῖν τοὺς πρεσβυτέρους.—Chrysost. Op. Par. 1718-38. In I. Epist. ad Tim. cap. iii. Hom. xi. Tom. XI. p. 604.]

[2 See before, page 411.]

your own example: although your foot is not your hand, yet (I am sure) you would be sorry if one man might not have both feet and hands.

But what need I labour anything in proving this? for you yourself confess more than I affirmed, and as much as I require, that is, that "election and ordination are sometimes confounded in ecclesiastical writers," and therefore the one taken for the other. I do not deny but that sometimes also they be distinguished; although the Admonition, in this place that I do now confute, doth utterly confound them[3].

Chapter vii. The Third Division.

T. C. Page 41, Sect. 1.

Upon the sixth of the Acts the gloss hath, that that which was done there of the twelve apostles, in willing the brethren to look out fit men, was done to give us example, and "must be observed in those that are ordained; for," saith the gloss, "the people must choose; and the bishop must ordain[4]." And that St Hierome must be so understood, it appeareth not only that it hath been so expounded, but also it may be easily proved; for that St Hierome's sentence and judgment appeareth in other places that he would have nothing here done without the people; as, in his Epistle ad Rusticum Monachum, *he willeth that the people should have power and authority to choose their clerks and their ministers[5]. And in his epistle to Neopotian, of the Life of the Clerks, he hath this distinction manifestly: " They run," saith he, " unto the bishops' suffragans certain times of the year, and bringing some sum of money they are anointed and ordained, being chosen of none; and afterward the bishop, without any lawful election, is chosen in hugger-mugger of the canons and[6] prebendaries only, without the knowledge of the people[7]." And so you see that, although that St Hierome saith that the bishop had the ordaining of the ministers, yet he had not the election; for the ordaining was nothing else but an approving of the election by putting on of hands; and consequently, having made your vaunt that all the learned fathers were of this judgment, that the bishop should elect the minister, you shew not so much as one.*

Hierome's words falsified.

An untruth, proceeding of gross ignorance; for these are Musculus his words, and not Hierome's.

[3 Cartwright rejoins: "What either godliness or honesty is in him which dare so barefaced deny things so openly untrue, I will leave to be judged of that which is said touching that the election doth not belong unto the bishop alone but unto the church." He then produces several testimonies to prove that a bishop must be ordained by at least three other bishops, and afterwards accuses Whitgift of seeking "starting-holes," and of "false conclusions," concluding, "your hookie is greater than your harvest."—Sec. Repl. pp. 274, &c.]

[4 Hic ordo servandus est in ordinandis: eligat populus: ordinet episcopus.— Bibl. cum Gloss. Ord. et Expos. N. de Lyra, Basil. 1502. Act. Apost. cap. vi. Gloss. Ord. Pars vi. fol. 174. 2.]

[5 See below, page 442, note 1.] [6 Or, Repl. 1 and 2.]
[7 See below, page 442, note 2.]

Jo. Whitgift.

What gloss saith so? where shall a man find it? or where is it? This is too large a scope that you take unto yourself. But I must pardon you; for Illyricus, of whom you have borrowed it, doth not otherwise quote the place. Howbeit the words, as Illyricus doth report them (which I think are taken out of *glossa ordinaria*), make nothing against anything that I have said: for, if you will thus reason, The bishop must "ordain;" *ergo*, he may not "elect," I deny your argument: the reason I have shewed before, one man may both "ordain" and "elect."

*T. C. falsi-
fieth Hie-
rome.* You have utterly falsified Hierome's words *ad Rusticum monachum*, and much more declined from the true interpretation of them than I would have suspected; especially seeing you would be thought to have entrapped me in the like not long before. For the words of Hierome be these: *Cum ad perfectam ætatem veneris, si tamen vita comes fuerit, et te vel populus vel pontifex civitatis in clerum elegerit, agito quæ clerici sunt*[1]: "When thou shalt come to perfect age, if thy life be answerable, and either the people or the bishop of the city shall choose thee into the clergy, do such things as belong to a clerk." He doth not here "will that the people should have authority to choose their clerks and their ministers," as you say; but he saith unto Rusticus the monk, that, "if either the people or the bishop of the city choose him to be clerk, that then he must do those things that pertain to a clerk." He saith, *Vel populus, vel pontifex, &c.*, signifying that it was a thing indifferent to be chosen either by the people, or by the bishop: which maketh for me against you; for I say that a bishop may choose a minister, and you deny it.

*T. C. father-
eth that upon
Hierome,
which is not
to be found
in him, but
is in Mus-
culus.* The place that you allege out of the epistle of Hierome, *ad Nepotianum de Vita Clericorum*, is not to be found in Hierome. They be Master Musculus his own words, *Tit. de Verbi Ministris*[2]. And, because that he doth adjoin them to a place which he hath alleged out of Hierome, therefore you think them to be alleged of him as Hierome's words: which is a gross oversight, and argueth that you have not read the

[1 Hieron. Op. Par. 1693-1706. Ad Rust. Monach. Epist. xcv. Tom. IV. Pars II. col. 776; where *in clericum*.]

[2 Curritur ad suffraganeos episcoporum certis anni temporibus, et allata qualicunque pecunia unguntur et ordinantur a nemine electi. Et episcopi citra legitimam electionem a solis canonicis in latebris citra conscientiam plebis eliguntur.—Wolfg. Muscul. Loc. Comm. Theol. Basil. 1599. De Ministr. Verb. Dei, p. 199.]

authors themselves. O how would you have triumphed if the like could have been espied in my book! There is a manifest place to the contrary in that epistle to Nepotian; for thus he saith: *Gloria patris est filius sapiens: gaudeat episcopus judicio suo, cum tales Christo elegerit sacerdotes*[3]: "A wise son is the glory of the father: let the bishop rejoice and be glad of his judgment, when he hath chosen unto Christ such priests." Here might I triumph over you (both for corrupting of Hierome's words, and fathering that upon him which is not to be found in him), if I were disposed to deal with you so profanely in a divine and serious matter. Only this I wish, that by these gross oversights you would learn one point of wisdom, that is, to be modest, and to know yourself[4].

Hier. ad Nepot.

Chapter vii. The Fourth Division.

T. C. Page 41, Sect. 2.

Now will I shew you the clean contrary of that you say, not that I gladly travail this ways; for, if you had not constrained me, you should not have heard one voice that[5] *way. And would to God that you would be content, especially when you meet with those that will be tried by the scriptures, to seek no farther strength than they give you. But I am loth you should oppress the truth, and make all men afraid of it, by making them believe that it is so desolate and forsaken of her friends, as you pretend. You confess St Cyprian is against you herein; and he was a learned father, and a martyr also, which did not only use this form of election, but also taught it to be necessary and commanded; and therefore methinketh you should not have said "all the learned fathers" without exception: you see also St Jerome is of another judgment. St Augustine also, when he speaketh how he appointed Eradius to succeed him, shewed*[6] *how it was the approved right and custom that the whole church should either choose or consent of their bishop*[7]. *And Ambrose saith that that is truly and certainly*

82. Epist. *a divine election to the office of a bishop, which is made of the whole church*[8]. *Gregorius Nazianzene, in the oration which he had at*

We have seen it smally to your credit.

[3 Hieron. Op. Ad Nepot. De Vit. Cler. Epist. xxxiv. Tom. IV. Pars II. col. 262.]

[4 Cartwright says: "I grant that I took Musculus' words for Jerome's; yet, if that make to the purpose, I had read the place. And Jerome himself in another place hath a sentence not much unlike." He denies also that the disjunctive has any such meaning as Whitgift attributed to it, and also asks: "And how cometh it to pass that you send Musculus here without all answer?"—Sec. Repl. pp. 276, 7.]

[5 This, Repl. 1, 2, and Def. A.]   [6 Sheweth, Repl. 1 and 2.]

[7 See below, page 445, note 4.]

[8 Ambros. Op. Par. 1686-90. Epist. Class. I. Ad Vercell. Eccles. Epist. lxiii. 2. Tom. II. col. 1023. See below, page 446.]

the death of his father, hath divers things which prove that the election of the minister pertained to the church, and confuteth those things which should seem to hinder it[1]. *These were "learned fathers," and yet thought not that the election of the pastor or bishop pertained to one man alone, but that the church had also her interest; therefore you see " all the learned fathers" are not of that mind you say they are.*

> This is an untruth; for he maketh no such confutation there.

Jo. Whitgift.

To Cyprian I have answered before: the people gave their consent in his time; but yet was he bold sometime to elect clerks without them; as it appeareth *Lib. ii. Epist.* 5, which he writeth unto the clergy and people, signifying unto them that it was not necessary to have their consent in choosing one Aurelius a clerk: his words be these: *In ordinandis clericis, fratres carissimi, solemus vos ante consulere, et mores et merita singulorum communi consilio ponderare. Sed exspectanda non sunt testimonia humana, cum præcedunt divina suffragia, &c.*[2]: "In the election of clerks, beloved brethren, we were wont to take your advice before, and to weigh with common advice every man's manners and deserts; but the testimonies of men are not to be looked for, when divine suffrages have gone before." In these words also it appeareth what interest the people then had in elections, even to bear witness, and to testify of the good life and conversation of such as should be admitted into the clergy.

> Cyprian chooseth without the consent of the people.
>
> Cypr. Lib. ii. epist. 5.
>
> What interest the people had in Cyprian's time.

Jerome himself (whatsoever your counterfeit Jerome doth affirm) agreeth with me.

Did not Illyricus tell you where Augustine speaketh these words, neither in what tome, nor in what book, nor in what epistle? Surely Augustine's works[3] are far larger than Musculus' Common-places. But the treatise you mean of is in his second tome among his epistles, in number 110. I would wish the learned reader to peruse it; then shall he soon perceive how little it maketh for your purpose, and how aptly it serveth mine. First, he doth not shew that "it was the approved right and custom that the whole church should either choose or consent of their bishop:" if he do, lay down his words; if you cannot, then hath Illyricus his collection deceived you. Secondly, although it may there appear that

> The testimony of Augustine cited by T. C. serveth not his purpose.

[1 See below, page 447.]
[2 In ordinationibus clericis, &c. mores ac merita, &c.—Cypr. Op. Oxon. 1682. Ad Cler. et Pleb. Epist. xxxviii. p. 74.]
[3 Words, Def. B.]

the people used to give their consents, yet Augustine, both by his own act, and by the act of Severus bishop of Milleum, declareth that not to be so necessary, or such a right, but that it may be, upon just considerations, altered. Last of all, the words of Augustine be plain; which I will only set down, and leave them to the consideration of the reader. Augustine, shewing his reasons why he did appoint Eradius to succeed him, saith thus: *Scio post obitus episcoporum, &c.*[4]: "I know that churches use, after the deaths of bishops, to be much troubled through ambitious or contentious persons; and it is my duty (so much as lieth in me) to provide for this city, lest that thing (whereof I have oftentimes had experience to my grief) should happen." Then he sheweth what a stir there was a little before in the church of Milleum about their bishop, at what time he was sent for unto them to appease the controversy; and, declaring how in the end they willingly embraced him whom Severus their bishop, whilst he was alive, appointed unto them, he saith: *Minus tamen aliquid factum erat, unde nonnulli, &c.:* "Yet was there somewhat less done, whereby divers were offended, because my brother Severus thought it sufficient to appoint his successor in the presence of the clergy, and spake not thereof unto the people; by occasion whereof some grief was conceived. But what needs more words? it pleased God; the grief was expelled, joy came in place; and he was admitted bishop whom the predecessor had appointed." And it followeth immediately: *Ergo ne aliqui de me querantur, voluntatem meam, quam credo Dei esse, in omnium vestrum notitiam profero,*

Aug. 2 Tom. 110.

Contention in popular elections.

Bishops appoint their successors.

[4 Scio post obitus episcoporum per ambitiosos aut contentiosos solere ecclesias perturbari; et quod sæpe expertus sum et dolui, debeo quantum ad me adtinet, ne contingat, huic prospicere civitati. Sicuti novit caritas vestra, in Milevitana ecclesia modo fui: petierunt enim me fratres, et maxime servi Dei qui ibi sunt, ut venirem; quia post obitum beatæ memoriæ fratris et coepiscopi mei Severi nonnulla ibi perturbatio timebatur. Veni, et quomodo voluit Dominus, adjuvit nos pro sua misericordia, ut cum pace episcopum acciperent, quem vivus designaverat episcopus eorum. Hoc enim eis cum innotuisset, voluntatem præcedentis et decedentis episcopi sui libenter amplexi sunt. Minus tamen aliquid factum erat, unde nonnulli contristabantur, quia frater Severus credidit posse sufficere ut sucessorem suum apud clericos designaret, ad populum inde non est locutus; et erat inde aliquorum nonnulla tristitia. Quid plura? Deo placuit; tristitia fugata est, gaudium successit. Ordinatus est episcopus, quem præcedens episcopus designaverat. Ergo ne aliquis de me queratur, &c....notitiam perfero: presbyterum Eraclium, &c. Adhuc in corpore posito beatæ memoriæ patre et episcopo meo sene Valerio, episcopus ordinatus est, et sedi cum illo, &c.—August. Op. Par. 1679-1700. Act. Ecclesiast. seu Epist. ccxxiii. 1, 4. Tom. II. col. 789, 90.]

presbyterum Eradium mihi successorem volo, &c.: "Therefore, lest any should complain of me, I do here signify unto you all my will (which I think to be the will of God): I will have Eradius the minister to be my successor, &c." Lastly, he sheweth how he himself was appointed bishop, his predecessor being yet alive.

Notes out of
the testimony
of Augustine. Here it is to be noted, first, what stir began to be in Augustine's time about such elections made by the people; which was the cause why he and others appointed unto themselves successors whilst they yet lived. Secondly, that Severus appointed to himself a successor, and thought it not necessary therein to require the consent of the people; which he would not have neglected, if it had been either necessary or usual. Last of all, that Augustine pronounceth Eradius to be his successor in the presence of the people, that they might know his mind, but yet without asking their voices, although they did willingly of themselves consent; for that which afterward he requireth them to subscribe unto was the petition that he made unto them, no more to trouble him with their civil matters, but that they would resort unto Eradius his successor for such causes. When the reader hath well considered these circumstances, which he shall better learn in the place itself, then let him judge how much it serveth for your turn.

Contention
about popu-
lar elections. It may appear by that epistle of Ambrose, what contention there was in *Vercellensi ecclesia* (to the which he wrote) about the election of their bishop; for they had been long destitute of one, as it there appeareth. Wherefore he exhorteth them to agreement by the example of their predecessors, who so well agreed in choosing of Eusebius; whereupon he saith: Ambros.
Ep. lxxxii. *Merito vir tantus* (meaning Eusebius) *evasit, quem omnis elegit ecclesia; merito creditum, quod divino esset electus judicio, quem omnes postulavissent*[1]: "He worthily proved a notable man, whom the whole church elected: he was rightly thought to be chosen by God's appointment, whom every one desired." And who doubteth but that he is called of God, whom the whole church, without suit, without sinister affection, without intent to maintain factions and schisms, doth desire? This proves that in Ambrose his time in that church the people desired their bishop; which is not

[1 Ambros. Op. Par. 1686-90. Epist. Class. i. Ad Vercell. Eccles. Epist. lxiii. 2. Tom. II. col. 1023.]

TO THE ADMONITION.   447

to be denied : but it also sheweth that in the same time there were marvellous contentions about such elections; which is to be considered.

Nazianzene in that oration hath not one argument to "prove that the election of the minister doth pertain to the church;" neither doth he "confute" those things which should seem to hinder it, for there is none alleged: only he declareth what a marvellous stir and sedition there was, at two sundry times, in the church of Cesaria, about the election of the bishop, what violence was used about the same, how the people were divided among themselves first, and after against their ministers; likewise, how they suddenly misliked their own choice, and would have disannulled it, if they had not been restrained of their wills by Nazianzene his father; how the emperor also, and the ruler of the city, taking part with the factious company, were by him pacified[2]. Surely this maketh very little to the commendation of popular elections. Nay, in the second contention that he there reciteth, declaring who were the especial authors of it, he saith: *Ecclesiæ enim a malo erant immunes, pariter et opulentiores et potentiores; sed omnis impetus ac seditio inter plebem erat, ac præcipue vilissimam*[3]: "For the churches (meaning the clergy) were clear from that mischief; so were the richer sort also, and they which were of greater authority: but all the violence and sedition was among the common people, and among them especially which were of the basest sort." And a little after, telling how his father pacified that sedition, he saith that his father writ unto them, admonished them, *populum, sacerdotes, necnon alios, et quotquot qui ad gradum pertinebant, obtestabatur, eligebat, calculum ferebat, &c.*[4]: "He humbly entreated the people, the priests, and others which pertained to that order, he elected, chose, &c." What is here spoken, that maketh not rather against you than with you? No man denieth

Nazianzene performeth not that for the which he is avouched.

Contention in popular elections.

The common people especial authors of tumults in elections.

ἐχειροτό-νει.

[2 Gregor. Naz. Op. Par. 1778-1840. In Patr. Fun. Orat. xviii. 33, &c. Tom. I. pp. 353, &c.]

[3 Οὐ γὰρ ἠγνοεῖτο τὸ ὑπεραῖρον, ὥσπερ οὐδ' ἐν ἄστρασιν ἥλιος, ἀλλὰ καὶ λίαν ἐπίδηλον ἦν, τοῖς τε ἄλλοις ἅπασι, καὶ τοῦ λαοῦ μάλιστα τῷ ἐγκρίτῳ τε καὶ καθαρωτάτῳ, ὅσον τε περὶ τὸ βῆμα, καὶ ὅσον ἐν τοῖς καθ' ἡμᾶς Ναζιραίοις, ἐφ' οἷς ἔδει τὰς τοιαύτας προβυλὰς κεῖσθαι μόνοις, ἢ ὅτι μάλιστα, καὶ οὐδὲν ἂν ἦν ταῖς ἐκκλησίαις κακὸν, ἀλλὰ μὴ τοῖς εὐπορωτάτοις τε καὶ δυνατωτάτοις, ἢ φορᾷ δήμου καὶ ἀλογίᾳ, καὶ τούτων αὐτῶν μάλιστα τοῖς εὐωνοτάτοις.—Id. ibid. 35. p. 356.]

[4 Id. ibid. 36. p. 357.]

but that the people at this time had interest in the election of the minister in divers churches; but that doth not prove that they ought to have so now, or that the bishop hath no interest in the same: nay, inconveniences of popular elections did then manifestly appear.

<small>T. C. reasoneth not *ad idem*, and defendeth not the Admonition.</small>

There is not as yet one authority brought in to prove that "the ordering of ministers doth at no hand appertain to the bishop;" which the Admonition affirmeth, and I have improved: but you have not replied unto it, keeping your old accustomed manner still, not to reason *ad idem*; for, whereas you should conclude thus, "The ordering of ministers doth at no hand pertain to a bishop," you conclude thus: "The election of a pastor or bishop pertaineth not to one man alone."

<small>T. C. letteth slip that which he should prove, and yet proveth not that which he would.</small>

And yet you have not proved that, only you bring in examples of popular elections; and so have I brought in both examples and authorities for the sole election of the bishop; for they be both true. But you ought to prove these two propositions, if you will justify the Admonition: first, "that popular elections ought to be perpetual;" and secondly, "that the ordaining of ministers doth at no hand pertain to the bishop." But you subtilly pass these over, and cast a mist before your reader's eyes, in heaping up out of Illyricus needless proofs[1].

<small>The propositions that should have been defended.</small>

Chapter vii. The Fifth Division.
T. C. Page 41, Sect. 3.

And that this election continued in the church until within a ccc. years, at what time there was more than Egyptiacal and palpable darkness over the face of the whole earth, it may appear in a treatise of Flaccus Illyricus, which he calleth an addition unto his book that he intituleth, The Catalogue of the Witnesses of Truth; of whom I confess myself to have been much holpen in this matter of the choice of the church touching the ministers, especially in the emperors' edicts which are before cited. For, lacking opportunities divers ways, I was contented somewhat to use the collection to my commodity, for the more speedy furtherance and better proceeding in other matters, which I will leave off, because they may be there read of those that be learned, whom I will also refer to the sixth and seventh[2]

<small>Not only much, but almost altogether.</small>

[1 Cartwright rejoins: "Cyprian is wholly ours in this cause," and proceeds to charge Whitgift with "open violence done unto Augustine's words," declaring that "this wresting of the example of Eradius......was taken from Pighius." He maintains also that Gregory Nazianzene is on his side.—Sec. Repl. pp. 278, &c.]

[2 Six and seven, Repl. 1 and 2.]

books of Eusebius, where both the forms of the elections in those times are described, and where, besides that the customs of the people's choice is set forth, there are examples of the election of the people and clergy, which were confirmed by the christian magistrate, namely, in the bishop of Constantinople. And these may suffice for the other that have not that commodity of books, nor ability nor skill to read them, being in a strange tongue, to know that, besides the institution of God in his word, this manner of electing[3] *did continue so long as there was any sight*[4] *of the knowledge of God in the church of God.*

An untruth; for there is no such thing to be found in these books of Eusebius. This is untrue; for Eusebius maketh not mention of confirmation of elections by any christian magistrate, nor of any bishop of Constantinople.

Jo. Whitgift.

"Illyricus his treatise" that you speak of doth nothing prejudice the cause that I have in hand, touching the authorities there alleged; for the question is not, whether it hath been so or no, but whether it be convenient and profitable for the church to have it so now. The reasons that Illyricus useth, beside his authorities, are of no great force to prove either necessity or conveniency of such elections in the church, as the state is now.

You do well to confess the help that you had by Illyricus; for it could not have been unespied, seeing you have, almost *verbatim*, drawn all the authorities and reasons that you use in this cause out of him. And truly I marvel with what face you can so opprobriously object unto me "other men's collections," and "lack of reading the ancient writers," when as it is evident that your whole book consisteth of other men's notes and collections, and that you yourself have scarce read any one of the authors that you have alleged: 18. authorities at the least you have borrowed of Illyricus in this cause, besides certain other reasons[5].

The reply of T. C. consisteth of other men's collections.

You refer the reader to the 6. and 7. book of Eusebius; where you say, "both the forms of elections in those times are described, and the customs of the people's choice set forth, and divers examples of the elections of the people and clergy, &c." But the reader should have been something beholding to you, if you had named the chapters as well as you have done the books. Howbeit you do very politicly to refer your readers to the whole books, which you are sure the most of them cannot, and of those that can many will not, peruse: but you have not dealt faithfully; for it is not to be found in any part of these two books, where "the customs of

T. C. sendeth his reader to Eusebius for that which he shall not find in him.

[3 Election, Repl. 1 and 2.]   [4 Light, Repl. 1 and 2.]
[5 The treatise referred to is that cited before, p. 398, note 1; 400, note 1.]

[WHITGIFT.]   29

the people's choice is set forth, or any example of the people and clergy's election confirmed by the christian magistrate;" nor yet any example of any "bishop of Constantinople." The contrary rather may be collected in sundry places.

Euseb. Lib. vi. cap. 10.

In the sixth book Eusebius declareth that "in the absence of Narcissus (because it was not known where he was) the governors of the churches adjoining ordain another bishop[1]." And after Narcissus' return, because he was aged, the story saith: *Dictum Alexandrum alterius parœciæ, &c.*[2]: "That the ordinance of God called the said Alexander, being bishop of another parish, to undertake that charge with Narcissus, according to a vision which was in the night revealed unto him." And in the next chapter he sheweth how that those of Hierusalem received the said bishop courteously, and would not suffer him to return to the place where he was bishop before, they being admonished by a vision in the night, which signified unto them that they should go out of the city-gates, and receive their bishop appointed unto them by God; which thing they also did by the consent *vicinorum episcoporum*, "of the bishops adjoining." What form or manner of electing can you gather of this place? except you will admit visions, and call them from one bishoprick to another to help some that is grown in age. Neither is here any mention made of the election of the people; for this that he saith, "Hierusalem went out, &c.," it may rather be understanded of the ministers and deacons of Hierusalem than of the people.

In the vii. book, chap. 30, it appeareth that the ministers and pastors had then authority to choose bishops[3]. Only in

[1 Τοῦ δὲ Ναρκίσσου ἀνακεχωρηκότος, καὶ μηδαμῶς ὅπη ὧν τυγχάνοι γινωσκομένου, δόξαν τοῖς τῶν ὁμόρων ἐκκλησιῶν προεστῶσιν, ἐφ' ἑτέρου μετίασιν ἐπισκόπου χειροτονίαν.—Euseb. in Hist. Eccles. Script. Amst. 1695-1700. Lib. VI. cap. x. p. 171.]

[2 ...τὸν εἰρημένον Ἀλέξανδρον ἐπίσκοπον ἑτέρας ὑπάρχοντα παροικίας οἰκονομία Θεοῦ ἐπὶ τὴν ἅμα τῷ Ναρκίσσῳ λειτουργίαν ἐκάλει, κατὰ ἀποκάλυψιν νύκτωρ αὐτῷ δι' ὁράματος φανεῖσαν... φιλοφρονέστατα οἱ τῇδε ὑπολαβόντες ἀδελφοί· οὐκέτ' οἴκαδε αὐτῷ παλινοστεῖν ἐπιτρέπουσι, καθ' ἑτέραν ἀποκάλυψιν καὶ αὐτοῖς νύκτωρ ὀφθεῖσαν, μίαν τε φωνὴν σαφεστάτην τοῖς μάλιστα αὐτῶν σπουδαίοις χρήσασαν· ἐδήλου γὰρ προελθόντας ἔξω πυλῶν τὸν ἐκ Θεοῦ προωρισμένον αὐτοῖς ἐπίσκοπον ὑποδέξασθαι. τοῦτο δὲ πράξαντες μετὰ κοινῆς τῶν ἐπισκόπων οἳ τὰς πέριξ διεῖπον ἐκκλησίας γνώμης, ἐπάναγκες αὐτὸν παραμένειν βιάζονται.—Id. ibid. cap. xi. p. 172.]

[3 In the place referred to, there is the copy of a letter written by the synod that deposed Paul of Samosata, in which they say: ἠναγκάσθημεν οὖν, ἀντιτασ-

the vi. book there is one example that may seem something to make for your purpose, until it be well considered. It is of one Fabianus, who was chosen bishop of Rome (as it is there reported) in this manner: *Cum fratres omnes ad or-* Lib. vi. *dinandum futurum episcopum in ecclesia congregati essent,* cap. 29. &c.[4]: "The report goeth, when as all the brethren were assembled together in the church, to choose him which should be bishop, and many of them determined of divers worthy and notable men, Fabianus himself being present with the rest, and no man minding to choose him, that a dove falling from above (like as the Holy Ghost descended upon our Saviour in likeness of a dove) did light upon his head; and so the whole people, being with one spirit much moved, did together with great joy and with one consent proclaim him worthy to be bishop, and immediately took him and placed him in the bishop's seat." Here we may learn that Fabianus was miraculously chosen to his bishoprick, and that the people moved with this miracle did burst out into commendation of him, and thought him worthy to be bishop: doth it therefore follow that they elected him? for it may be doubted whether those "brethren" that came together to ordain the bishop were of the clergy or of the people.

It is not denied but at this time the people did sometimes, and in some places, give their consents in the electing of their bishop: yet doth not this example prove it, being (as it may appear) extraordinary; neither is there in these two books "any form of such elections described, nor any customs of the people's choice set forth;" much less any "examples of the elections of the people and clergy, which were confirmed by the christian magistrate," as you affirm. And surely I marvel what you mean, to speak of any such confirmation by the

σόμενον αὐτὸν τῷ Θεῷ καὶ μὴ εἴκοντα ἐκκηρύξαντες, ἕτερον ἀντ' αὐτοῦ τῇ καθολικῇ ἐκκλησίᾳ καταστῆσαι ἐπίσκοπον Θεοῦ προνοίᾳ ὡς πεπείσμεθα. κ.τ.λ.—Id. ibid. Lib. VII. cap. xxx. p. 230.]

[4 Τῶν γὰρ ἀδελφῶν ἁπάντων χειροτονίας ἕνεκεν τῆς τοῦ μέλλοντος διαδέξεσθαι τὴν ἐπισκοπὴν ἐπὶ τῆς ἐκκλησίας συγκεκροτημένων, πλείστων τε ἐπιφανῶν καὶ ἐνδόξων ἀνδρῶν τοῖς πολλοῖς ἐν ὑπονοίᾳ ὑπαρχόντων, ὁ Φαβιανὸς παρών, οὐδενὸς μὲν ἀνθρώπων εἰς διάνοιαν ᾔει· ὅμως δ' οὖν ἀθρόως ἐκ μετεώρου περιστερὰν καταπτᾶσαν ἐπικαθεσθῆναι τῇ αὐτοῦ κεφαλῇ μνημονεύουσι, μίμηκα ἐνδεικνυμένην τῆς ἐπὶ τὸν Σωτῆρα τοῦ ἁγίου Πνεύματος ἐν εἴδει περιστερᾶς καθόδου. ἐφ' ᾧ τὸν πάντα λαὸν ὥσπερ ὑφ' ἑνὸς πνεύματος θείου κινηθέντα ὁμόσε προθυμίᾳ πάσῃ καὶ μιᾷ ψυχῇ ἄξιον ἐπιβοῆσαι· καὶ ἀμελλήτως ἐπὶ τὸν θρόνον τῆς ἐπισκοπῆς λαβόντας αὐτὸν ἐπιθεῖναι.—Id. ibid. Lib. VI. cap. xxix. p. 186.]

christian magistrate, seeing it is manifest that as yet there was no christian magistrate mentioned by Eusebius, except only one Philip, emperor of Rome, of whom he speaketh very little, and maketh no mention of any elections made in his time; so far off is he from expressing examples of any confirmation of such elections by any christian magistrate.

<small>A gross oversight of T. C.</small> "Namely (you say) in the bishop of Constantinople;" and yet there is no such example in either of those books, no, not so much as one word of any bishop of Constantinople. And, that it may appear how far you are overseen in this place, you shall understand that the last emperor, of whom Eusebius maketh any mention in these books, is Dioclesian, who came to the empire *anno* 288; but Constantinople was builded *anno* 335. So that by your assertion the bishop of Constantinople was confirmed above 40. years before Constantinople was[1].

Chap. vii.   The Sixth Division.

T. C. Page 42, line 2, and Sect. 1.

<small>Parturiunt montes, &c.</small> *I will add only one place, which if it be more bitter than the rest, and cut the quick more near, you shall not be angry with me, but first with those that were the authors of it, and then with him that wrote it.*

Eusebius, in the sixth book, speaking[2] *of Origen, which was* <small>Lib. vi. cap. 20.</small>[3] *admitted, not of one bishop, but of many bishops, to teach,*

<small>An untruth; as will appear.</small> *sheweth how the bishops were reprehended by the bishop of Alexandria called Demetrius, because they had admitted him without the election of the presbytery of the church, which were the chief in the election in every church, and unto the which the churches did commit the government of themselves in every several town and city, and saith, that it hath not been heard that* λαϊκοὺς *should* ὁμιλεῖν παρόντων τῶν ἐπισκόπων, *which is,* "*that the laymen should teach when the bishops were present.*" *Whereby it is*

<small>Untruth; for Origen was yet a layman, and not admitted minister by any.</small> *evident that he counted him a layman, which was only admitted by the bishops, although they were many, not being first elected by the presbytery of that church whereof he was the teacher.*

Jo. Whitgift.

The terrible preface that is here prefixed would make any

[1 Cartwright, in excuse for his mistake, says: "As in certain other places, so in this, instead of that I should have taken the quotation which came after, I taking the quotation in my paper book which went before was deceived; and for the 6. and 7. of Socrates, set down the 6. and 7. of Eusebius." He contends that the examples there are to his purpose, and complains of Whitgift as eluding what he finds in Eusebius.—Sec. Repl. pp. 281, 2.]

[2 Eusebius speaking, Repl. 2.]

[3 This reference is inserted from Repl. 2.]

man quake that is not acquainted with such vain brags. But soft, man, awhile, you do but dream; for there is no such matter in that book of Eusebius. Did you never hear tell of any, that labouring to smite at another have deadly wounded themselves? I believe it will fall so out with you in this bitter and sharp place; and then shall not I need " to be angry with" you : you shall have more cause to chafe with yourself.

T. C. smiteth at others, but woundeth himself.

For answer to the place, I say it is altogether by you falsified, and most untruly alleged. The only thing that Demetrius found fault with was because Origen, being a layman, did teach in the church, bishops being present; for he saith, "it was never heard that laymen should teach in the churches, bishops being present." But what is said to this? *Nescimus quomodo, &c.*[4]*:* "Wherein he affirmeth (we know not how) that thing which is not true; seeing there may be found divers, who, when they were able to profit the brethren, and that the holy bishops had exhorted them to instruct the people, did after this sort teach in the church: as Euelpis was required to do at Laranda by Neon; and Paulinus at Iconium by Celsus; and at Synada Theodorus by Atticus; which were all blessed brethren. And it is very likely that this thing was done also in other places, which we know not of." Yea, Demetrius himself suffered him to do the like in Alexandria; as it is manifest in sundry places of that book, and even in the end of the same chapter : " He returneth to Alexandria, and doth again employ himself to his accustomed diligence in teaching." But, because this place is so confidently

Eusebius falsified by T. C.

Euseb. Lib. vi. cap. 20.

[[4] Χρόνου δὲ μεταξὺ διαγενομένου, οὐ σμικροῦ κατὰ τὴν πόλιν ἀναρριπισθέντος πολέμου, ὑπεξελθὼν τῆς Ἀλεξανδρείας, καὶ μηδὲ τὰς κατ᾽ Αἴγυπτον διατριβὰς ἀσφαλεῖς ἑαυτῷ ἡγούμενος, ἐλθὼν ἐπὶ Παλαιστίνης, ἐν Καισαρείᾳ τὰς διατριβὰς ἐποιεῖτο· ἔνθα καὶ διαλέγεσθαι, τάς τε θείας ἑρμηνεύειν γραφὰς ἐπὶ τοῦ κοινοῦ τῆς ἐκκλησίας οἱ τῇδε ἐπίσκοποι, καίτοι τῆς τοῦ πρεσβυτερίου χειροτονίας οὐδέ πω τετυχηκότα αὐτὸν ἠξίουν. ὃ καὶ αὐτὸ γένοιτ᾽ ἂν ἔκδηλον, ἀφ᾽ ὧν περὶ τούτου Δημητρίῳ γράφοντες Ἀλέξανδρος ὁ Ἱεροσολύμων ἐπίσκοπος καὶ Θεόκτιστος ὁ Καισαρείας ὧδέ πως ἀπολογοῦνται. προσέθηκε δὲ τοῖς γράμμασιν, ὅτι τοῦτο οὐδέ ποτε ἠκούσθη, οὐδὲ νῦν γεγένηται, τὸ παρόντων ἐπισκόπων λαϊκοὺς ὁμιλεῖν· οὐκ οἶδ᾽ ὅπως προφανῶς οὐκ ἀληθῆ λέγων. ὅπου γοῦν εὑρίσκονται οἱ ἐπιτήδειοι πρὸς τὸ ὠφελεῖν τοὺς ἀδελφούς, καὶ παρακαλοῦνται τῷ λαῷ προσομιλεῖν, ὑπὸ τῶν ἁγίων ἐπισκόπων· ὥσπερ ἐν Λαράνδοις Εὔελπις ὑπὸ Νέωνος, καὶ ἐν Ἰκονίῳ Παυλῖνος ὑπὸ Κέλσου, καὶ ἐν Συνάδοις Θεόδωρος ὑπὸ Ἀττικοῦ, τῶν μακαρίων ἀδελφῶν. εἰκὸς δὲ καὶ ἐν ἄλλοις τόποις τοῦτο γίνεσθαι, ἡμᾶς δὲ μὴ εἰδέναι..... εἰς τὴν Ἀλεξάνδρειαν ἀφικόμενος τὰς συνήθεις ἐπετέλει σπουδάς.—Euseb. in Hist. Eccles. Script. Amst. 1695-1700. Lib. vi. cap. xix. p. 180.]

avouched, and so untruly, I will set it down as it is in Eusebius, *Lib. vi. cap.* 20; where he, speaking of Origen, saith thus: " In the mean time (by reason of a great war begun in that city) leaving Alexandria, and thinking that he could not safely abide in Egypt, he went into Palestina, and remained at Cesaria; where also he was requested of the bishops of that country, that he would dispute, and expound the holy scriptures before the whole church, when as yet he was not ordained minister. The which thing is hereby manifest; for that Alexander the bishop of Hierusalem, and Theoctistus bishop of Cesaria, writing to Demetrius of him, do after this sort render an account of that deed. Furthermore he addeth this also in his letters, that it was never heard of, neither yet at any time seen, that laymen did teach in the church, bishops being present: wherein (we know not how) he affirmeth that thing which is not true, &c.;" as it is set down before. What one word is there here that sheweth " how the bishops were reprehended by the bishop of Alexandria called Demetrius, because they had admitted Origen, without the election of the presbytery of the church, which were the chief in the election in every church, and unto the which the churches did commit the government of themselves in every several town and city, &c.;" as you affirm? Nay, is there any thing sounding that way? The only cause why Demetrius reproveth them (as I have said) is, because they suffered Origen in their presence to interpret the scriptures in the church, being as yet but a layman. And yet you see how Demetrius is reproved for that also, and how by sundry examples it is there shewed that it is no rare thing for a layman to interpret the scriptures in the church, the bishop being present, if he be thereunto called by the bishop.

<small>Origen was then indeed a layman.</small>

Is this your bitter place? is this that terrible cutter? Indeed it maketh your doings uncyphered, and shrewdly woundeth you, if you can well consider it.

But to make the matter yet more plain. Eusebius, in the same book and 23. chapter, sheweth how Origen afterwards *accepit presbyterii gradum in Cæsaria Palestinæ ab ejus loci episcopis*[1]: " was made minister in Cesaria Palestinæ of the bishops of that country." The which thing Demetrius misliked also, not for any just cause, but only of malice; for,

<small>Euseb. Lib. vi. 23.</small>

[1 Id. ibid. cap. xxiii. p. 182.]

although Demetrius at the first esteemed well of Origen, and bare good-will unto him, yet afterward, when he saw him marvellously to prosper, and to become very famous and well-accounted of, he then sought means, not only to discredit him, but those also which had preferred him to the ministry, laying to his charge that which he had done being a boy (that is, gelding of himself); as Eusebius doth at large declare, *Lib. vi. cap.* 8.[2] You see therefore how untruly you have reported Eusebius, and that there is no such cause by him expressed why Demetrius reproved the bishops, as you feign to be.

But I partly smell your meaning, which I suppose to be this, that all we, which are admitted into the ministry by the bishops without your presbytery, are but laymen; whereby you would insinuate that all those which have been baptized by us are not baptized, because you say that it is of the substance or "being of baptism, whether he be minister or no that ministereth that sacrament," page 114. And this is that mystery, which you and your fellows will not as yet openly utter, but craftily dissemble, until you see better opportunity. The truth is, your intent is rebaptization, and flat anabaptism. But I have declared sufficiently the vanity of your collection in this place, and the weakness of your reasons touching this matter, where you have given me more especial occasion to speak of it, Tract. ix.[3]

Pag. 114, sect. 1.

Chapter vii.   The Seventh Division.

T. C. Page 42, Sect. 2, 3.

Seeing then that the scripture doth teach this order, that there should be no minister thrust upon the church but by the consent thereof, and reason persuadeth that ways, and the use of the church hath been so from time to time, both in peace and in time of persecution, both under tyrants and godly princes, it cannot be without the high displeasure of Almighty God, the great hurt and sore oppression of the church, that one man should take this unto him which pertaineth to so many, or one minister which per-

[2 Id. ibid. cap. viii. pp. 169, 70.]

[3 Cartwright maintains his own view of Origen's case. "The D." he says, "confesseth that Origen taught being a layman in the church publicly: he cannot deny if he would but that he taught by the appointment of bishops. These two being put, what followeth but that in those days he was counted a layman which took upon him the ministry upon the bishops' appointing only? &c."—Sec. Repl. pp. 282, 3.]

No certain form of electing ministers in the scriptures.

taineth to more than one, especially where the advice of learned ministers may concur with the people's election or consent.

Now, if any man will rise up and say that this doctrine bringeth in disorder; and by this means children, boys[1], and women should have their voices, which is unseemly; all men understand that, where the election is most freest and most general, yet only they have to do which are heads of families; and that this is but a mere cavil to bring the truth in hatred, which is unworthy to be answered, and requireth rather a censor than a disputer to suppress it.

Jo. Whitgift.

"The scripture doth" not "teach any such order:" it hath examples to the contrary: it prescribeth herein no certain rule to be perpetual: there is better "reason" to the contrary, if the diversity of the time and other circumstances be considered: the church also hath not at all times, nor in all places, used one form and manner of election; not in the apostles' time, as it hath been declared: wherefore "the church" is neither "hurt" nor "oppressed," if the godly[2] magistrate alone do appoint in it bishops, and take such order for admitting other inferior pastors, as shall be thought to him most convenient; neither is "God displeased" with them for so doing, if they seek his glory therein, the godly peace and quietness of the church, and have respect to the end of the apostles in appointing ministers. But he is greatly displeased with those that make a necessity where none is, and trouble the churches with their own devices, and make contention for external matters.

¶ It is not necessary that the people should have interest in the election of ministers; but the contrary is convenient.

Chap. viii. The First Division.

Jo. Whitgift.

Now that you have uttered all your authorities and reasons, to prove that the people ought to have interest in the electing of their ministers, and that I have sufficiently (I trust) answered the same, let it not be troublesome unto you if summarily I collect my reasons that move me to think the contrary.

[[1] Children and boys, Repl. 1 and 2.]   [[2] Goodly, Def. B.]

1. And, first, I will prove that there is no certain form of electing prescribed in scripture, but that the same is left free for the churches to appoint, as shall be thought most convenient for their states and times.

No certain form of electing ministers in the scriptures.

2. Secondly, I will shew that there hath been great diversity, from time to time, used in the church touching elections, and that the people at all times, and in all places, have not been admitted thereunto.

3. Last of all, I will set down the reasons why the people have been debarred from such elections, and why they ought still so to be.

Touching the first, these be my reasons.

1. Christ (whose facts and deeds we ought especially to follow) did of himself alone, without the consent of any, call and choose his apostles, and likewise the 70. disciples whom he sent to preach.

Matt. x.
Luke x.

2. The apostles, Acts i., altered this manner and form; for they presented two, and the one of them was chosen by lot.

3. In the vi. of the Acts they clean altered this also; for the people presented seven to the apostles, and they were all chosen without lots: the apostles also laid on their hands upon them.

4. In the xiv. of the Acts this form is likewise changed; for Paul and Barnabas ordained ministers in every city, without either presentment by the people or casting of lots.

5. In the xiii. of the Acts it is manifest that Paul and Barnabas were sent only by the prophets and doctors, without any consent of the people either given or required: read the beginning of the chapter; it is plain enough of itself.

6. Paul sent Timothy and Titus, and gave them authority to ordain other: so that it is certain that here is no prescript manner and form appointed to be observed for ever; seeing that the apostles themselves did not bind or tie themselves to any such rule; which both M. Bullinger, Zuinglius, and Beza, do likewise confess; as I have before declared. And there M. Calvin (as I told you before) saith that of that example in the first of the Acts no certain rule can be gathered of electing and choosing ministers[3]. And M. Beza is of the

1 Tim. v.
2 Tim. i.
Tit. i.

[3 See before, page 296, note 4; page 303, notes 1, 2; and page 343, notes 5, 6.]

No certain form of electing ministers in the scriptures.
Beza, Lib. Conf. cap. 5.

same judgment, both for that example, Acts i., and the other also of deacons, Acts vi.; as I have likewise declared before. And, in that book of confession and v. chapter, he hath this saying worthy to be noted: "Because the multitude is for the most part ignorant and intractable, and the greater part doth oftentimes prevail against the better, not in a popular state lawfully appointed are all things committed to the unbridled multitude; but certain magistrates are appointed, by the consent of the people, to rule and govern them: if this wisdom be in worldly affairs, much more is a moderation to be had in those matters wherein men be oftentimes blinded. Neither is there any cause why any man of sound judgment should exclaim that in such matters there is no place for policy, except he can shew this policy, whereof I speak, to be repugnant to the word of God, which I think he cannot[1]." Hitherto M. Beza; and he speaketh of the electors of minis-

Idem.

ters. And a little after he saith that "we must not always look what the apostles did in ecclesiastical policy or in the government of the church; seeing there is so great diversity of circumstances, that a man cannot without preposterous zeal reduce all things, in all places and times, to one and the same form; but it is sufficient if respect be had to their end and purpose, which is not variable, and that manner and form

The end of the apostles in ecclesiastical policy must be regarded, and not their deeds.

used which leadeth thereunto, &c.[2]" Whereupon also I conclude, that in the scriptures there is no certain form prescribed of electing ministers, and that the doings of the apostles in that matter are not at all times of necessity to be followed; but it is sufficient to respect their end and purpose, that is, that there be meet ministers; and therefore M. Beza

Ibidem.

saith: "No man may here prescribe any certain rule; but, if the conscience be good, it is an easy matter to determine

[1 Quoniam enim plerumque multitudo et imperita est et intractabilis, et major pars sæpe meliorem vincit, ne in democratia quidem legitime constituta omnia permissa sunt effræni vulgo, sed constituti sunt ex populi consensu certi magistratus qui plebi præeant, et inconditam multitudinem regant. Quod si hæc prudentia in negotiis humanis requiritur, multo sane magis opus est certa moderatione in iis rebus in quibus homines prorsus cæcutiunt. Neque causa est cur quisquam sani judicii homo clamitet nullum hic esse prudentiæ locum, nisi hanc prudentiam, de qua loquor, ostendat cum Dei verbo pugnare, quod sane non arbitror.—Th. Bezæ Confess. Christ. Fid. Genev. 1587. cap. v. 35. pp. 151, 2.]

[2 Neque &c.: sed potius spectandus est eorum finis et scopus invariabilis, et ea deligenda forma ac ratio rerum agendarum quæ recta eo deducat. &c.—Id. ibid. p. 152. See before, page 254, note 2.]

Chap. viii. The Second Division.

2. Touching the second, that is, for the diversities of elections afterward used in the church, and that the people were not always admitted to the same, I refer you to that which hath been spoken before out of Eusebius and Zuinglius, of the apostles appointing of James to be bishop of Hierusalem[5]; of Cyprian, *Lib. i. Epist.* 4.; where he plainly confesseth that electing by the people was not then general, in that he saith, *Et fere per provincias universas tenetur*[6], and doth the contrary himself in choosing one Aurelius without the consent of the people, *Lib. ii. Epist.* 5[7]; likewise of the 18. canon of the council of Ancyrane[8]; 18. canon of the council of Antioch[9]; 12. and 13. can. *Con. Laodiceni*[10]: all which canons and councils I have alleged before.

In the first of the canons attributed to the apostles it is decreed that a bishop should be ordained of two or three bishops; and the Greek word is χειροτονείσθω[11].

In the second of the same canons the ordaining of priests, deacons, and other clerks, is committed to the bishop alone; and the Greek word there is χειροτονείσθω likewise[12].

In the 35. or 36. of the same canons it plainly appeareth that bishops were chosen without the consent of the people[13].

[3 Id. ibid. 37, p. 154. See before, page 303, note 2.]

[4 Cartwright rejoins that "the most part" of the authorities alleged in this section "have been brought before," and proved of no value; and that it may be "seen that the rest are no better than their fellows."—Sec. Repl. pp. 283, 4.]

[5 Euseb. in Hist. Eccles. Script. Amst. 1695-1700. Lib. II. cap. xxiii. p. 50; H. Zvingl. Op. Tigur. 1581. Ecclesiast. Pars II. fol. 48. 2.]

[6 Cypr. Op. Amst. 1682. Ad Pleb. et Cler. Hisp. Epist. lxvii. p. 172. See before, page 362, note 1.]

[7 Id. ibid. Ad Pleb. et Cler. Epist. xxxviii. pp. 74, 5.]

[8 Concil. Ancyr. can. 18. in Concil. Stud. Labb. et Cossart. Lut. Par. 1671-2. Tom. I. cols. 1461, 4.]

[9 Concil. Antioch. can. 18. ibid. Tom. II. col. 569.]

[10 Concil. Laod. cans. 12, 13. ibid. Tom. I. col. 1497. See before, page 366, note 6.]

[11 Ἐπίσκοπος χειροτονείσθω ὑπὸ ἐπισκόπων δύο ἢ τριῶν.—Can. Apost. 1. ibid. Tom. I. col. 25.]

[12 Πρεσβύτερος ὑπὸ ἑνὸς ἐπισκόπου χειροτονείσθω, καὶ διάκονος, καὶ οἱ λοιποὶ κληρικοί.—Can. 2. ibid.]

[13 Can. 35. ibid. col. 33. See before, page 366, note 3.]

In the 4. canon of the council of Nice the election of bishops is appointed only to bishops[1].

It appeareth plainly in the 19. can. *Con. Antiocheni*, that only the metropolitan and other ministers had interest in the ordaining and appointing of bishops[2].

It is manifest by Euseb. *Lib. vi. cap.* 8. and 23, that Origen was admitted and ordained minister only by bishops[3].

Hierome, in his epistle *ad Nepotianum*, in the words before recited, signifieth that the election of priests doth pertain to the bishop[4].

Gratian, Distinct. 62., hath this canon made by Leo who was bishop of Rome: *Nulla ratio sinit, &c.*[5]: "No reason permitteth that they should be accounted amongst the bishops, which are neither chosen of the clerks, nor desired of the people, nor consecrated of the bishops of that province with the judgment and allowance of the metropolitan." The gloss, expounding what this is, to be "desired of the people," saith that it is "to give testimony unto them[6]." And no man denieth but that such as are to be admitted into the ministry ought to have a testimony of their life and conversation, and that it should be lawful for any man to except against them, if there be just cause; but yet the judgment not to rest in the people.

And, Distinct. 63., there is this law: *Laici nullo modo se debent inserere electioni*[7]: "The lay-people ought by no means to thrust themselves into the election, or to meddle with the election." There are certain canons collected out of the Greek synods by Martin *Bracaren. Episc.*; and they

[1 Ἐπίσκοπον προσήκει μάλιστα μὲν ὑπὸ πάντων τῶν ἐν τῇ ἐπαρχίᾳ καθίστασθαι.—Concil. Nic. can. 4. ibid. Tom. II. col. 29.]

[2 Ἐπίσκοπον μὴ χειροτονεῖσθαι δίχα συνόδου καὶ παρουσίας τοῦ ἐν τῇ μητροπόλει τῆς ἐπαρχίας· κ.τ.λ. εἰ δὲ ἄλλως παρὰ τὰ ὡρισμένα γίγνοιτο, μηδὲν ἰσχύειν τὴν χειροτονίαν.—Concil. Antioch. can. 19. ibid. Tom. II. col. 569.]

[3 ...ὅτε τῶν κατὰ Παλαιστίνην οἱ μάλιστα δόκιμοι καὶ διαπρέποντες Καισαρείας τε καὶ Ἱεροσολύμων ἐπίσκοποι, πρεσβείων τὸν Ὠριγένην καὶ τῆς ἀνωτάτω τιμῆς ἄξιον εἶναι δοκιμάσαντες, χεῖρας εἰς πρεσβυτέριον αὐτῷ τεθείκασι.—Euseb. in Hist. Eccles. Script. Amst. 1695-1700. Lib. vi. cap. viii. p. 170.]

[4 Hieron. Op. Par. 1693-1706. Ad Nepot. De Vit. Cler. Epist. xxxiv. Tom. IV. Pars ii. col. 262. See before, page 443.]

[5 Nulla ratio sinit, ut inter episcopos habeantur, qui nec a clericis sunt electi, nec a plebibus expetiti, nec a provincialibus episcopis cum metropolitani judicio consecrati.—Leo Papa in Corp. Jur. Canon. Lugd. 1624. Decret. Gratian. Decr. Prim. Pars, Dist. lxii. cam. 1. col. 312. Conf. Leon. Magni Op. Lut. 1623. Ad Rust. Epist. xcii. cap. i. col. 475.]

[6 Consensus plebis requiritur in electione: et eo ipso consentiunt, quod perhibent ei testimonium.—Gloss. ibid.]

[7 Laici vero nullo &c.—Ibid. Dist. lxiii. ibid. This is the rubric of the distinction.]

are to be found *Tom. Conc. ii.* The first of the canons is this, the which Gratian also hath, Distinct. 63: *Non licet populo*, &c.[8]: "It is not lawful for the people to make the election of them which are preferred to priesthood; but it is in the judgment of the bishops that they should prove him which is to be ordained, whether he be instructed in the word, and in faith, and in spiritual conversation." The same may be also proved by the 2.[9] and 3.[10] canons following.

The people not always admitted to the election.

In the same Distinct. there is this canon, taken out of the 8. general council: *Consecrationes et promotiones*, &c.[11]: "This holy and general council, agreeing with former councils, hath decreed and enacted, that the consecrations and promotions of bishops should be made by the election of the clergy, and by the decree and college of the bishops."

Theodoret, *Lib. iv. cap.* 5, saith that, when Auxentius, being an Arian, was deprived of the bishoprick of Millain, Valentinian the emperor called together the bishops, and "willed them to place such a one in that bishoprick as he might safely commit himself unto, &c.;" and, when as they desired the emperor that he himself would choose one whom he thought meet, the emperor told them again, "that it were much better for them to elect one, because they were best able to judge of his meetness." And, although the people, being divided tumultuously, requested the bishops, some for one, some for another, and at the length all desired to have Ambrose; yet it may evidently appear that the interest of the election was in the bishops, and the confirmation and allowing of the same in the emperor[12]. And, in that the

Theod. Lib. iv. cap. 5.

[8 Non licet populo electionem facere eorum, qui ad sacerdotium promoventur: sed in judicio episcoporum est, ut ipsi eum, qui ordinandus est, probent, si in sermone et fide et in vita spirituali edoctus sit.—Capit. Græc. Synod. Interp. S. Martin. Episc. Bracaren. cap. 1. in Crabb. Concil. Col. Agrip. 1551. Tom. II. p. 222. Conf. Decret. Gratian. Decr. Prim. Pars, Dist. lxiii. can. 8. col. 316.]

[9 Episcopum oportet maxime quidem ab omni concilio constitui, &c.—Ibid. cap. 2.]

[10 Non debet ordinari episcopus absque consilio et præsentia metropolitani episcopi. &c.—Ibid. cap. 3.]

[11 ...Consecrationes et promotiones episcoporum concordans prioribus conciliis, clericorum electione, ac decreto episcoporum collegii fieri sancta hæc et universalis synodus diffinit, et statuit: &c.—Ex Oct. Syn. Act. prim. in Corp. Jur. Canon. Decret. Gratian. Decr. Prim. Pars, Dist. lxiii. can. 2. cols. 313, 4.]

[12 ...Αὐξεντίου γάρ, ὃς τὴν Ἀρείου μὲν εἰσεδέξατο λώβην, Μεδιολάνου δὲ τὴν ἐκκλησίαν πεπιστευμένος ἐν πλείσταις ἀπεκηρύχθη συνόδοις, τὸν βίον ὑπεξελθόντος, μεταπεμψάμενος τοὺς ἐπισκόπους ὁ βασιλεὺς, τοιοῖσδε πρὸς αὐτοὺς ἐχρήσατο λόγοις...τοιοῦτον δὴ οὖν καὶ νῦν τοῖς ἀρχιερατικοῖς ἐγκαθιδρύσατε θώκοις, ὅπως καὶ ἡμεῖς οἱ τὴν βασιλείαν ἰθύνοντες εἰλικρινῶς αὐτῷ τὰς ἡμετέρας ὑπο-

The people not always admitted to the election. bishops would have committed the whole matter to the emperor, it may appear that it greatly skilleth not who do choose; so that such be chosen as be fit for the place.

Distinct. 63. In the 63. Distinct. of Gratian it is also to be seen, that sometime the election and allowing of bishops was wholly given to the emperor; as we may read in the decree of Adrian the pope there mentioned[1]; and in the decree of Leo the first, where he sheweth how that the dissensions, heresies, and schisms, that were in the church, was the cause why that both the election of the Roman bishop, and of other also, was committed to the emperor[2].

Whereby it is evident that the people have not at all times, nor in all places, had interest in the elections of ministers. I know that Gratian in the same distinction saith as much in the behalf of the people[3]; but thereby we may gather that this election hath been variable, and from time to time used according to the place, time, and persons. For further proof hereof, I could recite the variety that now is, and heretofore also hath been, even in reformed churches; but, to avoid tediousness, I refer that to every man's own search.

This is most certain, that the form prescribed in the Second Admonition, and in this Reply of T. C. also, if it be considered, will appear to have in it *nihil apostolicum*, "nothing apostolical," but to differ as much from any form that was then used, as this doth that we retain in the church of England at this day, and a great deal more[4].

κλίνωμεν κεφαλάς....ταῦτα τοῦ βασιλέως εἰρηκότος, αὐτὸν ἡ σύνοδος ἠξίου ψηφίσασθαι, σοφόν τε ὄντα καὶ εὐσεβείᾳ κοσμούμενον. ὁ δὲ ἔφη, μεῖζον ἢ καθ' ἡμᾶς τὸ ἐγχείρημα. ὑμεῖς γὰρ τῆς θείας ἠξιωμένοι χάριτος, καὶ τὴν αἴγλην ἐκείνην εἰσδεξάμενοι, ἄμεινον ψηφιεῖσθε...οἱ δὲ τὴν πόλιν ἐκείνην οἰκοῦντες ἐστασίαζον, οἱ μὲν τοῦτον, οἱ δὲ ἐκεῖνον προβληθῆναι φιλονεικοῦντες· κ.τ.λ.—Theod. in Hist. Eccles. Script. Amst. 1695-1700. Lib. iv. capp. vi. vii. pp. 156, 7.]

[1 Imperator jus habet eligendi pontificem.—Corp. Jur. Canon. Lugd. 1624. Decret. Gratian. Decr. Prim. Pars, Dist. lxiii. can. 22. col. 322. This is the rubric of the canon.]

[2 Principibus vero atque imperatoribus electiones Romanorum pontificum atque aliorum episcoporum referendas, usus et constitutio tradidit pro schismaticorum atque hæreticorum dissensionibus, quibus nonnunquam ecclesia Dei concussa periclitabatur.—Ibid. can. 27. col. 326. This part of the canon is not, like the preceding portion, by Leo.]

[3 Ibid. cans. 9, &c. cols. 316, &c.]

[4 Cartwright in his rejoinder to this division says, that "the canons called the apostles', that of Antioch, Eusebius, and others which speak of ordaining, make nothing to this question which is of election;" accuses Whitgift of "having changed the words of the council" of Nice, "and instead of ordination put election;" makes light of Gratian; declares that "that which is gathered of Ambrose's

Chapter viii. The Third Division.

The reasons why the people have been secluded from such elections, and so ought to be, are these.

1. First, the marvellous contentions that have been in such kind of elections by the sinister affections of the people, being easily moved to division and parts-taking upon every light occasion. Examples whereof there be infinite almost in every election, as it may evidently appear to every one that hath but lightly run over any ecclesiastical history.

Why the people have been, and now ought to be, debarred from the election. Contention about the election of ministers.

When Damasus was chosen bishop of Rome, there was one Ursicinus, a deacon, set up against him; and the contention was so vehement betwixt them, and the rage of the people so intemperate, that they fell from voices to blows; insomuch that there was many slain, even in the place of election[5].

Plat. in vita Damasi.

What sedition was there moved in the election of Boniface the second, when Dioscorus contended with him for the bishoprick! the people were so divided that the contention could not be ended but with the death of Dioscorus[6].

Platina.

The like brawl was in the elections of Conon, Sergius, Paulus I., Constantinus[7], and almost in every election made in that seat; as it is evident in such stories as especially entreat of the lives of the bishops of Rome.

Platina.

The like stir there hath been in other places also, especially after that the churches were divided with heresies and sects. At Constantinople, after the death of Alexander their bishop, there was a marvellous uproar for his successor, some desiring to have Paul, a catholic, and some Macedonius, an Arian: this contention was so vehement, that the whole city was disturbed and many slain on both parties, yea, even the emperor's officer that was sent to appease it. Sozom. *Lib. iii. cap.* 4. and 7.[8]

Sozom. Lib. iii. cap. 4, and 7.

election out of Theodoret is most untrue," and concludes that, if there had been anything of value in Chrysostom's 3rd book *De Sacerdotio* (see below, page 466, note 3), Whitgift would have alleged it more particularly.—Sec. Repl. pp. 281, &c.]

[5 Damasus autem electus ad pontificatum obeundum Ursicinum diaconum competitorem habuit in basilica quæ Sicinini appellatur, ubi multi utrinque cecidere in ipso templo, cum res non suffragiis tantum, sed vi et armis tractaretur. —Plat. De Vit. Pont. Col. 1551. Damas. I. pp. 47, 8.]

[6 Hujus itaque tempore Bonifacius pontifex creatur, non sine contentione tamen: nam et Dioscorus, diviso bifariam clero, in demortui Felicis locum subrogatur. Exagitatus autem clerus hac seditione diebus octo et viginti, morte Dioscori a tanta perturbatione tandem liberatur.—Id. ibid. Bonifac. II. p. 66.]

[7 Id. ibid. Conon, Serg. I., Paul. I., Steph. III. pp. 88, 9, 90, 102, 3.]

[8 Soz. in Hist. Eccles. Script. Lib. III. capp. iv. vii. pp. 408, 12, 13.]

Why the people ought, and have been debarred from elections.

The strife that was in the same place, after the death of Atticus (Philip, Prochis, and Sisinius, striving for the bishoprick at one time), Socrates testifieth, *Lib. vii. cap.* 26[1]: the same doth he write also to have been betwixt Philip and Prochis, after the deprivation of Nestorius, *Lib. vii. cap.* 35[2].

Socrat. Lib. vii. cap. 26. Lib. vii. cap. 35.

After Eudoxius removed from Antioch to Constantinople, there was in Antioch great strife for a successor; as the same Sozomen sheweth, *Lib. iv. cap.* 28; where he addeth these words: "As in such things it cometh to pass, that there are divers contentions and seditions betwixt the clergy and betwixt the people[3]."

Sozom. Lib. iv. cap. 28.

Socrates, *Lib. v. cap.* 9, declareth the like tumults to have been about the election of Flavianus; and he addeth: *Atque ita Antiochena ecclesia denuo, non propter fidem sed propter episcopos, scinditur*[4]*:* "And so the church of Antioch is again divided, not for matters of faith, but for their bishops."

Socrat. Lib. v. cap. 9.

I declared before out of Nazianzene, in his funeral oration at the burial of his father, what great trouble and danger was at Cesarea in his time about the election of their bishops[5].

Nazianzen.

The same also I noted out of Augustine, *Epist. cx.:* it was the cause why both he and his predecessor in their life-times did provide to themselves successors; as it is there manifest[6].

Augustin. Tom. II. Ep. 110.

Socrates, *Lib. vi. cap.* 11, declareth what contention there was at Ephesus about the election of their bishop, the people being divided into sundry factions; insomuch that Chrysostom was himself enforced to appoint unto them one Heraclis his deacon[7].

Socrat. Lib. vi. cap. 11.

[1] Ἐγένετο δὲ μετὰ τὴν τελευτὴν Ἀττικοῦ πολλὴ φιλονεικία περὶ χειροτονίας ἐπισκόπου, ἄλλων ἄλλον ζητούντων· τινὲς μὲν γάρ, φησι, Φίλιππον τὸν πρεσβύτερον ἐζήτουν· τινὲς δὲ Πρόκλον· καὶ οὗτος δὲ πρεσβύτερος ἦν· κοινῇ δὲ πᾶς ὁ λαὸς ἐπόθει γίνεσθαι Σισίννιον, κ.τ.λ.—Socr. in eod. Lib. VII. cap. xxvi. p. 300.]

[2] Πάλιν περὶ ἐπιλογῆς ἐπισκόπων ζήτησις ἦν· καὶ πολλοὶ μὲν Φίλιππον,... πλείους δὲ τὸν Πρόκλον ἐπελέγοντο· κ.τ.λ.—Id. ibid. cap. xxxv. p. 308.]

[3] Ἐν δὲ τῷ τότε Εὐδοξίου κατασχόντος τὴν Κωνσταντινουπόλεως ἐκκλησίαν, πολλοὶ τὸν ἐν Ἀντιοχείᾳ θρόνον περιποιεῖν ἑαυτοῖς ἐσπούδαζον, καὶ ὡς εἰκὸς ἐπὶ πράγμασι τοιούτοις, φιλονεικίαι καὶ στάσεις διάφοροι τοῦ κλήρου καὶ τοῦ λαοῦ συνέβησαν.—Soz. in eod. Lib. IV. cap. xxviii. p. 477.]

[4] ...πάλιν τε ὁ λαὸς ἄνωθεν διεκρίνετο· οὕτως αὖθις διὰ τοὺς ἐπισκόπους, οὐ μὴν διὰ τὴν πίστιν, ἡ Ἀντιοχέων ἐκκλησία διῄρητο.—Socr. in eod. Lib. v. cap. ix. p. 218.]

[5] Gregor. Naz. Op. Par. 1778-1840. In Patr. Fun. Orat. xviii. 33, &c. Tom. I. pp. 353, &c. See before, page 447.]

[6] August. Op. Par. 1679-1700. Act. Ecclesiast. seu Epist. ccxxiii. 1, 4. Tom. II. coll. 789, 90. See before, pages 444, 5.]

[7 ...συνιδὼν ὁ Ἰωάννης ἀμφότερα τὰ μέρη φιλονείκως διακείμενα,...αὐτὸς

The same author, *Lib. vii. cap.* 7, testifieth the like contention to have been in Alexandria; whilst some desired Timothy an archdeacon, other some Cyril⁸. *Why the people ought, and have been debarred from elections.*

Evagrius, *Lib. ii. cap.* 5, writeth thus: *Cum autem hic Proterius &c.*⁹: "When this Proterius was placed in the bishop's seat of Alexandria, there arose a great and intolerable tumult among the people, which were tossed with divers sentences: for (as it often falleth out in such cases) some would have Dioscorus again; others stuck stoutly to Proterius; so that many incurable mischiefs were committed. For Priscus the rhetorician writeth that the governor of Thebes came the same time to Alexandria, and saw the people wholly to set themselves against the magistrates; and that, when the garrison of soldiers would have kept back the sedition, they beat them back with stones into the temple, which was in times past called the temple of Serapis: then the people coming thither with speed took the temple and burned the soldiers quick. But when the emperor understood hereof, he sent thither two thousand new soldiers, who, having a prosperous wind and passage, arrived the sixth day after at the great city of Alexandria, and so raged against the wives and daughters of the men of Alexandria, that much more mischief was now wrought than before." *Socrat. Lib. vii. cap. 7. Evagrius, Lib.ii. cap. 5.*

To what further inconvenience this intolerable contention came afterwards, the same Evagrius writeth, *cap.* 8, where *Evagrius, Lib.ii. cap. 8.*

τοίνυν Ἡρακλείδην τινὰ διάκονον ἑαυτοῦ, γένει Κύπριον, εἰς τὴν ἐπισκοπὴν προεβάλλετο· κ.τ.λ.—Socr. in Hist. Eccles. Script. Amst. 1695-1700. Lib. VI. cap. XI. p. 259.]

[⁸ ...ἐπιμάχου δὲ γενομένης καὶ ἐνταῦθα τῆς ἐπισκοπῆς, οἱ μὲν ἐζήτουν ἐνθρονισθῆναι Τιμόθεον ἀρχιδιάκονον· οἱ δὲ Κύριλλον, κ.τ.λ.—Id. ibid. Lib. VII. cap. vii. p. 280.]

[⁹ ...ὃς [Προτέριος] ἐπειδὴ τὸν οἰκεῖον κατειλήφει θρόνον, μέγιστος καὶ ἀνυπόιστος τάραχος τῷ δήμῳ διανέστη πρὸς διαφόρους κυμαινομένῳ γνώμας. οἱ μὲν γὰρ Διόσκορον ἐπεζήτουν, οἷάπερ εἰκὸς ἐν τοῖς τοιούτοις γίνεσθαι· οἱ δὲ Προτερίου μάλα γενικῶς ἀντείχοντο, ὡς καὶ πολλὰ καὶ ἀνήκεστα προελθεῖν. ἱστορεῖ δ' οὖν Πρίσκος ὁ ῥήτωρ, φθῆναι τηνικαῦτα τὴν Ἀλεξάνδρου τῆς Θηβαίων ἐπαρχίας, ἰδεῖν τε τὸν δῆμον ὁμόσε κατὰ τῶν ἀρχόντων χωροῦντα. τῆς τε στρατιωτικῆς δυνάμεως τὴν στάσιν διακωλύειν βουλομένης, λίθων βολαῖς αὐτοὺς χρήσασθαι· τρέψασθαί τε τούτους καὶ ἀνὰ τὸ ἱερὸν τὸ πάλαι Σαράπιδος ἀναδραμόντας ἐκπολιορκῆσαι, καὶ πυρὶ ζῶντας παραδοῦναι· ταῦτά τε τὸν βασιλέα μαθόντα δισχιλίους νεολέκτους ἐκπέμψαι· καὶ τοῦ πνεύματος ἐπιτυχόντας οὐριοδρομῆσαι, ὡς ἀνὰ τὴν ἕκτην τῶν ἡμερῶν τῇ μεγάλῃ τῶν Ἀλεξανδρέων προσχεῖν πόλει. κἀκεῖθεν τῶν στρατιωτῶν παροινούντων ἔς τε τὰς γαμετὰς καὶ θυγατέρας τῶν Ἀλεξανδρέων, τῶν προτέρων πολλὰ δεινότερα προελθεῖν.—Evagr. in eod. Lib. II. cap. v. p. 295.]

[WHITGIFT.]

The people not always admitted to the election.

he also describeth the manners and conditions of the people at large, and declareth how easily they are moved to contentions and tumultuous dealing, how willingly led by any factious person that pretendeth liberty, &c. In the end he sheweth how villanously and cruelly they murdered Proterius, appointed to be their bishop[1].

What should I speak of that hurly-burly that was in Millain before the election of Ambrose? whereof Theodoret speaketh, *Lib. iv. cap. 6.*[2]

Theod. Lib. iv. cap. 6.

Chrysost. Lib. iii. de Sacerdotio.

I shall desire the learned reader to peruse Chrysostom, in the iii. book that he writeth *de Sacerdotio*, where he speaketh of this matter plentifully, and declareth the marvellous partiality and the intolerable contentions that the people used, and was the cause of, in such elections[3].

If I were disposed to heap up examples, I could fill a large volume; but these (being almost in the best time of the church, under christian princes) manifestly declare what intolerable inconvenience ensueth such elections as are committed to the people, especially in these matters.

The election of ministers by the people an impediment to the civil magistrate in ecclesiastical matters.

2. My second reason is that, if such elections should be committed to the people, the civil magistrate (who hath the chief government of the church, and to whom the especial care of religion doth appertain) should not be able to procure such reformation, nor such consent and agreement in matters of religion, as he is when he hath himself the placing of bishops, and such as be the chief of the clergy: for the people (who are commonly bent to novelties and to factions, and most ready to receive that doctrine that seemeth to be contrary to the present state, and that inclineth to liberty) would usually elect such as would feed their humours; so that the prince neither should have quiet government, neither could be able to preserve the peace of the church, nor yet to plant that religion that he in conscience is persuaded to be sincere. As for the authority of disallowing their elections which you give unto him, it is but an intolerable trouble; and, besides that, he shall not understand their doings; or, if he doth, yet may he not deprive them of their liberty in choosing; so that you make his authority in effect nothing. Moreover, his churches

[1 Id. ibid. cap. viii. pp. 299, &c.]
[2 Theod. in eod. Lib. IV. cap. vii. p. 157.]
[3 Chrysost. Op. Par. 1718-38. De Sacerdot. Lib. III. cap. xv. Tom. I. pp. 392, &c.]

and whole kingdom should be filled with anabaptists, libertines, papists, puritans, and an hundred sects more, or ever he were aware; for who will complain of him whom the people do fancy, be he never so unmeet a person?

The people not always admitted to the election.

3. My third reason is taken out of your own book, fol. 25; where you say that the archdeacon may not be "judge of the aptness and ableness of the pastor, because he is inferior to the pastor, both in calling and gifts[4]:" which if it be true, then surely may not the people have anything to do in the election of the pastor, being in all respects much more inferior unto him than the archdeacon is; for to have interest in electing is to be admitted to judge of his meetness and aptness that is to be admitted.

If the people should choose, the inferior in gifts should be judge of the superior. Page 25, line 3.

4. It would be a cause why many churches should be longer destitute of their pastors than is convenient: for, if an unmeet man were chosen, and an appeal made to the next pastors, and from them to the next synod provincial, and then the parishioners that will not yield excommunicated, and after excommunication complained of to the prince, and then driven to a new election, and in the same peradventure as wayward as they were before; whilst, I say, all this were in doing (besides the marvellous schisms, contentions, brawlings, and hatred that must of necessity in the mean time be among them), two or three years might soon be spent (for all these things cannot be in due order well done in less time); all which time the parishes must be destitute of a pastor, and burn with those mischiefs that I have before recited.

Popular elections a cause of long want of pastors, &c.

5. It would make the government of the church popular; which is the worst kind of government that can be. For it is true that M. Calvin saith, *cap.* 20, *Instit.: Proclivis est a regno &c.*[5]*:* "The fall from a kingdom into a tyranny is very ready, and the change from the government of the best into the factions of a few is not much harder; but the fall from a popular state into a sedition is of all other most easy."

Popular election a cause of a popular government.

6. The people (as I have said before), through affection and want of judgment, are easily brought by ambitious persons to give their consent to unworthy men: they are soon moved by the request of their friends, and of such as they

The people easily led by affection.

[4 See before, page 304.]

[5 Proclivis est a regno in tyrannidem lapsus: sed non multo difficilior ab optimatum potestate in paucorum factionem: multo vero facillimus, a populari dominatione in seditionem.—Calvin. Op. Amst. 1667-71. Inst. Lib. IV. cap. xx. 8. Tom. IX. p. 399.]

either fear or love, to do anything; as may appear in sundry things committed unto them of great importance, yea, sometime when by oath they are bound to deal without all affection or partiality.

The people not always admitted to the election.

7. By this means they would think to have their pastor bound unto them, so that they would take it disdainfully to be reproved by him, according as his duty would require. Again, the pastor, considering their good-will in preferring of him, would not so freely reprehend them, nor willingly displease them.

A hinderance to the pastor in doing his duty.

8. To conclude, the people are for the most part rude and ignorant, careless also in such matters, and more meet to be ruled than to rule. For, as Chrysostom defineth, *Populus est quiddam tumultus &c.*[1]: "The people is a certain thing, full of tumult and stirs, consisting and rashly compacted for the most part of folly, oftentimes tossed with variable and contrary judgment, like to the waves of the sea, &c."

The people unfit to be judges in such cases.

Chrys. ii. in Joh.

These and a great number more reasons may be alleged, why the people are to be secluded from the election of their pastors: and yet do I not so utterly seclude them from such elections, but that, if they have anything to object against him that is to be ordained, they might be heard; which order is prescribed in the book of making ministers; and that is as much as can be required. Although I do not condemn those churches wherein this is safely committed unto them; for I only speak of the present estate of this church of England.

The reason why I do think the bishops to be the fittest to have both the allowing and ordaining of such as are to be ministers, I have expressed in my Answer to the Admonition. And they are not as yet by better reasons confuted[2].

[1] Εἰ δὲ πάλιν ἔροιό τί δήποτε ὁ δῆμός ἐστιν, ἐροῦσι, πρᾶγμα θορύβου γέμον καὶ ταραχῶδες, καὶ ἐξ ἀνοίας τὸ πλέον συγκείμενον, ἁπλῶς φερόμενον κατὰ τὰ τῆς θαλάττης κύματα πολλάκις, καὶ ἐκ ποικίλου καὶ μαχομένης συνιστάμενον γνώμης.—Chrysost. Op. Par. 1718-38. In Joan. Hom. iii. Tom. VIII. p. 23.]

[2 Cartwright replies that the apostles, when there was a contention, never thought of " cutting away the church's liberty;" that, "if the church's elections should be taken away because of contentions," "monarchies which oft have declined into tyranny...should have had an end long ago;" that the examples of contentions alleged by Whitgift, if the circumstances be considered, really make rather for the church's right of election; that the people have often been more orthodox than their governors; and that Whitgift, "defending the same cause which the papists, useth the very self-same armour, burnished by the names of Zuinglius, Calvin, Beza, &c.:" he therefore concludes " that both the church ought to have her consent in the election of her ministers; and that the sole authority of bishops creating ministers is unlawful."—Sec. Repl. pp. 288, &c.]

¶ Of ministers having no pastoral charge; of ceremonies used in ordaining ministers; of apostles, evangelists, and prophets.

Tract. IV.
Of ministers admitted, a place being not void.
Chapter i. The First Division.
Admonition.
The Seventh:

Then none admitted to the ministry, but [u] *a place was void* [u Acts i. 25.] *aforehand* [3], *to which he should be called* [4].

Answer to the Admonition, Page 47, Sect. 1, 2.

To prove this you cite in the margent the first of the Acts, where it is declared how Matthias was chosen in [5] the place of Judas, to make up the number of the xii. apostles. Surely this is but a slender reason: Matthias was chosen into the place of Judas; *ergo*, no man must be admitted into the ministry, except a place beforehand be void to the which he should be called. Every mean sophister will laugh at the childishness of this argument.

Matthias was chosen to be an apostle, and not to any certain cure; and therefore this example proveth nothing.

T. C. Page 42, Sect. 4.

The reason is of greater force than you would seem to make it: for, as the xii. place was to Matthias, so is a certain church unto a pastor or minister; and, as the apostles ordained none unto that place before it was void, so ought not the bishop ordain any until there be a church void and destitute of a pastor. And, as the apostles ordained not any apostle further than they had testimony of the word of God, as it appeareth [Acts i. 20.] *that St Peter proceedeth by that rule to the election, so ought no bishop ordain any to any function which is not in the scripture appointed. But there are by the word of God at this time no ordinary ministers* [6] *ecclesiastical which be not local and tied to one congregation; therefore this sending abroad of ministers which have no places is unlawful.*

[3 Beforehand, Adm.]
[4 The remainder of the sentence which appears below, page 485, is placed here in Answ.]
[5 Into, Answ.]   [6 Ministeries, Repl. 1 and 2.]

Jo. Whitgift.

<small>Ministers having no pastoral charge.</small>

As their reason is far from good reason, so are your similitudes far from proving the same; and the logicians say, *Solvitur similitudo, ostensa dissimilitudine.* First, there is great difference betwixt the office of an "apostle" and the office of a "pastor;" as you must needs confess. Then is there also difference in the number: for the apostles, which were chosen of Christ to be witnesses of his resurrection, were twelve, and therefore the number certain; but the number of preachers and pastors is not limited, but the more the better. Thirdly, there was one chosen in the place of Judas, that the scripture might be fulfilled, as Peter saith, Acts i.; but there is no such thing in the election of pastors and other ministers. Moreover, it was the twelfth place in number that Matthias was chosen unto, and not any local place such as pastors take charge of. Wherefore, except you can make a certain number, and no certain number; a local prescript and definite cure, and a general charge without prescription of any certain place, all one, or at the least very like; this argument, "Matthias was chosen into the place of Judas; *ergo*, no man must be admitted into the ministry except he have a cure," must of necessity be a very childish and fond argument. And how oft shall I tell you, that to reason *a facto ad jus*, "of an example to make a general rule," is a very unskilful kind of reasoning, except there be some general rule and commandment according to that example?

<small>Some admitted to the ministry, a place being not void.</small>

But was not Paul added to the number of the apostles, though there were no place void? Were not also Barnabas, Acts xiv., Epaphroditus, Phil. ii., Andronicus and Junia, Rom. xvi., called apostles? I might therefore as well reason thus, Paul, Barnabas, &c., were called to be apostles when there was no place void; *ergo*, some may be called to the preaching of the gospel, though they have no certain cure. But let us see how you will justify this assertion, that "there are no ordinary ministers ecclesiastical which be not local, and tied to one congregation, &c." For I utterly deny it in that sense that you speak it[1].

[[1] Cartwright rejoins that Whitgift "in heaping up certain differences between the office of an apostle and pastor answereth nothing to the matter." He further says that "he should have known that" Paul and Barnabas "were added by the Lord, and not by the church," and declares that "that which he objecteth

Chapter i. The Second Division.

T. C. Page 42, Sect. 5.

Marginal note: Ministers having no pastoral charge.

And, that it may the better appear that those functions do only remain which are appointed to one certain place, and that the reader may have the clearer and plainer understanding of all this matter, all the whole ecclesiastical function may be well divided, first, into extraordinary, or those that endured for a time, and into ordinary, which are perpetual. Of the first sort are the apostles and evangelists, which the Lord used for a time, as it were, for chief masons and principal builders of his church, as well to lay the foundations of churches where none were, as also to advance them to such forwardness and height until there might be gotten for the finishing of the building and house of the church fit pastors, elders, and deacons. And, that being done, they went from those places into others; which thing may be perceived by the continual story of the Acts of the Apostles, and by divers sentences which are found in the epistles of St Paul. And therefore also, when the churches have been by antichrist even rased from the foundations, God hath stirred up evangelists, even immediately by his Spirit, without any calling of men, to restore his churches again; of which sort was Master Wickliffe in our country, M. Hus and Hierome of Prague in Bohemia, Luther and Zuinglius in Germany, &c. And after this sort God may at his good pleasure work, when he purposeth to set in his gospel in any nation, where the whole face of the earth is covered with the darkness of ignorance and want of the knowledge of God.

Jo. Whitgift.

Although you cannot warrant by the scriptures this distinction of "ordinary" and "extraordinary" ecclesiastical functions, yet I think the apostolical function was extraordinary, in respect that it had for the time certain especial properties, as to bear witness of the resurrection of Christ, and of his ascension, which they did see with their eyes; also to plant and to found churches; likewise to go throughout the whole world. These, I say, were temporal and extraordinary; and so was the apostleship in this respect, but yet ordinary in respect of their chief function, which was to preach the gospel, and to govern the churches which they had planted. Likewise evangelists have an ordinary function, neither is there any cause why it should be called a temporal office, but only in respect of writing the gospel; for there is none that thinketh the office of preaching to be either extraordinary or temporal.

Marginal note: In what respect the apostolical function was extraordinary.

of Epaphroditus, &c. to be apostles...is an absurd begging of the question."— Sec. Repl. pp. 294, 5.]

Ministers having no pastoral charge.

But, I pray you, let me ask you one question, Why should not the office of seniors be as well extraordinary and temporal as the office of an apostle or an evangelist? for, as you say that "the apostleship and evangelistship remained until there might be gotten for the finishing of the building and house of the church fit pastors, &c.;" so say I that the office of seniors and elders might remain in the church until there were christian princes and magistrates, by whom the people of God might be kept in peace and quietness, and the churches of Christ more perfectly governed. And well assured I am that there are as good reasons for this as there are for the other: for, as in the place of the apostles, evangelists, &c. are succeeded bishops, pastors, doctors; so I may say that in the place of elders and seniors are come christian princes and magistrates.

What part of the apostles' function remaineth.

As for this part of the apostles' function, to visit such churches as were before planted, and to provide that such were placed in them as were virtuous and godly pastors, I know it remaineth still, and is one of the chief parts of the bishops' function; as shall hereafter more at large appear.

I grant that Master Hus, Hierome of Prague, &c., were stirred up even by God to preach his truth, and open the door of his word again; yet were they called to some function of the church before, although that function were for the most part wicked, and the church almost wholly corrupted with superstition and errors. But why you should rather call them "evangelists" than apostles, prophets, pastors, or doctors, I know not; especially seeing some of them had ordinary charges[1].

Chapter i. The Third Division.

T. C. Page 43, Sect. 1.

Of this sort of extraordinary functions are the prophets also, which, besides a singular dexterity and readiness of expounding the scriptures, had also the gift of telling things to come; which, because it is not now ordinarily, I think there is none will deny but it is an extraordinary calling: for the other two of the apostles and evangelists, it shall appear more at large hereafter (by occasion given by M. Doctor), that they are but for a time.

[[1] Cartwright censures Whitgift's "speeches" in this and the next division as "absurd."—Ibid. p. 295.]

Jo. Whitgift.

Ministers having no pastoral charge.

If you mean "prophets," in the respect of the gift of telling things to come, such as Agabus was, then be they temporal, but yet ordinary for the time wherein they were. But, if you mean prophets in respect of their dexterity and readiness in expounding the scriptures, such as Barnabas was, and Simon, Lucius, &c., and Saul; likewise such as Judas and Silas, Acts xv., and such as the apostle St Paul speaketh of, 1 Corinth. xiv.; I see no cause why either the calling should be extraordinary, or the office and gift temporal; except you have a liberty to make temporal and perpetual, ordinary and extraordinary, what you please. But, seeing you would have all things proved by scripture, I pray you, prove this that you have said either of the apostles, evangelists, or prophets, by the scripture; seeing you teach that of them which seemeth to be contrary unto the scripture.

Acts xi.
Prophets in some respect ordinary.
Acts xiii.
Acts xv.
1 Cor. xiv.

Chapter i. The Fourth Division.

T. C. Page 43, Sect. 2.

The ordinary and continual functions of the church are also divided into two parts; for either they are they that govern or take charge of the whole church, as are those which are called elders, or they which take charge of one part of the church (which is the poor of every church), as are those which are called deacons. Those again that be called presbyteri[2], *which we term elders of the church, and have to do with the whole church, are either those which teach and preach the word of God, and govern too, or else which govern only, and do not teach or*[3] *preach. Of the first kind are pastors and doctors: of the second are those which are called by the common name of elders or ancients. Of all this ordinary function I shall have occasion to speak, and of every one shall appear that (which I have said before), that they are no uncertain and undefinite ministries, but such as are limited unto a certain church and congregation. And first of all, for the pastor or bishop which is here mentioned, which name soever we consider of them, they do forthwith, as soon as they are once either spoken or thought of, imply and infer a certain and definite charge, being, as the logicians term them, actual relatives. For what shepherd can there be unless he have a flock? and how can he be a watchman unless he have some city to look unto? Or how can a man be a master unless he have a servant? or a father unless he have a child? Now if you will say that they have a charge, and they have flocks and cities to attend and watch upon; for a whole shire, or province, or realm, are their flocks, and their cities, and their charges.*

[2 That are presbyteri, Repl. 1 and 2.]   [3 Nor, Repl. 1 and 2.]

Jo. Whitgift.

Ministers having no pastoral charge.

This division also is of your own inventing; neither have you any mention of "seniors" (as you call them), or of "deacons," in that fourth chapter to the Ephesians, which you would have to be so perfect a rule of ecclesiastical functions. As for "pastors" and "doctors," you know that divers both ancient and late writers, as namely Hierome, Augustine, Chrysostom, Musculus, and Bucer, &c.[1], do confound them; and the reason that Hierome useth cannot be well denied, because the apostle saith not as he did before of the other, *alios pastores, alios doctores,* "some pastors, and other some doctors;" but he joineth them together, and saith, *alios pastores et doctores,* "some pastors and doctors." Moreover, I see not how you can justify your division of "seniors" by the word of God, as I shall further declare in that place where you more largely speak of them: in the mean time, I see no reason why your unpreaching and unministering "seniors" should have any perpetuity in the church more than apostles, for the cause that I have before alleged; neither have you yet proved that the deacons' office is only to provide for the poor: you have examples to the contrary; as I have declared in my Answer. To be short, I understand not how you can make "doctors" governors of any several parishes and churches, except you will make them pastors.

Eph. iv.

Tract. xvii.

But, because you only speak here, and prove nothing, I will defer a further answer until I hear more sound arguments.

You say, "a shepherd cannot be unless he have a flock, &c.;" all which is true; but he is also a shepherd, that hath more flocks, and he is a shepherd that hath a general care and oversight of many shepherds and many flocks. For he that hath many flocks and many shepherds may have one master-shepherd to see that all the rest do their duties, and that the sheep be kept in good order. And, though every several

[¹ Non enim ait, alios autem pastores, et alios magistros; sed, alios pastores et magistros; ut qui pastor est, esse debeat et magister.—Hieron. Op. Par. 1693-1706. Comm. Lib. II. in Epist. ad Ephes. cap. iv. Tom. IV. Pars I. col. 365.

August. Op. Par. 1679-1700. Ad Paulin. Epist. cxlix. cap. ii. 11. Tom. II. cols. 507, 8.

Chrysost. Op. Par. 1718-38. In Epist. ad Ephes. cap. iv. Hom. xi. Tom. XI. p. 83.

Wolfg. Muscul. Comm. in Epist. ad Ephes. Basil. 1561. cap. iv. p. 106. Conf. Loc. Comm. Theol. Basil. 1599. De Ministr. Verb. Dei, p. 195.

M. Bucer. Prælect. in Epist. ad Ephes. Basil. 1562. cap. iv. p. 107.]

city have several watchmen, which watch by course, yet may there be one that hath an especial care over all, and is appointed to see the rest do their duties: so one master may have many servants, one father many children. Wherefore, if you use this reason to improve the office of a bishop, it lacketh might; if to prove that a pastor must have a flock, no man doth deny it; but if to conclude that no man may preach unless he have a certain flock, there is no sequel at all in it; for first you must prove that the only office of a pastor is now remaining in the church, and that no man can be minister of the word and sacraments, except he be a pastor of some certain flock; for that do I constantly deny[2].

Ministers having no pastoral charge.

Chapter i. The Fifth Division.
T. C. Page 43, Sect. 3.

First of all, in your reading ministers that is untrue; for they go not to read in all churches, but tarry till[3] they be hired in one. And therefore, when the bishop hath laid his hand of them, they are no more ministers than before his hand came upon them, because they have no charges; and therefore the patron or person that hireth them to read, and setteth them a work, are their bishops, and make them ministers, and not the bishop of the diocese.

Petitio principii.

Jo. Whitgift.

These be but words grounded upon this false principle, that none ought to be admitted into the ministry but such as have a certain cure and charge; which you are never able to prove, either by scripture or good reason; but the contrary is manifest by both[4].

Chapter i. The Sixth Division.
T. C. Page 43, Sect. 4.

Secondarily, for those that preach to have a whole diocese, or province, or realm, to be their flock, or city to attend upon, is contrary to the policy or good husbandry of all those that would either have their city safe, or their flocks sound. For who are they which would appoint one for the

[2 Cartwright says that Whitgift "trifleth with his reader," and maintains at length that there is a difference between doctors and pastors.—Sec. Repl. pp. 295, &c.]
[3 Until, Repl. 1 and 2.]
[4 "... his answer is unsufficient."—pp. 297, 8.]

<small>Ministers having no pastoral charge.</small> watch of a thousand towns or cities, when as all they which love their safety would rather have for every city many watchmen, than for many cities one? Or what is he, that is so watchful and circumspect, whose diligence and watchfulness one city assaulted with enemies will not wholly occupy and take up? Or what is he, whose sight is so sharp, that he can see from one end of the diocese, or province, or realm, to the other end thereof? Or what is he, that will commit the keeping of twenty thousand sheep to one man, that looketh for any good or increase of them? How shall all these hear his whistle, how shall all know his voice, when they cannot hear it? How shall they acknowledge him, when they cannot know him? how shall they follow him, when they cannot see him go before? how shall he heal their diseases, when he cannot possibly know them? But some man will say that these are human reasons, and likelihoods, which may be overthrown with other similitudes. These notwithstanding are analogies drawn from the nature of those things which the ministers are likened unto, and are of the most part used of the Holy Ghost himself expressly.

Jo. Whitgift.

It is a great point of good husbandry and policy also to have, besides the several shepherds over several flocks, and sundry watchmen over sundry cities, divers other to feed the sheep, as occasion serveth, and to admonish the watchmen and the cities of their duties: else why did the apostles, after they had planted the churches, and placed shepherds and watchmen over them, so diligently afterwards visit them, and so carefully look unto them; as we read Acts xiv., xv., xviii.? Was the watch, think you, the worse kept, or the sheep the negligentlier looked unto? The policy that Darius used, Daniel vi., when he appointed a hundred and twenty governors over all his realm, and over them three to oversee them, and take an account of their doings, is greatly commended; and why may not this policy be necessary in the ecclesiastical state also? But you here run smoothly away with the matter, and suppose that there may not be for several cities and several flocks several watchmen and shepherds, because there be some that have a general care over many flocks and cities. If a thousand towns or cities have a thousand watchmen appointed unto them, to have the particular care over them, and also one, two, or more, to have a general care both over the watchmen, and over the cities also, do you not think that all shall be in better order and in much more safety?

<small>Similitudes are but weak arguments.</small> But your similitudes fail marvellously in sundry points,

which I must admonish you of, because you glory so much in them, and think that you have reasoned strongly, when you have used the weakest kind of argument that can be to prove anything; for, as the logicians say, *Similitudo rem illustrat, sed non probat:* "A similitude maketh a matter plain, but proveth it not." And it is easily overthrown by shewing the unlikelihood. In this the similitude agreeth that, as every city must have a watchman, and every flock a shepherd, so every church or parish must have a watchman or a pastor; and, as the watchman and shepherd his office is to watch and feed, and to have a necessary care over their charges, so must also the spiritual watchman and shepherd have a care over the people committed unto them. All this is true, and neither proveth nor improveth anything that is in question. I might as well say that, if the city be well watched, and the flock carefully looked unto, though it be not by the watchman or shepherd himself, but by his means and procurement, there can be no just fault found with either of them: likewise, that, when the shepherd hath brought his sheep into a pasture where they may both be sure from all danger, and have meat sufficient, then his presence is not so necessary for them, so that he do sometimes visit them: also that there is no one watchman that either doth or can watch continually, but must of necessity have his rest, so that some other supply his absence; and likewise, that there is no master-shepherd, but that he hath some under him, either boy, or man, to supply his absence whilst he is about other matters: to be short, that one shepherd hath care over sundry men's sheep, sundry flocks of sundry towns and parishes, &c. Divers other such similitudes of shepherds and watchmen might I also use, to prove many things contrary to your meaning. I might also shew unto you the dissimilitudes betwixt a temporal shepherd and a spiritual shepherd; unreasonable sheep that cannot feed themselves, or by any means provide for themselves, nor have any charge to look to themselves, and reasonable sheep, such as God hath endued with knowledge, to whom he hath left his word, which containeth in it sufficient to salvation, whom he hath charged to read it, and to hear it, who shall also answer for themselves, &c.; finally, what difference there is betwixt temporal meat and drink, which is soon digested, and therefore daily to be renewed, and spiritual food which continueth, and whereof he that hath once

Ministers having no pastoral charge.

*Ministers having no pastoral charge.*sufficiently tasted shall not hunger or thirst, &c.—these, I say, and a great number of other dissimilitudes, could I bring, to overthrow all that you can build upon these similitudes.

Jer. xxiii. Ezek. xxxiv.I might further say, that in the prophets and other places of the scriptures kings and mighty princes that have ample and large dominions be called both shepherds and watchmen, as namely in Jeremy xxiii., Ezekiel xxxiv. &c.; and therefore all those your reasons might as well be alleged against them; and of them also might you say, "What is he, whose sight is so sharp, that he can see from one end of the diocese, province, or realm, to another?" For these names be as common and as usual to kings and princes as they be to ministers of the word and bishops. And truly, if these similitudes sink once in the people's heads, and be applied unto civil government (against which they be as forcible as against the ecclesiastical), they will as easily, and far more easily, stir them up to seek alteration in that also[1].

Chapter i. The Seventh Division.

T. C. Page 43, Sect. 4, 5.

*No man doubteth what a flock is; and yet you have invented a strange definition.**But, that there be not[2] controversy left in this point, what is a flock? St Paul defineth it plainly, when he saith, "Appoint pastors," or elders, or bishops (for these words are indifferently used), through not every shire, or province, or realm, but "through every city, or town." And, lest that any man should here take occasion to conclude that then it is lawful for one man to be bishop or pastor of a whole city, such as London, or York, &c.; St Luke in the Acts doth declare the meaning of this place, where he saith that "they appointed elders throughout every congregation;" so that, if the city or town be great, and the professors of the gospel in it be more than will make conveniently a* *You have no word of God for this; and the practice of the primitive church doth confute it; as it is proved Tract. viii.**congregation, then there must be, by the rule of God, more pastors and bishops. Whereupon it appeareth that both no pastor or bishop ought to be made without there be a flock, as it were a void place for him; and that a flock is not a realm, or province, or diocese (as we now call a diocese), but so many as may conveniently meet in one assembly or congregation. And that this is the meaning of St Paul, it appeareth by the practice of the churches from time to time, which have both decreed against and found fault with these wandering and roving ministries.*

Tit. i. 5.[3]

Chap. xiv. 23.[3]

[1 Cartwright rejoins that Whitgift's arguments are unsatisfactory, and that his "reasons of the apostles' visiting and of Darius' policy lead to Rome."—Sec. Repl. pp. 298, 9.]

[2 No, Repl. 1, 2, and Def. A.]

[3 These references are inserted from Repl. 2.]

Jo. Whitgift.

Ministers having no pastoral charge.
Tit. i.

It is manifest that St Paul willed Titus to appoint *presbyteros* (for that word he useth) "in every city;" for so doth he also say. But what can you hereof conclude? What sequel is there in this argument: St Paul willed Timothy to appoint ministers in every city; *ergo,* "there must be none admitted to the ministry of the word but such as have some certain cure?" or, therefore one man may not have the oversight and direction of many cures? Indeed, if St Paul had said to Titus, Thou shalt appoint no ministers of the word, or seniors, but to a certain cure, or admit none to preach the gospel, except he have some one place certainly appointed unto him; then your reason had been something. But now it hath no shew of any argument.

The place, Acts xiv., tendeth to the same purpose; neither is there one word there to prove that such may not preach the word as have no certain charge committed unto them; but the contrary rather; for Paul and Barnabas, though they did appoint in every church ministers, yet did they preach themselves also. And I hear no reason yet why both these may not be true, that every church should have a pastor, and yet that some may be admitted to preach the word that have no several churches. This I am sure was usual in the apostles' time, and it is now most profitable; neither is there one tittle in the whole scripture against it. And you yourself have been in that case ever since you were preacher, and remain so still, for anything that I know [4].

Chapter i. The Eighth Division.

T. C. Page 44, Sect. 1.

The great council of Chalcedon decreed that no elder or deacon, or any
Cap. vi. Act. *other in the ecclesiastical order, should be ordained ἀπολελυμέ-*
15. *νως, that is, loosely and as it were let go at random whither he*
himself listed[5]; which he also interpreteth by and bye more plainly, when he
addeth that he should not be ordained, εἰ μὴ ἰδικῶς ἐν ἐκκλησίᾳ πόλεως
ἢ κώμης[6]; that is, "unless it be specially in a congregation of some city or
town." And in the council of Urban (as Gratian reporteth, Distinction lxx.)

The council of Chalcedon maimed.

[4 "...it is shameful injury done to Titus once to think that he made kinds of ministries, whereof he had no commission by the apostle. The rest is nothing but a manifest begging of that which is in question."—Ibid. p. 300.]

[5 Listeth, Repl. 2.]   [6 See below, page 479, note 3.]

Ministers having no pastoral charge.

You still stumble upon Hierome instead of Musculus.

it was decreed that the ordination that was made without any title should be void; and what that meaneth is shewed by and bye, when it is said, "And in what church any is intitled, there let him always remain[1].*" And this is also St Hierome his complaint, in that men were ordained unto the ministry when they were chosen by no church, and so went round about, having no certain place*[2]. *Ad Nepot.*

And therefore this, that none ought to preach unless he have some pastoral charge, ought not to have been so strange a thing unto you as you make it, if either the scriptures, or the councils, or the ancient fathers, had been so well known unto you, as either your name requireth, or you take upon you, which dare so boldly pronounce that there can be shewed no text of scripture for the matter.

Jo. Whitgift.

You are notable in falsifying and corruptly alleging of the authorities of fathers and councils; and a singular grace you have both in ascribing that unto them which they have not, and in otherwise reporting that which they have, as you do now in this place deal with the council of Chalcedon; for you say: "That council decreed that no elder or deacon, &c. should be ordained ἀπολελυμένως, that is, loosely, &c.:" and you add that "he interpreteth this more plainly, when he addeth that he should not be ordained, εἰ μὴ ἰδικῶς ἐν ἐκκλησίᾳ πόλεως ἢ κώμης, that is, unless it be specially in a congregation of some city or town." But you have craftily left out that which maketh against you, and plainly openeth the meaning of the council, which is this, ἢ μαρτυρίῳ, ἢ μοναστηρίῳ, &c.

Con. Chalced. cap. 6. Act. 15.

The whole canon is this: *Nullum absolute ordinari debere presbyterum aut diaconum, nec quemlibet in gradu ecclesiastico, nisi specialiter in ecclesia civitatis aut pagi, aut in martyrio, aut monasterio, qui ordinandus est, pronuncietur. Qui vero absolute ordinantur, decrevit sancta synodus, irritam haberi hujusmodi manus impositionem, et nusquam posse ministrari ad ordinantis ignominiam*[3].

[1 Sanctorum canonum statutis consona sanctione decernimus, ut sine titulo facta ordinatio irrita habeatur, et in qua ecclesia quilibet titulatus est, in ea perpetuo perseveret.—Ex Concil. Urban. II. hab. Placent. in Corp. Jur. Canon. Lugd. 1624. Decret. Gratian. Decr. Prim. Pars, Dist. lxx. can. 2. col. 348.]

[2 See before, page 442.]

[3 Μηδένα δὲ ἀπολελυμένως χειροτονεῖσθαι, μήτε πρεσβύτερον, μήτε διάκονον, μήτε ὅλως τινὰ τῷ ἐν ἐκκλησιαστικῷ τάγματι· εἰ μὴ ἰδικῶς ἐν ἐκκλησίᾳ πόλεως ἢ κώμης, ἢ μαρτυρίῳ, ἢ μοναστηρίῳ, ὁ χειροτονούμενος ἐπικηρύττοιτο. τοὺς δὲ ἀπολύτως χειροτονουμένους ὥρισεν ἡ ἁγία σύνοδος ἄκυρον ἔχειν τὴν τοιαύτην χειροθεσίαν, καὶ μηδαμοῦ δύνασθαι ἐνεργεῖν ἐφ' ὕβρει τοῦ χειροτονήσαντος.—

Whereby it is plain, that the meaning of the council is, to have none admitted into any ecclesiastical degree, except he have something to live upon, and not that he must of necessity have some cure; for then would not the council have said, *aut in martyrio, aut monasterio;* for these be no pastoral charges; neither yet would it have added, *aut diaconum aut quemlibet in gradu ecclesiastico,* " deacons or any other in ecclesiastical degree;" because every one admitted *in aliquem gradum ecclesiasticum,* "into any ecclesiastical degree[4]," is not admitted to a cure. Wherefore the gloss in Gratian doth well interpret the meaning of this canon, when it saith that none is to be ordained *sine titulo,* " without a title,"... *ne dicatur, mendicat in plateis infelix clericus*[5]: " lest it be said, an unhappy clerk beggeth in the streets;" and further addeth thus: *Colligitur etiam hic ex eo quod dicit, sive possessionis, argumentum, quod si quis habet patrimonium sufficiens, ordinari potest sine titulo*[6] : " An argument may also here be gathered, in that it saith (or of possession) that if any have sufficient patrimony, he may be ordained without a title." But these words, *sive in martyrio, sive in monasterio,* do manifestly declare that the council would have none admitted to any ecclesiastical function without some stay of living, either of some benefice, monastery, college, chapel, his own possessions, or such like; as the practice of the church under the pope is at this day. And yet, if any man should say that out of this canon there can be nothing gathered but only this, in what places those that are called to the ministry are to be admitted and ordained, I know not how you could answer it; for the words of the canon admit that sense properly.

That decree of Urban hath the same meaning; and that which followeth, " of remaining continually in that church in the which he is intituled," doth but signify that he must be assured of his living, whereunto he is intituled, during his life; for the same canon doth permit one man to have two churches,

Ministers having no pastoral charge.

Dist. 70. Ne-minem.

Concil. Calched. in Concil. Stud. Labb. et Cossart. Lut. Par. 1671-2. Act. xv. can. 6. Tom. IV. col. 758.]

[4 The twelve preceding words are omitted in Def. B. They form one line in Def. A.]

[5 Corp. Jur. Canon. Decret. Gratian. Decr. Prim. Pars, Dist. lxx. Gloss. in can. 1. col. 347.]

[6 Ibid. cols. 347, 8. The words *sive possessionis* occur in the canon as given by Gratian.]

but yet that he ought not to be *canonicus prebendarius*, but only of one church whereof he is intituled. But I cannot but marvel that you will use the testimony of this council of pope Urban, which was holden at the least *anno* 1090. after Christ, even in the most corrupt time, when as antichrist had fully possessed the see of Rome; in the which council among other things he confirmed the acts of pope Hildebrand against Henry the emperor[1]. This Urban also was the confirmer of superstitious[2] orders of the Cistercian friars and Carthusian monks[3]: he likewise deposed deacons that were married from their orders[4], and forbade (by the counsel of the traitorous archbishop Anselm) that any clerk should receive *beneficiorum investituram*, or any ecclesiastical dignity, of any prince or layman, but only of the pope[5]. And, that you may yet further understand what a worthy patron you have gotten for your cause, this Urban was he that was author of the "Canonical Hours," commonly called our "Lady's Psalter[6]."

Certainly Hierome saith no such thing in that epistle: you are disposed to father that of him that he never spake. His complaint was, that "much cost was bestowed upon churches in adorning and decking of them, and little regard to the choice of ministers[7];" meaning that they had more care

[1] Acta Gregorii vi[i]. contra ipsum Henricum probavit in concilio Placentino, favente Matilde comitissa...Hoc item tempore ordo Cartusiensium initium cepit.—R. Volaterr. Comm. Urban. Par. 1603. Lib. xxii. col. 799. Conf. J. Balæi Act. Rom. Pont. Franc. 1567. Lib. v. Urban. II. p. 189.]

[2] Of the superstitious, Def. A.]

[3] Cisterciensem autem ordinem primo in Burgundia excitatum, sua auctoritate confirmavit. Sunt etiam qui scribant Carthusienses religiosos hujus pontificis tempore originem habuisse.—Plat. De Vit. Pont. Col. 1551. Urban. II. p. 157. Conf. Centur. Eccles. Hist. Basil. 1560, &c. Cent. xi. cap. x. col. 542.]

[4] Eos qui post subdiaconatum uxoribus vacare volunt ab omni sacro ordine removemus, officioque atque beneficio ecclesiæ carere decernimus.—Urban. 2. in Corp. Jur. Canon. Lugd. 1624. Decret. Gratian. Decr. Prim. Pars, Dist. xxxii. can. 10. col. 161.]

[5] ...Dominus papa Urbanus...hæc quæ sequuntur capitula constituit............ Ut episcopi vel abbates, vel aliquis de clero, aliquam ecclesiasticam dignitatem de manu principum vel quorumlibet laicorum, non recipiat.—Matt. Paris. Hist. Major. Lond. 1640. Will. Sec. Tom. I. p. 22; Henr. Prim. ibid. p. 58. Conf. Centur. Eccles. Hist. Cent. iv. cap. viii. De Primat. cols. 549, &c.]

[6] Ut totidem etiam horæ in honorem deiparæ virginis quotidie recitarentur, instituit Urbanus secundus in concilio, quod in Gallis ad Claromontem habuit.— Polyd. Verg. De Invent. Rer. Amst. 1671. Lib. vi. cap. ii. p. 369.]

[7] Multi ædificant parietes, et columnas ecclesiæ substruunt; marmora nitent, auro splendent laquearia, gemmis altare distinguitur, et ministrorum Christi nulla electio est.—Hieron. Op. Par. 1693-1706. Ad Nepot. De Vit. Cler. Epist. xxxiv. Tom. IV. Pars ii. col. 263.]

to have gorgeous churches than good ministers. But what is this to your purpose? {Ministers having no pastoral charge.}

Thus have you proved neither by scripture, nor by council, nor doctor (truly alleged and understanded), that none may preach unless he have some pastoral charge: and I still affirm that you have not one text of scripture sounding that way; where there are to the contrary sundry examples, as I have alleged[8].

Chapter i. The Ninth Division.
Answer to the Admonition, Page 47, Sect. 2.

If you had used more reasons, I would have answered them. What certain cure had Paul, Barnabas, Philip, Epaphroditus, Andronicus, Junius; and yet they were not of the twelve apostles? It is a strange doctrine to teach that a man may not preach out of his own cure: it is more strange to say, that it is not lawful for him to preach, except he have some pastoral cure, being of himself able to live, and not minding to be burdensome to the church. If you seek for any text in the scripture[10] to confirm this doctrine, you can find none: if you seek for examples to the contrary, you shall find plenty. {To preach out of his own cure[9].}

T. C. Page 44, Sect. 2, 3, 4.

But you ask, what place Paul and Barnabas had appointed them. What, mean you thereby to conclude that, because Paul and Barnabas the apostles had no place appointed them, therefore a pastor or bishop should not? when this is one difference between the apostle and bishop, that the one hath no certain place appointed, and the other hath. But I think I smell out your meaning, which is, that we may make apostles also at these days, and that that function is not yet ceased; for otherwise your reason is nothing worth. Likewise also you ask of Philip, which was an evangelist. And so you think that these running ministers are lawful, because they are apostles and evangelists: against which I shall have occasion to speak

---

[8 Cartwright maintains that he has "set down the true meaning of" the council of Chalcedon, and cites Calvin as viewing it in the same light as himself (Inst. iv. Lib. cap. v. sect. 4). He goes on: "The council of Urban ought to make the D. blush; and the corruptions which he to so small purpose chargeth his book with cause it to speak so loud that the very deaf ears ought to hear. For this divinity of the later popery which he maintaineth, being condemned of the former, hath thereby a brand of corruption whereby it may be known, &c." —Sec. Repl. pp. 300, &c.]

[9 This marginal note is inserted from Answ. 2.] [10 In scripture, Answ.]

<small>Ministers having no pastoral charge.</small> *shortly after in the 50. page*[1]. *But, if a man be able to live of himself, and mind not to be burdensome to the church, it seemeth unreasonable unto you that he may not go about and preach throughout all churches.*

Did you never read any learned disputation[2], *and that of learned writers in our days, about this question, whether (although it be lawful) it be expedient that a man, being able and willing to live of himself, ought to take wages of the church, for inconveniences which might ensue of taking nothing? I do but ask you the question, because you make so great a wonder at this; for I will not take upon me here the defence of it, because I will not multiply questions.* <small>P. Martyr upon the 1 Cor. ix.[3] thinketh it more expedient for one to take wages of the church, although he be able to live of himself.[4]</small>

And why, I pray you, may not that man that is so able, and will be content to live of himself, why, I say, may not he teach and be the pastor of some church? Do you think that for his forbearing the wages of the <small>What laws and orders? where are they established?</small> *church he may break the laws and orders that God hath established?*

Jo. Whitgift.

It is a good reason to prove that there may be preachers of the word, which have no certain cure, and doth clean overthrow your former answer to the place Acts i.: for Paul and Barnabas were not chosen into any vacant place, as Matthias was; and therefore that reason is no reason. I do not say a bishop or pastor should not have a place appointed unto them (for I know bishops and pastors have their cures limited); but this I say, that some may be preachers and ministers of the word, which have no certain cure. Neither is this true, that all such as be admitted to the preaching of the word be either bishops or pastors.

Against apostles and evangelists we shall understand what you have to say, when we come to that place.

You ask me whether I "ever read any learned disputations, &c." I might ask you the same question; for you utter no great reading here, only you allege Peter Martyr upon 1 Cor. ix.; where he speaketh little of this matter. For the question is not whether a man, having a pastoral cure and sufficient of his own to live, may cease to take the ordinary stipend of his church or no; which is that that Peter Martyr

---

[[1] See below, pages 529, &c.] [[2] Disputations, Repl. 1 and 2.]
[[3] First to the Corinth. 9 chapter, Repl. 1 and 2.]

[[4] Hic diligenter ponderandæ sunt utræque offensiones, ut illam tandem evitet quam viderit evangelio et saluti proximorum gravius obstare. Sed expeditissimum videretur, ut consuetos proventus acciperet, quos, cum aliunde victum habeat, pauperibus distribuat.—P. Martyr. Comm. in D. Pauli prior. ad Corinth. Epist. Tigur. 1572. cap. ix. 12. fol. 116.]

handleth in that place, and whereof he maketh this resolution, that "he should do that therein that may most profit the church, and further the gospel, and yet to be most expedient to take the accustomed stipend⁴;" although St Ambrose, *Lib. i. Off. cap.* 36⁵, and divers other, be of the contrary judgment. But this is our controversy, whether a man having sufficient to live of by himself may not be admitted to the preaching of the gospel, except he have some pastoral cure. St Paul in that chapter glorieth that he took nothing of the Corinthians; and Peter Martyr, in the same place, saith that "Paul would take nothing, that he might the more freely reprehend⁶."

Ministers having no pastoral charge.

P. Martyr in 1 Cor. ix.

You ask me also, "why that man, that is so able, and will be content, may not teach, and be the pastor of a church, &c." I answer, that he may and if he will. But I ask you again, what if he be persuaded that he shall do more good by going to such places where there is greater want of preaching? What "law or order is there established by God" to the contrary? where is that law or that order? Set it truly down; and I yield unto it: else can I not but dissent from you, seeing I see manifest examples in the scripture to the contrary; and even your own example also in your own person, which ought to have moved you to a public confession, if you have all this while usurped an unlawful vocation; as certainly you have done, if this your assertion be true.

Of ceremonies used in ordaining Ministers.
Chapter ii. The First Division.
Admonition.

But now bishops (to whom the right of ordering ministers doth at no hand appertain) do make 60. 80. *or* 100.⁷ *at a clap, and send them abroad into the country like masterless men*⁸.

[⁵ Etenim si is qui imperatori militat, a susceptionibus litium, actu negotiorum forensium, venditione mercium prohibetur humanis legibus ; quanto magis qui fidei exercet militiam, ab omni usu negotiationis abstinere debet, agelluli sui contentus fructibus, si habet; si non habet, stipendiorum suorum fructu!— Ambros. Op. Par. 1686-90. De Offic. Ministr. Lib. I. cap. xxxvi. 184. Tom. II. col. 49.]

[⁶ At Paulus nihil ab eis volebat accipere, ut liberius posset reprehendere.— P. Martyr. Comm. in D. Pauli prior. ad Corinth. Epist. cap. ix. 12. fol. 115.]

[⁷ Or a 100, Adm.]

[⁸ This is the completion of the sentence of which the former clause appears page 469.]

Answer to the Admonition, Page 47, Sect. 3.

Ordering of ministers pertaineth to bishops.

That the ordering of ministers doth appertain to bishops properly, which you here utterly deny, I have proved before: they be best able to judge of men's ability to that function. It is their especial charge to see that there be meet ministers in the church, and therefore good reason that they should have the chief stroke in ordering of them: and yet in that business they trust not themselves alone; they have other godly and learned ministers to assist them in examining such as are to be admitted; they also require a testimonial of life and conversation from that place wherein those that are to be ministers have been latest and longest remaining.

Page 48, Sect. 1, 2.

If such numbers as you say be admitted at one time, and sent abroad "like masterless men," that is the fault of the person, not of the law; neither is it a sufficient cause to debar any learned, godly, and meet man from the ministry, able to live of himself, or having any other ecclesiastical living, as prebend, fellowship in some college of either university, or such like, though he have no pastoral charge and cure; neither shall you ever be able to prove, but that a man disposed and able to do good in the church of Christ may be admitted into the ministry, although he have no ecclesiastical living at all.

I mislike runagates and "masterless men," and such as are compelled to seek up and down to get them services, as well as you; and I hope the redress thereof is already determined.

T. C. Page 44, Sect. 4.

For the rest contained in those pages touching the ordaining of ministers and[1] bishops, I have before spoken at large.

Jo. Whitgift.

You have not answered to the most of this, that is in this portion contained, and especially touching the ordaining of bishops and ministers.

[1 O., Repl. 1, 2, and Def. A.]

Chapter ii. The Second Division.

Admonition.

The Eighth:

Then, after just trial and vocation, they were admitted to their function ▼1 Ti.iv.14. *by laying on of the hands of the company of the* ᵂ*eldership only*².

Answer to the Admonition, Page 49, Sect. 1, 2.

Of trial and vocation I have spoken before. To prove laying on of hands, &c., is alleged the first of⁴ Timothy, the fourth chapter: this is but a ceremony, and it is now used; for the bishop and other learned and grave ministers there present do lay their hands upon such as are admitted into the ministry. {Of³ laying on of hands.}

Now, if you would know what is here meant by seniors, you may learn if you please of Œcumenius, a learned and old writer, who expoundeth this place of Timothy⁶ on this sort: πρεσβυτέρους τοὺς ἐπισκόπους φησίν⁷: "By seniors he meaneth bishops." And so saith Chrysostom in like manner. {Œcumenius⁵. Seniors expounded⁵.}

T. C. Page 44, Sect. 5.

Œcumenius and Chrysostom say that by elders he meaneth bishops, not thereby to sever those that had the government of the church together with the pastor and minister of the word, which were called ancients, as you seem to mean; but to put distinction between those which are elders by age and elders by office: besides that it is before alleged that it may be that the pastor or bishop did in the name of all the elders lay on his hands upon him that was ordained. And, lastly, you know, and cannot deny, that St Paul in one or two places confoundeth the bishop and the elder. {An untruth: for Chrysostom maketh a manifest distinction.}

Jo. Whitgift.

The words of Chrysostom and Œcumenius be evident; as you might have perceived, if you would have taken pains to read the places. For the words of Chrysostom be these: Οὐ περὶ πρεσβυτέρων ἔφη ἐνταῦθα, ἀλλὰ περὶ ἐπισκόπων· "He speaketh not here of elders, but of bishops:" οὐ γὰρ {Chrysost. in ¹ Tim. iv.}

[² The remainder of the sentence (see below, page 488) is added here in Answ.]
[³ *Of* is not in Answ.]   [⁴ To, Answ.]
[⁵ These marginal notes are inserted from Answ. 2.]
[⁶ Paul, Answ.]
[⁷ Œcumen. Op. Lut. Par. 1631. Comm. cap. ix. in I. Epist. ad Tim. Tom. II. p. 234.]

δὴ πρεσβύτεροι τὸν ἐπίσκοπον ἐχειροτόνουν[1] : "for certainly the elders did not ordain the bishop." How say you? be not these words plain, that he meaneth bishops, and not other ministers? And M. Beza in his notes upon this place saith thus: *Presbyterii, i. ordinis presbyterorum, quo nomine probabile est cœtum omnium illorum significari, qui verbo laborabant in Ephesiorum ecclesia*[2]: "Of the eldership; that is to say, of the order of elders; by which name it is likely that the company of them which laboured in the word in the church of Ephesus are signified." *Ut Acto.* xx. Whereby it is certain that he secludeth your unministering seniors.

Beza.

Chapter ii. The Third Division.

Admonition.

A slanderous untruth.

Now there is (neither of these being looked unto) required an alb, a surplice, a vestment[3], a pastoral staff.

Answer to the Admonition, Page 49, Sect. 3.

In the book now allowed of making deacons and ministers, and consecrating of bishops, there is neither required alb, surplice, vestment[4], nor pastoral staff: read the book from the beginning to the ending. And therefore this is a false and untrue report.

An untrue reports.

Jo. Whitgift.

This is confessed by silence; and therefore here the Admonition containeth a manifest untruth, and wanteth a proctor.

Chapter ii. The Fourth Division.

Admonition.

Beside that ridiculous and (as they use it to their new creatures) blasphemous saying, " Receive the Holy Ghost."

[1 Chrysost. Op. Par. 1718-38. In I. Epist. ad Tim. cap. iv. Hom. xiii. Tom. XI. p. 618; where φησὶν for ἔφη.]

[2 Nov. Test. cum Th. Bezæ Annot. H. Steph. 1565. Epist. ad Tim. I. cap. iv. 14. p. 467; where *Presbyterii,* τοῦ πρεσβυτερίου. *Id est, ordinis,* and *qui in verbo.*]

[3 Required a surplice, a vestiment, Adm.; which has a note added: *These are required by their pontifical.* Answ. and Def. A. have *vestiment.*]

[4 Vestiment, Answ. and Def. A.]

[5 This marginal note is inserted from Answ. 2.]

Answer to the Admonition, Page 46, Sect. 4, and ult.

To use these words, "Receive the Holy Ghost," in ordering of ministers, which Christ himself used in appointing his apostles, is no more ridiculous and blasphemous than it is to use the words that he used in the supper; but it is blasphemy thus outrageously to speak of the words of Christ. The bishop by speaking these words doth not take upon him to give the Holy Ghost, no more than he doth to remit sins, when he pronounceth the remission of sins; but by speaking these words of Christ, "Receive the Holy Ghost; whose sins soever ye remit, they are remitted, &c.," he doth shew the principal duty of a minister, and assureth him of the assistance of God's Holy Spirit, if he labour in the same accordingly. *Receive the Holy Ghost* [6].

You call them his "new creatures:" these be but words of scurrility, to be hissed at, not to be answered. *Scurrility* [6].

T. C. Page 44, Sect. ult.

To say that the bishop may as well say: "Receive the Holy Ghost," as to say the words used in the supper, or to say that the sins of those which do believe are forgiven, is δὶς διὰ πασῶν, *as far as York and London. For there are commandments to the ministers to do that which they do, and here is none; and there the minister doth not command that the bread be the body of Christ, but he saith that it is: neither doth he command that sins should be forgiven, but pronounceth in the behalf of God that they are forgiven. It is not unlawful also that he with the congregation should make a prayer for the assistance or increase of God his gifts upon him that is ordained, but to command that he should receive it is merely unlawful. For these words, "Receive the Holy Ghost," are the imperative mood, and do expressly signify a commandment. And so the bishop may as well say to the sea, when it rageth and swelleth, "Peace, be quiet," as to say, "Receive the Holy Ghost." And, if you think it so good reason to use this in the making of ministers, because you use the words of our Saviour Christ, why may not you as well blow upon them as he did? For, seeing that our Saviour Christ confirmed his word there with a sacrament, or outward sign, and you think you must therefore do it because he did it; you are much to blame to leave out the outward sign, or sacrament of breath, whereby the faith of him that*[7] *is ordained might be the more assured of such gifts and graces as are requisite in his function. I heap not up here the judgment of writers*[8]: *you know, I think, it might easily be done, if I liked to follow that way.*

[6 These marginal notes are inserted from Answ. 2.]
[7 Which, Repl. 1 and 2.]   [8 Of the writers, Repl. 1 and 2.]

Jo. Whitgift.

Christ used these words, "This is my body," in the celebration of his supper; but there is no special commandment that the minister should use the same; and yet must he use them, because Christ used them: even so, when Christ did ordain his apostles ministers of the gospel, Joh. xx., he said unto them, "Receive the Holy Ghost, &c.;" which words, because they contain the principal duty of a minister, and do signify that God doth pour his Spirit upon those whom he calleth to that function, are most aptly also used of the bishop (who is God's instrument in that business) in the ordaining of ministers. St Paul speaking to Timothy, 1 Tim. iv., saith: "Neglect not the gift that is in thee, which was given unto thee by prophecy, with the laying on of the hands of the eldership." In which words the apostle signifieth that God doth bestow his gifts and Spirit upon such as be called to the ministry of the word; whereof imposition of hands is a token, or rather a confirmation: and therefore saith M. Calvin that "it was not a vain ceremony; because God did fulfil with his Spirit that consecration, which men did signify by imposition of hands[1]." And surely, as that is no vain ceremony, though it be done by men, so these be no vain words, though they be spoken by men.

Neither doth the bishop speak them as though he had authority to give the Holy Ghost, but he speaketh them as the words of Christ used in the like action; who (as I said before) doth most certainly give his Holy Spirit to those whom he calleth to the ministry. And surely, if any pattern either in calling or ordaining of ministers is to be followed, this of Christ is to be followed especially; and it is not unlike but that the apostles, when they laid on their hands, used the same words; because (as I have said) laying on of hands is a sign, or rather a confirmation of the same. That which you speak of commanding is a mere cavil; you know in your conscience that there is nothing less meant.

To recite the words of Christ in the name of Christ, in the self-same manner that Christ did speak them, is as lawful in this action as it is in the supper: for the bread is not the

---

[1 Unde colligimus non inanem fuisse ritum; quia consecrationem quam homines impositione manuum figurabant, Deus Spiritu suo implevit.—Calvin. Op. Amst. 1667-71. Comm. in Epist. i. ad Tim. cap. iv. 14. Tom. VII. p. 458.]

minister's body, but the sacrament of Christ his body; and yet he saith, "Take and eat: this is my body:" so, in reciting God's commandments, we say, "Thou shalt have no other gods but me;" and yet we mean not that we are their gods, but we speak the words of God in his person, and in the self-same manner and form that he hath left them unto us. But it is now no marvel though such as wickedly forsake their calling do also impiously deride and jest at the manner and form thereof.

Christ, when he said to the sea, "Peace, be quiet," shewed a miracle to confirm his divinity; but, when he said, "Receive the Holy Ghost, &c.," he did institute a ministry which should be used by man: and therefore there is no similitude betwixt these two. Christ, when he breathed upon them, did an action proper unto himself; for he thereby signified that he had authority to give unto them his Holy Spirit, and that the same Spirit did not only proceed from the Father, but from himself also: when he spake these words, he made a perpetual promise that all such should receive his Spirit, as from time to time were by him called to the office of the ministry.

I think you would surely use some authority of writers here, as you do in other places, if you had any; but I suppose you have not one that misliketh this form as it is used in this church of England. I know they do justly condemn the foolish imitation of the papists, who follow Christ in breathing; but that there is any great misliking of these words, "Receive the Holy Ghost" (except only when they speak of the papistical abusing of them), I cannot perceive.

Of Apostles, Evangelists, and Prophets.

Chapter iii. The First Division.

Admonition.

The Ninth:

˟ *Acts xx.* 28.
Eph. iv. 11.
Tit. i. 5.
1 *Pet. v.* 2.

Then every pastor ˟*had his flock*[2]*.*

[[2] The remainder of the sentence which appears below, page 528, is placed here in Answ.]

Answer to the Admonition, Page 50, Sect. 2.

To prove this you allege the xx. of the Acts, the iv. to the Ephesians, the i. to Titus, the v. chapter of the 1. of Peter: which places declare that there were pastors which had flocks; but they prove not that every pastor had a flock: nevertheless, howsoever you prove it, true it is that, if he be a pastor, he must have a certain flock; for therein doth a pastor differ from the rest of the degrees of ministers in Christ's church, mentioned in the[1] fourth chapter to the Ephesians. But you must learn that there be not only pastors in the church, but also apostles, prophets, evangelists, doctors, Ephes. iv., 1 Cor. xii.; who all are called ministers, and have their place in the church of Christ; as it shall be proved, if you deny it.

T. C. Page 45, Sect. 1.

This passeth all the divinity that ever I read, that there are now apostles, and evangelists, and prophets. You shall assuredly do marvels if you prove that, as you say you will, if any deny it: I deny it; prove you it.

Jo. Whitgift.

Apostles.

Then have you not read much "divinity;" for, if it be true that the apostle St Paul, in the fourth to the Ephesians, doth make a perfect platform of a church, and a full rehearsal of the offices therein contained (as you say he doth), then can I not understand how you can make those offices rather temporal, than the office of the pastors and doctors. And, forasmuch as you so greatly contemn authority, and would have all things proved by scripture, let me hear one word of the same that doth but insinuate these offices to be temporal. The place itself seemeth to import a continuance of these

Eph. iv.

functions, until the coming of Christ. For he saith: "He therefore gave some to be apostles, and some prophets, and some evangelists, and some pastors and teachers, for the gathering together of the saints, for the work of the ministry, &c.; until we all meet together in the unity of faith and knowledge of the Son of God, unto a perfect man, and unto the measure of the age and fulness of Christ, &c." I am persuaded that you cannot shew any like place, which doth so plainly import the abrogating of them, as this doth make

[1 That, Answ.]

for their continuance. I have, beside that place to the Ephesians, the twelfth of the first to the Corinthians, and the xiv.; where he speaketh of prophets as of perpetual ministers in the church of Christ. {1 Cor. xii. and xiv.}

I know that there were certain things in the apostles which were proper unto themselves, as their calling, which was immediately from God, their commission to go into the whole world, the power of working miracles, to be witnesses of the resurrection and of the ascension, &c.; but to preach the word of God in places where need requireth (though the same be not peculiarly committed to them), or to govern churches already planted, I see no cause why it should not be perpetual.

Likewise the office of the "evangelist," if it be taken for the writing of the gospel, then it is ceased. But, if it be taken for "preaching to the people plainly and simply[2]," as Bullinger thinketh; or generally for "preaching the gospel[3]," as Musculus supposeth, in which sense also Paul said to Timothy, 2 Tim. iv., "Do the work of an evangelist;" or for "preaching more fervently and zealously than other[4]," as Bucer saith; then I see no cause at all why it may not still remain in the church. {Evangelists. Bull. in iv. ad Ephes. Musc. Tit. de Ver. Minist. in Locis Com. Bucer in iv. Ephes.}

Moreover, prophets, if they be taken for such as have the gift of foreshewing things to come, then be they not in all times of the church; but, if they be such as St Paul speaketh of, 1 Cor. xiv., such, I say, as have an especial gift in interpreting the scriptures, whether it be in expounding the mysteries thereof to the learned, or in declaring the true sense thereof to the people, I understand not why it is not as perpetual as the pastor or doctor[5]. {Prophets. 1 Cor. xiv.}

[2 Evangelistæ autem dicebantur, qui plebe potissimum erudienda incumbebant, atque evangelium huic quam simplicissime annunciabant.—H. Bullinger. Comm. in Omn. Apost. Epist. Tigur. 1558. In Epist. ad Ephes. cap. iv. p. 430.]

[3 *Evangelistam* esse quid sit, varie exponitur. Breviter, vel est qui prædicat, vel qui literis mandat historias et doctrinam evangelii. Priore sensu Timotheo dicit apostolus: Opus fac evangelistæ, 2 Tim. iv. &c.—Wolfg. Muscul. Loc. Comm. Theol. Basil. 1599. Tit. de Verb. Ministr. Dei, p. 194.]

[4 Evangelistæ dicti sunt initio, quibus datus fuit ardor insignis evangelii annunciandi, et in eo magna facultas. Tales hodie quoque inveniuntur, &c.—M. Bucer. Prælect. in Epist. ad Ephes. Basil. 1562. cap. iv. p. 107.]

[5 Cartwright declares that Whitgift is maintaining an "anabaptistical dream;" that "impudently he hath abused the authority both of elder and later writers to cover this frenzy;" that "he is unworthy of any answer at all;" and that what he says of "the gift of foretelling things to come" is "senseless."— Sec. Repl. p. 303.]

Thus you see that I have both scripture and reason on my side ; and, to the end you may perceive that I am not destitute of the consent also of learned men in this matter, I will set down the opinions of one or two. Ambrose, upon these words, *Ad Ephes. iv., Et ipse dedit quosdam quidem apostolos, &c.* saith thus : " The apostles are bishops ; prophets be interpreters of the scriptures : although in the beginning there were prophets, as Agabus, and the four virgins prophetesses, as it is in the Acts of the Apostles, &c. ; yet now interpreters be called prophets, evangelists be deacons, as Philip ; for, although they be no priests, yet may they preach the gospel without a chair, as both Stephanus and Philip before named[1]." Bucer upon the same place saith that there be "evangelists" now[2]; and you yourself, fol. 42, confess that " Hus, Jerome of Prague, Luther, Zuinglius, &c. were evangelists[3]." Peter Martyr, in his Commentaries upon the xii. to the Romans, saith that " the apostle there describeth those functions and gifts which are at all times necessary for the church[4];" and in that place the apostle mentioneth prophesying. M. Calvin, in his *Institut. cap.* 8., doth confess that " God hath stirred up apostles and evangelists since that time of the primitive church, and that he hath done so likewise even now in this time[5]."

M. Bullinger, upon the place of the fourth to the Ephesians, saith that " the words be confounded, and that an apostle is also called a prophet, a doctor, an evangelist, a minister, and a bishop ; and a bishop an evangelist, and a prophet, &c.[6]"

[1 Apostoli episcopi sunt : prophetæ vero explanatores sunt scripturarum ; quamvis inter ipsa primordia fuerint prophetæ, sicut Agabus, et quatuor virgines prophetantes, sicut continetur in Actibus apostolorum &c. nunc autem interpretes prophetæ dicuntur. Evangelistæ diaconi sunt, sicut fuit Philippus ; quamvis non sint sacerdotes, evangelizare tamen possunt sine cathedra, sicut et beatus Stephanus et Philippus memoratus.—Ambros. Op. Par. 1686-90. Comm. in Epist. ad Ephes. cap. iv. vv. 11, 12. Tom. II. Append. col. 241.]

[2 M. Bucer. Prælect. in Epist. ad Ephes. cap. iv. p. 107. See before, page 493, note 4.]

[3 See before, page 471.]

[4 Prophetia hic sumitur a quibusdam pro facultate, qua multi in ecclesia futura divinitus prædicebant....Nos tamen illam significationem hoc loco non sequimur. Paulus enim hic vim illam edendi miracula non enumerat ; sed munera tantum describit, quæ omni tempore sint in ecclesia necessaria.— P. Martyr. Comm. in Epist. ad Rom. Basil. 1568. cap. xii. p. 624.]

[5 Calvin. Op. Amst. 1667-71. Inst. Lib. IV. cap. iii. 4. Tom. IX. p. 282. See below, page 496.]

[6 Nemo autem est qui non videat hæc vocabula invicem confundi et alterum

To be short, it is thus written in the confession of the churches in Helvetia: "The ministers of the new testament be called by sundry names; for they are called apostles, prophets, evangelists, bishops, &c." And (speaking of prophets) it saith: "The prophets in time past, foreseeing things to come, were called seers, who were expounders of the scriptures also; as some be even now-a-days. Evangelists were writers of the history of the gospel, and preachers also of the glad tidings of Christ his gospel; as Paul bid Timothy do the work of an evangelist, &c.[7]" So that to say that there is in the church "apostles, prophets, and evangelists," in such sense as I have declared, is no strange "divinity" to such as be divines indeed. But let us hear your reasons.

Confess. Helvetica.

Chapter iii. The Second Division.

T. C. Page 45, Sect. 1, 2, 3, 4.

And, that you may have something to do more than, peradventure, you thought of when you wrote these words, I will shew my[8] reasons why I think there ought to be none, nor can be none, unless they have wonderful and extraordinary callings. It must first be understanded that the signification of this word "apostle," when it is properly taken, extendeth itself not only to all the ministers of God, being sent of God, but to the embassador of any prince or nobleman, or that is sent of any public authority, and is used of the scripture by the trope of synecdoche for the twelve that our Saviour Christ appointed to go throughout all the world to preach the gospel; unto the which number was added St Paul and, as some think, Barnabas, which are severed from all other ministers of the gospel by these notes:

First, that they were immediately called of God; as St Paul to the Galatians proveth himself to be an apostle, because he was not appointed by men.

Gal. i. 1.[9]

accipi pro altero. Nam apostolus etiam propheta, doctor, evangelista, presbyter atque episcopus est. Et episcopus evangelista et propheta est, propheta doctor, presbyter, et evangelista.—H. Bullinger. Comm. in Omn. Apostol. Epist. Tigur. 1558. In Epist. ad Ephes. cap. iv. p. 431.]

[7 Porro ministri novi populi variis nuncupantur appellationibus. Dicuntur enim apostoli, prophetæ, evangelistæ, episcopi, &c. Prophetæ quondam præscii futurorum vates erant: sed et scripturas interpretabantur: quales etiam hodie adhuc inveniuntur. Evangelistæ appellabantur scriptores evangelicæ historiæ, sed et præcones evangelii Christi: quomodo et Paulus Timotheum jubet implere opus evangelistæ, &c.—Confess. et Expos. Fid. Christ. cap. xviii. in Corp. et Syntagm. Confess. Fid. Genev. 1654. p. 37.]

[8 Shew you my, Repl. 1 and 2.]

[9 The verse is added from Repl. 2.]

How apostles, &c. are said to be now.

Then that they saw Christ; which argument St Paul useth in the ix. 1 Cor.[1] *"Am I not an apostle? have I not seen Christ?"*

Thirdly, that these had the field of the whole world to till; whereas other are restrained more particularly, as to a certain plough-land, wherein they should occupy themselves: whereupon it followeth that, as we conclude against the pope truly that he can be no successor of the apostles, not only because he neither teacheth nor doth as they did, but because the apostles have no successors, neither any can succeed into the office of an apostle; so may we likewise conclude against those that would have the apostles now-a-days, that there can be none, because there is none unto whom all these three notes do agree; as that he is both sent of God immediately, or that he hath seen Christ, or that he is sent into all the world.

JO. WHITGIFT.

M. Calvin, upon the sixteenth to the Romans, saith that this word "apostle," in proper and usual signification, doth only comprehend that "first order which Christ in the beginning did appoint in his twelve disciples;" which is directly contrary to your saying.

I grant that in such respects as you now put down there be no "apostles;" although Matthias was not immediately called by God, as it appeareth, Acts i., and you before have confessed; neither can you prove by the scripture that Barnabas was so called, but the contrary rather doth appear in the xi. of the Acts, and yet he was an "apostle." St Paul in the first to the Corinth. ix. doth not say that he saw Christ, to prove that he was an "apostle," but to declare that he was in that respect nothing inferior to the rest of the apostles. I have before declared in what sense I say that there be apostles in the church, neither is it a matter so strange, seeing that M. Calvin saith as much in this place before recited:

Calv. in xvi. Rom. Instit. cap. 8. Quanquam non nego, quin apostolos postea quoque, vel saltem eorum loco evangelistas interdum excitarit Deus, ut nostro tempore factum est[2]: "Although I do not deny, but that God hath afterwards also stirred up apostles, or at the least evangelists instead of them, as it is done in our days[3]."

[1 Repl. 2 omits the words after *useth*, and places 1 *Cor. ix.* 1. in the margin.]

[2 Qui ergo salutis doctrinam huc et illuc circumferendo plantabant ecclesias, eos generaliter vocat apostolos hoc quidem loco. Nam alibi ad primarium illum ordinem restringit, quem Christus initio instituit in duodecim discipulis, &c.— Calvin. Op. Amst. 1667-71. Comm. in Epist. ad Rom. cap. xvi. 7. Tom. VII. p. 105. Conf. Inst. Lib. IV. cap. iii. 4. Tom. IX. p. 282.]

[3 Cartwright rejoins that Whitgift "declareth himself but a trifler. For, unless he be at defiance with his grammar, he shall be constrained will he nill he to confess it to be true which I have set down."—Sec. Repl. p. 303.]

Chap. iii. The Third Division.

T. C. Page 45, Sect. 5.

And, although some ecclesiastical writers do call sometimes good ministers successors of the apostles, yet that is to be understanded because they propound the same doctrine that they did, not because they succeeded into the same kind of function, which they could not do. St Paul doth use this word[4] *sometimes, in his proper and native signification, for him that is publicly sent from any to other; as when he speaketh of the brethren that were joined with Titus, which were sent by the churches with relief to the poor church in Jerusalem and Jewry, and where he calleth Epaphroditus an apostle. But that is with addition, and not simply; as in the first place he calleth the brethren "the apostles of the churches," that is, not the apostles of all churches, or sent to all churches, but the apostles which certain churches sent with the relief to other certain churches; and Epaphroditus he calleth not an apostle simply, but the apostle of the Philippians, that is, which the Philippians sent with relief to Paul, being in prison at Rome; as it appeareth in the same epistle.*

2Cor.viii.23.[5]

Phil. ii.25.[5]

Jo. WHITGIFT.

The writers of the *Magdelburgica* history call Epaphroditus an apostle in the same sense that they call Paul, and the rest of the apostles[6]; and M. Calvin thinketh the name of an apostle to be taken in that place generally, *pro quolibet evangelista*[7], "for any preacher of the gospel." Ambrose saith: *Erat eorum apostolus a Paulo factus, dum illum ad exhortationem eorum mittebat ad eos*[8]: "He was made their apostle of Paul, when as at their request he sent him unto them." And Theodoret in plain words doth call him an apostle, because he was bishop of the Philippians[9]. If these say true, as no doubt they do, then is not Epaphroditus called an apostle only in that signification that you say he was. In that he calleth them apostles, with an addition "of

Epaphroditus an apost. Cent. i. Lib. ii. cap. 7.

Calvin in ii. Philip.

Ambros. in Philip. ii.

Theo. 1 Tim. iii. & Philip. ii.

[4 Here Repl. 2 adds in *apostle.*]
[5 The verses are added from Repl. 2.]
[6 ... et Act. 14. Paulus et Barnabas apostoli dicuntur. Epaphroditus apostolus Philippensium dicitur, Philip. 2. et Andronicus et Junias insignes inter apostolos dicuntur Rom. 16.—Centur. Eccles. Hist. Basil. 1560, &c. Cent. i. Lib. ii. cap. vii. col. 507.]
[7 Calvin. Op. Comm. in Epist. ad Philip. cap. ii. 25. Tom. VII. p. 371.]
[8 Erat enim eorum apostolus ab apostolo factus &c.—Ambros. Op. Par. 1686-90. Comm. in Epist. ad Phil. cap. ii. vv. 25, 6, 7. Tom. II. Append. col. 258.]
[9 Οὕτω Φιλιππησίων ἀπόστολος ὁ 'Επαφρόδιτος ἦν· ὑμῶν γάρ, φησιν, ἀπόστολον καὶ συνεργὸν τῆς χρείας μου.—Theod. Op. Lut. Par. 1642-84. In Epist. i. ad Tim. cap. iii. Tom. III. p. 474. Ἀπόστολον δὲ αὐτὸν κέκληκεν αὐτῶν, ὡς τὴν ἐπιμέλειαν αὐτῶν ἐμπεπιστευμένον.—Id. in Epist. ad Phil. cap. ii. p. 333.]

the churches," not of all churches, he confirmeth my saying; for it argueth that there may be apostles, though they have commission but for one kingdom or province only; as Epaphroditus was the apostle of the churches of the Philippians, because he was sent unto them to preach. Thus doth both Ambrose, Theodoret, Calvin, and others, write[1].

Chapter iii. The Fourth Division.
T. C. Page 46, Sect. 1.

T. C. shifteth off a direct answer with this 'belike.'

And, as for Andronicus and Junius which are by you recited, belike to prove that we may have more apostles, because it is said of St Paul that they were "famous and notable amongst the apostles," Rom. xvi. 7.[2] *it cannot be proved by anything I see there, whether they had any function ecclesiastical or no. For St Paul calleth them his kinsfolks[3] and fellow-prisoners, and doth not say that they were his fellow-labourers; but[4] a man may be well notable and famous amongst the apostles, and well known unto them, which is no apostle. And, if the apostles would have had this order of the apostles to continue in the church, there is no doubt but that they would have chosen one into James his room, when he was slain, as they did when they supplied the place of Judas by* Acts xii. 2.[5] *choosing Matthias; and so ever, as they had died, the other would have put other in their places. So it appeareth that this function of the apostles is ceased.*

Jo. Whitgift.

Andronicus and Junia apostles. Cent. 1. Lib. ii. cap. 7.

Calvin.in xvi. Rom.

The foresaid authors of the story called *Magdelburgica* do also reckon these two among the apostles, even as they do Paul and Barnabas[6]. M. Calvin upon that place to the Romans saith, that "the name of an apostle there doth extend to all those which teach not one church only, but many, &c.[7];" and seemeth to account Andronicus and Junius such.

Beza in xvi. Rom.

M. Beza in the same place writeth thus: *Inter apostolos, &c. i. quorum nomen inter apostolos viget, vel qui et ipsi sunt insignes apostoli; sic enim accipitur interdum hoc nomen in genere pro his, qui Christi nomine funguntur*

[1 Cartwright accuses Whitgift in this division of self-contradiction and begging the question.—Sec. Repl. pp. 303, &c.]
[2 The verse is added from Repl. 2.]
[3 Kinsfolk, Repl. 1 and 2.]   [4 And, Repl. 1, 2, and Def. A.]
[5 This reference is inserted from Repl. 2. Repl. 1 does not give the verse.]
[6 See before, page 497, note 6.]
[7 Dum tertio loco *apostolos* nominat, hanc vocem non accipit in significatione propria et usitata, sed latius extendit ad eos omnes qui non unam tantum ecclesiam instituunt, sed promulgando ubique evangelio impendunt operam.—Calvin. Op. Amst. 1667-71. Comm. in Epist. ad Rom. cap. xvi. 7. Tom. VII. p. 105.]

legatione[8]: "That is, whose name is famous among the apostles, or which are themselves notable apostles; for so is this name sometime generally taken for those which are sent in embassage in the name of Christ." Bullinger doth think that they were in the number of the 72. disciples[9]. P. Martyr upon that place: "They are called notable amongst the apostles; not because they were of the college of the twelve apostles, but because (as it is credible) they had spread the gospel through many places, and had planted many churches." And a little after, speaking of your interpretation, he saith: "This sense doth not displease me, if the words themselves be not contrary thereunto[10]." So that he seemeth to doubt whether the words will bear your interpretation or no. Gualter and Bullinger also suppose it not to be unlikely that they were the first planters of christian religion at Rome[11]. And I can read of none that doubteth, whether they had any function ecclesiastical or no, as you do.

<small>Bull. in xvi. Rom.</small>

<small>Martyr in xvi. Rom.</small>

<small>Gualter in xvi. Rom.</small>

I brought them in before, *pagina* 47,[12] to prove that some may be chosen to preach the word which have no certain cure; and you, to avoid a direct answer, have shifted them off to this place, and now you say, that "belike" I bring them "to[13] prove that we may have more apostles:" which thing indeed they prove manifestly; but I brought them in to declare that a man may be admitted to preach, though he have no certain cure; and to that you have not answered.

There is nothing expressed in scriptures, whether the apostles did choose any into the room of James or no; but

[[8] Inter apostolos, ἐν τοῖς ἀποστόλοις. Id est, Quorum nomen apud ipsos etiam apostolos &c. pro iis qui &c.—Nov. Test. cum Th. Bezæ Annot. H. Steph. 1565. Epist. ad Rom. cap. xvi. 7. p. 225.]

[[9] Conjectura est hos duos e numero fuisse lxxii. discipulorum Domini, quorum mentio est in evangelio secundum Lucam. Horum fortassis institutione primum credidit Romanorum ecclesia. —H. Bullinger. Comm. in Omn. Apostol. Epist. Tigur. 1558. Ad Rom. cap. xvi. p. 119.]

[[10] ...appellantur insignes inter apostolos: non quod essent ex collegio duodecim apostolorum, sed quod, ut est credibile, evangelium per multa loca disseminassent, et ecclesias complures extruxissent....Fortasse dicuntur insignes inter apostolos, quasi illis probe noti, et minime obscuri in ecclesia Christi. Iste sensus mihi non displicet, modo verba ipsa non repugnent.—P. Martyr. Comm. in Epist. ad Rom. Basil. 1568. Rom. xvi. p. 681.]

[[11] At illum [Petrum] Romanæ ecclesiæ fundatorem esse, et illic episcopi munus obivisse, constanter nego. Nam si quis conjecturis locus est, hæc laus Aquilæ potius, vel Andronico et Juniæ, aut etiam multis simul debetur, &c.— R. Gualther. in Epist. ad Rom. Hom. Tigur. 1590. cap. xvi. Hom. xciv. fol. 220.]

[[12] See before, page 483.]   [[13] Them in to, Def. A.]

How evangelists may be said to be in our time.

I am persuaded they did not, neither was it necessary. For who ever said that there must be continually twelve apostles, and neither more nor less?

I told you before out of M. Calvin, that this word "apostle" in his proper and usual signification comprehendeth only the twelve apostles appointed by Christ. Wherefore in this signification there are now "no apostles," neither was there any since that time: but it signifieth also generally such as preach the gospel in sundry places; and, although they go not through the whole world, as the twelve did, yet are they not bound to any one place certainly. And, according to this signification, there both hath been and are apostles.

Chapter iii. The Fifth Division.
T. C. Page 46, Sect. 2, 3.

You ask further[1], that if a man should not preach before he have a pastoral charge, what they will answer unto Philip and Epaphroditus; whereby your meaning is, belike, that, although they be no pastors, yet they may be evangelists, which go about the country here and there. But this office is ceased in the church, as the apostles' is, saving that sometime the Lord doth raise up some extraordinarily for the building up of the churches which are fallen down, and pulled up by the foundations; as I have shewed somewhat before. And that it is ceased, it may appear by these reasons.

First, for because all those that the scripture calleth precisely evangelists (which are only Philip and Timothy) had their callings confirmed by miracle; and so it is like that Titus, and Silvanus, and Apollos, and if there were any other, had their vocations after the same manner confirmed: but there is no such miraculous confirmation now, therefore there is no such vocation. *Acts viii. 39. 1 Tim. i. 18.*

[For, albeit those that God hath raised up in those dark times and overthrows of the church whereof mention is made before, as M. Luther, &c., had not their callings always confirmed by direct and manifest miracles of healing or raising up from the dead; yet the marvellous success and blessing that the Lord gave unto their labours were sufficient seals unto all men, that, although they had no ordinary calling, nor by men, yet they were sent of God—that I speak nothing of the miraculous deliverances that some of them had out of dangers, by warning given of perils by those which were never seen before nor after, and by such like wonderful means as are to be seen in stories.][2]

Jo. Whitgift.

I have declared both before by scripture, reason, and other authority, that, though the name of an "evangelist" be changed, yet the office remaineth. The scripture nowhere

---

[1 Farther, Repl. 1 and 2.]
[2 The portion between brackets is added from Repl. 2.]

calleth Timothy an "evangelist;" only, 2 Tim. iv., St Paul willeth him to "do the work of an evangelist," which is to preach the gospel. But of this matter I have at large spoken in another place.

How evangelists may be said to be in our time.
2 Tim. iv.

It passeth to see how boldly you do abuse the scripture. Where do you read that either Timothy or Philip were ordained or confirmed evangelists by miracle? There can be no such thing imagined: in the 39. verse, Acts viii., the words be these: "And, as soon as they (that is Philip and the eunuch) were come out of the water, the Spirit of the Lord caught away Philip, that the eunuch saw him no more, &c." Was this the miracle that confirmed Philip an evangelist? Lord God, what mean you? This was rather done to confirm the eunuch: as for Philip, it is manifest that before this miracle he was an evangelist; for in the same chapter we read that before this time Philip had preached in Samaria, and converted them, being before seduced by Simon the sorcerer; and that he had also baptized them. Moreover, he had converted the eunuch and baptized him before this miracle was shewed: wherefore it could not be a confirming of his evangelistship.

Acts viii.

That in the 1 Tim. i. verse 18. insinuateth that divers prophecies had gone before of Timothy; whereby it was revealed that he should be a worthy minister of the church, or, as Calvin saith, " which had commended him to the church³;" although there be sundry interpretations of that place more like to be true than that. But how proveth it that he was made an evangelist by miracle? First, Timothy was now a bishop; as hereafter is proved. Secondly, here is no mention made of any calling to an evangelistship. Thirdly, a prophecy is not a miracle. Last of all, though this were true both in Philip and Timothy (as it is in neither), yet doth it not follow that whosoever is called to be an evangelist must also be confirmed by miracle; for particular examples make no general rule: Timothy was ordained minister of the gospel, *per impositionem manuum,* "by the laying on of hands," 1 Tim. iv., 2 Tim. i. And therefore his vocation was ordinary, and needed no such confirmation by miracle.

1 Tim. iv.
2 Tim. i.

[³ Proinde ex ejus verbis colligimus, plures fuisse editas prophetias de Timotheo, quæ ipsum ecclesiæ commendarent.—Calvin. Op. Amst. 1667-71. Comm. in Epist. I. ad Tim. cap. i. 18. Tom. VII. p. 443.]

Chapter iii. The Sixth Division.

How evangelists may be said to be in our time.

T. C. Page 46, Sect. 4.

Now again, if there should be any evangelist, who should ordain him? You will say, the bishop; but I say that cannot be, that the greater should be ordained of the less: for the evangelist is a higher degree in the church than is the bishop or pastor. And, if he be so, why hath he not his estimation here in the church above the bishop or archbishop either? for the archbishop is but a bishop; or why doth he not[2] ordain bishops, as Timothy and Titus did, which were evangelists, being one point of their office; as Eusebius declareth[3]?

Heb. vii. 7.[1]

Euseb. Lib. iii. cap. 27.

Jo. Whitgift.

You do but try my patience in so often offending in "the petition of the principle:" for neither can you prove an evangelist to be a higher degree in the church than is a bishop, neither is it true that Timothy and Titus were evangelists, and not bishops; and in that point have you all the writers both old and new, stories and other, one or two only excepted, flatly against you; besides the evident reasons that may be collected out of the scripture.

Heb. vii.

I know not to what purpose you quote the vii. to the Hebrews, except it be for this text: "The less is blessed of the greater;" in which place blessing is not taken for ordaining or consecrating; for Melchisedech did no such thing to Abraham: but it is there taken as it is Num. vi.; where the priests are commanded to bless the people; and therefore serveth not your turn for anything here spoken.

Numb. vi.

Vain quotations.

I understand not to what end you quote "Eusebius in his third book and 27. chapter." For there is not in that place one word spoken of an evangelist, or any part of his office.

[¹ The verse is added from Repl. 2.]
[² Doth not he, Repl. 1, 2, and Def. A.]
[³ There is a mistake here; for, as Whitgift afterwards observes, nothing to the point occurs in the place named. But as Cartwright afterwards, in the second edition of his Reply, corrected 27 to 37, the following is doubtless the passage intended: ...ἔπειτα δὲ ἀποδημίας στελλόμενοι, ἔργον ἐπετέλουν εὐαγγελιστῶν,... οὗτοι δὲ θεμελίους τῆς πίστεως ἐπὶ ξένοις τισὶ τόποις αὐτὸ μόνον καταβαλλόμενοι, ποιμένας τε καθιστάντες ἑτέρους, τούτοις τε αὐτοῖς ἐγχειρίζοντες τὴν τῶν ἀρτίως εἰσαχθέντων γεωργίαν, ἑτέρας αὐτοὶ πάλιν χώρας τε καὶ ἔθνη μετῄεσαν, κ.τ.λ.—Euseb. in Hist. Eccles. Script. Amst. 1695-1700. Lib. III. cap. xxxvii. p. 88.]

Chapter iii. The Seventh Division.
T. C. Page 46, Sect. 5.

Again, if there be in every church a pastor, as St Paul commandeth, what should the evangelists do? for either that pastor doth his duty, and then the evangelist is superfluous; or, if he do it not, then he is no lawful pastor, and so ought he to be put out, and another to be put in his stead. And, where the pastor doing his duty cannot suffice, there the scripture hath given him an aid of the doctor, which for because his office consisteth in teaching doctrine, to this end that the pastor might not be driven to spend so much time in propounding the doctrine, but might have the more time to employ in exhorting and dehorting, and applying of the doctrine to the times and places and persons, it is manifest that he also is tied to a certain church. For how could he be an aid unto the pastor to whose help he is given, unless he were in the same church where the pastor is? And that the evangelist's office hath been so taken as a function that endured but _{Lib. v. cap.} *for a time, it may appear, first, by that which Eusebius writeth,* _{10.[4]} *speaking of Pantenus: "for," saith he, "there were until that time evangelists, &c.[5];" which was about the year of our Lord 162. Whereby he giveth to understand that about that time they ceased, and that in his time there was none, when notwithstanding there were bishops or pastors, and*[6] _{Lib. i. Offic.1.} *elders and deacons. And Ambrose saith that there be no apostles but those which Christ himself did appoint*[7]: *whereby it appeareth that of all the ecclesiastical functions that preach the word there are but the pastor and doctor only left unto us, and the same also restrained to particular charges.*

Jo. Whitgift.

But what if there be not in every church such a pastor, neither can be? is the "evangelist" then necessary? You must of necessity confess that; for the people must not be deprived of the word, when by such means they may have it. Howbeit, though every church had his pastor, and every pastor did his duty, yet might preaching by other do good, as well for the confirmation of the doctrine and the more frequent preaching, as also for that it pleaseth God sometimes to work that by one that he doth not by another. But what scripture have you to prove that "the doctor" is added to "the pastor," as "an aid," or that the doctor is tied to a certain place? You have no licence to coin new scriptures; and in the old I am sure you cannot find it. As for your bare word, it is but a very bare proof.

[4 Lib. v. cap. 9, 10, Repl. 2.]
[5 See below, page 504, note 4.] [6 *And* is not in Repl. 2.]
[7 Ambros. Op. Par. 1686-90. De Offic. Ministr. Lib. I. cap. i. 3. Tom. II. cols. 2, 3. See below, page 504, note 5.]

I told you before that Hierome, Augustine, Chrysostom, Musculus, and divers other upon good reason confound "pastor" and "doctor," and think them to be but diverse names of one office[1]. And, whereas you say that "the doctor's office consisteth in teaching doctrine to this end, that the pastor might not be driven to spend so much time in propounding the doctrine, &c.," I would gladly know whence you learn that. Ambrose saith, "they be such as see good rule kept in the church, or such as teach children[2]."

<small>Ambrose in iv. Eph.</small>

<small>Lib. v. cap. 9.</small>

Eusebius' words, speaking of Pantenus, be these: "There were as yet at that time many evangelists which were prest[3] and ready to this, that they might with a godly zeal, according to the apostles' example, promote and plant the word of God[4]." Which prove that there were then evangelists good store, which were zealous, &c. But there is no mention made of any ceasing of their office: it rather proveth a continuance of the same, being so long after the apostles' time. There is now no such evangelists as go from kingdom to kingdom, or through the world, because the miraculous gift of tongues is now ceased. Neither is any now lawfully called to any such ecclesiastical function but by man, and therefore they must go no further than his authority extendeth that hath called them.

Ambrose saith truly, if he should say that there are no apostles but such as Christ himself appointed, if we speak properly and usually (as I have before declared); but that is no hinderance to anything that I have affirmed. And yet surely the words of Ambrose sound nothing that way; for Ambrose, abasing and disabling himself, saith thus: *Non igitur mihi apostolorum gloriam vendico; quis enim hoc, nisi quos ipse Filius elegit Dei, &c.*[5] "I therefore challenge not to myself the glory of the apostles; for who can do this

[1 See before, pages 474, 94.]

[2 Magistri vero exorcistæ sunt, quia in ecclesia ipsi compescunt et verberant inquietos: sive ii qui literis et lectionibus imbuendos infantes solebant imbuere. —Ambros. Op. Par. 1686-90. Comm. in Epist. ad Ephes. cap. iv. vv. 11, 12. Tom. II. Append. col. 241.]

[3 Prest: prepared.]

[4 ... ἦσαν γὰρ ἦσαν εἰσέτι τότε πλείους εὐαγγελισταὶ τοῦ λόγου, ἔνθεον ζῆλον ἀποστολικοῦ μιμήματος συνεισφέρειν ἐπ' αὐξήσει καὶ οἰκοδομῇ τοῦ θείου λόγου προθυμούμενοι.—Euseb. in Hist. Eccles. Script. Amst. 1695-1700. Lib. v. cap. x. p. 142.]

[5 Ambros. Op. De Offic. Ministr. Lib. I. cap. i.3. Tom. II. cols. 2, 3. Ambrose goes on: Non prophetarum gratiam, non virtutem evangelistarum, non pastorum circumspectionem.]

but they whom the Son of God did choose?" And what can you hereof conclude? He saith afterwards also, that he doth not challenge to himself " the circumspection of pastors;" yet was he then a bishop, as it is in that place evident. Gladly would you have some authority for your purpose if you could tell where to find it [6].

[6 Cartwright ridicules what Whitgift says of Ambrose abasing himself, and adds: "He might as well say, that it is a point of great modesty for a man to profess that he cannot climb up into heaven without a ladder." He then goes on at very great length, referring to various parts of the Defence, to controvert what Whitgift says of the continuance of the offices of apostles, prophets, and evangelists.—Sec. Repl. pp. 307, &c.]

¶ Of the Residence of the Pastor.
Tract. v.
Chapter i. The First Division.
T. C. Page 46, Sect. 6.

Now that I have proved that there are no evangelists, prophets, or apostles, and that the ministries of the[1] *word which remain are limited unto certain places; I will take that which you grant, that is, that the pastor or bishop ought to have a special flock, and demand of you wherefore he should have it. Is it not to attend upon it? And can he attend upon it, unless he be resident and abiding upon it? But he cannot be abiding upon it, if he go from place to place to preach where he thinketh necessary. Therefore, being pastor or bishop of a congregation allotted unto him, he may not go from place to place to preach where he thinketh good, much less to have a mastership of a college in one corner of the land, a deanery in another, and a prebend in the third, and so be absent from his pastoral charge in such places where either he preacheth not, or needeth not to preach; those places being otherwise furnished without him. For then how is this difference kept between the pastor and other ministers, that the one is tied to a place, and the other is not? For, if you say that it is in that he shall preach more at his flock than at other places, I answer that the evangelists and apostles did tarry longer in one place than in another, and taught some congregations years, when they did not other some months. And therefore they say nothing which allege for the non-residence of pastors, that St Paul called Timothy and Titus from Ephesus* 2 Tim. iv. 12.[2] *and Crete: for, first, they were evangelists and no pastors; then,* Tit. iii. 12.[2] *they went not of their own heads, but called of the apostle, which was a chief governor of the church: and, thirdly, they went not, but having other sufficient put in their place, as it appeareth in their several epistles; so*[3] *that, if that place make anything, it maketh not to prove the non-residency, but rather whether a minister may be translated from one church to another.*

A digression from the matter to the persons.

Jo. Whitgift.

Your reader, if he judge indifferently, cannot but acknowledge this, that you so confidently speak of proofs, to be but a vain brag, and nothing so.

There is no man that denieth but that a pastor ought so to attend upon his flock as he may be well able to do his duty towards the same, and with a good conscience answer his doings before the chief Pastor, to whom he shall give his account. In the mean time, if he be godly, if he preach

How a pastor ought to be resident.

[1 Def. B. repeats *the.*]
[2 These references are inserted from Repl. 2. They are misplaced and erased with a pen in Repl. 1.]
[3 *So* is placed after *thing* in Def. B.]

among them as often as he is persuaded to be convenient, if he have a care over them, that they be not destitute of that which is necessary, if he have such as are honest, learned, and diligent, to supply his absence, he may be bold to say to his unlawful judges, *Tu quis es, qui judicas alienum servum?* Rom. xiv. *proprio domino stat, aut cadit :* " Who art thou, which condemnest another man's servant ? he standeth or falleth to his own master." Whether a pastor having a flock may also preach out of his own charge, is another question. And, although it be by you denied, yet, because your words without proof weigh not much, I will (for the avoiding of confusion) speak nothing thereof in this place, but this only, that, as the opinion is strange, so is it most untrue, and not to be justified either by scripture, ancient fathers, or reasons.

But, O T. C., who seeth not the mark you shoot at? Why T. C. slideth from who perceiveth not how you slide from the matter to the the matter to the person. person ? To what end do you here recite "a mastership of a college, a deanery, a prebend," but that your meaning is to note some one particular man, whom (because he hath withstood your erroneous and contentious doctrine, hath not exalted you, as it is well known you have desired, hath executed those laws upon you which, for the avoiding of manifest and wilful perjury, you ought to have executed of yourself) you seek by all means possible to deface[4]? Is this conscience ? Is this *præbere te benevolum magistro, non solum dum in eo* The oath of the fellows of *vixeris, sed etiam postea pro virili, &c.*[5] *?* The Lord forgive Trin. Coll. in Cambridge. you, and give you grace to know yourself!

If he that hath this mastership, deanery, prebend, and benefice, neglect his duty in any one of them, if he do not that that both God's laws and man's laws require of him, if he be a loiterer, if he seek his ease, if he be not able to give an account of his doings when he shall thereunto be called, then let him sustain both the shame and the blame also.

The pastor is not so tied to any place, that he may not The pastor may be absent upon from the same be bodily absent upon occasion; as I am ready sent upon occasion. to prove by sufficient both reason and authority, when I shall be urged thereunto. The examples of the "evangelists" and of the "apostles" do verify the same ; for they fully instructed the churches wherein they preached in all things necessary to

[[4] Whitgift himself is meant. He had licence to hold several prefferments: master of Trinity College, dean of Lincoln, prebendary of Ely. See Strype, Whitgift, Book I. chapp. v. viii. x.]

[[5] Liber Statut. Coll. Trin. cap. xii. *De Sociorum electione.* See before, page 15.]

salvation, though they did not continually remain with them, but now and then visit them. And therefore the pastors may so do in like manner.

<small>Timothy being a pastor was absent from Ephesus.</small>

Touching Timothy and Titus (whom you so oft without any kind of proof deny to be pastors) I have spoken elsewhere at large: notwithstanding, because your too too bold asseverations may appear what they are, I will in a few words even in this place declare both that Timothy and Titus were pastors, and that their examples do evidently prove that a pastor may be upon occasions absent from his flock. And for this time I will be content with that only that M. Calvin

<small>In the treatise of archbishops, &c. Tract. viii. Calvin.</small>

writeth touching the same matter, referring the reader for further proof to that that I have in more ample manner written of the same. M. Calvin, 1 Tim. i., doth call Timothy "pastor of the church of Ephesus[1]." And in the 1 Tim. iv., expounding these words, *ne donum quod in te est, &c.*, he saith that "the Holy Ghost had by oracle appointed Timothy to be received into the order of pastors[2];" and, 2 Tim. iv., that "he did excel vulgar and common pastors[3];" meaning that he was an excellent pastor, endued with more singular and notable gifts, and of greater authority than the common sort of pastors be. And in the same chapter, speaking of Paul's sending for Timothy from Ephesus to Rome, he saith that "there was no small cause why Paul sent for Timothy from that church which he ruled and governed, and that so far off: hereby we may gather (saith he) how profitable conference is with such men; for it might be profitable to all churches, which Timothy might learn in a small time; so that the absence of half a year, or of one whole year, is nothing in comparison of the commodity that cometh thereby[4]."

[1 In eo quod Timotheo Ephesi mandaverat suas partes, observanda est pia ejus sollicitudo. Sic enim satagebat in colligendis pluribus ecclesiis, ut priores non relinqueret destitutas pastore.—Calvin. Op. Amst. 1667-71. Comm. in Epist. I. ad Tim. cap. i. 3. Tom. VII. p. 438.]

[2 ...scilicet Spiritus sanctus oraculo Timotheum destinaverat ut in ordinem pastorum cooptarent.—Id. ibid. cap. iv. 14. p. 458.]

[3 Jam vero probabilius est Timotheum, quem sibi Paulus proximum in omnibus collegam adsciverat, gradu et officii dignitate antecelluisse vulgares pastores, quam fuisse unum quemlibet ex eorum numero.—Id. in Epist. II. ad Tim. cap. iv. 5. p. 490.]

[4 Non erat certe levis causa cur eum ab ecclesia cui præerat evocaret: et quidem tam procul. inde licet colligere quantum habeant momenti talium virorum colloquutiones. Nam omnibus ecclesiis diu profuturum erat, quod brevi temporis spatio didicisset Timotheus: ut levis esset dimidii vel totius anni jactura præ compensatione.—Id. ibid. 9. p. 491.]

Whereby it is manifest that Calvin both took him to be a pastor, and also excuseth his absence. So that the example of Timothy maketh much for the purpose: the like may be said of Titus, and of sundry other in the scriptures.

Now, if the apostle being a chief governor of the church might call Timothy and Titus so far from their cures, and that for no great nor yet common matters of the church, but for his own private business, as it appeareth, 2 Tim. iv.; then I trust you will also think it lawful that such as be rulers and governors of the church may do the like. There is no man that writeth so exactly of "non-residence," but he confesseth certain necessary causes of absence: as if it be for the commodity of the church whereof he is pastor, or for the commodity of the whole church of that kingdom, or for the commodity of other particular churches in the same, or for necessity, or upon commandment of higher authority; in all these and such like cases the absence of a pastor is lawful, and it is *præsentia* rather than *absentia*, if you will believe learned writers. Now, if you will demand of me who shall allow these causes, I answer, no one private man, of what calling soever he be, but the magistrates, to whom the government of the church is committed: if they allow the absence, and the pastor satisfy his own conscience, there is no man of God, no good conscience, no modest spirit, that dare presume to judge him, much less to condemn him. *Lawful causes of the pastor's absence.*

That he ought in his absence to provide a sufficient deputy, I confess, and that example of Tychicus doth prove that; for he was Timothy's deputy, and not his successor, as you seem to insinuate. M. Calvin saith that "St Paul sent Tychicus to Ephesus, when he sent for Timothy to Rome, in the mean time to supply his absence[5]." So that he was but Timothy's deputy. Moreover, it is manifest that Timothy was oft absent from Ephesus, twice with Paul at Rome, and that he returned thither again this last time, as well as he did at other times; as both M. Calvin's words before mentioned do declare, and I also have evidently proved in that place where I prove Timothy to be bishop of Ephesus[6]. *Calv. in 2 Tim. iv.* *Timothy oft absent from Ephesus.* *Tract. viii.*

[5 Imo ne Timotheo absente destituta aut nudata maneat Ephesiorum ecclesia, *Tychicum* illuc *mittit.*—Id. ibid. 10. ibid.]

[6 Cartwright accuses Whitgift of flying "from the judgment of the word of God unto his own conscience," and calls his arguments "absurd."—Sec. Repl. pp. 330, &c.]

Chap. i. The Second Division.

T. C. Page 47, Sect. 1.

This is to sit in men's consciences as God.

But I will never weary my pen to confute those whom their own consciences are too strong for, and confuteth every night when they go to bed; for that were nothing else but to reason with the belly that hath no ears to hear, or with the back that hath no eyes to see. Those that think that they, having charges of their own, yet may go from place to place where they think it necessary, and that it skilleth not where they preach, so they preach, must consider that, if they think that God is the author of their placing in their flocks, then that either their abode there is needful and expedient, or else that God did not see well and clearly what was meet to be done in placing them over that congregation, and appointing that that congregation should hang and depend upon them for their nourishment and good government.

Jo. Whitgift.

The pastor may preach in more places.

A sore judgment and presumptuous: still I say, *Tu quis es, &c.*: "Who art thou which condemnest, &c." The rest of that section is builded upon the petition of the principle; for there is no man (I think) that so regardeth preaching in other places, that he neglecteth it in his own. But I am fully persuaded that God hath so called no man to one place, that he hath restrained him from doing good in other places also; and I constantly believe that, in the more places he laboureth and doth good, the more his service to be accepted unto God. And it is a token that he is truly called, when he hath an hearty desire to profit many.

All congregations of Christians are dear unto God; wherefore he doth not so much incline to any one, that he would have the other altogether neglected. And therefore, if there be but one good man placed in a whole shire, I think that he is there placed to do good in the country round about him, and that he ought so to do, because they be all sheep pertaining to one fold; but yet so must he labour generally, that he have an especial care of his own particular flock[1].

[1 Cartwright rejoins that it "is not the question" whether a man who "is called to one place" be "restrained from doing good in other." He argues that Whitgift is here contrary to himself; for he had previously (see before, page 484) said "that pastors and bishops have their cures limited;" and that it is wholly unjustifiable for a man to be "going to other churches of his own head," under pretence of some divine calling "to that place where he may do most good." Whitgift, he says, "by this reason must take shipping over to Rome and Constantinople, and to whatsoever place he shall understand to have need of his help."—Ibid. pp. 334, &c.]

Chapter i. The Third Division.
T. C. Page 47, Sect. 2.

And you see that, if I would follow those noble metaphors of watchman and shepherd, which the scripture useth to express the office of a minister with, what a large field is opened unto me. For then I could shew you how that cities besieged, and flocks in danger of the wolves, are watched continually night and day; and that there is no city so sore and so continually besieged, nor no flocks subject to so manifold diseases at home, or hurtful and devouring beasts abroad, and that without any truce or intermission, as are the churches, the shepherds and watchmen whereof are pastors or bishops.

Luke ii. 8.[2]

Jo. Whitgift.

I have shewed before what your metaphors of "watchmen" and "shepherds" can prove; what dissimilitudes there is betwixt them and spiritual watchmen and pastors[3]. I think your meaning is not, that the pastor should preach both night and day, or that there is no continual watching but continual preaching. If I were disposed to dally with you in your metaphors, I could say unto you that "watchmen" must of necessity oftentimes have their deputies, or else that there must be many of them, and so watch by turns. I could also say that, as soon as the "watchman" hath told the city of the enemy's approaching, and hath descried them unto it, he may depart from his station and take his rest: likewise that the "watchman" hath least to do when his enemies are nighest, especially when they have invaded the city; for then are the soldiers to drive them away by force. Wherefore by these metaphors this only can you prove, that the pastors ought to admonish their flocks of their enemies, descry them in time, and will them to be vigilant. The enemies are known, the armour is certain, the citizens reasonable: wherefore, if they neglect the admonitions given in due time and order, if they be not vigilant, their blood be upon their own pates; the "watchman" hath done his duty. The like in all respects may be said of "shepherds" and sheep.

Tract. iv. cap. 1. divis. 6. The metaphors of watchmen and shepherds.

To what purpose you have quoted in your margent the ii. of Luke, I know not, except it be because it is there said that "the shepherds were watching their sheep in the night." Luke ii.

[² The verse is inserted from Repl. 2.] [³ See before, pages 476, &c.]

The which how you can apply to your purpose I would gladly learn; for these shepherds went from their sheep, and left them in great danger[1].

Chapter i. The Fourth Division.
T. C. Page 47, Sect. 3.

But I will leave that to their considerations, and will shew that the parts and duties of the minister be such and so many in his own flock, that, if he were as wise as Salomon was, as great in counsel as Joseph, as well learned as St Paul, as active as Josue, which fought so many battles in small space, yet all were little enough, or too little, to perform to the full that which his charge requireth of him. Of the pastors therefore is required, not[2] only the preaching of the word and ministering of the sacraments, whereof the preaching of the word and ministering of the sacrament of baptism ought to be continually, and as oft as the church may conveniently assemble; the other sacrament of the Lord his supper, although not so continually (for that the church shall hardly have so much leisure from their necessary affairs of this life, as that they may celebrate it as often as the other), yet so often as that we remember that too rare and seldom celebrating it argueth a mind too too much forgetful of the unspeakable benefit of our redemption, and argueth also that we are far behind the primitive church in zeal, which did celebrate it every Sabbath—I say, beside the preaching of the word and ministering of the sacraments, there is required of him that he should admonish privately, and house by house, those that are under his charge. Acts xx. 20.[3]

Jo. Whitgift.

Certain it is that the charge of a pastor is great, and that he which doth the best must confess and say that he is but an unprofitable servant: and yet, if he occupy his talents, be they more or be they fewer, and gain with them more or less, he hath a merciful Master, who will embrace him with mercy, and will accept of his service. And therefore, though he be much inferior to Salomon in wisdom, to Joseph in counsel, to Paul in learning, and to Josua in activity, yet may he be a faithful servant, and hear of his Lord and Master, *Euge, serve bone et fidelis, &c.* : "It is well done, good servant and faithful."

Matt. xxv.

If you should thus straitly deal with the pastors, and

[[1] Cartwright censures Whitgift for dallying here not with his "but with the Holy Ghost's metaphors of pastor and watchman."—Sec. Repl. pp. 336, &c.]

[[2] *Not* is not in Def. B.]   [[3] The verse is inserted from Repl. 2.]

leave them no consolation, you should not follow our Saviour Christ his mildness and mercy.

But let the bitterness of your speeches go, and let us come to the weight of your reasons. You say that "there is required of the pastors preaching of the word, and ministering of the sacraments, and private admonition, and that the preaching of the word and ministering of the sacrament of baptism ought to be continual;" and private exhortations likewise; and therefore the pastor may not be absent. Touching "the preaching of the word," I have spoken before something: it must be according to the conscience and discretion of the pastor, who hath to consider what is best for that congregation whereof he hath the charge, both for the often preaching and for the manner of preaching also. "The sacraments" may be administered by other than by the pastor; as they were in the apostles' time, 1 Cor. i., and Acts x. "Private exhortation" must also be used as occasion serveth, according to the discretion of the minister. But I marvel that you say, "the ministering of the sacrament of baptism ought to be continually, &c." You know that in Victor his time it was celebrated but once in the year, at Easter[4]; and in Tertullian's time at Easter and Pentecost[5]. And in many parishes in England there is no such daily need of administering that sacrament. To conclude, both the sacraments may be as well ministered by another, if occasion serve. And therefore of all other reasons this is the slenderest.

Baptism ministered but once in the year.

St Paul's meaning in the xx. of the Acts is not that he daily went into their houses to exhort them, but that he did so as occasion served[6].

Chapter i.   The Fifth Division.
T. C. Page 47, Sect. 3.

Now tell me how this can be done profitably without a diligent marking and looking into their manners. How can either public preachings

[4 Eodem vero tempore [paschæ] baptisma celebrandum est catholicum. Sed tamen, si necesse fuerit,...quocunque loco vel momento....baptizentur.—Victor Papa in Corp. Jur. Canon. Lugd. 1624. Decret. Gratian. Decr. Tert. Pars, De Consecr. Dist. iii. can. 22. col. 1971.]

[5 Diem baptismo solenniorem pascha præstat; cum et passio Domini, in quam tinguimur, adimpleta est...Exinde pentecoste ordinandis lavacris latissimum spatium est, quo et Domini resurrectio inter discipulos frequentata est, et gratia Spiritus sancti dedicata, &c.—Tertull. Op. Lut. 1641. De Bapt. 19. p. 264.]

[6 Cartwright rejoins that Whitgift's reply is "from the purpose;" and that "the cavil of baptism is utterly unworthy of answer."—Sec. Repl. p. 339.]

or private admonitions have their effect and working, unless the word of God be applied according to the disposition or state of that people unto which it is preached? And undoubtedly hereof it cometh that the word of God is no more effectual in this realm than it is, for because it is preached hand over head, without knowledge and understanding the estate of the people. For so oftentimes the promises and glad tidings of the gospel of our Saviour are preached unto those that, being before secure in their sins, are after the hearing of the promises rocked into a dead sleep thereof; and[1] they that are overthrown with the conscience of their sin, and confounded in themselves, are, by the sharpness of the law and hearing of the judgment of God, broken into pieces and driven to desperation. And so likewise the people are taught sometimes how to lead their lives in honest conversation, when all that doctrine falleth to the ground, because they have no knowledge of Christ, nor of faith in him: and, to be short, it is as much as if either the surgeon should apply his plaster, or the physician his medicine, when they neither know of the wound or disease of their patients. But this knowledge of their estate cannot be without a continual abode amongst them; therefore a continual residence is necessary.

Jo. Whitgift.

A man may profit them by preaching whom he knoweth not.

The apostles and other in their time did not long continue in one place to learn the people's manners, and yet did they much prevail by preaching; neither is it so hard a matter to know the people's manners and conditions, though a man be not perpetually resident among them.

The word of God (his name be praised therefore!) hath been effectual in England; and numbers are by the same converted from superstition, blindness, and ignorance, to the true knowledge of God. But this is an old and usual objection of *The usual objection of the anabaptists.* the anabaptists against the church of Christ, that "in their churches there is a manifest amendment of life, but in other churches, which seem to profess the gospel, there appeareth no such fruit; and that the gospel is preached, but no man the better[2]." This, I say, is the slanderous speech of the anabaptists against those churches from the which they have divided themselves, and it is very oft used by you.

You must think that there be pastors and preachers in England that understand the state of the people, and know what discretion to use in their sermons and exhortations, as well as you can teach them. But this is most true that, as you think none learned but yourself, so do you also judge all men to lack both wit and discretion but yourself. And here in this place have you taken upon you this censure most confidently, I will not say arrogantly.

[¹ Sleep of them and, Repl. 2.]   [² See before, page 363, note 6.]

In the end of this division you conclude thus: "The knowledge of the estate of the people cannot be known without a continual abode with them; therefore a continual residence is necessary." You must prove the antecedent; for it is false. The apostle knew (so far as it was necessary for him to know) the Romans, the Corinthians, Galatians, and other churches to whom he wrote; and yet was he not continually resident among them. And so did the other apostles and preachers, which were not resident in any one place: and yet a preacher may do good in preaching among them whom he knoweth not; for it is God that directeth him in his words and matter. And, forasmuch as he cannot but know that every congregation consisteth of divers minds and affections, therefore (except he be void of discretion) he will so moderate and temper his sermon or exhortation, that it may profit all, and hurt none but such as do not accordingly receive it. And therefore both these propositions are false; that a man by preaching cannot profit such as he knoweth not, and that he cannot know them except he be perpetually resident with them[3].

The pastor may know the estate of the people without a continual abode amongst them.

Chapter i. The Sixth Division.
T. C. Page 48, Sect. 1.

1 Sam. i. 9.[5] *Moreover, as in the law the priests were ready in the temple to answer to all[4] the doubts and questions that any of the people should come to ask, so the ministers in their several parishes should be ready to dissolve the difficulties that either one hath with another, or with himself, touching the conscience; for want whereof the consciences of many, after doubtful and dangerous wrestling with the devil and with despair, are strangled. And thereupon some hang or drown themselves, some other, putting away all care or conscience of sinning, and labouring to have no sense nor feeling of their sin, close up the wound unhealed, which after either breaketh out more dangerously, or else, every day more and more waxing senseless and without feeling, treasure up unto themselves the wrath of God against the day of judgment. For, although the judgment of God doth not for the time follow them so hard as them which, through terror of conscience, untaught and uncomforted, kill themselves; yet their estate is never the less dangerous therefore, but rather more, forasmuch as, by a longer*

[3 Cartwright replies that the example of the apostles is not to the point; and that Whitgift is mistaken in thinking it easy "to know the people's conditions: all wise men see the contrary: yea, the experience of men, deceived in the natures of their friends, wives, and children, best known unto them, might have taught him otherwise."—Sec. Repl. pp. 339, &c.]

[4 Answer all, Repl. 1 and 2.]

[5 This reference is inserted from Repl. 2.]

line of sin drawn out, they also pull upon themselves a heavier condemnation. Which things when they see oftentimes before their eyes, that will consider it, it is easy to judge that it cometh to pass a great deal oftener than we can see.

JO. WHITGIFT.

You do not refer me to any place where I might read that "the priests in the law were ready in the temple to answer all the doubts and questions that any of the people should come to ask, &c.:" and I do not remember any such place in the scripture; except you mean that which is written in the xvii. of Deut. verse 9, &c.; where there is no such attendance mentioned, but only the people are willed to bring their controversies to the priests and the judge. If you mean the 12. verse of that chapter, where it is said of the priest that "he standeth before the Lord to minister there," you have also missed the cushion[1]. For the meaning of that place is, that whosoever presumptuously refuseth to hearken unto the priest (so long as the priest is the true minister of God, and pronounceth according to his word) shall die, &c. The priest here had to do in civil and judicial matters together with the judge; the priest was but in the chief place where judgment was heard, and not in every particular congregation. Wherefore, if you would conclude any thing of this place, it must be that the priest must be joined with the judge, and have to do in civil and judicial matters, and remain in some chief place of the country where judgments are to be heard. You can by no means hereof conclude that every particular congregation should have a pastor continually remaining with them.

There is not now any such general ignorance but that there may divers be found able to answer all such doubts as you speak of sufficiently, though the pastor be absent. The scriptures also are publicly read in every man's house, which are, as St Paul saith, 2 Tim. iii., "profitable to teach, to improve, to correct, to instruct in righteousness; that the man of God may be absolute, being made perfect in all good works;" and, as Chrysostom calleth them, they be an apothecary his shop, where every man may find remedy for his diseases[2].

[1 Missed the cushion: failed in your attempt; an allusion, probably, to archery. See Nares' Glossary.]

[2 Ἂν λύπη συμβῇ, ὥσπερ εἰς ἀποθήκην φαρμάκων ἔγκυψον· λάβε παραμυθίαν ἐκεῖθεν τοῦ δεινοῦ, ἂν ζημία, ἂν θάνατος, ἂν ἀποβολὴ οἰκείων.—Chrysost. Op. Par. 1718-38. In Epist. ad Coloss. cap. iii. Hom. ix. Tom. XI. p. 391.]

Moreover, the sufficiency of his curate may be such that he shall be as well able to answer all such questions as if he himself were present. Neither are those cases you put usual (God be thanked!), and they oftentimes happen where there is least cause to complain of any absence of the pastor[3].

Chapter i. The Seventh Division.

T. C. Page 48, Sect. 1.

When as therefore the only preaching of the word of God being continual is a bond strong enough to hold the pastor to his flock, then the inquiry of the manners and behaviour of his flock, the private admonitions and consolations, the dissolving of doubts when any riseth, as a three or fourfold cord ought much more to hold him; so that he which shall break all these things willingly and wittingly cannot easily be thought to break them as Sampson did his, by the strength of God, but rather by some other power not of God.

Jo. Whitgift.

I would not have any man to think that I take upon me to maintain careless and slothful pastors: I speak only of such as be vigilant, and occupy themselves profitably in the church, visit their several flocks, and teach them to the satisfying both of the parishes, and of their own consciences also: such I am persuaded may do as much in all those points here by you mentioned, to the commodity of their flock, being sometimes absent, as if they were continually present, besides the good they may do to the whole church generally, whereof they are also members and ministers. *Careless and slothful pastors be not defended.*

But I muse with what face you can thus seek to deface true pastors that do good in the church, though not so much as you think they should do, seeing you yourself and a number more do no good at all in any place, but only range up and down, live at other men's tables, disturb the church, and think that you have done your duties when you have defaced *Some men delight to deface good men, that do no good themselves.*

[3 Cartwright thinks Whitgift's memory very short; else he might have remembered many places in scripture which prove "continual residence of the pastor." But he will be content, he says, to refer to St Paul, "the best expounder of the law; who, setting forth the priests' function, by that part of it which consisted in sacrifices, useth a word of great strength (προσεδρεύοντες, 1 Cor. ix. 13) to bind them to a continual residence, and signifieth in effect a continual sitting at their charge." He adds that what is said of there being "divers beside the pastor," and "help by reading of the scriptures," is unsatisfactory, and little to the purpose.—Sec. Repl. pp. 342, 3.]

all other men's doings. I am verily persuaded that he which preacheth at his cure but one sermon in a year offendeth God less than you do, that have forsaken your calling.

Chapter i. The Eighth Division.
T. C. Page 48, Sect. 1.

Besides that, St Paul commandeth that the pastor should be a pattern or example in all goodness and holiness of life unto his flock; and our Saviour Christ saith that, when the shepherd hath led forth his sheep, he "goeth before them;" but, if the pastor be not amongst his flock, and have not his conversation there, they cannot follow him. If they have not the example before their eyes, they cannot make the like unto it. Therefore this commandment also bindeth them to residency[2] amongst their flocks. St Peter willeth the pastors of the churches that they should feed the flocks. What flocks? Not every one, but those which are committed to their faith or trust, or which dependeth upon them. And St Paul, speaking to the ministers or bishops of Ephesus, willeth them that they should "take heed unto the flocks over the which the Holy Ghost had made them overseers;" where he restraineth, as St Peter did, their oversight and watch unto their particular flock. St Paul saith that he took it heavily that he was separated from them but a small time. If therefore the apostle was away with grief from them whom he had taught, whom his calling compelled to be away, and[3] would not suffer to be always there; what shall be thought of the pastors, whose callings[4] is to be with their flocks, and which are consecrated unto them, even as the apostles were unto the whole world? what, I say, shall be thought of them that are away months and years?

1 Tim. iv. 12.[1]

John x. 4.[1]

1 Pet. v. 2.[1]

Acts xx. 28.[1]

1 Thess. ii. 17.[1]

Jo. Whitgift.

A man may follow the example of him that is not always present.

Christ is a pattern and an example to us in all goodness, whom we must follow; and yet we never saw him, but have only heard of him by his word. St Paul willed the Corinthians, 1 Cor. iv. and xi., and the Philippians, chap. iii., to follow him; and yet was he not perpetually resident among them. A man may be throughly known, touching his external conversation, of those with whom he is divers times conversant, although he be not always abiding with them. I think there be pastors very well known to their flocks both for their life

---

[1 The verses of the first two and last two references and the other altogether are inserted from Repl. 2.]
[2 Residence, Repl. 1 and 2.]
[3 Away from and, Repl. 2.]   [4 Calling, Repl. 2.]

and doctrine, and yet do not continually remain with them: you and I have not been long nor much conversant together; and yet surely I suppose that I know you both touching your religion, conversation, and affection, as well as if I had been twenty years companion in your chamber with you. And therefore this is no good argument, to say that "the pastor must be an example to his flock;" and therefore he must of necessity be continually among them: for he may so be, and that perfectly, if he be sundry times among them, and likewise if they hear of his good conversation in place where he remaineth, when he is not among them.

The same answer serveth for that which is alleged out of the x. of St John.

St Peter, 1 Epist. chap. v., doth not only exhort pastors, and such as be addicted to some certain place, but all other also to whom this word *presbyter* doth reach; as it may appear in that he himself saith, *qui sum et ipse presbyter:* 1 Pet. v. "which am also myself an elder." Wherefore it is an exhortation general to all preachers and ministers of the word, and not only proper to pastors. The words that follow be diversly expounded: some say, "feed the flock of God which dependeth upon you," some, "which is committed unto you," and other some, "as much as lieth in you," which is the most common interpretation; and it is as much as though he should say, according to the talent that God hath given unto you. But, howsoever it be interpreted, the meaning is, that every man labour in teaching, instructing, and governing the church of Christ, and the charge committed unto him, faithfully and diligently. Which exhortation of Peter may be obeyed of him that is not continually remaining in one place, if he do as I have said before.

The words of St Paul, Acts xx., tend to the same end. A minister of the word and pastor must be diligent in his calling, not slothful, and ought to seek by all means possible to profit the church of Christ, and especially in such places whereunto he is especially called: all this I grant.

The place of St Paul, 1 Thess. ii., is far from the purpose. For Paul declareth his singular good-will and affection that he had to the Thessalonians: he doth not express any duty of his ministry; and therefore a learned man interpreting that place saith: *Hinc colligimus, quod sancti etiam se videre secundum carnem gestiunt:* "Hereof we gather that the saints also do gladly desire to see one another bodily." A man, to express his singular affection towards his friend, will say that it grieveth him to be out of his company one hour. But how followeth this argument: Paul was desirous to be corporally present with the Thessalonians, and to remain with them; *ergo,* a pastor must never be absent from his flock? If it be lawful to make such arguments, I will conclude anything[1].

Chapter i. The Ninth Division.
T. C. Page 48, Sect. 1.

And indeed those that feed their flocks faithfully according to the commandment of God, do see what a great wisdom and mercy of God it is to appoint every flock his pastor, and every pastor his flock. They can tell of a wonderful love that God worketh in them towards their flocks, and in their flocks towards them. A great encouragement unto them, and as it were a prick to stir up their dulness it is, when they see the blessing of God upon their labours, and thereof a marvellous care and thought to turn all such things away as should hinder the increase of that blessing, which they cannot have any feeling or experience of, which are not conversant with their flocks: besides, a[2] familiarity between the pastor and the flock is profitable to this, that every one may[3] be emboldened to come and demand to be satisfied of those things they doubt of; which they will never do unto those whom they are not by continual conversation acquainted with.

Jo. Whitgift.

How can you tell? You have no such experience, for you never had flock; or what boasting pastor hath so bragged of himself? Peradventure because some troublesome persons, delighted with contentions and strange opinions, made much of him, and the rest gave him some countenance, he thought they loved him, when as peradventure it was nothing so. But be it true of those whom you mean: I doubt not but there be flocks that have that "love towards their pastors," and pastors that have that "love towards their flocks" (though they do not continually remain with them), which

[[1] Cartwright replies that his reasons are still "unanswered;" that what Whitgift says is "senseless;" and that, "if St Peter and Paul cry never so high in this language of continual residence, yet the D. is deaf and will not hear."—Sec. Repl. pp. 343, &c.]

[[2] Besides this a, Repl. 2.]

[[3] Profitable that they may, Repl. 2.]

ought to be in the children of God, and which never will be removed, deface you them as much as you can.

Chapter i.   The Tenth Division.
T. C. Page 49, line 2.

And it is not nothing that Aristotle disputeth against Plato his community, which would have all things common, and that all men indifferently should have care of all things, and should have nothing which he should say to be his own.   For therein Aristotle said very well, that that which was cared for of all men was neglected of all, and cared for of none; so that the preservation of wife, or children, or of any other possession, was then the best and surest when as every man had a certain possession committed unto him, which he should care for and take charge of.   And so the Lord his wisdom was, for the better surety and salvation of his church, not to make many ministers, which should in common and indifferently take care of all, but ordained that the church should be divided in divers[4] *parts, and that every one should have a piece to care for and to give account for.*

You speak contraries.

Jo. Whitgift.

What hath Aristotle to do with "non-residence?" Authority is scarce when his help is required. But what saith he? forsooth, "that that which was cared for of all men was neglected of all." I think that you report not Aristotle's words truly; for, as far as I remember, he saith that "that which is common to all is neglected of all[5]." The other cannot be true; for "that which is cared for of all men" cannot "be neglected of all" (for "to care for," and "to neglect," be contraries), but must of necessity be well provided for and looked unto[6]. But to what purpose do you allege this? Because I say that no man must so look to his private charge that he neglect the other parts of the church, do I therefore say that there is no private charge, but all things are in common? It is the duty of every member in the commonwealth so to look to his own private affairs and business, that he neglect not the common state of his country: are all things therefore common? Neither did Aristotle ever teach that a man should so care for his "certain possession" that he preferred not the

Aristotle not rightly alleged.

A man having a private charge ought to care for the whole.

[4 Divided into divers, Repl. 1 and 2.]
[5 "Ηκιστα γὰρ ἐπιμελείας τυγχάνει τὸ πλείστων κοινόν.—Aristotl. Op. Lut. Par. 1629. De Rep. Lib. ii. cap. iii. Tom. II. p. 314.]
[6 "...a wrangling cavil."—Sec. Repl. p. 346.]

common utility before it; and so likewise Christ hath divided to every man a portion of his church to care for, but yet not so, that he should think himself no longer bound to the whole, or that he must now cease from profiting the whole.

Chapter i. The Eleventh Division.
T. C. Page 49, Sect. 1.

Now, if any man will say that in such great scarcity of pastors it is good, that when a man hath travailed in one place, and removed them from superstition, and brought them to believe in God through Christ, to go to another place, and assay also to draw them from idolatry; first, I urge that which I did before, which is the calling wherein every man must abide, and without the which no man ought to attempt any thing. Then, I say that it is as hard a province, and as painful a thing unto the pastor, as acceptable and precious a work unto the Lord, to keep those which are gotten, as to get those which are not gotten; and that that saying is fulfilled here, if in any thing else: Non minor est virtus, quam quærere, parta tueri[1].

Jo. Whitgift.

This objection is of greater force than you are able to withstand. For the same God, that hath called him to the one place to plant his true religion there, hath also called him to the other, that he may do the like; even as he did the apostles, prophets, and evangelists, and pastors also, who have been even immediately after the apostles' time transferred from one place to another, for the greater commodity of the church: neither can it be proved that any man should be so tied to one place, that he may not be transferred to another to profit more.

It is true that the devil most grievously assaulteth those which have embraced the truth, because now they are become his professed enemies, and openly withstand him; but they are sufficiently armed with faith, and with the word of God; so that, although they be tempted, yet can they not be overcome. The other that remain in ignorance he wholly possesseth, and, because they have yielded themselves unto him, he doth suffer them to be quiet: therefore to deliver such out of his servitude and bondage, and so to arm and

[1 Here Repl. 2 adds: *It is as great a virtue to keep that which is already gotten as to have got it.*]

instruct them, that they are not only able to withstand, but to put to flight the devil also, must of necessity be both the "hardest," and the most "acceptable work unto God;" except you will say that it is more commendable to help him who is sufficiently armed and able to resist, than him that is altogether unarmed and as it were under the foot of his enemy. Certainly the most "acceptable work unto God" is to convert sinners unto repentance, and to heal such as be sick: and therefore Christ himself said that he "came to Luke xix. seek that which was lost;" and the parable of the lost groat, Luke xv. and of the prodigal son, doth with might and main overthrow your sayings: so do the whole dealings of the apostles, and the whole course of the scriptures[2].

Chapter i. The Twelfth Division.

T. C. Page 49, Sect. 2.

For we know that, after that the devil perceiveth that men are pulled out of the power of darkness into the glorious light of the gospel, he sweateth and laboureth by a thousand means to destroy them, and bestirreth himself more then than in the time of their ignorance; and, instead of that one chain of ignorance, and want of the knowledge of God, he layeth a thousand traps for them, to snare them with. So that the continual danger that the church is in doth as it were speak unto the pastor in the common proverb, Σπάρτην ἣν ἔλαχες κόσμα : *that is, look diligently* κόσμει. *to that charge which thou hast received. For, if the watchman should forsake the city whereunto he is appointed, and go and watch in another where he is not called, although he save that, if he lose the other, he shall not therefore escape the punishment of betraying the other city where he was placed watchman.*

Jo. Whitgift.

So it is; but all the devils in hell cannot prevail against them: therefore said St Paul to the Ephes. chap. vi., "Put Eph. vi.

[2 Cartwright rejoins to that which Whitgift says, "although they be tempted, yet they cannot be overcome," that this "is confuted not only by divers examples of most excellent saints, Noe, David, Peter, &c., but by whole churches of Galatia, &c., which have been carried away by false teachers;" and that, "if he speak of the final victory, it is absurd, considering that that dependeth of the election of God, unknown unto him, and may be as well said of the elect which have not yet believed." He adds that, although any thing "be never so good a work in itself, yet it is not good, much less the best, unto him which hath no calling thereunto."—Sec. Repl. pp. 346, 7.]

on the whole armour of God, that ye may be able to resist in the evil day, &c." Every Christian is in this case, yea, the pastor himself; but wot you what Christ saith, John x., "My sheep hear my voice; and no man shall take them out of my hands?" The scriptures, as Chrysostom saith, be "continual schoolmasters[1];" and he that hath understanding may therein learn how to withstand Satan and all his assaults. And therefore said the apostle to the Colos. iii., "Let the word of God dwell in you abundantly, in all wisdom, teaching and admonishing your ownselves in psalms and hymns, &c."

John x.

Chrysost. in iii. Col.

Col. iii.

If "the watchman" hath sufficiently admonished "the city," and hath ministered weapons unto them, brought them out of the bondage of their enemy, and leave some other behind him to supply the rest, and then "go to another" city to deliver it also from the like slavery; if in the mean time the former city be lost, or revolted (which is not like), their blood be upon themselves: the watchman hath done his duty. When Jonas had told Ninive her offences, and shewed his message for the which he was sent, was there any more required of him? Moreover, I am persuaded that, wheresoever the preacher may do most good, thither is he "called" of God; neither is this to forsake his station, but to follow his calling, and to do good.

The preacher is called thither where he may do most good.

Chapter i.   The Thirteenth Division.
T. C. Page 49, Sect. 3.

Touching the behalf of God and his glory, if any man will say that they cannot perish which once have believed, and therefore those may be left, and others attempted; I can say of those that are in ignorance and blindness, that they cannot perish that be elected, although they never have the gospel preached. And therefore we must walk in those ways that God hath appointed to bring them to salvation, which is to feed them continually, and watch over them so long as they are in danger of hunger, in danger of wolves, in danger of the enemies within and without; which is so long as the church is here upon the earth.

Jo. Whitgift.

God forbid that any man should use any such kind of

[1 ...κτᾶσθε βιβλία φάρμακα τῆς ψυχῆς. εἰ μηδὲν ἕτερον βούλεσθε, τὴν γοῦν καινὴν κτήσασθε, τῶν ἀποστόλων τὰς πράξεις, τὰ εὐαγγέλια, διδασκάλους διηνεκεῖς.—Chrysost. Op. Par. 1718-38. In Epist. ad Coloss. cap. iii. Hom. ix. Tom. XI. p. 391.]

excuses, to take away the means whereby God useth to call such as be his: but it is a comfort to the pastor, when he is in conscience persuaded that he hath not omitted to open unto his flock those ways and means, and that he ceaseth not still to admonish them of the same in time convenient. St Paul, Acts xx., saith to the ministers of the church of Ephesus, that he was "free from the blood of them all, and *Acts xx.* that he had opened unto them the whole counsel of God, &c.:" and yet he had not been much with them; and after that time he thought that he should not see the most of them any more. Wherefore a man may do his duty, and open all things and means necessary unto salvation, although he be not continually remaining in one place. Chrysostom expounding the place in the third to the Colossians, "Let the word of God dwell in you, &c.," after that he hath willed them to "prepare them *Chrysost. in iii. Col.* bibles," and told them that "it especially pertaineth to them to read the scriptures," he addeth, "cast not all upon our shoulders. You are sheep, but yet reasonable: the apostle hath committed many things unto you. Those that are to be instructed must not always learn, &c.²" And again he saith: *Habes oracula Dei: nemo te docebit quemadmodum illa*³: "Thou hast the word of God: no man can teach thee like unto it."

Chapter i.   The Fourteenth Division.

T. C. Page 49, Sect. 4.

Upon all which things I conclude that the residence of the pastor is necessary; and to doubt whether the pastor ought to be resident amongst his flock is to doubt whether the watchman should be in his tower, the eye should be in the head, or the soul in the body, or the shepherd amongst his flock, especially where the sheep are continually in danger of wolves, as in the land of Jewry, from whence this similitude or manner of speech was taken, where they watched their flocks night and day; as I observed before out of St Luke.

Jo. Whitgift.

The question is not, "whether the pastor ought to be

[² Μᾶλλον δὲ μὴ ἔγκυπτε, ἀλλὰ ἀνάλαβε πάντα. ἔχε ἐπὶ τῆς διανοίας...ἀγαπητὸν μετὰ τούτων σωθῆναι, μήτιγε χωρὶς τούτων. μὴ τὰ πάντα ἐφ' ἡμᾶς ῥίπτετε, πρόβατά ἐστε· ἀλλ' οὐκ ἄλογα, ἀλλὰ λογικά· πολλὰ καὶ ὑμῖν ὁ Παῦλος ἐπιτρέπει. οἱ διδασκόμενοι οὐ διαπαντὸς ἐπὶ τὸ μαθεῖν διατρίβουσιν, ἐπεὶ οὐ διδάσκονται.—Id. ibid.]

[³ Id. ibid.]

resident" or no, but of the time, the manner, and kind of residence. No man must continually be absent; for that were altogether to neglect his flock: neither is it required that he be continually present; for that cannot be. But, if he neglect not his duty in preaching, and perform other things requisite, although he be sundry times absent upon the occasions before specified, yet is he not to be condemned; seeing it oftentimes cometh to pass that such kind of men do most good, both in their churches particularly, and in the church generally.

<small>Tract. iv. cap. 1. divis. 6, and Tract. v. cap. 1. divis. 3.</small> Of "the watchman" and of "the shepherd" I have spoken before[1], and shewed wherein the similitude holdeth, and wherein it holdeth not: no one "watchman" is continually in the tower; neither is it possible that he should be: it is sufficient if the tower be watched, and the chief watchman neglect not his duty: "the shepherd" also is not always present with his sheep, but sometime he leaveth them alone, when he hath folded them, or brought them into a safe pasture, and sometimes he committeth them to his servant, or to some other to be kept in his absence. The similitude of "the eye" and of "the soul" in some points may be aptly applied, but not in this of residence; for, if either "the eye" be plucked out of "the head," or "the soul" separated from "the body," neither of them both can be restored again. But you must confess that there be causes why a pastor may be absent from his flock without any such uncurable danger; and therefore these similitudes in these cases of absence hold not[2].

T. C. Page 49, Sect. 5.

If any will[3] hereupon conclude that they have no space given them to sleep, to eat, to drink, &c., they are cavils which I will not vouchsafe to answer.

Jo. Whitgift.

A very modest and short answer.

[1 See before, pages 476, &c., 511, 12.]
[2 "If this be a sufficient exception, there be few similitudes in the scripture, which are able to hold out; and he might as well say that, as the eye waxeth worse and worse through age, so the pastor may wax every day more fool than other."—Sec. Repl. pp. 347, 8.]
[3 If any man will, Repl. 2.]

Chapter i.   The Fifteenth Division.
T. C. Page 49, Sect. ult.

Again, if he will say that then they may not go forth of the town to Here you overthrow *do their necessary business for their families, I desire them, in the name* all your former *of God, that they abuse not his graces, in devising cloaks to cover their dis-* building. Joh. xxi.15, *orders; but that they would set before them the love of Christ,* 16, 17.[4] *which shall be found to be so much, as they shall shew themselves diligent in continual feeding their flocks, and to fear the judgment of God, before whom no feigned or coloured excuse will stand. And so I trust they will make no longer absence[5] than must needs; and, if upon any occasion at any time they be somewhat longer, that the same be not without the leave of their churches, whose they are, and which they for the Lord his sake serve, and then also that in such rare and necessary absence* Here you admit cu- *they provide them of some able man to teach in the mean season, which* rates; which is contrary to *the church by her governors will allow of.* your former assertion.

Jo. Whitgift.

Yet such doubts would be directly resolved, for they seem something to trouble you: and in very deed they cause you to overthrow whatsoever you have hitherto gone about to build; for now you confess that the pastor may be absent of his own private "business[6]," if he have leave of his parish, and if he "provide some able man to teach in the mean season, &c." I pray you, let me ask you a few questions: may not a man be as well absent for public affairs, or at the commandment of the prince or chief magistrate, as he may be for his own private "business?" Is not his flock in as great danger when their pastor is absent with their "leave," as when he is absent without their "leave?" Or where do you find it in scripture, that the pastor ought to ask "leave" of his parish, when he hath occasion to be absent? Or how shall he get "an able man in the mean season" to teach his flock, when as you affirm that "no man may be admitted into the Page 42, &c. ministry except he have a certain flock committed unto him[7]?" and that then "it is not lawful for him to preach out of his own cure[8]?" These questions would be answered, and these

---

[4 The verses are inserted from Repl. 2.]   [5 Absences, Repl. 1 and 2.]
[6 "His triumphs, upon that I confess that the pastor may for some business, with leave of his church, with an able deputy be absent...are beggarly."—Ibid. p. 353.]
[7 See before, pages 469, 78.]
[8 "As though in such necessity, for so small a time, the supply may not be made by the pastors hard by."—Ibid. p. 356.]

Of plural-
ities.
contrary speeches of yours reconciled, if it be possible. For undoubtedly they do not agree with your former talk.

Of Pluralities, or having more benefices than one.
Chapter ii. The First Division.
Admonition.

Then had every flock¹ his shepherd, or else ʸshepherds: ʸActs xiv. 23. *now they do not only run fisking² from place to place (a miserable disorder in God's church), but ᶻcovetously join living to living, making* ᶻIsai. v. 8. *shipwreck &of their own consciences, and being but one shep-* &1Tim. i.14. ³ *herd (nay, would to God they were shepherds, and not wolves!) have many flocks.*

Answer to the Admonition, Page 50, Sect. 3, 4; and Page 51, Sect. 1.

You say also, that "every flock had his shepherd, or else shepherds." And, to prove that one flock had more shepherds, you cite Acts xiv.; which maketh nothing for your purpose: yet I deny not but one flock may have more pastors; for I see nothing in the word of God against it.

To be short, you say now they go "fisking from place to place, and covetously join living to living, &c.; and being but one shepherd have many flocks." If you mean, by "fisking from place to place," such as preach in divers places, and not in their own cures only, your phrase of
Scurrility⁴.
To preach from place to place⁴.
"fisking" is too light and scurrilous. When you allege any reason why men may not go "from place to place" to preach, where they think it necessary, you shall either be answered or yielded to. In the mean time I think it agreeable both to God's word and conscience.

Against covetously joining of "living to living" you allege the v. of Esay; which is far from your purpose; for the prophet speaketh there of such as oppress the poor, and will not suffer them to have a place to dwell in: yet I do not allow such as covetously "join living to living," of what kind or degree of men soever they be.

[¹ And every flock, Adm. and Answ. See before, page 491.]
[² Fisking: dancing.]   [³ Adm. has 1 *Tim. i.* 19.]
[⁴ These marginal notes are inserted from Answ. 2.]

Jo. WHITGIFT.   *Of pluralities.*

To the abusing of the xiv. of the Acts by the Admonition, nothing is answered by T. C., nor to the v. of Esay.

Chapter ii. The Second Division.
Answer to the Admonition, Page 51, Sect. 1.

But I see no cause why one good and diligent pastor may not rather be credited with more flocks, than a slothful, unskilful, or negligent with one. You think (I suppose) that there be divers parishes in England which might be joined in one, and so committed to one man; and why may they not be so in like manner, when they be distinct? *Why may not one man have divers parishes⁴.*

T. C. Page 50, Sect. 1.

And hereupon also is ended another question that the answerer maketh, whether one may have many flocks; which is, whether one shepherd may be many shepherds, one watchman many watchmen. For, if his residence be necessary in one place, then he ought to content himself with one.

Jo. WHITGIFT.

My question is this: "Why one man may not as well have divers parishes when they be distinct, as he may when they be joined together?" For the compass, the number, and the distance of place, is all one. You confess that the one may be, and the reformed churches in France did so use it, where (as I am credibly informed and you before seem to affirm⁵) six towns or more were committed to one pastor. This being lawful, I see not why the other should not be so in like manner; neither have you answered to any one word in this part⁶. *Pag. 34, lin. 10.*

Chap. ii. The Third Division.
Answer to the Admonition, Page 51, Sect. 2.

I speak not this to encourage any man to take more upon him than with a good conscience he may well discharge. And I would wish you to abstain from judging

[⁵ See before, page 379.]

[⁶ Cartwright declares that what Whitgift has said "is unworthy any answer. As if a thousand sheep in one pasture were not easilier and with more commodity tended than three in three sheep-gates." He goes on to complain of untrue statements being made.—Sec. Repl. p. 356.]

530 THE DEFENCE OF THE ANSWER [TRACT. V.

Of pluralities. too far, when you see a man that hath more livings use himself uprightly and carefully in them all, and otherwise profitably to the whole church[1].

T. C. Page 50, Sect. 2.

And, whereas you would have men charitably[2] judge of those which take many livings; surely if so be that he taketh many flocks, not to the intent to have more living to maintain an ambitious pomp, or to satisfy a greedy desire of having more than enough, but to this end, that he may bring in a more plentiful harvest unto the Lord; it were good that he would be content to take but that living of all his flocks, which he now hath of one, especially where one is able to keep and maintain him and his family honestly. Else let him hear what councils and others have thought of those which have more benefices than one.

You might have spoken in the singular number, for any plurality you have used.

Jo. Whitgift.

You keep no order in answering my book, but place and displace at your pleasure, only to this end, as it should seem, that you would not have your reader perceive what you omitted unanswered. But I will follow you, and examine "what councils and other have thought of such as have more benefices than one;" for in this portion you utter but words, and take upon you to judge men's intents and purposes, and to prescribe them their stipend.

Chap. ii. The Fourth Division.

T. C. Page 50, Sect. 3.

T. C. useth a most corrupt council for his defence.

In the 15. canon of the council of Nice it is commanded that "no clerk should be placed in two churches;" and he addeth the reasons: whereof "the first is, that it is a point of merchandise and of filthy gain; the second, that no man can serve two masters; the third, that every one ought to tarry in that calling wherein he is called[4]." Matt. vi. 24.[3] 1 Cor. vii. 24.[3]

Jo. Whitgift.

T. C. allegeth the second council of Nice to determine controversies.

It should seem that you would gladly make men believe (and it is very like that you yourself are also persuaded), that

[1 This paragraph in Answ. follows that in page 534.]
[2 Profitably, Def. B.]
[3 The verses are added from Repl. 2.]
[4 Κληρικὸς ἀπὸ τοῦ παρόντος μὴ κατατασσέσθω ἐν δυσὶν ἐκκλησίαις· ἐμπορίας γὰρ καὶ αἰσχροκερδείας ἴδιον τοῦτο·...ἠκούσαμεν γὰρ ἐξ αὐτῆς τῆς κυριακῆς φωνῆς, ὅτι οὐ δύναταί τις δυσὶ κυρίοις δουλεύειν...ἕκαστος οὖν κατὰ τὴν ἀποστολικὴν φωνὴν, ἐν ᾧ ἐκλήθη, ἐν τούτῳ ὀφείλει μένειν, καὶ προσεδρεύειν ἐν μιᾷ ἐκκλησίᾳ.— Concil. Nic. ii. Act. viii. can. 15. in Concil. Stud. Labb. et Cossart. Lut. Par. 1671-2. Tom. VII. col. 609.]

this council was the first "council of Nice." For else why do you in the next section place Damasus, and name the second tome of the councils, when as Damasus was long time before this your council of Nice; and the same council is in the second tome of the councils? Lest therefore the reader may be deceived, I let him to understand, that this canon here by you alleged is a canon of the second council of Nice, holden about *anno* 795. or 781., and one of the corruptest councils that ever was; wherein not only praying to saints and adoring of relics, but also worshipping of images, &c., was confirmed[5].

Of pluralities.

But yet let us examine this canon of that council. In the end of that same canon it is thus written: *Et hæc quidem in hac regia civitate; in his autem quæ extra sunt locis, propter hominum inopiam permittitur*[6]*:* "And these things are to be understood in this regal city; for in those places that be without, it is permitted for the scarcity of persons." Whereby it is plain that the meaning of the canon is, that no one man should have committed unto him more great cities than one; but that he might have more towns or villages committed to his charge, it is manifest by those words of that canon that I have rehearsed. And therefore Gratian himself doth thus expound that canon: *Sed duæ ecclesiæ intelliguntur ecclesiæ duarum civitatum, in quibus nullus debet conscribi*[7]*:* "But by two churches are meant the churches of two cities; wherein no man ought to be appointed." And for the proof thereof he allegeth this canon of the council of Chalcedon: *Clericum in duarum ecclesiis civitatum conscribi non oportet*[8]*:* "A clerk may not be appointed in the churches of two cities." And the gloss upon that place saith that "one man may be intituled in two churches, if the churches be poor; or if the bishop do dispense and think it convenient; or if the number of clerks be few; or if he be intituled to the one, and have the other *in commendam*; or if the one be near to the

The canon of the second council of Nice examined.

Caus. xxi. q. 1. Clericus.

[5 " I cannot precisely say whether the leaving out of second were my fault or the fault of some other; but that I meant to deceive none, there be which can witness, by that that in the second edition (howsoever it was omitted) I gave a note whereby that should be corrected."—Sec. Repl. p. 357.]

[6 Concil. Nic. II. Act. viii. can. 15. in Concil. Stud. Labb. et Cossart. Tom. VII. col. 609.]

[7 Corp. Jur. Canon. Lugd. 1624. Decret. Gratian. Decr. Sec. Pars, Caus. XXI. Quæst. i. Not. ad can. 1. col. 1231.]

[8 Ibid. can. 2; where *civitatum eodem tempore conscribi*. Conf. Concil. Calched. in Concil. Stud. Labb. et Cossart. Act. xv. can. 10. Tom. IV. col. 759.]

Of pluralities. other[1]." And the authority of this gloss is as sufficient as the credit of that "council of Nice," if the canon did not expound itself. I omit the absurd allegation of the scriptures to confirm this their purpose. For the place, Matt. vi., is to be understood of contrary masters; and that in the 1 Cor. vii. of the kind of vocation, and not of the place. He that doth his duty in more places is lawfully called to them all; as I have said before[2].

Chapter ii.   The Fifth Division.

T. C. Page 50, Sect. 4.

An oversight; for it is in the first tome.   And in the second tome of the Councils, Damasus, in his fourth epistle, likeneth those that set over their charges unto other unto "harlots, which, as soon as they have brought forth their children, by and bye give them to be nourished of others, to the intent that they might the sooner fulfil their inordinate lusts[3]."

Jo. Whitgift.

You are deceived: it is in the first "tome of councils;" and therefore the more like it is that you take the former council to be the first "council of Nice." But such dealing is usual with you: if you had meant plainly, you would have said, "the second council of Nice," and not simply, "the council of Nice;" which argueth either that you were deceived yourself, or else sought to deceive others.

Damasus alleged to a wrong purpose.   This place of Damasus is nothing at all to your purpose; which you might easily have perceived, if you had read that epistle. For he only there speaketh against such as were called *chorepiscopi*, who were in degree inferior to bishops, and yet did they despise to be counted no better than priests. There were certain bishops in Damasus' time that gave them-

[1 ...quæritur, an clericus possit intitulari, in quibus [*al.* duabus] ecclesiis? respondet, quod non, nisi in sex casibus. Unus est, cum ecclesiæ pauperes sunt... Secundus est, propter dispensationem episcopi...Tertius est, propter paucitatem clericorum...Quartus est, cum habet unam intitulatam clericus, et aliam commendatam...Quintus est, si papa hoc concedit...Sextus est, cum una adhæret alteri, vel dependet ex altera.—Ibid. Gloss. col. 1230.]

[2 Cartwright censures Whitgift for producing Gratian's exposition, and concludes: "he is not so much a shepherd which hath many flocks, as the D. saith, as a thief."—Sec. Repl. pp. 357, 8.]

[3 Illi nanque episcopi, qui talia sibi præsumunt, videntur mihi esse meretricibus similes, quæ statim, ut pariunt, infantes suos aliis nutricibus tradunt educandos, ut suam citius libidinem explere valeant.—Damas. Papæ Epist. iv. de Chorepisc. in Crabb. Concil. Col. Agrip. 1551. Tom. I. p. 388. For the degree of credit to be attached to this and other decretal epistles of the early Roman bishops, see Oudin's Dissertation, Comm. de Script. Eccles. Lips. 1722. Tom. II. cols. 46, &c.]

selves wholly to idleness and pleasure, and committed their office to such as were called *chorepiscopi*; as it is evident in that epistle : neither doth he mean any other charge than consecrating of priests, deacons, and virgins, imposition of hands, blessings, erecting of altars, dedicating of churches, and such like, which were taken properly to pertain to the bishop, and yet notwithstanding was by some bishops passed over to such *chorepiscopi*. This negligence of bishops in such matters Damasus condemneth, together with the office of *chorepiscopus*. And this is the whole drift of Damasus in that epistle; as it is most evident. And therefore saith Leo (as Gratian reporteth) Dist. lxviii. : *Hi* (meaning *chorepiscopi*) *propter insolentiam suam, qua officia episcoporum sibi usurpant, ab ecclesia prohibiti sunt*[4]: "These men for their insolency, whereby they usurp the office of bishops, are excluded from the church." So that here is not one word in this whole epistle against curates, and such as are left to supply the pastor's absence. Moreover, you yourself in the beginning of this page confess, that a man being absent may leave his deputy in his place[5]. But yet here you have forgotten your purpose, that is, to prove that one man may not have more benefices; in which cause also it appeareth that you are destitute of proofs, being compelled to use only corrupt authorities[6].

Of pluralities.

Distinct. 68.

Pag. 50, line 1.

Chapter ii. The Sixth Division.

T. C. Page 50, Sect. 5.

Whether it were better that one diligent pastor should have many flocks, than a negligent and unskilful pastor one, is not the question; for we say neither is lawful, nor ought to be done.

Jo. Whitgift.

You say much, but prove little. I think it much better that one man have divers, than that any should be untaught. For I speak of that time wherein there is not a competent number of preachers to be had for all places.

[4 Hi vero propter &c. sibi usurpabant, ab ecclesia hodie prohibiti sunt.—Corp. Jur. Canon. Lugd. 1624. Decret. Gratian. Decr. Prim. Pars, Dist. lxviii. can. 4. col. 345. This appears to be Gratian's note, and not a part of Leo's epistle.]

[5 See before, page 527.]

[6 Cartwright declares that he had no opinion of any "good meaning" in Damasus, but his "comparison" "being apt," he took it "as a good stone set in an evil place."—Sec. Repl. p. 358.]

It passeth to see how you have dismembered my book, even of purpose to avoid the answering of divers things, and even very here you have omitted one principal point. For I ask also this question, "Why that parishes being distinct may not as well be committed to one man, as the same might be if they were made all one;" as you would have them? for the distance of places, and the number of persons is not altered; only the ease of the pastor and greater pains of the people is procured. For, whereas the pastor before came to them, now must they take pains to come to him. But such things you will not vouchsafe the answering, because indeed you cannot.

Chapter ii. The Seventh Division.

Answer to the Admonition, Page 50, Sect. 1.

Of the division of parishes[1].

For who divided parishes? and who hath authority to join them? did not Dionysius, a monk, and pope of Rome? For it is thus written of him, *Tom. i. Concil.*:

Dionysius[2].

Dionysius monachus papa presbyteris ecclesias divisit et cœmeteria, parochiasque et diœceses constituit[3]: "Dionysius, a monk and pope, divided to priests churches and churchyards, and appointed parishes and dioceses."

T. C. Page 50, Sect. 6, 7.

Do you believe that which you set down of Denis the monk and pope, that he devised and divided parishes? If you do not, why would you have us believe it? If the law doth condemn him that turneth a blind man out of the way, or layeth a block before him, what doth Deut. xxviii. 18.[4]

Assertions without proof.

it him which would put out the eyes of them that see their way already? I have shewed, and the matter is plain, that the Lord divided national churches into parishes and congregations: so that, if St Paul have not the word of parish, yet he hath the thing. And those that have read stories know that διοίκησις (*which we call a diocese, and which containeth with us numbers of parishes*) *was at the first taken to be the same that parish is, and used a great while before Denis was born, or monkery begotten.*

And as for cœmeteria, or churchyards, if you mean those places that lie next round about the churches, as they came in with the monk, they

[1 Division of parish is human, Answ. 2.]
[2 This is inserted from Answ. 2.]
[3 Hic presbyteris &c.—Ex Lib. Pont. Damasi in Crabb. Concil. Col. Agripp. 1551. Tom. I. p. 164.]
[4 This marginal reference is inserted from Repl. 2.]

might well have gone out with him, for any profit either to the church or Of plural-
commonwealth by[5] them. But if you mean, as the Greek word which ities.
*is there used signifieth, a fit place where the bodies of men sleep and are
buried, attending the time of their rising up again in the last and general
day of judgment, then these churchyards were in the time of the law, and
in the primitive church in all[6] times, when there was any outward policy*
Luke vii. 12.[7] *of the church, and especially when the church had quietness*
Euseb. vii.
Lib. 13. *and peace, that it might without danger bury their dead in
some certain convenient place thereunto appointed[8]; which was, for fear of
the infection, commonly, as it may be gathered, in the field out[9] of the town:
unto the which use and custom (if it might be done conveniently) it were
well that we were restored, both because it is more safe for the preservation
of the towns and cities in their health, as also for that through the
superstition which hath been of being buried rather in the church than
in the churchyard, in the chancel rather than in the church, nearer the
high altar than further off, the remnants whereof are in a great number
of men's hearts yet, which might much be helped by the bringing in of
that custom again, of burying the dead in some honest place out of the
town thereto appointed.*

Jo. Whitgift.

I have told you my author; and, if you will not credit one That Denis
witness, you shall have more. Denis himself doth testify it in parishes.
an epistle that he writ to Severus a bishop[10]. Damasus saith
the same, so doth Marianus Scotus, Platina[11], and others.
Polydore Vergil doth something plainly open the matter in
these words: *Circiter annum Domini* 267, *Dionysius tam* Pol. Virg.
presbyteris urbis Romæ, quam aliarum gentium, templa, de Invent.
*cœmeteria et parochias quas dicunt, divisit: præterea epi-
scopis diœceses distribuit, mandavitque ut unusquisque suis
finibus ac limitibus contentus esset: parochias (ut hoc demon-
stremus) nostri appellant singula templa diœcesis, et eorum
territorium certis terminis distinctum, &c.*[12]: "About the 267.
year of our Lord, Dionysius divided churches, churchyards,

[5 Commonwealth cometh by, Repl. 2.]
[6 Church and at all, Repl. 2.] [7 The verse is added from Repl. 2.]
[8 ...καὶ ἄλλη δὲ τοῦ αὐτοῦ διάταξις φέρεται, ἣν πρὸς ἑτέρους ἐπισκόπους πεποίηται, τὰ τῶν καλουμένων κοιμητηρίων ἀπολαμβάνειν ἐπιτρέπων χωρία.—
Euseb. in Hist. Eccles. Script. Amst. 1695-1700. Lib. vii. cap. xiii. p. 214.]
[9 Field and out, Repl. 2.]
[10 Ecclesias vero singulas singulis presbyteris dedimus, parochias et cœmeteria eis divisimus, et unicuique jus proprium habere statuimus, &c.—Dionys. Papæ Epist. ii. ad Sever. Episc. in Crabb. Concil. Tom. I. p. 166.]
[11 Marian. Scot. Chronic. Basil. 1559. Lib. ii. Æt. vi. col. 294. Plat. De Vit. Pont. Col. 1551. Dionys. p. 31.]
[12 ...circiter annum salutis cclxvii. Dionysius, &c.—Polyd. Verg. De Invent. Rer. Amst. 1671. Lib. iv. cap. ix. p. 261.]

Of pluralities.

and parishes (as they call them), as well to the priests of Rome as of other nations: furthermore, he distributed dioceses unto bishops, and commanded that every one should content himself with his own bounds and limits: our men call parishes (that we may make this plain) the several churches of a diocese, and their territory limited within certain bounds, &c." Wherefore take heed lest you cast dust in your own eyes, and blind yourself; for this of Denis is not denied of any that I can read.

Where hath "the Lord divided national churches into parishes and congregations?" Why do you not note the place? Or where hath "St Paul the thing, though not the word" or name? or what stories say that "διοίκησις was taken to be the same that we call now a parish?" Here is much spoken, but nothing proved.

How parishes are by man distinguished.

This Denis was bishop of Rome about the year of our Lord 263.; which peradventure you have not considered. But, to put all this matter out of doubt, and to open that, the ignorance whereof maketh you so hot in this matter, there was divers congregations and churches in the apostles' time, but yet was there not any limitation of place, or certain compass of ground certainly appointed; for that was left to the discretion of man to enlarge, or to contract, as it should be thought from time to time most convenient: and who can once imagine or suppose that Christ or his apostles did appoint the limits of dioceses or parishes? or who knoweth it not that it is in the power of such as have authority to enlarge or diminish dioceses or parishes, as they shall see it expedient? I know nothing to the contrary, but that the parish, whose bonds and limits be but one mile compass, may be made ten mile compass, and contrariwise. It is well said of one, that *distributio gregis nunc extenditur, nunc coarctatur pro hominis arbitrio*: "The distribution of a flock is sometime enlarged, and sometime made less, according to the judgment of man." And this matter needeth not to seem so strange unto you; for, if you had been so diligent a reader of the book of Acts and Monuments, as you boast yourself to be, then might you have read there that the council of Nice did appoint to certain bishops the limits and bounds of their provinces and dioceses[1]. But what should I labour in a matter so manifest?

[1 See Fox, Acts and Mon. Lond. 1684. Vol. I. p. 11.]

If by *cœmeteria* or churchyards those places be meant {Of pluralities.} that be about the churches, where we use to bury the dead (as it is most like they be), then hear I no reason at all why you should in such manner speak of them, except you will pluck down whatsoever hath beforetime been appointed, be it never so ancient, and the use thereof convenient and necessary. There is no doubt but by *cœmeteria* are meant places of burial, which because they have been (as you confess) "at all times certain, especially in the peace of the church," it is meet that they should so still remain. And, forasmuch as the places now used, if they were appointed by Denis (as it is most like), are fitly appointed, and most conveniently in most places, you have alleged no cause as yet why they should be removed, but the self-same cause, that may be in like manner used to remove the church, and whatsoever else hath been devised by any man, be it otherwise never so necessary, convenient, or comely.

But I will not follow you in these digressions, where you only spend paper with words void of proof. If you quote Eusebius, *vii. Lib.* 13. to prove that the place of burial was "in the fields," there can be no such thing gathered of his words; and, if you quote him to prove that the word signifieth a place of burial, you go about to prove that which no man denieth[2].

[[2] Cartwright makes a long answer to this division, discrediting the witnesses brought to prove that Denis "first divided parishes." He afterwards in reply to the question "where it appeareth that the scripture divided national churches into congregations and parishes?" says, "of that the scripture willeth elders to be chosen for every competent congregation and particular body of church, and also that these assemblies (as all other things in the church) should be with the greatest convenience. &c." He adds that bishops had originally the charge only of parishes, and maintains that he is right in taking the place of burial mentioned by Eusebius to have been "in the field."—Sec. Repl. pp. 358, &c.]

¶ Of Ministers that cannot preach, and of giving licences to preach.

Tract. VI.

Some may be Ministers that cannot preach.

Chapter i. The First Division.

Admonition.

The Tenth:

Then the ministers were *preachers; now bare readers[1]. * Phil. ii. 20, 25. Col. i. 7. Luke ix. 2.

Answer to the Admonition, Page 52, Sect. 2, 3.

<small>Unapt proofs of the Admonition[2].</small> Your places of scripture alleged to prove that ministers were then preachers prove not that all were then preachers. The place in the second to the Philippians, 20. verse, is this: "For I have no man like-minded, who will faithfully care for your matters." And in the 25. verse: "But I suppose it necessary to send my brother Epaphroditus to you, my companion in labour and fellow-soldier, even your messenger, and he that ministered unto me such things as I wanted." Colossians i. verse 7: "As ye also learned of Epaphras, our dear fellow-servant, which is for you a faithful minister of Christ." *Quorsum hæc?*

How prove these places that all ministers then preached? That of Luke, chapter ix., proveth as well that they cured diseases, as that they preached; and therefore out of that place you might as well conclude that all ministers ought to be curers of sicknesses, as well as preachers. This I write only to let you understand your vanity and ignorance in quoting so many scriptures to so small purpose.

Jo. Whitgift.

Ad hæc ne verbum quidem; but only to the place of the ninth of Luke, and that out of place.

[[1] Answ. places here the sentence of the Admonition which appears below, page 544.]

[[2] This marginal note is not in Answ. 2.]

Chapter i. The Second Division.

Answer to the Admonition, Page 52, Sect. ult.

Of ministers that cannot preach.

I wish that every minister were a preacher; but, that being unpossible as the state is now, I see not how you can condemn reading ministers, seeing reading is necessary in the church, and faith cometh as well by reading the scriptures in the book, as by rehearsing of them without book. In the xxxi. of Deuteronomy it is thus written: *Leges verba legis hujus coram omni Israel, &c.:* "Thou shalt read the words of this book before all Israel, &c." St Paul saith in the xv. to the Romans: *Quæcunque scripta sunt &c.:* "Whatsoever is written &c." But I never heard reading of the scriptures, reading of prayers, reading of homilies taken out of the scripture, condemned, but only by the authors of this book, and by the Zuinfildians.

Faith cometh by reading.

The Zuinfildians condemn[3] reading of scripture.

T. C. Page 50, Sect. ult.; Page 51, Sect. 1.

If you should beget and be a father of many books, and all your children like their eldest brother, you would (without better advice) shake many grounds of our religion. For here again you wish that all pastors were able to teach; but, "that being unpossible (as the state[4] is now)," you are content with pastors or ministers that can do nothing but read. You throughout your whole book make this a marvellous good estate, and always turn the best side outward; and, when men go about to urge the deformities thereof, to the end they might be remedied, then you lay open the shame and nakedness of it, and make it greater than it is indeed. For, as I have shewed before, the church standeth not so much in need of your reading ministers, as you would make the world believe. And, although it be a great deformity and sore plague of the church, which you here speak of, and confess at unwares, yet you will let no man come near to heal it. There be some make a gain by sores and sore legs, and therefore they have a medicine to keep their wounds always green, that they should not heal.

I hope you do not of purpose keep the church in this estate; but this I dare say, that the chief of your gain and of your honour consisteth and is grounded in the ruins of the church, and therefore I desire you to look unto it.

Jo. Whitgift.

I omit whatsoever you here speak against my person, for I am purposed to abstain from requiting you in like sort; only

The causes of the lack of able ministers.

[3 Condemned, Answ. 2.]   [4 Estate, Repl. 1 and 2.]

Of ministers that cannot preach.

I will answer for myself where you labour to slander me. The cause of lack of a sufficient number of meet ministers in this church is neither the religion professed, nor the government that is used, nor yet the governors; but partly the cruelty of the times past, wherein numbers of meet ministers have been consumed; partly the unwillingness of men in this present time, which have not that zeal to enter into this calling that is to be wished; and partly (nay, chiefly and principally) you and your schisms, which have caused some to cast off their ministry wholly, some to forsake their pastoral charges, and yet to keep their prebends and other livings, some to deprave the ministry, condemn it, and by all means possible alienate as many from it as they can. And therefore nothing that I confess of the scarcity of meet and able ministers derogateth anything either from the doctrine professed in this church, or from the kind of government, or the magistrates, but rather commendeth the same; because, notwithstanding all the former impediments, yet hath it a number of excellent ministers, and doth continually breed more.

If my confession tend to the condemnation of any, it is of you and your adherents, who have more hindered and slandered the gospel in this realm of England, than the papists either have done, or could possibly do. And I am fully persuaded that one of the greatest deformities suffered in this church is lack of discipline towards you, who be so far from "healing any sore" in the church, that the more you be suffered, the greater do you wound it. And in very deed the reformation you pretend is nothing but a mere confusion, or rather subversion both of the church and commonwealth also.

My "honour and gain" is but very small, yet it is more than I am worthy of: but I trust the time will come, when as such boiling affections, uttered in so spiteful a manner, will be made manifest; and I pray God it be not imputed unto you in that day. If my "honour and gain" be other than may stand with the good and prosperous estate of the church, I am ready to yield it up whensoever I shall by due authority be required. In the mean time, God be judge betwixt you and me.

Chapter i. The Third Division.

T. C. Page 51, Sect. 1, 2, 3, 4, 5, 6, 7.

Of ministers that cannot preach.

But what if the estate of the church be such as you speak of, that it will scarce yield three preaching pastors and bishops in some dioceses; may you therefore make reading ministers? Indeed, if the apostle had made this a counsel only, and no commandment, that pastors of churches should be able to teach, then your saying might have been borne.

1 Tim. iii. 2.[1]
Tit. i. 9.[1]

But, seeing that St Paul hath commanded expressedly, that he should be "able to teach, and to convince the gainsayers," I would learn of you gladly, what necessity there is which can cause a man to break the moral law of God, to bring in a tradition of man. You may as well break any other commandment of God for necessity's sake, as break this, being comprehended in the first table.

And to say that these that can only read must be tolerated in the church as ministers is to say, because you can have no pastors in the churches, you will have idols; for so will I not doubt to call them, although, through ignorance of that which they do, some may be good men: but yet, in respect of the place that they occupy, they are idols; for they stand for that, and make shew of that, which they are not; and, admit you them as often as you will, the Lord pronounceth that they shall be no ministers to him, which have no knowledge.

Osee vi.[2]

But let us hear your reason: there must be reading in the church; therefore there must be ministers which can do nothing else. Then we may reason thus too: There must be breaking of bread, and distributing of the cup in the church, and pouring on water; therefore whosoever is able to break a loaf of bread, or to lift a cup of wine, or to pour on water on the body of the child, may be made a minister.

It is your own reason.

And did you never read that there were readers in the church, when there were no reading ministers? But of that of reading[3] *of the scriptures and prayers in the church, there will be a fitter place to speak afterward, where it shall be shewed how unjustly you surmise these things of them.*

Touching homilies shall be spoken more hereafter, where further occasion is given.

Jo. Whitgift.

St Paul, 1 Tim. iii. and Tit. i., sheweth what qualities a bishop or a pastor ought to have; but he doth not say that, if none can be found, or not a sufficient number, in whom all these qualities do concur, that then the church shall rather be destitute of ministers than have such: for there were in his time that swerved from this rule; and yet was he glad they preached.

[[1] The verses are added from Repl. 2.]
[[2] Osee iv. 6, Repl. 2.]   [[3] But of reading, Repl. 2.]

<small>Of ministers that cannot preach.</small>

Of the ministers of this church of England, though divers be ignorant, yet may they by study and diligent reading of the scriptures, catechisms, homilies, and other godly and necessary books, so profit in knowledge, that, although they be not able publicly to preach, yet may they be able privately to exhort, and otherwise also by reading the scriptures and homilies, according to the order appointed, greatly profit the people of God. But what should I contend with you in this matter? This church of England in this point professeth nothing that is not allowed by the general confession of the churches in Helvetia; from the which I think you will not dissent. That confession, as I told you before, hath these words: "We condemn all unmeet ministers not endued with gifts necessary for a shepherd that should feed his flock: howbeit we acknowledge that the harmless simplicity of some shepherds in the old church did sometimes more profit the church than the great, exquisite, and fine or delicate, but a little too proud, learning of some others. Wherefore we reject not now-a-days the good simplicity of certain; so that they be not altogether unskilful of God and his word."

<small>Confess. Helvet.</small>

There is nothing in that sixth of Osee that serveth your turn. You say that I reason thus: "There must be reading in the church; therefore there must be ministers that can do nothing else." You know what is written, *Sapient. i.: Os quod mentitur, &c.:* "The mouth that speaketh lies slayeth the soul, &c." I would it were not so usual with you. My argument is this, that, forsomuch as there cannot be a sufficient number of preachers to furnish this church of England in all places, therefore there may be reading ministers, that is, such ministers as, by reading the scriptures and other books appointed unto them, may profit the people and instruct them; "for reading is necessary in the church, &c." This is my reason. That which you use is a child of your own begetting, it is none of mine; as the reader cannot choose but perceive. The reason that followeth "of breaking bread, and distributing the cup, &c." is used but for a jest, which ought not to be in serious matters; and therefore I leave it to them that are disposed to laugh, when they should rather weep.

I know there were readers of old in the church; but they

[¹ Confess. et Expos. Fid. Christ. cap. xviii. in Corp. et Syntagm. Confess. Fid. Genev. 1654. p. 38. See before, page 338, note 1.]

had not authority to administer the sacraments, as our minis- *Of ministers that* ters have, and of necessity must have, and lawfully may have *cannot preach.* also; as it shall be hereafter declared. *Tract. ix. cap. i. The 15. division*

Chapter i. The Fourth Division.

T. C. Page 51, Sect. 7.

I do not use to maintain the places which are quoted, although they be truly alleged, for the causes which I have before mentioned; but yet I — Nay, it is because you *Luke ix. 2.*[2] *cannot but speak of this place of St Luke, for fear of the* cannot, for you want no *danger that may ensue. For, if this be a good reason, that* good will. *the place of St Luke may not be used to prove that preaching is perpetually annexed to the ministry, because in the same place is made mention of curing of diseases, which is but a temporal thing, and followed the ministry but for a time, then the commandment of St James, that the* *James .14.*[2] *elders of the church should pray for those that are sick, is now no commandment, because putting on of hands, and anointing of them, that they might recover their health, hath no place: and by this means you will pull from us as many* [3] *places of the new testament, as you did before of the old.*

Jo. Whitgift.

You would no doubt "maintain" all "their places," if you could; for the quotations be the substance of that book, and the thing that most persuaded the reader, which credited all things there written without examination, and thought it must of necessity be true, being so confirmed by the scriptures. And surely you could not have greatlier condemned the authors of that Admonition, than in suffering so many quotations of theirs to pass without defence. For what wickedness can there be greater than to abuse the scriptures in maintaining of sects and errors?

The place of Luke is not answered; the words of the text be these: "And he sent them to preach the kingdom of God, *Luke ix.* and to cure the sick, &c." No man living can conclude of this place the one more than he can do the other; and your words be but your own. There be other places a number that be more general than this, to prove preaching by: this was peculiar and proper to the disciples, as the whole circumstances

[² The first reference altogether and the verse of the second are inserted from Repl. 2.]

[³ From us many, Repl. 2.]

Of ministers that cannot preach.

of the place declare; for they are also commanded "to take nothing with them in their journey, neither staves, &c." To preach is perpetual; but it cannot be gathered of this place that none ought to be admitted into the ministry but such as can preach, because it was peculiarly spoken to the apostles; as the other circumstances do prove. The commandment of St James is general; for he telleth what all sick men ought to do, and the ministers likewise that resort to the sick; and therefore, though the anointing with oil, which was a sign of the gift of healing, be taken away, because the gift is ceased, yet doth praying remain still, and is perpetual, and not only proper to some ministers of the church, but common to all. Wherefore the places be not like; the one being spoken peculiarly to the disciples, the other generally to all ministers.

Of Licences to preach. Chapter ii.
Admonition.

And, if any be so well disposed to preach in their own charges, they may not without my lord's licence[1].

Answer to the Admonition, Page 53, Sect. 1, 2, 3.

Not to preach without licence[2].

You here find fault that, if a preacher be disposed to preach in his cure, he may not do it without my lord's licence.

Where the word of God is professed, and christian magistrates govern, there it is meet that no man should take upon him any function except he be by the magistrate (to whom it doth appertain) thereunto admitted. And, forasmuch as there be always in the church hypocrites, heretics, schismatics, and other evil-disposed persons, which study for nothing more than to disquiet the state of the church, and to occupy the people with their factions; it is necessary that none should be admitted to preach in any place, without he be thereunto licensed by the bishop, who ought to have a diligent care in that matter.

I suppose you are not of that mind, that men may now in this church under christian magistrates preach without licence: it hath always been the opinion of

[1 See before, page 538.]
[2 Answ. 2 adds *of a christian magistrate*.]

wise, learned, and godly men, that since the apostles' time none were ordinarily called to the office of preaching, but such as were called of God by man: only anabaptists, and some other sect of heretics, teach the contrary.

T. C. Page 51, Sect. 8, 9; and Page 52, Sect. 1, 2.

What dealing is this, to bring men in[3] suspicion of that which they never thought of? as though there were any word that sounded to this, that a man should put himself into the office of preaching, without the approbation of those men to whom it doth pertain. A doubtful saying.

Their complaint is, that those which are ordained pastors, and therefore to preach, cannot do it without further licence; as if a man should be charged to do a thing forthwith, and then he that chargeth him bindeth him hand and foot, that he cannot do it unless he will loose him.

The bishops enable him to teach, and point him a place to teach in; and yet they will not let him teach, unless he have a further licence. If he be an heretic or schismatic, or suspected of any such thing, why is he admitted, or, being admitted, why is he suffered to be so much as a reader in the church? And, because you could not answer this, therefore you set up a fancy of yours to confute. And thus you fight without an adversary, and you make triumphs where there is no victory.

They will say unto you, that not only under a godly magistrate, but not in the time of persecution, any man ought to take upon him any function in the church, unless he be thereunto called by men, except he have a wonderful calling, which is rare, and must be diligently examined by them which have it, lest under pretence of the Spirit of God, whom they make author of their calling, it fall out that it be but their own headlong affection that hath thrust them in: so far they are from the frenzy of anabaptists, which you, by a confutation of that which they never affirmed, would seem to stain them with.

Jo. Whitgift.

This reply consisteth partly of equivocations, and partly of false suppositions. For, where you say that "no man should put himself into the office of preaching, without the approbation of those men to whom it doth appertain," you speak ambiguously, and therefore you must explicate what you mean by "those to whom it doth appertain;" whether the people and seniors, as you call them, or the bishops, or the civil magistrate, or such to whom the civil magistrate doth commit the judging of such matters. For the anabaptists confess that they must be called of their

[3 Into, Repl. 1 and 2.]

churches, but they deny the authority of the civil magistrate herein, and the authority of such also as he doth appoint for that end and purpose. Again, you here suppose that no man may preach out of his own cure; and therefore, being once admitted to preach there, he needeth no further licence. Likewise you do suppose that none may be admitted to preach except he have a cure; to be short, that hypocrites, heretics, schismatics, may be known forthwith, or, " being suspected," by and bye removed out of the ministry; all which suppositions be untrue, and therefore this reply full of great absurdities. Their meaning is plain, and[1], though there be just cause why the bishop should inhibit them from preaching, both for their contentions, and also for their errors, yet would they preach whether the bishop will or no; for the case is their own. They were admitted to preach in their cures, and elsewhere, so long as they used themselves modestly, quietly, and taught sound doctrine; but, after they began to divide the church, and make contention in it, they were restrained from preaching, until such time as, upon their submission and reformation, they should be thereunto admitted again: *hinc illæ lacrymæ*, this is the matter; and hereto you answer *ne gry quidem*[2].

[1 That, Def. A.]

[2 οὐδὲ γρῦ. Aristoph. Demosth. &c.—Cartwright says he will dispatch "the chapter entitled, Of licences to preach," in a word or two: he calls Whitgift's reasoning "silly sophistry," and declares him "spoiled of all both conscience and judgment."—Sec. Repl. pp. 361, 2. But he afterwards adds a long rejoinder which he denominates " Of preaching ministers" to Whitgift's 5th and 6th tractates; and in this he remarks on both what has been said here and also in other parts of the Defence.—Ibid. pp. 363, &c.]

www.ingramcontent.com/pod-product-compliance
Lightning Source LLC
Chambersburg PA
CBHW052012040526
R18239600001BA/R182396PG44108CBX00004BA/7